Transforming Physical Assets to Cognitive Enterprises With Digital Twins

Zornitsa Yordanova
https://orcid.org/0000-0002-6056-8445
University of National and World Economy, Bulgaria

Hamed Nozari
https://orcid.org/0000-0002-6500-6708
University of National and World Economy, Bulgaria

IGI Global Scientific Publishing
Publishing Tomorrow's Research Today

Vice President of Editorial	Melissa Wagner
Director of Acquisitions	Mikaela Felty
Director of Book Development	Jocelynn Hessler
Production Manager	Mike Brehm
Cover Design	Jose Rosado

Published in the United States of America by
IGI Global Scientific Publishing
701 East Chocolate Avenue
Hershey, PA, 17033, USA
Tel: 717-533-8845 | Fax: 717-533-7115
Website: https://www.igi-global.com E-mail: cust@igi-global.com

Library of Congress Cataloging-in-Publication Data

LCCN: 2026014516 (CIP Data Pending)
ISBN13: 979-8-3373-9998-0
Isbn13Softcover: 979-8-3373-9999-7
EISBN13: 979-8-2600-0005-2
British Cataloguing in Publication Data
A Cataloguing in Publication record for this book is available from the British Library.

Editorial Advisory Board

Table of Contents

Detailed Table of Contents

The development of cyber-physical systems, artificial intelligence, and big data infrastructures has altered how organizations operate with respect to physical assets. The use of digital twins, or virtual copies of actual systems, is one of the primary changes, as these systems tend to receive and analyze real-time sensor data to track performance, run simulations, and enhance performance. Digital twins were originally intended for monitoring and predictive maintenance; nowadays, they are being integrated into larger intelligent enterprise systems. These systems are now being developed to detect trends, forecast interruptions, and support sophisticated decision-making as organizations use more and more data to inform their decisions. Digital twins are slowly becoming the infrastructure of cognitive enterprises that learn from data, adapt to change, and enable organizations to operate more proactively.

This research explains multi-agent digital twin architectures for achieving real-time adaptability at the enterprise level. By moving from centralized models to distributed cognitive ecosystems, each physical asset becomes a semi-autonomous digital agent capable of local analysis, prediction, and decision-making. Through coordination mechanisms, multi-objective optimization, and distributed intelligence between the edge and the cloud, these agents create collective behavior that is consistent and aligned with the strategic goals of the organization. Also, scenario modeling and multi-level feedback loops provide the basis for the formation of emergent dynamics and systemic learning. The presented framework provides a foundation for designing self-regulating and co-evolving cognitive enterprises.

Industry 4.0 and lean management are reshaping enterprise competition. Lean has traditionally depended on human observation and retrospective analysis to eliminate waste, but predictive analytics and simulation now offer greater precision, speed, and scalability. With real-time data, machine learning models, and advanced simulation tools, organisations can anticipate equipment failures, optimise production schedules, test process changes virtually, and align supply chains with dynamic market demand. This chapter examines how predictive analytics and simulation within Industry 4.0 frameworks enhance lean practices. It reviews methods such as discrete event simulation, agent-based modelling, machine learning-based demand forecasting, and digital twin-enabled value stream analysis. Their integration with lean tools value stream mapping, kaizen, just-in-time production, and total productive maintenance is analysed. Drawing on theory, empirical studies, and global cases, the chapter provides a practical guide for using data-driven intelligence to achieve operational excellence.

The rapid advancement of digital technologies in recent years has led to a fundamental transformation in the structure and management of industrial manufacturing systems. Smart manufacturing assets, relying on technologies such as the Industrial Internet of Things, artificial intelligence, cyber-physical systems, and digital twins, have paved the way for the formation of a new generation of smart industrial organizations. These technologies enable continuous monitoring of equipment, predictive data analysis, and data-driven decision-making in manufacturing environments. This chapter reviews the evolution of manufacturing assets, key enabling technologies, the role of digital transformation in smart asset management, and their industrial applications, and finally analyzes the path of industries moving toward autonomous industrial organizations.

The increasing complexity of industrial systems and the rapid spread of digital technologies have revolutionized the way organizations manage physical assets. Digital Twin technology has emerged as an effective tool for connecting physical systems to digital models, enabling real-time monitoring, predictive analytics, and intelligent decision-making. In this chapter, an integrated Digital Twin-based framework for intelligent asset management is presented, which enables the interaction between physical assets, operational data, analytical models, and decision-support systems. The applications of this technology in optimizing asset performance and moving toward cognitive management are also examined.

Artificial Intelligence (AI), Internet of Things (IoT), Digital Twins, and Predictive Analytics are transforming modern organizations into intelligent and adaptive systems. However, most existing studies examine these technologies individually, limiting understanding of their combined impact. This chapter addresses this gap by proposing an Integrated Cognitive Enterprise Framework that unifies data acquisition, intelligent processing, virtual simulation, and predictive decision-making. The framework enables real-time responsiveness, continuous learning, and proactive optimization through a closed-loop feedback mechanism. The study also explores applications across industries such as manufacturing, healthcare, smart cities, and supply chains. Key challenges including data security, integration complexity, and skill gaps are discussed. The findings highlight that true organizational intelligence emerges from the integration of technologies, offering both theoretical and practical insights for adaptive digital transformation.

The emergence of Artificial Intelligence and advanced data ecosystems is transforming traditional organizations into cognitive enterprises. This paper examines the evolution from Digital Twins to AI-driven intelligent decision ecosystems, where real-time data, predictive analytics, and machine learning enable adaptive, resilient, and self-learning organizational systems. Digital Twins are no longer limited to physical assets but are increasingly applied to business processes, supply chains, and customer interactions to enhance strategic and operational decision-making. The study proposes a conceptual framework for AI-enabled organizational transformation, highlighting the role of human–AI collaboration, automation, and intelligent platforms in improving agility, innovation, and sustainability. It also discusses challenges related to governance, ethics, data security, and workforce readiness. The paper contributes to the understanding of cognitive enterprises as a foundation for competitive advantage in the era of Industry 5.0.

The chapter analyzes the role of rule design in the strategy and strategic behavior of game-theoretic models, equilibrium, and efficiency of decisions and then generalizes findings to digital twin-driven cognitive enterprises. Digital twins are becoming smart decision-support systems, which mimic real-world situations and demand powerful rule-based systems to direct strategic engagements between agents. Based on combinatorial and economic game theory, this paper is going to examine how the differences in information structures, payoff mechanisms, action space and rules of enforcement influence strategic behavior. The article uses a systematic literature review. The results point to the fact that flexible rule systems are helpful in the process of strategic richness, but they also make computation more difficult. The

Preface

ABOUT THIS BOOK

In recent decades, the rapid convergence of digital technologies has fundamentally transformed the way we understand, manage, and develop physical assets. What was once a static approach based on historical data and reactive decision-making is now moving towards a dynamic, intelligent, and learning ecosystem. At the heart of this transformation is the concept of the "digital twin," no longer limited to simulation or monitoring, but as a cognitive decision-making layer that will play a key role in shaping the organizations of the future.

This book is an attempt to explain this fundamental transition from traditional asset management to "cognitive organizations." This book brings together a collection of theoretical perspectives, conceptual frameworks, and applied studies to demonstrate how digital twins, in conjunction with artificial intelligence, multi-agent systems, multi-objective optimization, and cyber-physical architectures, can lead to the creation of self-regulating, predictive, and decision-supporting systems.

The chapters in this book cover a wide range of applications and domains, from intelligent asset management and production optimization in smart factories to modern agriculture, smart cities, data-driven marketing, and complex organizational systems. This diversity of topics demonstrates the high potential of digital twins to transform different industries, as well as their ability to integrate data, models, and decisions at different organizational levels.

One of the main themes of this book is the move from "digital twins" to "cognitive organizations"; Where systems not only represent the current situation, but are also able to predict the future, evaluate different scenarios, and make optimal decisions automatically or semi-automatically. In this direction, concepts such as agent-based intelligence, adaptive learning, closed-loop feedback loops, and human-digital twin coexistence play a central role.

Also, this book specifically addresses the challenges of sustainability, resilience, and crisis management in complex systems. By using digital twins, predictive analysis, risk management, and the design of systems resistant to disruptions are possible; a topic that has become doubly important in today's volatile and uncertain world.

This work is useful not only for researchers and students in the fields of industrial engineering, management, data science and information technology, but also for industrial managers, policymakers and innovation activists as a strategic guide on the path to digital transformation. An attempt has been made to create a bridge between theory and practice by providing coherent frameworks and practical examples.

Finally, it is hoped that this book can act as an effective step towards developing the knowledge and application of digital twins at the organizational and inter-organizational levels and pave the way for the formation of a new generation of intelligent, adaptable and sustainable enterprises; enterprises that not only react to data, but also learn from it, evolve with it and actively shape the future.

Zornitsa Yordanova
University of National and World Economy, Bulgaria

Hamed Nozari
University of National and World Economy, Bulgaria

Chapter 1
Business Process Intelligence and Digital Twins

Gautam Shivaraj
http://orcid.org/0009-0000-5184-8448
Adarsh Institute of Management and Information Technology, Bengaluru, India

G. Silambarasan
http://orcid.org/0009-0004-6233-4943
Periyar University, Salem, India

ABSTRACT

The chapter discusses the use of Digital Twins in various industries, including manufacturing, healthcare, logistics, and supply chain management, demonstrating their potential to improve process design, optimize resource allocation, and enhance customer experiences. It also addresses the integration challenges and the need for robust data architectures, cybersecurity considerations, and scalability for widespread adoption.By synthesizing case studies, technological trends, and research findings, this chapter provides a comprehensive view of how Business Process Intelligence and Digital Twins together can drive digital transformation, foster innovation, and create competitive advantages for businesses. The chapter emphasizes the future potential of these technologies, their impact on the evolving business landscape, and the importance of aligning them with strategic business goals.

DOI: 10.4018/979-8-3373-9998-0.ch001

1. INTRODUCTION

In a world that is rapidly turning digital, businesses have been continually under the pressure to enhance the efficiency of operations, innovation in response to market changes, and deliver superior value to the consumers. Conventional ways of process management and decision making processes tend to fail in complex, data-driven environments. New technologies and approaches have been developed in response to the need to remain competitive as organizations strive to be competitive. Business Process Intelligence (BPI) and Digital Twins are among the most promising as these two concepts have been transforming the manner in which businesses observe, analyze, and optimize their operations.(Ibrahim et al., 2026)

In its simplest definition, Business Process Intelligence (BPI) concerns the power of using data to enhance business processes. It is the application of data analytics, process mining, and performance monitoring tools to give an insight into how business processes are performed. With the help of BPI, organizations will be able to see how their processes are performing, find out inefficiency, and keep on upgrading them. BPI aims at making business operations clearer, predictable, and responsive, thus allowing organizations to react to any changes in the internal and external environment much faster.(Feng et al., 2025)

Digital Twins on the other hand is a revolutionary concept that will bridge the physical and digital worlds. A Digital Twin is a simulated or virtual object, system or process. Digital Twins provide businesses with a real-time virtual representation, which is capable of analysis, testing, and optimization by employing real-time data of physical entities (machines, devices, or the whole production lines) and advanced simulation models. The idea was originally created in the manufacturing sector but has since been used in other industries such as healthcare industry, energy and logistics and even smart cities.(Teng et al., 2025)

The combination of BPI and Digital twins gives organizations a unique chance to streamline and control their processes with a greater level of precision and insight. BPI provides a structure with which the workflow of a business can be evaluated and optimized, whereas Digital Twins can be used as a real-time interactive simulation that can forecast future events, experiment with potential new conditions, and pinpoint the processes in order to optimize them. Using both of these technologies together business is able to gain a greater insight into its operations, make well-informed decisions and make preventive actions to mitigate risks or inefficiencies before it becomes an expensive issue.(Schink et al., 2026a)

An example is that of a manufacturing company that implements BPI along with a Digital Twin of its production line. Key performance indicators (KPIs) that the BPI system may continuously monitor included throughput, cycle time, and quality indicators, and the Digital Twin simply gave it a dynamic model of the production line operations, using real-time data which was provided by sensors on machines, materials and workers. Through the combination of these two systems, the company is able to virtually test how the various operational situations will be, the bottlenecks, as well as the equipment failure and the workflow optimization all on the virtual front before making any real world changes. This is a forecasting based, data-oriented methodology that assists companies to achieve efficiency, cost-cutting, and overall performance.

Simulation, monitoring, and optimization of business processes with the help of BPI and Digital Twins allows not only to gain a competitive advantage but also to become one of the essential enablers of digital transformation. With companies moving towards more nimble, data-driven organizations, the combination of these technologies will be important in making sure that companies are resilient, responsive and able to adjust to the ever-evolving market forces.(He, 2026a)

This chapter will discuss Business Process Intelligence and Digital Twins concepts, their respective potentials, and how their combination can enhance smarter decisions and processes optimization and business innovation. We are going to discuss the advantages, difficulties, and major uses of these technologies in various industries providing the examples of how they may be utilized to change the way businesses work and develop new conditions to grow and be able to last.(Loia et al., 2026a)

2. BACKGROUND: GETTING TO KNOW BUSINESS PROCESS INTELLIGENCE

Business Process Intelligence (BPI) is an interdisciplinary field that involves data analytics, process management, and performance optimization to offer actionable knowledge about processes that can be performed within an organization. It is the exploitation of information produced by different systems in an organization, the analysis of the information and the eventual utilization of the information to make well-informed decisions with the aim of enhancing operational performance, quality, and standards. In its simplest form, BPI is based on ongoing monitoring, analysis, and enhancement of the business processes by using sophisticated technologies, including data mining, machine learning, and artificial intelligence (AI).

The importance of BPI is getting very critical in the modern business environment where organizations are overwhelmed with information that is of different sources. When optimally used and analyzed, this data can be of great benefit as it allows uncovering inefficiencies, streamlining workflows, improving decision-making, and reinforcing the continuous improvement efforts. To a large extent, BPI forms the foundation of the transformation of operations within an organization and thus helps in making businesses more responsive to challenges and opportunities.(Ivanov & Gusikhin, 2026a)

BPI is an extensive process that normally consists of a number of steps all of which play a role in the ultimate objective of enhancing business processes. To deconstruct the most important elements and methodologies that characterize Business Process Intelligence, we can start by identifying the following:

Process Discovery and Mapping

The Business Process Intelligence process discovery is the initial step, which involves the analysis of the available data to learn how business processes are actually operating. This step can entail process mining which is a method that is employed to obtain data of different systems (including Enterprise Resource Planning (ERP), Customer Relationship Management (CRM), or Supply Chain Management (SCM) systems) to recreate process flows. Process mining algorithms process the event logs of the IT system and help organizations see their processes on screen and plot them as they are being implemented.(Wickremasinghe et al., 2025a)

With this visualization we can see a clear and data driven picture of the way work is flowing through the organization, the various steps, activities and actors involved. It is also capable of showing the difference in the way the processes are implemented as per the desired or the probable workflows and give information on the possible inefficiencies or deviation that should be dealt with.

It could be used in a manufacturing firm as a process discovery could reveal what is being done in the production process, where the delay is caused, or how much time machines are waiting but the managers are able to know the bottlenecks that are causing delays in the whole process.(Kookalani et al., 2026a)

Process Monitoring and Performance Management

After mapping processes and understanding processes, the process monitoring is the next undertaking of BPI. This entails monitoring of the key metrics in real-time to determine how the business processes are actually performing. The Key Performance Indicators (KPIs) are put in place to quantify the effectiveness and efficiency of every process. These KPIs may be a very diverse set of metrics, including cycle time, cost per unit, customer satisfaction, throughput rate, error rates, and adherence to regulatory standards.(Barbuto et al., 2026)

BPI tools help organizations to monitor the processes constantly, and to inform the managers about the deviations and inefficiency occurring during the process. As an illustration, BPI tools in an e-commerce business can be used to monitor the duration that an order has taken in passing through the cart to shipping. In case the process becomes delayed, managers can be informed and they might put corrective action that will not affect customer satisfaction.

BPI is also used to have a holistic perspective of the performance of interdependent processes in an organization besides tracking of individual processes. The managers can be able to see how various processes interact with each other and in the process they can see which processes can be improved in some areas at the same time.(Tonelli et al., 2026)

Process Analysis and Identification of Root Causes

The other fundamental aspect of BPI is process analysis. It does not merely monitor the performance metrics but also explores the factors behind inefficiencies, delays or under-optimal performance. Organizations are also able to dive deeper into data to make patterns, trends and root causes out of the data using data analytics and process mining.

As an illustration, what happens to a sales team that is performing poorly. The conventional approaches may merely imply that the sales process should be improved. Nevertheless, using BPI and process analysis, it may be revealed that the bottleneck does not actually lie with the sales team, but rather in the lead qualification process which delays the process of potential sales. The managers can also focus on particular areas of work to make improvements instead of making blanket and ineffective modifications by determining the source of the inefficiency.

Moreover, it is possible to incorporate enhanced predictive analytics in BPI to anticipate the performance of the process in the future. Through historical data, machine learning algorithms can forecast their risks, including supply chain or customer churn, and suggest preventive measures to address those before they affect the business.(Hasan & Nguyen, 2026)

Process Optimization and Continuous Improvement

Business Process Intelligence is ultimately aimed at optimization of business. When the inefficiency or performance gaps have been realized, BPI tools are found to give recommendations on how to improve. Such improvements may include workflow adjustments, automatization of some functions or restructuring of resources. In addition, BPI is combined with business rules management systems to make sure that the processes are in line with the organizations objectives and compliance requirement.

Automation is another trend that can be applied in process optimization in BPI. Repetitive and time-consuming processes can be automated by applying Robotic Process Automation (RPA) or AI-based systems so that employees can work on more valuable processes. As an illustration, an HR department may employ BPI to detect time spoilage in the process of onboarding employees and introduce an automated workflow that simplifies the process of submitting documents, granting authorizations and training schedules.

Another feature of BPI is continuous improvement. Businesses will be able to constantly optimize their processes by using feedback loops provided by monitoring and analysis. It is in line with the idea of Lean or Six Sigma approach that is aimed at minimizing waste and enhancing quality in the long term. The organizations that apply BPI are able to gain a progressive approach, with every process tracking and optimization cycle resulting in a more efficient and streamlined process.(Das et al., 2026)

Greater Decision-Making by Data-Driven Insights

Among the greatest advantages of BPI, it is possible to mention its power to deliver data-driven decision-making. Organizations are able to make decisions based on objective data and analytics rather than relying on the power of intuition or anecdotal evidence. BPI provides managers with insights that are real time and inform strategic and operational decisions.

As an example, BPI could be used to analyze workflow in order to approve or disapprove loans within a financial services firm. With the discovery of inefficiencies and delays, the management is able to make decisions, which are based on resources allocation, or, the management can implement new systems, which are faster to process. By using BPI, the decision-makers have the right information that is up-to-date and helps in making smarter and more effective decisions.(Abdessadak et al., 2025a)

BPI Tools and Technologies

BPI is implemented in an organization through a number of tools and technologies. These include:

Process Mining Tools: These are the tools that lie at the core of BPI. They assist organizations to map out their processes, detect inefficiencies and track performance. According to the definitions, such popular tools of process mining are Celonis, Disco, and UiPath Process Mining.

Data analytics and Business Intelligence (BI) Tools: BI tools like Tableau, Power BI, or Qlik Sense can be attached to BPI systems to help to provide visual dashboards, reports, and detailed analytics of business processes.

Robotic Process Automation (RPA): Robotic process automation (RPA) software, such as Blue Prism and Automation Anywhere is typically applied alongside BPI to automate repetitive processes, making them leaner.

Machine Learning and Predictive Analytics: It is possible to use machine learning algorithms to process data to determine future trends, what risks may be present, and what the process should be improved.

Business Rules Management Systems (BRMS): These systems enable business organizations to define, administer and implement rules that regulate the manner in which processes ought to be carried out.(Cappiello et al., 2026)

3. THE RISE OF DIGITAL TWINS

Conceptual Framework for Integrating BPI and Digital Twins

1. BPI Data Collection and Monitoring:
    - o Process Discovery: Identifying how business processes are currently being performed, including flow, steps, and interactions between various functions (e.g., manufacturing, logistics).
    - o Performance Monitoring: Real-time tracking of KPIs such as cycle time, error rates, cost per unit, customer satisfaction, and throughput. These data points are continuously captured by BPI tools like process mining and business intelligence (BI) software.
    - o Analysis and Reporting: BPI provides organizations with detailed insights into the operational gaps, inefficiencies, and performance discrepancies in business processes.
2. Digital Twin Simulation and Forecasting:
    - o Real-Time Data Integration: Digital Twins rely on data from sensors and IoT devices to create a dynamic model of physical systems, such as machines, production lines, or entire supply chains. This model is continuously updated based on real-world data.
    - o Simulation of Operations: Digital Twins allow businesses to simulate different scenarios and process changes (e.g., how changing the production schedule affects throughput or how a machine failure might impact the entire system).
    - o Predictive Insights: Digital Twins forecast potential future events, such as equipment breakdowns, bottlenecks, or system failures, by analyzing historical and real-time data.(Kookalani et al., 2026b)
3. Integration of BPI and Digital Twin:

- o Feedback Loop: The integration of BPI and Digital Twins creates a feedback loop. BPI tracks the real-time performance of business processes and feeds this data into the Digital Twin. The Digital Twin, in turn, simulates and analyzes future scenarios using this data and sends actionable insights back to the BPI system.
- o Scenario Testing and Decision Support: By combining BPI's real-time insights with Digital Twin's predictive simulations, organizations can test different scenarios (e.g., process changes, machine replacements, or resource allocation) in a virtual environment before applying them in the real world.
- o Optimization and Continuous Improvement: The system continuously adapts based on performance data and simulations, allowing businesses to optimize operations proactively. BPI's analytics tools enable real-time monitoring and continuous improvement, while Digital Twin technology enables predictive maintenance and long-term optimization. (Fonseca i Casas & Pi i Palomes, 2026a)

Visualizing the Integration of BPI and Digital Twins

Here is a diagram illustrating how BPI and Digital Twins integrate in a business environment:

1. BPI (Process Discovery & Performance Monitoring) → Real-Time Data
   - → Digital Twin (Simulation & Prediction) → Predictive Insights & Scenario Testing
   - → Feedback Loop to BPI (Optimization) → Continuous Improvement

Figure 1. the Integration of BPI and Digital Twins

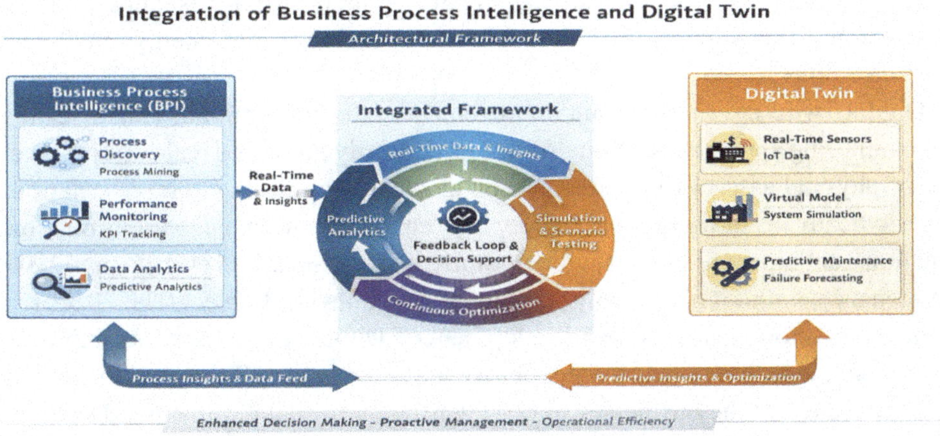

This flow shows the complementary roles of both systems, where BPI continuously provides real-time data for operational tracking, and Digital Twins leverage this data to simulate various scenarios and predict future outcomes. The insights gained from simulations inform real-time process optimization, thereby improving operational performance(Iglesias et al., 2026a)

Why This Framework is Important

Introducing this conceptual model will help the reader better understand how BPI and Digital Twins work in tandem to improve organizational performance. It moves beyond theoretical descriptions of each technology and demonstrates their practical application within an integrated system. The model serves as a foundation for understanding how businesses can leverage both technologies to optimize processes, predict risks, and make informed decisions in a dynamic and data-driven environment.

Moreover, the feedback loop between BPI and Digital Twins is crucial for continuous process improvement, making it easier for organizations to stay adaptable, proactive, and resilient in the face of changing market conditions. By adding this conceptual model, the chapter not only explains the individual benefits of BPI and Digital Twins but also highlights how their integration creates greater value than the sum of their parts.(Pavleska, 2026a)

Digital Twins as a concept has been very active over the last couple of years, particularly with industries trying to realize the strength of digital transformation. A Digital Twin is a simulated physical object, system or process. These virtual models are driven by real-time data through sensors, IoT devices and so on and hence can mirror the real behavior and performance of the real-life counterparts. This idea was initially elaborated in the manufacturing industry but has quickly spread to numerous other spheres, including healthcare and transport, energy, intelligent cities, and others.

Digital Twins are an important improvement of the conventional design, testing and monitoring approaches. Digital Twins provide a dynamic and real-time perspective of physical assets or systems, instead of only using the static representations or periodically performing checks. They help companies to model various possible situations, anticipate future behavior, optimize performance, and even do predictive maintenance, without necessarily touching the real physical object.(He, 2026b)

Several factors influence the development of Digital Twins, such as improved data collection technologies, the popularity of the Internet of Things (IoT), and the rising demands of the businesses to consider the use of data in making decisions. Here, we discuss the history of Digital Twins, major aspects of the Digital Twin, and their application in industries to accelerate innovation and operational effectiveness.(Banad et al., 2025)

History and Development of Digital Twins

Digital Twin was initially coined by Michael Grieves in 2002 when he was working at the University of Michigan. In the early days Digital Twins were mostly applied to product lifecycle management (PLM) which concerned the development of digital models of physical products to be designed, tested, and analysed. Such models would enable engineers and designers to know how a product would perform in the real world, possible problems that may arise and adjust the design to a better design prior to production.

Nonetheless, the idea changed considerably in the next decades. The introduction of Internet of Things (IoT) technology allowed sensors to be cheaper and more advanced, allowing the collection of data on physical assets in real-time. This was an opportunity to build more dynamic and real time Digital Twins that were not just able to simulate the design of the product but also track its performance, maintenance requirements, and overall efficiency over the course of its existence.

Digital Twins are now not just products and machines but are now applied to entire systems, processes, and even cities. As an example, city planners can now simulate traffic trends, energy consumption, and waste management, and other city processes using Digital Twins, and plan them better and more sustainably. In manufacturing, the whole supply chain and production line can be modeled as a Digital Twin, and companies can discover inefficiencies, anticipate downtimes, and time-optimize the workflow.(Fornari et al., 2025)

The Most Important Digital Twins Components

Digital Twin production and application is dependent on multiple fundamental aspects that enable it to reproduce its physical counterpart in flawless and real-time fashion. These components include:

Physical Object or System: The masterpiece of a Digital Twin is the physical object or system represented in it. This may consist of a machine in a factory floor to an entire city or a process involved in industry. The physical object produces data that is measured with the help of different sensors and IoT gadgets.

Data Collection Infrastructure: The data collection infrastructure is a major element of Digital Twins, which collects real-time information through the sensors fitted on the physical system. The parameters that these sensors are used to measure include temperature, pressure, vibration, speed, location, among other performance parameters. The information is sent to a central repository where the information can be processed and analyzed.

Digital Model/Simulation: The digital model refers to the representation of the physical object, system or process in a virtual form. It is developed with the help of the latest modeling programs and simulation programs. CAD (Computer-Aided Design) data, system blueprint and other specifications in engineering can be used in the model, however, it also takes real time data to make it a mirror-mirror image of the actual situation of the physical system.

Data analytics and AI Algorithms: Data analytics is an important step in Digital Twin technology. The processing and analysis of the real-time data obtained through the physical system will help the companies pinpoint on patterns, detect anomalies, and predict the future behavior. These predictions are often improved with the help of AI algorithms to deliver more useful insights. As an example, predictive analytics can determine when a machine will break down based on its performance and companies can plan to have their machine serviced before/before it breaks down. (Marfoglia et al., 2026)

User Interface and Visualization Tools: Digital Twins are based on advanced user interfaces that provide the user with the capability to interact with a digital model and visualize the digital data. These interfaces usually have dashboards, 3D models and data visualizations that give real time information of the performance and well being of the physical system. These interfaces can help operators and decision-makers evaluate performance, find areas of inefficiencies as well as experiment with various scenarios.

Digital Twin Technology and the Role of Internet of Things (IoT)

One of the factors that contribute to the emergence of Digital Twins is the wide use of the Internet of Things (IoT) technology. Sensors, actuators, and embedded systems are IoT devices that are utilized to gather large volumes of data on physical assets in real-time. This information is the basis of Digital Twins development and operation.

As an illustration, IoT sensors can be used in a smart building to measure the quality of the air, temperature, humidity and energy use. This real-time data can be used in a Digital Twin of the building to simulate energy usage patterns, optimize heating and cooling systems and to guarantee that the building runs efficiently. On the same note, in the manufacturing sector, IoT-driven machines could feed real-time data into a Digital Twin of the production line, which would assist operators to detect and address bottlenecks, equipment health and enhance production efficiency.

Increasing the access to high-speed networks, edge computing, and cloud computing infrastructure is also important in facilitating the proper utilization of IoT devices in Digital Twin applications. Digital Twins get even more valuable with these improvements since organizations are able to process and analyze large amounts of real-time data quickly and effectively.(de las Morenas et al., 2025)

4. DIGITAL TWIN USAGE IN INDUSTRIES

Digital Twins have been used in many industries, all of which have been advantageous due to the option of simulating, tracking, and optimizing the physical systems in real time. Some of the most notable uses of Digital Twins are listed below:

4.1 Manufacturing and Industry 4.0

Digital Twins are also applied in the manufacturing industry to optimize the production line, enhance equipment maintenance, and design products. The whole manufacturing process can be simulated on digital Twins of production lines and can help to understand the possible bottlenecks, downtime, or quality problems. This enables the manufacturers to streamline their operations, cut costs and enhance the overall efficiency of their production systems.

One of the strongest uses of Digital Twins in the manufacturing process is predictive maintenance. Another advantage of constant equipment monitoring with Digital Twins is the ability of companies to anticipate when a machine may fail, so that they can perform their maintenance services before failing, preventing the expensive downtime.(Olawade et al., 2026)

4.2 Healthcare and Medical Devices

Digital Twins in healthcare are applied to the virtual patients, medical devices and even hospitals. The role of simulating patient conditions allows doctors to learn more about the progression of a disease and can analyze the treatment options and implement them in practice. In the case of medical devices manufacturers, Digital Twins offers a chance to test devices in the virtual environment which enhances the design process and guarantees improved functioning and safety.

Patient avatars or digital Twins can be used to track health conditions in real-time and combine information on medical records, wearables, and sensor equipment to form a digital representation of a patient. Such avatars may be applied to the individual treatment plans, predictive diagnostics, or even simulations of surgery.

4.3 Smart Cities and Management of Infrastructure

Smart cities are getting a lot of significance in the form of Digital Twins. Digital twins can be used by cities to simulate traffic flow, energy consumption, water supply and waste management systems. This enables the city planners and operators to maximise the use of resources, lower energy consumption, and enhance efficiency within the city.(Lin et al., 2025a)

As an illustration, a Digital Twin of a city traffic system can be used to simulate road traffic and congestion and assist city planners to make rational decisions regarding infrastructure improvement, transit routes, and city layout. In the same way, the Digital Twins of power grids and water supply systems can assist utilities to predict fluctuations in demand, optimize maintenance and minimise the disruptions in services.(Fonseca i Casas & Pi i Palomes, 2026b)

4.4 Energy and Utilities

Digital Twins are applied in the energy industry to optimize power production, distribution and consumption. The digital twins of wind farms, solar plants and power plants can give operators real-time information about the functionality of energy systems and allow them to anticipate maintenance, maximize energy generation and stability of grids.

As an illustration, a Digital Twin of a wind farm could use the influence of weather conditions on turbine performance, so the operators would be able to optimize the speed of turbines and enhance energy efficiency. In the same manner, the Digital Twins of power grids can be utilized to model different demand situations, detect possible areas of failure, and optimize power distribution throughout the grid. (Iglesias et al., 2026b)

4.5 Benefits of Digital Twins

Along with the emergence of Digital twins, a range of advantages is being introduced that can have an enormous impact on the work process and decision-making. These include:

Enhanced Decision-Making: Digital twins can empower organizations to make better decisions due to real-time, data-driven information, which can be used to make decisions based on actual performance metrics as opposed to assumptions and past information.

Predictive Maintenance: Digital Twins allow predictive maintenance as the assets are monitored in real-time and predicted when they will fail. This decreases the downtime, extends the life span of the assets and even reduces the cost of maintenance.

Better Product Design and Innovation: With Digital Twins, there is the ability to test and simulate new products, systems, or processes in the virtual world to a great extent. This saves the use of physical prototypes and shortens the innovation cycles.

Operation Optimization: Digital Twins offer an all-encompassing perspective of operations, which allows organizations to detect inefficiencies, simplify the workflow, and streamline the use of resources.

Cost Reduction: Digital twins prevent wastage of resources through forecasting failures, process optimization, and asset management to ensure companies cut cost and maximize ROI.

5. COMBINING BUSINESS PROCESS INTELLIGENCE WITH DIGITAL TWINS

The use of Business Process Intelligence (BPI) and Digital Twins has become the biggest breakthrough in the transformation of business by allowing organizations to streamline their practices with real-time information, as well as with predictive systems. Although Business Process Intelligence is a framework, which is used to analyze and optimize business processes on a continual basis by utilizing data and process management tools, Digital twins are real-time, dynamic simulations of physical systems, processes, and assets. With the integration of these two potent technologies, organizations can not only visualize their operations but also simulate various scenarios, predict further results and optimise performance even better.

This collaboration between BPI and Digital Twins is changing the way businesses address their operations and engage with them, which are becoming more responsive, predictive, and data-driven. This section discusses how the two technologies can be incorporated to have unprecedented visibility, improved decision making and increased efficiency in a number of industries.(Iglesias et al., 2026b)

5.1 Additional Strengths of BPI and Digital Twins

To see the strength of integration, first it is important to analyze the complementary worth of the two technologies.

Business Process Intelligence (BPI) deals with the analysis of data and optimization of processes. It gives a comprehensive insight of how business operations are executed, the areas of inefficiency and allows the continuous improvement. BPI enables business to monitor key performance indicators (KPIs), bottlenecks and enhance workflows by means of data analytics and process management software.

Digital twins on the other hand provide real time virtual depiction of physical systems or processes. The simulations enable companies to view assets, systems or whole environments in real time, simulate future conditions as well as carry out predictive analysis to avoid failures or inefficiencies. Digital Twins take the data generated by sensors and IoT devices during the operating work, and they form a dynamic and detailed model that mirrors the performance in reality.

BPI and Digital Twins give a combined perspective of the physical and operational aspects of a business when put together. Although BPI monitors performance in the data sense of the process, Digital Twins can model the performance of the process as it is performed in the real world providing a more in-depth understanding of how operations work and predictive performance optimization.(Iglesias et al., 2026b)

5.2.The Collaboration of BPI and Digital Twins

The use of BPI and Digital twins enables companies to close the loop between digital simulations and actual data in the operation room. This is the way this integration can be achieved:

Real-Time Data Flow: Since a Digital Twin constantly gets real time data through sensors and other IoT devices, it can be used to monitor the performance, analyze the efficiency of processes and keep track of KPIs using the data received by BPI tools. The ability of the Digital Twin to provide real-time information to BPI systems guarantees that the businesses can have the latest insights on the performance of the processes as well as the behavior of the assets.

Business Processes Simulation: Although BPI normally utilizes the past or aggregated data to examine the business processes, digital twins can simulate business processes in real time. By acting together, the Digital Twin is able to introduce a virtual space in which various process conditions can be experimented. This simulated environment allows BPI to study the effect of changes or changes in process, and give the managers a stronger means of making decisions.

Predictive Analytics and Forecasting: Digital twins are among the strongest features capable of predicting the further results on the basis of real-time data. Predictive analytics can be employed to forecast process interferences, maintenance, or inefficiencies before they happen when combined with BPI. To use the Digital Twin, as an illustration, in a manufacturing plant, BPI-tools may be used to track the various performance measures such as the throughput of production, whereas the Digital Twin simulates how the machine would behave on the floor. Should the Digital Twin anticipate the possible malfunctioning of a machine, the BPI systems can issue alerts to the operations team and recommend process changes to eliminate delays.

Process Optimisation through Scenario Testing: BPI and Digital Twins can help businesses optimise their processes by testing various scenarios of process optimisation in a virtual context before applying them in the real world. Through such a process, businesses are able to evaluate how the changes (e.g., changes in the production timing, staffing or allocation of resources) would affect the performance of processes, its cost-efficiency, and quality of output. This would help the decision-makers to test different paths and choose the best action to take and minimize the risks of trial and error in the real world operations.(Kreuzer et al., 2024)

6. SIGNIFICANT ADVANTAGES OF CO-LOCATION BETWEEN BPI AND DIGITAL TWINS

BPI and Digital Twins have a number of practical advantages that can assist companies to enhance the efficiency of their operations and their strategy:

6.1 Greater Transparency and Visibility of Processes

Through the combination of BPI and Digital Twins, companies will be able to have a holistic and live experience of their operations. Such a combined strategy provides visibility not only of the flow of work but also the performance of physical resources. To use the example of a supply chain, BPI tools can be used to monitor the flow of goods, whereas Digital Twins can be used to simulate the movement and the status of inventory across multiple sites. This allows the decision-makers to watch the health and the efficiency of the whole system and take decisive steps in order to resolve any problems that emerge.

As an illustration, in logistics, Digital Twins can deliver a live image of delivery trucks, cargo, and the general chain of supply. BPI can use this data to trace the delivery time, pinpoint areas of delays and will point out areas where improvements can be enhanced. It is also possible to respond to challenges more successfully and in a shorter time since both business processes and physical systems are fully transparent to organizations.(Kreuzer et al., 2024)

6.2 Improved Proactive Maintenance and Risk Management

The combination of BPI and Digital Twins can increase predictive maintenance. Traditional schedules in maintenance are based on reactive maintenance or time interval (Maintaining equipment when it fails). Nevertheless, with real-time information of Digital Twins and process performance indicators of BPI, organizations will have the opportunity to predict when a piece of equipment will soon experience a failure, depending on the variables, such as usage.

As an illustration, in a manufacturing facility, Digital Twins is able to simulate the wear and tear of a machine by examining the data of temperature, pressure, and vibration. In addition to the process monitoring tools of BPI, managers are able to know when a machine will need repairs and act to avoid unexpected downtimes. This proactive strategy reduces inconveniences, reduces expenses on maintenance and makes operations a lot easier.(Kreuzer et al., 2024)

6.3 Workflow and Resource Allocation is Optimized

With the help of both BPI and Digital Twins, the resources can be optimized by having a better insight of the way assets and resources are consumed by the business. An example in manufacturing is that BPI can be used to monitor the productivity of a production line, whereas Digital Twins can be used to simulate the functionality of single machines. When these insights are combined, the businesses will be able to resource more efficiently- they can adjust the staffing, equipment use and material distribution in real-time and based on preemptive scenarios.

Indicatively, where the BPI shows that a given production line is working below optimal capacity, Digital twins can be used to model possible changes, including changing machine speeds or rearranging the order of operations, to maximize throughput. This will allow managers to use the optimal mix of resource utilization and workflow design in order to achieve efficiency.(Iglesias et al., 2026b)

6.4. Accelerated Decisions and Greater Agility

By using BPI and Digital Twins, one can hasten the process of making decisions, as it allows receiving not only real-time information but also forecasts as well. With access to both present performance data (through BPI) and forecasts (through Digital Twins), decisions can be taken in an agile and informed manner by the decision-makers in an organization. It is particularly useful in industries with high velocity such as manufacturing, logistics, and energy where the decision-making process requires to be quick in order to prevent disruptions.

As an example, in case a manufacturing plant has an unforeseen supply chain very, then Digital Twins can predict how the disruption is going to impact production, whereas BPI can give real-time information on which resources or products would be impacted the most. This allows the decision-makers to make instant, informed decisions that can be adjusted, like the changes in production time, redistribution of the inventory, or finding other suppliers, to prevent the disruption and ensure that everything proceeds without a problem.(Ibrahim et al., 2026)

6.5 Cost-Saving and Process Optimization

The reduction of costs and enhanced operations are one of the primary accomplishments of combining BPI and Digital Twins. By using real-time monitoring, predictive analysis and simulation, businesses will be able to optimize all aspects of their operations. To illustrate, through Digital Twins to test various scenarios and forecast possible failures or inefficiency, companies can take preemptive measures to modify to avoid expensive downtime or squandering of resources.

BPI may be used to monitor the cost-effectiveness of different business operations, including production, inventory management, or logistics, whereas Digital Twins may be used to model the effects of a change in these processes on the bottom line. Through the testing process, the business can be able to determine the most cost-effective strategies and apply the same to the real life.(Pavleska, 2026b)

Real Life Case: Integration in Manufacturing

A manufacturing facility is another example that can be used to better comprehend how BPI and Digital Twins collaborate. Digital Twin of the production line would give real-time simulation of machines, workers, and materials in operation on the basis of the data provided by the IoT sensors. The BPI tools would study the main indicators of such aspects as the rate of production, use of resources, and condition of equipment and feed that information to the Digital Twin.

When a bottleneck or inefficiency is identified in the production cycle by BPI (a machine is not performing as well as it could or the allocation of resources is not optimal), the Digital Twin can be used to simulate the effect of various solutions-including altering machine speeds, addition of extra shifts, or the optimum allocation of resources- without actually making any physical change. These simulations can then be applied to the decision making process to result in greater process improvements and resource optimization.

Principles of Applying Business Process Intelligence and Digital Twins

The Business Process Intelligence (BPI) and Digital Twins are changing the way organizations operate in different industries. Real-time process data combined with predictive simulations and continuous optimization of businesses increases a clearer insight into its operations, enhanced decision-making, and significant efficiencies. Some of the major sectors and applications of BPI and Digital twins to drive business performance are listed below.(Feng et al., 2025)

7. MANUFACTURING AND INDUSTRY 4.0

The application of Industry 4.0 in the realms of manufacturing is defined by the adoption of smart technologies (the Internet of Things (IoT), artificial intelligence (AI) and automation in the production. The core of the elements of Industry 4.0 objectives such as improved productivity, flexibility and lowering of the cost are all achieved with BPI and Digital Twins.

Real-Time Monitoring and Performance Optimization: Digital Twins give a virtual view of the assets of manufacturing, including machines, robots, and complete production lines, where real-time measurement of sensors is reflected. BPI tools use such data to track the production process, detect inefficiencies, and measure such Key Performance Indicators (KPIs) as speed of production, quality rates, and energy consumption. This will help manufacturers make informed decisions that are aimed at maximizing performance.(Teng et al., 2025)

Predictive Maintenance: One of the most important areas of application of Digital Twins in manufacturing is predictive maintenance. With Digital Twins, businesses can monitor the state of the machines and equipment constantly and forecast when a machine will be a failure or not. Added to BPI, such predictive data can be used to send maintenance warnings, keeping unplanned downtime to a minimum and minimizing the cost of emergency maintenance.(Schink et al., 2026a)

Process Optimization and Resource Allocation: BPI and Digital twins used together enable manufacturers to test various production situations in a virtual environment. In the case of an example, manufacturability can experiment with alterations in machine configurations, employee rotations, or resource repositioning and determine its effects on the overall production process. Workflows, waste, and resource use can be optimized, minimum of waste and better use of resources can be achieved by simulating such changes using Digital Twins and using them in the real world.(Kookalani et al., 2026a)

7.1 Supply Chain and Logistics

Supply chain management refers to the process of coordinating complicated systems of suppliers, manufacturers and distributors. BPI and Digital Twins may be integrated to improve the functioning of any supply chain by offering a glimpse into all the stages of the process and providing opportunities to make better decisions and handle the risks.

End-to-End Supply Chain Visibility: The flow of goods, inventory levels, and lead times can be simulated by an end-to-end supply chain digital twin of the entire supply chain, including the source of raw materials, supply, and end customers. BPI instruments are able to monitor the supply chain performance of each part of the chain like delivery time, cost of transportation and product quality. This would give supply chain managers a holistic and real time view of their supply chain processes which would enable them to understand their bottlenecks, optimize their stocks and enhance efficiency of their supply chain.

Demand Forecasting and Inventory Management: The correct demand forecasting is one of the challenges of the supply chain management. Using Digital Twins in conjunction with BPI, the business is able to simulate the changes in demand and modify their supply chain. As an example, the BPI tools could be used to analyze the history of sales, whereas the Digital Twins can be used to model the effect of different demand levels on production, transportation, and inventory. This will enable the firms to maximize the stock, reduce stockouts, and minimize the chances of overstocking.(Fonseca i Casas & Pi i Palomes, 2026b)

Risk Management and Scenario Planning: Digital Twins allow companies to model possible risks, e.g. a transportation breakdown, a shipment delay, or a change in the performance of suppliers. The simulations enable the supply chain managers to experiment with various risk mitigation options and evaluate the effects of such options prior to their application in the real world. The active methodology assists companies to reduce the impacts of disruptions and enhance their robustness towards unexpected occurrences, like a natural calamity or a change in geopolitical circumstances.

7.2 Healthcare and Medical Devices

BPI and Digital Twins are revolutionizing the patient care, the management of operations, and the development of medical devices in the healthcare industry. With real-time data and virtual simulation, healthcare institutions are able to enhance patient results, streamline operations, and design and enhance the workability of medical equipment.

Personalized Medicine and Patient Monitoring: Digital Twins can simulate a virtual version of a single patient, which is a patient avatar, based on the data of medical record, wearables and sensor devices. Simulating the state of the patient, doctors get an opportunity to discuss various treatment alternatives and forecast the results of various treatments. This enables tailored and efficient treatment programs, enhancing patient care and minimizing the trial and error method, which is usually related to conventional interventions.

Predictive Diagnostics and Early Intervention: BPI tools may be utilized to monitor patient information, including vital signs, lab results, and medication adherence, whereas Digital Twins can be used to give a real-time simulation of health of the patient. This interaction allows the healthcare providers to anticipate the development of a disease or complication before beginning to show up so that they can intervene at an early stage and avoid an expensive medical crisis. Indicatively, a Digital Twin of a heart disease patient can imitate the impacts of various therapies and can point out the most successful therapy to that particular individual.(Lin et al., 2025a)

Medical Simulation and Design: Digital Twins Digital twins are applied to the design and testing of medical equipment, including pacemakers, prosthetics, or diagnostics equipment. Manufacturers are able to develop a virtual representation of a medical device and simulate its behavior in realistic conditions, e.g. how a pacemaker would react to various heart rhythms or how a prosthetic limb will fit the anatomy of a patient. Companies can also maximize product designs, decrease the development time, and enhance the product safety and reliability by integrating BPI and Digital Twins.(Iglesias et al., 2026b)

7.3 Smart City and Urban Planning

The digital technologies aspect of smart cities presupposes improving the quality of life of the inhabitants, maximizing the utilization of resources as well as increasing the efficiency of the city infrastructure. BPI and Digital Twins integration is central to the attainment of these objectives due to the ability to offer a holistic perspective of the urban systems and processes.

Urban Infrastructure Monitoring: Digital Twins has the ability to replicate the infrastructure of a smart city, such as transportation system, energy grid, water system, and garbage collection. The performance of each system can be tracked using BPI tools and measures the things such as the traffic flow, energy consumption, and resource usage. Such integration offers a real-time perspective to the city planners to know how the infrastructure systems are functioning and what can be done to streamline them.(Teng et al., 2025)

Traffic and Transportation Optimization: Traffic simulation and transportation system is one of the most effective uses of Digital Twins in smart cities. Having developed a Digital Twin of the transportation network of a city, the planners can model various traffic conditions, i.e. alterations in roadways, the launch of new public transport tracks, or the influence of special events. BPI tools would be able to monitor the performance indicators, including the congestion rates, travel rates, and emissions of vehicles, as this would allow to plan more efficient transportation systems and minimize traffic-related problems.(He, 2026a)

Energy and Resource Efficiency: Cities produce a huge volume of information concerning the use of energy, the usage of water, waste management, and other resources. Combining BPI and Digital Twins will enable the city administrators to optimize their resources by modeling demand patterns and finding their opportunities of efficiency enhancement. To take a recent example, an example of a Digital Twin of an energy grid in a city can be used to simulate the effect of introducing renewable energy or altering demand so that a city planner can determine how to allocate energy to the best of its abilities and the best of the energy is used efficiently.

7.4 Energy and Utilities

The energy industry is undergoing a significant revolution with the utilities shifting to a more sustainable and efficient way of producing and distributing energy. Digital Twins and BPI play a significant role in assisting energy companies to cope with and optimize their systems, minimize the cost of operations, and shift to renewable energy sources.(Ivanov & Gusikhin, 2026a)

Grid Management and Optimization: Digital Twins of power grids enable the generation, distribution, and consumption of energy in the energy industry in real-time. BPI tools monitor such vital measurements as power flow, voltage, and equipment performance. Through the combination of these technologies, the energy companies will be able to check the performance of the grid in real-time, anticipate the changes in demand, and optimize the power distribution to minimize energy waste, maintain the stability of the grid, and achieve a higher level of efficiency. (Wickremasinghe et al., 2025a)

Renewable Energy Integration: As the energy industry shifts to more eco-friendly energy sources such as solar and wind energy, the Digital Twins and BPI are necessary to manage the fluctuation of renewable energy generation. Digital Twins have the capability to emulate the behavior of renewable energy sources, including solar panels or wind turbines and forecast the effect of weather conditions on energy production. These predictions can then be analyzed using BPI tools to implement optimized energy storage, distribution and consumption strategies.

Predictive Maintenance of Energy Assets: In the energy industry, predictive maintenance is one of the largest uses of Digital Twins, just as in the case of manufacturing. Digital Twins will be able to anticipate when energy assets (turbines, transformers, generators, etc.) need to be serviced by constantly monitoring their health status and avoiding unexpected downtime and minimizing repair expenses. BPI tools are able to monitor the performance indicators, and give information on the time the assets need to be attended to so that the production of energy is reliable and cost effective.(Barbuto et al., 2026)

7.5 Food Production and Agriculture

Another sector that BPI and Digital Twins are being implemented in to maximize production processes, minimize waste, and enhance their sustainability is agriculture. Digital Twins are able to model the actions of a crop, livestock or a complete farming system, whereas the BPI tools evaluate performance by analyzing crop yield, water consumption and environmental impact.

Precision Farming: Digital Twins are able to predict soil conditions, weather conditions, and growth of crops by imitating the conditions of the fields and enabling a farmer to predict outputs and manage the subsequent irrigation and fertilization times. BPI tools have the ability to monitor such metrics as water usage, fertilizer efficiency, and labor productivity so that farmers could maximize waste and enhance crop yields.(Tonelli et al., 2026)

Supply Chain Optimization: BPI and Digital twins can optimize farm to table, a process of food production and distribution. The simulation of the whole food supply chain enables business to realize the inefficiencies, food waste reduction, and inventory optimization. The BPI tools can monitor indicators such as the rates of spoilages, transportation, and delivery time to deliver the food to the consumer in fresh and time-sensitive forms.(Abdessadak et al., 2025a)

8. ADVANTAGES OF BUSINESS PROCESS INTELLIGENCE AND DIGITAL TWINS INTEGRATION

Business Process Intelligence (BPI) and Digital Twins integration have a broad range of advantages that can help organizations streamline their business operations, make better decisions, and optimize their performance in general. With the predictive capabilities and simulations offered by Digital Twins and the real-time, data-driven insights of BPI, a business can have the entire, and dynamic knowledge about its operations. This synergy gives organizations the ability to act proactive to challenges, enhance efficiencies and make smarter decisions that create value. (Olawade et al., 2026)

In this part, we discuss the many advantages of combining BPI and Digital Twins and how such a potent combination can revolutionize the processes of business in any industry.

8.1 Better Decision-Making and Insight Generation

The enhancement of the decision-making is one of the most important advantages of the combination of BPI and Digital Twins. Under the conventional approaches of decision-making, decision-makers usually use stagnant reports, past reports or intuition in making their decisions. Nevertheless, BPI in combination with Digital Twins is expected to offer access to dynamic data, which is real-time and mirrors the reality of the performance of both processes and physical systems. This evidence-based practice will result in superior, quicker, and more precise decision-making. (Iglesias et al., 2026b)

Data-based Deliverables: BPI constantly tracks and analyses business processes in order to identify key performance indicators (KPIs) of throughput, cycle times, and resource usage. Combined with Digital Twins, this information is complemented by real-time models of physical processes that enables decision-makers to have a real-time picture of the whole business environment. Indicatively, within a production plant, the BPI tools can reveal the areas of inefficiency, whereas Digital Twin will provide an overview of the running of the equipment in real-time, allowing managers to make evidence-based decisions to solve bottlenecks or optimize processes. (Kreuzer et al., 2024)

Predictive Decision Support: Digital Twins based on real-time data are simulated to recreate different scenarios, which can then be used to provide predictive analytics to anticipate possible events. With the insights offered by BPI to optimize the process and predictive capabilities of the Digital Twin, decision-makers have an opportunity to experiment with various strategies and determine their effects before the implementation. This enables companies to be proactive in decision-making and avoid problems that will emerge.(Iglesias et al., 2026b)

8.2 Efficiency in Operations and Process Optimization

BPI combined with Digital Twins improves business operational efficiency because it gives businesses an overall picture of their processes, systems, and assets.

Companies are able to determine areas of inefficiency, streamline and run more efficient workflows, and budget resources effectively.

Real-Time Control and Optimization: Organizations can use the continuous optimization of business processes with the assistance of the Digital Twin (which simulates physical assets in real-time) and BPI (which monitors business processes in real-time). To provide an example, in manufacturing, BPI is able to monitor production information and performance measures whereas Digital Twins model the behavior of machines, employees, and materials. Through constant examination of operational data and the physical simulations, organizations are able to detect inefficiencies, adjust in real time as well as keep on improving performance.

Scenario Testing and Optimization: Simulation of different scenarios through Digital Twins enables businesses to test modification of business processes prior to actual physical changes being made. To illustrate, a Digital Twin model can be used to evaluate how alterations in a production schedule, resource allocation or process flow may influence an organization. The results can then be analyzed using BPI tools and suggested as the best strategies to use in making the operations more efficient to enable the businesses optimize their operations with minimum risks.

Resource Utilization: BPI in combination with Digital Twins can help businesses to become more efficient in the usage of resources, including labor, equipment, and materials. Through real-time data analysis and simulation of the effects of different operational changes, businesses are able to allocate their resources more efficiently, minimize waste, and maximize their productivity.(Pavleska, 2026b)

8.3 Improved Maintenance Prognostics and Less Down Time

The advantages of combining BPI and Digital Twins in the predictive maintenance area are one of the most influential. With the help of Digital Twins that constantly track the condition of equipment and BPI that analyze the data on operations, organizations will be able to anticipate the time when machines or systems will fail and take appropriate measures to avoid the failure of equipment before it takes place. This minimises unplanned downtime, minimizes maintenance expenses and maximises asset life.

Proactive Maintenance: Digital Twins monitor the health of assets in real time through the provision of information via sensors attached to machines and vehicles, as well as infrastructure. This data can be combined with BPI to determine when an asset will need a maintenance or repair. As an example, the performance of equipment can be analyzed with the help of BPI tools to monitor wear and tear and compare them with operating standards. Through this analysis, Digital Twin will be able to predict possible failure scenarios and suggest maintenance schedules without downtime and with better life expectancy.

Cost Savings: Owing to the transition to proactive maintenance over reactive maintenance, organizations will be able to limit expensive repairs, avoid disastrous failures and increase the lifespan of assets. Predictive maintenance aids in the company to save the expenses involved in unplanned downtimes and emergency repairs and hence saving a lot of money.(Ivanov & Gusikhin, 2026a)

8.4 Economy of Scale and Improved Redistribution of Resources

The synergy of BPI and Digital Twins is beneficial to businesses in that it assists business in cutting down costs without compromising inefficiency, optimization of processes, and allocation of resources in all areas of business. This leads to improved decisions regarding investments, human resources, energy consumption, and other important operation expenses.

Less Wasting: BPI also helps businesses reduce their wastage by constantly analyzing data regarding operations, and thus they can determine sections where resources (e.g. materials, labor, or time) are wasting. By using Digital Twins, organizations are able to simulate different changes that can be made to workflows and processes to determine their effects on the utilization of resources. As an illustration, a manufacturer can take advantage of Digital Twins to model various production processes and study their implications on the usage of resources. BPI can then monitor the cost of every scenario thus allowing the businesses to choose the most efficient and cost effective alternative.(Kookalani et al., 2026a)

Energy and Utilities Optimization: BPI and Digital Twins integration can help reduce costs significantly in the energy-intensive industries in the areas of energy use and utility utilization. Digital Twins can assist businesses in determining areas of inefficiency and improve the use of energy by mimicking energy flows and tracking consumption patterns, which will decrease the total operating cost.(Wickremasinghe et al., 2025a)

More effective Division of Resources: The synergy between BPI and Digital Twins will enable organizations to maximize resource allocation (people, machinery, raw materials, etc.). To illustrate that, in logistics, BPI could be used to analyze the productivity of warehouses, whereas Digital Twins could be used to simulate the movement of inventory. Through simulation, by determining the best warehouse pattern and optimizing inventory by simulation, firms can minimise the operation costs and maximise the throughput.(Hasan & Nguyen, 2026)

8.5 Accelerated Innovation and Risk-Free Testing

BPI and Digital Twins will make innovation faster because a business can test new ideas, products or processes in the virtual world and then apply them to reality. This does not only accelerate the process of innovation but also minimizes the risks of trial and error experimentation.

Simulation of New Processes: Digital Twins give organizations the opportunity to simulate the effect of a new process design, manufacturing process, or change in operations inside the organization. This simulation can be evaluated in conjunction with BPI, and therefore, the businesses could experiment with various situations and choose the most appropriate course of action without having to budget on physical prototypes or real-life implementations.(Das et al., 2026)

Product Development and Testing: Digital twins can be utilized in product development to develop virtual product models and simulate how they behave in various conditions. The progress of the development could be traced using BPI tools and measure the time to market, utilization of resources, and cost. With the two technologies, organizations are able to optimize product designs, test new concepts in a short period of time and therefore, have faster time-to-market and improved products.(Abdessadak et al., 2025a)

Less Risk: Digital Twins enable companies to explore alternative changes in a safe virtual environment, and in this way, the risk of failure in the real world is also reduced. The capacity to simulate scenarios whether it concerns testing of new business strategies, changes in production, or even designs of the products means that businesses can be able to innovate with more confidence.(Cappiello et al., 2026)

8.6 Better Customer Experience and Service Delivery

Customer experience is also improved by the integration of BPI and Digital Twins, which help businesses to comprehend and anticipate customer behavior more, better the quality of products, and provide a more personalized experience.

Individual Customer Experiences: With the help of Digital Twins, one can simulate the various experiences and relationships with customers by creating virtual versions of the customer journeys. Given this, customer behavior, preferences, and feedback can be analyzed using BPI tools in order to assist organizations to customize their products or services to satisfy individual needs. This one-on-one treatment results in more customer satisfaction and loyalty.

Quality Control and Assurance: BPI and Digital Twins are used together in the industries like manufacturing to maintain the quality of products. Digital Twins are used to simulate the behaviour of machines and production lines in real-time, BPI measures performance metrics of processes like defect rates, cycle times and quality of output. This combination will assist businesses to detect quality problems early in time and make corrective measures before the products are released to the customer hence enhancing the quality of products and minimizing returns. (Marfoglia et al., 2026)

8.7 Operations Flexibility and Scalability

With the growth and expansion of organizations, BPI and Digital Twins integration allow them to scale their operations efficiently and remain flexible and adaptable.

Scalable Operations: Digital Twins can be used to simulate various scenarios in the operation of the enterprise and hence enables businesses to test how varying a single aspect of the process will impact the whole system. This flexibility is also helpful in that as businesses grow in size, they are able to easily modify their operations to suit higher levels of production, new markets or extra product lines without ruining their current processes.

Adaptation to Change: in a rapidly changing industry, like retail or technology, BPI and Digital Twins together offer the adaptability needed to keep up with the competition. Real-time data and predictive simulations enable businesses to constantly optimize their processes, experiment with new approaches and innovations, so that the business is well-equipped to evolve in accordance with changing market conditions.(de las Morenas et al., 2025)

Case Study

1. Manufacturing: General Electric's Digital Twin Implementation

General Electric (GE), a global leader in industrial manufacturing, has effectively implemented Digital Twin technology in its gas turbine manufacturing process. GE uses sensors installed in their turbines to collect real-time data on parameters such as temperature, vibration, and pressure. This data is then used to create a dynamic simulation or Digital Twin of each turbine. With the help of BPI tools, GE constantly monitors key performance indicators (KPIs) like efficiency, fuel consumption, and maintenance needs. By integrating BPI with Digital Twins, GE can predict potential failures before they happen, schedule preventative maintenance, and improve turbine performance by making adjustments in real-time.

The combined use of BPI and Digital Twins has led to significant cost savings, as it helps GE minimize unplanned downtime, optimize fuel consumption, and reduce maintenance costs. In addition, the technology enhances decision-making by providing engineers with a more accurate understanding of turbine performance, which directly contributes to improved efficiency across GE's entire fleet of turbines. For example, GE reported a 10-15% increase in operational efficiency and a reduction in downtime by 20% after implementing this technology.

This case study demonstrates how the integration of BPI and Digital Twins can transform a traditionally heavy industry like manufacturing, making it more responsive, data-driven, and cost-efficient.(Ivanov & Gusikhin, 2026b)

2. Healthcare: Philips Healthcare's Personalized Patient Care

Philips Healthcare has been at the forefront of integrating Digital Twin technology into the healthcare sector. One notable application is in the development of personalized patient avatars. By creating a Digital Twin of an individual patient, healthcare providers can simulate how different medical treatments or interventions will affect the patient's condition in real-time. For instance, Philips created a Digital Twin for heart disease patients to predict how their condition would evolve with various treatments.(Lin et al., 2025b)

The Digital Twin receives continuous updates from the patient's medical records, wearables, and diagnostic devices, allowing it to provide accurate forecasts on treatment efficacy, recovery times, and risks. BPI tools are used to monitor and analyze key metrics such as heart rate, blood pressure, and medication adherence, feeding real-time insights into the patient's digital avatar. This enables healthcare providers to fine-tune treatment plans based on individual responses, reducing trial and error in the treatment process and enhancing patient outcomes.

Philips also uses this technology to improve the design and testing of medical devices. By simulating how medical equipment will perform under various conditions, the company can optimize device performance and safety before mass production. This results in faster time-to-market, lower costs, and higher-quality healthcare products.

This example illustrates the value of BPI and Digital Twin integration in healthcare, especially in providing tailored treatments, optimizing device design, and enhancing patient care.

3. Logistics: DHL's Supply Chain Optimization with Digital Twins

DHL, a global leader in logistics, has implemented Digital Twin technology to enhance its supply chain management. By creating a Digital Twin of its global logistics network, DHL can simulate and monitor every aspect of the supply chain in real-time. This includes tracking shipments, optimizing routes, and managing inventory levels across warehouses and distribution centers.

BPI tools are used to analyze data on delivery times, fuel costs, and shipment delays, allowing DHL to identify inefficiencies in its logistics operations. The Digital Twin helps to visualize the entire supply chain process and predicts disruptions caused by factors such as weather, traffic, or geopolitical events. By running simulations in a virtual environment, DHL can test different scenarios, such as route changes or alternative suppliers, to see how they would affect the overall performance of the supply chain.

As a result, DHL has significantly improved its ability to respond to supply chain disruptions. The company has reduced transportation costs by 15% and enhanced customer satisfaction by improving delivery accuracy and speed. In one case, DHL used this technology to reroute deliveries during a major snowstorm, ensuring that shipments were delivered on time despite the extreme weather conditions.

DHL's use of BPI and Digital Twin technology in logistics underscores the value of real-time visibility and predictive analytics in optimizing global supply chains.

4. Smart Cities: Singapore's Smart Traffic Management with Digital Twins

Singapore is known for its smart city initiatives, and Digital Twin technology plays a crucial role in its urban planning and traffic management systems. The city has developed a Digital Twin of its entire transportation network, which includes roads, traffic lights, public transport systems, and pedestrian walkways. Sensors embedded throughout the city collect real-time data on traffic flow, congestion, and transit usage.(Loia et al., 2026b)

Using BPI tools, city planners monitor and analyze traffic performance metrics such as average speed, congestion levels, and public transport utilization. This data is fed into the Digital Twin, which simulates different traffic scenarios and helps decision-makers optimize traffic light timings, manage public transport schedules, and improve road infrastructure. By modeling different conditions (e.g., rush hour, accidents, or public events), the city can predict traffic bottlenecks and proactively implement measures to avoid them.

The integration of BPI and Digital Twin technology has led to significant improvements in traffic management, reducing congestion by 20% and travel time by 10%. The system also provides a more responsive approach to city management by enabling planners to adjust in real-time to changing conditions.

Singapore's smart city initiative is an excellent example of how BPI and Digital Twins can improve urban living by enhancing transportation systems, optimizing resource allocation, and minimizing disruptions.

9. ANALYTICAL SUMMARY: STRATEGIC ADVANTAGES OF INTEGRATING BPI AND DIGITAL TWINS

The integration of Business Process Intelligence (BPI) and Digital Twin technologies offers organizations a powerful toolkit to drive operational excellence, improve decision-making, and enhance overall business performance. This chapter has explored how each of these technologies contributes to data-driven insights and real-time process optimization, but their combined impact is where the real value lies.

1. Enhanced Decision-Making and Predictive Insights

BPI provides the data analytics and performance monitoring capabilities that allow organizations to see their processes in action. However, it is the Digital Twin that takes this data to the next level by simulating potential future scenarios and offering predictive insights. This predictive capability allows decision-makers to not only understand current inefficiencies but also forecast risks, anticipate failures, and proactively optimize their processes. As a result, companies can move from reactive to proactive management, making faster, more informed decisions that enhance business agility and responsiveness.(Schink et al., 2026b)

2. Process Optimization and Efficiency Gains

By integrating BPI and Digital Twins, organizations can optimize business processes in real-time, ensuring that they run at peak efficiency. While BPI helps organizations continuously monitor KPIs and process performance, Digital Twins create a virtual replica of the physical systems, enabling businesses to test various operational scenarios without real-world consequences. This virtual testing helps companies experiment with changes, evaluate the impact of those changes, and choose the most optimal approach—reducing trial-and-error costs and minimizing operational risks. The result is optimized workflows that enhance productivity and efficiency.

3. Cost Reduction and Predictive Maintenance

One of the most immediate benefits of combining BPI and Digital Twins is cost reduction. Traditional maintenance schedules are often based on fixed intervals or reactive measures, leading to unnecessary downtime and inflated maintenance costs. By combining real-time data from BPI with the predictive capabilities of Digital Twins, organizations can adopt predictive maintenance strategies. This allows them to anticipate when equipment will fail or when a process will experience inefficiencies, enabling businesses to take corrective action before issues arise. Predictive maintenance, in turn, reduces downtime, unplanned maintenance costs, and resource waste, ultimately leading to substantial cost savings and improved asset utilization. (Wickremasinghe et al., 2025b)

4. Real-Time Visibility and Transparency

The integration of BPI and Digital Twins offers unparalleled visibility into both business processes and the physical systems that drive those processes. BPI continuously monitors the flow of information within processes, while Digital Twins provide a real-time digital representation of the physical assets or systems. This integration allows organizations to track the performance of systems in real-time, identify potential bottlenecks, and optimize resource allocation with precision. For example, in logistics, companies can track the status of inventory and shipments, while simultaneously simulating how changes in one part of the supply chain affect the entire system. This holistic visibility ensures that decision-makers can act quickly and efficiently when disruptions occur.

5. Accelerated Innovation and Competitive Advantage

Organizations that integrate BPI and Digital Twins gain a significant competitive advantage. By leveraging real-time data, predictive insights, and simulation capabilities, businesses can accelerate the innovation cycle. Digital Twins allow companies to test new products, processes, or designs virtually before committing to costly real-world changes. Whether it's adjusting the production schedule, testing new features in a product, or simulating market responses, businesses can iterate and innovate faster, reducing time-to-market and improving product quality. As a result, these companies are better positioned to respond to shifting market conditions and stay ahead of competitors.(Abdessadak et al., 2025b)

6. Digital Transformation and Organizational Resilience

The integration of BPI and Digital Twins is a cornerstone of digital transformation. Organizations that adopt these technologies are better equipped to navigate the complexities of today's data-driven and fast-paced business environment. The ability to monitor, predict, and optimize operations in real-time ensures that businesses can adapt to changes quickly—whether they're driven by market trends, technological advancements, or external disruptions (e.g., supply chain crises, economic shifts). As businesses continue to evolve digitally, the use of BPI and Digital Twins will play a pivotal role in shaping resilient, data-driven organizations that are prepared to meet both present and future challenges.

Actionable Insights for Businesses

To successfully implement BPI and Digital Twin technologies, organizations should:

- Identify key processes: Start by pinpointing areas in the business where optimization will yield the highest impact. For example, in manufacturing, focus on production lines, while in logistics, prioritize inventory and shipment management.
- Ensure robust data collection: Invest in a strong data collection infrastructure that includes IoT devices, sensors, and process monitoring tools. This will enable accurate and real-time data for the Digital Twin simulations.
- Align technologies with business objectives: BPI and Digital Twin technologies should be deployed in alignment with organizational goals, ensuring that the data insights and predictions generated directly contribute to strategic decision-making.
- Promote a culture of continuous improvement: Foster an environment where data-driven insights are consistently used to challenge existing practices and implement more efficient solutions.

CONCLUSION: BUSINESS PROCESS INTELLIGENCE AND DIGITAL TWINS

Business Process Intelligence (BPI) and Digital Twins integration is the new milestone of Business management, optimization, and innovativeness. These two technologies contribute to the table distinct advantages: BPI is oriented to continuous monitoring of processes, their analysis and optimization based on facts, and Digital Twins provide a dynamic and live virtual ecosystem of physical objects, systems, and processes that allow to simulate, conduct predictive analytics, and test scenarios. Together, these technologies give organisations a comprehensive perspective of the inner process of their organizations and the actual operations to make smarter and more informed decisions.

With growing complexity, competition, and demands of swift adaptation among industries, BPI and Digital Twins combined can enable companies to handle these issues more suitably. This integration has increased operational efficiency, optimization of resources and risk management, and, at the same time, promotes innovation and continuous improvement. Establishing a business environment can now model and forecast results prior to implementation into the real world and therefore not only does this minimize the risk involved in application of trial-and-error methods, but also the turnaround time in the innovation process is much faster and an organization is able to respond more rapidly to changes in the market and customer needs.

There are several advantages of the real-time insights that Digital Twins can provide, combined with the process optimization opportunities that can be offered by BPI, in a broad range of industries, including manufacturing, supply chain management, healthcare, smart cities, energy, and agriculture. With the combination of the two technologies, companies can establish more resilient, flexible, and data-driven operations that are in a position to react to arising challenges and opportunities.

In addition, these technologies are not limited to improved operations, in fact, they directly add to customer experiences, product quality, and service provision. This is achieved through better design of products, predicting service requirements, and offering customised services, which put the businesses in a better position to address the changing requirements of customers.

After all, to keep optimizing the operations, innovating at a greater pace, and using the data in a way that would matter are the keys to future business success. Since BPI and Digital Twins are still developing and growing in various industries, integration will become a pillar of digital transformation as companies can keep pace with the trends, create efficiencies, and produce better results in an ever-competitive world.

REFERENCES

Abdessadak, A., Ghennioui, H., Thirion-Moreau, N., Elbhiri, B., Abraim, M., & Merzouk, S. (2025a). Digital twin technology and artificial intelligence in energy transition: A comprehensive systematic review of applications. In *Energy Reports* (Vol. 13, pp. 5196–5218). Elsevier Ltd., DOI: 10.1016/j.egyr.2025.04.060

Abdessadak, A., Ghennioui, H., Thirion-Moreau, N., Elbhiri, B., Abraim, M., & Merzouk, S. (2025b). Digital twin technology and artificial intelligence in energy transition: A comprehensive systematic review of applications. In *Energy Reports* (Vol. 13, pp. 5196–5218). Elsevier Ltd., DOI: 10.1016/j.egyr.2025.04.060

Banad, Y. M., Sharif, S. S., & Rezaei, Z. (2025). Artificial intelligence and machine learning for smart grids: from foundational paradigms to emerging technologies with digital twin and large language model-driven intelligence. In *Energy Conversion and Management: X* (Vol. 28). Elsevier Ltd., DOI: 10.1016/j.ecmx.2025.101329

Barbuto, V., Savaglio, C., Lee, E. A., & Fortino, G. (2026). Engineering opportunistic digital twins with lingua franca. *Future Generation Computer Systems, 178*, 108262. DOI: 10.1016/j.future.2025.108262

Cappiello, G., Casoli, D., Tuan, A., & Visentin, M. (2026). From digital tools to sustainable change: How change agents enable the twin transition in hospitality. *International Journal of Hospitality Management, 134*, 104591. Advance online publication. DOI: 10.1016/j.ijhm.2026.104591

Das, P., Woods, O., & Kong, L. (2026). Modelling nature? The digital twinning and untwinning of urban farms. *Geoforum, 170*, 104539. DOI: 10.1016/j.geoforum.2026.104539

de las Morenas, J., Belmonte, L. M., & Morales, R. (2025). Designing an AI-driven digital twin architecture for building energy prediction. *Journal of Building Engineering, 113*, 113966. Advance online publication. DOI: 10.1016/j.jobe.2025.113966

Feng, C., Reed, K. F., Giordano, J. O., & You, F. (2025). Precision decarbonization for clean dairy farming with digital twin and edge intelligence. In *Nexus* (Vol. 2, Number 4). Cell Press. DOI: 10.1016/j.ynexs.2025.100105

Fonseca i Casas, P., & Pi i Palomes, X. (2026a). Building Society 5.0: A foundation for decision-making based on open models and digital twins. *Advanced Engineering Informatics, 69*, 103970. Advance online publication. DOI: 10.1016/j.aei.2025.103970

Fonseca i Casas, P., & Pi i Palomes, X. (2026b). Building Society 5.0: A foundation for decision-making based on open models and digital twins. *Advanced Engineering Informatics, 69*, 103970. Advance online publication. DOI: 10.1016/j.aei.2025.103970

Fornari, F., Compagnucci, I., Callisto De Donato, M., Bertrand, Y., Beyel, H. H., Carrión, E., Franceschetti, M., Groher, W., Grüger, J., Kilic, E., Koschmider, A., Leotta, F., Li, C. Y., Lugaresi, G., Malburg, L., Mangler, J., Mecella, M., Pastor, O., Riss, U., . . . Valderas, P. (2025). Digital Twins of Business Processes: A Research Manifesto. In *Internet of Things (The Netherlands)* (Vol. 30). Elsevier B.V. DOI: 10.1016/j.iot.2024.101477

Hasan, A., & Nguyen, D. T. (2026). Integrating agentic AI and digital twins for intelligent decision-making systems. *Array (New York, N.Y.), 29*, 100721. DOI: 10.1016/j.array.2026.100721

He, Y. (2026a). Rewiring industrial futures: The role of AI-enabled digital twins in energy productivity transitions. *International Review of Economics & Finance, 105*, 104898. Advance online publication. DOI: 10.1016/j.iref.2026.104898

He, Y. (2026b). Rewiring industrial futures: The role of AI-enabled digital twins in energy productivity transitions. *International Review of Economics & Finance, 105*, 104898. Advance online publication. DOI: 10.1016/j.iref.2026.104898

Ibrahim, N. I., Vering, C., Giannetti, N., & Kim, M. Sholahudin, Storek, T., Müller, D., & Saito, K. (2026). State-of-the-art of the digital twin concept in HVAC+R systems for thermal management of buildings. In *Renewable and Sustainable Energy Reviews* (Vol. 229). Elsevier Ltd. DOI: 10.1016/j.rser.2025.116601

Iglesias, F., Ros, F., Hoang, L., Thuy, V., Gourcy, L., Moquet, J.-S., Daële, V., & Dupraz, S. (2026a). *A conceptual architecture for AI-assisted Digital Twins in natural resource management*. https://doi.org/DOI: 10.48436/b615a

Iglesias, F., Ros, F., Hoang, L., Thuy, V., Gourcy, L., Moquet, J.-S., Daële, V., & Dupraz, S. (2026b). *A conceptual architecture for AI-assisted Digital Twins in natural resource management*. https://doi.org/DOI: 10.48436/b615a

Ivanov, D., & Gusikhin, O. (2026a). Supply chain digital twin design and implementation at scale: A case study at the Ford Motor Company and generalizations. *Omega, 139*, 103447. Advance online publication. DOI: 10.1016/j.omega.2025.103447

Ivanov, D., & Gusikhin, O. (2026b). Supply chain digital twin design and implementation at scale: A case study at the Ford Motor Company and generalizations. *Omega, 139*, 103447. Advance online publication. DOI: 10.1016/j.omega.2025.103447

Kookalani, S., Green, S., Luo, P., Alavi, H., Parn, E., Sun, Z., & Brilakis, I. (2026a). Mapping digital twin applications in infrastructure and the built environment across research types, methods, sectors, phases, and scales. *Automation in Construction, 182*, 106778. DOI: 10.1016/j.autcon.2026.106778

Kookalani, S., Green, S., Luo, P., Alavi, H., Parn, E., Sun, Z., & Brilakis, I. (2026b). Mapping digital twin applications in infrastructure and the built environment across research types, methods, sectors, phases, and scales. *Automation in Construction, 182*, 106778. DOI: 10.1016/j.autcon.2026.106778

Kreuzer, T., Papapetrou, P., & Zdravkovic, J. (2024). Artificial intelligence in digital twins—A systematic literature review. *Data & Knowledge Engineering, 151*, 102304. Advance online publication. DOI: 10.1016/j.datak.2024.102304

Lin, T. Y., Ming-Fang Yen, A., Li-Sheng Chen, S., Hsu, C. Y., Yeh, Y. P., & Hsiu-Hsi Chen, T. (2025a). Artificial intelligence for precision viral surveillance of emerging infectious disease (EID): Data-driven digital twin metaverse-envisioned study. *Computers in Biology and Medicine, 196*, 110877. Advance online publication. DOI: 10.1016/j.compbiomed.2025.110877 PMID: 40773996

Lin, T. Y., Ming-Fang Yen, A., Li-Sheng Chen, S., Hsu, C. Y., Yeh, Y. P., & Hsiu-Hsi Chen, T. (2025b). Artificial intelligence for precision viral surveillance of emerging infectious disease (EID): Data-driven digital twin metaverse-envisioned study. *Computers in Biology and Medicine, 196*, 110877. Advance online publication. DOI: 10.1016/j.compbiomed.2025.110877 PMID: 40773996

Loia, F., Perillo, C., & Gravili, G. (2026a). Unleashing the power of digital twin and big data as a new frontier for smart mobility: An ecosystem perspective. *Big Data Research, 43*, 100576. Advance online publication. DOI: 10.1016/j.bdr.2025.100576

Loia, F., Perillo, C., & Gravili, G. (2026b). Unleashing the power of digital twin and big data as a new frontier for smart mobility: An ecosystem perspective. *Big Data Research, 43*, 100576. Advance online publication. DOI: 10.1016/j.bdr.2025.100576

Marfoglia, A., D'Errico, C., Mellone, S., & Carbonaro, A. (2026). A Knowledge Graph-Driven Framework for Deploying AI-Powered Patient Digital Twins. *Future Generation Computer Systems, 108380*, 108380. Advance online publication. DOI: 10.1016/j.future.2026.108380

Olawade, D. B., Oisakede, E. O., Bello, O. J., Analikwu, C. C., Egbon, E., & Ojo, A. (2026). Digital twins in oncology: From predictive modelling to personalised treatment strategies. *Critical Reviews in Oncology/Hematology, 220*, 105171. Advance online publication. DOI: 10.1016/j.critrevonc.2026.105171 PMID: 41621635

Pavleska, T. (2026a). Taxonomy of digital twins for power grids. *Advanced Engineering Informatics, 70*, 104124. DOI: 10.1016/j.aei.2025.104124

Pavleska, T. (2026b). Taxonomy of digital twins for power grids. *Advanced Engineering Informatics, 70*, 104124. DOI: 10.1016/j.aei.2025.104124

Schink, A., Gutmann, T., & Brenk, S. (2026a). Transforming B2B platforms through interconnected digital twins: Enhancing situation awareness for decision-making. *Technovation, 149*, 103368. Advance online publication. DOI: 10.1016/j.technovation.2025.103368

Schink, A., Gutmann, T., & Brenk, S. (2026b). Transforming B2B platforms through interconnected digital twins: Enhancing situation awareness for decision-making. *Technovation, 149*, 103368. Advance online publication. DOI: 10.1016/j.technovation.2025.103368

Teng, X., Shen, Z., & Zhang, Y. (2025). Rule-based symbolic AI computing-driven digital twin model for ex-ante energy evaluation of task-ambience air conditioning systems in zero-energy buildings. *Sustainable Cities and Society, 134*, 106947. Advance online publication. DOI: 10.1016/j.scs.2025.106947

Tonelli, F., Paolucci, M., Giovannetti, A., Mosca, M., & Torterolo, L. (2026). Integrated 3D Simulation and Digital Twin Framework for Collaborative Production Process Design and Planning in Small and Medium Enterprises: A Use Case Analysis. *Procedia CIRP, 138*, 48–53. DOI: 10.1016/j.procir.2026.01.010

Wickremasinghe, G., Frost, S., Rafferty, K., & Sharma, V. (2025a). Sustainable business decision modelling with blockchain and digital twins: A survey. *Blockchain: Research and Applications, 100312*. Advance online publication. DOI: 10.1016/j.bcra.2025.100312

Wickremasinghe, G., Frost, S., Rafferty, K., & Sharma, V. (2025b). Sustainable business decision modelling with blockchain and digital twins: A survey. *Blockchain: Research and Applications, 100312*. Advance online publication. DOI: 10.1016/j.bcra.2025.100312

KEY TERMS AND DEFINITIONS

Business Process Intelligence (BPI): Business Process Intelligence refers to the use of data analytics, process mining, and performance monitoring tools to provide organizations with insights into their business processes. The goal of BPI is to monitor, analyze, and optimize business processes in real-time, helping organizations identify inefficiencies, improve decision-making, and enhance operational performance.

Continuous Optimization: Continuous Optimization refers to the ongoing process of improving business operations by using real-time data and simulations to identify areas for improvement. With the integration of BPI and Digital Twins, continuous optimization allows businesses to adapt and refine processes dynamically as new data becomes available.

Digital Twin: A Digital Twin is a virtual replica of a physical object, system, or process. It leverages real-time data from sensors, IoT devices, and other sources to create a dynamic, data-driven simulation of the real-world counterpart. This virtual model allows organizations to visualize, simulate, and analyze the behavior and performance of physical assets or systems, enabling predictive maintenance, scenario testing, and process optimization.

Key Performance Indicators (KPIs): KPIs are measurable metrics that organizations use to track and evaluate the success of their business processes. Examples include cycle time, throughput rate, cost per unit, customer satisfaction, and error rates. BPI tools monitor these KPIs in real-time to provide insights into the effectiveness of operations.

Predictive Analytics: Predictive Analytics is the use of historical data, statistical algorithms, and machine learning techniques to predict future events or trends. In the context of BPI and Digital Twins, predictive analytics helps organizations forecast performance issues, maintenance needs, or process inefficiencies before they occur.

Process Mining: Process Mining is a method used to analyze and visualize business processes by extracting data from IT systems (e.g., ERP, CRM, and SCM). It helps to map out how processes are executed in reality, highlighting deviations from expected workflows and identifying inefficiencies or bottlenecks.

Chapter 2
Cyber-Physical Architecture for Digital Twin-Enabled Intelligent Enterprises

Hossein Abdi
http://orcid.org/0009-0003-6528-3662
Bio10, Australia

Naser Heidari
Bio10, Dubai, UAE

ABSTRACT

In recent years, digital twins have emerged as one of the key technologies in the digital transformation of organizations. This research examines architectures based on cyber-physical systems for the development of intelligent organizations based on digital twins. In this framework, the layered structure of the architecture including physical infrastructure, data collection, communications, digital modeling, data analysis, and decision-making systems has been analyzed. The role of data synchronization, analytical engines, and integration with enterprise platforms in improving system performance has also been investigated. The results show that digital twins can help increase the efficiency, flexibility, and intelligence of organizations by providing a comprehensive view of operations and supporting data-driven decision-making.

DOI: 10.4018/979-8-3373-9998-0.ch002

1. INTRODUCTION

In recent years, organizations around the world have faced a wave of technological developments that have fundamentally changed the way industrial and service systems are designed, managed, and operated. The spread of digital technologies, the development of data infrastructures, and the increase in the power of information processing and analysis have led organizations to move towards new models of management and decision-making. In this context, the concept of the digital twin has emerged as one of the most important tools for digital transformation; a concept that allows the creation of a dynamic virtual representation of physical systems and through which the behavior of real systems in digital environments can be observed, analyzed, and even predicted (Li et al., 2026).

A digital twin is not just a simple simulation model of a physical system, but a dynamic, data-driven structure that continuously interacts with the real system. This interaction is formed through data streams collected from sensors, industrial equipment, and operational systems. With the help of this data, the digital model is able to reflect the state of the physical system in real time and at the same time evaluate different operational scenarios. Such a capability has made digital twins a key component in the management of complex systems, especially in advanced industries, smart manufacturing and supply chains (Bordbar et al., 2026).

Along with the development of this concept, the emergence of cyber-physical systems has also played an important role in the formation of intelligent enterprise infrastructures. Cyber-physical systems refer to structures in which physical components, computing infrastructures and communication networks interact with each other in an integrated manner. In such an environment, data generated in the physical space is quickly transferred to cyberspace and, after analysis and processing, decisions and control commands are returned to the operational systems. This two-way interaction between the physical and digital worlds enables continuous feedback loops that ultimately lead to improved system performance and increased organizational intelligence (Leng et al., 2019).

In this context, leading organizations are gradually moving towards the model of intelligent organizations. In such organizations, decision-making is not based solely on experience or static analysis, but real-time data, analytical models, and predictive tools play a decisive role in process management. The use of digital twins alongside cyber-physical infrastructures allows systems to be continuously monitored and management decisions to be made based on accurate, data-driven analysis. The result of such an approach is increased operational efficiency, reduced uncertainty in decision-making, and improved organizational ability to cope with environmental changes (Yordanova & Nozari, 2026).

Despite significant advances in digital technologies, one of the fundamental challenges in the development of intelligent organizations is the lack of coherent architectures to integrate the various components of this ecosystem. In many cases, data systems, analytical models, communication infrastructures, and decision-making systems have been developed in a fragmented manner, with insufficient structural coordination between them. As a result, achieving an architectural framework that can organize the interaction between the physical, data, analytical, and management layers in a systematic manner has become one of the fundamental needs in designing organizations based on digital twins.

Cyber-physical architectures can serve as a framework for organizing these interactions. By defining the different layers of the system, from physical infrastructure and sensors to digital models, analytical engines, and decision-making systems, such architectures enable the creation of a coherent structure for managing the flow of data and knowledge in the organization. In this structure, data collected from physical systems is transferred to digital twin models, then processed through analytical tools and intelligent algorithms, and finally converted into management and control decisions. Such a process can pave the way for the formation of organizations that are not only capable of continuous monitoring of operations, but also have the ability to predict and optimize their performance.

Accordingly, the main goal of this chapter is to present an architectural framework for intelligent organizations based on digital twins in the context of cyber-physical systems. This framework attempts to explain the relationship between different layers of the system, from physical and data infrastructure to analysis and decision-making layers, in a structured manner. It also examines the interaction between digital twins and operational systems in the form of data and feedback loops. Such an approach can provide a more comprehensive understanding of the role of cyber-physical architectures in the development of intelligent organizations and clarify the path to designing data- and model-based organizational systems.

2. DIGITAL TWINS AND THE EMERGENCE OF INTELLIGENT ENTERPRISES

The spread of digital technologies in the last decade has led to the formation of new patterns in the management of organizations. Today's organizations are no longer managed solely on the basis of traditional decision-making structures and static analyses, but have gradually moved towards models in which data, advanced analytics and digital models play a central role in guiding operations. In such circumstances, the concept of digital twin has been proposed as one of the most important tools for organizational transformation; a concept that allows the creation of a dynamic representation of real systems in the digital environment and through which the performance of physical systems can be monitored, analyzed and even predicted in real time (Bordbar et al., 2026).

Digital twin in its simplest definition refers to a dynamic digital model of an asset, process or physical system that is connected to the real system through a continuous flow of data. This connection allows the digital model to be continuously updated and can reflect the real state of the system with high accuracy. Unlike traditional simulation models, which are usually based on historical data or static assumptions, digital twins are able to receive real-time data and analyze system behavior based on it. Such a capability has made this technology one of the key tools in the management of complex systems, especially in areas such as smart manufacturing, industrial asset management, and supply chains (Hasan & Nguyen, 2026).

One of the important features of digital twins is their ability to create a link between the physical and digital space. In this framework, data collected by sensors and operational equipment is transferred to a data infrastructure and then analyzed in the form of digital models. The results of these analyses can be fed back to operational systems in the form of management recommendations, optimization scenarios, or even control commands. This feedback loop enables organizations to continuously evaluate the performance of their systems and, if necessary, make necessary changes to operational processes (Tao et al., 2019).

In such a context, the concept of an intelligent organization is gradually taking shape. An intelligent organization refers to an organization whose management decisions are made based on real data, advanced analytics, and predictive models. In this type of organization, information generated in different parts of the system is collected and analyzed in an integrated manner, and the results of these analyses are made available to managers and decision-support systems. In this way, the organization is able not only to understand the current state of its operations, but also to predict and plan for future trends.

Digital twins play an important role in realizing such a structure. By providing a digital environment for analyzing and evaluating real systems, this technology allows for virtual experiments, analyzing different scenarios, and identifying areas for improvement. For example, in a manufacturing system, a digital twin can simulate the behavior of equipment and production lines and examine the impact of various changes in operating parameters. The results of these analyses can be used to optimize processes, reduce operating costs, and increase productivity.

To better understand the role of digital twins in the formation of intelligent enterprises, it is necessary to examine the key concepts related to this area in a structured manner. Table 1 shows the most important concepts related to this area and their role in the development of intelligent enterprises.

Table 1. Core Concepts in Digital Twin–Enabled Intelligent Enterprises

Concept	Description	Role in Intelligent Enterprises
Digital Twin	A dynamic digital representation of a physical system that is continuously updated using real-time operational data	Enables real-time monitoring, analysis, and predictive evaluation of system behavior
Cyber-Physical Systems	Integrated systems where physical components interact with computational and communication infrastructures	Facilitates seamless integration between physical processes and digital platforms
Data-Driven Decision Making	An organizational approach where managerial decisions are guided by analytical insights derived from operational data	Improves decision accuracy, responsiveness, and strategic planning
Intelligent Enterprise	An enterprise that systematically leverages data, advanced analytics, and digital technologies to optimize operations and decision processes	Enhances operational efficiency, adaptability, and organizational intelligence

As shown in Table 1, the digital twin is only one component of a broader ecosystem that includes cyber-physical systems, data infrastructures, and analytics tools. The combination of these elements provides a platform in which organizations can transform information generated in operational processes into knowledge that can be used in decision-making. In such an environment, the boundary between physical operations and digital analytics is largely erased, and management processes are continuously influenced by real-world data.

In addition, the use of digital twins can help organizations increase their flexibility in the face of changing environmental conditions. Organizations equipped with such technologies are able to more quickly detect changes in market conditions, customer demand, or the state of operational systems and design appropriate responses. This capability is especially important in complex and dynamic environments that require rapid management responses (Nozari, 2026).

In summary, the emergence of digital twins can be considered one of the key factors in the transformation of organizations towards intelligent structures. By enabling continuous monitoring of systems, analyzing operational data, and evaluating different scenarios, this technology plays an important role in enhancing organizational awareness and improving decision-making processes. As a result, digital twins are not only a tool for modeling physical systems, but have gradually become a central component in the architecture of intelligent organizations that can create an effective link between data, analysis, and decision-making.

3. FOUNDATIONS OF CYBER-PHYSICAL ENTERPRISE SYSTEMS

Technological developments in recent years have led to the formation of a new generation of organizational infrastructures in which the boundary between physical and digital systems has gradually blurred. In this context, the concept of cyber-physical systems has been proposed as one of the main foundations of digital transformation in organizations. These systems are integrated structures in which physical components, computing infrastructures, communication networks and data analysis systems interact with each other in a coordinated manner. The main goal of such a structure is to create an operational environment in which data generated in real systems is quickly transferred to the digital space and, after analysis and processing, is converted into management decisions or control commands (Lian et al., 2026).

Cyber-physical systems actually provide a framework through which the interaction between the physical world and cyberspace can be managed in a structured manner. In an industrial or service organization, equipment, machinery, operational infrastructure, and even logistics processes are considered as physical parts of the system. These components are connected to communication networks through sensors and data collection devices and continuously record information about the performance status, environmental conditions, and operating parameters. The collected data is then transferred to the processing infrastructure and analyzed there. The results of these analyses can be returned to the executive systems in the form of management reports, operational alerts, or control commands (Qu et al., 2026).

One of the important features of cyber-physical systems is the two-way interaction between the physical system and the digital space. Unlike traditional information systems that were usually limited to only recording and processing past data, cyber-physical systems are able to monitor the status of operational systems in real time and make appropriate decisions based on the analysis of current data. This feature is especially important in environments where rapid changes in operational conditions occur, as organizations can react more quickly to environmental changes.

In the meantime, digital twins play an important role in complementing the architecture of cyber-physical systems. The digital twin acts as a dynamic model of the physical system that is continuously updated with real data. This model can reflect the behavior of the real system while allowing for the analysis of different operational scenarios. As a result, the combination of digital twins with cyber-physical infrastructure creates a platform in which organizations can more accurately monitor the performance of their systems and improve decision-making processes (Nozari & Yordanova, 2026).

From an enterprise architecture perspective, cyber-physical systems usually consist of several different layers, each of which has a specific task in managing data and information flows. At the lowest level, there is the physical layer, which includes operating equipment, machinery, production infrastructure, and other real system components. This layer is connected to the data collection layer, which is responsible for recording and transmitting information about the system status, using sensors and measurement equipment. Next, the collected data is transferred to the data processing and analysis layer through communication infrastructure. In this layer, analytical algorithms, predictive models, and decision-making tools are used to extract knowledge from the data. Finally, the results of these analyses are provided to management and control systems so that they can make appropriate decisions (Filinis et al., 2026).

To better understand how the various components of cyber-physical systems interact in organizational environments, Figure 1 shows a conceptual framework of this structure.

Figure 1. Cyber-Physical Interaction Framework in Intelligent Enterprises

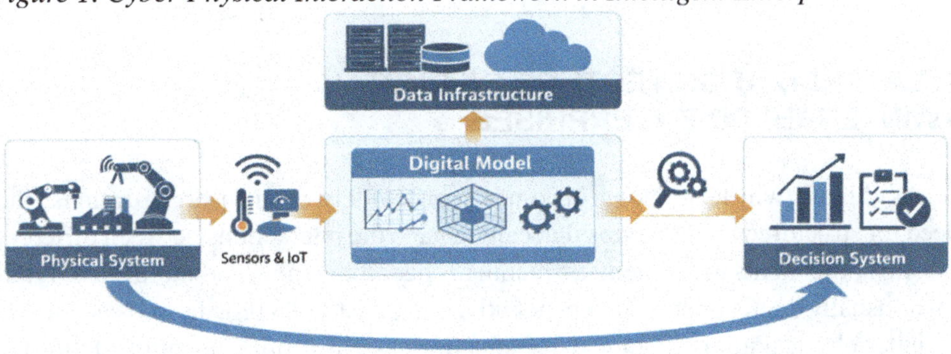

This figure illustrates the relationship between the main components of cyber-physical systems in intelligent enterprises. In this framework, the physical system is at the lowest level and communicates with the digital infrastructure through sensors and data collection equipment. The data collected from these systems is transferred to a data platform and then analyzed in the form of digital models. The results of these analyses are transferred to decision-making systems and can ultimately be returned to operational systems in the form of control commands.

As can be seen in Figure 1, the data flow in this architecture operates as a feedback loop. Data generated in physical systems is transferred to the digital space and, after analysis, the resulting information is returned to the operational environment. This feedback loop allows organizations to continuously evaluate the performance of their systems and make necessary changes if necessary.

The importance of such a structure has increased increasingly in modern organizational environments. Organizations that use cyber-physical infrastructures are able to analyze information generated in different parts of the operation in an integrated manner and make more accurate decisions based on it. In addition, such a structure can help increase transparency in organizational processes, reduce uncertainty in decision-making, and improve coordination between different parts of the organization.

In summary, cyber-physical systems can be considered one of the most important infrastructures for the formation of intelligent organizations. By creating a link between operational data, digital models and decision-making processes, these systems pave the way for the development of organizations that are able to manage their activities dynamically and data-driven. Combining these infrastructures with digital twin technology can be an important step towards creating organizations that are not only able to monitor and analyze operations, but also have the ability to predict and optimize their performance.

4. LAYERED ARCHITECTURE OF DIGITAL TWIN–ENABLED ENTERPRISES

As digital twin technology becomes more widely used in organizations, the need for structured architectures that can manage the interactions between different system components in a systematic manner is becoming more and more felt. Digital twins usually do not operate independently, but are part of a broader ecosystem that includes physical infrastructure, data collection systems, communication platforms, analytical models, and decision-making systems. For this reason, designing a layered architecture for digital twin-based organizations can play an important role in integrating these components and managing data flows across the organization (Fu et al., 2026).

Layered architectures help organizations divide complex systems into a set of independent but related layers. Each layer performs a specific task in data management, information processing, or decision-making support. Such a structure not only increases transparency in system design, but also allows for the gradual development of digital infrastructure and the addition of new capabilities. In organizational environments where large volumes of operational data are generated, this type of architecture can help improve data management and increase the efficiency of analytical systems (Nozari, 2026).

In the framework of smart organizations based on digital twins, the system architecture usually includes several key layers, each of which plays a specific role in the data cycle and decision-making. At the lowest level, there is the physical infrastructure layer, which includes operational equipment, industrial machinery, production lines, logistics infrastructure, and other real components of the system. This layer is the main source of data generation in the organization and reflects the real state of operations. To transfer the data generated in this layer, the sensor and data acquisition layer is used. This layer includes a variety of sensors, measuring devices, and Internet of Things equipment that continuously record information about the performance of the systems.

In the next step, the collected data is transferred to the communication and edge processing layer. This layer is responsible for transferring data from physical equipment to digital infrastructure and usually includes industrial communication networks, IoT platforms, and edge processing systems. Using edge processing at this stage can help reduce data transmission latency and increase system responsiveness. The processed data is then fed into the digital twin modeling layer. In this layer, digital models of physical systems are created and continuously updated with real-world data. These models can simulate system behavior and allow for the analysis of various operational scenarios (Paul et al., 2026).

Above this level is the analytics and intelligence layer, where advanced data analysis tools, machine learning algorithms, and predictive models are used. The main goal of this layer is to extract knowledge from the collected data and provide management insights. For example, this layer can identify hidden patterns in data, predict equipment status, or analyze system performance under different conditions. The output of these analyses is provided to the decision-making and control layer. This layer is responsible for converting the results of the analyses into operational decisions or control commands that can be used to improve system performance.

Finally, at the highest level of the architecture is the enterprise applications layer, which includes management systems, monitoring dashboards, and enterprise planning platforms. This layer provides managers and decision makers with the information obtained from data analysis in the form of reports and performance indicators. In this way, organization managers can make decisions based on accurate and up-to-date information about the status of the systems (Qian et al., 2022).

To better understand how these layers are interconnected, Figure 2 shows an overview of the layered architecture of digital twin-based organizations.

Figure 2. Layered Cyber-Physical Architecture for Digital Twin–Enabled Enterprises

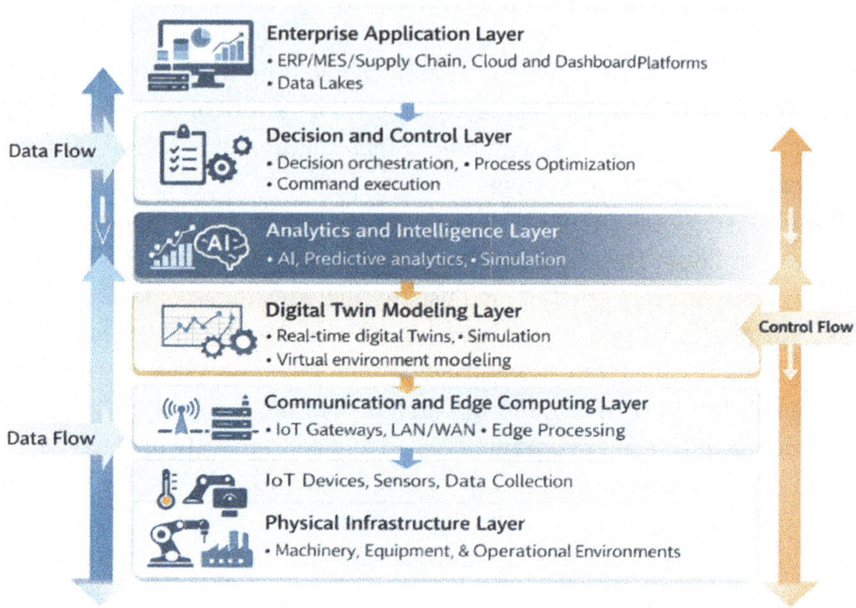

This figure shows the overall structure of the architecture as a set of interconnected layers. At the lowest level, there are physical systems and operational equipment that generate raw data. This data is transmitted to higher layers through sensors and communication networks, where it is processed by digital models and analytical tools. The results of these analyses are ultimately transmitted to the decision-making and management layers and can help improve operational processes.

As can be seen in Figure 2, the communication between the different layers of the architecture is formed as a continuous data flow. The data generated in the physical layers is gradually transferred to higher layers and, after processing, is transformed into knowledge that can be used in decision-making. In some cases, this data flow also acts as a feedback loop, so that the results of the analysis can be fed back to operational systems in the form of control commands. Such a structure enables dynamic, data-driven management of operations.

The importance of layered architectures in digital twin-based organizations is because they enable the integration of different technologies into a coherent framework. In the absence of such architectures, data systems, analytical models, and management systems may be developed separately and not effectively communicated between them. However, in a layered architecture, each part of the system is placed in a specific place and the interaction between different components is managed in an organized manner.

Overall, layered architecture is one of the key elements in the development of intelligent organizations based on digital twins. By providing a platform for integrating data, models, and decision-making, this architecture helps organizations exploit the full potential of digital technologies and manage their operational processes dynamically and intelligently.

5. DATA SYNCHRONIZATION AND DIGITAL TWIN DYNAMICS

One of the most important elements in the effective functioning of digital twins is their ability to continuously synchronize with physical systems. A digital twin can be used as a reliable tool for analysis and decision-making when its digital representation is continuously synchronized with the real state of the system. This synchronization is achieved through a process called data synchronization, a process in which data generated in the operational environment is transferred to the digital model in real time or near real time and updated in its structure. As a result, the digital twin is able to reflect changes in the physical system in the shortest possible time and provide an accurate picture of the current state of the system (Nozari, 2026).

In complex organizational environments, a significant amount of data is generated from various sources. Industrial equipment, environmental sensors, process control systems, and management systems all continuously produce information about the performance of the systems. This data can include operating parameters, environmental conditions, equipment status, and performance indicators. For a digital twin to function properly, it is necessary to collect, process, and transfer this data to the digital model through an appropriate data infrastructure. This process is usually carried out through IoT platforms, data management systems, and data stream processing infrastructures (Jarzyńska et al., 2026).

Data synchronization is not limited to transferring information from the physical system to the digital model. In many applications, the digital twin also acts as an analytical tool that can predict future system behavior or evaluate different operational scenarios based on the received data. The results of these analyses can be fed back to the operational systems in the form of management recommendations or control commands. In this way, the interaction between the physical system and the digital model takes the form of a feedback loop in which data, analysis, and decisions are continuously exchanged between the two spaces (Chen et al., 2026).

In such a framework, the concept of digital twin dynamics is introduced. Dynamics here refers to the ability of the digital model to adapt to changes in the real system. In other words, the digital twin is not a static model, but a dynamic structure that is constantly updated based on new data. This feature is especially important in environments where operating conditions change rapidly. For example, in a manufacturing or logistics system, changes in demand, equipment conditions, or supply chain status can affect the system's performance. By receiving new data, the digital twin is able to identify these changes and adapt its model to the new conditions.

Another important aspect of digital twin dynamics is the processing of data streams in real time. In many industrial applications, data is generated at a high rate and needs to be analyzed in the shortest possible time. The use of technologies such as data stream processing, real-time analytics, and edge processing can help reduce the latency in data transmission and analysis. Such infrastructures allow the digital twin to be updated almost simultaneously with the real system and provide more accurate information about the system status (Nozari & Yordanova, 2025).

To illustrate how the physical system and the digital twin interact in the data synchronization process, Figure 3 shows a conceptual view of this interaction cycle.

Figure 3. Bidirectional Synchronization Between Physical Systems and Digital Twins

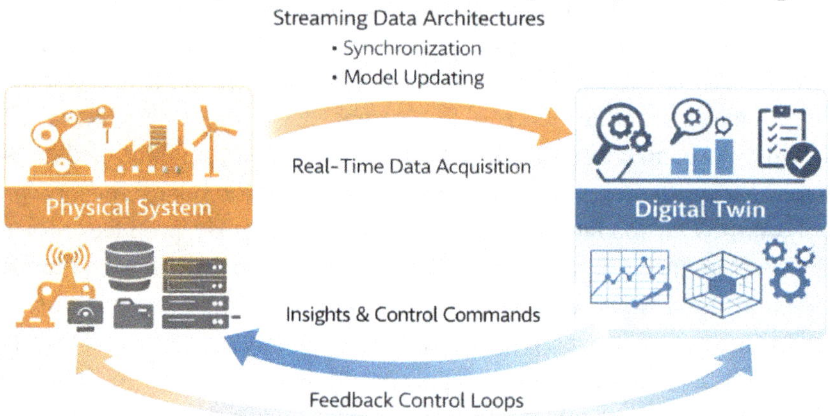

This figure shows the structure of the bidirectional interaction between the physical system and the digital twin. In this framework, data generated in the equipment and sensors of the real system are first collected and transferred to a data infrastructure. This data is then fed into the digital twin model and used to update the model's state. Next, analytics tools and predictive algorithms in the digital environment analyze the data and produce results in the form of management insights or control decisions. These results can ultimately be fed back to the physical system to improve its performance.

As shown in Figure 3, the data synchronization process operates in a continuous feedback loop. Real data is fed into the digital model, the model performs analyses based on this data, and the results of the analyses are fed back to the operational system. This loop enables organizational systems to dynamically adapt to changing environmental conditions.

This cycle of interaction is increasingly important in modern organizations. Organizations that use digital twins are able to analyze information generated in operational processes in real time and make more accurate decisions based on it. In addition, digital twins allow for testing different scenarios in a digital environment; meaning that changes can be examined in a digital model before they are implemented in the real system. Such a capability can help reduce the risk of operational decisions and increase organizational efficiency.

Ultimately, data synchronization and digital twin dynamics are two essential elements in the functioning of this technology. Without a proper mechanism for data transfer and processing, the digital model cannot provide an accurate representation of the real system. However, when this mechanism is properly designed, the digital twin can become a powerful tool for monitoring, analyzing, and optimizing organizational systems and play an important role in the development of intelligent organizations.

6. INTELLIGENCE AND ANALYTICAL ENGINES IN DIGITAL TWIN ARCHITECTURE

In digital twin architectures, data alone does not provide much operational value; the real value is created when this data is transformed into knowledge that can be used in decision-making. For this reason, in many advanced digital twin architectures, a dedicated layer is considered for data analysis and production of operational intelligence. This layer, commonly known as the analytics and intelligence engine, is responsible for processing data collected from physical systems and extracting usable patterns, relationships, and predictions. In fact, this layer is considered the connecting link between raw operational data and organizational decision-making processes (Amirkhanova et al., 2026).

Analytics engines in digital twin architectures use a set of advanced methods and tools for data analysis. These tools can include machine learning algorithms, predictive models, statistical analysis methods, and simulation systems. The main goal of these tools is to identify hidden patterns in data and convert them into insights that can help improve system performance. For example, in an industrial environment, data on equipment performance can be used to predict potential failures. Such analysis can help an organization take the necessary measures to maintain equipment before a failure occurs and prevent sudden shutdowns (Hamza, 2026).

One important application of analytics engines in digital twins is predictive analytics. In this type of analytics, historical and current data are used to predict the future behavior of the system. For example, in a manufacturing system, data on production speed, energy consumption, and equipment operating conditions can be analyzed to predict the future performance of production lines. The results of such analytics can help managers make better decisions about production planning, resource management, and process optimization (Jagatheesaperumal & Rahouti, 2023).

In addition to predictive analytics, the analytics engines in the digital twin architecture also use anomaly detection methods. The goal of these methods is to identify unusual behaviors in the system that may indicate a problem or change in operating conditions. For example, a sudden change in the energy consumption pattern of a device can indicate a malfunction. Anomaly analysis systems are able to quickly identify such changes and send the necessary alerts to managers or control systems.

Another important capability in this layer is the use of simulation and scenario analysis. Digital twins allow various changes in operating conditions to be tested first in the digital environment. For example, an organization can examine the effect of changes in production parameters, changes in demand patterns, or even disruptions in the supply chain in the digital model. Such analysis allows managers to evaluate the consequences and choose the best option before applying changes to the real system (Nozari & Szmelter-Jarosz, 2025).

To better understand the role of analytics engines in a digital twin architecture, Table 2 shows the most important analytics capabilities used in this architecture.

Table 2. Analytical Capabilities in Digital Twin Architectures

Analytical Capability	**Function**	**Enterprise Benefit**
Predictive Analytics	Uses historical and real-time data to forecast future system behavior	Improves planning and proactive decision-making
Machine Learning Models	Learns patterns from large datasets to improve prediction and system understanding	Enhances adaptive system intelligence
Anomaly Detection	Identifies abnormal patterns or deviations in operational data	Enables early detection of system failures
Simulation and Scenario Analysis	Tests operational scenarios in a virtual environment	Reduces operational risk and supports strategic planning

As can be seen in Table 2, analytics engines can provide a wide range of capabilities to the organization. These capabilities range from predictive analytics to scenario simulation. Combining these tools with digital twins allows organizations to use their operational data more effectively and make more accurate decisions.

Another important point is that analytics engines in a digital twin architecture usually operate as an integrated system. In other words, data collected from physical systems is first stored in the data base and then made available to analytical algorithms. The results of these analyses can be presented in the form of management dashboards, operational alerts, or decision-making recommendations. In some cases, these results can even be transmitted directly to control systems and automatically used to adjust operational parameters.

In intelligent organizations, such a structure can play an important role in increasing productivity and improving management processes. When data is continuously analyzed and its results are used in decision-making, the organization will be able to identify environmental changes more quickly and respond more appropriately. In addition, the use of advanced analytics can help identify opportunities for improvement in operational processes and pave the way for optimizing system performance.

In summary, analytics and intelligence engines are one of the key components in the digital twin architecture. These engines play an important role in creating data-driven and intelligent organizations by transforming raw data into actionable insights. Without such a layer, data generated in physical systems cannot be effectively used in management processes. But when this data is processed by appropriate analytical tools, the digital twin can become a powerful platform for analyzing, predicting, and optimizing organizational operations.

7. ENTERPRISE INTEGRATION AND PLATFORM CONNECTIVITY

In many organizations, digital twin technology can only show its true value when it is effectively integrated with other organizational systems. In fact, digital twin as a standalone technology cannot provide all the expected capabilities in organizational operations management. Rather, it is necessary for this technology to communicate with the organization's information systems, data platforms, and management infrastructure to receive operational data and use the results of the analysis in organizational decision-making processes. For this reason, organizational integration and connection to digital platforms are considered as one of the key components in the digital twin architecture (Leng et al., 2026).

In modern organizational environments, multiple information systems are used to manage different parts of operations. These systems can include enterprise resource planning systems, production management systems, supply chain management platforms, asset management systems, and data analytics tools. Each of these systems has a specific role in managing organizational processes and usually produces valuable data about the organization's performance. A digital twin can provide a comprehensive picture of the organization's state when it can communicate with these systems and integrate their data into its digital models (Pu et al., 2024).

One of the most important systems that is usually integrated with a digital twin is an enterprise resource planning (ERP) system. This system maintains information related to the organization's financial resources, production planning, inventory management, and operational activities. Connecting a digital twin to such a system can enable more detailed analysis of organizational processes. For example, production data recorded in operational systems can be analyzed alongside financial and management data, providing a more comprehensive view of the organization's performance.

Along with ERP systems, manufacturing execution systems (MES) also play an important role in integrating digital twins with organizational operations. These systems are typically deployed at the factory or production line level and manage information related to equipment performance, production line status, and operational planning. Connecting digital twins to such systems can enable more accurate monitoring of production processes and analysis of equipment performance.

In addition, many organizations use supply chain management platforms to coordinate logistics, distribution, and inventory management activities. Integrating digital twins with these platforms can help organizations better understand the flow of materials and information in the supply chain and analyze the impact of various changes in demand or supply. In such situations, digital twins can be used as an analytical tool to simulate different scenarios in the supply chain.

In recent years, cloud platforms and data lakes have also played an important role in integrating enterprise digital systems. These platforms enable the storage and processing of large volumes of data and allow organizations to manage data generated in different parts of the system on a common platform. The use of such infrastructures can facilitate the process of integrating digital twins with other enterprise systems and enable large-scale data analysis (Nozari & Yordanova, 2025).

To better understand how digital twins interact with different enterprise systems, Figure 4 shows a conceptual view of this integrated architecture.

Figure 4. Integration of Digital Twin Architecture with Enterprise Systems

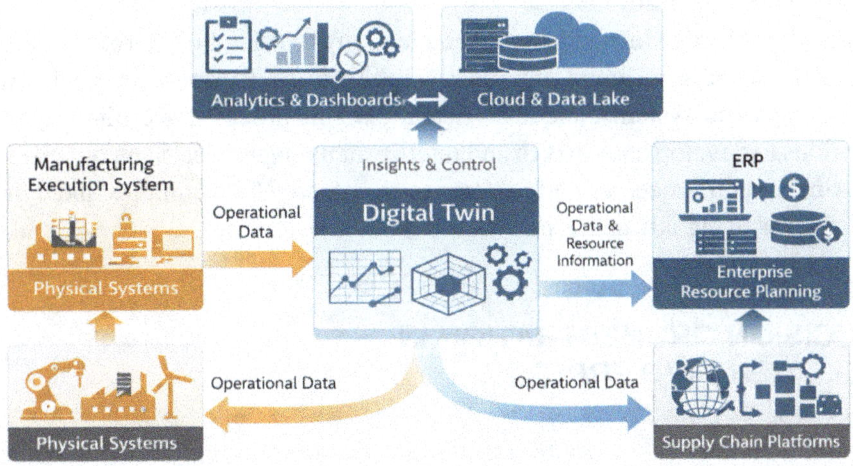

This figure shows how a digital twin can be placed as an analytical core among a set of enterprise systems. In this framework, operational data is collected from physical systems and production management systems and transferred to the digital twin model. In addition to this data, information related to organizational resources, production planning, and logistics activities is also entered into the digital model from ERP systems and supply chain platforms. This data is analyzed in the digital environment and the results are provided to the organization's managers in the form of reports, performance indicators, and management recommendations.

As can be seen in Figure 4, the digital twin in this architecture plays the role of a bridge between operational data and management decisions. Data generated in various organizational systems is transferred to the digital model and analyzed there in an integrated manner. The results of these analyses can be used to improve production planning, optimize resource consumption, and increase the efficiency of operational processes.

One of the key benefits of such a unified architecture is that organizations can gain a more comprehensive view of how their systems are performing. In many organizations, data is scattered across multiple systems, making it difficult to get a complete picture of the state of operations. But when this data is integrated into a digital twin, it becomes possible to analyze the relationships between different parts of the system.

In addition, integrating digital twins with enterprise platforms can help improve coordination across different parts of an organization. When data and analytics are available on a common platform, managers and experts can make decisions based on more accurate and up-to-date information. Such an approach can led to increased transparency in organizational processes and reduced uncertainty in decision-making (Garro & Sorrenti, 2026).

Overall, enterprise integration and connectivity to digital platforms are key elements in the success of digital twin-based architectures. By connecting operational data, management systems, and analytical tools, this process paves the way for organizations to develop data-driven and intelligent management. Such organizations can optimize their processes and perform more effectively in complex and dynamic environments using advanced analytics.

8. DECISION ORCHESTRATION IN INTELLIGENT ENTERPRISES

With the expansion of digital technologies and the increase in the volume of operational data in organizations, the decision-making process has also undergone a transformation. In the past, many management decisions were made based on individual experience or limited information analysis, but in modern organizations, decision-making has increasingly become dependent on data, analytical models, and intelligent systems. In such circumstances, the concept of decision orchestration has emerged as one of the key elements in the management of intelligent organizations. This concept refers to a process in which various organizational decisions at different levels and departments are managed in a coordinated and data-driven manner to improve the overall performance of the system (Sheean et al., 2026.

In complex organizations, decisions are made at different levels. Some of these decisions are made at the operational level and within the framework of daily activities, while others are at the tactical or strategic level. For example, in a manufacturing organization, decisions such as adjusting equipment operating parameters or scheduling production activities are made at the operational level, while decisions such as planning production capacity or developing new production lines are made at the strategic level. Coordination of these decisions at different levels is of great importance, because lack of coordination between them can lead to reduced system efficiency and conflict in organizational processes.

In the meantime, digital twin technology can play an important role in coordinating organizational decisions. By providing a comprehensive representation of operational systems, digital twin enables analysis of relationships between different parts of the organization. This digital model can collect data generated in physical systems, information recorded in management systems, and the results of advanced analytics on a single platform. As a result, decision makers can have a more accurate picture of the organization's status and make their decisions based on more comprehensive information.

One of the important advantages of using digital twins in the decision-making process is the possibility of coordinating decisions in real time. In dynamic operational environments, system conditions may change rapidly and there is a need for rapid management response. By receiving real-time data from operational systems, a digital twin can identify changes in the system state and provide the results of the analysis to managers or control systems. In this way, the necessary decisions can be made in the shortest possible time.

In addition, digital twins also provide the possibility of evaluating different decision-making scenarios. For example, an organization can examine the effect of changes in production planning, resource allocation or distribution routes in the digital model and then choose the best option. Such an approach can help reduce the risk of management decisions and increase the efficiency of organizational processes. In fact, a digital twin acts as a digital laboratory environment in which different decisions can be evaluated before being implemented in the real system.

In intelligent organizations, decision coordination is typically achieved through a combination of data analytics, predictive models, and optimization algorithms. These tools can analyze the complex relationships between different system variables and provide suggestions for improving performance. For example, in a logistics network, analysis of transportation data, inventory, and customer demand can help determine the best distribution routes or optimize inventory planning. When such analyses are performed within the framework of a digital twin, their results can be used in a coordinated manner across the entire organization (Nozari & Nassar, 2025).

Another important point in decision coordination is the integration between the organization's information systems. In many organizations, data is stored in different systems, and communication between these systems is limited. Such a situation can be an obstacle to coordinated decision making at the organization level. But when these systems are connected through a unified digital architecture, it becomes possible to share data and coordinate decisions. In this context, the digital twin can serve as the central core of data analysis and decision support.

From a management perspective, decision coordination can lead to increased transparency and coherence in organizational processes. When different decisions are made within a data-driven and integrated framework, the likelihood of conflict between different parts of the organization is reduced. In addition, such an approach can help improve coordination between operational, management, and strategic units, ultimately increasing the overall efficiency of the organization.

Overall, decision coordination is considered one of the key characteristics of intelligent organizations. This process, using operational data, analytical models, and technologies such as the digital twin, enables coordinated management of decisions at different levels of the organization. As a result, organizations can respond faster and more effectively to environmental changes and dynamically improve their performance by relying on accurate analytics and up-to-date information.

9. STRATEGIC VALUE OF CYBER-PHYSICAL DIGITAL TWIN ARCHITECTURES

Digital twin architectures based on cyber-physical systems have become a key element in the digital transformation of organizations in recent years. These architectures enable the observation, analysis, and management of complex processes in industrial and organizational environments by creating a dynamic connection between physical systems, operational data, and analytical models. In such a framework, the digital twin is not simply a simulation model, but acts as an information infrastructure that combines real data with analytical and decision-making models. This capability has led to digital twins playing an important role in increasing productivity, improving asset management, and improving the quality of decision-making (Alam & El Saddik, 2017).

In cyber-physical architectures, physical systems are connected to the digital environment through sensors and communication infrastructure. The data generated in these systems is continuously collected and used in processing and analytical layers. This data can include information about equipment performance, operating conditions, energy consumption, or process status. Next, this data is organized into digital models to provide an accurate picture of the actual state of the system. Such a structure allows organizations to monitor the performance of complex systems in real time and take the necessary corrective actions in case of changes or disruptions.

One of the most important strategic values of digital twin architectures is increasing operational transparency in organizations. In many industrial systems, process information is scattered across different parts of the organization, and managers do not have a comprehensive view of the performance of the entire system. By integrating data from different sources, digital twins provide a comprehensive picture of the state of the system. This helps managers to better understand the relationships between different parts of the organization and make their decisions based on more accurate information.

In addition, cyber-physical architectures enable predictive analytics and scenario evaluation. When operational data is continuously captured in a digital model, this data can be used to analyze trends and predict the future state of the system. For example, organizations can predict the probability of equipment failure and plan preventive maintenance measures by analyzing equipment performance data. Such an approach can help reduce operating costs and increase system reliability (Ellahi et al., 2026).

From a strategic perspective, another important benefit of digital twins is supporting data-driven decision-making. In complex organizations, management decisions often require analyzing large amounts of data and examining the possible consequences of different options. By providing a comprehensive analytical environment, digital twins enable the evaluation of different decision-making options. In this way, organizations can examine the effects of a decision in the digital environment before implementing it in the real system and choose the option that is most efficient.

Within the framework of cyber-physical architectures, various layers are considered for data management and information analysis. These layers usually include the data collection layer, the communication layer, the digital modeling layer, and the analysis and decision-making layer. The interaction between these layers causes the data generated in physical systems to be quickly converted into usable information. Such a structure allows organizations to respond quickly to environmental changes and helps improve the flexibility of operational systems.

In this regard, Table 3 provides an overview of some of the strategic values of digital twin architectures in cyber-physical environments.

Table 3. Strategic Benefits of Cyber-Physical Digital Twin Architectures

Strategic Dimension	Description
Operational Transparency	Provides a comprehensive view of physical system performance and operational processes through integrated real-time data streams.
Predictive Analytics	Enables forecasting of system behavior and early detection of potential failures using continuous monitoring and data analysis.
Decision Support	Supports data-driven managerial decisions by evaluating different operational scenarios within the digital twin environment.
Resource Optimization	Improves allocation and utilization of resources by analyzing system performance and identifying inefficiencies.
System Resilience	Enhances the ability of systems to respond and adapt to disturbances, uncertainties, and changing operational conditions.

As shown in Table 2, digital twin architectures can create multiple values for organizations. These values are not limited to improving operational performance, but can also lead to the formation of new management approaches. When organizations have access to accurate data and advanced analytics, they can make their decisions in a more systematic and evidence-based manner.

On the other hand, cyber-physical architectures can also help increase organizational agility. In competitive and dynamic environments, organizations must be able to respond quickly to changes in the market or operational conditions. By providing up-to-date information and real-time analytics, digital twins enable rapid identification of changes and appropriate decisions. This feature can help organizations perform better in complex and uncertain environments.

Ultimately, the strategic value of digital twin architectures goes beyond their technical applications. They are increasingly becoming the infrastructure for intelligent management of complex systems. By combining operational data, analytical models, and decision-making tools, digital twins can help organizations manage their processes seamlessly and continuously improve their performance. For this reason, it is expected that the use of these architectures will expand across industries in the coming years, and their role in the digital transformation of organizations will become more prominent.

10. CONCLUSION

The rapid developments in digital technologies in recent years have led organizations and various industries to move towards using new approaches to managing complex systems. In the meantime, the concept of digital twins has been proposed as one of the most important tools of digital transformation. By creating a virtual representation of physical systems and connecting it to real data, digital twins enable monitoring, analysis, and optimization of operational processes. This capability has led many organizations to use this technology to improve efficiency, increase operational transparency, and enhance the quality of decision-making.

The present study attempted to explain the role of this technology in the intelligent management of organizations and industrial processes by examining digital twin architectures within the framework of cyber-physical systems. The results of the studies showed that digital twins can act as an integrated infrastructure for collecting, analyzing, and interpreting operational data. In such architectures, data generated in physical systems is transferred to the digital environment through sensors and communication networks, where it is examined by analytical models and data processing tools. This process allows for a more detailed understanding of the behavior of systems and the identification of performance patterns.

One of the most important achievements of using digital twins is increasing transparency in organizational processes. In many complex systems, information related to the performance of different parts of the organization is stored scattered in different systems, and it is difficult to obtain a comprehensive picture of the state of the system. By integrating data from different sources, digital twins provide the ability to observe and analyze the overall state of the system. This feature helps managers and decision makers to better understand the relationships between different parts of the organization and make their decisions based on more accurate information.

In addition, digital twins can play an important role in improving decision-making processes. In dynamic operational environments, management decisions often have to be made under conditions of uncertainty and with multiple variables in mind. By providing a dynamic analytical environment, digital twins enable the evaluation of different decision-making scenarios. In this way, organizations can examine the possible consequences of a decision in the digital environment before implementing it in the real system and choose the option that has the highest efficiency and lowest risk.

From a strategic perspective, the use of digital twin architectures can also help increase the flexibility and resilience of organizations. In industrial and organizational environments, operating conditions may change rapidly and systems face numerous challenges. By providing real-time data and predictive analytics, digital twins enable the rapid identification of changes and appropriate response to them. This feature can help organizations perform better in complex and uncertain conditions and prevent widespread disruptions in operational processes.

On the other hand, the studies showed that the successful development and implementation of digital twins requires attention to several key factors. First, the existence of appropriate infrastructure for collecting and transmitting operational data is of great importance. Without access to accurate and up-to-date data, digital models cannot provide a true picture of the state of the system. Second, integration between different information systems of the organization is essential, because the data required for analyzing the performance of systems is usually stored in multiple systems. Third, the use of advanced analytical tools to process data and extract knowledge from them plays an important role in increasing the operational value of digital twins.

Overall, the findings of this study show that digital twin architectures based on cyber-physical systems can be used as a key infrastructure for the intelligent management of complex systems. By combining operational data, analytical models, and decision-making tools, these architectures provide a better understanding of system behavior and improve management processes. Given the rapid expansion of digital technologies and the increasing importance of data in the management of organizations, the use of digital twins is expected to play a more prominent role in the digital transformation of various industries in the future.

Finally, it can be said that digital twins are not only a tool for monitoring and analyzing systems, but are also gradually becoming a platform for intelligent decision-making in organizations. Combining this technology with advanced data analysis and decision-making models can pave the way for the formation of a new generation of intelligent organizations that are able to dynamically manage their processes and continuously improve their performance.

REFERENCES

Alam, K. M., & El Saddik, A. (2017). C2PS: A digital twin architecture reference model for the cloud-based cyber-physical systems. *IEEE Access : Practical Innovations, Open Solutions*, *5*, 2050–2062.

Amirkhanova, G., Adilkyzy, S., Amirkhanov, B., Baizhanova, D., & Chen, S. (2026). A Digital Twin Architecture for Integrating Lean Manufacturing with Industrial IoT and Predictive Analytics. *Information (Basel)*, *17*(2), 196.

Bordbar, A., Tadros, M., Nazemian, A., Aung, M. Z., Georgoulas, K., Louvros, P., & Boulougouris, E. (2026). Digitalisation of shipyard production planning: A review of simulation, optimisation, AI, and digital twin methods (2010–2025). *Journal of Marine Science and Engineering*, *14*(4), 396.

Bordbar, A., Tadros, M., Nazemian, A., Aung, M. Z., Georgoulas, K., Louvros, P., & Boulougouris, E. (2026). Digitalisation of shipyard production planning: A review of simulation, optimisation, AI, and digital twin methods (2010–2025). *Journal of Marine Science and Engineering*, *14*(4), 396.

Chen, J., Wang, Z., Gao, H., He, Q., Mou, J., & Wang, W. (2026). The Role of Digital Twin in Advancing Industrial Internet of Things: Insights, Applications, and Future Directions. IEEE Internet of Things Journal.

Ellahi, R. M., Ali, M., Ali Shah, S. A., Qureshi, M. A., Gulzar, S., Wood, L. C., & Ahmed Bekhit, A. E. D. (2026). Harnessing digital twins: transforming livestock supply chain management: a comprehensive review. *Cogent Food & Agriculture*, *12*(1), 2611196.

Filinis, N., Spatharakis, D., Dimolitsas, I., Fotopoulou, E., Vassilakis, C., Zafeiropoulos, A., & Papavassiliou, S. (2026). A Scalable and Modular Open-Source Stack for Computing Continuum Digital Twins. *Future Generation Computer Systems*, •••, 108411.

Fu, X., Qin, M., Pace, P., Savaglio, C., Li, W., & Fortino, G. (2026). Generative AI-Driven Digital Twin in the Manufacturing Internet of Things: A Comprehensive Survey. *IEEE Internet of Things Journal.*

Garro, A., & Sorrenti, A. (2026). Designing an ISO 23247-compliant Hybrid Digital Twin Architecture for industry. *Information and Software Technology*, •••, 108039.

Hamza, M. F. (2026). Cloud, Edge, and Digital Twin Architectures for Condition Monitoring of Computer Numerical Control Machine Tools: A Systematic Review. *Information (Basel)*, *17*(2), 153.

Hasan, A., & Nguyen, D. T. (2026). Integrating agentic AI and digital twins for intelligent decision-making systems. *Array (New York, N.Y.)*, •••, 100721.

Jagatheesaperumal, S. K., & Rahouti, M. (2023). Building digital twins of cyber physical systems with metaverse for industry 5.0 and beyond. *IT Professional*, *24*(6), 34–40.

Jarzyńska, M., Nierychlok, A., & Olender-Skóra, M. (2026). The Concept of a Hierarchical Digital Twin. *Applied Sciences (Basel, Switzerland)*, *16*(2), 605.

Leng, J., Zhang, H., Yan, D., Liu, Q., Chen, X., & Zhang, D. (2019). Digital twin-driven manufacturing cyber-physical system for parallel controlling of smart workshop. *Journal of Ambient Intelligence and Humanized Computing*, *10*(3), 1155–1166.

Leng, S., Yang, X., Jiang, Z., Wei, Y., & Wang, C. (2026). Dynamic simulation and optimization approach for coevolutionary intelligent manufacturing cell with digital twin. *International Journal of Advanced Manufacturing Technology*, •••, 1–16.

Li, M., Yang, C. M., Lo, W., & Kao, Y. W. (2026). A Digital-Twin-Enabled AI-Driven Adaptive Planning Platform for Sustainable and Reliable Manufacturing. *Machines (Basel)*, *14*(2), 197.

Lian, M., Li, L., Wang, S., Wang, C., & Li, M. (2026). Design and research of IIoT intelligent automatic production line security monitoring system based on digital twin. *International Journal of Computer Applications in Technology*, *78*(1), 13–24.

Nozari, H. (2026). Digital twin-based predictive maintenance in cold chain logistics. *Operations Research*, *60*(1), 481–499. DOI: 10.1051/ro/2025167

Nozari, H. (2026). Urban Digital Twins and Data-Centric Architectures for the Emergent Economy 5.0. In Industry 5.0's Impact on Economic Innovation (pp. 51-70). IGI Global Scientific Publishing.

Nozari, H., & Nassar, S. (2025). Real-time data-driven multi-objective optimization in B2B marketing using digital twins. OPSEARCH, 1-27.

Nozari, H., & Szmelter-Jarosz, A. (2025). A Predictive Maintenance Approach for Composting Plants Based on ERP and Digital Twin Integration. *Machines (Basel)*, *13*(12), 1123.

Nozari, H., & Yordanova, Z. (2025). A fuzzy–digital twin optimization framework for simultaneous management of waste and energy consumption in sustainable manufacturing. An International Journal of Optimization and Control: Theories & Applications, 25360152.

Nozari, H., & Yordanova, Z. (2025). An intelligent digital twin approach for optimizing multi-channel supply chains in uncertain environments. Green Technologies and Sustainability, 100309.

Nozari, H., & Yordanova, Z. (2026). An Adaptive Fuzzy Multi-Objective Digital Twin Framework for Multi-Depot Cold-Chain Vehicle Routing in Agri-Biotech Supply Networks. *Logistics (Basel)*, *10*(2), 27.

Paul, S., Manna, N., Roy, S., & Jana, T. K. (2026, January). A Machine Tool Digital Twin to Implement Smartness in Discrete Production Environment. In Recent Advances in Industrial and Systems Engineering: Selected Papers from International Conference on Industrial Engineering and Analytics (ICONIEA) 2024 (pp. 223-247). Singapore: Springer Nature Singapore.

Pu, Y., Pan, X., Shang, X., Li, M., & Zhang, M. (2024). Cyber Physical Integrated Digital Twin Network Model for Enterprise Producing High-Performing Logistics. *Wireless Personal Communications*, •••, 1–18.

Qian, C., Liu, X., Ripley, C., Qian, M., Liang, F., & Yu, W. (2022). Digital twin—Cyber replica of physical things: Architecture, applications and future research directions. *Future Internet*, *14*(2), 64.

Qu, Y., Zhao, N., & Zhang, H. (2026). Digital Twin-Driven Joint predictive and optimization scheduling Method for Parcel Sorting Systems. Digital Engineering, 100092.

Tao, F., Qi, Q., Wang, L., & Nee, A. Y. C. (2019). Digital twins and cyber–physical systems toward smart manufacturing and industry 4.0: Correlation and comparison. *Engineering*, *5*(4), 653–661.

Yordanova, Z., & Nozari, H. (2026). An Agentic Digital Twin Framework for Fuzzy Multi-Objective Optimization in Dynamic Humanitarian Logistics. *Algorithms*, *19*(3), 198. DOI: 10.3390/a19030198

Chapter 3
From Digital Twins to Cognitive Enterprises:
Frameworks for Intelligent Organizational System

Aadi Goyal
http://orcid.org/0009-0009-6907-9566
Christ University, India

Vijayalaxmi Rajendran
http://orcid.org/0000-0002-8378-9750
Christ University, India

Pankaj Dhaundiyal
http://orcid.org/0000-0002-4815-1647
Christ University, India

ABSTRACT

The development of cyber-physical systems, artificial intelligence, and big data infrastructures has altered how organizations operate with respect to physical assets. The use of digital twins, or virtual copies of actual systems, is one of the primary changes, as these systems tend to receive and analyze real-time sensor data to track performance, run simulations, and enhance performance. Digital twins were originally intended for monitoring and predictive maintenance; nowadays, they are being integrated into larger intelligent enterprise systems. These systems are now being developed to detect trends, forecast interruptions, and support sophisticated decision-making as organizations use more and more data to inform their decisions. Digital twins are slowly becoming the infrastructure of cognitive enterprises that learn from data, adapt to change, and enable organizations to operate more proactively.

DOI: 10.4018/979-8-3373-9998-0.ch003

1. CONCEPTUAL FOUNDATIONS: DIGITAL TWINS AND THE COGNITIVE ENTERPRISE PARADIGM

1.1 Introduction

Companies across all sectors are experiencing a radical shift in their decision-making, moving from traditional managerial judgments based on experience to real-time, data-driven, and responsive forms of organizational intelligence. The most crucial piece of this transformation is the introduction of the so-called digital twin (DT), which has been produced in less than 20 years since that highly specific aerospace simulation tool, a strategic infrastructure with the capability to model and optimize complex organizational frameworks. Consequently, the concern of researchers and practitioners today is no longer whether digital twins are critical to managing organizations, but whether existing conceptual frameworks will be sufficient to guide and control their implementation of the technology at the enterprise level (Barata & Kayser, 2024; Iliu ă, et al., 2022).

Even with the rapid growth of studies on digital twins, the scholarly literature is divided across multiple fields. The main directions of engineering and information systems scholarship have been technical architectures and system-level implementations. In contrast, the primary focus of management and organizational studies has been on digital transformation. However, there is no clear formulation of how digital twin technologies can be embedded in organizational cognition and responsive decision-making. Such fragmentation has led to conceptual inconsistencies and the absence of integrated frameworks that explain how digital twins can become infrastructures that support enterprise-level intelligence as opposed to being operations simulation tools.

This gap is addressed in this chapter by suggesting an interlaced conceptual framework that relates digital twin maturity, AI-enabled cognition, enterprise architecture alignment, and governance capability. Instead of exploring these dimensions individually, the chapter integrates results from studies on digital twins, artificial intelligence, enterprise architecture, and industry case studies, describing how digital twins can be used as a decision-support infrastructure in the cognitive enterprise. The aim of the chapter is thus to explain the development of digital twins that start as technical depictions of physical systems and evolve into organizational platforms that support continuous observation, anticipatory reasoning, and adaptive choices throughout the enterprise.

To support this point, the chapter's initial section explores the theory of digital twins and its history. It then examines definitional arguments and typological categorizations in the literature, and examines the organizational implications of digital twins using archetypal and scalar theories. This theoretical foundation lays the groundwork for the following sections, which examine how artificial intelligence and enterprise architecture can enable digital twins to work together within a cognitive enterprise transformation.

1.2 Historical Evolution of Digital Twin Technology

1.2.1 Origins: Product Lifecycle Management and the Grieves Model

The conceptual origins of the digital twin can be traced to (Grieves & Vickers, 2017), who first proposed the concept as part of product lifecycle management (PLM). They suggested their model, in which every physical product should be matched by a virtual one capable of reporting its current status, past performance, and future actions. The resulting conceptual framework, comprising a physical and a virtual object and a two-way data channel between them, became the design principle for most subsequent instances of digital twins in the literature (Tao, Zhang, Liu, & Nee, 2019; Fuller, Fan, Day, & Barlow, 2020).

The discussion had a significant empirical basis in parallel advances in aerospace engineering. Specifically, NASA developed high-fidelity simulations of spacecraft to monitor structural integrity and operational performance when physical inspection was not possible. These early systems bore more of the characteristics of advanced simulation environments than of complete analog-digital twins. However, they proposed continuously updating virtual images with real-world information. However, the entirely independent closed-loop interaction, i.e., in which the knowledge produced by the virtual model directly affects the actions of the physical system, was not yet achieved in the early implementations (Rasheed, San, & Kvamsdal, 2020).

Later studies have understood the evolution of the digital twin technology as a generational advance. (Iliu ă, et al., 2022) present the earliest generation (1990-2010), which is mainly comprised of model-based digital representations utilized in aerospace engineering and other extremely technical fields. The second generation (2010-2015) established a real-time data connection via the Internet of Things, enabling monitoring of all physical assets along the way. Machine learning and predictive analytics were integrated into the third generation (2015-2020) to make digital twins more anticipatory in their decision-making. The latest generation (around 2020) has some cognitive abilities, including autonomous perception, reasoning, and adaptive behavior of the system, which are frequently referred to in the literature as cognitive digital twins (Rathore, Shah, Shukla, Bentafat, & Bakiras, 2021). This generational change implies that digitized twins adoption could be realized not as a dichotomous decision based on technology but as a maturity process in two phases by which organisations gradually build more sophisticated analytical and decision-making systems.

1.2.2 The Industry 4.0 Inflection and Expansion Toward Organizational Applications

The Industry 4.0 initiative, launched in Germany in 2011, significantly expanded the use of digital twin technology beyond individual assets. Industry 4.0 focused on the adoption of hybridization of cyber-physical frameworks, real-time information transfer, and digital systems in factory Settings. In this context, digital twins became necessary instruments to connect the physical systems of production with digital models that enable continuous monitoring, simulation, and optimization. Consequently, after a short period of time, the digital twins shifted their focus from a niche engineering tool to a broader niche in operations management and information systems (Alcácer & Cruz-Machado, 2019) (Warke, Kumar, Bongale, & Kotecha, 2021).

This change also broadened the concept of the digital twin in its use, since it was no longer limited to monitoring assets but extended to applications across the organization and the system as a whole. Surveys of digital twin applications in infrastructure management indicate that the principle can be applied to any system whose behavior may be characterized and studied using virtual representations (Qiu, et al., 2025). This ontological extension enables the application of the digital twin structures to organizational activities, decision packages, and enterprise architecture.

More recent studies place digital twins within the new Industry 5.0 paradigm, which focuses on human-centric, intelligent, and sustainable production systems. Here, the cognitive enterprise has become a popular principle for organizations seeking to combine innovative digital technologies with flexible learning and decision-making (Barata & Kayser, 2024). Digital twins are gaining widespread recognition as the structural support for this transformation, enabling organizations to maintain an ever-fresh virtual representation of their business, simulate potential strategic or operational scenarios, and then test them in practice.

1.3 Definitional Analysis: Toward Conceptual Precision

1.3.1 The Definitional Fragmentation Problem

Although digital twin technologies are increasingly being adopted, a problem of fragmented definitions persists in the literature. The term digital twin is used in many studies with varying assumptions, including whether a digital twin is connected, at what level of intelligence, whether data are synchronized, and whether the physical system is represented. According to (Botín-Sanabria, et al., 2022), this failure to achieve definitional consistency is one of the greatest impediments to cumulative development of theory in the area.

According to (Jones, Snider, Nassehi, Yon, & Hicks, 2020), one of the most popular attempts to produce such a synthesis of definitions is the six major features common to most definitions of digital twins:

1. the existence of a physical entity,
2. a corresponding digital representation,
3. a data connection between the two,
4. real-time synchronization,
5. simulation capability, and
6. decision-support functionality.

It is based on these points that this chapter takes the following working definition:

A digital twin is an active, harmonized digital representation of a physical, process, or organizational entity that facilitates the two-way flow of data, real-time observation, simulation, and informed decision making.

In this definition, the concept of digital twins has more to do with the aspect of representation, but it can also support adaptive decision-making in organizational settings (Fuller, Fan, Day, & Barlow, 2020; Rasheed, San, & Kvamsdal, 2020).

1.3.2 The Kritzinger Taxonomy: Digital Models, Shadows, and Twins

The digital twin literature is significantly conceptually differentiated, with (Kritzinger, Karner, Traar, Henjes, & Sihn, 2018) distinguishing between a digital shadow and digital models. The character of data connectivity and the level of automation between physical and virtual systems determine the main distinction between these categories. A digital model does not entail an automated process for exchanging data; it is updated by hand. A digital shadow enables automatic one-way transfer of the physical system to the virtual model, enabling real-time monitoring without reverse actuation. In contrast, a digital twin is a form of autonomous data exchange, in which the virtual model is not only reflexive but also responsive to the physical system, engaging in two-way communication (Tao, Zhang, Liu, & Nee, 2019; Rasheed, San, & Kvamsdal, 2020), with the important differences being as shown in Table 1.1.

Table 1. Typological Differentiation of Digital Models, Digital Shadows, and Digital Twins

Construct	Data Flow	Automation	Real-Time	Primary Function
Digital Model	None (manual)	None	No	Static design & scenario analysis
Digital Shadow	Physical → Virtual	Automated	Yes	Live monitoring; predictive maintenance
Digital Twin	Physical ↔ Virtual	Full	Yes	Closed-loop optimization; autonomous decision support

(Kritzinger, Karner, Traar, Henjes, & Sihn, 2018; Jones, Snider, Nassehi, Yon, & Hicks, 2020; Rasheed, San, & Kvamsdal, 2020)

1.4 Archetypes and Scalar Typologies

1.4.1 DT Archetypes: From Standalone Assets to Networked Ecosystems

It has been found that the digital twins have several archetypal configurations distinguished by the degree of integration, connectivity, and intelligence. These configurations are synthesized by (Botín-Sanabria, et al., 2022) into four major archetypes.

The Standalone Twin encompasses a single digital language for a single property, with automated piece of data gathering and robust framework for more overall enterprise integration. The Integrated Twin leverages digital twins with enterprise systems such as ERP, MES, or PLM, enabling cross-functional data analysis and operational coordination (Leng, et al., 2021). The hierarchy twin integrates more than two digital twins into composite models that are models of complex systems or production environments. Lastly, the Networked Twin also takes this architecture beyond organizational boundaries by enabling joint intelligence on shared digital twin systems within companies and ecosystems (Sacoto-Cabrera, Perez-Torres, Tello-Oquendo, & Cerrada, 2025).

Combined, the archetypes demonstrate the rise of digital twin capabilities from established secluded operational facilities to interdependent infrastructures to facilitate inter-organizational wisdom and optimization at the ecosystem level.

1.4.2 Scalar Hierarchy: From Component-Level to Organizational Twins

The scalar hierarchy model is another helpful tool for explaining the maturity of digital twins, as it describes the progressive development of digital twins applications in several levels of system complexity. There are four main levels: component-level twins, system-level twins, system-of-systems twins, and organizational twins, which reflect enterprises as a whole. (Li, 2025)

The Digital Twin of an Organization (DTO) is the highest level of these developments. A DTO combines operational data of enterprise information systems, semantic process models, and analytical tools based on AI. It generates a continually updated picture of the organization's actual activities. The DTOs, unlike conventional organizational models, which tend to present a comparatively inert set of documentation, are representations of the real-time dynamics of decision-making.

However, technical integration alone is not enough to achieve this kind of maturity. According to studies on enterprise interoperability and cognitive systems, the DTO implementation requires significant transformations in data governance frameworks, organizational learning processes, and human-AI collaboration models (Ali, Gaffinet, Panetto, & Naudet, 2024). The scalar hierarchy is hence an indication not just of a transformation in technology but of a wide-ranging change in how organizations share knowledge, make decisions, and engage in adaptive learning.

1.5 Synthesis and Transition

The discussion above demonstrates three main propositions about the development of digital twin technologies. To begin with, the creation of digital twins must be seen as a matter of scale, not a bifurcated state of technology, with increasingly sophisticated forms of predictive and adaptive intelligence provided by greater maturity. Second, the organizational value of digital twins is inherent to the solution's technical architecture and to its connectivity with enterprise systems, organizational decision processes, and organizational learning structures (Ali, Gaffinet, Panetto, & Naudet, 2024; Rossmann & Hertweck, 2022). Thirdly, a Digital Twin of an Organization (DTO) is the key to mediating the representation of physical assets and enterprise-level cognitive intelligence.

These lessons provide the conceptual background for the following part of the chapter, which discusses how artificial intelligence and machine learning technologies enable cognitive functions that support intelligent decision-making processes within organizations.

2. AI, MACHINE LEARNING, AND ANALYTICS IN COGNITIVE DIGITAL TWINS

2.1 Introduction

The above part has already established that digital twins have progressed to encompass technical models of physical properties and have developed into more intelligent infrastructures capable of facilitating the monitoring of organizations, the simulation of actions, and intelligent decision-making. The following analysis explains why this change is achievable. Specifically, the cognitive digital twin will emerge through the interactions of artificial intelligence, machine learning, and more sophisticated knowledge representation processes, making the digital twins not only reflect reality but also interpret, predict, and act on it.

This section of the paper will argue that cognitive digital twins cannot be seen as data-intensive simulation systems, but rather as smart systems that integrate sensing, modeling, analytics, and learning to facilitate increasingly autonomous forms of reasoning and action. The conversation takes place in three phases. To start with, it analyses the architectural principles of cognitive digital twins and the stacked architectures that structure data, models, services, and connectivity are structured. Second, it examines how machine learning paradigms can transform digital twin information into predictive, diagnostic, and adaptive intelligence. Third, it argues for the use of predictive analytics, ontologies, and knowledge graphs to help digital twins shift away from asset-level optimization toward organizational knowledge integration.

2.2 Cognitive Digital Twin Architecture

The architecture of a cognitive digital twin provides the structural framework for integrating sensing, modeling, analytics, and feedback into a functioning decision-support system. Whereas the literature provides several architectural definitions, the majority of them all amount to a similar notion: the appearance of cognitive ability when digital twins merge real-time data acquisition, virtual depiction, analysis, and continuous connectivity through a coordinated system. Organizational-wise, this architecture is significant because it will determine whether a digital twin serves as a monitoring tool or evolves into an adaptable infrastructure that can trigger intelligent action.

2.2.1 Layered Frameworks and Five-Dimensional Models

Another common trend in digital twin literature is that many authors adopt layered or multidimensional models to describe the structure of the digital twin system. Although the terms vary in different studies, their fundamental elements are mostly similar. Majority of them have a physical layer where assets, processes or operational activities create data; a virtual layer where these entities are modeled or simulated; a service or analytics layer where prediction, optimization and monitoring functions are realized; and a connectivity or data layer where the coordination of information flows takes place. There are five-dimensional formulations that treat data and connection mechanisms as dimensions and emphasize the importance of interoperability and real-time synchronization across the architecture.

These models are important not because of the labels applied to each layer, but because of the general conceptual understanding they offer. A digital, physical object copy is not sufficient as a cognitive digital twin. They rely on a framework in which data capture, representation, analysis, and service provision are part of a single whole. This integration ensures that digital twins can help with operational visibility, as well as simulation, diagnosis, and decision support. The issue of layered frameworks in relation to organizational decision-making is that they facilitate understanding of how intelligence is assembled, aligned, and graded across both technical and managerial environments.

2.2.2 Closed-Loop Optimization: From Sensing to Adaptive Learning

The second distinguishing characteristic of cognitive digital twin architecture is the presence of a closed-loop logic that mediates between the physical data sensed and interpreted in the digital environment and the actions or recommendations that, in turn, impact the actual physical system. This is what makes cognitive digital twins different from static or unidirectional digital representations. In a closed-loop architecture, sensing technologies measure current functionality in real time; analytical models analyze it; and the response is delivered through outputs that modify behavior, optimize processes, or provide intervention guidance. The digital twin thus enters into a continuous loop of perception, thinking, and reaction.

This closed-loop structure is important because it supports adaptive learning. With constant feedback from the physical environment to the digital twin, the models of the latter may be optimized, and its suggestions may advance with time. This brings optimization out of the realm of a one-time analysis and an undertaking that is a process of learning and adaptation. At the managerial level, closed-loop optimization is important because it enables organizations to avoid retrospective analysis in favor of proactive, responsive control. It is not only important that the system senses and simulates, but also that it gathers Community Feedback and uses it to make better future decisions under varying conditions.

Collectively, layered structures and closed-loop systems indicate that cognitive digital twins are best understood as technological systems. Its smartness is not in disaggregated algorithms, but in the concerted action of seeing, modeling, analytics, connectivity, and feedback. That is what makes them applicable not only to asset management but also to the overall organizational decision-making.

2.3 Machine Learning Paradigms for Organizational Intelligence

The main process in developing digital twins beyond representation towards organizational intelligence is machine learning. As more real-time and historical data are generated in digital twin spaces, machine learning can be used to identify system patterns, detect anomalies, forecast outcomes, and inform decision-making under dynamic conditions. The value of machine learning in enterprise digital twins lies not only in technical automation but also in converting operational data into predictive, diagnostic, adaptive, and more accessible forms of decision support.

2.3.1 Supervised, Unsupervised, and Reinforcement Learning in Enterprise DTs

There are three general paradigmatic pathways through which machine learning has advanced to digital twin systems: supervised, unsupervised, and reinforcement learning. Both have distinct abilities in organizational intelligence, and together they form the analytical heart of the cognitive digital twin.

Supervised learning is the most common paradigm deployed in enterprise digital twin applications due to its relative suitability for data-rich operational settings where historical records can be labeled and a model trained. In practice, it is usually applied to predictive maintenance, classifying defects, quality monitoring, and predicting demands. What is valuable to it as an organization is that it has enabled companies to foresee potential consequences and act before things are lost in the whirlwind. In that regard, supervised learning reinforces the predictive capabilities of digital twins by enabling decisions that account for future outcomes, rather than relying solely on retrospective analysis.

Unsupervised learning helps augment this role by discovering trends and anomalies in cases with incomplete or unavailable labeled data. It can be really helpful in the digital twins setting, especially in terms of grouping operating conditions, identifying unusual states, and exposing latent representations of data in complex datasets. This makes it especially useful in novel or changing operational environments, where failure categories may still be unknown. The value of its managerial implications is that it helps organizations enhance diagnostic performance: they can identify silent, inefficient operations, peculiar activities, or unforeseen threats that would be harder to detect under rule-based supervision alone.

The most adaptive of the three paradigms is reinforcement learning, as it enables systems to discover optimal policies through dynamic interaction with the environment. This is of particular concern in enterprise digital twin applications, since in the virtual setting, it is possible to experiment, test policies, and optimize without risking the physical system to the dangers and expenses of exploratory action. As a result, reinforcement learning is increasingly applied to scheduling, process control, logistics optimization, and other dynamic decision-making environments. The relevance of its organizational aspect is that it supports adaptive action in the face of uncertainty, bringing digital twins nearer to ongoing optimization by supporting and not centering on analytical assistance at a single point.

A combination of supervised, unsupervised, and reinforcement learning can help digital twins transform enterprise data streams into predictive, diagnostic, and adaptive intelligence. The three of them are useful to organizational management, enhancing foresight, detecting problems, and increasing the firm's ability to act intelligently in changing operational circumstances.

2.3.2 Federated Learning for Distributed Digital Twin Environments

Since the implementation of digital twins is no longer confined to single facilities but is now distributed across the supply chain, smart cities, and networked inter-organizational platforms, the issue of learning from distributed, privacy-sensitive data is becoming increasingly relevant. In these environments, there are instances where enterprise intelligence cannot rely on centralized information consolidation, as ownership restrictions, regulatory constraints, competitive factors, or distributed infrastructure may control information. Federated learning can solve this issue by enabling models to be trained across many digital twin nodes, with raw data remaining local.

In a federated learning system, all nodes produce model updates based on the data they hold, and only those updates are transferred to a coordinating device rather than the original datasets. This has significant implications on digital twins environments which span organizational boundaries. It enables joint predictive, optimization, or anomaly detection without losing data sovereignty or exposing to the dangers of direct data exchange. With digital twins becoming more of an ecosystem, as opposed to an organization, federated learning will become highly essential to the scalability of cognitive capability without compromising privacy, trust, or compliance.

Organizationally, federated learning will be significant because it will bring digital twin intelligence at the network level instead of just the enterprise. It provides a means of collective prediction and decision support in situations where no single actor has full visibility and control of the system. Federated learning thus advances a more decentralized model of organizational intelligence, one that is in line with the realities of cross-enterprise coordination and platform-based ecosystems.

2.3.3 Generative AI and Large Language Models as Cognitive DT Enablers

Additional cognitive digital twin capability now presents a new dimension, introduced by the development of generative artificial intelligence, particularly large language models and multimodal foundation models. The initial stages of digital twin studies focused on sensing, simulation, prediction, and optimization. Compared to it, generative AI adds an interface to digital twin systems and human decision-makers by making analytics outcomes more readable, interactive, and accessible at all levels.

The translation of sophisticated analytical findings into natural-language descriptions and recommendations is one of the most important tasks for digital twins using LLMs. This reduces the technical gap between elite digital twin analytics and managers' decision-making; rather than being interpreted only by specialists whose tasks involve engineers or data scientists per se, the outputs of digital twins can gradually be conveyed in languages that are understandable to executives, middle managers, and frontline workers. This democratization of access helps to expand the organizational applicability of digital twins and improve their chances to be part of the real decisions instead of being limited to the technical team companies.

Entering new ways of human-AI interaction into digital twin environments is also possible through generative AI. These include conversational scenario analysis, natural-language questioning of system behavior, anomaly description, and easy specification of optimization constraints. The reason why such capabilities are significant is that they transform the digital twin into an interactive cognitive system as opposed to a strictly analytical infrastructure. Organizational-wise, it implies that model accuracy ceases to be a defining determinant of the value of digital twins, and that the degree to which intelligence can be conveyed, understood, and used by the various decision-makers is a more defining factor.

The value of generative AI to enterprise digital twins lies in its role as a layer of accessibility and interaction with organizational intelligence. It not only enables the systems associated with digital twins to produce insights but also to share them in a way that enables broader engagement, quicker interpretation, and more integrated decision-making across the enterprise.

2.4 Predictive Analytics and Real-Time Decision Intelligence

By this stage, the conversation has moved away from AI as a constellation of analytical instruments to AI as an organizational knowledge infrastructure, which establishes the foundation for integrating enterprise architecture. Predictive analytics, anomaly detection, ontologies, and knowledge graphs are significant not because they focus on enhancing technical performance, but because they enable digital twins to bridge the gap between operational intelligence and organizational reasoning.

2.4.1 Predictive Maintenance and Anomaly Detection

By this stage, the conversation has moved away from AI as a constellation of analytical instruments to AI as an organizational knowledge infrastructure, which establishes the foundation for integrating enterprise architecture. Two of the most common use cases of AI-enabled digital twins are predictive and condition-based maintenance, which are the most mature and most widespread, as they demonstrate how sensor data can be converted into real-time decision intelligence that can be acted upon within an organization.

Wireless sensors can be trained on past sensor streams using machine learning models that capture vibration patterns, temperature trends, acoustic emissions, and current draw to extract patterns linked to imminent component failure. These predictions in digital twin environments enable organizations to plan their maintenance processes at the optimal stage between early replacement and costly unplanned failures. In that regard, predictive maintenance is the broader trend in digital twin development, from descriptive monitoring to predictive and prescriptive organizational intelligence.

The empirical evidence supports this position. According to (Warke, Kumar, Bongale, & Kotecha, 2021), predictive maintenance using digital twins can reduce unplanned downtime by 30-50 percent compared to preventive maintenance based on time in high-value manufacturing settings. Similarly, (Alcácer & Cruz-Machado, 2019) point to predictive maintenance as the most delimited source of value generation in Industry 4.0 digital twin integration, and it often serves as the entry point for the organization through which companies expand the digital twin.

In addition to maintenance, anomaly detection adds value to this reasoning by enabling digital twins to detect unexpected changes in operational behavior in real time. It is significant because this ability will allow an organization to shift its decision-making approaches from responding to the problem to intervening early in advance, which substantially enhances the value of DT systems as permanent decision-support frameworks.

2.4.2 Kowledge Graphs and Ontology-Based Cognitive Representation

Although predictive analytics can provide asset-scale intelligence, enterprise-scale cognitive digital twins need a more robust representational structure to interconnect assets, processes, units within the organization, and strategic goals. The conversation thus shifts beyond the individual analysis aptitude to the knowledge base that is needed to support the larger organizational thought.

The most popular technology for this purpose is knowledge graphs. Since knowledge graphs are semantic network structures where nodes represent objects and edges are typed relationships, they can be used to encode machine-readable correlations between the occurrences of operational events, business functions, and governance rules, as well as between the knowledge of the context and digital twins. This also makes them particularly relevant to digital twin organizations (DTO)-level analysis, in which the role of such analysis does not just rely on tracking single assets, but rather on logic between systems that form the organization.

Reviewing the knowledge of cognitive systems and enterprise interoperability (Ali, Gaffinet, Panetto, & Naudet, 2024), they find that knowledge graph integration is a major difference between asset-level and enterprise-level cognitive DT realizations. Unlike asset-level DTs, which mainly rely on sensor-data integration, enterprise-level DTs must also model organizational processes, decision logic, governance structures, and contextual relations that cannot be described using raw operational data alone.

Ontology-based representation serves as the semantic foundation of a knowledge graph. Ontologies give formal expression to the concepts, properties, and relationships that characterize an organizational field, enabling AI logical reasoning within the digital twin to be conducted with respect to semantically consistent and organizationally appropriate structures. This is especially critical when DT systems make decisions that cross operational, managerial, and strategic lines.

It has also been indicated that ontology-based DT systems have the potential to enhance the quality of decision advice in complex settings. Concretely (Li, 2025), the author of a study on AI-based digital twins in smart-energy management in the city demonstrates that ontology-based DT structures are better at responding to multi-objective optimization problems than their purely data-driven counterparts. It has a strong implication on the design of enterprise DTs. Since DT systems are no longer merely asset analytics but enterprise cognition, knowledge representation is necessary to provide reliable, explainable decision support.

By doing so, knowledge graphs and ontologies represent the conceptual mapping of the AI's ability and integration within the enterprise architecture. They allow digital twins to forecast not just activities but also place those forecasts in the broader context of the organization, interrelationships, and organizational goals.

2.5 Synthesis and Transition

This part also shows that the cognitive abilities of digital twins result from the combination of layered architectures, closed-loop feedback mechanisms, machine learning paradigms, predictive analytics, and knowledge representation systems. Collectively, they enable digital twins to transform from mere surveillance systems into smart structures capable of intelligence, predictability, diagnosis, and adaptive support for decision-making.

Technological capability, however, is not sufficient to create organizational value. Although the analytical foundations of cognitive digital twins are provided by artificial intelligence, machine learning, and knowledge representation, these functions should be integrated into organizational structures to provide a means of influencing actual decision-making. Digital twins are required to be situated at enterprise-wide levels of data, applications, processes, and strategies to be decision support infrastructures, and not isolated analysis tools. Section 3 thus explores enterprise architecture as the organizational mechanism through which digital twin intelligence is implemented into action.

3. INTEGRATING DIGITAL TWINS INTO ENTERPRISE ARCHITECTURE AND DECISION MAKING

The technical capability of digital twins (DTs) to reason, sense, and model physical systems is required, but not enough to develop organizational value. Although Section 2 showed how artificial intelligence, machine learning, and knowledge representation enable digital twins to acquire cognitive capabilities, they are only useful when embedded in organizational decision structures. In practice, the value of DT systems is created when analytical outputs are conveyed to the operational, tactical, and strategic levels of decision-making at the right pace and level.

Enterprise architecture (EA) provides the mechanism through which this integration occurs within the organization. By aligning technology infrastructure, data resources, business procedures, and strategic goals, EA serves as the connective tissue that transforms DT intelligence into practical organizational knowledge. This section thus discusses how digital twin systems are integrated into the enterprise architecture and how this integration can support the decision making and strategic intelligence.

3.2 Enterprise Architecture Frameworks for Digital Twin Integration

3.2.1 Aligning DTs Across Data, Application, Process, and Strategy Layers

Digital twin systems run on information architectures in organizations, which need to be aligned on four key layers: data, application, process, and strategy. The fact that misalignment between these layers is one of the most annoying organizational factors that have contributed to the failure of DT implementations, even when the underlying technology works, is quite well known (Rossmann & Hertweck, 2022; Botín-Sanabria, et al., 2022).

Data Layer

At the data layer, DT integration involves integrating non-homogeneous enterprise data. These and others are enterprise resource planning (ERP) and manufacturing execution system (MES) records, semi-structured IoT sensor telemetry, unstructured maintenance logs, and foreign supply-chain data. One of the most commonly mentioned barriers to the value production of DT is fragmentation across these data sources.

In (Leng, et al., 2021) review of digital twin based smart manufacturing architecture, data layer fragmentation is found to be the most widespread technological impediment to successful DT implementation. More than 60% of the analyzed implementation failures are attributable to siloed, non-interoperable data sources within organizations, underscoring the need for integrated enterprise data architectures.

Application Layer

At the application level, DT systems should be integrated with existing enterprise software platforms to prevent the emergence of parallel information environments that operate without a preconceived workflow. Rather, DT platforms are to be used to supplement the current enterprise applications.

The architecture fails to suggest any specific digital transformation of smart-city digital infrastructure, instead suggesting. However, it does not mandate the SiMiTi architecture for smart-city digital transformation, which proposes bidirectional API connectivity between digital twin systems and enterprise platforms such as ERP, CRM, and supply-chain management systems. In the absence of such application-layer integration, DT outputs cannot trigger workflow activity, update enterprise records, or feed the dashboards that operational managers use. (Zakaria, Akil, Dhiana, & Prayitno, 2025)

Process Layer

The process layer involves formally aligning DT-generated insights with business processes. This often requires mapping current workflows and redesigning them to ensure that digital twin outputs serve as active decision-making inputs rather than passive monitoring inputs.

The process-layer integration is the most complex challenge in DT adoption within the organization. This integration will require inter functional collaboration among IT, operations, and strategic management functions, which may be difficult in a highly departmentalized organization. (Rossmann & Hertweck, 2022)

Strategy Layer

At the stratum, the executive must decisively consider the use of DT intelligence in strategic planning. This involves applying digital twin insights to operations such as scenario analysis, capital investment planning, long-term operational strategy, and portfolio management.

According to the analysis of Industry 5.0 strategy formation presented by (Barata & Kayser, 2024), companies that limit the implementation of digital twins to operational monitoring do so in a systematic way that prevents them from realizing the greater strategic value of DT investments.

Synthesis

By combining these four layers, we begin to appreciate the importance of full integration, such that, despite having technically advanced DT systems, one would still fail to achieve enterprise value. Not until digital twins are aligned at the levels of data, application, process, and strategy can this analytical functionality be converted into valuable organizational decision support.

3.2.2 IoT, Cyber-Physical Systems, and Edge-Cloud Architectures as DT Enablers

The digital twin systems are based on Industrial Internet of Things (IoT) sensor networks embedded in cyber-physical systems that integrate computing, communication, and control technologies with physical processes. These sensing systems provide real-time data flows necessary to keep virtual models of physical assets on course.

Indicating the maturity of the IoT sensors as the predominant technological aspect in the transition of a simple digital shadow into a full-scale digital twin, (Alcácer & Cruz-Machado, 2019) list the maturity of IoT sensors as a component of the Industry

4.0 technological platform in the review. Streams of high-frequency sensor data keep virtual models continuously aligned with their real-life counterparts.

The structure by which this data is measured into DT systems has a significant impact on latency, bandwidth consumption, and computing requirements. This has led to edge-cloud architectures becoming the primary paradigm for the massive deployment of DT.

In the edge-cloud model, the sensor (edge) and central cloud infrastructure are distributed across multiple layers, with the latter handling the computing tasks. Round-trip delays to cloud servers will introduce unacceptable latency to high-bandwidth, time-sensitive DT tasks with edge computing at the sensor, including anomaly detection, safety monitoring, and real-time process optimization. (Sacoto-Cabrera, Perez-Torres, Tello-Oquendo, & Cerrada, 2025)

By contrast, cloud infrastructure is better suited to computationally intensive data tasks (such as training AI models, cross-horizon simulations, and cross-site DT federation).

Smart-city energy management, hybrid edge-cloud DTs have much shorter response times and lower infrastructure costs than solely cloud-based systems. These architectural choices directly affect system scaling, operational costs, and how quickly the information provided by DT can be used to make organizational decisions in a managerial context. (Li, 2025)

Table 2. Edge-Fog-Cloud Tier Differentiation in Enterprise Digital Twin Architectures

Tier	Processing Location	Latency Profile	Primary DT Function	Typical Use Cases
Edge	At or adjacent to sensor / actuator	Milliseconds	Real-time control, safety monitoring, immediate anomaly response	CNC machine control, safety shutdowns, real-time quality checks
Fog	Local gateway / plant-level server	Seconds	Local DT model sync, short-horizon prediction, IoT data aggregation	Predictive maintenance, production scheduling, KPI dashboards
Cloud	Centralized / multi-cloud	Minutes–hours	AI model training, long-horizon simulation, cross-enterprise DT federation	Strategic scenario planning, DTO analytics, federated learning

(Sacoto-Cabrera, Perez-Torres, Tello-Oquendo, & Cerrada, 2025; Li, 2025)

3.2.3 Interoperability Standards and Digital Twin Ecosystems

Interoperability is a precondition for scaling value creation as these single-asset implementations develop over time into enterprise-wide, cross-organizational eco-systems of DT deployments. Interoperability is the property of heterogeneous DT systems to interact with each other and perform coordinated actions without having to integrate at a notable scale.

The interoperability challenge in enterprise DT ecosystems operates across three dimensions:

- Syntactic interoperability – common data formats and communication protocols
- Semantic interoperability – shared meanings and ontological structures for data
- Organizational interoperability – aligned governance frameworks and data-sharing agreements

Semantic interoperability is the most challenging dimension in their review of enterprise interoperability (Ali, Gaffinet, Panetto, & Naudet, 2024). Many domain-specific ontologies have been developed, including manufacturing ontologies, building information modeling standards, smart-city data frameworks, and health-care models, resulting in fragmented semantic ecosystems that are challenging to combine through cross-domain DT.

Advances have occurred more at the syntactic front. The Asset Administration Shell (AAS) standard emerged in the Platform Industry 4.0, and the Industrial Internet Consortium provides a framework for the digital representation of physical assets that enables plug-and-play interoperability across vendor platforms.

Research surveys of sustainability-oriented implementations of DT (Pater & Stadnicka, 2021) demonstrate that organizations implementing AAS-compliant architecture incur lower integration costs and shorter deployment schedule, a finding corroborated by more extensive technology surveys (Botín-Sanabria, et al., 2022).

Recent strategies centered on knowledge-graph interoperability models, in which domain ontologies are networked via common upper ontologies, e.g., SOSA/SSN, are promising for addressing semantic interoperability. Nevertheless, the adoption of these frameworks by enterprises is low.

Finally, interoperability standards are also necessary to support multi-site coordination and enterprise-level decision support, especially in distributed supply chains, smart-city infrastructures, and cross-organization DT ecosystems.

3.3 Digital Twin-Driven Decision Support and Strategic Intelligence

3.3.1 Decision Support Architectures: From Operational to Strategic Enterprise DTs

In cases where digital twins have been effectively incorporated into enterprise architecture, their analytical outputs would inform decision making at various levels of the organization. The literature identifies three decision layers for applying DT intelligence: operational, tactical, and strategic.

DT decision support at the operational level has been described as high frequency, short time horizons, and a high level of automation. Virtual models continuously compare the actual state of physical systems against a set of performance limits and generate automatic responses or warnings.

They note that operational DT applications have been the most impactful so far and provide quantifiable value in predictive maintenance, quality control, and energy optimization in manufacturing and logistics settings (Tao, Zhang, Liu, & Nee, 2019) in their state-of-the-art review.

On the tactical level, DT decision support supports medium-term planning spanning days to months. These are used in production scheduling, maintenance planning, and resource allocation. When digital twins are integrated with enterprise systems such as ERP and MES, planners can use operational data from these systems in real time to make planning decisions.

Empirical research (Warke, Kumar, Bongale, & Kotecha, 2021) supports the idea that such integrations can reduce production planning time by 25-40% and improve decision-making.

At the strategic level, DT decision-making involves long-term organizational decisions, capital investment planning, market strategy, sustainability governance, and organizational restructuring. This layer is not as developed due to technical difficulties and organizational obstacles.

Companies that incorporate DT insights into their strategic decisions gain dynamic capabilities, enabling them to detect changes, simulate strategic responses, and quickly reallocate resources in uncertain markets. (Barata & Kayser, 2024)

3.3.2 Simulation-Based Scenario Planning and Organizational Agility

Among the greatest benefits of enterprise digital twins is their ability to test potential operational and strategic alternatives in high-fidelity, contestable virtual environments.

Conventional scenario planning approaches tend to rely on qualitative arguments or streamlined informational analyses. Conversely, scenario simulation based on a DT relies on continuously updated virtual models derived from observed operational data. This facilitates realistic, data-driven decision-making.

The concept of simulation-as-a-service thus became a central architectural principle of advanced DT systems (Fuller, Fan, Day, & Barlow, 2020). Quantitative simulation models can be used to quickly assess hypothetical situations, such as changes in production capacity or the protection of the supply chain or infrastructure.

The Journal of Business Research indicates that business model innovation is also facilitated by DT simulations, especially in the circular economy context, where organizations should test their service models and resource flows before investing in their physical implementation. (Kristoffersen, Blomsma, Mikalef, & Li, 2020)

The capabilities of DT-driven simulation, in turn, increase organizational agility, enabling companies to perceive shifts in the environment, consider possible strategies, and execute them more quickly (Zakaria, Akil, Dhiana, & Prayitno, 2025).

3.3.3 Process Mining, Process Prediction, and Real-Time Monitoring

One important analytical tool that enables digital twins to reflect organizational processes is process mining.

Process mining produces formal process models based on event logs generated by enterprise information systems, such as ERP transaction logs, workflow management system logs, and IoT event streams. This enables DT systems to capture real-life operational processes rather than the formal documents that describe them.

There is often a discrepancy between the formal process definition and the actual architecture in large organizations. These deviations would go undetected with traditional auditing and manual analysis tools. Process mining can be used to identify and analyze such variations in real time in digital twins.

Process mining is perceived as a key gap in the construction of enterprise DT infrastructures because it renders organizational processes intelligible to AI-based inference within these infrastructures. (Ali, Gaffinet, Panetto, & Naudet, 2024)

Process mining may be further extended to process prediction, where machine learning models use historical execution data to guide the future progression of current process instances. Examples of risks that can be identified from these predictions include delayed customer orders, maintenance delays, or breaches of procurement rules.

One of the AI applications with the greatest value in enterprise DT settings is process prediction, which is directly related to cost management, service levels, and risk management in organisations (Rathore, Shah, Shukla, Bentafat, & Bakiras, 2021).

Real-time monitoring of processes is an addition to the closed-loop process intelligence cycle, as it continuously compares current processes to performance benchmarks predefined by DT and initiates corrective organizational measures in the event of deviations.

3.4 Summary

In this section, the enterprise architecture and decision-making have been looked into.

Support structures turn digital twin systems from simple technical monitoring devices into providers of organizational intelligence and competitive advantage.

The literature yields three major conclusions.

To begin with, digital twins are equally architectural and technological issues regarding organizational value. It is only where DT systems are coordinated between data, application, process, and strategy layers and integrated into the process of making decisions in the organization that the analysis capabilities of the system can translate into quantifiable business results (Leng, et al., 2021; Barata & Kayser, 2024; Rossmann & Hertweck, 2022).

Secondly, the technological platform of enterprise DT integration, such as IoT sensor networks, edge-cloud computing platforms, and interoperability standards, is progressively maturing. Hybrid edge-cloud models and new standardization models are gradually being adopted to address technical impediments to enterprise-scale DT implementation (Sacoto-Cabrera, Perez-Torres, Tello-Oquendo, & Cerrada, 2025; Alcácer & Cruz-Machado, 2019).

Third, currently, there are advanced DT decision-support capabilities available technically: simulation-based scenario planning, process-mining, and real-time predictive monitoring, which are difficult to institutionalize in organizational governance frameworks (Fuller, Fan, Day, & Barlow, 2020; Rathore, Shah, Shukla, Bentafat, & Bakiras, 2021; Ali, Gaffinet, Panetto, & Naudet, 2024).

4. EMPIRICAL EVIDENCE AND INDUSTRY CASE STUDIES

4.1 Introduction

Conceptual frameworks can provide a good understanding of the architecture and theoretical basis of digital twin (DT) systems. Still, they cannot fully inform us about how these systems can be deployed in an organizational context constrained by resources, legacy infrastructure, and institutions. To overcome this weakness, this section considers empirical case studies across fields such as manufacturing, healthcare, smart cities, and supply chain systems, where DT implementations have resulted in documented, quantifiable outcomes.

Analysis aims at achieving three ends. To start with, it identifies performance dimensions where the adoption of DT has been determined to generate quantifiable organizational value regularly. Second, it studies in which cases increased benefits are not expected. Third, it isolates cross-case knowings that can be deployed across industries rather than being tied to a particular industry setting. Notably, the section does not make DT adoption uniformly successful. Rather, it also emphasizes good outcomes and the contradictions, implementation barriers, and trade-offs that emerge from empirical findings.

To explain the interaction between the technological and organizational aspects discussed throughout the chapter, Figure 1 presents a conceptual framework showing the layered architecture through which digital twin systems will develop into cognitive enterprise capabilities. To clarify how the technological and organizational dimensions discussed throughout the chapter interact in practice, Figure 1 presents a conceptual framework illustrating the layered architecture through which digital twin systems evolve into cognitive enterprise capabilities.

Figure 1. Depicts the integrated framework proposed in this chapter, demonstrating how digital twin infrastructures evolve into cognitive enterprise systems through the interaction of AI, enterprise architecture, and governance mechanisms.

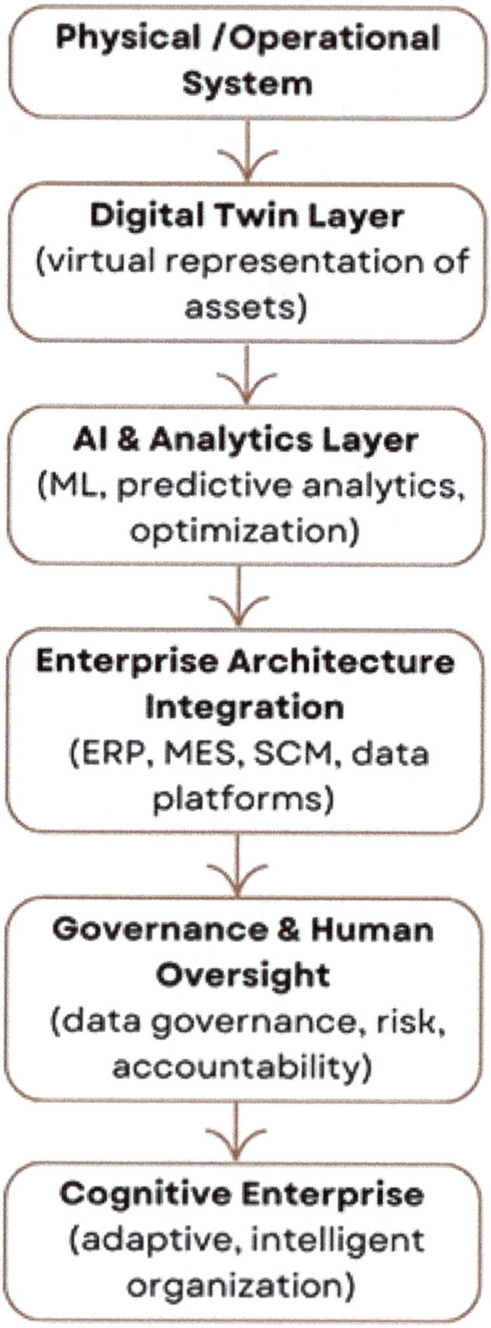

Digital twin architectures, as depicted in Figure 1, are used as an intermediate layer between physical operational systems and advanced analytics and enterprise decision structures. Sensors capture real-time data of physical assets, and then they are incorporated into the digital twin layer that offers a moving virtual representation of operational environments. This data is consumed by the AI and analytics layer, which uses machine learning and predictive models to generate operational insights and optimization suggestions. Such insights are then incorporated into enterprise architecture applications such as ERP, MES, and supply chain applications, so that the data used can serve as the basis for decision-making across different organizational processes. Governance systems, such as data governance, accountability systems, and human controls, will guarantee responsible and strategic utilisation of AI-based insights. When these layers work together in a coordinated fashion, organizations no longer operate through monitoring but instead create cognitive enterprises that can make decisions adaptively, intelligently, and autonomously.

4.2 Manufacturing and Industry 4.0 / 5.0 Applications

4.2.1 Cognitive DTs for Intelligent Production Systems and Smart Factories

The field of manufacturing is the most advanced in implementing digital twins, and its empirical base is large enough to support successful generalization. As the evidence suggests, full DT deployments - with artificially intelligent-driven analytics or feedback systems, defined by bi-directional data flows - would always perform better than simple “digital shadow systems” that can replicate physical processes but do not engage in active interventions. A study found that facilities with fully implemented DT systems achieved quantifiable improvements in the main operational indicators. (Leng, et al., 2021)

In the fourteen manufacturing case studies reviewed, organizations with cognitive DT architectures showed improvements in defect counts of 18-34 percent and an increase in overall equipment effectiveness (OEE) of 22-41 percent on average. These gains were highest in organizations that incorporated the output of DT in the enterprise workflow by utilizing manufacturing execution infrastructure (MES) and enterprise resource planning (ERP) systems. Conversely, companies that used DT dashboards as monitoring tools recorded only partial performance improvements.

Cognitive DTs integrate machine learning, geometry, and real-time operational data to facilitate adaptive decision-making in production settings. Such systems have been found to spot and correct process drift 6 to 8 times faster than systems that rely on humans to detect quality issues in semiconductor manufacturing environments, preventing classes of quality failures that are hard to detect through periodic quality inspection. (Ali, Gaffinet, Panetto, & Naudet, 2024)

Nevertheless, empirical evidence shows that the best implementations are not necessarily those that maximize full automation. Effective deployments of the smart factory are often based on hybrid human-DT decision-making models, in which human capabilities are supplemented with the use of algorithms. This type of collaborative system has been found to perform better than fully automated systems and purely operator-driven processes, across combined performance factors such as operational efficiency, safety, and strategic flexibility. (Barata & Kayser, 2024)

4.2.2 Predictive Maintenance and Supply Chain Resilience

One of the most well-documented benefits of DT deployment is predictive maintenance. According to an analysis of 31 independent industrial implementations, (Warke, Kumar, Bongale, & Kotecha, 2021) report that DT-based predictive maintenance systems resulted in lower mean time-to-repair costs (by almost 28 percent) and unplanned downtime costs (by 35-50 percent). Similar findings have been made in infrastructure management. As an illustration report a 38-52 percent decrease in the expenses involved in emergency maintenance in civil infrastructure systems with the help of DT-enabled monitoring and predictive analytics. (Qiu, et al., 2025)

The quality of products produced by the DT systems, however, hinges heavily on the level of automation applied to operational processes. The insurance of quality improvement was statistically significant only when DT predictions were used to automate parameter changes in the production system. Conversely, there was a significant decrease in performance gains when DT alerts were routed through manual review processes before operational adjustments were made. These results suggest that incorporating DT analytics into organizations' decision loops should not be overlooked. (Warke, Kumar, Bongale, & Kotecha, 2021)

Digital twin technology has also shown great potential to enhance supply chain resilience. According to a review published in the Journal of Industrial Information Integration (Sharma, Kosasih, Zhang, Brintrup, & Calinescu, 2022), organizations with supply chain DT systems saved up to forty to sixty times in response to disruptions in comparison to other companies that have not adopted the system. The most significant factor enabling this has been simulation speed. New DT-enabled environments enable managers to model a variety of supply chain scenarios in several hours rather than weeks, enabling rapid decision-making during disruptions.

These advantages of resilience, however, were noted to be experienced mainly in companies that realized multi-tiered access to supply chains, beyond the short-term, Tier-1 suppliers to Tier-2 and Tier-3 supply chains. Generally, DT implementations provided accurate representations of local supply chain networks but could not capture systemic weaknesses emerging in the upper supplier ecosystems. (Ali, Gaffinet, Panetto, & Naudet, 2024)

4.3 Healthcare, Smart Cities, and Cross-Sector Applications

In other fields beyond the manufacturing industry, digital twins are being applied to healthcare and urban infrastructure, yet there is still relatively little empirical evidence. The Healthcare DT Application shows great potential but will face significant implementation challenges due to information fragmentation, privacy policies, and interoperability issues among clinical information systems. The healthcare industry is one of the areas where the gap between the anticipated DT value and actual performance is particularly significant. (Rathore, Shah, Shukla, Bentafat, & Bakiras, 2021)

However, some of the reported applications exhibit actual advantages. Simulation systems based on DT have been used in hospital capacity management (such as elective procedure cancellations), leading to 25-40 per cent fewer cancellations due to more accurate predictions of bed occupancy and staffing. In addition to clinical operations, DT-based facility management processes have also yielded environmental and operational gains. Hospitals equipped with environmental control systems can reduce consumption and the number of healthcare-associated infections by optimizing their use. (Bibri & Huang, 2025)

Another fast-expanding area of usage is urban digital twins. A literature review of 87 urban DT implementations by (Sacoto-Cabrera, Perez-Torres, Tello-Oquendo, & Cerrada, 2025) has identified a common pattern wherein urban areas first implement an operational monitoring system that works via DT, and later attempt to incorporate those systems into strategic governance operations. Cities that reduced DT systems to running dashboards saw small efficiency gains but showed no significant improvement in policy outcomes over the long term. Conversely, those municipalities that incorporated simulated urban planning and policy modelling processes with DT data demonstrated quantifiable improvements in the quality of infrastructure investment decisions and policy efficiency.

On the same note, (Li, 2025) indicates that digital twins of energy-environment models in the city have led to reductions in energy waste of 18-31 percent and to the development of carbon-footprint analysis, which would be hard to provide with traditional management methods.

4.4 Cross-Case Synthesis and Summary

In the four areas reviewed in this section, three cross-case trends are clear enough to justify more generalizations about the circumstances in which digital twins can create organizational value.

First, in implementing the benefits of DT, the presence of closed feedback loops between physical operations and virtual models is critical. The enhancements that are realized in organizations that operate developing DT systems as monitoring devices are usually limited. In comparison, companies that introduce DT analytics to the mechanisms of automated feedback of operations write statistically higher returns on performance (Leng, et al., 2021).

Second, non-technical organizational factors have a determining effect on implementation outcomes. The evidence, provided by several industries, suggests that aspects of data governance organization, top management dedication, and corporate culture explain a higher rate of variation in DT performance than technical features alone. This finding can be explained by the meta-review by (Rossmann & Hertweck, 2022), which emphasizes the role of managerial and institutional conditions in shaping digital transformation outcomes.

Third, the value created by digital twin systems is likely to grow over time rather than being realized immediately after initial use. Empirical research has cited the greatest gains in performance in organizations that have evaluated three to seven years of experience in building DT capabilities, indicating that it takes organizations three to seven years to modify processes, data infrastructure, and governance systems around the technology.

Combined, these results indicate that technological limitations are not the key factors limiting the creation of DT values, but organizational and governance-related issues are. The second section therefore examines how governance forms, strategic management, and institutional frameworks shape the development of digital twin systems into the full manifestation of cognitive enterprise capabilities.

5. MANAGERIAL, ORGANIZATIONAL, AND STRATEGIC IMPLICATIONS

5.1 Introduction

Based on the empirical evidence examined in the foregoing section, it is observed that when the digital twin (DT) implementation fails to deliver the perceived value, the root cause is rarely in sensor technical constraints, quality, or algorithms. Instead, repetitive constraints arise on the managerial and organizational level. These encompass systems of governance that are not compatible with machine-assisted decision-making, cultures within organizations that limit information sharing, leadership teams that are not long-term and strategic about DT maturity journeys, and workforces that lack the hybrid skills required for human-AI collaborative systems.

These issues prove that the shift towards the models of the cognitive enterprise is not a technological issue but an inherently management and organizational change issue.

This part will bring together the above conceptual and empirical discussion with the organizational problems that senior managers should address as they proceed with the enterprise's cognitive deployment.

5.2 Strategic Management of Digital Twin Adoption

5.2.1 Dynamic Capabilities and Governance Structures

One theoretical framework that helps one understand how digital twin systems can create strategic value in organizations is the dynamic capabilities framework (Teece, 2018). Dynamic capabilities enable an organization to perceive new opportunities, capture them through viable resource allocation, and adapt to a changing environment. The mechanisms are closely associated with the technical functionalities of the developed DT systems, which involve real-time sensing, simulation, and adaptive optimization.

Empirical data, however, indicate that the connection between DT adoption and development is conditional rather than automatic. (Youssef & Adel, 2025) reveal that DT investments enhanced dynamic capabilities only in organizations that already had excellent absorptive capacity, such as internal knowledge management systems and other learning infrastructure, which could capture the intelligence generated. On the same note, similar results were reported by (Kristoffersen, Blomsma, Mikalef, & Li, 2020), who found a statistically significant increase in capabilities in manufacturing firms only when DT systems were applied in a setting with a pre-established data analytics culture.

These results indicate that digital twins cannot generate dynamic capabilities; rather, they enhance the capabilities already formed by the organization.

Managerial implication: Senior leaders should thus not see adoption of DT as a solo technological upgrade, but rather as a component of a larger, broader capabilities-building strategy that is inclusive of analytics maturity, data governance, and knowledge management systems.

A second challenge is that of an increasing mismatch between how DT systems generate strategic insights and the organizational governance structures to convert those insights into operational choices. In most organizations, DT intelligence is generated faster than governance systems can receive and take action to address it. Consequently, decision bottlenecks arise despite organizations' technically advanced DT infrastructures. (Barata & Kayser, 2024)

This governance gap is one of the biggest impediments to the adoption of DT at the enterprise level, often more important than technical integration issues (Rossmann & Hertweck, 2022). This argument is corroborated by empirical evidence provided by (Pater & Stadnicka, 2021),who found that organizations that had clear governance frameworks regarding the execution of the DT, including the establishment of the ownership structure, decision-making rights, and performance metrics, performed 2.3 times higher than those organizations that considered the implementation of the DT as decentralized IT projects.

The role of governance structures is especially evident at the enterprise level. Whereas a domain-based digital twin can work well within a distributed mechanism of governance, high-scale systems DT systems need centralized strategic coordination to track cross-functional data integration and value attribution.

Managerial implication: To achieve cognitive enterprise transformation, organizations should develop formal management systems for DTs, such as explicit accountability systems, enterprise architecture, and decision-making systems that can respond to real-time intelligence.

5.3 Organizational Learning, Competencies, and Change Management

5.3.1 Competency Frameworks and Learning Loops

Whereas the technical architecture of digital twin systems has been explored in the scholarly literature, little attention has been paid to human abilities to interpret and manage such systems. This gap is also a significant organizational risk because the performance of DT deployments will eventually rely on human capacity to interpret and respond to system outputs. (Jones, Snider, Nassehi, Yon, & Hicks, 2020)

According to empirical research on DT implementation, we can identify four major areas of capability as particularly significant for an organization's development of cognitive enterprise capabilities.

The former is data literacy, which is defined as employees at various levels of organizations' ability to comprehend and share information based on DT analytics. The second one is AI critical evaluation, which would entail monitoring the credibility and practicality of algorithmic suggestions in particular operating conditions. The third competence that is usually least practiced is human-AI teaming, meaning working jointly by human specialists and automated systems to make decisions. Lastly, the field of DT governance literacy is gaining increasing significance as organizations implement systems that raise complex issues of data confidentiality, responsibility, and moral control (Ali, Gaffinet, Panetto, & Naudet, 2024; Rathore, Shah, Shukla, Bentafat, & Bakiras, 2021).

All these competencies, combined, are the pillars of effective human interaction with cognitive DT systems.

Managerial implication: Organizations must allocate funds to systematic training initiatives that not only develop technical skills in DT but also expand skills in AI assessment, data analytics, and governance literacy.

Digital twins also change the pace of learning in an organization. Growth: With complete DT, it can take hours to recreate learning cycles that previously took months to analyze the data. Although this ability to accelerate learning can yield impressive performance gains, new managerial problems arise. (Leng, et al., 2021)

There are instances in which the improvement recommendations generated by DT systems exceed the organization's ability to act on them, especially in the manufacturing setting of a circular economy. The distribution of unwritten recommendations over time damaged the managerial confidence in the system and undermined the perceived validity of DT-generated judgments. (Kristoffersen, Blomsma, Mikalef, & Li, 2020)

Managerial implication: To ensure successful DT governance, there is a need to balance the pace of data-driven learning and the capacity of implementation within an organisation. In the absence of this alignment, the gains from rapid intelligence creation can be lost due to overload in operational functions.

5.3.2 Change Management and Workforce Resistance

The workforce's opposition to DT use is uniform across sectors and organizational environments. Nevertheless, this resistance can be regarded as irrational technophobia, which is more easily interpreted than the actual organizational forces and can negatively affect implementation strategies.

According to qualitative research, the issues expressed by employees are often grounded in legitimate concerns about skills obsolescence, the responsibility for making AI-assisted decisions, professional autonomy, and surveillance systems developed by sensors. These issues provoke wider aspects of privacy, dignity, and justice in the digitally monitored workplaces.

The researchers conclude that organizations that take these issues into consideration through proactive practices, including involving employees in system design (setting up open accountability frameworks and investing in workforce reskilling), adopt DT faster and show better system performance (Barata & Kayser, 2024).

These results show why the social contract between organizations and their labor force is significant during the digital transformation process. When employees perceive that the DT systems do not pose a threat but are support tools, there is an increased likelihood that they will share tacit knowledge on how to operate the system, exhibit model constraints, and be engaged in the quest to enhance the performance of the system.

Managerial implication: Change management strategies that address issues of power, accountability, and fairness should be employed to ensure the successful implementation of DT rather than relying on communication campaigns or training.

Finally, the building of organizational competencies and learning. Mechanisms, workforce trust has a direct impact on the maturity of DT governance structures and on the sustainability of long-term enterprise transformation.

5.4 Summary

Moving to cognitive enterprise systems is not an easy managerial and organizational issue, but it is not a technological upgrade either. According to empirical data, digital twin systems mostly enhance, rather than form, organizational capabilities (Teece, 2018; Kristoffersen, Blomsma, Mikalef, & Li, 2020).

Effective enterprise-wide implementation of DT thus necessitates clear governance models to organize cross-functional data flows and address issues of value attribution (Rossmann & Hertweck, 2022; Pater & Stadnicka, 2021). Meanwhile, organizations should invest in developing competencies beyond technical operations in DT, including data literacy, AI evaluation, human-AI interaction, and governance awareness (Jones, Snider, Nassehi, Yon, & Hicks, 2020; Ali, Gaffinet, Panetto, & Naudet, 2024).

The digital twins also accelerate organizational learning, which creates new managerial dilemmas regarding decision-making capacity and execution bandwidth. Moreover, employee opposition to DT systems is often a sign of legitimate issues of responsibility, autonomy, and equity that require organizations to address through inclusion efforts in the direction of governance and reskilling.

These management and organizational aspects underscore the importance of having well-developed governance and ethical rules and measures that can inform Ioanthro-AI cooperation in the more autonomous organizations of the future. In the following section, the governance systems, integrity norms, and institutional arrangements necessary to facilitate the conscientious use of cognitive enterprise technologies are reviewed.

6. GOVERNANCE, ETHICS, TRUST, AND HUMAN-AI COLLABORATION

The managerial and organizational issues described in Section 5 cannot be resolved only with the help of better technology or sophisticated strategic planning. They need institutional systems that delineate accountability for decisions made by digital twins (DTs), establish data control regulations, and specify the circumstances under which autonomous machine activities can occur within organizations. Governance and ethics are not thus peripheral issues that can be adopted once the DT systems are mature. On the contrary, they are structural design requirements. When left inadequately developed during initial system development, organizations can be exposed to a lot of risks, including regulatory liability, loss of stakeholder trust, and operational uncertainty.

This part explores governance, ethical theories, and people-AI collaboration strategies to foster the responsible creation of cognitive enterprises. In particular, it seeks to: (1) discuss how the AI ethics principles can be applied to the cognitive DT settings; (2) discuss the data privacy, security, and sovereignty as the key governance variables; and (3) discuss the human-AI collaboration frameworks that would not sacrifice human agency, facilitate the proper calibration of trust, and deal with cognitive implications of the DT-enhanced work settings..

6.2 Ethical Frameworks and Responsible Digital Twin Governance

6.2.1 AI Ethics Principles, Data Privacy, and the Regulatory Landscape

The most common principles of AI ethics, as outlined in the literature on governance, including transparency, fairness, accountability, and human oversight, all have operational implications for the consideration of DT arrangements. Transparency means that, in addition to the structure of DT systems being documented, the rationale behind the AI models running in systems should be readable by the organizational actors whose decisions depend on the outputs of such systems. The reason is that (Rathore, Shah, Shukla, Bentafat, & Bakiras, 2021) in a review of AI and big data in digital twins, the most frequently discussed governance issue among practitioners of enterprise DT is the AI decision logic ambiguity, more acute in their survey results, than data security or computational reliability. Interpretability does not simply represent a question of ethical plausibility; when the recommendations generated by the DT are to be used to make a safety-related or otherwise legally meaningful decision, it becomes a minimum operational requirement. Responsibility-who is the agent organization that can take a negative result in an autonomous DT decision- is perhaps the least discussed issue of governance in the current literature. The accountability gap, which is a structural feature of prevailing enterprise DT deployments, is not a unique event but an extension of the accountability structures that existed before, based on human action and decision-making, and poorly aligned with autonomous or semi-autonomous machine action (Ali, Gaffinet, Panetto, & Naudet, 2024).

The governance issues related to data privacy and sovereignty continue to grow as the scale of DT implementation increases. The challenge of asset-level DT data governance can often be addressed by extending existing enterprise data protection mechanisms. In the organizational domain, where DT systems can integrate employees' personal information, commercially sensitive operational information, and information shared across organizational boundaries in networked twin ecosystems, privacy regulation requires exclusive architectural and contractual solutions that most organizations have not yet formulated. Regarding the governance risks that may jeopardize cross-enterprise investments in DT integrations, (Botín-Sanabria, et al., 2022) explain that the data sovereignty conflicts, or disagreements over which organizational entity can be entitled to access data generated by the joint physical resources within multi-party industrial ecosystems, are an emerging and underreported governance risk that can sabotage investments. The regulatory environment is also evolving rapidly in that respect: the EU AI act and the ramifications of GDPR on automated decision-making, industry-specific regulation in healthcare and critical infrastructure are also gradually limiting under what circumstances autonomous DT decision-making can be legally operated, and the corresponding compliance obligations should be engineered into the framework of the DT systems and not as an addition to them once the deployment is made. As stated by (Youssef & Adel, 2025), organisations that perceive regulatory compliance as a negative influence on the establishment of DT capability and an alternative to regulatory compliance as a governing mechanism promoting institutional trust systematically lower their performance outcomes at both the regulatory and business levels.

When managers implement enterprise digital twins, all these ethical principles need to be translated into operational governance practices, such as explainable AI models, well-specified accountability, and written decision-making guidelines for autonomous system recommendations.

6.3 Human-AI Collaboration in Cognitive Enterprise Systems

6.3.1 Augmentation vs. Automation, Operator 5.0, and Trust Calibration

The fundamental design dilemma of human-AI interaction in the cognitive enterprise systems is not the question of whether to use a human or machine agent to make organizational decisions, but the allocation of decision power between the human and machine agent within the decision architectures to afford the best composite performance across the dimensions of efficiency, safety, accountability, and human dignity. In Technovation, which covers the role of DT in Industry 5.0 (Barata & Kayser, 2024), formulate the thesis of augmentation in a highly aggressive manner: the most effective uses of cognitive enterprise include the introduction of DT intelligence to enlarge rather than supplant human cognitive capability, and the consequences of machine error are finite and can be repaired. The mass of the empirical evidence considered in Section 4 does not support the thesis of automation that the more the DT autonomy, the higher the organizational value; and the governance model it implies that the human control is viewed as a friction to be eliminated is increasingly becoming incongruent with the new regulatory imperatives in the AI decisions regarding the consequences of the consequential decisions.

The organizational role concept in the literature on Industry 5.0, called Operator 5.0, describes the human agent as a partner rather than a passive consumer of machine proposals in a cognitive enterprise setting. The proposal of the SiMiTi intelligent enterprise architecture by (Zakaria, Akil, Dhiana, & Prayitno, 2025) in Smart Cities is intended to explicitly implement human-AI collaboration interfaces in the system architecture, not as an afterthought when it comes to the design of a DT system (e.g., the design of a Smart Cities system) which is not a design philosophy but is also consistent with empirical evidence that the contribution of the workforce to the design of a DT system predicts the performance of the system under implementation. Trust calibration In the Journal of Industrial Information Integration, (Sharma, Kosasih, Zhang, Brintrup, & Calinescu, 2022) summarize the state of the art of the field of DT and single out both over-trust (automation bias, where human agents act upon the recommendations of a deployed system without critically evaluating them) and under-trust (automation resistance, where human agents disregard reliable outputs of a deployed system) as the reported failure modes of deployed systems. Trust calibration is governed by the system design: Quantification of trust with DT advice, development of guides for structured human scrutiny of critical decisions, and provision of periodic operational reports to human operators. It is a governance task for organisations to articulate their DT strategies.

6.4 Summary

Governance and ethics cannot be considered bottom-up provisions in cognitive enterprise formation, but rather design provisions that form the core of how digital twin systems create sustainable organizational value. Concepts like transparency, accountability, data sovereignty, and human oversight must thus be translated into tangible governance structures incorporated into enterprise architectures (Rathore, Shah, Shukla, Bentafat, & Bakiras, 2021; Botín-Sanabria, et al., 2022).

Reviewed evidence indicates that the following human-oriented methods of governance, including the augmentation-over-automation design philosophy, the Operator 5.0 role model, and institutionalized mechanisms of trust calibration, can be used to help companies find a balance between technological efficiency and human agency and institutional trust (Barata & Kayser, 2024; Zakaria, Akil, Dhiana, & Prayitno, 2025; Sharma, Kosasih, Zhang, Brintrup, & Calinescu, 2022).

The following section discusses new technology frontiers that will shape the further development of cognitive enterprises, including organizational digital twins, predictive enterprise systems, and the integration of digital twin architecture into the industrial metaverse.

7. EMERGING TRENDS: DTOS, PREDICTIVE ENTERPRISES, AND AUTONOMOUS DECISION SYSTEMS

7.1 Introduction

Three new fields are discussed: The Digital Twins of Organizations (DTOs) that extend the intelligence of DT to the scale of an enterprise; the idea of predictive enterprise architecture that transforms the organization into an anticipatory and partially autonomous decision system; and the integration of the DT technologies with the industrial metaverse and sustainability governance platforms. This segment does not examine speculative forecasts; rather, through its interpretation, it examines the emerging empirical and theoretical trends that continue to build on the framework established earlier in the chapter.

7.2 Digital Twins of Organizations: From Asset Intelligence to Enterprise Cognition

7.2.1 Graph-Based Knowledge Representation and Organizational Agility

A Digital Twin of an Organization (DTO) is a significant development in Digital Twins, understood as the physical object within the enterprise. A DTO is a constantly evolving, machine-readable computational embodiment of an organization that models its processes, resources, systems, and relationships. In contrast to asset-level digital twins, which are mostly interested in tracking and simulating the operational conditions of physical systems, DTOs focus on recording the structure and dynamics of processes and decision environments within the organization.

Use of knowledge graph architectures is one of the most common technical foundations for enabling DTO capability, as they represent the organization's processes, roles, assets, systems, and external partners as nodes in a semantic network. The association among these components is not only defined and structured in a manner that enables artificial intelligence facilities to examine dependencies, simulate business conditions, and assess the consequences of possible strategic actions. The literature on cognitive enterprise interoperability demonstrates that these graph-based representations help organizations go beyond observing operational conditions to comprehend the interactions among different processes and systems about the larger messages of an organization (Ali, Gaffinet, Panetto, & Naudet, 2024).

The shift between asset-level intelligence and organizational-level intelligence has significant ramifications for organizational agility and strategic experimentation. In Industry 5.0 architectures incorporating DTOs, enterprise-level digital twins enable organizations to continuously assess how well strategic goals and operational performance are located in a variety of dimensions (Barata & Kayser, 2024). Organizations can also test potential structural or strategic changes virtually, using a scenario simulation within a DTO environment, before rolling them into real operations, thereby minimizing the cost and risk of strategic experimentation (Youssef & Adel, 2025).

Despite the promise of DTO architectures for developing cognitive enterprises, large-scale implementations remain limited. A significant part of the existing literature remains theoretical, and empirical data are mostly culled from case-based research rather than from results determined statistically. The organizations thus experience major issues with the governance framework, data integration, and the capabilities needed to operate enterprise-level digital twins.

By doing so, DTO architectures can be viewed as the logical extension of the integrated framework described in the chapter, in which digital twin-based infrastructures, AI-based analytics, and enterprise architectures come together to facilitate higher cognitive decision-making within the organization.

7.3 Predictive Enterprises and Autonomous Decision Systems

7.3.1 From Forecasting to Autonomous Action and Industry 5.0 Contexts

The logical extension of the closed-loop cognitive DT architecture exhibited in Section 2 is the predictive enterprise, which is an archetype of organizational structure where AI-enabled DT systems not only monitor the current state of an organization but also predict the future, in addition to pre-programming organizational response to problems even before they appear in the real world. Authors of (Rathore, Shah, Shukla, Bentafat, & Bakiras, 2021) in their systematic review categorize predictive enterprise capability, i.e., descriptive analytics (what happened), predictive analytics (what will happen), and prescriptive analytics (what should be done). Most current deployments of DT by enterprises are in the descriptive-to-predictive boundary; the prescriptive analytics layer, where AI systems do not merely predict conditions but generate, evaluate, and suggest or even implement the optimal organizational response, is the boundary capability where the next generation of cognitive DT systems is being developed, and is yet to be developed on an enterprise scale. Having looked at the design of smart manufacturing systems, in the Journal of Manufacturing Systems, (Leng, et al., 2021) report that DT-based prescriptive analytics on production settings, which reconfigures production schedules, resource assignments, and process settings based on forecast conditions and autonomously is technically demonstrated to work with controlled manufacturing systems, however has faced serious governance and reliability issues that have slowed their incorporation to large-scale enterprises. The Industry 5.0 context also offers a third dimension. An autonomous DT decision system in Industry 5.0 environments must be set to achieve human-machine symbiosis, and not human replacement, to give prescriptive advice that human actors will make decisions on and approve under the assumed tendencies of autonomous, pre-authorised routine optimisation as autonomous decisions are made. (Zakaria, Akil, Dhiana, & Prayitno, 2025)

In the broader context of the cognitive enterprise addressed in this chapter, predictive enterprise architectures are where digital twin analytics can transform into consumption and predictive capabilities, and be promoted to structured decision support and directed autonomous optimization.

7.4 Convergence with Emerging Technologies: Metaverse and Sustainability

7.4.1 Industrial Metaverse and DTs for Environmental and Social Governance

Although not yet a core part of the cognitive enterprise engine described in this chapter, several new technological convergences are broadening the range of applications of digital twins, specifically within immersive collaboration environments and sustainability governance.

Among the most explicit processes is the combination of digital twins and the industrial metaverse. Geographically dispersed teams are able to visualize and interact with digital forms of physical assets in virtual settings, as well as processes and organizational systems. In addition to being visualized, these environments facilitate joint scenario planning, operator training through realistic simulations, and coordination of complex operations across locations. Empirical studies of AI-based digital twins in smart buildings show that immersive environments of digital twins have the potential to positively influence decision-making in multifaceted control tasks by offloading cognitive processing associated with conventional dashboard interfaces (Bibri & Huang, 2025), which can inform the human-AI collaboration models preceding in the chapter.

The other fast-growing application is related to sustainability governance. Digital twins at the organizational and system levels can be used to measure and optimize environmental performance, including energy consumption, emissions, waste management, and indicators of the circular economy. Similarly, DT-enforced SCS provides companies with the opportunity to test circular business models, including remanufacturing or material recovery loops, prior to implementation and to minimise the risks posed by sustainability transitions (Kristoffersen, Blomsma, Mikalef, & Li, 2020).

7.5 Summary

The three new technology fronts presented in this section, which include the DTO-level organizational intelligence, predictive enterprise analytics, and metaverse-sustainability convergence of digital twins, have a similar developmental trajectory. Each brings into scope the digital twin intelligence application in established, small, limited-scope operational settings and extends it to more generalized organizational settings, including increased analytical complexity and governance requirements. DTO architectures build on the previous augmented capabilities of digital twins, but at the organizational level rather than at the asset level ((Ali, Gaffinet, Panetto,

& Naudet, 2024; Barata & Kayser, 2024). Predictive enterprise systems advance the descriptive monitoring of DT analytics to predictive and prescriptive decision support (Rathore, Shah, Shukla, Bentafat, & Bakiras, 2021; Leng, et al., 2021). The interfaces provided by the metaverse turn DTC environments into realms of organizational interaction where organizations can collaborate and experience the spaces in the most immersive manner (Bibri & Huang, 2025). Meanwhile, the applications of DT that are sustainability-oriented expand the applications of digital twins in environmental governance and circular economy planning (Ali, Gaffinet, Panetto, & Naudet, 2024; Kristoffersen, Blomsma, Mikalef, & Li, 2020). With the proliferation of DT applications, which are increasingly application-focused, there is similarly greater governance complexity regarding cognitive enterprise systems.

8. SYNTHESIS AND CONCLUSION: TOWARD AN INTEGRATED FRAMEWORK FOR COGNITIVE ENTERPRISE TRANSFORMATION

8.1 An Integrated Cognitive Enterprise Framework

The seven sections above have discussed digital twin technology and cognitive enterprise transformation through a series of analytical lenses, including conceptual, technical, architectural, empirical, managerial, governance-oriented, and prospective. The synthesis of these perspectives shows that there is a system of relations that a single analytical frame cannot describe. The cognitive enterprise is not a technology but a capability of the organization: the state that succeeded in inoculating DT sensing, AI reasoning, organizational decision-making, and governance systems into a stable system capable of continuous learning and self-directed adaptation. The synthesized framework resulting from this analysis has three major dimensions.

The technical maturity dimension characterizes progress in the Kritzinger taxonomy of digital models through digital shadow up to full cognitive twin, and of the scalar hierarchy component to organizational DT. The majority of the organizations nowadays are already in the digital shadow to integrate twin range the breadth of their operations, close enough to cognitive enterprise capability to make the voyage real, but far enough away to make the governance and organizational investments necessary visible and meaningful (Kritzinger, Karner, Traar, Henjes, & Sihn, 2018; Iliu ă, et al., 2022). The dimension of organizational integration explains the fit between DT intelligence and enterprise architecture in data, application, process, and strategy layers. The dimension on which the empirical evidence of the underperformance of organizations relative to their technical capabilities in the field of DT is epistemic (Leng, et al., 2021; Rossmann & Hertweck, 2022). The aspect of governance maturity discusses the way in which accountability systems, ethical codes, trust-building machinery, and schemes of human-AI collaboration are developed to act responsibly and sustainably with the intelligent capabilities of the organizations powered by DT (Ali, Gaffinet, Panetto, & Naudet, 2024; Barata & Kayser, 2024; Botín-Sanabria, et al., 2022). Organizations that develop the three dimensions simultaneously succeed in bringing about cognitive transformation within the enterprise; investments in technical maturity, coupled with disregard for the integration of organization and governance, bring a fraction of the available value.

8.2 Implications, Limitations, and Future Research

The integrated framework identifies three areas of gap in the existing body of research which are of priority to the researcher: longitudinal empirical research on the maturity process of DT that can determine causal other than merely correlational relationships between DT investment and organizational performance; development of governance framework that is in harmony with the autonomous decision capability that fourth-generation cognitive DTs is approaching and research on DTO level organizational intelligence that cuts across the technical knowledge graph literature and the management science community formulated independently literatures of organizational learning and dynamic capabilities. The most applicable implication of the analysis on the practitioners is that sequencing assumes the organizations that invest in the organizational aspect of the integration and governance aspect of the DT capability before or alongside their technical investments in the infrastructure of the corresponding technology are always faster than these organizations that view governance and organizational alignment as a downstream phenomenon (Pater & Stadnicka, 2021; Warke, Kumar, Bongale, & Kotecha, 2021). The regulation by the governance analysis reveals to policymakers a regulatory course as follows: compliance with AI Acts, implication of automated organizational decision-making in the GDPR, and regulation toward the specific sector will gradually embed the situation in which autonomous cognitive enterprise DT conversion can be lawful, and pro-active regulation will be a strategic priority over compliance-protective reaction (Youssef & Adel, 2025). The great shortcoming of the analysis is that the literature, on which they are founded, is still in its early stages: some of the empirical claims that are offered on behalf of DTO-level organizational intelligence and predictive enterprise prescriptive analytics are founded on a thinner evidence base than the manufacturing and infrastructure DT performance statements, and scholars and practitioners have to take this into account. The cognitive enterprise is that destination whose arrival does not necessarily send one down a particular roadmap, since it is an organizational direction toward the realization of which no technology can substitute institutional choices, governance investments, and human-AI systems of relationships, however advanced.

8.3 Conclusion

This chapter discussed how digital twin (DT) technologies have evolved from asset-level engineering models to enterprise-scale decision infrastructures that enable cognitive organizational systems. The discussion has shown that the shift to a cognitive enterprise is not only tied to technological advancement but also to the combination of digital twin designs with artificial intelligence, enterprise architecture, and governance systems.

There are some important lessons learnt during the analysis. To begin with, digital twins have the greatest organizational value when they are transformed into decision-support architectures linked to AI-based analytics. Second, enterprise architecture is important in facilitating organization-wide implementation by harmonizing data, applications, and decision processes at both operational and strategic levels. Third, the system of governance, such as ethical frameworks, accountability pipelines, and models of human-AI collaboration, is needed to ensure that the use of the digital twin intelligence is responsible and sustainable.

The concept of an integrated framework presented in this chapter adds value to the progressive literature by connecting technological maturity, organizational integration, and governance capability into a single model of cognitive enterprise transformation. It is important to note that this framework identifies that, to achieve the maximum value from digital twin technologies, organizations must work on these dimensions simultaneously.

Pragmatically, the results imply that organizational integration and governance design, along with technological investment, are key considerations for organizations undertaking digital twin initiatives. Further longitudinal studies of digital twin adoption and DTO-level organizational intelligence architectures, as well as governance models that can host increasingly autonomous enterprise decision systems, should be undertaken.

REFERENCES

Alcácer, V., & Cruz-Machado, V. (2019). Scanning the Industry 4.0: A Literature Review on Technologies for Manufacturing Systems. *Engineering Science and Technology, an International Journal, 3*(3), 899–919. https://linkinghub.elsevier.com/retrieve/pii/S2215098618317750. DOI: 10.1016/j.jestch.2019.01.006

Ali, J. A., Gaffinet, B., Panetto, H., & Naudet, Y. (2024). Cognitive systems and interoperability in the enterprise: A systematic literature review. *Annual Reviews in Control, 57*, 100954. Advance online publication. DOI: 10.1016/j.arcontrol.2024.100954

Barata, J., & Kayser, I. (2024). How will the digital twin shape the future of industry 5.0? *Technovation, 134*, 103025. Advance online publication. DOI: 10.1016/j.technovation.2024.103025

Bibri, S. E., & Huang, J. (2025). AI and AI-powered digital twins for smart, green, and zero-energy buildings: A systematic review of leading-edge solutions for advancing environmental sustainability goals. *Environmental Science and Ecotechnology, 28*, 100628. DOI: 10.1016/j.ese.2025.100628 PMID: 41244699

Botín-Sanabria, D. M., Mihaita, A. S., Peimbert-García, R. E., Ramírez-Moreno, M. A., Ramírez-Mendoza, R. A., & Lozoya-Santos, J. (2022). Digital Twin Technology Challenges and Applications: A Comprehensive Review. *Remote Sensing (Basel), 14*(6), 1335. DOI: 10.3390/rs14061335

Fuller, A., Fan, Z., Day, C., & Barlow, C. (2020). Digital Twin: Enabling Technologies, Challenges and Open Research. *IEEE Access : Practical Innovations, Open Solutions, 8*, 108952–108971. Advance online publication. DOI: 10.1109/ACCESS.2020.2998358

Grieves, M., & Vickers, J. (2017). Digital Twin: Mitigating Unpredictable, Undesirable Emergent Behavior in Complex Systems. In *F.-J. Kahlen, S. Flumerfelt, & A. Alves, Transdisciplinary Perspectives on Complex Systems* (pp. 85–113). Springer International Publishing. DOI: 10.1007/978-3-319-38756-7_4

Iliu ă, M. E., Moisescu, M. A., Pop, E., Ionita, A. D., Caramihai, S. I., & Mitulescu, T. C. (2022). Digital Twin—A Review of the Evolution from Concept to Technology and Its Analytical Perspectives on Applications in Various Fields. *Applied Sciences (Basel, Switzerland), 12*(8). Advance online publication. DOI: 10.3390/app14135454

Jones, D., Snider, C., Nassehi, A., Yon, J., & Hicks, B. (2020). Characterising the Digital Twin: A systematic literature review. *CIRP Journal of Manufacturing Science and Technology, 29*, 36–52. DOI: 10.1016/j.cirpj.2020.02.002

Kristoffersen, E., Blomsma, F., Mikalef, P., & Li, J. (2020). The smart circular economy: A digital-enabled circular strategies framework for manufacturing companies. *Journal of Business Research, 120*, 241–261. DOI: 10.1016/j.jbusres.2020.07.044

Kritzinger, W., Karner, M., Traar, G., Henjes, J., & Sihn, W. (2018). Digital Twin in manufacturing: A categorical literature review and classification. [Elsevier.]. *IFAC-PapersOnLine, 51*(11), 1016–1022. DOI: 10.1016/j.ifacol.2018.08.474

Leng, J., Wang, D., Shen, W., Li, X., Liu, Q., & Chen, X. (2021). Digital twins-based smart manufacturing system design in Industry 4.0: A review. *Journal of Manufacturing Systems, 60*, 119–137. DOI: 10.1016/j.jmsy.2021.05.011

Li, Y. (2025). AI-Enhanced Digital Twins for Energy Efficiency and Carbon Footprint Reduction in Smart City Infrastructure. *Applied and Computational Engineering*, 42-47.

Pater, J., & Stadnicka, D. (2021). Towards Digital Twins Development and Implementation to Support Sustainability Systematic Literature Review. *Management and Production Engineering Review*, 63-73.

Qiu, S., Zaheer, Q., Ali, F., Wajid, S., Chen, H., Ai, C., & Wang, J. (2025). EXPLORING THE IMPACT OF DIGITAL TWIN TECHNOLOGY IN INFRASTRUCTURE MANAGEMENT: A COMPREHENSIVE REVIEW. *Journal of Civil Engineering and Management, 31*(4), 395–417. Advance online publication. DOI: 10.3846/jcem.2025.23718

Rasheed, A., San, O., & Kvamsdal, T. (2020). Digital Twin: Values, Challenges and Enablers From a Modeling Perspective. *IEEE Access : Practical Innovations, Open Solutions, 8*, 21980–22012. Advance online publication. DOI: 10.1109/ACCESS.2020.2970143

Rathore, M. M., Shah, S. A., Shukla, D., Bentafat, E., & Bakiras, S. (2021). The Role of AI, Machine Learning, and Big Data in Digital Twinning: A Systematic Literature Review, Challenges, and Opportunities. *IEEE Access : Practical Innovations, Open Solutions, 9*, 32030–32052. Advance online publication. DOI: 10.1109/ACCESS.2021.3060863

Rossmann, A., & Hertweck, D. (2022). Digital Twins: A Meta-Review on Their Conceptualization, Application, and Reference Architecture. *Hawaii International Conference on System Sciences.* DOI: 10.24251/HICSS.2022.550

Sacoto-Cabrera, E. J., Perez-Torres, A., Tello-Oquendo, L., & Cerrada, M. (2025). IoT, AI, and Digital Twins in Smart Cities: A Systematic Review for a Thematic Mapping and Research Agenda. *Smart Cities*, 175.

Sharma, A., Kosasih, E., Zhang, J., Brintrup, A., & Calinescu, A. (2022). Digital Twins: State of the art theory and practice, challenges, and open research Questions. *Journal of Industrial Information Integration, 30,* 100383. Advance online publication. DOI: 10.1016/j.jii.2022.100383

Tao, F., Zhang, H., Liu, A., & Nee, A. (2019). Digital Twin in Industry: State-of-the-Art. *IEEE Transactions on Industrial Informatics, 15*(4), 2405–2415. Advance online publication. DOI: 10.1109/TII.2018.2873186

Teece, D. J. (2018). Business models and dynamic capabilities. *Long Range Planning, 51*(1), 40–49. DOI: 10.1016/j.lrp.2017.06.007

Warke, V., Kumar, S., Bongale, A., & Kotecha, K. (2021). Sustainable Development of Smart Manufacturing Driven by the Digital Twin Framework: A Statistical Analysis. *Sustainability (Basel), 13*(18), 10139. Advance online publication. DOI: 10.3390/su131810139

Zakaria, L., Akil, I., Dhiana, A., & Prayitno, E. (2025). Designing the SiMiTi Architecture: A Framework for Sustainable Digital Transformation in Intelligent Enterprises. *Jurnal ilmiah Sistem Informasi dan Ilmu Komputer, 5*(3). DOI: 10.55606/juisik.v5i3.1775

Zheng, X., Lu, J., & Kiritsis, D. (2022). The emergence of cognitive digital twin: Vision, challenges and opportunities. *International Journal of Production Research, 60*(24), 7610–7632. DOI: 10.1080/00207543.2021.2014591

Chapter 4
Multi-Agent Digital Twin Architectures for Real-Time Enterprise Adaptation

Hamed Nozari
http://orcid.org/0000-0002-6500-6708
University of National and World Economy, Bulgaria

K. Tanya
Birla Institute of Technology and Science Pilani, Dubai, UAE

Seema P. Suthar
Birla Institute of Technology and Science Pilani, Dubai, UAE

ABSTRACT

This research explains multi-agent digital twin architectures for achieving real-time adaptability at the enterprise level. By moving from centralized models to distributed cognitive ecosystems, each physical asset becomes a semi-autonomous digital agent capable of local analysis, prediction, and decision-making. Through coordination mechanisms, multi-objective optimization, and distributed intelligence between the edge and the cloud, these agents create collective behavior that is consistent and aligned with the strategic goals of the organization. Also, scenario modeling and multi-level feedback loops provide the basis for the formation of emergent dynamics and systemic learning. The presented framework provides a foundation for designing self-regulating and co-evolving cognitive enterprises.

DOI: 10.4018/979-8-3373-9998-0.ch004

1. INTRODUCTION

In recent years, the concept of the digital twin has evolved beyond a tool for monitoring and simulating physical assets into a strategic infrastructure for redefining the nature of organizations. What was initially conceived as a digital model to represent the state of an industrial equipment or process is now evolving into a distributed cognitive system that is capable of analyzing data in real time, making decisions, and dynamically adapting to changing environmental conditions (Galuzin et al., 2022).. This conceptual transition, along with the development of artificial intelligence, the industrial Internet of Things, and edge computing, has paved the way for the formation of a new generation of organizations that can be called "cognitive enterprises."

In such a context, the main issue is no longer simply the digital representation of physical assets, but the design of architectures that can achieve organizational adaptability at a large scale and in real time. Today's organizations operate in environments that are faced with extreme demand fluctuations, supply chain disruptions, energy shifts, operational risks, and complex competitive pressures. In these circumstances, centralized and hierarchical responses are often slow, inefficient, and prone to decision-making bottlenecks. Therefore, there is a need for structures in which intelligence is distributed not in a single center, but in a network of semi-autonomous digital entities (Kalyani & Collier, 2024)..

Multi-agent architectures in the context of digital twins have emerged precisely in response to this need. In this approach, each physical asset or subsystem has a digital counterpart that not only reflects its state, but is also capable of making local decisions using predictive models, optimization algorithms, and learning mechanisms. These digital agents align their local goals with the larger goals of the organization through coordination and negotiation protocols, resulting in a kind of collective intelligence at the enterprise level. Such a structure enables rapid response to unexpected events and dynamic reconfiguration of operational policies (San et al., 2026)..

Real-time adaptability in this context does not simply mean fast response, but also requires continuous cycles of sensing, analyzing, making decisions, and exercising control at different levels of the organization. These cycles must be designed in such a way as to strike a balance between system stability and decision-making agility. On the one hand, the system should not become unstable in the face of every minor fluctuation; on the other hand, delay in decision-making can lead to missed opportunities or increased losses. Digital twin multi-agent architectures provide a platform for managing this balance by distributing computation at the edge of the network and strategic coordination at the cloud level (Hasan & Nguyen, 2026)..

At a conceptual level, the transition from centralized digital twins to multi-agent ecosystems can be seen as a move from "representation" to "cognition." In early models, the twin played more of a digital mirror role; but in the new generation, each twin becomes a decision-making entity that is in continuous interaction with other twins. These interactions lead to the formation of emergent behaviors at the organizational level; behaviors that emerge not through central command, but through the co-evolution of agents. In such a structure, the organization can be imagined as a living digital system that has the ability to learn, reconfigure, and redefine its strategies in response to environmental changes.

From an operational perspective, realizing this vision requires the design of specific architectural layers, inter-agent coordination mechanisms, multi-objective optimization models, and synchronization mechanisms between the edge and the cloud. Also, the precise definition of local and macro goals and the way information is exchanged between them will play a decisive role in the efficiency of the system. In fact, the main question of this chapter is how to build a framework in which organizational adaptability is not an ad hoc response, but an inherent and internal capability of the system, relying on multi-agent digital twin architectures.

This chapter, by explaining the conceptual foundations and architecture of multi-agent digital twins, examines distributed decision-making mechanisms, goal alignment, and adaptive dynamics at the enterprise level. Its goal is to provide a coherent framework for the transition from physical asset management to the design of cognitive enterprises; enterprises in which the boundary between physics and cyber is blurred and intelligence flows throughout the structure of the organization.

2. FROM CENTRALIZED TWINS TO MULTI AGENT COGNITIVE ECOSYSTEMS

In early digital twin architectures, the main focus was on creating a comprehensive, centralized model of the physical asset that aggregated all operational data into a single analytical core. This structure, based on central processing and hierarchical control, enabled monitoring, predictive failure, and limited optimization. However, this model was challenged when organizations became networks of highly interdependent, dynamic assets interacting with unpredictable environments. The increase in data volume, the decrease in tolerance for decision-making delays, and the need for immediate responses at the operational level showed that the centralized model was not sufficient to manage organizational adaptability at large scale (Marah & Challenger, 2024)..

In such circumstances, the concept of a multi-agent cognitive ecosystem was proposed as the next step in the evolution of digital twins. In this approach, each asset, process, or subsystem has a semi-autonomous digital twin that not only reflects the physical state, but also has the ability to analyze, predict, and make local decisions. These twins act as “digital agents” that have specific goals, constraints, and behavioral models and can interact with each other in a distributed framework (Li et al., 2026).. In this way, intelligence is transferred from a central core to a network of cognitive entities.

The fundamental difference between a centralized architecture and a multi-agent ecosystem lies in the logic of coordination and control. In a centralized structure, the decision-making flow is mainly top-down and based on an overall organizational model; whereas in a multi-agent ecosystem, decisions are made at the local level and reach macro-alignment through coordination mechanisms. These mechanisms can include consensus protocols, multi-objective negotiation, internal pricing mechanisms, or distributed convergence algorithms. The result of such interactions is the formation of emergent behavior at the organization level, which is the result of the synergy of agents rather than the direct command of a control center (Mohammed et al., 2026)..

From a structural perspective, the transition to a cognitive ecosystem requires a redefinition of the concept of “organizational control”. In this framework, control does not mean the exercise of centralized command, but rather the design of interaction rules, the definition of common goals, and the creation of a stable communication infrastructure between agents. Each twin, as a cognitive unit, analyzes local data, predicts its own state, and makes decisions that are valid within the framework of the organization’s macro-policies. At the same time, it also considers the impact of its decisions on the entire system through continuous information exchange with other twins (Ivanov, 2026)..

This transformation transforms the organization from a linear, hierarchical structure to a dynamic network of digital entities that are capable of self-organization and reconfiguration. In such an ecosystem, disruption in one sector can be quickly detected by relevant actors and managed by redistributing operational workloads or changing local policies, without the need for immediate intervention from a single center. This feature is especially important in environments with high volatility or unpredictable risks.

Finally, multi-agent cognitive ecosystems can be considered an advanced stage in the maturation of digital twins, in which the focus shifts from “precise modeling of an asset” to “designing distributed intelligence at the enterprise level.” This transition not only increases the capacity for real-time adaptation, but also provides the foundation for the formation of self-regulating, learning, and co-evolving organizations; Organizations in which the boundary between analysis, decision, and execution is defined continuously and through interaction between digital agents.

3. STRUCTURAL ARCHITECTURE OF MULTI AGENT DIGITAL TWIN ENTERPRISES

The design of architecture in multi-agent digital twin-based enterprises is not merely a technical issue, but rather a reflection of how intelligence, decision-making authority, and coordination mechanisms are distributed across the organization. In this context, the architecture should be designed in a way that, on the one hand, preserves the autonomy of local agents and, on the other hand, ensures strategic alignment at the macro level. Such a balance can only be achieved if the system structure is defined in a layered, modular, and at the same time dynamic manner (San et al., 2026)..

At the first layer, there is the cyber-physical interface layer, which is responsible for connecting physical assets, sensors, actuators, and control systems to the digital infrastructure. This layer provides real-time data flow and transmits the operational status of equipment, energy consumption, production quality, or environmental conditions to higher layers. Accuracy, reliability, and low latency in this layer play a fundamental role in the quality of decision-making of the entire system (Kulkarni et al., 2019)..

The second layer is the local intelligence layer of the twins. At this level, each asset or subsystem has a digital twin with independent cognitive capabilities. These capabilities include state estimation, future behavior prediction, local optimization, and risk assessment. Each twin makes operational decisions based on data received from the physical layer as well as information shared from other agents. This layer is the transition point from mere representation to active decision-making.

At the third layer, there is the inter-agent coordination layer. This layer includes communication protocols, consensus mechanisms, multi-objective negotiation, and distributed convergence algorithms. At this level, digital agents align their local goals with the goals of other agents and the macro-policies of the organization. The result of these interactions is the formation of adaptive collective behavior and the prevention of systemic conflicts. The correct design of this layer will determine the sustainability and efficiency of the entire ecosystem (Fan et al., 2026)..

At the highest level is the strategic enterprise intelligence layer, which includes macro goals, performance indicators, adaptive policies, and macro feedback mechanisms. This layer is not necessarily a centralized control center, but can be implemented in a distributed manner in the cloud or in a hybrid edge-cloud environment. The role of this layer is to provide a framework within which local decisions of agents are guided in line with the organization's mission and strategy (Nozari & Szmelter-Jarosz, 2025).. The location of these layers and their interaction are shown in Figure 1.

Figure 1. Multi-agent digital twin layered architecture for real-time enterprise adaptability

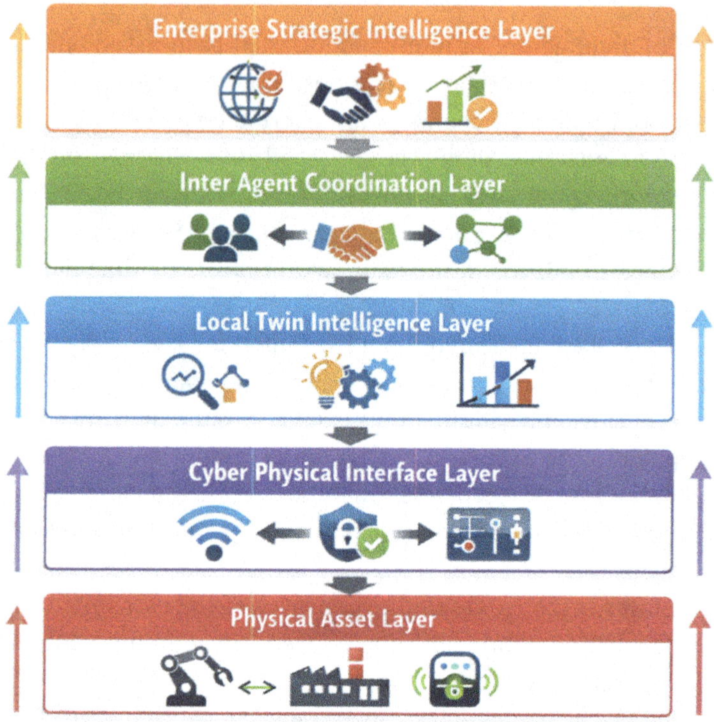

As can be seen in Figure 1, the flow of information starts from the bottom up, but the flow of decisions and policies can also be propagated top down or horizontally among agents. This bidirectional and networked structure allows for rapid feedback and dynamic reconfiguration. Also, the existence of horizontal communication between twins in the coordination layer indicates that organizational convergence is not necessarily achieved through a central point, but rather the result of multilateral interactions between cognitive agents.

A key feature of this architecture is the ability to separate the decision-making level based on time sensitivity. Low-latency and operational decisions are made in the lower layers and near the edge, while macro-policy setting and goal redefinition are done in the strategic layer. This separation, in addition to reducing the computational burden of the center, increases the system's resilience to network disruptions.

Finally, the structural architecture of multi-agent digital twin enterprises can be considered a platform in which adaptability is designed not as a sectional response, but as an inherent feature of the system. Logical layering, distributed intelligence, and the design of coordination mechanisms are the three main pillars of this architecture that provide the basis for the formation of cognitive, self-regulating, and co-evolutionary organizations.

4. REAL TIME ADAPTATION MECHANICS

Real-time adaptability in multi-agent digital twin architectures is not just about speed of response, but also about designing continuous and distributed decision-making cycles that can structurally absorb, analyze, and reconfigure environmental changes. In this framework, the system operates not as a linear chain of sensing and control, but as a network of cognitive agents, each of which assesses its own state in real time and makes decisions in interaction with other agents (Okegbile et al., 2026)..

The first component of this mechanism is event-driven detection. Unlike traditional systems that operate based on fixed time intervals, in multi-agent architectures, significant changes in operational data act as triggers for the initiation of the adaptation cycle. These events can include deviations from the optimal range, sudden increases in demand, equipment efficiency drops, or changing energy conditions. Rapid and accurate detection of these events is a prerequisite for activating the analytical and decision-making layers (Lin et al., 2026).

The second component is local inference and prediction at the level of each twin. Each digital agent estimates the possible consequences of changes on its performance using predictive models, learning algorithms, and defined objective functions. These analyses can include failure prediction, cost estimation, capacity analysis, or risk assessment. The importance of this stage is that the initial decision is made at the level closest to the data source, avoiding complete dependence on the center.

The third stage is decision propagation and inter-agent coordination. In a multi-agent ecosystem, the decision of one agent is rarely independent of the others. A change in the production schedule of a piece of equipment may affect energy consumption, delivery time, or logistical capacity. Therefore, local decisions are transmitted to other related agents through the coordination layer and are adjusted in the form of multi-objective consensus or negotiation processes. These interactions are designed to reduce systemic conflicts and achieve convergence to a stable state (Clemen et al., 2021).

The fourth component is control propagation and operational reconfiguration. Once an agreement or optimal policy is reached, control signals are sent to the cyber-physical layer to implement changes at the equipment or process level. These actions can include adjusting production parameters, changing resource allocation, redistributing operational workload, or activating backup capacities. The feedback from implementing these decisions is fed back into the sensing loop, completing the adaptation process.

A fundamental challenge in this loop is the balance between stability and agility. If the system is too sensitive, it may become unstable to small fluctuations; on the other hand, if it is too conservative, opportunities for optimization or crisis prevention will be missed. For this reason, dynamic thresholds, data smoothing filters, and prioritization policies are used in the design of adaptive mechanisms to adjust responses according to the severity and importance of the event (Nozari & Yordanova, 2025)..

Also, in hybrid edge-cloud architectures, the division of decision-making tasks plays an important role in the efficiency of real-time adaptation. Time-sensitive decisions are made at the edge and close to the asset, while strategic analysis and macro-goal redefinition are performed at the cloud level. This separation, in addition to reducing latency, increases the system's resilience in the face of communication disruptions.

In summary, real-time adaptation mechanisms in multi-agent digital twin-based enterprises can be defined as a continuous cycle of detection, analysis, coordination, and execution, in which intelligence is distributed across the network of agents. In such a structure, adaptation is not an emergency response, but a continuous and structured process that allows the system to operate in a stable and co-evolving manner in dynamic environments.

5. DISTRIBUTED MULTI OBJECTIVE ENTERPRISE OPTIMIZATION

In multi-agent digital twin architectures, optimization is no longer a centralized problem with a single objective function, but a distributed, multidimensional process in which each digital agent has its own goals, constraints, and performance metrics. In such an environment, optimization must be designed to both maintain local efficiency and ensure macro-organizational coherence. This requires a shift from single-centered optimization to a multi-objective, networked framework in which conflicts and trade-offs between different objectives are dynamically managed (Gupta et al., 2026)..

At the local level, each twin has an objective function that can include minimizing operating cost, maximizing efficiency, reducing energy consumption, increasing reliability, or reducing risk. These objectives are often in conflict with each other; for example, increasing production speed may increase energy consumption or accelerate equipment depreciation. Thus, even at the level of a single agent, the optimization problem is multi-objective in nature and requires the determination of a set of Pareto solutions that represent the trade-offs between objectives (Nozari et al., 2025).

At the inter-agent level, the complexity increases. The objectives of one twin may have a direct or indirect impact on the performance of other twins. For example, the decision of a manufacturing unit to increase capacity may impose a greater burden on the energy or logistics system. Therefore, it is necessary to define a mechanism to align local objectives with the macro-goals of the firm. This alignment can be achieved through dynamic weighting of objectives, definition of combined utility functions, or the use of multi-objective consensus algorithms (Dobai et al., 2022)..

One of the key approaches in this field is the use of the concept of distributed Pareto surfaces. In this framework, each agent generates a set of locally optimal solutions, and then, through information exchange with other agents, these sets are refined to reach a level of optimality that is also acceptable at the macro scale. This process can be performed iteratively until relative convergence among the agents is achieved. The advantage of this approach is that the need to completely transfer raw data to a single center is eliminated and the computational load is distributed across the network (Nozari et al., 2025)..

In designing this framework, the correct definition of organizational constraints is of particular importance. Some constraints are local in nature, such as the capacity of a piece of equipment or the technical limitations of a process; while others are defined at the macro level, such as the energy consumption ceiling of the entire enterprise or environmental sustainability goals. Distributed optimization must be able to take these constraints into account at different levels and prevent the emergence of local solutions that conflict with macro policies.

Also, the dynamic and real-time nature of the system requires that optimization be performed adaptively, not statically. Changes in market conditions, energy costs, or equipment status can change the structure of the objective function and the relative weights of the criteria. Therefore, digital agents must be able to adjust the parameters of their optimization model based on environmental feedback. This feature transforms optimization from a periodic calculation into a learning and co-evolutionary process (Rojek et al., 2025)..

In summary, distributed multi-objective optimization in multi-agent digital twin-based enterprises can be defined as a mechanism for balancing local efficiency and systemic efficiency. In this framework, optimal decisions are formed not at a central point, but in the continuous interaction between cognitive agents. The result of this interaction is the formation of a flexible and scalable decision-making structure that is able to keep the organization's performance within optimal boundaries in complex and dynamic environments.

6. INTELLIGENCE DISTRIBUTION ACROSS EDGE AND CLOUD

In multi-agent digital twin architectures, the distribution of intelligence between the edge and the cloud is not simply an infrastructure choice, but a strategic decision in designing adaptation and optimization mechanisms. If all processing is centralized at the cloud level, the system will face latency, network dependency, and bottleneck risk; and if all decisions remain at the edge level, the macro-alignment and strategic coherence of the organization will be weakened. Therefore, the main issue is not to choose one of the two, but to design a distributed and complementary pattern in which each level has a specific and coordinated role (Nozari, 2025)..

At the edge level, the focus is on decisions that are highly time-sensitive and dependent on local conditions. These decisions include real-time control of equipment, adjustment of operating parameters, response to rapid fluctuations, or early detection of errors. The proximity of computation to the data source reduces latency and increases resilience to communication disruptions. In addition, local processing can reduce the load of data transmission to the cloud and prevent network saturation (Andruccioli et al., 2026).. At this level, digital twins play the role of operational agents that generate immediate responses using lightweight, updatable models.

In contrast, the cloud layer is the home of strategic intelligence and macro analytics. At this layer, aggregated data from multiple agents is analyzed to identify long-term patterns, systemic trends, and cross-functional optimization opportunities. More sophisticated machine learning algorithms, macro forecasting models, and multi-objective optimization are implemented at this level. Also, macro policies and control parameters that should be applied to edge agents are redefined at this level (Bakliwal et al., 2018)..

A key element in this architecture is the model synchronization mechanism. Models used at the edge should be periodically or event-driven aligned with the cloud macro models. This synchronization can include updating the weights of the learning model, adjusting decision thresholds, or modifying the coefficients of the objective functions. At the same time, this process should not disrupt the instantaneous performance of local agents. Designing optimal synchronization cycles plays a decisive role in maintaining the balance between model stability and innovation.

Also, in more advanced frameworks, approaches such as distributed or federated learning are used, in which the raw data remains at the edge and only the model parameters are exchanged between the edge and the cloud. In addition to reducing the data transmission burden, this approach also helps to maintain information security and privacy. In industrial environments where data sensitivity is high, such mechanisms can create a competitive advantage (Pratitajati et al., 2026)..

From a scalability perspective, intelligent division between the edge and the cloud allows the system to operate on two different time scales. In the short-term, the edge provides fast and stable responses; In the long term, the cloud modifies macro policies and sets the direction of the system. These two levels, in continuous interaction with each other, create a cycle of learning and reconfiguration that allows the organization to be both resilient to momentary shocks and adapt to structural changes in the environment.

Finally, the distribution of intelligence between the edge and the cloud can be considered one of the main pillars of the cognitive enterprise architecture. This distribution not only increases the computational efficiency and scalability of the system, but also provides the basis for the formation of multi-level adaptability; adaptability in which operational, tactical, and strategic decisions act in a converged and coordinated network.

7. ENTERPRISE SCALE ADAPTIVE SCENARIO MODELING

In multi-agent digital twin architectures, adaptability becomes meaningful when the system can reconfigure its behavior not only in response to current data, but also in the face of possible future scenarios. Enterprise-scale adaptive scenario modeling means designing a framework in which digital twins can simulate the impact of potential events and evaluate alternative decision paths before they fully occur. This approach elevates adaptability from a reactive to a predictive level (Amirkhanov et al., 2026)..

In this framework, scenarios can include supply chain disruptions, sudden demand fluctuations, energy price increases, key equipment failures, or policy changes. Each scenario is defined as a set of changed parameters that affect the operational state of one or more agents. Digital twins analyze the consequences of these changes at the local and systemic levels using predictive and optimization models and generate a set of possible responses (Márquez & Fernández, 2026)..

A key feature of scenario modeling in a multi-agent architecture is the propagation of effects across a network of agents. In a complex enterprise, the impact of a disruption is not limited to one department. For example, the failure of a manufacturing facility can reduce delivery capacity, increase pressure on other units, and ultimately affect customer satisfaction. In the multi-agent digital twin framework, these effects are simulated through defined relationships between agents and their propagation paths are analyzed. Such analysis allows the organization to identify vulnerabilities and system bottlenecks in advance (Skobelev, 2020)..

Scenario modeling also provides a platform for performing “if-then” analyses at the enterprise scale. Digital agents can simulate multiple decision paths in parallel and evaluate the performance of each path based on multi-objective indicators. These indicators can include total cost, service level, energy consumption, operational risk, or sustainability indicators. The result of this process is the selection of a strategy that is not only efficient in the short term, but also remains robust to different scenarios (Kabashkin & Saveljevs, 2026)..

From a structural perspective, implementing scenario modeling at the enterprise scale requires an infrastructure that allows for simultaneous local and macro simulations. Here, the role of the edge-cloud architecture is highlighted again; fast, local simulations can be performed at the edge, while hybrid analytics and strategic evaluation of scenarios are performed at the cloud. The interaction between these two levels allows for a dynamic evaluation cycle in which scenarios are continuously updated based on real-world data.

Another important point is the link between scenario modeling and organizational learning. Each time a scenario is simulated or experienced, the resulting data can be used to improve the prediction models and adjust the objective functions. In this way, the system not only reacts to events, but also learns from them and increases its adaptive capacity over time (Santos et al., 2024).

In summary, adaptive scenario modeling at the enterprise scale can be seen as a tool for transforming uncertainty into operational knowledge. In this context, multi-agent digital twins allow the organization to analyze possible paths and make more informed decisions before it fully faces a crisis or opportunity. The result of this approach is the formation of an enterprise that not only responds to changes, but also anticipates and manages them; an enterprise in which adaptability has become a structural and sustainable capability.

8. EMERGENT COGNITIVE ENTERPRISE DYNAMICS

In multi-agent digital twin architectures, organizational behavior is not simply the result of executing predetermined instructions, but rather the result of continuous interactions, mutual feedback, and co-evolution of digital agents. When each twin acts as a semi-autonomous cognitive entity while also being embedded in a network of dependencies, patterns of behavior emerge at the macro level that are not directly observable in any of the individual agents. This phenomenon, referred to as "emergent behavior," underlies the formation of true cognitive enterprises (Nozari, 2025)..

Emergent behavior occurs when local decisions, through coordination and feedback mechanisms, become systemic patterns that are stable. For example, if several production agents independently decide to increase capacity, this may lead to pressure on the energy system or a decrease in profit margins at the macro level. But in a cognitive ecosystem, the interaction between agents and the existence of moderating mechanisms cause the system to move towards a balanced and adaptive state. This balance is achieved not by a central command, but by the gradual convergence of local behaviors (Elshafei et al., 2025).

Emergent dynamics are also tied to the concept of multilevel feedback. In this framework, feedback is not only transmitted from the environment to the agent, but also flows between agents and between architectural layers. Operational decisions at the edge can affect macro-policies, and policy modifications can in turn change the behavior of local agents. These feedback loops create a nonlinear and dynamic structure in which the system is constantly adjusting itself (Wu et al., 2021). To understand these dynamics, Figure 2 shows a conceptual representation of the emergent interaction loop in the cognitive enterprise.

Figure 2. The cycle of emergent dynamics in a cognitive enterprise based on a multi-agent digital twin

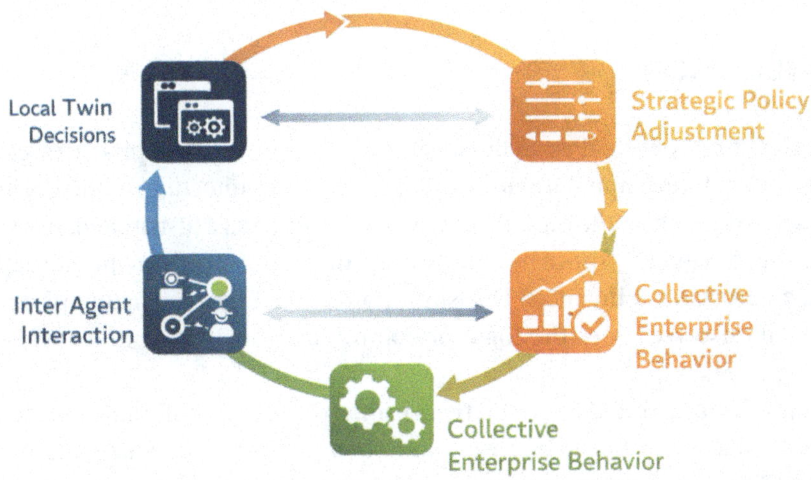

As can be seen in Figure 2, the local decisions of the twins are transformed into collective behavior through inter-agent interaction. This collective behavior affects macro performance indicators and leads to the modification of strategic policies. Then, the new policies return to the local agents and complete the adaptation cycle. This circular and feedback structure is the basis for the formation of emergent dynamics.

One of the important consequences of these dynamics is the ability of organizational self-regulation. In such a system, even in the event of sudden disruption or change, agents can form a new state of equilibrium by relying on local information and network interactions. This self-regulation is especially important in high-risk and uncertain environments, because it reduces the dependence on external intervention or centralized decision-making.

Furthermore, emergent dynamics provide the basis for the formation of systemic learning. When successful or unsuccessful patterns are identified at the macro level, they can be applied in the form of adjusting model parameters, modifying objective functions, or redefining interaction rules in the network. In this way, the system not only adapts in the moment, but also evolves over time and expands its cognitive capacity (Lehmann et al., 2023).

Finally, the cognitive enterprise can be considered as a system in which the boundary between local decision and macro strategy is dynamically redefined. Organizational behavior is not the result of a command center, but rather the result of a network of intelligent interactions that are continuously shaping and reshaping performance patterns. This feature transforms the organization from a reactive structure to a co-evolving ecosystem that is able to act sustainably and creatively in the face of complexity and uncertainty.

9. CONCLUSION

The shift from physical asset management to cognitive enterprise design is one of the most profound transformations in enterprise architecture in the digital age. This chapter shows how the digital twin, when designed as a distributed, multi-agent architecture, can evolve from a monitoring and modeling tool to an infrastructure for shaping enterprise intelligence. This shift not only changes the nature of decision-making, but also redefines the logic of control, coordination, and learning at the enterprise level.

In centralized architectures, the twin primarily acts as a digital representation of the asset that collects and analyzes data. In a multi-agent framework, however, each twin becomes a semi-autonomous cognitive entity that can assess its own state, predict the future, and make decisions in interaction with other agents. This paradigm shift distributes intelligence from a central core to a network of digital agents, enabling real-time adaptability at the enterprise scale.

The layered architecture introduced in this chapter demonstrated that organizational adaptability results from the structural interaction between cyber-physical layers, local intelligence, inter-agent coordination, and strategic policy. These layers are interconnected vertically and horizontally, forming multi-level feedback loops. In such a system, data flows from the bottom up, while policy and strategic direction can be disseminated from the top down or across agents. This networked structure frees the organization from dependence on centralized decisions and increases the capacity for rapid and sustained responsiveness.

The real-time adaptive mechanisms explained in this chapter showed that responding effectively to environmental changes requires a continuous cycle of event detection, local analysis, network coordination, and operational reconfiguration. This cycle not only increases the speed of decision-making, but also allows for a balance between stability and agility. The design of dynamic thresholds, the division of tasks between the edge and the cloud, and the definition of consensus protocols all play a key role in shaping this balance.

Distributed multi-objective optimization was also introduced as one of the fundamental pillars of the cognitive enterprise. In this framework, each agent has local goals that may conflict with the goals of other agents or with macro policies. Through multi-objective alignment and negotiation mechanisms, these conflicts are transformed into a set of Pareto-optimal solutions at the macro level. The result of this process is the formation of a boundary of optimal performance that is not the result of a central point calculation, but the result of the continuous interaction of digital agents.

Intelligent distribution between the edge and the cloud also showed that adaptability operates on two time scales. In the short term, operational decisions are made close to the asset to reduce latency and increase resilience. In the long term, macro analytics and policy redefinition are performed at the cloud level to adjust the direction of the organization's movement. This intelligent division not only increases computational efficiency, but also maintains strategic coherence.

Enterprise-scale adaptive scenario modeling strengthens the predictive dimension of this architecture. Multi-agent digital twins can simulate the impact of potential disruptions or opportunities before they fully occur and evaluate alternative paths. This capability transforms the organization from a reactive structure to a predictive and forward-looking system. As a result, uncertainty becomes a platform for continuous learning and improvement, rather than a mere threat.

Finally, the concept of emergent dynamics showed that organizational behavior in such an architecture is the result of nonlinear interactions and multilevel feedback. Performance patterns observed at the macro level are not necessarily predictable at the level of individual agents. This feature turns the cognitive enterprise into a co-evolving system in which local decisions and macro policies continuously shape each other. Such a structure is not only adaptive, but also learning and self-regulating.

In general, multi-agent digital twin architectures can be considered as the infrastructure for the transition from reactive to cognitive enterprises. In this framework, physical assets are no longer simply production resources, but become nodes in an intelligent network that can analyze, make decisions, and reconfigure itself in real time. This transformation transforms the organization from a static, hierarchical structure to a dynamic, convergent ecosystem that can maintain its performance within optimal boundaries in complex and changing environments.

Therefore, the future of industrial and service enterprises lies not in the mere increase in automation, but in the design of cognitive architectures; architectures in which multi-agent digital twins act as the core of the organization's intelligence, making adaptability an inherent and sustainable capability.

REFERENCES

Amirkhanov, B., Kunelbayev, M., Amirkhanova, G., Nurgazy, T., Tyulepberdinova, G., & Tletay, S. (2026). Development of a Digital Twin for a Bakery Line With Predictive Analytics and Adaptive Control Functions. *IET Collaborative Intelligent Manufacturing*, *8*(1), e70056. DOI: 10.1049/cim2.70056

Andruccioli, M., Girau, R., Mirri, S., & Salomoni, P. (2026, January). Towards declarative deployment and lifecycle orchestration of digital twin ecosystems. In 2026 IEEE 23rd Consumer Communications & Networking Conference (CCNC) (pp. 1-6). IEEE.

Bakliwal, K., Dhada, M. H., Palau, A. S., Parlikad, A. K., & Lad, B. K. (2018). A multi agent system architecture to implement collaborative learning for social industrial assets. *IFAC-PapersOnLine*, *51*(11), 1237–1242. DOI: 10.1016/j.ifacol.2018.08.421

Clemen, T., Ahmady-Moghaddam, N., Lenfers, U. A., Ocker, F., Osterholz, D., Ströbele, J., & Glake, D. (2021, May). Multi-agent systems and digital twins for smarter cities. In *Proceedings of the 2021 ACM SIGSIM conference on principles of advanced discrete simulation* (pp. 45-55). DOI: 10.1145/3437959.3459254

Elshafei, B., Chaplin, J. C., Sanderson, D., & Ratchev, S. (2025). Facilitating interoperability in manufacturing systems using digital twins: A multi-asset AAS system. *International Journal of Advanced Manufacturing Technology*, •••, 1–18. DOI: 10.1007/s00170-025-17178-z

Fan, H., Chow, E., Lu, T., Fuh, J. Y. H., Lu, W. F., & Li, B. (2026). A unified framework for large language model-guided reinforcement learning in digital twin industrial environments. *Robotics and Computer-integrated Manufacturing*, *99*, 103215. DOI: 10.1016/j.rcim.2025.103215

Galuzin, V., Galitskaya, A., Grachev, S., Larukhin, V., Novichkov, D., Skobelev, P., & Zhilyaev, A. (2022). Autonomous digital twin of enterprise: Method and toolset for knowledge-based multi-agent adaptive management of tasks and resources in real time. *Mathematics*, *10*(10), 1662. DOI: 10.3390/math10101662

Gupta, B., Namireddy, V., Quraishi, A., Begum, A. Y., Rao, K. B., Sundaram, A., & Smerat, A. (2026). Adaptive Resource Scheduling for Digital Twin-Based 6G Communication on Intelligent Computing-Integrated Network. IEEE Communications Standards Magazine.

Hasan, A., & Nguyen, D. T. (2026). Integrating agentic AI and digital twins for intelligent decision-making systems. *Array (New York, N.Y.)*, *29*, 100721. DOI: 10.1016/j.array.2026.100721

Ivanov, D. (2026). Agentic digital twins: Bridging model-based and AI-driven decision-making support for a new era of supply chain and operations management. *International Journal of Production Research*, •••, 1–17. DOI: 10.1080/00207543.2026.2630277

Kabashkin, I., & Saveljevs, A. (2026). Mathematical Framework for Airport as Cognitive Digital Twin of Aviation Ecosystem. *Mathematics*, *14*(3), 558. DOI: 10.3390/math14030558

Kalyani, Y., & Collier, R. (2024). The role of multi-agents in digital twin implementation: Short survey. *ACM Computing Surveys*, *57*(3), 1–15. DOI: 10.1145/3697350

Kulkarni, V., Barat, S., & Clark, T. (2019). *Towards adaptive enterprises using digital twins. In 2019 winter simulation conference (WSC).* IEEE.

Lehmann, J., Lober, A., Häußermann, T., Rache, A., Ollinger, L., Baumgärtel, H., & Reichwald, J. (2023). The anatomy of the internet of digital twins: A symbiosis of agent and digital twin paradigms enhancing resilience (not only) in manufacturing environments. *Machines (Basel)*, *11*(5), 504. DOI: 10.3390/machines11050504

Li, M., Yang, C. M., Lo, W., & Kao, Y. W. (2026). A Digital-Twin-Enabled AI-Driven Adaptive Planning Platform for Sustainable and Reliable Manufacturing. *Machines (Basel)*, *14*(2), 197. DOI: 10.3390/machines14020197

Lin, C. Y., Tseng, T. L., & Tsai, T. H. (2026). Adaptive Reinforcement Learning-Driven Digital Twin for Multi-Objective and Multi-Machine Process Optimization. *IEEE Transactions on Artificial Intelligence*, 1–15. DOI: 10.1109/TAI.2026.3655629

Marah, H., & Challenger, M. (2024). Adaptive hybrid reasoning for agent-based digital twins of distributed multi-robot systems. *Simulation*, *100*(9), 931–957. DOI: 10.1177/00375497231226436

Márquez, A. C., & Fernández, J. F. G. (2026). Agentic AI for autonomous preventive maintenance policy governance: A multi-agent framework for dynamic industrial environments. *Expert Systems with Applications*, *314*, 131767. DOI: 10.1016/j.eswa.2026.131767

Mohammed, S. K., Singh, S., Mizouni, R., Otrok, H., & Damiani, E. (2026). Digital Twins Paradigm: A Systematic Review from the Reinforcement Learning Perspective. *ACM Computing Surveys*, *58*(7), 1–33. DOI: 10.1145/3777367

Nozari, H. (2025). *Artificial Intelligence of Everything and Sustainable Development.* Springer. DOI: 10.1007/978-981-96-7202-8

Nozari, H., Nassar, S., & Szmelter-Jarosz, A. (2025). Fuzzy multi-objective optimization model for resilient supply chain financing based on blockchain and IoT. *Digital*, *5*(3), 32. DOI: 10.3390/digital5030032

Nozari, H., & Szmelter-Jarosz, A. (2025). A Predictive Maintenance Approach for Composting Plants Based on ERP and Digital Twin Integration. *Machines (Basel)*, *13*(12), 1123. DOI: 10.3390/machines13121123

Nozari, H., Szmelter-Jarosz, A., & Weiland, D. (2025). A Fuzzy Multi-Objective Sustainable and Agile Supply Chain Model Based on Digital Twin and Internet of Things with Adaptive Learning Under Environmental Uncertainty. *Applied Sciences (Basel, Switzerland)*, *15*(19), 10399. DOI: 10.3390/app151910399

Nozari, H., & Yordanova, Z. (2025). An intelligent digital twin approach for optimizing multi-channel supply chains in uncertain environments. Green Technologies and Sustainability, 100309.

Okegbile, S. D., Cai, J., Niyato, D., & Shen, X. (2026). Leveraging Knowledge-Driven Large Language Models-Enabled Intent-Based Security Architectures for Human Digital Twin Networks. *IEEE Network*, 1–9. DOI: 10.1109/MNET.2025.3649156

Pratitajati, E., Lestari, Y. D., & Okdinawati, L. (2026). Reframing innovation adoption in high compliance sectors: A multi-level perspective on digital twins for circular economy in pharmaceuticals. *International Journal of Innovation Science*, •••, 1–26. DOI: 10.1108/IJIS-07-2025-0344

Rojek, I., Mikołajewski, D., Dostatni, E., Cybulski, J., & Kozielski, M. (2025). Personalization of ai-based digital twins to optimize adaptation in industrial design and manufacturing. *Applied Sciences (Basel, Switzerland)*, *15*(15), 8525. DOI: 10.3390/app15158525

San, O., Rasheed, A., Bozdemir, E., & Deng, J. (2026). The evolution of digital twins from reactive to agentic systems. *Nature Computational Science*, *6*(1), 6–10. DOI: 10.1038/s43588-025-00944-0 PMID: 41612013

San, O., Rasheed, A., Bozdemir, E., & Deng, J. (2026). The evolution of digital twins from reactive to agentic systems. *Nature Computational Science*, *6*(1), 6–10. DOI: 10.1038/s43588-025-00944-0 PMID: 41612013

Santos, R., Piqueiro, H., Dias, R., & Rocha, C. D. (2024). Transitioning trends into action: A simulation-based Digital Twin architecture for enhanced strategic and operational decision-making. *Computers & Industrial Engineering*, *198*, 110616. DOI: 10.1016/j.cie.2024.110616

Skobelev, P., Laryukhin, V., Simonova, E., Goryanin, O., Yalovenko, V., & Yalovenko, O. (2020, September). Multi-agent approach for developing a digital twin of wheat. In 2020 IEEE international conference on smart computing (SMARTCOMP) (pp. 268-273). IEEE.

Wu, J., Zhou, M., Xu, M., Zhang, J., Guo, Y., Zhang, Y., & Zhang, C. (2021, October). Research and design of a digital twin-based enterprise architecture digital control platform for provincial electrical power company. In 2021 6th international conference on control, robotics and cybernetics (CRC) (pp. 186-191). IEEE. DOI: 10.1109/CRC52766.2021.9620120

Chapter 5
Predictive Analytics and Simulation in Enterprise Environments for Industry 4.0 and Lean Management

Rupayan Roy
http://orcid.org/0000-0002-8118-431X
Department of Fashion Technology, National Institute of Fashion Technology, Kannur, India

Aprajita Singh Parihar
Department of Fashion Technology, National Institute of Fashion Technology, Kannur, India

Manoj Tiwari
http://orcid.org/0000-0001-8949-0330
Department of Fashion Technology, National Institute of Fashion Technology, Kannur, India

ABSTRACT

Industry 4.0 and lean management are reshaping enterprise competition. Lean has traditionally depended on human observation and retrospective analysis to eliminate waste, but predictive analytics and simulation now offer greater precision, speed, and scalability. With real-time data, machine learning models, and advanced simulation tools, organisations can anticipate equipment failures, optimise production schedules, test process changes virtually, and align supply chains with dynamic market demand. This chapter examines how predictive analytics and simulation

DOI: 10.4018/979-8-3373-9998-0.ch005

within Industry 4.0 frameworks enhance lean practices. It reviews methods such as discrete event simulation, agent-based modelling, machine learning-based demand forecasting, and digital twin-enabled value stream analysis. Their integration with lean tools value stream mapping, kaizen, just-in-time production, and total productive maintenance is analysed. Drawing on theory, empirical studies, and global cases, the chapter provides a practical guide for using data-driven intelligence to achieve operational excellence.

1. INTRODUCTION

Over the past century, industrial enterprise management has evolved from Henry Ford's mass production theories to the Toyota Production System's waste elimination principles to Industry 4.0's data-saturated, algorithmically governed reality. The current combination of digital intelligence and lean principles is the most significant change of operational excellence. Any firm intending to compete in an era of volatility, complexity, and rapid technological change must understand how predictive analytics and simulation have become crucial lean enterprise tools (Liker, 2004; Schwab, 2016).

Womack and Jones (1996)'s synthesis of the Toyota Production System codifies lean management with five core principles: precisely defining value from the customer perspective, mapping and optimizing the value stream, enabling the continuous flow of products and services, establishing pull-based production driven by actual demand, and relentlessly pursuing perfection through continuous improvement. These ideas were applied for decades through direct observation, manual data gathering, paper-based kanban systems, and kaizen seminars. These technologies produced significant performance improvements, but they were limited by human analysis speed, measurement cycle frequency, and cognitive restrictions of operating extremely complex, multi-variable production systems (Womack & Jones, 1996; Shah & Ward, 2007).

The German government coined Industry 4.0 to define the fourth industrial revolution powered by cyber-physical systems, the Internet of Things, artificial intelligence, and advanced robots, which has changed these limits. Sensors in production lines, distribution networks, and supplier facilities generate high-resolution operational data continuously. Machine learning algorithms can recognize patterns, predict problems, and optimize schedules in real time from data streams faster than humans. Enterprises can test process modifications in virtual environments like digital twins, discrete event simulators, and agent-based models before investing in physical implementation. The effects on lean management are significant (Kagermann et al., 2013; Hermann et al., 2016).

While powerful, traditional lean approaches have well-documented limits in dynamic, high-variability corporate systems. Value stream mapping cannot represent the stochasticity of manufacturing processes under changing demand situations. Manual kanban systems cannot quickly adjust to supply or demand changes without causing inventory or production stoppages. Kaizen workshops, while culturally valuable, use retrospective data and may overlook failure patterns that predictive models may spot weeks in advance. Exactly where predictive analytics and simulation transform, these gaps (Rother & Shook, 1998; Netland & Powell, 2017).

This chapter advances a focused central argument: that the transformative value of predictive analytics and simulation in lean enterprise management is realized not through the piecemeal adoption of individual technologies, but through their systematic integration into a closed-loop improvement architecture in which data acquisition, analytical inference, virtual experimentation, and lean intervention are mutually reinforcing and continuously updated. This argument is developed across three analytical layers. The first establishes how the data and analytical foundations of Industry 4.0 extend the diagnostic reach of lean methods beyond what manual observation can achieve. The second examines how digital twins and simulation environments provide the de-risked experimental space that kaizen has always required but rarely achieved at speed. The third critically evaluates the conditions under which these claimed benefits are realized, acknowledging the limitations, boundary conditions, and generalizability constraints that a balanced academic assessment demands. Global case studies and emerging evidence through 2026 ground claims in verifiable operational experience.

2. CONCEPTUAL FOUNDATIONS: INDUSTRY 4.0, LEAN MANAGEMENT, AND DATA INTELLIGENCE

Industry 4.0 is the convergence of nine technical pillars that enable intelligent, self-optimizing industrial systems. Internet of Things, big data analytics, AI/ML, cloud computing, additive manufacturing, autonomous robotics, simulation and digital twins, augmented and virtual reality, and cybersecurity are these pillars. Researchers call their operation cyber-physical systems: production environments where digital machines monitor, operate, and optimize physical machinery. The McKinsey Global Institute believes that Industry 4.0 technologies could generate \$3.7 trillion to \$11 trillion in manufacturing, supply chain, and operational value by 2025 (Rusal et al., 2019; Manyika et al., 2013).

Figure 1. Predictive Analytics Maturity Model for Lean Enterprise

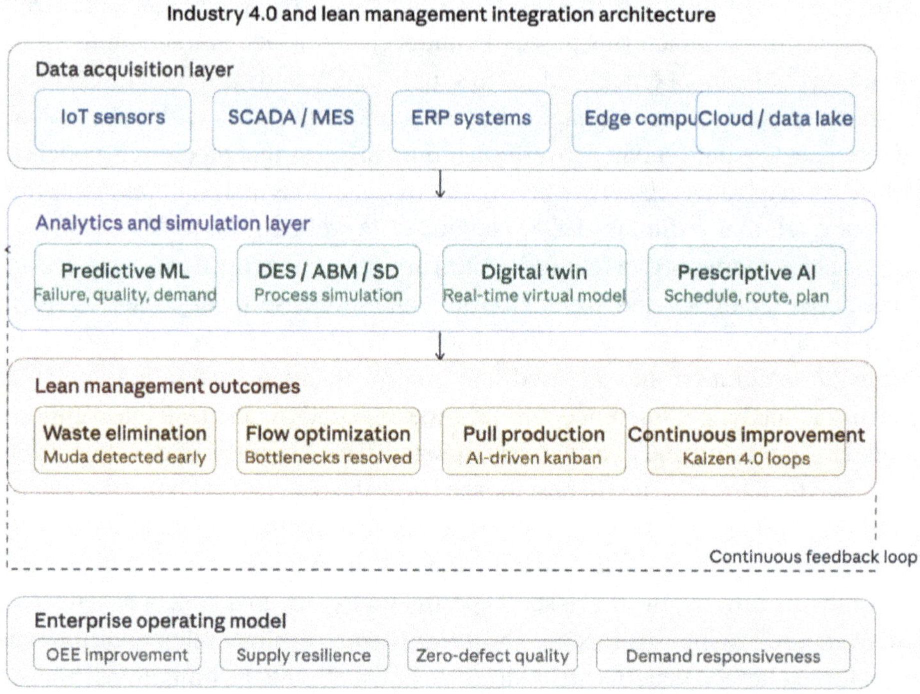

Figure 1 presents the three-layer architecture that underpins the integration of Industry 4.0 technologies with lean management practice. The base layer captures the data acquisition infrastructure, encompassing industrial IoT sensors, SCADA and MES systems, ERP platforms, edge computing devices, and cloud data lakes. The central analytics and simulation layer processes the data streams generated by the acquisition layer through four principal analytical capabilities: predictive machine learning models for failure, quality, and demand forecasting; discrete event simulation, agent-based modelling, and system dynamics tools for process and supply chain simulation; digital twin environments for real-time virtual modelling; and prescriptive AI systems for scheduling, routing, and operational planning. The output layer translates analytical insights into the lean management outcomes of waste elimination, flow optimisation, pull production, and continuous improvement. A continuous feedback loop connects operational results back to the analytics and acquisition layers, ensuring that model accuracy improves iteratively as operational data accumulates.

Lean management, which originated from the Toyota Production System created by Taiichi Ohno and Shigeo Shingo during Japan's post-war reconstruction, is based on five concepts that continue to be pertinent today, as described by Womack and

Jones in the mid-1990s. Value is only determined from the customer's viewpoint; everything the consumer is unwilling to pay for is deemed waste, or muda, and must be eradicated. The value stream includes all operations, both value-adding and non-value-adding, necessary to deliver a product from conception to the client. Flow denotes the continuous progression of products along the value stream, devoid of interruptions, flaws, or delays. Pull signifies that production is initiated by genuine customer demand instead of conjectural forecasting. Perfection is the pursuit of perpetual incremental enhancement without conclusion. Although these concepts are easy to express, they are remarkably challenging to maintain in intricate, high-variability enterprise settings without the use of advanced analytical techniques (Ohno, 1988; Womack & Jones, 1996; Shingo, 1989).

The interplay between lean management and Industry 4.0 is not merely additive; it is multiplicative. Lean offers the conceptual foundation for determining what to optimize and the rationale behind it, but Industry 4.0 technologies deliver the analytical capabilities and accuracy necessary to identify, measure, and optimize with a level of detail and speed unattainable by manual approaches. IoT sensors obviate laborious data collecting and deliver constant, objective assessment of value stream performance. Machine learning algorithms reveal waste patterns that would need months for human observers to identify. Digital twins enable engineers to evaluate lean solutions in virtual settings prior to their use on actual production lines, significantly mitigating the risk and expense associated with improvement trials. The resultant capability is a business that can pursue excellence not only aspirationally but also operationally, in near real-time (Sanders et al., 2016; Buer et al., 2018).

Predictive analytics functions at four tiers of analytical sophistication: descriptive, diagnostic, predictive, and prescriptive. Descriptive analytics aggregates historical data to elucidate past events, as demonstrated by manufacturing efficiency dashboards and defect rate trend reports. Diagnostic analytics examines the reasons behind events through root cause analysis methods and multivariate process diagnostics. Predictive analytics employs statistical models and machine learning to anticipate future events, encompassing equipment failure prediction, demand forecasting, and quality outcome modeling. Prescriptive analytics advances by suggesting specific activities to be undertaken, utilizing optimization algorithms and simulations to determine the optimal course of action within established limitations. Each level is contingent upon the prior one, and the most advanced Industry 4.0 lean firms function concurrently across all four levels (Gandomi & Haider, 2015; Davenport, 2006).

Figure 2. Industry 4.0 and Lean Management Integration Architecture

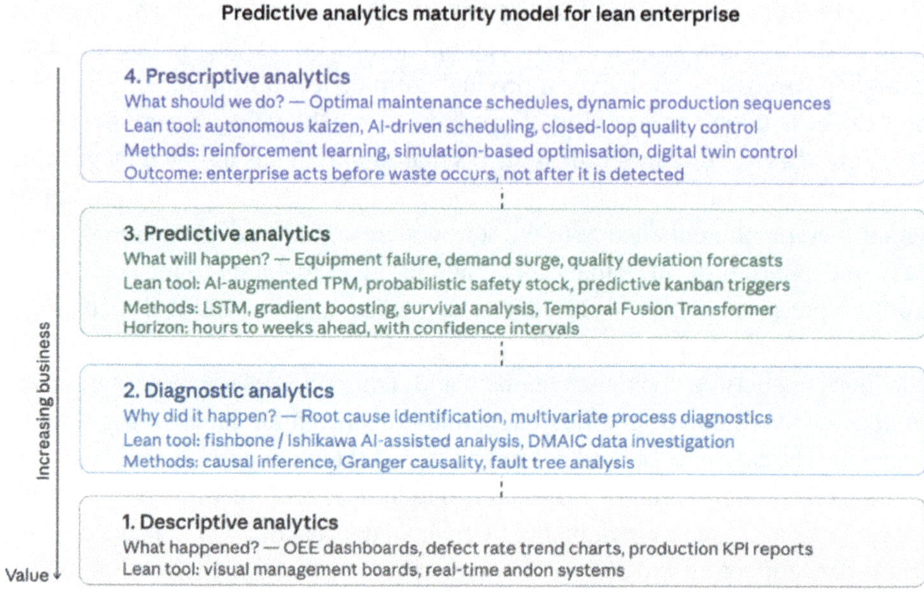

Figure 2 maps the four-level predictive analytics maturity model to the specific lean management tools, industrial methods, and operational outcomes associated with each level of analytical capability. The model progresses from descriptive analytics at the base, which summarises historical performance data through OEE dashboards and real-time andon systems, through diagnostic analytics, which investigates root causes of operational failures using causal inference and fault tree methods, to predictive analytics, which anticipates future equipment failures, demand surges, and quality deviations using LSTM networks, gradient boosting models, and Temporal Fusion Transformers. The apex of the model is prescriptive analytics, at which level AI-driven scheduling, autonomous kaizen systems, and closed-loop quality control enable the enterprise to act before waste occurs rather than detecting it retrospectively. The vertical axis represents increasing business value, reflecting the progressive shift from retrospective observation to proactive, autonomous operational management.

Simulation modeling paradigms employed in Industry 4.0 lean scenarios encompass four primary techniques. Discrete event modeling describes systems as sequences of events delineated by time intervals, rendering it optimal for evaluating production line performance, buffer dimensions, and changeover scheduling. System dynamics modeling elucidates the feedback loops, accumulations, and delays that induce oscillatory behavior in supply chains and manufacturing processes, proving especially beneficial for comprehending inventory instability. Agent-based modeling replicates the interactions of autonomous agents, including production cells, suppliers, and logistics providers, facilitating the examination of emergent behavior within intricate industrial networks. Monte Carlo simulation incorporates randomness into model parameters, facilitating probabilistic evaluation of results amid uncertainty. Collectively, these methodologies provide business analysts with a comprehensive array of tools necessary to comprehend, anticipate, and enhance intricate lean systems (Law, 2015; Sterman, 2000; Macal & North, 2010).

Much of the material on Industry 4.0 and lean management fails to explain conceptual integration by providing a tangible operational design that shows how the component technologies work together. A five-phase integration logic that converts the abstract convergence of lean, analytics, and simulation into a step-by-step decision and implementation architecture is proposed in this chapter to fill this gap. The five phases Predict, Analyze, Simulate, Execute, and Improve match the analytical and lean management layers in this chapter.

IoT sensor networks and industrial data platforms collect operational signals from assets, processes, and supply chains during Predict. This data allows machine learning models to predict equipment degradation, demand variations, quality deviations, and supply disruptions, taking the organization from retrospective awareness to anticipatory readiness. Diagnostic analytics and causal inference tools analyze predictive layer outputs to discover value stream components that cause expected performance deficits in the Analyze phase. This phase plugs the gap between generic failure signals and maintenance or process decisions.

Before any physical change is performed, digital twins and discrete event or agent-based simulation environments are utilized to simulate and assess candidate lean interventions under historical variability settings. The traditional kaizen workshop becomes a continuous, data-rich virtual experimentation process at this phase. The Execute phase implements the simulation's highest-value intervention: a maintenance operation, kanban parameter adjustment, schedule re-optimization, or supply route diversification. In the enhance phase, operational outputs are fed back into predictive models and simulation environments as new training data, allowing the system to learn from each cycle and enhance prediction accuracy and intervention quality. PASEI's closed-loop feedback separates it from linear technology deployment models and makes integration systemic rather than sequential. The framework provides a decision architecture that organizations can enter at different phases depending on their data maturity, analytical capability, and lean culture readiness, not a universal deployment order or requirement that all five phases be implemented simultaneously. (Sanders et al., 2016; Buer et al., 2018; Nozari & Yordanova, 2026b).

3. DATA INFRASTRUCTURE FOR PREDICTIVE ANALYTICS IN INDUSTRY 4.0 ENTERPRISES

A solid, scalable, and well-governed data infrastructure underpins all predictive analytics and simulation capabilities. In Industry 4.0 firms, this infrastructure initiates at the shop floor with industrial IoT sensor networks that incessantly collect operational data from machinery, production lines, material handling systems, and environmental conditions. Contemporary manufacturing plants may utilize tens of thousands of sensors to measure vibration, temperature, pressure, electrical current, acoustic emissions, and optical properties, with sampling rates varying from milliseconds to seconds. The volume, pace, and variety of data produced by these sensor networks clearly constitute big data, and efficient management necessitates architectural decisions that conventional enterprise IT systems were not meant to support (Lee et al., 2015; Xu et al., 2018).

Enterprise data architecture in Industry 4.0 businesses generally incorporates several levels of systems: Enterprise Resource Planning systems like SAP S/4HANA or Oracle Cloud ERP, which oversee financial, procurement, and master data; Manufacturing Execution Systems that monitor and regulate production on the shop floor; Supervisory Control and Data Acquisition systems that connect directly with industrial control apparatus; and Computerized Maintenance Management Systems that document equipment history and maintenance timelines. The integration of heterogeneous technologies into a cohesive industrial data platform that facilitates real-time analytics across operational and business data is a significant technological barrier in the deployment of Industry 4.0. Contemporary Industrial IoT solutions like PTC ThingWorx, Siemens MindSphere, and GE Predix are explicitly engineered to address these integration deficiencies (Delsing, 2017; Zhong et al., 2017).

Time-series databases have become an essential element of Industry 4.0 data architectures, tailored for the high-frequency, timestamp-indexed data produced by industrial sensors. Platforms like InfluxDB, OSIsoft PI System, TimescaleDB, and cloud-native solutions such as AWS Timestream offer the necessary storage efficiency and query performance for large-scale operational analytics. Data lakes, constructed on platforms like Apache Hadoop, Databricks, or cloud object storage, function as repositories for both structured and unstructured operational data, facilitating batch analytics, model training, and cross-domain integration that traditional relational databases cannot achieve. The architectural notion of decoupling storage from computation, as shown in contemporary cloud data platforms, allows organizations to autonomously grow their analytical capabilities relative to their data quantities (Russom, 2011; Inmon & Linstedt, 2014).

The integration of operational technology and information technology networks, commonly known as OT/IT convergence, is essential for uninterrupted data transfer from the factory floor to business analytics platforms. Historically, operational technology (OT) networks functioned independently from information technology (IT) infrastructure, employing proprietary communication protocols like Modbus, PROFIBUS, and EtherNet/IP, which were specifically built for deterministic real-time control rather than data transmission. The implementation of open industrial communication standards like OPC Unified Architecture and MQTT has markedly expedited OT/IT integration by offering vendor-neutral, secure, and semantically robust data exchange methods. Edge computing devices, situated at the intersection of operational technology (OT) and information technology (IT) domains, execute local pre-processing, data normalization, and protocol translation, thereby diminishing the bandwidth and latency requirements on central analytics infrastructure (Serpanos & Wolf, 2018; Sisinni et al., 2018).

Data quality management is an essential although frequently undervalued topic in industrial analytics implementations. Industrial time-series data is often compromised by sensor drift, communication interruptions, calibration inaccuracies, and measurement noise, which can substantially impair the efficacy of predictive models developed on flawed signals. Enterprise-level data quality pipelines must integrate automated anomaly detection to identify questionable readings, interpolation methods to address missing values, calibration correction procedures, and feature engineering systems that convert raw sensor signals into the statistically sound inputs necessary for machine learning models. The lack of stringent data quality management is a primary factor contributing to the failure of predictive analytics projects in industrial environments, highlighting the necessity for specialized data engineering practices within Industry 4.0 enterprises (Batini & Scannapieco, 2006; Janssen et al., 2017). The core components of a robust Industry 4.0 data infrastructure, along with their enabling technologies and specific roles in supporting lean analytics, are summarised in Table 1.

Table 1. Key Data Infrastructure Components for Industry 4.0 Predictive Analytics

Component	Key Technologies	Role in Lean Analytics
Industrial IoT Sensors	MEMS accelerometers, thermal cameras, acoustic sensors	Continuous real-time data acquisition from production assets
Industrial Communication	OPC UA, MQTT, EtherNet/IP	Secure, standardized data transport from OT to IT layers
Time-Series Database	InfluxDB, OSIsoft PI, AWS Timestream	High-frequency operational data storage and retrieval
Edge Computing	AWS Greengrass, Azure IoT Edge	Local pre-processing and low-latency predictive insights

continued on following page

Table 1. Continued

Component	Key Technologies	Role in Lean Analytics
Data Lake	Databricks, Apache Hadoop, Azure Data Lake	Unified storage for cross-domain analytics and model training
Streaming Analytics	Apache Kafka, Apache Flink, Spark Streaming	Real-time event processing and anomaly detection

4. PREDICTIVE MAINTENANCE AND ASSET PERFORMANCE MANAGEMENT

The economic rationale for shifting from reactive and preventive maintenance practices to predictive maintenance is persuasive. Reactive maintenance, wherein equipment is fixed solely post-failure, incurs the highest overall costs due to unanticipated downtime, emergency labor premiums, hurried parts acquisition, and subsequent output losses. Time-based preventative maintenance decreases the incidence of catastrophic failures but incurs considerable over-maintenance expenses by substituting components that possess considerable remaining useful life. Condition-based and predictive maintenance, in contrast, activate solely when sensor data and prediction models suggest an impending breakdown, hence maximizing the equilibrium between operational uptime and maintenance costs. Industry analyses suggest that predictive maintenance can reduce maintenance costs by 10 to 25 percent and unplanned downtime by 35 to 45 percent under favorable conditions. However, these figures warrant critical scrutiny: they are typically derived from pilot deployments on well-instrumented assets with mature failure mode libraries. Hamadache et al. (2019) found that performance gains vary substantially across industry sectors and asset types, and that results from controlled single-asset studies frequently overstate gains achievable in complex multi-asset production environments. Realization of these benefits is conditional on adequate data quality, sufficient failure event samples for model training, and robust integration between predictive outputs and maintenance execution systems. Nozari (2026) demonstrates this concretely in cold chain logistics, where digital twin-based predictive maintenance delivered measurable reliability improvements specifically because sensor coverage, failure data, and execution integration were systematically co-designed rather than retrofitted. (Mobley, 2002; Scheffer & Girdhar, 2004; Besnard & Bertling, 2010).

Machine learning methodologies for failure prediction encompass many algorithmic categories tailored to distinct types of failure data and operational limitations. Survival analysis models, such as Cox proportional hazards regression and Weibull distribution fitting, assess the likelihood of failure over time by utilizing historical failure data and are especially useful in fleet-level maintenance planning when substantial samples of failure incidents are accessible. Gradient boosting algorithms, such XGBoost and LightGBM, are proficient at discerning intricate non-linear correlations between operational parameters and failure indicators derived from tabular sensor data. Long Short-Term Memory neural networks are especially adept in processing sequential sensor data, effectively capturing temporal relationships that reveal degradation patterns over hours or days prior to failure. Models for estimating Remaining Useful Life, which forecast the remaining running cycles or hours before a component necessitates replacement, are increasingly utilized in aerospace, rail transportation, and semiconductor manufacturing to inform condition-based maintenance scheduling (Jardine et al., 2006; Lee et al., 2014; Ren et al., 2018).

Historically, vibration analysis has been the primary method for monitoring the health of rotating machinery, utilizing spectrum analysis of accelerometer signals to identify early-stage faults in bearings, shaft imbalances, gear tooth wear, and rotor eccentricities. The utilization of deep learning in vibration signal analysis has markedly enhanced the diagnostic potential of vibration monitoring by extracting feature representations directly from raw waveforms, eliminating the need for human feature engineering. Infrared cameras facilitate the identification of hotspots in electrical switchgear, refractory linings, and heat exchanger tubes using thermal imaging. Acoustic emission monitoring detects the high-frequency stress waves produced by crack propagation and material fatigue. Oil debris monitoring analyzes the morphology of wear particles in lubrication systems. The amalgamation of signals from several sense modalities via data fusion and multi-modal deep learning models significantly enhances diagnostic accuracy compared to single-modality methods, especially for intricate machinery with numerous potential failure modes (Hamadache et al., 2019; Lei et al., 2020).

Prognostics and Health Management frameworks, as delineated by ISO 13381, offer a systematic methodology for amalgamating condition monitoring, fault diagnosis, and prognosis into a unified asset intelligence capability that links to maintenance planning, spare parts management, and operational decision-making. The amalgamation of PHM outputs with Computerized Maintenance Management Systems and ERP procurement modules facilitates the automated creation of maintenance work orders, spare parts purchase requisitions, and updates to maintenance schedules predicated on anticipated failure timelines, thereby bridging the gap between asset health analytics and operational maintenance execution (Peng et al., 2010; *ISO 13381-1, 2015*).

The incorporation of predictive maintenance functionalities into Total Productive Maintenance frameworks constitutes a logical progression of the lean methodology in asset management. The principal statistic of TPM, Overall Equipment Effectiveness, disaggregates equipment performance into availability, performance efficiency, and quality rate. Predictive analytics immediately improves OEE by minimizing unanticipated downtime, detecting slow-speed and minor stoppage trends, and associating equipment deterioration with product quality results. AI-enhanced TPM platforms may dynamically prioritize maintenance work orders based on anticipated failure likelihood, business effect, and the availability of maintenance resources, assuring optimal deployment of resources for maximum return. AI-assisted inspection checklists on mobile devices facilitate autonomous maintenance tasks, hence enhancing condition monitoring beyond the limitations of centralized systems (Nakajima, 1988; McKone et al., 1999).

5. DEMAND FORECASTING, INVENTORY OPTIMIZATION, AND JUST-IN-TIME PRODUCTION

Precise demand forecasting is fundamental to just-in-time production, inventory optimization, and supply chain coordination. Traditional statistical forecasting techniques, including ARIMA, exponential smoothing, and seasonal decomposition, have been significantly augmented in high-volume enterprise contexts by machine learning methodologies that can integrate extensive predictor variables, identify non-linear demand patterns, and dynamically adjust to structural shifts in demand behavior. Ensemble forecasting techniques amalgamate the predictions of various models, such as gradient boosting regressors, random forests, and neural networks, to yield forecasts that are more precise and resilient than those generated by any individual model. Amazon's demand forecasting infrastructure, which generates probabilistic predictions for hundreds of millions of product-location combinations using ensemble models, illustrates the scale at which ML forecasting now operates. It is important, however, to acknowledge the boundary conditions on these methods: the M4 forecasting competition (Makridakis et al., 2018) demonstrated that statistical baseline methods frequently match or outperform complex ML models on shorter time horizons and for products with stable, low-volume demand histories. ML forecasting advantages are most pronounced in high-volume, high-frequency, and promotion-influenced environments where the volume of training data justifies model complexity. For SMEs with limited data histories, simpler ensemble methods may provide equivalent accuracy at lower cost and with greater interpretability for operational planners. Nozari and Yordanova (2026a) illustrate this boundary explicitly in metaverse-based retail environments, demonstrating that fuzzy multi-objective digital twin frameworks outperform deterministic ML approaches specifically where demand uncertainty is structural and multi-dimensional rather than merely statistical (Box et al., 2015; Makridakis et al., 2018; Fildes et al., 2022).

Long Short-Term Memory networks and their architectural successors, including Temporal Fusion Transformers and N-BEATS, have exhibited robust efficacy in demand forecasting tasks marked by intricate seasonality, trend disruptions, and external influencing factors such as promotions, weather phenomena, and macroeconomic indicators. The Temporal Fusion Transformer, created by researchers at Google DeepMind, explicitly simulates temporal attention across several time horizons and input types, facilitating interpretable multi-horizon probabilistic forecasting that is especially beneficial for supply chain planning applications. The incorporation of external signals, like web search patterns, social media sentiment indexes, rival price data, and satellite imaging of parking lots and shipping ports, has significantly broadened the informational scope accessible to enterprise demand forecasting algorithms (Lim et al., 2021; Oreshkin et al., 2020).

Probabilistic demand forecasting, which produces a comprehensive prediction distribution rather than a singular estimate, is widely acknowledged as the suitable foundation for safety stock optimization and service-level-oriented inventory management. Conventional deterministic forecasting, when paired with static safety stock formulas, consistently undervalues the expenses associated with demand variability in multi-echelon inventory systems, resulting in either excessive working capital allocated to safety stock or intolerable stockout rates. Quantile regression forests, conformal prediction intervals, and deep probabilistic forecasting models like DeepAR allow inventory planners to establish safety stock levels that directly align with target service levels, balancing holding costs against stockout costs with mathematical accuracy (Huber et al., 2017; Salinas et al., 2020).

Just-in-time and just-in-sequence production systems, which depend on meticulously planned material delivery to production cells with minimum buffer inventory, are inherently susceptible to demand unpredictability and supply uncertainty. AI-driven kanban systems substitute static reorder points and preset order quantities with dynamic replenishment signals derived from real-time consumption rates, anticipated future demand, and upstream supply availability. Takt time optimization, which aligns production tempo with customer demand, can be dynamically modified in intelligent production settings according on real-time order intake data and resource availability indicators. Multi-echelon inventory optimization approaches, utilizing stochastic dynamic programming and reinforcement learning, allow organizations to concurrently ascertain appropriate base stock levels at each node within intricate supply networks (Hopp & Spearman, 2011; Simchi-Levi et al., 2014; Oroojlooy & Nazari, 2021).

The principal forecasting approaches deployed in Industry 4.0 lean environments, spanning classical statistical methods through to deep probabilistic models, are compared in Table 2 across their algorithmic family, core strength, and specific application in just-in-time production contexts. Predicting supplier lead time using machine learning models is a vital aspect of demand-supply integration in lean situations. Models utilizing historical purchase order data, supplier performance metrics, logistics tracking details, and external variables like port congestion indices and commodity price trends can forecast lead time distributions for specific supplier-material combinations with significantly enhanced precision compared to static lead time assumptions. The predictive lead time distributions inform safety stock calculations and dynamic reorder point models, allowing procurement teams to uphold target service levels while substantially reducing inventory investment compared to static lead time models (Simchi-Levi et al., 2018; Tang, 2006).

Table 2. Forecasting Approaches and Their Application in Lean Just-in-Time Environments

Method	Algorithmic Family	Strength	Lean Application
ARIMA / ETS	Statistical	Transparency, interpretability	Stable, mature product demand
Gradient Boosting	Ensemble ML	Non-linear patterns, feature richness	Promotional and seasonal demand
LSTM / GRU	Deep Learning	Sequential temporal patterns	High-frequency production demand
Temporal Fusion Transformer	Attention-based DL	Multi-horizon probabilistic	Supply chain inventory planning
DeepAR	Probabilistic DL	Full predictive distributions	Safety stock optimization

6. PRODUCTION SCHEDULING AND SHOP FLOOR OPTIMIZATION

Production scheduling in contemporary manufacturing firms constitutes a highly complex optimization challenge in operations research, generally categorized as NP-hard due to the combinatorial explosion of potential assignment and sequencing choices involving numerous jobs, multiple machines, and various operational constraints such as setup durations, tooling availability, operator qualifications, and energy tariffs. Advanced Planning and Scheduling systems tackle this complexity using constraint-based optimization engines, such as mixed-integer linear programming solvers, genetic algorithms, and simulated annealing metaheuristics, which produce near-optimal schedules within reasonable computational timeframes. Contemporary APS solutions like Asprova, DELMIA Ortems, and Siemens Opcenter synchronize with real-time MES data to facilitate dynamic re-scheduling in response to production variations, machine malfunctions, or urgent orders that interrupt the established timetable (Pinedo, 2016; Blazewicz et al., 2019).

Reinforcement learning has emerged as a highly promising method for production scheduling, owing to its capacity to derive scheduling policies via trial-and-error interactions with production environment simulators, without necessitating explicit mathematical formulations of the objective function. Within a reinforcement learning paradigm, a scheduling agent monitors the present state of the shop floor, chooses an action, such as allocating a job to a machine, receives a reward signal indicative of the outcomes of that decision concerning makespan, tardiness, and resource utilization, and progressively refines its scheduling policy to optimize cumulative reward. Deep Q-Network and Proximal Policy Optimization algorithms have exhibited competitive efficacy on benchmark job shop scheduling challenges, and their implementation in real-world flexible manufacturing settings with dynamic job arrivals is a prominent focus of industrial research (Mnih et al., 2015; Zhang et al., 2020; Liu et al., 2022).

Digital shop floor management enhances the real-time visibility and analytical functions of conventional factory execution systems through the incorporation of AI-driven anomaly detection, computer vision surveillance, and operator decision support interfaces. Real-time production monitoring dashboards display important performance indicators such as cycle time, queue lengths, work-in-progress inventory, and machine utilization with a level of detail and refresh rate unattainable by paper-based shop floor management systems. Automated anomaly detection algorithms identify departures from typical work cycle times, unanticipated machine stoppages, and quality anomalies within seconds of their occurrence, allowing supervisors to intervene before minor disruptions progress into significant production losse (Mourtzis, 2020; Lu et al., 2022).

The Theory of Constraints, formulated by Eliyahu Goldratt, offers a supplementary framework to lean scheduling by directing improvement efforts towards the singular system restriction, or bottleneck, that restricts total throughput. AI-assisted bottleneck identification evaluates real-time queue length data, machine utilization metrics, and workflow dependency graphs to dynamically pinpoint the current throughput-limiting constraint in intricate production networks, which may transition from one resource to another as production mix and volumes fluctuate. Drum-Buffer-Rope scheduling, a methodology derived from the Theory of Constraints, can be dynamically implemented in digital environments where the drum pace is determined by real-time machine data, buffer sizes are calculated using predictive queue length models, and the rope regulates the release rate of raw materials to align with bottleneck throughput (Goldratt, 1990; Watson et al., 2007).

Energy-conscious production scheduling is becoming a crucial aspect of lean waste reduction within the Industry 4.0 framework, as companies encounter escalating energy expenses, carbon pricing strategies, and sustainability reporting requirements. The combination of real-time power pricing signals, carbon intensity data from grid operators, and equipment energy consumption profiles allows production schedulers to relocate energy-intensive processes to times of reduced cost and carbon intensity, while maintaining delivery promises. Research in automotive and chemical industry has shown that intelligent energy-aware scheduling can yield energy cost reductions of 10 to 20 percent, significantly contributing to operational cost reduction and sustainability performance (Gahm et al., 2016; Duflou et al., 2012).

7. SIMULATION TECHNOLOGIES FOR ENTERPRISE PROCESS OPTIMIZATION

For over forty years, discrete event simulation has been the principal computational instrument for lean value stream analysis in industrial engineering, allowing engineers to model production systems as networks of queues and servers while examining their behavior under diverse loading conditions, process time distributions, and configuration options. Within the framework of Industry 4.0, discrete event simulation (DES) has been markedly improved due to the accessibility of extensive operational data for model parameterization, real-time model updating functionalities, and the incorporation of optimization algorithms that can methodically explore the configuration space for opportunities for lean enhancement. Platforms like Simio, Arena, AnyLogic, and FlexSim facilitate the development of intricate factory models that integrate stochastic process durations, machine failure and repair distributions, operator schedules, material handling limitations, and shift patterns, thereby allowing for the virtual evaluation of process modifications, layout redesigns, and capacity investment decisions with a precision unattainable by analytical models alone (Law, 2015; Kelton et al., 2015).

System dynamics modeling tackles a category of industrial issues that discrete event simulation (DES) inadequately represents: the medium- and long-term dynamic behavior of production and supply chain systems influenced by feedback loops, accumulations, and information delays. The quintessential example of system dynamics in supply chain scenarios is the bullwhip effect, a phenomena where minor variations in retail demand escalate into significant swings in supplier order amounts when orders propagate upstream through multi-echelon supply chains. System dynamics models demonstrate how ordering policies, information-sharing practices, and supply chain structural characteristics influence these oscillations, allowing firms to reconfigure their supply chain governance for enhanced stability.

In lean environments, system dynamics is especially useful for simulating the long-term effects of alterations in inventory policies, capacity investment choices, and supplier development strategies (Sterman, 2000; Forrester, 1961; Lee et al., 1997).

Agent-based modeling enhances the simulation toolkit by allowing the depiction of intricate industrial systems as collections of autonomous, interacting agents, each governed by distinct behavioral norms and local decision-making abilities. In supply chain applications, agents may denote separate suppliers, logistics providers, distribution facilities, and retail outlets, each functioning according to their distinct ordering processes and reacting to localized demand and inventory signals. The collective behavior of these interacting agents can generate intricate macro-level phenomena, including supply chain disruption cascades, cluster formation among rival suppliers, and adaptive re-routing of material flows around disrupted nodes, which cannot be anticipated solely from individual behavioral rules. Agent-based modeling (ABM) has been utilized in the design of robust supply network topologies, the assessment of epidemic risk transmission within supply chains, and the simulation of multi-tier supplier relationship dynamics (Macal & North, 2010; Tordecilla et al., 2021).

Monte Carlo simulation serves as the statistical foundation for risk and uncertainty analysis in enterprise planning, allowing analysts to substitute single-point estimates of uncertain parameters with probability distributions and to propagate uncertainty through intricate models to produce probabilistic distributions of outcome variables. In project planning applications, Monte Carlo simulation of task duration distributions generates probabilistic project completion timeframes that more accurately reflect the spectrum of potential outcomes compared to deterministic critical path assessments. Monte Carlo simulation of supplier lead time distributions, demand variability, and disruption probability in supply chain risk assessment facilitates the quantitative analysis of inventory buffer needs, dual sourcing methods, and supply chain insurance choices (Kroese et al., 2011; Kleijnen, 2015).

Simulation-based optimization integrates discrete event simulation or agent-based models with metaheuristic search algorithms, including genetic algorithms, simulated annealing, and particle swarm optimization, to facilitate the systematic identification of optimal design configurations within extensive solution spaces that exhaustive enumeration cannot feasibly investigate. This methodology is especially effective for multi-objective lean optimization challenges, such as concurrently minimizing cycle time, work-in-progress inventory, and changeover frequency while upholding service level objectives, where the interrelations among decision variables create non-linear trade-off frontiers that analytical techniques cannot delineate. Real-time simulation and hardware-in-the-loop testing, which directly links simulation environments to physical control systems, facilitates the validation of automation logic and control algorithms in virtual settings prior to physical implementation, thereby minimizing the risk and expense associated with lean automation investments (Kleijnen, 2015; Garcia-Sabater et al., 2017).

8. DIGITAL TWINS FOR LEAN ENTERPRISE MANAGEMENT

The digital twin concept, initially proposed by Michael Grieves about product lifecycle management, has evolved into a fundamental framework for Industry 4.0 enterprise management. An industrial digital twin is a real-time, bidirectionally linked virtual version of a physical asset, process, or system, consistently synchronized with its physical counterpart via sensor data streams and actuator feedback loops. In contrast to conventional simulation models that are created, executed, and subsequently discarded, digital twins are dynamic models that perpetually represent the real-time condition of their physical equivalents, facilitating the generation of operational insights, hypothesis testing, and real-time control decision-making. The significance of a digital twin transcends mere monitoring, incorporating prediction, optimization, and virtual experimentation that facilitates lean improvement without physical interference. This potential, however, is highly sensitive to implementation maturity. Negri et al. (2017) distinguish between four levels of digital twin fidelity ranging from basic asset monitoring through to fully autonomous bidirectional control, and the majority of industrial deployments as of the mid-2020s operate at the lower fidelity levels where synchronization is periodic rather than continuous and the twin's simulation environment is not yet coupled to live control decisions. Claims about digital twins enabling real-time kaizen and closed-loop process optimization therefore apply with full force only to a small subset of leading adopters with mature sensor infrastructure, high-fidelity physics-based models, and established data governance. For most manufacturers, the digital twin is currently better characterized as a decision-support tool than as an autonomous operational system, and the investment and capability requirements for ascending the fidelity ladder are substantial. Nozari and Yordanova (2026b) address this gap directly by proposing a self-deciding adaptive digital twin framework using agentic AI for fuzzy multi-objective optimization, demonstrating that the path from monitoring to autonomous decision-making requires not only sensor integration but a fundamentally different control architecture built around agentic reasoning under uncertainty *(Negri et al., 2017; Nozari & Yordanova, 2026b)*(Grieves & Vickers, 2017; Tao et al., 2018).

Figure 3. Digital Twin Feedback Loop for Lean Enterprise Improvement

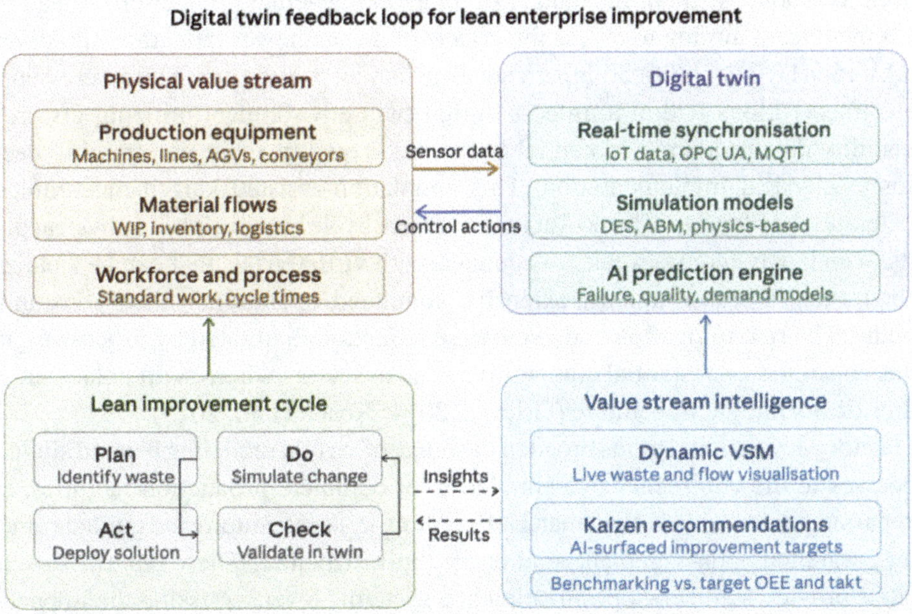

Figure 3 illustrates the bidirectional coupling between the physical value stream and its digital twin that forms the operational core of lean enterprise management in Industry 4.0 environments. The upper half of the figure depicts the physical value stream, containing production equipment, material flows, and workforce processes, alongside the digital twin, which maintains real-time synchronisation through IoT and industrial communication protocols, runs continuous simulation models using discrete event simulation and agent-based approaches, and operates an AI prediction engine for failure, quality, and demand forecasting. Digital twins for value stream mapping signify a revolutionary improvement of a crucial diagnostic tool in lean management. Conventional value stream mapping generates a static visual depiction of the current-state value stream, reflecting data gathered through manual observation within a restricted time frame. A digital twin-based value stream map is consistently updated with real-time data from production systems, quality sensors, inventory management systems, and logistics tracking platforms, offering a dynamic representation of value stream performance that uncovers variability, bottlenecks, and waste patterns that static maps cannot reveal. The capacity to replicate historical value stream behavior, analyze specific periods of subpar performance, and superimpose enhancement possibilities on the current-state model significantly expedites the lean improvement cycle (Rother & Shook, 1998; Negri et al., 2017).

Process digital twins provide virtual experimentation, which is essential to the kaizen technique, without the danger of interrupting actual production. A lean improvement team aiming to assess the effects of a changeover reduction initiative, a workstation layout modification, or a novel quality inspection procedure can evaluate these interventions within a process digital twin environment utilizing historical variability data to identify potential bottlenecks, quality risks, and training needs prior to physical implementation. This simulation-assisted kaizen methodology accelerates the Plan-Do-Check-Act improvement cycle by substituting physical pilot tests, which may require weeks to conduct, with virtual trials that can be finalized in hours and assessed against extensive simulated operational history spanning months. The risk mitigation and cycle time reduction facilitated by process digital twins constitute a substantial competitive edge in sectors where swift enhancement is a critical strategic imperative (Grieves, 2014; Rosen et al., 2015).

Factory-level digital twins broaden the range of virtual modeling beyond singular processes to the comprehensive simulation of complete production facilities, encompassing production layout, material handling systems, automated guided vehicle fleets, warehouse management, and energy infrastructure. These enterprise-scale models provide lean flow optimization at a systemic level, assessing the impact of alterations in production sequencing, buffer dimensions, and facility configuration throughout the entire manufacturing system. Supply chain digital twins broaden this reach to include comprehensive supply network modeling, facilitating the simulation of multi-tier supplier interruptions, logistics network redesigns, and demand shock scenarios throughout the whole supply chain. The amalgamation of digital twin platforms with MES and ERP systems via bidirectional data APIs facilitates automatic performance assessment against objectives, real-time detection of value stream deterioration, and AI-generated continual improvement suggestions (Stark et al., 2019; Schluse et al., 2018).

9. QUALITY MANAGEMENT AND DEFECT PREDICTION

Statistical process control, pioneered by Walter Shewhart and enhanced by W. Edwards Deming, has served as a fundamental element of lean quality management for more than seventy years. Conventional Statistical Process Control (SPC) evaluates process outputs against control limits established from historical process capability data, indicating when a process displays non-random variation that requires examination. The constraint of traditional Statistical Process Control (SPC) in high-velocity, intricate Industry 4.0 manufacturing settings is its focus on discrete quality attributes in isolation, its utilization of control limits derived from historical process behavior that may no longer be applicable, and its dependence on human operators to analyze control charts and implement corrective measures. Machine learning-enhanced Statistical Process Control (SPC) mitigates these limitations by facilitating multivariate surveillance of numerous process parameters concurrently, dynamically adjusting control limits as process capability develops, and automating the identification and categorization of process anomalies using supervised learning algorithms trained on historical fault signatures (Montgomery, 2019; Shewhart, 1931; Qiu, 2014).

AI-driven defect identification with computer vision and convolutional neural networks has revolutionized automated optical inspection in manufacturing across various sectors, including semiconductor fabrication, printed circuit board assembly, automobile surface finish inspection, and food quality assessment. Deep learning models trained on annotated picture datasets of defective and conforming components can attain inspection accuracy levels that equal or surpass those of human inspectors, while functioning at production line speeds unattainable by human visual inspection. Transfer learning methodologies, which refine pre-trained image classification models on production-specific defect datasets, significantly alleviate the data collection demands necessary for implementing efficient inspection systems, thereby rendering this technology attainable for manufacturers with constrained defect sample repositories (LeCun et al., 2015; Weimer et al., 2016).

Root cause analysis in intricate manufacturing processes poses a formidable analytical challenge: discerning the upstream process circumstances that led to a downstream quality failure among numerous possibly linked process variables assessed at various stages of production. Causal inference methodologies, such as Granger causality analysis, directed acyclic graph modeling, and structural equation models, facilitate the identification of authentic causal linkages between process parameters and quality outcomes, differentiating them from misleading correlations. Predictive quality models, which link upstream process parameters to downstream product quality outcomes, allow lean practitioners to intervene at the process parameter level prior to defect production, rather than identifying them through end-of-line inspection. The amalgamation of predictive quality analytics with lean Six Sigma DMAIC methodologies establishes a data-driven continuous improvement framework that markedly enhances cycle time during the Analyze and Improve phases (Pearl, 2009; Bastian et al., 2014).

Zero-defect manufacturing, a goal that has guided lean and Six Sigma quality philosophies for decades, is becoming operationally feasible in high-technology production settings through the incorporation of predictive quality analytics, closed-loop process control, and AI-assisted inspection. The digital thread concept establishes a comprehensive electronic record that connects product design specifications, manufacturing process parameters, inspection results, and field performance data for each manufactured unit, thereby facilitating traceability, warranty analysis, and regulatory compliance in industries such as aerospace, medical devices, and automotive safety components. The integration of digital thread data with machine learning quality models facilitates continuous learning systems that enhance predicted accuracy as the quantity of field performance feedback increases during the product lifetime (Grieves, 2014; Stark et al., 2019).

10. SUPPLY CHAIN RESILIENCE AND RISK ANALYTICS

Supply chain resilience has become a paramount strategic necessity due to a series of significant interruptions that exposed the vulnerabilities inherent in highly efficient, lean, low-buffer supply chains. The COVID-19 pandemic resulted in concurrent demand shocks, supply disruptions, and logistics network failures, revealing the weaknesses of single-source supplier methods, inadequate safety stock approaches, and concentrated geographic production bases. The semiconductor shortage of 2021, the Suez Canal blockade, and persistent extreme weather disruptions have shown the insufficiency of static supply chain models in a context marked by escalating geopolitical instability, climatic risk, and systemic fragility. The challenge for lean practitioners is to reconcile the structural tension between lean's efficiency imperative and resilience's redundancy requirements, a tension that is not resolved by technology alone but demands a deliberate strategic reconfiguration of the supply chain design logic itself. It is analytically important to acknowledge that the post-pandemic disruptions cited here exposed a specific failure mode: excessive optimization of single-metric efficiency at the expense of systemic robustness. The appropriate policy response is not the wholesale abandonment of lean principles but a more nuanced, risk-adjusted application of them that distinguishes between value-stream waste and strategic resilience buffers. This distinction, which analytics can quantify but cannot determine without managerial judgment about acceptable risk levels and competitive trade-offs, represents the irreducible human dimension of supply chain strategy in the Industry 4.0 era (Chopra & Sodhi, 2004; Sheffi, 2005; Tang, 2006).

Predictive supply chain risk monitoring utilizes machine learning algorithms to offer advance notice of supply disruptions prior to the occurrence of material shortages or delivery failures. Models utilizing financial statement data, credit rating histories, payment behavior, news sentiment analysis, and macroeconomic indicators can predict the likelihood of supplier financial distress weeks or months prior to public disclosure, allowing procurement teams to proactively qualify alternative sources or augment safety stock. Natural language processing models consistently analyze news feeds, regulatory announcements, and social media for indicators of geopolitical tensions, labor conflicts, natural disasters, and logistical delays that may impact supplier availability. Satellite imaging analytics offer impartial, real-time evaluations of supplier manufacturing activity, port congestion, and agricultural production circumstances (Zsidisin et al., 2004; Hendricks & Singhal, 2005; Simchi-Levi et al., 2018).

Scenario planning and simulation-based stress testing of supply chain resilience allow organizations to quantify the financial and operational impacts of disruption scenarios prior to their occurrence, hence guiding risk mitigation expenditures with empirical facts rather than guesswork. Digital twins of supply chains, integrated with actual supplier lead time distributions, capacity limitations, and network topology data, can model the effects of disruption scenarios such as the loss of a vital single-source supplier, a port closure impacting 30 percent of inbound volume, or a 20 percent increase in demand. The results of these scenario studies, quantified as predicted revenue loss, inventory costs, and customer service decline, furnish the empirical foundation for board-level investment decisions on supply chain risk (Kleindorfer & Saad, 2005; Schmitt & Singh, 2012).The principal supply chain risk categories confronting lean enterprises operating in Industry 4.0 environments, together with their observable indicators, corresponding predictive analytics approaches, and recommended lean mitigation strategies, are consolidated in Table 3.

Table 3. Supply Chain Risk Categories and Predictive Analytics Approaches

Risk Category	Risk Indicators	Analytics Approach	Lean Mitigation Strategy
Supplier Financial Distress	Credit ratings, payment delays, news sentiment	ML classifier on financial data	Dual sourcing, safety stock increase
Lead Time Inflation	Historical lead time trends, port congestion	Time-series anomaly detection	Dynamic safety stock, buffer adjustment
Demand Volatility	Forecast error, order variability	Probabilistic demand forecasting	Pull system, flexible capacity
Logistics Disruption	Carrier reliability, weather alerts, port data	NLP news monitoring, IoT tracking	Multi-modal routing, nearshoring
Geopolitical Risk	Trade policy, sanctions, conflict indicators	Country risk scoring models	Supply chain diversification

The restructuring of supply chains following the epidemic has yielded lasting strategic insights that are transforming lean supply chain philosophy for the next decade. The notion of strategic inventory differentiates between waste-producing operating inventory and resilience-enhancing buffer stock maintained for recognized risk scenarios, representing a significant refinement to the lean principle of inventory reduction. Strategies for nearshoring and regional supply chain diversification, which forgo certain unit cost benefits of global low-cost sourcing in favor of diminished logistics risk and abbreviated lead times, are being assessed via supply chain network design models that quantify the total landed cost and risk-adjusted value of various sourcing configurations. Analytics-driven resilience planning integrates real-time risk assessment with established contingency processes and supplier relationship management, allowing firms to respond to disturbances more swiftly and effectively than those employing only reactive strategies (Tang & Musa, 2011; Simchi-Levi et al., 2018).

11. HUMAN FACTORS, WORKFORCE ANALYTICS, AND LEAN CULTURE

The human aspect of Industry 4.0 lean management transcends mere technological implementation, encompassing the evaluation, assistance, and advancement of the workforce functioning within progressively automated and data-driven production settings. Workforce analytics platforms, utilizing wearable sensor technology such as accelerometers, heart rate monitors, electromyography sensors, and smart helmets, facilitate the objective evaluation of worker productivity, fatigue levels, and ergonomic risk exposure, thereby enhancing the subjective assessments that have traditionally underpinned lean standard work and ergonomic enhancement initiatives. Predictive models utilizing wearable sensor data can detect the initial indicators of cumulative weariness or musculoskeletal strain prior to their emergence as errors, near-misses, or injuries, facilitating proactive intervention via task rotation, break scheduling, or workstation redesign (Romero et al., 2016; Yoon et al., 2020).

Augmented reality and AI-assisted operator guidance systems signify a substantial progression in the lean principle of standard labor, which delineates the most efficient sequence of activities for executing a certain operation. Augmented reality headsets, including Microsoft HoloLens and smart glasses, integrated with real-time AI quality inspection feedback, provide operators with sequential work instructions, visual assembly guidance, torque wrench verification, and quality check prompts superimposed on their field of vision, thereby diminishing dependence on paper-based instructions and significantly expediting the training of new operators. Poka-yoke, or mistake-proofing systems, a fundamental lean tool, can be executed in an AI-enhanced manner via computer vision systems that identify incorrect component orientation, absent parts, or erroneous assembly sequences, delivering immediate corrective feedback prior to the propagation of defects downstream (Nee et al., 2012; Palmarini et al., 2018).

The emergence of collaborative robots, or cobots, is redefining human-machine collaboration in lean contexts by enabling them to operate alongside human operators instead of completely replacing them. Cobots produced by Universal Robots, FANUC, and ABB are engineered to perform physically strenuous, repetitive, or ergonomically risky tasks, allowing human operators to concentrate on activities that necessitate dexterity, judgment, quality evaluation, and problem-solving—functions that yield the greatest cognitive and creative value in lean production systems. The ideal allocation of responsibilities between human operators and collaborative robots constitutes an analytical challenge suitable for time-and-motion analysis, simulation, and ergonomic modeling, and serves as a significant application area for lean engineering within Industry 4.0 contexts (Romero et al., 2016; Becker, 2016).

The effective incorporation of predictive analytics and simulation into lean companies necessitates intentional change management techniques that confront the cultural conflicts arising from the shift from intuition-based, manual enhancements to data-driven, algorithmically supported decision-making. Lean cultures are defined by a reverence for the expertise and insights of frontline employees, an inclination for direct observation and gemba visits, and a critical stance towards remote or abstract assessments that are detached from operational realities. Effective change management in this context necessitates the involvement of frontline workers in the co-design of analytical tools, ensuring that algorithmic insights are conveyed in formats comprehensible to operators lacking data science expertise, and illustrating through initial successful deployments that predictive analytics augments rather than supplants the judgment of seasoned lean practitioners (Holweg, 2007; Becker, 2016).

12. GLOBAL CASE STUDIES AND REAL-WORLD DEPLOYMENTS

12.1 Toyota: Adaptive Just-in-Time with Digital Kanban

Toyota's incorporation of real-time production data and digital kanban systems signifies a logical progression of the Toyota Production System for the Industry 4.0 age, rather than a deviation from its core principles. Toyota's worldwide manufacturing network utilizes sophisticated IoT sensor systems to monitor production line conditions, inventory quantities, and quality indicators in real time throughout its facilities in Japan, North America, Europe, and Asia. Digital kanban signals supplant paper-based replenishment cards with electronically generated signals from MES-integrated consumption monitoring, facilitating more accurate and timely material replenishment that diminishes buffer inventory without heightening the risk of production interruptions. Toyota has articulated its implementation of AI-driven demand signal processing to dynamically modify production takt times and staffing allocations based on real-time order intake patterns, a capability that enhances the responsiveness of just-in-time production to a degree of precision unattainable by manual kanban systems (Liker & Meier, 2006; Toyota Motor Corporation, 2023).

12.2 Siemens Amberg: Near-Zero Defect Manufacturing

Siemens' Electronics Manufacturing Plant in Amberg, Germany, is esteemed as one of the most sophisticated Industry 4.0 manufacturing facilities globally, producing SIMATIC programmable logic controllers with a defect rate of roughly 11.5 parts per million across a portfolio of over 1,000 variants. The facility attains this efficiency via an extensive MES-driven production intelligence framework, wherein machines and products autonomously interact, production orders are monitored from raw materials to finished goods at the component level using product-embedded RFID tags, and real-time statistical process control is implemented for over 1,000 process parameters. Predictive quality models associate upstream process signatures with downstream test failures, facilitating process modifications prior to defect occurrence. The plant's digital twin environment, connected with its MES infrastructure, is utilized consistently for capacity planning, process optimization, and lean improvement experimentation *(*Siemens AG, 2019*;* Hausladen & Schosser, 2021*)*.

12.3 General Electric: Predix Platform for Industrial Asset Intelligence

General Electric's creation of the Predix industrial IoT platform exemplified one of the most ambitious initial endeavors to establish an enterprise-level predictive analytics framework for industrial asset management. Implemented throughout GE's aviation, energy, and healthcare sectors, Predix linked numerous gas turbines, wind turbines, jet engines, and medical imaging systems to cloud-based analytical models that forecasted component failures, enhanced maintenance schedules, and produced fuel efficiency recommendations. The platform showcased the revolutionary capabilities of predictive maintenance on an industrial scale; GE indicated that insights from predictive analytics via Predix allowed customers to circumvent billions in unanticipated downtime expenses. GE's subsequent restructure facilitated the commercialization of the Predix platform, although the technical and operational insights derived from its implementation continue to have significant influence within the industrial analytics sector *(GE* Digital, 2016*;* Iansiti & Lakhani, 2014*)*.

12.4 Bosch: Connected Manufacturing and Lean Digital Transformation

Bosch's lean digital transformation initiative, executed throughout its extensive network of over 250 manufacturing facilities, exemplifies how a substantial multinational manufacturer can methodically amalgamate Industry 4.0 analytics competencies with its established lean management ethos. Bosch's connected manufacturing platform, Bosch IoT Suite, consolidates machine data from production lines within its automotive components, power tools, and home appliances sectors, facilitating cross-plant benchmarking of Overall Equipment Effectiveness (OEE), the dissemination of predictive maintenance models, and the propagation of lean best practices on a network scale that would be unfeasible through manual benchmarking methods. Bosch has announced that its predictive maintenance implementations have decreased maintenance expenses by as much as 25 percent at pilot facilities, while its AI-driven quality inspection systems have attained defect detection rates that surpass those of human inspection in high-velocity production settings (Bosch Group, 2022; Riedl et al., 2017).

12.5 Amazon: Reinforcement Learning and Lean Logistics at Hyperscale

Amazon's fulfillment network exemplifies an unparalleled integration of machine learning and lean logistics principles at an operational scale unprecedented in the annals of manufacturing and distribution. Amazon's demand forecasting system produces probabilistic demand predictions for numerous product-location combinations to inform inventory placement decisions, utilizing ensemble machine learning models that integrate historical sales data, search trend indicators, promotional schedules, and seasonal patterns. Reinforcement learning algorithms dictate the sequencing and routing choices of several robotic systems in fulfillment centers, enhancing picking path efficiency in real time as inventory locations and order batches fluctuate during the operational day. Amazon's supply chain digital twin infrastructure facilitates the simulation of network-level disruption scenarios, guiding resilience investments and contingency planning through quantitative risk assessments based on past disruption data (MacCormack et al., 2020; Meller & Dobson, 2022).

12.6 SME Adoption in Europe and Asia

Small and medium-sized enterprises encounter unique obstacles in adopting Industry 4.0, such as restricted capital budgets, insufficient internal data science expertise, and the challenge of rationalizing substantial digital infrastructure investments relative to the operational returns attainable at lower production volumes. Government-backed initiatives in Germany, such as the Mittelstand 4.0 initiative, in Singapore through the SMEs Go Digital program, and in South Korea via the Smart Factory Support Program, have mitigated these obstacles through subsidized technology trials, collaborative competence centers, and vendor ecosystem development programs tailored for SMEs. The German Mittelstand 4.0 initiative has created a network of competence centers in key industrial areas, offering SMEs access to

Industry 4.0 demonstration environments, technological consulting, and workforce training programs, thereby reducing the barriers to digital lean transformation for manufacturers lacking internal Industry 4.0 transformation teams (BMBF, 2019; IMDA, 2022; MOTIE, 2021).

13. CHALLENGES AND BARRIERS TO IMPLEMENTATION

The incorporation of predictive analytics and simulation into lean enterprise settings, however promising, encounters a multifaceted array of technological, organizational, and strategic obstacles that must be methodically resolved for implementations to yield expected benefits. Data silos and legacy system integration constitute the most significant technical challenge; the existing operational technology in manufacturing facilities globally comprises equipment from various decades, utilizing proprietary communication protocols and lacking the necessary data interfaces for contemporary analytics integration. Integrating sensor technology and communication middleware into brownfield assets is theoretically achievable but operationally intricate and often costly, necessitating meticulous change management to prevent production disruption during the commissioning of new equipment (Lasi et al., 2014; Alcacer & Cruz-Machado, 2019).

Organizational resistance to data-driven decision-making constitutes a substantial obstacle in lean firms characterized by robust cultures of operator empowerment and experiential knowledge. Seasoned lean practitioners, possessing a profound intuitive comprehension of their production systems acquired via extensive observation, may exhibit skepticism towards algorithmic advice that they cannot directly scrutinize or intuitively verify. The conflict between algorithmic authority and human competence is not solely cultural but also epistemological: in safety-critical production settings, operators are accountable for decisions that algorithms may affect but cannot take responsibility for. Establishing corporate trust in predictive analytics necessitates a synthesis of transparent model elucidation, sustained accuracy, and cultural change management strategies that frame analytics as a decision-support instrument rather than a substitute for human discernment (Davenport & Patil, 2012; Sharda et al., 2018).

Model interpretability and operator trust exemplify a particular aspect of this overarching difficulty in deep learning implementations. The superior predictive accuracy of deep neural networks compared to simpler, more interpretable models like decision trees and logistic regression is accompanied by diminished clarity on the reasoning behind individual predictions. In production settings where operators must determine whether to respond to a machine failure prediction that would lead to a planned maintenance interruption with considerable production cost ramifications, comprehending the rationale behind the model's specific prognosis is operationally crucial. Explainable AI tools, such as SHAP value analysis, LIME, and attention visualization methods, are progressively integrated into industrial predictive maintenance implementations to tackle this difficulty (Doshi-Velez & Kim, 2017; Lundberg & Lee, 2017).

The justification for investment and measurement of return on investment for predictive analytics and simulation initiatives poses a distinctive challenge, because the primary benefits, including avoided downtime, reduced inventory costs, and prevented quality failures, are counterfactual and difficult to attribute unambiguously. This measurement problem is compounded by the systemic interdependence of the PASEI cycle: when predictive models, simulation environments, and lean improvement programs interact over time, isolating the marginal contribution of each component to aggregate performance improvement is methodologically demanding. The talent and skills gap represents a further structural constraint. Professionals with combined expertise in lean operations, data science, and industrial systems engineering are exceptionally scarce, and the gap is widening as technology deployment outstrips practitioner supply. Critically, the documented performance gains from leading adopters such as Siemens Amberg and Bosch are not straightforwardly replicable by organizations lacking equivalent analytical talent, organizational change capability, and data infrastructure maturity. Benchmarking against these leaders without accounting for such capability differentials produces analytically misleading conclusions for organizations planning adoption (Westerman et al., 2014; Frey & Osborne, 2017).

Cybersecurity in interconnected industrial settings constitutes a significant concern that must be clearly addressed in the design of Industry 4.0 architecture. The integration of operational technology networks, which govern physical production processes and safety systems, with enterprise IT networks and cloud platforms significantly amplifies the attack surface vulnerable to malicious entry. The 2021 assault on the Oldsmar water treatment facility, the 2017 NotPetya ransomware incident that significantly impaired manufacturing processes across various multinational corporations, and the 2021 Colonial Pipeline ransomware attack collectively exemplify the potentially disastrous ramifications of insufficient operational technology cybersecurity. Defense-in-depth designs that include network segmentation, anomaly detection for operational technology traffic, privileged access control, and industrial cybersecurity monitoring platforms are vital elements of any prudent Industry 4.0 data infrastructure implementation (Lee & Seshia, 2017; Stouffer et al., 2015).

14. STRATEGIC IMPLICATIONS FOR ENTERPRISE LEADERS, ENGINEERS, AND POLICYMAKERS

Operations and manufacturing executives must create cohesive lean-digital roadmaps that synchronize predictive analytics investments with strategic operational enhancement priorities, rather than adopting technology for its own merit. The most successful Industry 4.0 lean transformations are grounded in a precise identification of the most valuable improvement opportunities within the enterprise value stream, encompassing asset availability, demand responsiveness, quality performance, or supply chain resilience, and are structured to implement analytics capabilities that directly target these opportunities. Investment in data infrastructure, model development, and organizational capacity must be appropriately scaled and timed to yield quantifiable operational benefit at each phase, therefore enhancing organizational confidence and technical proficiency necessary for increasingly ambitious implementations (Porter & Heppelmann, 2014; Westerman et al., 2014)

Industrial engineers and lean practitioners must prioritize the development of data literacy and simulation skills to effectively lead the co-design of AI-enhanced lean improvement initiatives. The lean engineer in the Industry 4.0 era must effectively collaborate with data scientists and software engineers to convert operational domain knowledge into model features, validate predictive model outputs against actual processes, interpret simulation results within the framework of lean value stream analysis, and convey analytical insights to operational stakeholders. Academic programs in industrial engineering, operations management, and lean manufacturing must swiftly adapt to integrate data science, machine learning, and simulation modeling into their core curricula, equipping graduates for the interdisciplinary roles required for successful Industry 4.0 lean transformation (Frey & Osborne, 2017; Autor, 2015).

IT and OT architects face the challenge of designing scalable, secure, and interoperable Industry 4.0 data infrastructures that fulfill both operational control and analytics requirements while maintaining the safety and dependability of production systems. This necessitates a profound comprehension of the technical attributes of industrial communication protocols alongside the statistical and computational demands of machine learning and simulation tasks, a rare amalgamation of skills typically absent in conventional IT or OT engineering teams. Policymakers and industry organizations must invest continuously in digital infrastructure, establish interoperability standards to minimize integration complexity and vendor lock-in, create extensive workforce reskilling programs to bridge capability gaps, and develop regulatory frameworks that promote responsible industrial data usage while safeguarding intellectual property and operational security (OECD, 2019; World Economic Forum, 2020).

15. FUTURE DIRECTIONS AND EMERGING FRONTIERS

The most revolutionary immediate frontier in lean enterprise analytics is the notion of the autonomous lean enterprise: a production and supply chain framework wherein AI perpetually detects waste patterns, formulates improvement hypotheses, simulates intervention outcomes, and executes solutions within established authority parameters with minimal human involvement in the enhancement process. Initial expressions of this concept are evident in closed-loop quality control systems that autonomously modify process parameters based on real-time quality sensor data, in demand-responsive production planning systems that perpetually re-optimize schedules in reaction to order intake modifications, and in predictive maintenance platforms that automatically create and prioritize maintenance work orders. The gradual expansion of autonomous decision-making capacity from strictly regulated process control environments to wider operational planning areas will characterize the forthcoming decade of lean business capabilities advancement (Russell & Norvig, 2020; Brynjolfsson & McAfee, 2014).

Foundation models for industrial processes signify a novel paradigm influenced by the achievements of massive language models in natural language tasks. Pretrained on a variety of industrial datasets, including production records, maintenance logs, quality inspection data, and supply chain event histories from various sectors, industrial foundation models offer a versatile foundation for analytics applications that presently necessitate costly, customized model development for each new deployment scenario. The capacity of these models to facilitate few-shot adaptation to novel production environments, cross-industry knowledge transfer, and natural language interfaces for operational analytics inquiries could substantially reduce the technical obstacles to advanced analytics implementation in small and medium-sized enterprises and manufacturing sectors in emerging economies (Brown et al., 2020; Bommasani et al., 2021).

Quantum computing signifies a future-oriented yet potentially transformative ability for efficient corporate optimization. A significant number of critical optimization problems in production scheduling, inventory management, and supply chain network design are computationally intractable at the scales seen in major enterprises, compelling practitioners to resort to approximation or heuristic solutions. Quantum optimization techniques, such as the Quantum Approximate Optimization Algorithm and variational quantum eigensolvers, have the potential to address specific categories of combinatorial optimization problems with greater scale and solution quality than classical algorithms can achieve. As of the mid-2020s, practical quantum advantage for industrial optimization problems is still a research frontier rather than a deployable capability; however, enterprises with extended planning horizons are starting to invest in quantum readiness evaluations and the development of hybrid classical-quantum algorithms (Preskill, 2018; Farhi et al., 2014).

Sustainable lean 4.0 is becoming a strategic necessity that incorporates carbon footprint assessment, energy consumption optimization, and circular material flow analysis into lean value stream management. The incorporation of real-time energy monitoring into production scheduling facilitates intelligent load shifting to reduce energy expenses and carbon intensity, so extending lean waste elimination to energy and environmental resource management. Principles of the circular economy aim to eradicate waste by designing products and processes for material recovery and reuse. These principles can be enhanced by IoT-enabled material traceability systems that monitor the composition, quality, and location of materials throughout their lifecycle, facilitating the optimization of reverse logistics and recycling processes with the same analytical rigor applied to forward supply chains (Bocken et al., 2016; Geissdoerfer et al., 2017).

Human-AI collaboration in lean management will target cognitive task allocation between humans and AI technologies. Humans will frame creative problems, make ethical decisions, manage stakeholders, and lead organizational change, while AI systems will recognize patterns in large datasets, optimize in complex constraint environments, and simulate improvement scenarios at speeds beyond human cognitive abilities. In this collaborative model, human-AI interfaces, decision frameworks, and governance structures must be intentionally designed to retain human accountability for operational decisions while using AI to greatly improve decision-maker information. Lean management's experience developing work systems that promote human learning, engagement, and continuous improvement helps define these interfaces.

Generative AI for simulation scenarios could speed up simulation-based lean enhancement. Professional engineers must manually define failure modes, process parameter distributions, and disruption scenarios to build current simulation models, which slows simulation capability deployment in corporate improvement initiatives. Industrial simulation data and operational failure databases can be used to train generative AI systems to create realistic stress-test scenarios, innovative failure mode hypotheses, and experimental designs for enhancements, greatly improving enterprise simulation-based improvement initiatives. (Brown et al., 2020; Russell & Norvig, 2020).

16. CONCLUSION

Predictive analytics and simulation are integral components of a closed-loop improvement framework, wherein lean principles and digital intelligence are interdependent. The PASEI paradigm illustrates that Industry 4.0 enhances lean management solely when prediction, analytical diagnosis, virtual simulation, operational execution, and iterative learning operate as a cohesive system rather than as isolated technological endeavors. Sensor-rich environments produce the data necessary for models, predictive models reveal insights that inform efficient treatments, simulation environments mitigate risks associated with those interventions prior to implementation, and operational outcomes consistently enhance model precision. The global case studies provided here demonstrate that this architecture is an experimentally verifiable trend in successful lean transformations, rather than a theoretical assertion. Organizations that effectively integrated prediction, simulation, and execution realized sustainable performance improvements; conversely, those that implemented technologies without considering data governance, cultural integration, and organizational change continuously underachieved. Enabling environments, rather than technology, dictate the efficacy of the PASEI cycle in realizing its promise. Recent research by Nozari and Yordanova (2026a, 2026b) and Nozari (2026) indicates that autonomous, self-determining systems are expanding this framework into areas of operational complexity that were previously unattainable by computation. The future lean company will surpass its founders' expectations, while adhering to the fundamental belief that an unwavering, human-centered quest for perfection is the sole sustainable basis for operational excellence.

REFERENCES

Alcacer, V., & Cruz-Machado, V. (2019). Scanning the Industry 4.0: A literature review on technologies for manufacturing systems. *Engineering Science and Technology, an International Journal, 22*(3), 899–919. DOI: 10.1016/j.jestch.2019.01.006

Autor, D. H. (2015). Why are there still so many jobs? The history and future of workplace automation. *The Journal of Economic Perspectives, 29*(3), 3–30. DOI: 10.1257/jep.29.3.3

Batini, C., & Scannapieco, M. (2006). *Data quality: Concepts, methodologies and techniques*. Springer.

Becker, W. (2016). Digital transformation in manufacturing: Implications for lean management. *International Journal of Operations & Production Management, 36*(12), 1452–1469.

Besnard, F., & Bertling, L. (2010). An approach for condition-based maintenance optimization applied to wind turbine blades. *IEEE Transactions on Sustainable Energy, 1*(2), 77–83. DOI: 10.1109/TSTE.2010.2049452

Blazewicz, J., Ecker, K. H., Pesch, E., Schmidt, G., & Weglarz, J. (2019). *Handbook on scheduling: From theory to applications* (2nd ed.). Springer.

BMBF (Bundesministerium fur Bildung und Forschung). (2019). *Mittelstand-Digital: The program for SME digitalization*. Federal Ministry of Education and Research.

Bocken, N. M. P., de Pauw, I., Bakker, C., & van der Grinten, B. (2016). Product design and business model strategies for a circular economy. *Journal of Industrial and Production Engineering, 33*(5), 308–320. DOI: 10.1080/21681015.2016.1172124

Bommasani, R., Hudson, D. A., Aditi, E., ... (2021). On the opportunities and risks of foundation models. arXiv preprint arXiv:2108.07258.

Bosch Group. (2022). *Bosch annual report 2022: Connected manufacturing and sustainability*. Robert Bosch GmbH.

Box, G. E. P., Jenkins, G. M., Reinsel, G. C., & Ljung, G. M. (2015). *Time series analysis: Forecasting and control* (5th ed.). Wiley.

Brown, T. B., Mann, B., & Ryder, N.. (2020). Language models are few-shot learners. *Advances in Neural Information Processing Systems, 33*, 1877–1901.

Brynjolfsson, E., & McAfee, A. (2014). *The second machine age: Work, progress, and prosperity in a time of brilliant technologies*. W. W. Norton.

Buer, S. V., Strandhagen, J. O., & Chan, F. T. S. (2018). The link between Industry 4.0 and lean manufacturing: Mapping current research and establishing a research agenda. *International Journal of Production Research, 56*(8), 2924–2940. DOI: 10.1080/00207543.2018.1442945

Chopra, S., & Sodhi, M. S. (2004). Managing risk to avoid supply-chain breakdown. *MIT Sloan Management Review, 46*(1), 53–61.

Davenport, T. H. (2006). Competing on analytics. *Harvard Business Review, 84*(1), 98–107.

Davenport, T. H., & Patil, D. J. (2012). Data scientist: The sexiest job of the 21st century. *Harvard Business Review, 90*(10), 70–76.

Delsing, J. (Ed.). (2017). *IoT automation: Arrowhead framework*. CRC Press. DOI: 10.1201/9781315367897

Digital, G. E. (2016). *Predix: The industrial internet platform*. General Electric Company.

Doshi-Velez, F., & Kim, B. (2017). Towards a rigorous science of interpretable machine learning. arXiv preprint arXiv:1702.08608.

Duflou, J. R., Sutherland, J. W., Dornfeld, D., Herrmann, C., Jeswiet, J., Kara, S., Hauschild, M., & Kellens, K. (2012). Towards energy and resource efficient manufacturing: A processes and systems approach. *CIRP Annals, 61*(2), 587–609. DOI: 10.1016/j.cirp.2012.05.002

Farhi, E., Goldstone, J., & Gutmann, S. (2014). A quantum approximate optimization algorithm. arXiv preprint arXiv:1411.4028.

Fildes, R., Ma, S., & Kolassa, S. (2022). Retail forecasting: Research and practice. *International Journal of Forecasting, 38*(4), 1283–1318. DOI: 10.1016/j.ijforecast.2019.06.004

Forrester, J. W. (1961). *Industrial dynamics*. MIT Press.

Frey, C. B., & Osborne, M. A. (2017). The future of employment: How susceptible are jobs to computerisation? *Technological Forecasting and Social Change, 114*, 254–280. DOI: 10.1016/j.techfore.2016.08.019

Gahm, C., Denz, F., Dirr, M., & Tuma, A. (2016). Energy-efficient scheduling in manufacturing companies: A review and research framework. *European Journal of Operational Research, 248*(3), 744–757. DOI: 10.1016/j.ejor.2015.07.017

Gandomi, A., & Haider, M. (2015). Beyond the hype: Big data concepts, methods, and analytics. *International Journal of Information Management*, *35*(2), 137–144. DOI: 10.1016/j.ijinfomgt.2014.10.007

Garcia-Sabater, J. P., Maheut, J., & Marin-Garcia, J. A. (2017). A two-stage sequential planning scheme for integrated operations planning and scheduling system using MILP: The case of an engine assembler. *Flexible Services and Manufacturing Journal*, *24*(2), 171–209. DOI: 10.1007/s10696-011-9126-z

Geissdoerfer, M., Savaget, P., Bocken, N. M. P., & Hultink, E. J. (2017). The circular economy: A new sustainability paradigm? *Journal of Cleaner Production*, *143*, 757–768. DOI: 10.1016/j.jclepro.2016.12.048

Goldratt, E. M. (1990). *Theory of constraints*. North River Press.

Grieves, M. (2014). Digital twin: Manufacturing excellence through virtual factory replication. White Paper. Florida Institute of Technology.

Grieves, M., & Vickers, J. (2017). Digital twin: Mitigating unpredictable, undesirable emergent behavior in complex systems. In Kahlen, F. J., Flumerfelt, S., & Alves, A. (Eds.), *Transdisciplinary perspectives on complex systems* (pp. 85–113). Springer. DOI: 10.1007/978-3-319-38756-7_4

Hamadache, M., Daho, S., Begg, S., & Lotfi, A. (2019). A comprehensive review of near-zero downtime maintenance approaches for Industry 4.0 predictive maintenance. *IEEE Access : Practical Innovations, Open Solutions*, *7*, 77452–77464.

Hausladen, I., & Schosser, M. (2021). Towards a maturity model for digital lean management. *Total Quality Management & Business Excellence*, *32*(9-10), 1035–1053.

Hendricks, K. B., & Singhal, V. R. (2005). An empirical analysis of the effect of supply chain disruptions on long-run stock price performance. *Production and Operations Management*, *14*(1), 35–52. DOI: 10.1111/j.1937-5956.2005.tb00008.x

Hermann, M., Pentek, T., & Otto, B. (2016). Design principles for Industrie 4.0 scenarios. *Proceedings of the 49th Hawaii International Conference on System Sciences*, 3928-3937. DOI: 10.1109/HICSS.2016.488

Holweg, M. (2007). The genealogy of lean production. *Journal of Operations Management*, *25*(2), 420–437. DOI: 10.1016/j.jom.2006.04.001

Hopp, W. J., & Spearman, M. L. (2011). *Factory physics* (3rd ed.). Waveland Press.

Huber, J., Gossmann, A., & Stuckenschmidt, H. (2017). Cluster-based hierarchical demand forecasting for perishable goods. *Expert Systems with Applications*, *76*, 140–151. DOI: 10.1016/j.eswa.2017.01.022

Iansiti, M., & Lakhani, K. R. (2014). Digital ubiquity: How connections, sensors, and data are revolutionizing business. *Harvard Business Review*, *92*(11), 90–99.

IMDA (Infocomm Media Development Authority). (2022). *SMEs Go Digital programme report.* Singapore Government.

Inmon, W. H., & Linstedt, D. (2014). *Data architecture: A primer for the data scientist.* Morgan Kaufmann.

Janssen, M., van der Voort, H., & Wahyudi, A. (2017). Factors influencing big data decision-making quality. *Journal of Business Research*, *70*, 338–345. DOI: 10.1016/j.jbusres.2016.08.007

Jardine, A. K., Lin, D., & Banjevic, D. (2006). A review on machinery diagnostics and prognostics implementing condition-based maintenance. *Mechanical Systems and Signal Processing*, *20*(7), 1483–1510. DOI: 10.1016/j.ymssp.2005.09.012

Kagermann, H., Wahlster, W., & Helbig, J. (2013). *Recommendations for implementing the strategic initiative Industrie 4.0. National Academy of Science and Engineering*. Acatech.

Kelton, W. D., Sadowski, R. P., & Zupick, N. B. (2015). *Simulation with Arena* (6th ed.). McGraw-Hill.

Kleijnen, J. P. C. (2015). *Design and analysis of simulation experiments* (2nd ed.). Springer. DOI: 10.1007/978-3-319-18087-8

Kleindorfer, P. R., & Saad, G. H. (2005). Managing disruption risks in supply chains. *Production and Operations Management*, *14*(1), 53–68. DOI: 10.1111/j.1937-5956.2005.tb00009.x

Kroese, D. P., Taimre, T., & Botev, Z. I. (2011). *Handbook of Monte Carlo methods*. Wiley. DOI: 10.1002/9781118014967

Lasi, H., Fettke, P., Kemper, H. G., Feld, T., & Hoffmann, M. (2014). Industry 4.0. *Business & Information Systems Engineering*, *6*(4), 239–242. DOI: 10.1007/s12599-014-0334-4

Law, A. M. (2015). *Simulation modeling and analysis* (5th ed.). McGraw-Hill.

LeCun, Y., Bengio, Y., & Hinton, G. (2015). Deep learning. *Nature*, *521*(7553), 436–444. DOI: 10.1038/nature14539

Lee, E. A., & Seshia, S. A. (2017). *Introduction to embedded systems: A cyber-physical systems approach* (2nd ed.). MIT Press.

Lee, H. L., Padmanabhan, V., & Whang, S. (1997). Information distortion in a supply chain: The bullwhip effect. *Management Science*, *43*(4), 546–558. DOI: 10.1287/mnsc.43.4.546

Lee, J., Bagheri, B., & Kao, H. A. (2015). A cyber-physical systems architecture for Industry 4.0-based manufacturing systems. *Manufacturing Letters*, *3*, 18–23. DOI: 10.1016/j.mfglet.2014.12.001

Lee, J., Wu, F., Zhao, W., Ghaffari, M., Liao, L., & Siegel, D. (2014). Prognostics and health management design for rotary machinery systems. *Mechanical Systems and Signal Processing*, *42*(1-2), 314–334. DOI: 10.1016/j.ymssp.2013.06.004

Lei, Y., Yang, B., Jiang, X., Jia, F., Li, N., & Nandi, A. K. (2020). Applications of machine learning to machine fault diagnosis: A review and roadmap. *Mechanical Systems and Signal Processing*, *138*, 106587. DOI: 10.1016/j.ymssp.2019.106587

Liker, J. K. (2004). *The Toyota way: 14 management principles from the world's greatest manufacturer*. McGraw-Hill.

Liker, J. K., & Meier, D. (2006). *The Toyota way fieldbook*. McGraw-Hill.

Lim, B., Arik, S. O., Loeff, N., & Pfister, T. (2021). Temporal fusion transformers for interpretable multi-horizon time series forecasting. *International Journal of Forecasting*, *37*(4), 1748–1764. DOI: 10.1016/j.ijforecast.2021.03.012

Liu, C., Zhang, X., & Song, X. (2022). A survey of deep reinforcement learning for intelligent production scheduling. *Journal of Manufacturing Systems*, *64*, 579–596.

Lu, Y., Xu, X., & Wang, L. (2022). Smart manufacturing process and system automation: A critical review of the standards and envisioned scenarios. *Journal of Manufacturing Systems*, *56*, 312–325. DOI: 10.1016/j.jmsy.2020.06.010

Lundberg, S. M., & Lee, S. I. (2017). A unified approach to interpreting model predictions. *Advances in Neural Information Processing Systems*, *30*, 4765–4774.

Macal, C. M., & North, M. J. (2010). Tutorial on agent-based modelling and simulation. *Journal of Simulation*, *4*(3), 151–162. DOI: 10.1057/jos.2010.3

. MacCormack, A., Forbath, T., Brooks, P., & Kalaher, P. (2020). Innovation at Amazon: The art of developing business models. Harvard Business School Case 9-614-064.

Makridakis, S., Spiliotis, E., & Assimakopoulos, V. (2018). Statistical and machine learning forecasting methods: Concerns and ways forward. *PLoS One*, *13*(3), e0194889. DOI: 10.1371/journal.pone.0194889

Manyika, J., Chui, M., Bughin, J., Dobbs, R., Bisson, P., & Marrs, A. (2013). *Disruptive technologies: Advances that will transform life, business, and the global economy*. McKinsey Global Institute.

McKone, K. E., Schroeder, R. G., & Cua, K. O. (1999). Total productive maintenance: A contextual view. *Journal of Operations Management, 17*(2), 123–144. DOI: 10.1016/S0272-6963(98)00039-4

Meller, R. D., & Dobson, K. (2022). Optimizing Amazon fulfillment center layouts with simulation and machine learning. *IISE Transactions, 54*(5), 445–461.

Mnih, V., Kavukcuoglu, K., Silver, D., Rusu, A. A., Veness, J., Bellemare, M. G., Graves, A., Riedmiller, M., Fidjeland, A. K., Ostrovski, G., Petersen, S., Beattie, C., Sadik, A., Antonoglou, I., King, H., Kumaran, D., Wierstra, D., Legg, S., & Hassabis, D. (2015). Human-level control through deep reinforcement learning. *Nature, 518*(7540), 529–533. DOI: 10.1038/nature14236

Mobley, R. K. (2002). *An introduction to predictive maintenance* (2nd ed.). Butterworth-Heinemann.

Montgomery, D. C. (2019). *Introduction to statistical quality control* (8th ed.). Wiley.

MOTIE. (Ministry of Trade, Industry and Energy). (2021). Korea smart factory support program annual report. Government of the Republic of Korea.

Mourtzis, D. (2020). Simulation in the design and operation of manufacturing systems: State of the art and new trends. *International Journal of Production Research, 58*(7), 1927–1949. DOI: 10.1080/00207543.2019.1636321

Nakajima, S. (1988). *Introduction to TPM: Total productive maintenance*. Productivity Press.

Nee, A. Y. C., Ong, S. K., Chryssolouris, G., & Mourtzis, D. (2012). Augmented reality applications in design and manufacturing. *CIRP Annals, 61*(2), 657–679. DOI: 10.1016/j.cirp.2012.05.010

Negri, E., Fumagalli, L., & Macchi, M. (2017). A review of the roles of digital twin in CPS-based production systems. *Procedia Manufacturing, 11*, 939–948. DOI: 10.1016/j.promfg.2017.07.198

Netland, T. H., & Powell, D. J. (Eds.). (2017). *The Routledge companion to lean management*. Routledge.

Nozari, H. (2026). Digital twin-based predictive maintenance in cold chain logistics. *Operations Research, 60*(1), 481–499. DOI: 10.1051/ro/2025167

Nozari, H., & Yordanova, Z. (2026a). Fuzzy multi-objective digital twin framework for dynamic pricing and assortment optimization in metaverse-based retail environments. *Journal of Revenue and Pricing Management*. Advance online publication. DOI: 10.1057/s41272-026-00586-5

Nozari, H., & Yordanova, Z. (2026b). A self-deciding adaptive digital twin framework using agentic AI for fuzzy multi-objective optimization of food logistics. *Algorithms*, *19*(3), 218. DOI: 10.3390/a19030218

OECD. (2019). *OECD going digital: Shaping policies, improving lives*. Organisation for Economic Cooperation and Development.

Ohno, T. (1988). *Toyota production system: Beyond large-scale production*. Productivity Press.

Oreshkin, B. N., Carpov, D., Chapados, N., & Bengio, Y. (2020). N-BEATS: Neural basis expansion analysis for interpretable time series forecasting. *International Conference on Learning Representations (ICLR)*.

Oroojlooy, A., & Nazari, M. (2021). A review of cooperative multi-agent deep reinforcement learning. *Applied Intelligence*, *53*(11), 13677–13722. DOI: 10.1007/s10489-022-04105-y

Palmarini, R., Erkoyuncu, J. A., Roy, R., & Torabmostaedi, H. (2018). A systematic review of augmented reality applications in maintenance. *Robotics and Computer-integrated Manufacturing*, *49*, 215–228. DOI: 10.1016/j.rcim.2017.06.002

Pearl, J. (2009). *Causality: Models, reasoning, and inference* (2nd ed.). Cambridge University Press. DOI: 10.1017/CBO9780511803161

Peng, Y., Dong, M., & Zuo, M. J. (2010). Current status of machine prognostics in condition-based maintenance. *International Journal of Advanced Manufacturing Technology*, *50*(1-4), 297–313. DOI: 10.1007/s00170-009-2482-0

Pinedo, M. L. (2016). *Scheduling: Theory, algorithms, and systems* (5th ed.). Springer. DOI: 10.1007/978-3-319-26580-3

Porter, M. E., & Heppelmann, J. E. (2014). How smart, connected products are transforming competition. *Harvard Business Review*, *92*(11), 64–88.

Preskill, J. (2018). Quantum computing in the NISQ era and beyond. *Quantum : the Open Journal for Quantum Science*, *2*, 79. DOI: 10.22331/q-2018-08-06-79

Qiu, P. (2014). *Introduction to statistical process control*. CRC Press.

Ren, L., Cui, J., Sun, Y., & Cheng, X. (2018). Multi-bearing remaining useful life collaborative prediction: A deep learning approach. *Journal of Manufacturing Systems*, *43*, 248–256. DOI: 10.1016/j.jmsy.2017.02.013

Riedl, M., Zipper, H., Meier, M., & Diedrich, C. (2017). Cyber-physical systems alter automation architectures. *Annual Reviews in Control*, *38*(1), 123–133. DOI: 10.1016/j.arcontrol.2014.03.012

Romero, D., Bernus, P., Noran, O., Stahre, J., & Fast-Berglund, A. (2016). The operator 4.0: Human cyber-physical systems and adaptive automation. *IFIP Advances in Information and Communication Technology*, *488*, 677–686. DOI: 10.1007/978-3-319-51133-7_80

Rosen, R., von Wichert, G., Lo, G., & Bettenhausen, K. D. (2015). About the importance of autonomy and digital twins for the future of manufacturing. *IFAC-PapersOnLine*, *48*(3), 567–572. DOI: 10.1016/j.ifacol.2015.06.141

Rother, M., & Shook, J. (1998). *Learning to see: Value stream mapping to add value and eliminate muda*. Lean Enterprise Institute.

Rusal, A., Iqbal, M., Anwar, W., & Gul, M. (2019). Industry 4.0: Technological revolution and its impact on value chain. *International Journal of Supply Chain Management*, *8*(6), 921–935.

Russell, S., & Norvig, P. (2020). *Artificial intelligence: A modern approach* (4th ed.). Pearson.

Russom, P. (2011). Big data analytics. *TDWI Best Practices Report*, *19*(4), 1–34.

Salinas, D., Flunkert, V., Gasthaus, J., & Januschowski, T. (2020). DeepAR: Probabilistic forecasting with autoregressive recurrent networks. *International Journal of Forecasting*, *36*(3), 1181–1191. DOI: 10.1016/j.ijforecast.2019.07.001

Sanders, A., Elangeswaran, C., & Wulfsberg, J. P. (2016). Industry 4.0 implies lean manufacturing: Research activities in industry 4.0 function as enablers for lean manufacturing. *Journal of Industrial Engineering and Management*, *9*(3), 811–833. DOI: 10.3926/jiem.1940

Scheffer, C., & Girdhar, P. (2004). *Practical machinery vibration analysis and predictive maintenance*. Newnes.

Schluse, M., Priggemeyer, M., Atorf, L., & Rossmann, J. (2018). Experimentable digital twins: Streamlining simulation-based systems engineering for Industry 4.0. *IEEE Transactions on Industrial Informatics*, *14*(4), 1722–1731. DOI: 10.1109/TII.2018.2804917

Schmitt, A. J., & Singh, M. (2012). A quantitative analysis of disruption risk in a multi-echelon supply chain. *International Journal of Production Economics, 139*(1), 22–32. DOI: 10.1016/j.ijpe.2012.01.004

Schwab, K. (2016). The fourth industrial revolution. World Economic Forum.

Serpanos, D., & Wolf, M. (2018). *Industrial internet of things*. Springer.

Shah, R., & Ward, P. T. (2007). Defining and developing measures of lean production. *Journal of Operations Management, 25*(4), 785–805. DOI: 10.1016/j.jom.2007.01.019

Sharda, R., Delen, D., & Turban, E. (2018). *Business intelligence, analytics, and data science: A managerial perspective* (4th ed.). Pearson.

Sheffi, Y. (2005). *The resilient enterprise: Overcoming vulnerability for competitive advantage*. MIT Press.

Shewhart, W. A. (1931). *Economic control of quality of manufactured product. D.* Van Nostrand.

Shingo, S. (1989). *A study of the Toyota production system from an industrial engineering viewpoint*. Productivity Press.

Siemens, A. G. (2019). *Amberg electronics plant: Where digitalization meets reality*. Siemens Communications.

Simchi-Levi, D., Kaminsky, P., & Simchi-Levi, E. (2014). *Designing and managing the supply chain: Concepts, strategies, and case studies* (3rd ed.). McGraw-Hill.

Simchi-Levi, D., Wang, H., & Wei, Y. (2018). Increasing supply chain robustness through process flexibility and inventory. *Production and Operations Management, 27*(8), 1476–1491. DOI: 10.1111/poms.12887

Sisinni, E., Saifullah, A., Han, S., Jennehag, U., & Gidlund, M. (2018). Industrial internet of things: Challenges, opportunities, and directions. *IEEE Transactions on Industrial Informatics, 14*(11), 4724–4734. DOI: 10.1109/TII.2018.2852491

Stark, J., Anderl, R., & Schleich, B. (2019). Digital twin: Research and applications in manufacturing. *Procedia Manufacturing, 28*, 1–9.

Sterman, J. D. (2000). *Business dynamics: Systems thinking and modeling for a complex world*. McGraw-Hill.

Stouffer, K., Falco, J., & Scarfone, K. (2015). Guide to industrial control systems (ICS) security. NIST Special Publication 800-82 Revision 2. National Institute of Standards and Technology.

Tang, C. S. (2006). Perspectives in supply chain risk management. *International Journal of Production Economics, 103*(2), 451–488. DOI: 10.1016/j.ijpe.2005.12.006

Tang, C. S., & Musa, S. N. (2011). Identifying risk issues and research advancements in supply chain risk management. *International Journal of Production Economics, 133*(1), 25–34. DOI: 10.1016/j.ijpe.2010.06.013

Tao, F., Zhang, H., Liu, A., & Nee, A. Y. C. (2018). Digital twin in industry: State-of-the-art. *IEEE Transactions on Industrial Informatics, 15*(4), 2405–2415. DOI: 10.1109/TII.2018.2873186

Tordecilla, R. D., Juan, A. A., Montoya-Torres, J. R., Quintero-Araujo, C. L., & Panadero, J. (2021). Simulation-optimization methods for designing and assessing resilient supply chain networks under uncertainty scenarios: A review. *Simulation Modelling Practice and Theory, 106*, 102166. DOI: 10.1016/j.simpat.2020.102166

Toyota Motor Corporation. (2023). *Annual report 2023: Woven by Toyota*. Toyota Motor Corporation.

Watson, K. J., Blackstone, J. H., & Gardiner, S. C. (2007). The evolution of a management philosophy: The theory of constraints. *Journal of Operations Management, 25*(2), 387–402. DOI: 10.1016/j.jom.2006.04.004

Weimer, D., Scholz-Reiter, B., & Shpitalni, M. (2016). Design of deep convolutional neural network architectures for automated feature extraction in industrial inspection. *CIRP Annals, 65*(1), 417–420. DOI: 10.1016/j.cirp.2016.04.072

Westerman, G., Bonnet, D., & McAfee, A. (2014). *Leading digital: Turning technology into business transformation*. Harvard Business Review Press.

Womack, J. P., & Jones, D. T. (1996). *Lean thinking: Banish waste and create wealth in your corporation*. Simon & Schuster.

World Economic Forum. (2020). The future of jobs report 2020. World Economic Forum.

Xu, L. D., Xu, E. L., & Li, L. (2018). Industry 4.0: State of the art and future trends. *International Journal of Production Research, 56*(8), 2941–2962. DOI: 10.1080/00207543.2018.1444806

Yoon, S., Ye, W., Snell, J., Best, H., & Tarvainen, M. (2020). Wearable sensors for human activity recognition and health assessment. *IEEE Reviews in Biomedical Engineering, 14*, 45–62.

Zhang, C., Song, W., Cao, Z., Zhang, J., Tan, P. S., & Chi, X. (2020). Learning to dispatch for job shop scheduling via deep reinforcement learning. *Advances in Neural Information Processing Systems*, *33*, 1621–1632.

Zhong, R. Y., Xu, X., Klotz, E., & Newman, S. T. (2017). Intelligent manufacturing in the context of Industry 4.0: A review. *Engineering (Beijing)*, *3*(5), 616–630. DOI: 10.1016/J.ENG.2017.05.015

Zsidisin, G. A., Ellram, L. M., Carter, J. R., & Cavinato, J. L. (2004). An analysis of supply risk assessment techniques. *International Journal of Physical Distribution & Logistics Management*, *34*(5), 397–413. DOI: 10.1108/09600030410545445

Chapter 6
Smart Manufacturing Assets and the Digital Transformation of Intelligent Industrial Enterprises

Hossein Abdi
Bio10, Australia

Naser Heidari
http://orcid.org/0009-0002-5703-8731
Bio10, Dubai, UAE

ABSTRACT

The rapid advancement of digital technologies in recent years has led to a fundamental transformation in the structure and management of industrial manufacturing systems. Smart manufacturing assets, relying on technologies such as the Industrial Internet of Things, artificial intelligence, cyber-physical systems, and digital twins, have paved the way for the formation of a new generation of smart industrial organizations. These technologies enable continuous monitoring of equipment, predictive data analysis, and data-driven decision-making in manufacturing environments. This chapter reviews the evolution of manufacturing assets, key enabling technologies, the role of digital transformation in smart asset management, and their industrial applications, and finally analyzes the path of industries moving toward autonomous industrial organizations.

DOI: 10.4018/979-8-3373-9998-0.ch006

1. INTRODUCTION

In recent decades, manufacturing industries have been experiencing a wave of technological transformations that have fundamentally changed the way industrial assets are designed, operated, and managed. Rapid advances in digital technologies, including the Industrial Internet of Things, big data analytics, artificial intelligence, and cyber-physical systems, have blurred the boundaries between physical systems and digital environments. As a result, the concept of digital transformation in manufacturing industries has become one of the main axes of industrial development worldwide. In such a context, manufacturing assets are no longer simply passive physical equipment, but have become intelligent and connected elements that can generate data, report their status, and in some cases even participate in operational decision-making (Joshi et al., 2026).

In traditional manufacturing models, industrial assets such as machinery, production lines, and process equipment have largely operated as static, stand-alone systems. These assets were typically managed based on scheduled maintenance schedules, operator experience, and limited operational information. Such an approach often encountered challenges such as unplanned downtime, inefficient use of production capacity, and difficulty in monitoring equipment status. With the advent of digital technologies and increased capabilities for collecting and processing operational data, continuous monitoring of asset performance became possible, paving the way for a shift to intelligent approaches to manufacturing asset management (Yang et al., 2026).

In the context of new industrial developments, the concept of smart manufacturing assets has emerged as a key pillar of digital factories. Smart assets are equipment that, in addition to physical performance, also have communication, computing, and analytical capabilities. These assets can collect data related to operational status, environmental conditions, and process performance in real time and transmit it to analytical systems. Analyzing this data allows for the identification of performance patterns, prediction of equipment failure, and optimization of production processes. As a result, industrial organizations will be able to make their operational and management decisions based on accurate and up-to-date data (Huang & Liu, 2026).

One of the important technologies that plays a prominent role in realizing this transformation is the digital twin. A digital twin is a virtual model or profile of a physical asset that uses real-time data and analytical models to represent the behavior and status of the real system in the digital environment. This technology allows real-time monitoring of equipment performance, analysis of various operational scenarios, and even prediction of future system behavior. Through such a capability, industrial organizations can evaluate the effects of various decisions in the digital environment and choose optimal solutions before real problems occur in the physical environment.

Along with the development of smart assets and digital technologies, the concept of smart industrial organizations has also gradually taken shape. In these types of organizations, data is considered one of the most important strategic assets, and decisions are made based on data analysis, predictive models, and intelligent algorithms. The integration of manufacturing assets with enterprise information systems such as enterprise resource planning systems, production execution systems, and analytics platforms enables the creation of an integrated digital ecosystem. In such an ecosystem, information related to asset performance, production status, energy consumption, and other operational indicators are continuously collected and analyzed, which helps improve productivity, reduce costs, and increase the flexibility of the organization (Nozari, 2026).

Despite significant advances in digital technologies, the effective implementation of smart manufacturing assets and digital transformation in industrial organizations still faces challenges. Issues related to system integration, data security, managing large amounts of information, and organizational changes are among the issues that need to be addressed on the path to digital transformation. In addition, the successful use of smart assets requires the development of new management models and decision-making frameworks that can effectively manage the interaction between physical systems, operational data, and analytical tools.

Given these developments, examining the role of smart manufacturing assets in the digital transformation of industrial organizations has become increasingly important. The purpose of this chapter is to provide a comprehensive view of how manufacturing assets are evolving in the digital age and to explain the role of new technologies in creating smart industrial organizations. In this regard, the evolution of manufacturing assets in industrial environments is first examined, then the key technologies that enable the smartization of these assets are discussed. Next, the role of digital twins and analytical systems in industrial asset management is analyzed, and finally, the implications of these developments for the formation of smart industrial organizations are examined.

2. EVOLUTION OF MANUFACTURING ASSETS IN THE DIGITAL ERA

Production assets have always been considered one of the main elements in the performance and productivity of industrial systems. In the past, the concept of production assets was mainly limited to machinery, mechanical equipment, assembly lines and other physical components used in manufacturing processes. This equipment often operated independently and without extensive communication with other system components, and information about their performance was usually obtained through manual reports or periodic monitoring. In such conditions, asset management was more based on the practical experience of operators and preventive maintenance programs, and access to accurate and real-time data about the condition of the equipment was not very possible (Xu et al., 2026).

With the advancement of information and communication technologies, especially in the last two decades, the concept of production assets has gradually changed. The first stage of this change began with the increase in the connectivity of equipment. At this stage, industrial equipment was equipped with sensors and communication modules, and the possibility of transferring operational data from the physical environment to information systems was provided. This evolution enabled industrial organizations to systematically collect and analyze data on equipment status, production, energy consumption, and environmental conditions for the first time. As a result, decision-making processes in the field of equipment maintenance and operation became largely data-driven, and organizations were able to gain a more accurate view of the performance of their assets (Kumar et al., 2026).

Following this trend, a more advanced stage of the evolution of manufacturing assets was formed, in which industrial equipment was equipped with a form of operational intelligence in addition to connectivity. In this phase, often discussed in the context of smart factories and Industry 4.0, manufacturing assets are able to process the data generated locally or on analytical platforms and, based on the results of the analysis, provide suggestions for improving performance. For example, a manufacturing machine can predict the possibility of failure by analyzing its vibration patterns or operating temperature and send the necessary warnings before a production line stops. Such capabilities have elevated the role of manufacturing assets from mere execution equipment to active elements in the industrial decision-making process.

In recent years, with the development of technologies such as artificial intelligence, advanced data analytics, and digital twins, the concept of manufacturing assets has entered a new phase, which can be called the autonomous asset phase. At this stage, assets not only generate data and monitor their own status, but also are able to automatically change their operating settings or interact with other equipment in the production environment under certain conditions. This evolution has gradually led to the formation of ecosystems in which various equipment is connected in a smart network and operates in harmony to optimize the performance of the production system (Buccoliero et al., 2026).

To better understand this evolution, manufacturing assets can be classified into four main levels, including traditional assets, connected assets, smart assets, and autonomous assets. Each of these levels represents a stage in the evolution of technology and the increasing level of intelligence in industrial systems. Table 1 provides a comparison of the key characteristics of these four asset types and shows how the level of connectivity, data analytics capabilities, and autonomy have increased over time.

Table 1. Comparison of Traditional, Connected, Smart, and Autonomous Manufacturing Assets

Type of Asset	Connectivity	Data Capability	Intelligence Level	Decision Autonomy	Integration with Enterprise Systems
Traditional Assets	Very limited	Manual or periodic data collection	None	None	Low
Connected Assets	Sensor-based connectivity	Continuous data collection	Basic monitoring	Low	Moderate
Smart Assets	Networked and data-enabled	Real-time analytics	Advanced analytics and prediction	Moderate	High
Autonomous Assets	Fully networked	Real-time and historical data integration	AI-driven intelligence	High	Very high

As shown in Table 1, the most important difference between these four levels lies in the amount of data usage and the level of decision-making intelligence. In traditional assets, data is mostly collected in a limited and manual manner, and its role in decision-making is very limited. In contrast, connected assets are able to record operational data continuously using sensors and communication networks. This data allows for precise monitoring of equipment performance and paves the way for the development of intelligent monitoring systems.

At the next level, namely smart assets, the collected data is not only stored but also analyzed. The use of analytical algorithms and predictive models at this stage enables production systems to identify equipment performance patterns and take corrective actions before serious problems arise. Ultimately, autonomous assets represent an advanced stage in the evolution of industrial systems, in which operational decision-making is largely delegated to intelligent systems.

The transformation of manufacturing assets in the digital age is not limited to improving equipment performance, but also has far-reaching implications for organizational structure and industrial business models. Smart assets can provide valuable information about production processes, energy efficiency, and product quality, which helps organizational managers make more accurate strategic decisions. In addition, the widespread connection of assets to digital platforms allows for new models of collaboration between equipment, information systems, and human operators (Yordanova & Nozari, 2026).

Overall, the evolution of manufacturing assets from traditional equipment to intelligent and autonomous systems is one of the most important developments in modern industries. This transformation has not only increased productivity and reliability in manufacturing processes, but has also paved the way for the emergence of digital factories and smart industrial organizations. The rest of the chapter will examine the key technologies that have made this transformation possible.

3. CORE TECHNOLOGIES ENABLING SMART MANUFACTURING ASSETS

The proliferation of smart manufacturing assets in industrial environments is the result of the advancement of a set of digital technologies that have developed rapidly in recent years. These technologies have enabled the connection between physical equipment, information systems, and analytical tools, paving the way for the emergence of smart manufacturing systems. In such an environment, industrial assets are no longer simply mechanical equipment, but are transformed into digital-physical elements that can generate data, process it, and participate in operational decisions. The combination of these technologies has enabled manufacturing systems to dynamically adapt to operating conditions and optimize their performance (Zhang, 2026).

One of the most important technologies that plays a fundamental role in making manufacturing assets smart is the Industrial Internet of Things. In this technology, manufacturing equipment is connected to each other using sensors, controllers, and communication networks and is able to send its operational information in real time. This data can include parameters such as temperature, pressure, rotation speed, vibration, energy consumption, and other performance indicators. Connecting these equipment to industrial networks allows for large-scale production data collection and enables real-time monitoring of asset status. As a result, industrial managers can gain a more accurate picture of the performance of the production system and take corrective actions in a timely manner (Nozari, 2023).

Along with the Industrial Internet of Things, the concept of cyber-physical systems also plays an important role in the development of smart assets. Cyber-physical systems are a combination of physical and computational components that interact with each other through communication networks. In these systems, data from the physical environment is transmitted to digital systems and, after analysis, the results are returned to the physical equipment in the form of control commands. This continuous cycle of information exchange enables production systems to respond quickly to environmental changes and dynamically adjust their performance. Such a capability is particularly important in complex manufacturing environments that require coordination between multiple devices.

Another important technology in making manufacturing assets smart is artificial intelligence and data analytics. The data collected by sensors and industrial systems is usually very large in volume and cannot be analyzed manually. Machine learning algorithms and data analysis methods make it possible to identify hidden patterns in operational data. Through these analyses, it is possible to model the behavior of equipment, predict the probability of failures, and even determine the optimal conditions for operating the manufacturing system. The use of such methods has caused industrial asset management to move from traditional approaches based on reacting to problems to predictive and intelligent approaches (Padhamnath, 2026).

In addition, edge computing and cloud computing also play an important role in the architecture of smart manufacturing systems. In many industrial applications, data must be processed at high speed to make immediate decisions. In such situations, edge computing enables initial data processing close to the equipment, avoiding the delays caused by data transmission to remote processing centers. In contrast, cloud computing provides a suitable platform for storing large amounts of data and performing complex analytics. The combination of these two approaches allows industrial systems to use manufacturing data at both the local and enterprise levels.

To better understand how these technologies interact, the technology architecture for smart manufacturing assets can be considered as a multi-layer structure. This structure shows how data is collected from the physical environment and, after passing through various communication and analytical layers, is transformed into management and operational decisions.

Figure 1. Technology Architecture for Smart Manufacturing Assets

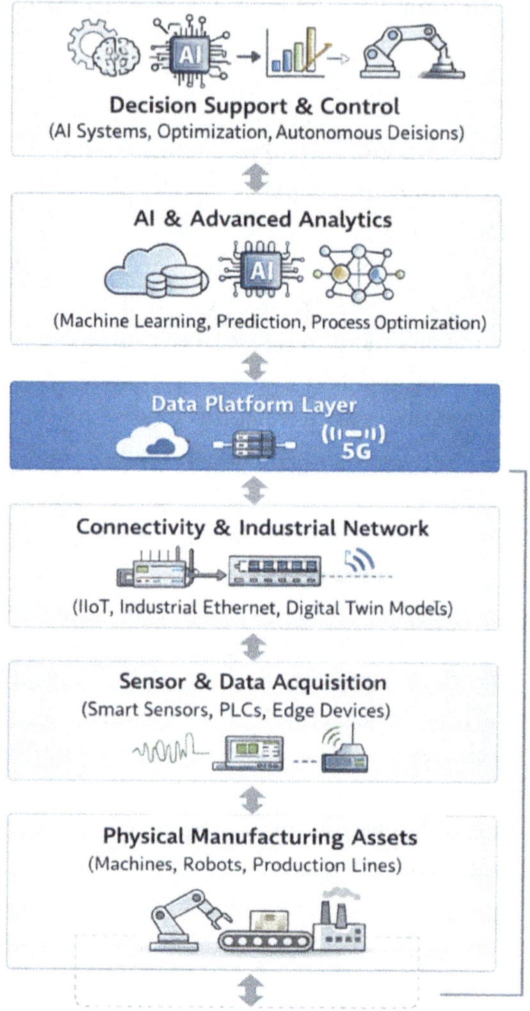

As shown in Figure 1, at the lowest level of this architecture is the physical asset layer, which includes machinery, production equipment, and other operational components of the system. Above this layer is the sensor and data acquisition layer, which is responsible for measuring various operational parameters. The data generated at this stage is transmitted to industrial networks through the communication layer and sent to data platforms.

At higher layers, the collected data is processed in data platforms and analytical systems. At this stage, data analysis algorithms and artificial intelligence are used to extract valuable information from the data. Finally, the results of these analyses are provided to industrial managers or control systems in the form of decision support systems so that they can take the necessary measures to improve the performance of equipment and production processes.

This multi-layer architecture shows that the smartization of production assets is the result of the interaction of a set of complementary technologies. Each of these technologies plays a specific role in the production and data analysis chain, and the elimination of any of them can reduce the efficiency of the entire system. As a result, the successful design and implementation of smart manufacturing assets requires the proper integration of these technologies into a coherent digital architecture (Nozari & Yordanova, 2026).

Overall, the advancement of digital technologies has made manufacturing assets active elements in industrial ecosystems. Extensive equipment connectivity, advanced data analytics, and the use of intelligent systems have enabled the creation of flexible and data-driven manufacturing environments. This transformation has not only increased the productivity of industrial systems, but also paved the way for the development of a new generation of intelligent industrial organizations.

4. DIGITAL TRANSFORMATION OF INDUSTRIAL ENTERPRISES

Digital transformation has become one of the most important topics in the management and development of industrial organizations in recent years. Increasing competition in global markets, increasing complexity of supply chains and rapid growth of digital technologies have led manufacturing organizations to look for ways to redesign their structures, processes and decision-making models. Meanwhile, digital transformation does not only mean the use of new technologies, but also a broader process that includes recreating operational models, improving information flow and creating intelligent mechanisms for decision-making in the organization (Khojasteh et al., 2026).

In traditional industrial environments, many management and operational processes were carried out separately and without effective communication between different parts of the organization. Production systems, asset management, production planning and supply chain management often operated as separate systems and data exchange between them was limited. This situation caused the organization's managers to face information limitations in analyzing the overall status of the production system, and management decisions were often made with delays or based on incomplete data. Digital transformation attempts to address these information gaps by creating an integrated digital ecosystem.

One of the most important features of digital transformation in industrial organizations is the integration of data flows at the organization level. In such an environment, information generated by equipment, sensors, and operational systems is continuously collected in data platforms and made available to analytical systems. This data can provide valuable information about the performance of machinery, the status of production lines, energy consumption, product quality, and process efficiency. Analyzing this information helps organizations identify weaknesses in the production system and develop optimal solutions to improve performance (Lin & Dang, 2026).

Another important dimension of digital transformation is the integration of operational systems with organizational information systems. In many modern factories, enterprise resource management systems, production execution systems, maintenance management systems, and data analytics platforms interact seamlessly with each other. This integration makes production information available in real time across the organization and management decisions can be made based on real-time data. For example, data on equipment status can be used directly in production planning systems to align production schedules with real-time system conditions.

In addition to information integration, digital transformation has also paved the way for the development of new data-driven decision-making models. In such models, management decisions are made not only based on experience or traditional analytics, but also on predictive models and intelligent algorithms. The use of advanced data analytics, machine learning models, and decision support systems helps organizations predict future trends in the manufacturing system and take necessary measures to prevent potential problems before they occur. This approach increases organizational resilience and reduces operational risks (Zhang & Xu, 2026).

To better understand the relationship between intelligent manufacturing assets and the digital transformation of industrial organizations, this process can be examined in the form of a conceptual framework that shows how manufacturing data is transformed into management knowledge and operational decisions. Figure 2 shows this framework in a simplified form.

Figure 2. Digital Transformation Framework for Intelligent Industrial Enterprises

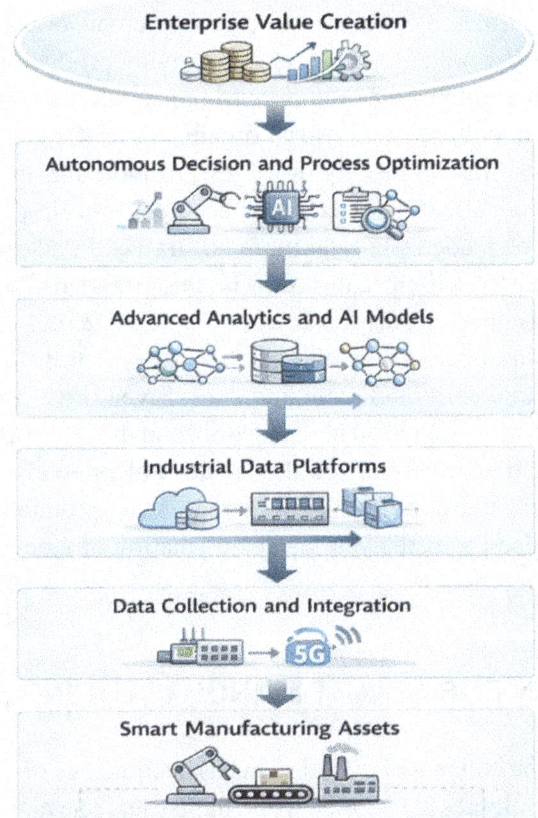

As shown in Figure 2, at the lowest level of this framework are smart manufacturing assets, which include machinery, equipment, and manufacturing systems equipped with sensors and communication capabilities. These assets continuously collect operational data related to manufacturing processes. Next, the generated data is collected in the data collection and integration layer and transmitted to analytical systems through industrial networks and data platforms.

At the next level, industrial data platforms play an important role in storing and managing manufacturing data. These platforms enable the aggregation of data from various sources in the organization and provide a suitable platform for performing advanced analytics. The data stored in these platforms is then processed in analytical models and artificial intelligence algorithms to identify performance patterns in the manufacturing system.

The results of these analyses are ultimately used in the form of intelligent decision-making systems. These systems can provide suggestions for optimizing production processes, improving equipment performance, and reducing resource consumption. In some cases, it is even possible to implement corrective decisions automatically. The ultimate goal of this process is to create organizational value by increasing productivity, reducing costs, and improving product quality.

Digital transformation also has important impacts on the organizational structure and management culture of industrial organizations. Organizations that move toward digital transformation usually move toward more flexible and data-driven structures. In such organizations, access to accurate and up-to-date information allows decisions to be made faster and more accurately. In addition, collaboration between different parts of the organization increases and management processes become more transparent (Nozari & Szmelter-Jarosz, 2025).

Overall, digital transformation plays a key role in transforming traditional industrial organizations into intelligent and data-driven organizations. The use of digital technologies, the integration of data flows, and the development of advanced decision-making models have enabled the creation of more efficient and flexible production systems. This trend not only increases the productivity of industrial organizations, but also paves the way for the formation of a new generation of intelligent industrial organizations.

5. DIGITAL TWIN FOR SMART MANUFACTURING ASSETS

In recent years, the concept of digital twin has become one of the most important transformative technologies in manufacturing industries. The rapid growth of sensor technologies, industrial communications, data analytics, and advanced modeling has made it possible to create digital profiles of physical assets. A digital twin is generally referred to as a model or digital representation of a physical asset, process, or system that is dynamically connected to the real system and continuously receives and analyzes operational data. This continuous connection between the physical system and the digital model allows the real state of the equipment to be reconstructed in a virtual environment and allows for accurate analysis of system performance (Fang et al., 2026).

In modern manufacturing environments, industrial assets such as machinery, production lines, industrial robots, and process equipment are equipped with sensors and communication systems. These sensors are capable of measuring various parameters such as temperature, pressure, vibration, speed, energy consumption, and other performance indicators. The data generated by these sensors is transmitted to data platforms, where it is used to create or update the digital twin model. In this way, the digital twin acts as a virtual version of the physical asset that represents the behavior of the real system in a digital environment.

One of the most important advantages of using digital twins in manufacturing systems is the ability to monitor equipment performance in real time. In traditional systems, equipment status checks were usually performed periodically, and many technical problems were only detected when they led to production stops or product quality degradation. In contrast, digital twins can analyze operational data in real time and identify abnormal changes in equipment behavior. This capability allows industrial organizations to take corrective actions before serious failures occur and prevent unwanted stops in production lines (Pan et al., 2026).

Another important application of digital twins in manufacturing industries is predicting the future behavior of systems. Using analytical models and machine learning algorithms, historical and real-time data from equipment can be used to predict performance trends. For example, if certain patterns of vibration or operating temperature are observed in an industrial machine, the digital twin model can predict the likelihood of a failure in the near future. Such a capability allows industrial managers to plan maintenance and repair programs intelligently and reduce maintenance costs.

In addition to monitoring and forecasting, digital twins also enable the analysis of different operational scenarios. In many cases, industrial managers need to examine the effects of various changes to a manufacturing system; for example, changing production speeds, adjusting process parameters, or using new equipment. Conducting such tests in a real-world environment can be costly and even dangerous. In contrast, digital twins allow these scenarios to be simulated in a digital environment, allowing managers to evaluate the possible outcomes of different decisions before implementing them in the real system (Alokdeh et al., 2026).

To better understand how physical assets and digital models interact, the digital twin architecture in manufacturing systems can be represented in the form of a conceptual framework. This framework shows how operational data is collected from the physical environment and, after analysis in the digital model, is transformed into management and control decisions. Figure 3 shows a simplified view of this architecture.

Figure 3. Digital Twin Architecture for Smart Manufacturing Assets

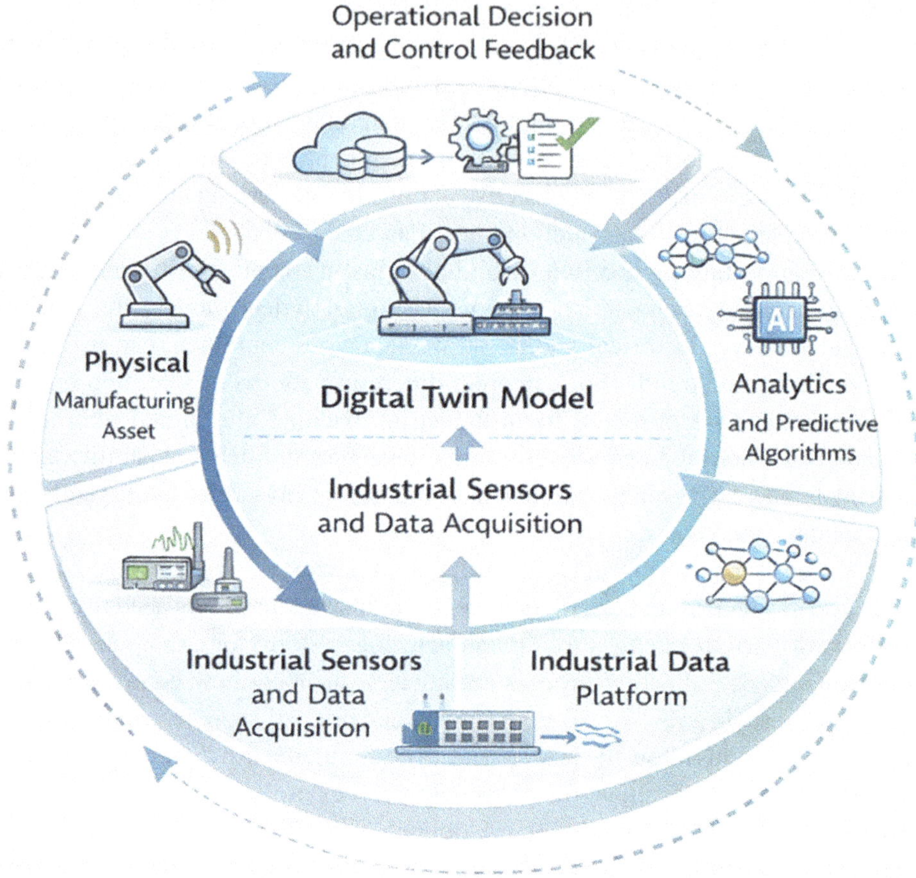

As shown in Figure 3, at the lowest level of the architecture is the physical production asset, which can include industrial machinery, production robots, or assembly lines. These devices are equipped with a set of sensors that continuously measure operational data. Next, the collected data is transferred to an industrial data platform that is responsible for storing and managing the data.

In the next layer, the operational data is used to create or update a digital twin model. This model creates a digital representation of the behavior and characteristics of the physical system, allowing for detailed analysis of the equipment's performance. The data and models created in the analysis phase and predictive algorithms are then processed to identify performance patterns and the likelihood of technical problems.

Finally, the results of the analysis are fed back to the physical system in the form of operational decisions and control commands. This process creates a feedback loop between the physical system and the digital model that helps to continuously improve the performance of the equipment. Such a loop is one of the key features of digital twins in industrial environments, allowing manufacturing systems to dynamically adapt to operating conditions.

The use of digital twins in manufacturing industries can also have significant impacts on the productivity and sustainability of industrial systems. Accurate analysis of equipment performance can help reduce energy consumption, optimize resource use, and extend the useful life of equipment. In addition, information from digital twins can also be used in strategic decision-making within the organization and help managers plan the development of manufacturing systems (Movahed et al., 2023).

Overall, digital twins are recognized as one of the key technologies in the digital transformation of manufacturing industries. By connecting physical assets with digital models, this technology enables real-time monitoring, predictive analysis, and optimization of manufacturing processes. For this reason, many industrial organizations are investing in the development and implementation of digital twins to benefit from its benefits in improving their performance and competitiveness.

6. INTELLIGENT ASSET MANAGEMENT AND DECISION AUTOMATION

Industrial asset management has always been a fundamental issue in the productivity and sustainability of manufacturing systems. In many industries, manufacturing equipment constitutes a significant portion of an organization's capital, and its proper functioning plays a decisive role in production quality, operating costs, and system reliability. In the past, asset management was mainly based on periodic maintenance schedules and the experience of technical specialists. Although this approach was efficient in many cases, as industrial systems became more complex and the volume of operational data increased, the need for more advanced methods for monitoring and managing equipment became more and more felt (Bagherian et al., 2026).

In recent years, the emergence of digital technologies and intelligent systems has led to the formation of a new approach to industrial asset management, which is referred to as intelligent asset management. In this approach, data from sensors, condition monitoring systems, and industrial platforms is continuously collected and analyzed to determine the real state of the equipment. This data can provide valuable information about machinery performance, operating conditions, and the likelihood of failures. Analyzing such data allows for the identification of equipment performance patterns and helps organizations make more informed decisions about the maintenance, repair, and operation of industrial assets (Nozari & Yordanova, 2025).

One of the most important applications of intelligent asset management is predictive maintenance. In this approach, instead of performing maintenance based on fixed time schedules, actual equipment data is analyzed to predict the likelihood of future failures. For example, an unusual increase in the vibration or temperature of an industrial machine can be an indication of a problem with mechanical components. Analytical algorithms can detect such changes and issue the necessary alerts to take corrective action. This method reduces unplanned downtime, increases equipment life, and reduces maintenance costs.

In addition to predictive maintenance, intelligent asset management also includes monitoring the condition of equipment. In this approach, information related to the performance of machinery is continuously monitored to quickly identify any changes in operating conditions. The use of advanced sensors and data analysis systems allows the condition of equipment to be monitored in real time. Such a capability helps industrial managers to prevent serious problems in the production system and take corrective actions in a timely manner.

In addition to these applications, the development of artificial intelligence and data analysis technologies has enabled decisions related to asset management to be made automatically. In many modern industrial systems, intelligent algorithms are able to analyze operational data and provide suggestions for optimizing equipment performance. For example, these systems can determine when a component needs to be replaced, or how the operating settings of a machine should be changed to increase its productivity. Such decisions can be implemented semi-automatically or even fully automatically, and the role of human operators is limited to monitoring the system performance (Li et al., 2026).

The various applications of AI in industrial asset management can be examined in different categories. Table 2 shows a sample of these applications and the technologies used in each.

Table 2. AI Applications in Intelligent Asset Management

Application	AI Technique	Data Required	Expected Benefits
Predictive Maintenance	Machine Learning	Sensor data, vibration, temperature	Reduced downtime and maintenance cost
Condition Monitoring	Data analytics	Real-time operational data	Early detection of equipment anomalies
Failure Prediction	Neural networks	Historical operational data	Prevention of unexpected equipment failures
Process Optimization	Optimization algorithms	Production and performance data	Improved efficiency and resource utilization

As can be seen in Table 2, the applications of AI in asset management cover a wide range of activities. One of the most important of these applications is the prediction of equipment failures. Machine learning algorithms can identify patterns that appear before failures occur by analyzing historical equipment performance data. Identifying these patterns allows organizations to take preventive measures before serious problems arise.

Another application of AI in this area is the optimization of operational processes. Analyzing equipment performance data can show what settings for machinery will produce the best performance. In some cases, optimization algorithms can dynamically adjust the operating parameters of the production system to increase productivity and reduce resource consumption. Such capabilities are especially important in complex production systems that include multiple equipment and different processes.

Intelligent asset management can also play an important role in increasing the sustainability of industrial systems. Accurate analysis of equipment performance can help reduce energy consumption, reduce production waste, and optimize resource utilization. In addition, information from intelligent monitoring systems can also be used in the organization's long-term planning and help managers make better strategic decisions about investing in new equipment (Lan et al., 2026).

In general, intelligent asset management and decision-making automation are considered one of the most important outcomes of the digital transformation in manufacturing industries. The use of advanced sensors, industrial data analysis, and intelligent algorithms has enabled industrial organizations to accurately monitor the performance of their equipment and make management decisions based on real data. Such an approach not only increases the efficiency of production systems, but also plays an important role in reducing operating costs and increasing equipment reliability.

7. INDUSTRIAL APPLICATIONS AND CASE EXAMPLES

The expansion of digital technologies in recent years has led many manufacturing industries to move towards the use of smart assets, industrial data analytics, and digital twins. This transformation is not limited to a specific industry sector, but encompasses a wide range of industries, including advanced manufacturing, energy, food, pharmaceuticals, and industrial logistics. The use of smart technologies in these areas has enabled organizations to monitor their production processes more accurately, increase system efficiency, and make management decisions based on real-time data (Nozari & Yordanova, 2025).

One of the most important areas that has benefited from smart asset technologies is advanced manufacturing plants. In such environments, industrial machinery, assembly lines, and production robots are equipped with sensors and communication systems that continuously record operational data. This data is stored in industrial data platforms and analyzed through analytical algorithms. The results of these analyses can lead to optimization of production processes, reduction of unintended downtime, and improvement of product quality. Many modern factories use these technologies to create flexible production systems that are able to adapt quickly to changes in market demand (Sivarethinamohan et al., 2026).

Another important area is the energy industry and industrial infrastructure. In power plants, refineries, and energy distribution systems, industrial equipment plays a vital role in the stability and performance of the system. The use of advanced sensors and intelligent monitoring systems has made it possible to monitor the status of equipment in real time and quickly identify any changes in operating conditions. Data analysis from these systems can help predict equipment failure and improve maintenance programs. This is especially important in energy systems, where equipment downtime can have far-reaching consequences.

The pharmaceutical and biotechnology industries are also among the areas that have widely used smart asset technologies in recent years. In these industries, precise control of process conditions such as temperature, pressure, and material composition is of great importance. The use of precise sensors and data analysis systems allows real-time monitoring of production processes and helps manufacturers maintain product quality at a high level. In addition, the use of digital models and simulation systems can help optimize drug production processes and reduce production costs (Meng & Song, 2026).

There are also wide applications for smart asset technologies in the food and industrial agriculture industries. In these areas, digital monitoring systems can collect information related to production conditions, the quality of raw materials, and the status of process equipment. This information helps production managers to control production processes more accurately and prevent problems such as contamination or product quality degradation. In addition, manufacturing data analysis can help optimize energy and resource consumption in food factories.

Another important application area of smart technologies is industrial logistics and supply chain systems. In these systems, transportation equipment, smart warehouses, and inventory management systems are connected to digital networks and generate operational data continuously. Analyzing this data can help improve transportation planning, reduce delivery times, and increase transparency in the supply chain. Many industrial organizations use these technologies to create smart supply chains that are able to respond quickly to market changes (Nozari, 2025).

To provide an overview of the different applications of smart manufacturing assets in different industries, Table 3 shows examples of these applications in various industrial areas.

Table 3. Examples of Smart Manufacturing Asset Applications Across Industries

Industry	Application Area	Smart Asset Application	Key Benefits
Advanced Manufacturing	Production lines	Smart sensors and predictive maintenance	Reduced downtime and improved productivity
Energy Systems	Power plants and energy networks	Real-time monitoring and equipment diagnostics	Increased reliability and operational safety
Pharmaceutical Industry	Bioprocess and drug manufacturing	Process monitoring and digital models	Improved quality control and process optimization
Food Processing	Industrial food production	Sensor-based quality monitoring	Enhanced product quality and reduced waste
Logistics and Supply Chain	Warehousing and transport systems	Smart tracking and automated logistics	Increased efficiency and supply chain visibility

As can be seen in Table 3, smart asset technologies are used in a wide range of industries. In advanced manufacturing industries, the main focus is on improving production line efficiency and reducing equipment downtime. In energy industries, the main goal is to increase system reliability and prevent critical equipment failures. In the pharmaceutical and food industries, digital technologies help improve product quality and precisely control production processes.

In addition, in logistics and supply chain systems, the use of smart technologies can lead to increased transparency and efficiency in managing the flow of goods. Such applications show that smart manufacturing assets are not limited to the factory environment, but can be used throughout the entire industrial ecosystem from production to distribution.

Overall, the industrial applications of smart technologies show that digital transformation is rapidly changing the nature of manufacturing and industrial systems. Organizations that are able to use these technologies effectively can gain a significant competitive advantage in global markets. On the other hand, the development of these technologies has paved the way for the emergence of a new generation of intelligent, data-driven industrial systems, in which decisions are increasingly based on data analysis and digital models.

8. TOWARD AUTONOMOUS INDUSTRIAL ENTERPRISES

Recent developments in digital technologies, especially in the field of artificial intelligence, industrial data analytics, industrial Internet of Things, and digital twins, have created a new direction in the development of industrial organizations, which can be described as a move towards autonomous industrial organizations. In such organizations, many operational decisions and even part of management decisions are made based on data analysis and intelligent algorithms. This development represents a transition from purely automated production systems to systems that are able to understand their own situation, analyze environmental changes, and dynamically implement appropriate corrective actions (Hu et al., 2026).

In traditional industrial organizations, decision-making was mainly carried out hierarchically and based on human experience. Although industrial automation systems played an important role in controlling production processes, these systems usually operated according to a set of predefined rules and had a limited ability to adapt to new conditions. In contrast, autonomous industrial organizations use intelligent systems and analytical models that are able to continuously analyze operational data and make appropriate decisions based on the results of these analyses.

One of the key elements in the formation of autonomous industrial organizations is the complete integration of data at the organizational level. In such an environment, information related to equipment performance, production line status, supply chain conditions, and even market data are continuously collected and analyzed. This data is used as input for analytical models and decision-making algorithms, allowing industrial systems to have a more comprehensive understanding of their operational situation. The result of this process is the creation of a dynamic decision-making system that can continuously optimize the organization's performance (Nozari et al., 2025).

Along with data integration, the use of advanced artificial intelligence algorithms also plays an important role in the development of autonomous industrial organizations. Machine learning and deep learning algorithms are able to identify complex patterns in industrial data and use this information to predict the behavior of manufacturing systems. Such capabilities help organizations identify potential problems before they occur and take preventive measures in a timely manner. In addition, intelligent systems can analyze different operating scenarios and choose the best option to optimize system performance.

Another important feature of autonomous industrial organizations is the ability to coordinate between smart assets. In modern manufacturing environments, various equipment such as machinery, robots, and industrial transportation systems are connected to communication networks and are able to share their operational information with each other. This communication allows the equipment to coordinate its behavior with the system conditions. For example, in a smart factory, if the production speed in one section increases, other sections of the production line can also automatically adjust their performance to maintain balance in the entire system.

In addition, autonomous industrial organizations use advanced digital models to simulate and analyze the performance of manufacturing systems. Digital twins play an important role in this area, as they allow for the creation of a digital profile of the entire manufacturing system. These models can simulate the behavior of the system under different conditions and help industrial managers to examine the effects of various decisions before implementing them in the real environment. The use of such tools makes the decision-making process in industrial organizations more accurate and efficient.

The move towards autonomous industrial organizations also has important implications for the management structure and human resources. In such organizations, the role of humans' changes from performing operational activities to monitoring the performance of intelligent systems and analyzing their results. Industrial operators and managers act more as data analysts and strategic decision makers, and intelligent systems perform many operational tasks automatically. This change can lead to increased organizational productivity and reduced human errors in production processes (Singamsetty et al., 2026).

Despite the many benefits, the development of autonomous industrial organizations also comes with challenges. Issues related to data security, integration of different systems, management of huge amounts of information, and development of digital infrastructure are among the issues that need to be considered in the digital transformation process. In addition, building trust among managers and employees towards intelligent decision-making systems is also an important factor in the success of this transformation.

Overall, the move towards autonomous industrial organizations can be considered one of the most important future trends in the development of manufacturing industries. The combination of digital technologies, industrial data analysis, and intelligent systems has enabled organizations to manage their production processes dynamically and automatically. Such organizations will be able to respond more quickly to environmental changes, increase the efficiency of production systems, and create a sustainable competitive advantage in global markets.

9. CONCLUSION

Technological developments in recent decades have fundamentally changed the way industrial systems are designed, operated, and managed. In the past, many manufacturing systems were based on individual physical equipment and traditional management processes, with limited access to accurate data about asset performance. In such an environment, management decisions were often made based on practical experience or incomplete information. With the advent of digital technologies and the expansion of data-driven infrastructures, new conditions have emerged in manufacturing industries in which data, advanced analytics, and intelligent systems play a central role in the management and optimization of industrial assets.

This chapter examines the transformation of manufacturing assets from traditional equipment to intelligent systems. This transformation shows that industrial assets are no longer simply mechanical components in manufacturing processes, but have become active elements in digital ecosystems. Equipping machinery with advanced sensors, developing industrial communication networks, and using data platforms has made it possible to collect and analyze a huge amount of operational data. This data provides a basis for developing analytical models and intelligent decision-making systems, enabling industrial organizations to manage the performance of their production systems more accurately.

Next, the key technologies that enable the development of smart production assets were examined. Technologies such as the Industrial Internet of Things, cyber-physical systems, artificial intelligence, industrial data analytics, and cloud computing platforms play a fundamental role in creating digital infrastructure in production environments. By creating connections between physical equipment and digital systems, these technologies have enabled the creation of integrated and data-driven production systems. The result of this transformation is the creation of smart production environments that are able to dynamically adapt to operating conditions and optimize their performance.

One of the most important tools developed in this area in recent years is digital twin technology. Digital twins allow the creation of virtual models of physical assets that can represent the behavior of the real system in a digital environment. The use of this technology allows industrial organizations to monitor equipment performance in real time, simulate different operating scenarios, and examine the effects of management decisions before implementing them in the real environment. Such a capability helps improve decision-making processes and increase the productivity of manufacturing systems.

In addition, intelligent asset management was examined as one of the important outcomes of the digital transformation in manufacturing industries. The use of advanced sensors, condition monitoring systems, and data analysis algorithms has enabled organizations to accurately monitor equipment performance and plan maintenance actions based on real system conditions. Approaches such as predictive maintenance and real-time monitoring of equipment can reduce unplanned downtime, extend asset life, and reduce operating costs.

A review of the industrial applications of these technologies shows that smart manufacturing assets are being used in a wide range of industries. Advanced manufacturing, energy systems, pharmaceuticals, food, and logistics are just a few of the areas where the use of digital technologies has led to significant improvements in system performance. In many of these industries, data from industrial equipment is used as a valuable resource for optimizing processes and improving product quality.

One of the important trends that was highlighted at the end of this chapter is the movement of industries towards autonomous industrial organizations. In such organizations, intelligent systems are able to analyze operational data and make the necessary decisions to improve system performance. This transformation represents a shift from purely automated manufacturing systems to systems that are able to understand their own situation, analyze environmental changes, and implement appropriate corrective actions. Such organizations can respond more quickly to market changes and increase the productivity of their manufacturing systems.

Despite significant progress in this area, the full development of intelligent manufacturing systems is still accompanied by challenges. Issues related to data security, industrial system integration, managing huge amounts of data, and developing digital infrastructure are among the issues that require serious attention on the path to digital transformation. In addition, the success of this transformation largely depends on the ability of organizations to create a data-driven organizational culture and develop new skills in their workforce.

Finally, it can be said that intelligent manufacturing assets and their associated technologies play an important role in the formation of a new generation of industrial organizations. The combination of digital technologies, industrial data analytics, and intelligent systems has enabled organizations to manage their manufacturing systems more efficiently, flexibly, and sustainably. In the near future, further development of digital technologies and increased use of intelligent systems are expected to pave the way for the emergence of fully intelligent factories and autonomous industrial organizations.

REFERENCES

Alokdeh, S. K., Al-Sulaiti, I., Shwedeh, F., Alzoubi, H. M., & Ahmed, G. (2026). Transforming Smart Manufacturing: The Pivotal Role of IOT and Data Integration in Enhancing Operational Efficiency in Manufacturing Sector.

Bagherian, A., Srivastav, A. L., & Mukherjee, S. (2026). Barriers and strategies of smart factory evolution in industry 4.0: An empirical study. *International Journal of Computer Integrated Manufacturing*, *39*(1), 65–97. DOI: 10.1080/0951192X.2025.2461055

Buccoliero, F. O., Corallo, A., Crespino, A. M., Del Vecchio, V., Lezzi, M., & Spennato, A. (2026). Modelling a Process Shop Floor Digital Twin in Smart Manufacturing: Best Practices from a Case Study. *IEEE Transactions on Engineering Management*, *73*, 1667–1680. DOI: 10.1109/TEM.2026.3657042

Fang, L., Shi, J., Wu, L., Tan, J., & Wan, J. (2026). Perspectives and prospects on embodied intelligence-empowered smart manufacturing. *Journal of Intelligent Manufacturing*, •••, 1–20. DOI: 10.1007/s10845-025-02763-6

Hu, R., Guoyong, M., Abbas, A., & Wattoo, M. U. (2026). Explorative industrial internet promotes open green innovation in manufacturing enterprises. *Scientific Reports*, *16*(1), 11312. DOI: 10.1038/s41598-026-40439-0 PMID: 41760707

Huang, D., & Liu, R. (2026). Research on the Technology–Organization–Environment Matching Mechanism in the Digital Transformation of the Manufacturing Industry: Evidence from Frontline Employees in the Guangdong–Hong Kong–Macao Greater Bay Area. *Administrative Sciences*, *16*(1), 43. DOI: 10.3390/admsci16010043

Joshi, S., Sharma, M., Gunasekaran, A., & Joshi, T. (2026). Sustainable smart manufacturing through digital Servitization: A systematic literature review using use cases. *International Journal of Computer Integrated Manufacturing*, •••, 1–38. DOI: 10.1080/0951192X.2026.2622987

Khojasteh, Y., Mousavi Jahan Abadi, S. M., & Ng, C. (2026). Leveraging digital transformation in supply chains: Strategies for agility, performance, and resilience. In *Digital Transformation of Supply Chains: Business Objectives and Applications* (pp. 3–39). Springer Nature Switzerland. DOI: 10.1007/978-3-032-01206-7_1

Kumar, D., Addula, S. R., Lind, M., Brown, S., & Odion, S. (2026). AI-Driven Hybrid Deep Learning and Swarm Intelligence for Predictive Maintenance of Smart Manufacturing Robots in Industry 4.0. *Electronics (Basel)*, *15*(3), 715. DOI: 10.3390/electronics15030715

Lan, X., Hu, Z., Pei, X., & Wen, C. (2026). Does Digital Infrastructure Promote the Upgrading of Manufacturing Enterprises? Evidence From China. *Growth and Change*, *57*(1), e70101. DOI: 10.1111/grow.70101

Li, J., Song, H., & Ma, Y. (2026). The mechanism and impact of digital transformation on supply chain resilience in the manufacturing industry. *Scientific Reports*, *16*(1), 7635. DOI: 10.1038/s41598-026-38930-9 PMID: 41652069

Lin, Y. C., & Dang, J. F. (2026). From product specifications to smart manufacturing: Generative AI-driven process innovation for BOM digitization and its applications. *Advanced Engineering Informatics*, *71*, 104451. DOI: 10.1016/j.aei.2026.104451

Meng, T., & Song, S. (2026). Environmental regulation, greenization pressure and enterprise digital transformation: The role of government subsidy policies in China. *Post-Communist Economies*, •••, 1–28. DOI: 10.1080/14631377.2026.2634634

Movahed, A. B., Aliahmadi, A., Parsanejad, M., & Nozari, H. (2023). A systematic review of collaboration in supply chain 4.0 with meta-synthesis method. *Supply Chain Analytics*, *4*, 100052. DOI: 10.1016/j.sca.2023.100052

Nozari, H. (Ed.). (2023). *Building smart and sustainable businesses with transformative technologies*. IGI Global. DOI: 10.4018/979-8-3693-0210-1

Nozari, H. (2025). Integrating Neuromorphic Intelligence with Fuzzy Multi-Objective Models in Resilient Green Supply Chain Design. Process Integration and Optimization for Sustainability, 1-14.

Nozari, H. (2026). Digital twin-based predictive maintenance in cold chain logistics. *Operations Research*, *60*(1), 481–499. DOI: 10.1051/ro/2025167

Nozari, H., & Szmelter-Jarosz, A. (2025). A Predictive Maintenance Approach for Composting Plants Based on ERP and Digital Twin Integration. *Machines (Basel)*, *13*(12), 1123. DOI: 10.3390/machines13121123

Nozari, H., Szmelter-Jarosz, A., & Weiland, D. (2025). A Fuzzy Multi-Objective Sustainable and Agile Supply Chain Model Based on Digital Twin and Internet of Things with Adaptive Learning Under Environmental Uncertainty. *Applied Sciences (Basel, Switzerland)*, *15*(19), 10399. DOI: 10.3390/app151910399

Nozari, H., & Yordanova, Z. (2025). A fuzzy–digital twin optimization framework for simultaneous management of waste and energy consumption in sustainable manufacturing. An International Journal of Optimization and Control: Theories & Applications, 25360152.

Nozari, H., & Yordanova, Z. (2025). An intelligent digital twin approach for optimizing multi-channel supply chains in uncertain environments. Green Technologies and Sustainability, 100309.

Nozari, H., & Yordanova, Z. (2026). An Adaptive Fuzzy Multi-Objective Digital Twin Framework for Multi-Depot Cold-Chain Vehicle Routing in Agri-Biotech Supply Networks. *Logistics (Basel)*, *10*(2), 27. DOI: 10.3390/logistics10020027

Padhamnath, P. (2026). AIoT-Driven Robotics System in Smart Manufacturing Sectors. In *AIoT-Driven Sustainable Manufacturing and Operational Initiatives* (pp. 174–193). CRC Press. DOI: 10.1201/9781003503323-10

Pan, Y., Huang, Z., Lev, B., Xu, L., & Olson, D. (2026). A literature review on the artificial intelligence in manufacturing systems under industry 5.0. *International Journal of Production Research*, •••, 1–42. DOI: 10.1080/00207543.2026.2623537

Singamsetty, S., Singamsetty, S., Satyanarayana, S., & Kumar, P. R. (2026, February). Next-Generation Digital Twin Analytics in Smart Manufacturing using Cross-Layered Edge Cloud Deep Learning. In 2026 IEEE 5th International Conference on AI in Cybersecurity (ICAIC) (pp. 1-6). IEEE. DOI: 10.1109/ICAIC67076.2026.11395731

Sivarethinamohan, R., Elamurugan, B., & Aranganathan, P. (2026). Benefits and Challenges of Industrial Robotics in Smart Manufacturing. In Industrial Robotics in Smart Manufacturing (pp. 119-136). CRC Press.

Xu, Z., Shan, X., Pan, R., Wu, W., & Liu, N. (2026). Nonlinear relationship between innovation input and intelligent manufacturing from an absorptive capacity perspective. *Scientific Reports*, *16*(1), 7269. DOI: 10.1038/s41598-026-37926-9 PMID: 41639162

Yang, M., Pu, Z., Tavera, C., & Liu, G. (2026). Digital transformation and corporate financialization: Evidence against the tech bubble hypothesis. *Financial Innovation*, *12*(1), 7. DOI: 10.1186/s40854-025-00800-0

Yordanova, Z., & Nozari, H. (2026). An Agentic Digital Twin Framework for Fuzzy Multi-Objective Optimization in Dynamic Humanitarian Logistics. *Algorithms*, *19*(3), 198. DOI: 10.3390/a19030198

Zhang, C., & Xu, Y. (2026). How Does Digital Intelligence Empower Green Transformation in Manufacturing Companies? A Case Study Based on FAW-Volkswagen. *Sustainability (Basel)*, *18*(2), 1045. DOI: 10.3390/su18021045

Zhang, H. (2026). Research on enterprise digital strategy in the context of intelligent manufacturing: The application and impact of AIGC. *Technology Analysis and Strategic Management*, •••, 1–15. DOI: 10.1080/09537325.2026.2620060

Chapter 7

An-Integrated Digital Twin Framework for Intelligent Asset Management

Hamed Nozari
http://orcid.org/0000-0002-6500-6708
University of National and World Economy, Bulgaria

Zornitsa Yordanova
http://orcid.org/0000-0002-6056-8445
University of National and World Economy, Bulgaria

ABSTRACT

The increasing complexity of industrial systems and the rapid spread of digital technologies have revolutionized the way organizations manage physical assets. Digital Twin technology has emerged as an effective tool for connecting physical systems to digital models, enabling real-time monitoring, predictive analytics, and intelligent decision-making. In this chapter, an integrated Digital Twin-based framework for intelligent asset management is presented, which enables the interaction between physical assets, operational data, analytical models, and decision-support systems. The applications of this technology in optimizing asset performance and moving toward cognitive management are also examined.

DOI: 10.4018/979-8-3373-9998-0.ch007

1. INTRODUCTION

The vast developments in digital technologies over the past decades have fundamentally changed the way organizations manage and operate physical assets. In the past, physical assets such as industrial equipment, manufacturing machinery, energy infrastructure, and logistics systems were mainly considered as operational components whose role was limited to performing specific tasks in production or service processes. The management of these assets was also often based on traditional maintenance and repair methods, scheduled service schedules, and expert-based decision-making. However, the increasing complexity of industrial systems, the growth of operational data, and the need to increase the productivity and reliability of assets have made traditional approaches no longer meet the needs of modern organizations (Wang, 2026).

In such circumstances, organizations have moved towards using advanced technologies to improve their asset management. The emergence of technologies such as the Internet of Things, big data analytics, cloud computing, and artificial intelligence has made it possible to collect, process, and analyze a huge amount of data generated by industrial equipment and systems. This data can provide valuable information about the performance status of assets, equipment failure patterns, and system operating conditions. Proper use of this information can play an important role in improving management decisions, increasing system reliability, and reducing operating costs (Aklashie et al., 2026).

Among the emerging technologies, the concept of Digital Twin has emerged as one of the most important tools for transforming physical asset management. Digital Twin can be defined as a dynamic digital representation of a physical asset that is continuously updated with real-world data from the system. This digital representation is usually a combination of sensor data, simulation models, analytical algorithms, and decision support systems that allow organizations to monitor the condition of assets in real time and predict their future behavior. Such a capability allows the Digital Twin to be used not only as a monitoring tool, but also as an analytical platform for improving asset performance (Nozari & Yordanova, 2026).

The importance of the Digital Twin in asset management becomes more apparent when organizations are faced with challenges such as sudden equipment stops, reduced system productivity, and increased maintenance costs. In many industries, unexpected equipment failures can have significant economic consequences and even disrupt supply chains and production processes. Using the Digital Twin allows organizations to analyze operational data and simulate system behavior, identify potential failures before they occur, and take appropriate preventive measures. For this reason, many industrial and high-tech companies have made significant investments in the development and implementation of Digital Twin systems (Cong et al., 2026).

On the other hand, the transformation in asset management is not limited to monitoring the condition of equipment. In today's complex industrial environments, organizations need systems that can play an active role in the decision-making process in addition to data analysis. In other words, the ultimate goal is to move from monitoring systems to intelligent and cognitive systems that are able to analyze operational data and provide optimal suggestions for asset management. In such an approach, Digital Twin can act as the central core of an intelligent asset management system that connects physical data and analytical models.

In this context, the concept of Intelligent Asset Management has been proposed as one of the new approaches in organizational asset management. This approach focuses on the use of digital technologies to improve decision-making related to the performance, maintenance, and operation of assets. Combining Digital Twin with data analytics and AI algorithms can enable organizations to continuously monitor the performance of their assets, identify system performance patterns, and adopt optimal strategies for equipment utilization.

Given the increasing importance of Digital Twin in asset management, the development of frameworks that can integrate this technology into organizational processes is of particular importance. Such frameworks must be able to manage the interaction between physical assets, operational data, analytical models, and decision support systems in a way that organizations can benefit from the full potential of Digital Twin to improve the performance of their assets. In this regard, this chapter examines an integrated Digital Twin-based framework for intelligent asset management and attempts to show how this technology can play an important role in the transformation of physical asset management in modern organizations.

2. EVOLUTION OF ASSET MANAGEMENT IN THE DIGITAL ERA

Asset management has always been a fundamental pillar in the performance of industrial and infrastructure organizations. In many industries, from manufacturing and energy to transportation and urban infrastructure, a significant portion of an organization's capital is embodied in physical assets such as machinery, equipment, production lines, and operational systems. For this reason, the way these assets are managed has a direct impact on the productivity, reliability, and economic performance of organizations. However, asset management approaches have evolved over time, and this evolution has accelerated, especially in the digital age (Daneshvar et al., 2026).

In the early stages of industrial development, asset management was largely based on reactive approaches. In this approach, often known as post-failure maintenance, equipment was repaired or replaced only when it failed. Although this approach was applicable in simple systems, it was associated with significant risks in complex industrial environments. Sudden equipment stoppages could lead to disruptions in production processes, increased operating costs, and reduced product quality. For this reason, organizations gradually moved towards preventive approaches to asset management.

In the next step, the concept of preventive maintenance was introduced. In this approach, maintenance activities were carried out based on scheduled schedules to prevent sudden failures. Although this method was more efficient than the reactive approach, it still had limitations. In many cases, equipment could require repair ahead of schedule or, conversely, parts that still had a significant useful life were replaced. This caused maintenance schedules to be suboptimal and unnecessary costs to the organization (Bhatia & Kumar, 2026).

With the advancement of information technologies and the increasing availability of operational data, the concept of condition-based maintenance was introduced as a new stage in the evolution of asset management. In this approach, maintenance decisions are made based on real data related to the condition of the equipment. The use of sensors and monitoring systems made it possible to collect data such as temperature, vibration, pressure, and other performance indicators. Analysis of this data could reveal early signs of equipment failure and help organizations take appropriate corrective actions before the problem occurs.

The next step in this direction was the development of the predictive maintenance approach. In this approach, operational data is analyzed using analytical models and machine learning algorithms to predict the future behavior of equipment. Predictive maintenance allows organizations to not only monitor the current condition of assets, but also estimate the likely time of equipment failure. Such a capability can significantly reduce maintenance costs and increase system reliability (Scolamiero & Boccardo, 2026).

With the emergence of digital technologies in recent decades, asset management has entered a new phase that can be called smart asset management. At this stage, technologies such as the Internet of Things, cloud computing, big data analytics, and artificial intelligence play an important role in asset management. Connecting industrial equipment to digital networks enables continuous collection of operational data, enabling organizations to monitor the performance of their assets in real time. In addition, advanced analytics systems can identify complex performance patterns and provide valuable information for management decisions.

One of the most important concepts at this stage is the use of digital models of physical assets. These models, which are usually implemented in the form of a Digital Twin, allow the representation of the actual behavior of equipment in a digital environment. Using such models, organizations can simulate different operational scenarios and evaluate the impact of different decisions on asset performance. This capability is especially important in complex industrial systems where management decisions can have far-reaching consequences (Sompolgrunk et al., 2026).

The transformation of asset management in the digital age is not limited to improving maintenance methods, but has also led to a change in the nature of management decisions. In the past, many decisions related to the operation of assets were made based on the experience of managers or limited data analysis. While in modern systems, decisions are increasingly made based on extensive data analysis and intelligent models. This change in approach has caused asset management to transform from an operational activity to a knowledge-based and data-driven process.

Finally, the evolution of asset management shows that organizations are moving towards creating systems that can seamlessly combine operational data, analytical models and decision-making tools. Such systems are not only able to monitor the condition of assets, but can also help optimize the performance of equipment throughout their life cycle. Meanwhile, Digital Twin technology has emerged as one of the most important tools for realizing intelligent asset management and is expected to play a more central role in the transformation of industrial systems in the coming years.

3. DIGITAL TWIN TECHNOLOGY FOR ASSET MANAGEMENT

The advancement of digital technologies in recent years has led to the emergence of concepts that can reduce the gap between physical systems and digital analytical environments. One of the most important of these concepts is the Digital Twin technology, which is recognized as one of the key tools in the transformation of physical asset management. The Digital Twin can be broadly defined as a dynamic digital representation of a physical asset that recreates the behavior of the system in a virtual environment using real-world data, analytical models, and simulation tools. This digital representation is usually continuously updated with operational data and can provide an accurate picture of the current and future state of the assets (Nozari & Yordanova, 2025).

The initial roots of the Digital Twin concept go back to the fields of systems engineering and industrial simulation, but with the expansion of the Internet of Things and the increase in the processing power of computing systems, this concept has gradually become one of the main pillars of digital transformation in various industries. In many advanced industries, the Digital Twin acts as a bridge between the physical and digital worlds, enabling more accurate analysis of asset performance. Such a capability helps organizations move their management processes from traditional experience-based approaches to data-driven decision-making (Barykin et al., 2026).

One of the key features of the Digital Twin in asset management is its ability to integrate operational data and analytical models. In a Digital Twin-based system, data generated by sensors and industrial equipment is continuously collected and transferred to the digital model of the asset. This data can include information about the operating conditions of the equipment, system performance indicators, and environmental parameters. Combining this data with analytical models and intelligent algorithms allows for the analysis of system behavior and the prediction of the future state of the asset.

From an asset management perspective, the Digital Twin can play several important roles. First, this technology enables real-time monitoring of equipment status. Using the digital asset model, managers and engineers can view the operational status of systems at any time and be aware of potential problems. Second, the Digital Twin enables the simulation of various operational scenarios. This capability helps organizations to examine their effects in the digital environment before implementing decisions in the real world. Third, the Digital Twin can play an important role in predicting equipment failures and planning maintenance, thereby reducing operational costs (Nozari, 2023).

To better understand the structure of Digital Twin technology in asset management, it is necessary to examine the main components of this system. A Digital Twin usually consists of several different layers, each of which has a specific task in the data management and system analysis process. At the lowest level, there is the physical asset that generates operational data. At the next layer, sensors and data acquisition systems record information related to the system's performance. This data is then transferred to the digital modeling layer, where analytical and simulation models are used to represent the system behavior. Finally, there is the analysis and decision-making layer, which transforms the processed data into usable information for managers and engineers (Edirisinghe et al., 2026).

To illustrate the overall structure of this technology in asset management, Figure 1 shows the conceptual framework of a Digital Twin system for physical assets. This figure shows the interaction between the physical asset, the data collection layer, the digital model, and the analysis and decision-making systems.

Figure 1. Conceptual Architecture of a Digital Twin System for Intelligent Asset Management

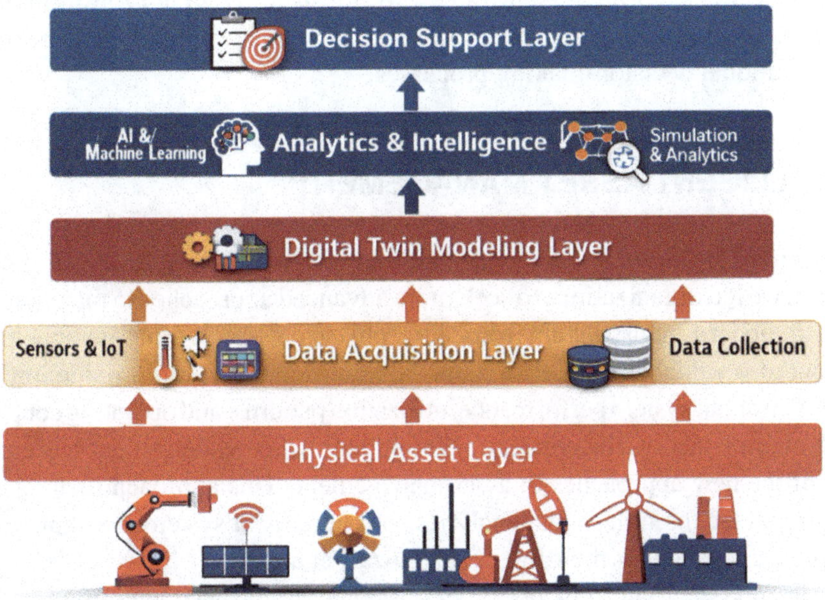

After observing this architecture, it can be seen that the Digital Twin is not just a simple simulation model, but a multi-layered system that connects real data, analytical models, and decision-making tools. In this architecture, the physical asset acts as the main data source, and the information generated by it is transmitted to the digital environment through sensors and communication infrastructure. In the modeling layer, the collected data is processed using analytical models and advanced algorithms to reconstruct the behavior of the system in the digital environment. This process allows the digital model to provide an accurate picture of the real state of the asset.

One of the important advantages of such an architecture is the possibility of two-way interaction between the physical and digital worlds. In an advanced Digital Twin system, the data flow is not limited to only from the physical system to the digital model, but the results of the analysis can also be fed back to the physical system and used in the decision-making process. This two-way interaction can help improve equipment performance, reduce system downtime, and increase asset productivity.

Overall, Digital Twin technology has provided a suitable platform for the transformation of physical asset management. By combining operational data, analytical models and decision-support tools, this technology enables more accurate monitoring of the condition of assets and optimization of their performance. For this reason, many organizations are moving towards implementing Digital Twin systems to benefit from the capabilities of this technology to improve their asset management. In the following sections, an integrated framework for using Digital Twin in intelligent asset management will be presented, showing how this technology can be applied in organizational decision-making processes.

4. INTELLIGENT ASSET MANAGEMENT

The spread of digital technologies and the increasing complexity of industrial systems have led organizations to seek more advanced approaches to managing their assets. In modern industrial environments, physical assets are not just operational tools, but also valuable sources of data and knowledge that can provide important information about system performance, utilization patterns, and operating conditions. In such circumstances, the concept of Intelligent Asset Management has emerged as one of the new approaches to asset management. This approach focuses on the use of digital technologies, data analytics, and intelligent systems to improve asset performance throughout their life cycle (Nozari et al., 2023).

Intelligent Asset Management can be considered an advanced stage in the evolution of organizational asset management, in which decisions are increasingly based on real-time data and advanced analytics. In this approach, data generated by industrial equipment is collected through sensors and monitoring systems and analyzed using analytical tools. Analyzing this data can reveal equipment performance patterns and provide valuable information for maintenance planning, operation optimization, and risk management. In this way, asset management is transformed from a limited operational activity into an analytical and knowledge-based process.

One of the main goals of intelligent asset management is to increase the reliability and productivity of systems. In many industries, equipment failure can have significant economic consequences and even cause complete shutdown of production processes. Using advanced analytical methods, organizations can continuously monitor the health of equipment and identify early signs of failure. This capability helps managers take appropriate preventive measures before serious problems occur and prevent sudden system shutdowns (Wu et al., 2026).

In addition to increasing system reliability, intelligent asset management plays an important role in optimizing equipment performance. In many industrial systems, the way equipment is operated can have a significant impact on energy consumption, process efficiency, and product quality. Analysis of operational data can show how changes in operating parameters affect system performance. This information can be used to adjust equipment operating conditions and improve their performance. As a result, organizations will be able to use their assets more efficiently.

Another important feature of intelligent asset management is the use of predictive models and machine learning algorithms to analyze system behavior. These models can identify equipment performance patterns and predict their future behavior by analyzing historical and operational data. For example, predictive models can estimate the probability of equipment failure in the near future and determine the appropriate time to perform repairs. Such a capability can significantly reduce maintenance costs and increase system productivity (Nozari & Yordanova, 2026).

In recent years, the combination of intelligent asset management with emerging technologies such as the Digital Twin has led to the formation of a new generation of management systems. In these systems, digital asset models are integrated with real system data, allowing for more accurate analysis of equipment performance. The Digital Twin can serve as the analytical core of intelligent asset management, combining operational data, simulation models, and decision-making algorithms into a single platform.

This integration between physical assets and digital models allows organizations to control their management processes more accurately. For example, managers can use the digital model of equipment to simulate different operating scenarios and evaluate the impact of different decisions on system performance. Such a capability helps organizations to examine the consequences of changes in the digital environment before implementing them in the real environment.

From a strategic perspective, intelligent asset management can play an important role in the transformation of organizations towards intelligent and data-driven systems. In such organizations, data generated by assets is considered as one of the main sources of decision-making, and the analysis of this data can provide valuable insights to improve the performance of the organization. This approach can also help to create closer communication between operational, engineering and management units and make decision-making processes more efficient (Reuther et al., 2026).

Finally, the move towards intelligent asset management represents a change in the nature of industrial systems management. In this approach, physical assets are considered not only as operational components of the system, but also as sources of data and knowledge that can play an important role in improving the performance of the organization. The use of digital technologies, analytical models, and decision support systems can enable organizations to elevate their asset management to a higher level of efficiency and productivity, paving the way for the development of intelligent industrial systems.

5. INTEGRATED DIGITAL TWIN FRAMEWORK FOR INTELLIGENT ASSET MANAGEMENT

With the expansion of digital technologies and the increase in the volume of data generated in industrial systems, organizations are increasingly in need of frameworks that can manage information related to physical assets in an integrated manner. Although Digital Twin technology is known as a powerful tool for digital representation of assets, effective utilization of this technology requires a coherent structure that can connect operational data, analytical models and organizational decision-making processes. In this regard, the development of an integrated Digital Twin framework for intelligent asset management can play an important role in improving the performance of industrial systems.

In many organizations, asset data is stored in various systems such as industrial control systems, operational databases and maintenance management systems. This data fragmentation can create a serious obstacle to comprehensive analysis of asset performance. Integrated Digital Twin frameworks are designed to create connections between these data sources and transform them into usable knowledge. Such a framework not only enables monitoring of equipment condition, but can also help analyze system behavior, predict failures, and optimize asset performance.

In an integrated Digital Twin framework, the interaction between the physical and digital worlds is continuous. Physical assets generate operational data through sensors and communication systems, and this data is transmitted to the digital environment. In the digital environment, analytical models and intelligent algorithms process this data and provide information about the current and future state of the system. This information can be used as a basis for management decisions.

In addition to monitoring and analyzing data, Digital Twin frameworks also allow for the simulation of various management scenarios. For example, managers can examine the effect of changes in equipment operating conditions or the implementation of various maintenance programs in the digital environment. This capability helps organizations assess the consequences of decisions before they are implemented in the real world. As a result, operational risks are reduced and the quality of decisions is increased.

To illustrate the overall structure of this framework, Figure 2 shows the architecture of an integrated Digital Twin framework for intelligent asset management. The figure shows the interaction between various system components, including physical assets, data infrastructure, analytical models, and decision-making systems, in a networked structure.

Figure 2. Integrated Digital Twin Framework for Intelligent Asset Management

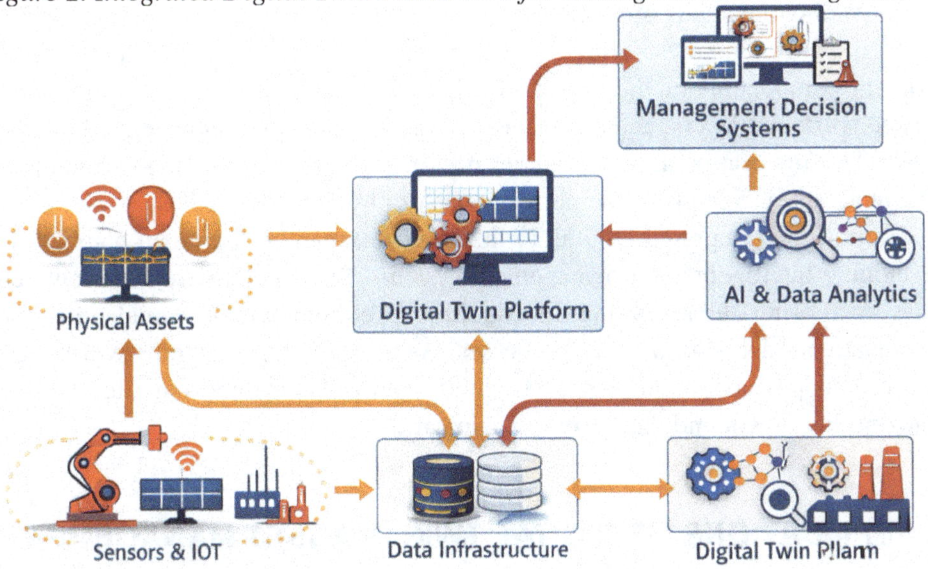

As can be seen in the figure, the proposed framework consists of several key components, each of which plays a specific role in the asset management process. At the lowest level, there are physical assets, which include industrial equipment, production machinery, and other operational infrastructure. These assets record their operational data through sensors and IoT systems and transmit it to the data infrastructure. The data collected at this stage can include information about operating conditions, performance indicators, and equipment health status.

In the next stage, the collected data is transmitted to the Digital Twin platform. This platform is responsible for creating and maintaining a digital model of the assets and combines real system data with analytical and simulation models. The result of this process is the creation of a digital representation of the assets that can reconstruct the behavior of the system under different operational conditions.

At the higher layer, there are data analysis and artificial intelligence modules that are responsible for analyzing the information generated by the Digital Twin. These modules can identify equipment performance patterns and provide predictions about the future behavior of the system. For example, machine learning algorithms can estimate the probability of equipment failure or determine the optimal conditions for asset utilization.

Finally, the output of these analyses is transmitted to management decision support systems. These systems provide managers with the analyzed information in the form of management dashboards, operational alerts, or decision-making suggestions.

Such a capability helps managers make more accurate and faster decisions by better understanding the status of assets.

An important feature of the proposed framework is the integration between the different components of the system. In this framework, data flows continuously between different layers, and each layer can use the information generated in other layers. This integration allows analytics performed in the digital environment to be effectively used to improve the performance of physical assets.

Overall, the integrated Digital Twin framework can be used as a platform for developing intelligent asset management systems. Such a framework not only enables monitoring and analyzing the condition of equipment, but can also improve organizational decision-making processes. As a result, organizations will be able to use their physical assets more efficiently and take an important step towards realizing intelligent and data-driven organizations.

6. APPLICATIONS OF DIGITAL TWIN IN ASSET MANAGEMENT

The development of Digital Twin technology in recent years has made this concept one of the key tools in physical asset management in various industries. Using Digital Twin, organizations are able to create a digital profile of their equipment and operational systems and thereby analyze asset performance more accurately. Such a capability provides a deeper understanding of system behavior and helps managers make more effective decisions in the field of asset operation, maintenance, and optimization. As a result, Digital Twin is gradually recognized as one of the key technologies in the evolution of industrial asset management (Nozari & Yordanova, 2026).

One of the most important applications of Digital Twin in asset management is predictive maintenance and repair. In many industries, sudden equipment failure can cause production processes to stop and impose significant costs on the organization. Using Digital Twin, equipment operational data is continuously collected and analyzed, and analytical models can identify system performance patterns. This information allows for the prediction of equipment failures before they occur. In this way, organizations can plan maintenance activities at the right time and prevent unexpected system shutdowns. Such an approach not only reduces maintenance costs, but also increases equipment reliability (Patel et al., 2026).

Another important application of Digital Twin in asset management is equipment health monitoring. In complex industrial systems, the health status of equipment can be affected by various factors such as operating conditions, system workload, and environmental factors. By combining sensor data and analytical models, Digital Twin enables continuous monitoring of equipment health status. In this framework, various performance indicators are continuously analyzed and any deviations from the normal conditions of the system are identified. This capability can help managers identify potential system problems at an early stage and take the necessary corrective actions.

Digital Twin also plays an important role in optimizing asset performance. In many industries, the way equipment is operated can have a significant impact on process efficiency and resource consumption. Using a digital asset model, organizations can simulate different operating scenarios and examine the effects of changes in operating parameters. These simulations can help identify optimal operating conditions for equipment. For example, in manufacturing systems, a Digital Twin can be used to determine the best operating conditions for machinery to increase process efficiency and reduce energy consumption (Nozari & Yordanova, 2026).

Another important application of the Digital Twin is asset lifecycle management. Industrial assets typically have long lifecycles, and their effective management requires careful planning throughout the various stages of the equipment's life. The Digital Twin can record information about asset performance over time and create a comprehensive database of equipment performance history. This information can be used in decisions related to major repairs, equipment upgrades, or asset replacement. As a result, organizations will be able to adopt more effective strategies for managing the lifecycle of their assets.

Digital Twin can also play an important role in risk management and increasing the resilience of industrial systems. In complex industrial environments, the occurrence of operational disruptions can have far-reaching consequences. Using digital asset models, organizations can simulate various disruption scenarios in the digital environment and examine their effects on system performance. Such a capability helps managers design appropriate strategies to deal with critical situations and prevent widespread damage.

Digital Twin applications in asset management are not limited to manufacturing industries, but have also been used in areas such as energy, transportation, urban infrastructure, and process industries. For example, in the energy industry, Digital Twin is used to monitor the performance of power plants and optimize equipment utilization. In transportation systems, digital models can be used to analyze infrastructure performance and improve maintenance planning. In process industries, Digital Twin can also help analyze the behavior of complex systems and optimize production processes (Dui et al., 2026).

Overall, the applications of Digital Twin in asset management show that this technology can play an important role in the transformation of industrial systems. The use of Digital Twin allows for more accurate monitoring of asset status, prediction of future system behavior, and optimization of management decisions. For this reason, many organizations are moving towards the development and implementation of Digital Twin-based systems in order to benefit from the capabilities of this technology to improve the performance of their assets.

7. TOWARD COGNITIVE ASSET MANAGEMENT: FROM DIGITAL TWINS TO AUTONOMOUS DECISION SYSTEMS

With the rapid development of digital technologies, the concept of Digital Twin has gradually gone beyond a tool for system simulation and monitoring and has become a platform for intelligent decision-making in organizations. In the early generations of Digital Twin, the main focus was on creating a digital representation of physical assets and analyzing operational data. These digital models could display the status of equipment in real time and enable simulation of system behavior under different operating conditions. However, recent advances in areas such as artificial intelligence, machine learning, and advanced data analytics have led Digital Twin to move towards systems that are able to not only analyze the status of systems, but also play an active role in the decision-making process (Nozari, 2026).

In this path of evolution, the concept of Cognitive Asset Management has been proposed as an advanced stage in the evolution of asset management. In cognitive asset management, digital systems do not only act as monitoring tools, but also generate new knowledge by analyzing operational data and learning from system performance patterns (Zhang et al., 2026). This knowledge can be used to predict future asset behavior, identify optimization opportunities, and provide management recommendations. In such an approach, the Digital Twin acts as the central core of a cognitive system that analyzes asset-related information and transforms it into actionable insights for decision-making.

One of the important features of cognitive asset management is continuous learning from operational data. In modern industrial systems, equipment continuously generates data about its performance. This data can include information about operating conditions, system workload, energy consumption, and other performance indicators. Machine learning algorithms can analyze this data and identify hidden patterns in system behavior. Over time, these algorithms will be able to create more accurate models of asset behavior and provide more reliable predictions.

The next step in this direction is the move towards automated decision-making systems. In many organizations, data analysis is still performed by digital systems, but the final decision-making remains the responsibility of human managers. However, recent advances in the field of artificial intelligence have made it possible for some operational decisions to be made automatically by intelligent systems. For example, an advanced Digital Twin can analyze equipment operating data to determine the optimal operating conditions of the system and provide suggestions for adjusting operating parameters.

In such a system, the interaction between the physical and digital worlds takes the form of an intelligent feedback loop. Data generated by physical assets is transmitted to the digital environment and analyzed there. The results of these analyses can be fed back to operational systems in the form of management recommendations or even control commands. This process enables industrial systems to respond adaptively to environmental changes and continuously improve their performance.

Realizing cognitive asset management requires an infrastructure that can manage industrial data, analytical models, and decision support systems in an integrated manner. In this framework, the Digital Twin acts as a central platform that combines sensor data, simulation models, and artificial intelligence algorithms in a common environment. This platform can act as an interface layer between operational systems and organizational decision-making systems, providing the information needed to manage assets.

Ultimately, the move from traditional Digital Twins to Cognitive Digital Twins represents a significant shift in how organizational assets are managed. In this new approach, physical assets are no longer considered merely operational resources, but become active components of an intelligent, self-decision-making ecosystem. Such a system can enable organizations to dynamically manage the performance of their assets and make operational decisions with greater accuracy and speed. As a result, cognitive asset management can play a significant role in shaping a new generation of organizations in which data, artificial intelligence, and digital systems are integrated to improve performance and increase productivity.

8. CONCLUSION

The digital transformation has had a profound impact on the way organizations manage physical assets in recent years. In today's complex and data-driven industrial environments, physical assets are no longer just operational components of systems, but have become important sources of data and knowledge that can play a significant role in improving organizational performance. In such circumstances, the use of technologies that can effectively connect the physical world and digital environments has become a necessity for organizations. Digital Twin technology is one of the most important tools that has been considered in recent years to achieve this goal.

This chapter first examined the evolution of asset management in the digital age and showed how traditional approaches to maintaining and operating equipment have gradually given way to data-driven and analytical methods. In this evolution, the use of operational data and advanced analytics plays a key role in improving management decisions. Using this data, organizations can gain a more accurate understanding of the behavior of their systems and adopt more effective strategies for asset utilization.

Next, Digital Twin technology was introduced as one of the most important tools for the transformation of physical asset management. By creating a dynamic digital representation of physical assets, Digital Twin enables equipment condition monitoring, system performance analysis, and simulation of various operational scenarios. Such a capability helps organizations analyze the behavior of their assets more accurately and make management decisions based on more accurate information. In addition, combining Digital Twin with technologies such as the Internet of Things, big data analytics, and artificial intelligence can create new capacities for asset management.

One of the main focuses of this chapter was to provide an integrated Digital Twin framework for intelligent asset management. In this framework, the interaction between physical assets, data infrastructure, digital models, and analytical systems was considered. This framework shows how data generated by industrial equipment can be transferred to a digital platform and processed there using analytical models. The results of these analyses can be used as a basis for management decisions and help organizations manage the performance of their assets more effectively.

This chapter also examined various applications of Digital Twin in asset management. These applications include predictive maintenance of equipment, system health monitoring, asset performance optimization, and equipment lifecycle management. The results of studies and industrial experiences show that the use of Digital Twin can significantly reduce operating costs and increase system reliability. In addition, Digital Twin can play an important role in improving organizational decision-making processes and help managers make more accurate and data-driven decisions.

In the final sections, the path of Digital Twin evolution from an analytical tool to a cognitive system was examined. Recent advances in artificial intelligence and machine learning have enabled the Digital Twin to move towards systems that are capable of not only analyzing data but also actively participating in the decision-making process. Such systems can learn from operational data and analyze system performance patterns, provide suggestions for improving asset performance, and even make some operational decisions automatically.

Overall, the results of this chapter show that Digital Twin technology can play an important role in the transformation of physical asset management and help organizations move towards intelligent and data-driven systems. Establishing a connection between physical assets and digital models allows for more accurate analysis of system performance and improved decision-making processes. In the future, with the advancement of artificial intelligence technologies and the development of digital infrastructure, Digital Twin is expected to become one of the main components of intelligent organizations and play an important role in the formation of a new generation of organizations, namely Cognitive Enterprises.

REFERENCES

Barykin, S., Shulga, A., Dinets, D., & Mikhaylov, A. (2026). Digital twin-enhanced credit risk prioritization in mortgage portfolios: A hybrid model approach. *Quality & Quantity*, *60*(2), 1–23. DOI: 10.1007/s11135-026-02579-3

Bhatia, M., & Kumar, V. (2026). The role of digital twin in urban infrastructure and building management: A global scientometric perspective. *Cluster Computing*, *29*(1), 38. DOI: 10.1007/s10586-025-05813-z

Cong, W., Tao, W., & Jinsong, B. (2026). Agentic digital twin-embedded maintenance methodology for energy equipment: A self-evolving operational paradigm. *Journal of Manufacturing Systems*, *84*, 100–116. DOI: 10.1016/j.jmsy.2025.11.020

Daneshvar, A., Golroo, A., Moghadas Nejad, F., Karbalaei, A., Hosseini, P., & Rasti, M. (2026). Cognitive Digital Twins for Pavement Management: A Comprehensive Review. *Archives of Computational Methods in Engineering*, *33*(3), 1–20. DOI: 10.1007/s11831-026-10503-z

Dui, H., Wang, H., & Xing, L. (2026). Digital Twin-Enabled Smart Operation and Maintenance Framework With Generative AI Design of Intelligent Manufacturing Systems. *IEEE Transactions on Reliability*, *75*, 504–517. DOI: 10.1109/TR.2025.3646186

Edirisinghe, E., Wu, G., Maggo, D., Cheng, C. T., Pang, T. Y., Rahman, A., Avery, A. L., Murphy, K. R., & Lora, C. A. (2026). A Digital Twin-Enabled Framework for Agrivoltaic System Design, Simulation, Monitoring and Control. *Machines (Basel)*, *14*(3), 254. DOI: 10.3390/machines14030254

Nozari, H. (Ed.). (2023). *Building smart and sustainable businesses with transformative technologies*. IGI Global. DOI: 10.4018/979-8-3693-0210-1

Nozari, H. (2026). Neuromorphic Computing and Cognitive Economics. In Industry 5.0's Impact on Economic Innovation (pp. 17-34). IGI Global Scientific Publishing.

Nozari, H., Ghahremani-Nahr, J., & Najafi, E. (2023). The role of Internet of things and Blockchain in the development of agile and sustainable supply chains. In *Digital supply chain, disruptive environments, and the impact on retailers* (pp. 271–282). IGI Global Scientific Publishing. DOI: 10.4018/978-1-6684-7298-9.ch015

Nozari, H., & Yordanova, Z. (2025). An intelligent digital twin approach for optimizing multi-channel supply chains in uncertain environments. Green Technologies and Sustainability, 100309.

Nozari, H., & Yordanova, Z. (2026). Digital twin–driven decision support for human capital management under uncertainty. Green Technologies and Sustainability, 100353.

Nozari, H., & Yordanova, Z. (2026). An Adaptive Fuzzy Multi-Objective Digital Twin Framework for Multi-Depot Cold-Chain Vehicle Routing in Agri-Biotech Supply Networks. *Logistics (Basel)*, *10*(2), 27. DOI: 10.3390/logistics10020027

Nozari, H., & Yordanova, Z. (2026). Green and Circular Supply Chain Finance Supported by Carbon-Twin Accounting. In Industry 5.0's Impact on Economic Innovation (pp. 99-116). IGI Global Scientific Publishing.

Patel, U. R., Ghaffarianhoseini, A., GhaffarianHoseini, A., & Burgess, A. (2026). Towards a well-being-oriented framework for urban digital twins. *Cities (London, England)*, *169*, 106579. DOI: 10.1016/j.cities.2025.106579

Reuther, A., Plesker, C., Bassauer, D., & Schleich, B. (2026). A Digital Twin Framework for Programmable Logic Controllers in Industrial Automation Systems. *Procedia CIRP*, *139*, 446–452. DOI: 10.1016/j.procir.2025.08.193

Scolamiero, V., & Boccardo, P. (2026). A BIM-Based Digital Twin Framework for Urban Roads: Integrating MMS and Municipal Geospatial Data for AI-Ready Urban Infrastructure Management. *Sensors (Basel)*, *26*(3), 947. DOI: 10.3390/s26030947

Sompolgrunk, A., Golzad, H., Liu, H., Banihashemi, S., & Najafi, M. (2026). The evolution of digital twins within the big BIM data landscape. Smart and Sustainable Built Environment, 1-28.

Wang, R. (2026). A Data-Driven Predictive Maintenance Framework for Smart Buildings: Integrating Digital Twin and Machine Learning in HVAC Systems. Journal of Building Engineering, 115416. Aklashie, S., Agyekum, K., Tchao, E. T., Adinyira, E., & Nani, G. (2026). Blockchain-digital twin integration in construction material passports: preparing for digital product passport implementation. Built Environment Project and Asset Management, 1-18. Nozari, H., & Yordanova, Z. (2026). Digital twin–driven decision support for human capital management under uncertainty. Green Technologies and Sustainability, 100353.

Wu, X., Yu, T., Liu, X., Yue, C., Jiang, X., Li, J., & Li, Z. (2026). Design of laser-assisted processing digital twin system. *Journal of Manufacturing Systems*, *85*, 155–174. DOI: 10.1016/j.jmsy.2026.01.001

Zhang, J., Sun, J., Zhao, H., Huang, F., Xu, B., & Wang, Q. (2026). Toward Smart and Green Energy Stations: A Cognitive Digital Twin Framework for Intelligent Management. *IEEE Internet Computing*, 1–10. DOI: 10.1109/MIC.2025.3649567

Chapter 8
An Integrated Cognitive Enterprise Framework Using Digital Twins, AI, IoT, and Predictive Analytics

S. Harish Alwar
http://orcid.org/0009-0002-0554-3760
Dr. G.U. Pope College of Engineering, India

T. Ganesan
http://orcid.org/0009-0006-9941-1935
Dr. G.U. Pope College of Engineering, India

K. Anish
http://orcid.org/0009-0004-8833-1804
Dr. G.U. Pope College of Engineering, India

I. Manickam
http://orcid.org/0009-0005-3635-7938
Dr. G.U. Pope College of Engineering, India

K. DanielRaj
http://orcid.org/0009-0001-9863-5682
Kalaignarkarunanidhi Institute of Technology, India

DOI: 10.4018/979-8-3373-9998-0.ch008

ABSTRACT

Artificial Intelligence (AI), Internet of Things (IoT), Digital Twins, and Predictive Analytics are transforming modern organizations into intelligent and adaptive systems. However, most existing studies examine these technologies individually, limiting understanding of their combined impact. This chapter addresses this gap by proposing an Integrated Cognitive Enterprise Framework that unifies data acquisition, intelligent processing, virtual simulation, and predictive decision-making. The framework enables real-time responsiveness, continuous learning, and proactive optimization through a closed-loop feedback mechanism. The study also explores applications across industries such as manufacturing, healthcare, smart cities, and supply chains. Key challenges including data security, integration complexity, and skill gaps are discussed. The findings highlight that true organizational intelligence emerges from the integration of technologies, offering both theoretical and practical insights for adaptive digital transformation.

1. INTRODUCTION

With the rapid evolution of digital technology, modern organizations are being transformed from traditional operational systems into intelligent and adaptive organizations. Technologies like Artificial Intelligence (AI), Internet of Things (IoT), Digital Twins, and Predictive Analytics are helping organizations improve decision-making and operational efficiency and respond to environmental changes(Porter & Heppelmann, 2014; Kagermann et al., 2013; Lu et al., 2020).

Although existing research has examined these technologies individually, the understanding of how these technologies can be integrated into a unified system to facilitate the development of cognitive organizations remains low. Most of the existing research has focused on the isolated technological capabilities rather than developing a systematic approach to the integrated implementation of these technologies(Tao et al., 2018; Atzori et al., 2010; Russell & Norvig, 2021; Provost & Fawcett, 2013).

This chapter aims to bridge the existing gap by proposing an integrated Cognitive Enterprise Framework consisting of the integrated implementation of the Internet of Things (IoT), Artificial Intelligence (AI), Digital Twins, and Predictive Analytics.

2. DIGITAL TWINS: CONCEPT AND ARCHITECTURE

The digital twin technology has become one of the cornerstones of the new intelligent systems allowing organizations to establish a smooth linkage between offline and online entities(Tao et al., 2018; Grieves & Vickers, 2017). A Digital Twin is a kind of a dynamic, virtual, aesthetically clear image of a real object, process, or system which is constantly modified with the help of real-time information(Rosen et al., 2015; Xu et al., 2021). The technology enables organizations to track, model and optimize the actions in a very effective risk-free virtual context(Kritzinger et al., 2018; Lu et al., 2020).

The Digital Twin concept is fundamentally based upon the desire to reflect real-world systems in the virtual reality(Grieves & Vickers, 2017; Tao et al., 2018). In comparison to the static models, Digital Twins are constantly updated with sensor and other interconnected devices data, thus the virtual model is always related to the current state of the existing physical object(Atzori et al., 2010; Gubbi et al., 2013). This real-time synchronization helps organizations to have in-depth understanding of system behavior, anticipate any possible problems and make sound decisions(Lee et al., 2015; Zhou et al., 2015).

2.1 Definition and Main Components

Digital Twin is made up of a number of important elements that interact to form an overall and smart system (Tao et al., 2018; Kritzinger et al., 2018; Fuller et al., 2020). The first is the physical entity, and this entity may be any actual object of the world, e.g. machine, vehicle, building, and even entire process in industry (Rosen et al., 2015; Grieves & Vickers, 2017). This physical object is fitted with sensors to determine and measure different parameters like the temperature, pressure, speed and performance measurements (Atzori et al., 2010; Gubbi et al., 2013).

The second element is the virtual model, which is an electronic model of the physical being (Tao et al., 2018; Xu et al., 2021). This model is developed based on the simulation tools, mathematical models, and history to recreate the behavior and features of the physical system (Fuller et al., 2020; Rosen et al., 2015). The truthfulness of the Digital Twin is determined by the ability of this virtual model to be a true reflection of the reality (Grieves & Vickers, 2017).

The third layer is the data integration layer that links the physical and digital world (Atzori et al., 2010; Xu et al., 2014). This layer is based on IoT technologies, communication networks, and cloud platforms that can relay intelligence about the real-time transmission of the physical entity to the virtual model (Gubbi et al., 2013; Zanella et al., 2014). It provides a flawless data flow and synchronization across the two environment (Shi et al., 2016; Satyanarayanan, 2017).

The fourth is the analytics and intelligence layer, processing the gathered information based on Artificial Intelligence and the use of advanced analytics methods (Russell & Norvig, 2021; Goodfellow et al., 2016; Provost & Fawcett, 2013). This layer facilitates the Digital Twin to create insights, anomalies, predict failures, and optimization of performance (Lu et al., 2020; Lee et al., 2015). All these discrete elements form a closed-loop system in which the insights of the digital model could be utilized in the improvement of real-life operations (Zhou et al., 2015; Xu et al., 2021).

Figure 1. Digital Twin Architecture

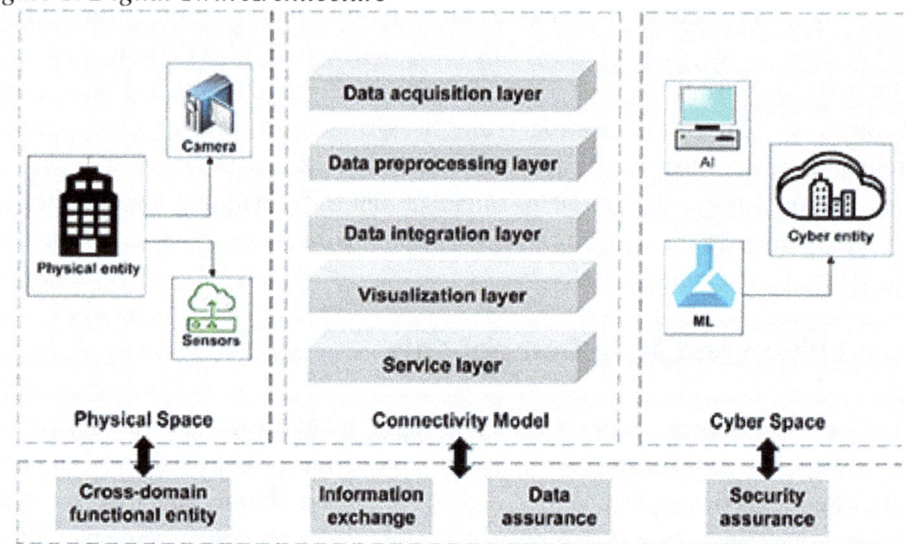

2.2 Types of Digital Twins

There are various types of Digital Twins regarding their scope and usage (Tao et al., 2018; Kritzinger et al., 2018; Fuller et al., 2020). Component Twins are the separate components in a system that can be sensors or mechanical components on which finer monitoring and detecting faults can be done (Rosen et al., 2015; Grieves & Vickers, 2017). Asset Twins uses various aspects to reflect a full-scale asset including machine or device to give a bigger picture on performance (Tao et al., 2018; Xu et al., 2021).

System Twins are inseparable resources in a system e.g. a complete production line or machine network (Kritzinger et al., 2018; Lee et al., 2015). These two twins aid organisations to comprehend the relationships among various assets and to maximise the performance of the system in general (Zhou et al., 2015; Lu et al., 2020). Lastly, Process Twins represent more complicated work processes and activities that include two or more systems (Fuller et al., 2020; Xu et al., 2021). They help in simulating and optimizing end-to-end processes; this helps the organization to enhance efficiency and productivity at the macro level (Porter & Heppelmann, 2014; Kagermann et al., 2013).

2.3 Applications Across Industries

Digital Twin technology has broad applications across multiple industries, including manufacturing, healthcare, smart cities, and energy systems. These applications enable real-time monitoring, predictive maintenance, and system optimization(Tao et al., 2018; Fuller et al., 2020). Use in Industries HPV can be applied in multiple industries such as photovoltaic, substrate molding, RFID, audiology, energy management, motorcycle, optical systems, and mobile devices but not limited to them (Kritzinger et al., 2018; Rosen et al., 2015).

The Digital Twin technology also has a wide impact and is applicable in numerous industries (Grieves & Vickers, 2017; Xu et al., 2021). Digital Twins have been applied in the manufacturing industry to monitor devices, to anticipate when they will need attention and to streamline the manufacturing process (Kagermann et al., 2013; Lee et al., 2015). This brings about lean time, quality and efficiency of operations (Zhou et al., 2015; Lu et al., 2020).

Digital Twins apply in healthcare to develop patient-centered models that can be used in the diagnosis of illnesses, treatment planning and prediction of health outcomes (Topol, 2019; Raghupathi & Raghupathi, 2014). This allows individualized therapy and better treatment of patients. Simulation of urban environments, control of traffic flow, energy consumption optimization, and better planning of infrastructures are all simulated in Digital Twins in the context of smart cities (Batty et al., 2012; Zanella et al., 2014; Mehmood et al., 2017).

Digital Twins also find applications in the energy sector where they are used to oversee power plants, anticipate equipment failures and distribution of energy (Waller & Fawcett, 2013; Shi et al., 2016). Applying the same method, Digital Twins can be used in transportation and logistics by optimizing routes, managing fleets, and also ensuring efficiency of supply chain by giving real-time information about the process (Porter & Heppelmann, 2014; Andrews et al., 2014).

3. DATA BACKBONE: INTERNET OF THINGS (IOT)

Internet of Things (IoT) is an important component of facilitating intelligent organizational change as it is the main source of real-time data (Atzori et al., 2010; Gubbi et al., 2013). It is the foundation block of contemporary digital ecosystems; it relates the physical world with the digital world in terms of connecting physical devices, systems and environments (Zanella et al., 2014; Ashton, 2009). IoT allows collecting, monitoring, and controlling data continuously via a system of sensors, actuators, and communication technologies, which are the key to developing intelligent and adaptive systems (Shi et al., 2016; Satyanarayanan, 2017).

IoT can be defined as a network of interconnected devices that are installed with sensors and software to respond to collect and share data via the internet (Atzori et al., 2010; Gubbi et al., 2013). Such equipment may include straightforward sensoric devices that detect humidity and temperature to complicated industrial machines that track performance and efficiency (Xu et al., 2014; Mehmood et al., 2017). IoT also allows organizations to get a real-time view of their operations and make informed decisions because it allows them to bridge physical and digital systems by ensuring smooth communication between these two systems (Waller & Fawcett, 2013; Provost & Fawcett, 2013).

Among the most important contributions of IoT, one must also mention the fact that the IoT is capable of producing vast amounts of real-time data (Davenport, 2006; Shmueli & Koppius, 2011). This information can give organizations information about the present physical systems and systems can be tracked to understand the performance of the organizations and see any anomalies and be able to act in accordance to the changes (Lee et al., 2015; Zhou et al., 2015). Real-time information is important in manufacturing, healthcare, and transportation fields in order to make the sectors efficient, safe, and reliable (Topol, 2019; Raghupathi & Raghupathi, 2014; Andrews et al., 2014).

3.1 IoT in Real-Time Data Collection

Real time data collection is the main activity of IoT in intelligent systems (Atzori et al., 2010; Gubbi et al., 2013; Xu et al., 2014). Physical devices also have sensors that constantly record information in the relation to different parameters like temperature, pressure, motion, energy use and location (Zanella et al., 2014; Mehmood et al., 2017). This data is sent to centralized systems or cloud development where it is processed and analyzed (Shi et al., 2016; Satyanarayanan, 2017).

The real-time collection of data is an attribute that allows organizations to keep track of activities within the organization in real-time without having to involve manual handwork (Davenport, 2006; Provost & Fawcett, 2013). To illustrate, in a manufacturing plant, IoT sensors will be able to monitor the performance of machines and identify abnormalities that could be signs of imminent failures (Lee et al., 2015; Zhou et al., 2015). This enables predictive maintenance which minimizes the downtime and enhances the productivity (Waller & Fawcett, 2013; Shmueli & Koppius, 2011).

Moreover, real-time information helps to make decisions quickly (Russell & Norvig, 2021; Jordan & Mitchell, 2015). Organizations are able to react instantly on events of change in the operational conditions thus reducing risks and maximizing performance (Lu et al., 2020; Porter & Heppelmann, 2014). This feature is critical when the delays may cause a lot of losses or damage (Andrews et al., 2014; Satyanarayanan, 2017).

Figure 2. IoT-Based Real-Time Data Flow

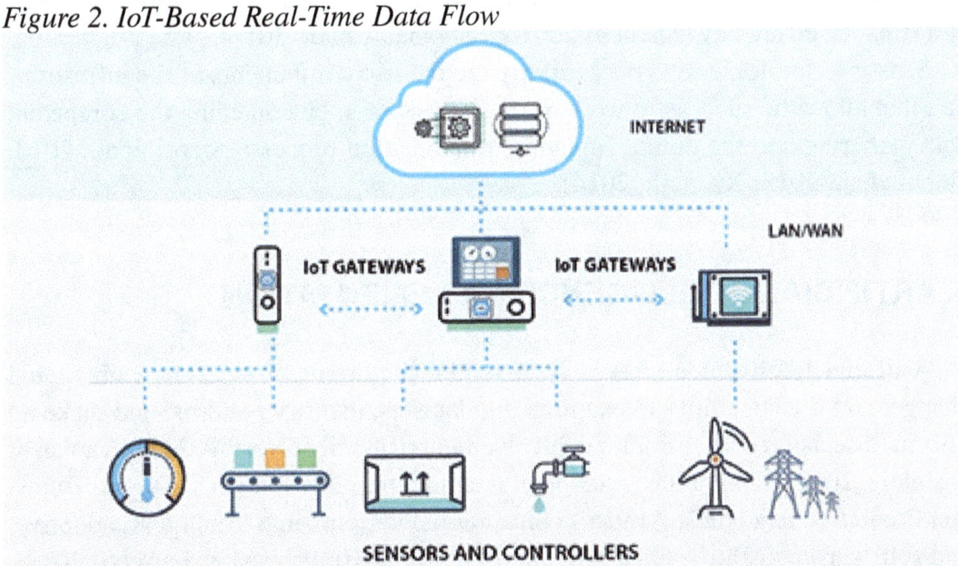

3.2 Sensor Technologies and Connection

It is the nature of sensors and the connectivity technologies that drive the transmission of data that determine the effectiveness of IoT systems (Atzori et al., 2010; Gubbi et al., 2013; Xu et al., 2014). The basic elements of the IoT are sensors, which detect information about the physical world (Zanella et al., 2014; Mehmood et al., 2017). The basic category of sensors is the temperature sensor, the pressure sensor, the motion sensor, the humidity sensor and the optical sensor. Further-developed systems can also be equipped with cameras, GPS devices and biometric sensors to collect more advanced data (Ashton, 2009; Xu et al., 2014).

The connectivity technologies will make sure that data saved by sensors is delivered effectively to processing systems (Gubbi et al., 2013; Zanella et al., 2014). Such technologies are Wi-Fi, Bluetooth, Zigbee, cellular networks, and the up-and-coming technology like 5G (Andrews et al., 2014; Shi et al., 2016). All of the connectivity options are advantageous based on the factors of range, speed, power consumption, and reliability (Satyanarayanan, 2017; Mehmood et al., 2017).

As an example, the 5G technology provides a high-speed data transmission and low-latency and is suitable in processes that need real-time communication like autonomous vehicle and smart cities (Andrews et al., 2014; Zanella et al., 2014). Another relevant development that supports and compliments the IoT is edge computing where the data processing is brought near the source to minimize latency and enhance efficiency (Shi et al., 2016; Satyanarayanan, 2017).

Sensor technologies and connectivity are the two components of the infrastructure that allow the successful work of the IoT systems, guaranteeing the competent data gathering and the uninterrupted communication process (Atzori et al., 2010; Gubbi et al., 2013; Xu et al., 2014).

4. ARTIFICIAL INTELLIGENCE IMPLEMENTATION

Artificial Intelligence (AI) is an essential facilitator of smart organizational change, and it is an ability to examine big datasets, identify patterns, and make an informed decision with less human involvement (Russell & Norvig, 2021; Kaplan & Haenlein, 2019). If combined with other technologies, including IoT, Digital Twins, and Predictive Analytics, AI turns conventional systems into intelligent, adaptive, and self-learning (Tao et al., 2018; Atzori et al., 2010; Provost & Fawcett, 2013). This integration enables the organizations to go farther in automation to actual intelligence whereby the systems can not only perform tasks but also learn and become better as time goes by (Jordan & Mitchell, 2015; Goodfellow et al., 2016).

Artificial intelligence ranges from a wide field of technologies, such as Machine Learning (ML), Deep Learning, Natural Language Processing (NLP), and Computer Vision (Goodfellow et al., 2016; LeCun et al., 2015; Nilsson, 2010). These technologies allow systems to work with both structured and unstructured information to discover relationships and create an actionable insight (Bishop, 2006; Murphy, 2012). The AI is becoming instrumental in the process of finding value in data and enabling the use of data to make decisions (as organizations continue to generate more data) (Davenport, 2006; Provost & Fawcett, 2013; Domingos, 2012).

4.1 Deep Learning and Machine Learning in Businesses

Machine Learning is a field of AI which allows a system to analyze data and become more functional without necessarily being coded to do so (Mitchell, 1997; Jordan & Mitchell, 2015; Bishop, 2006). Enterprise applications of the ML algorithms include demand prediction, customer relationship, fraud and predictive maintenance (Provost & Fawcett, 2013; Waller & Fawcett, 2013). ML models have the ability to make predictions based on real-time and historical data by detecting the patterns (Murphy, 2012; Domingos, 2012).

The more sophisticated type of ML is Deep Learning, which works with complex data, e.g., images, audios, and texts, and processes them using artificial neural networks (Goodfellow et al., 2016; LeCun et al., 2015; Schmidhuber, 2015). It can be applied especially in speech recognition, image classification and natural language understanding (Nilsson, 2010; Goodfellow et al., 2016). As an example, customer service chatbots, medical image analysis, and autonomous systems apply deep learning models (Topol, 2019; Russell & Norvig, 2021).

The implementation of ML and deep learning in businesses supports the decision-making process by supporting the provision of insights that are hard or impossible to derive within the available traditional approaches (Davenport, 2006; Provost & Fawcett, 2013). The technologies allow organizations to process large quantities of data effectively and reveal concealed patterns that facilitate innovation and productivity (Lu et al., 2020; Porter & Heppelmann, 2014).

4.2 AI-Driven Automation and Decision-Making

Probably one of the greatest advantages of AI integration is that it can automate the complex processes and assist in decision-making (Russell & Norvig, 2021; Kaplan & Haenlein, 2019; Lu et al., 2020). Auto-pilot AI is not only a form of rule-driven systems, but it also learns and modifies itself (Jordan & Mitchell, 2015; Goodfellow et al., 2016). Smart systems are able to process data in real-time, identify problems and do relevant steps without human intervention (Lee et al., 2015; Zhou et al., 2015).

AI has also been applied in business processes to automate repetitive business processes, including data entry, customer service, and inventory management (Davenport, 2006; Provost & Fawcett, 2013). This saves on the cost of operation and human error is minimized. More to the point, AI facilitates intelligent decision-making because it is able to predict and prescribe (Shmueli & Koppius, 2011; Domingos, 2012). As an illustration, AI systems may provide the best pricing measures, possible risk detection, and corrective measures (Waller & Fawcett, 2013; Porter & Heppelmann, 2014).

AI can also be used to help make decisions in real-time because it creates an opportunity to process data as it appears (Satyanarayanan, 2017; Shi et al., 2016). This capability enables organizations to react swiftly to any changes in a dynamic environment like a financial market or a supply chain thereby enabling the organization to stay ahead of competition (Andrews et al., 2014; Lu et al., 2020).

4.3 Enhancing Digital Twins With AI

The combination of AI and Digital twins boosts their abilities considerably and makes them not simple simulative tools but smart systems (Tao et al., 2018; Fuller et al., 2020; Lu et al., 2020). Digital Twins can analyze live data, learn based on past tendencies, and predict the future with the help of AI (Russell & Norvig, 2021; Goodfellow et al., 2016).

As an example, in factories, AI-based Digital Twins can be used to predict failures of equipment even before they happen, allowing to do prior maintenance and minimize downtime (Lee et al., 2015; Zhou et al., 2015). Moreover, it is also possible to optimize the performance of the systems through AI, which provides ongoing analysis and recommendations on how to improve (Provost & Fawcett, 2013; Waller & Fawcett, 2013).

Digital Twins can also be simulated to perform scenario simulation in which AI can be used to test various conditions and determine their effect on system performance (Kritzinger et al., 2018; Xu et al., 2021). This will enable the organizations to assess strategies, mitigate risks and make decisions that are informed without tampering with the real-world operation (Shmueli & Koppius, 2011; Domingos, 2012).

More than that, AI improves the scalability of Digital Twins, as they can support complex systems with many integrated elements (Fuller et al., 2020; Lu et al., 2020). It is especially relevant to large-scale usage, like smart cities and industrial ecosystems (Batty et al., 2012; Zanella et al., 2014).

5. PREDICTIVE ANALYTICS FOR PROACTIVE DECISION-MAKING

Predictive Analytics has now become one of the foundations of smarter organizational change, allowing businesses to preempt what is to come next and make decisions that are informed and proactive (Shmueli & Koppius, 2011; Siegel, 2016). Unlike conventional analytics which is concerned with either the knowledge of the past (descriptive) or the knowledge of why something occurred (diagnostic), predictive analytics responds to the key question: What is likely to happen next? (Provost & Fawcett, 2013; Domingos, 2012). Organizations are able to predict the future, streamline processes, and minimize uncertainty by using historical data, real time processes, statistical models and machine learning algorithms to forecast (Murphy, 2012; Waller & Fawcett, 2013).

The growing supply of massive amounts of data through the enterprise systems, the IoT devices, and the digital interactions has increased the significance of predictive analytics (Atzori et al., 2010; Gubbi et al., 2013; Xu et al., 2014). Organizations cannot be constrained by the lack of data today but how well they can derive value off it (Davenport, 2006; Provost & Fawcett, 2013). Predictive analytics converts raw information into proactive insights and helps to make smarter plans, achieve better efficiency, and increase competitiveness (Siegel, 2016; Waller & Fawcett, 2013; Lu et al., 2020).

5.1 Concepts and Techniques

Predictive analytics is developed on the basis of statistical approach, data mining, and machine learning models (Shmueli & Koppius, 2011; Provost & Fawcett, 2013; Murphy, 2012). The methods enable systems to discern patterns, relations, and trends in the data and utilize them to predict future results (Domingos, 2012; Bishop, 2006).

Regression analysis is one of the techniques on which the relationship between the dependent and independent variables is modeled (Murphy, 2012; Provost & Fawcett, 2013). It is commonly applied in forecasting continuous variables like sales revenue, level of demand or financial performance (Waller & Fawcett, 2013; Davenport, 2006). A typical retail organization can apply regression to predict sales in the future according to seasonal patterns and marketing expenditure (Siegel, 2016; Shmueli & Koppius, 2011).

The other important technique is time-series analysis that involves the data that is gathered over time (Murphy, 2012; Domingos, 2012). It is effective in determining trends, seasonality and cyclical tendencies and therefore has found application especially in demand forecasting, energy consumption prediction, and stock market analysis (Waller & Fawcett, 2013; Siegel, 2016). Most commonly applied techniques include ARIMA (AutoRegressive Integrated Moving Average) and exponential smoothing.

The techniques of classification are applied when the outcomes have prescribed categories (Provost & Fawcett, 2013; Bishop, 2006). Such algorithms include decision trees, logistic regression and support mechanisms of machines that aid the classification of information into a category, e.g. classifying a transaction as a fraud or legitimate transaction (Domingos, 2012; Murphy, 2012).

Machine learning has a major role in predictive analytics where it allows the models to learn with the data provided to it and later get more accurate as time progresses (Jordan & Mitchell, 2015; Goodfellow et al., 2016). Neural networks, random forests and gradient boosting are advanced and can capture the complicated and non-linear correlations in big data (LeCun et al., 2015; Schmidhuber, 2015). The techniques are particularly useful in processing large data and unstructured data, including text and images (Goodfellow et al., 2016; Bishop, 2006).

Also, preprocessing of data is an important component of predictive analytics (Provost & Fawcett, 2013; Davenport, 2006). Data cleaning, transformation and normalization of data guarantee that the models can give accurate and reliable results (Murphy, 2012; Domingos, 2012). Selections and engineering of the features also improve the model performance as they select the most significant variables (Bishop, 2006; Provost & Fawcett, 2013).

Figure 3. Predictive Analytics Workflow

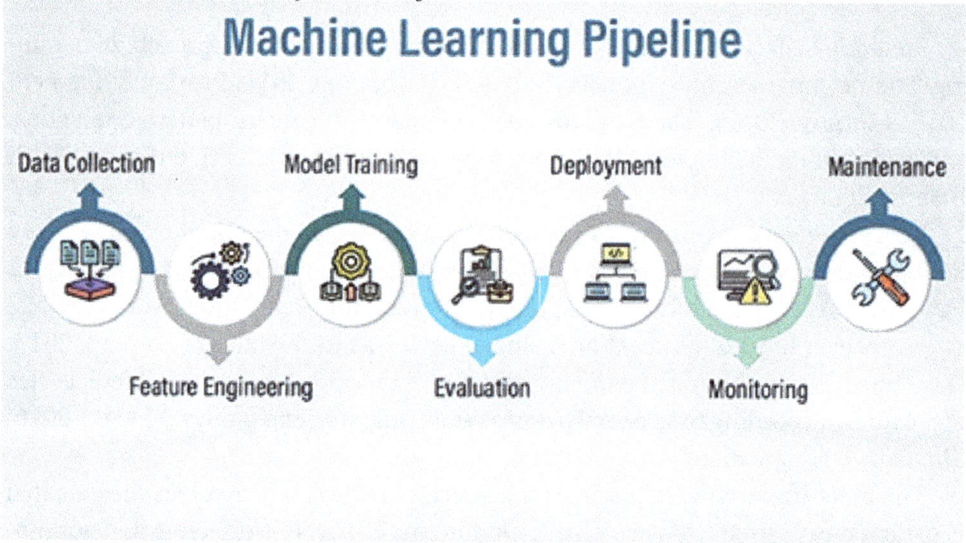

5.2 Forecasting and Risk Management

One of the most popular uses of predictive analytics is forecasting (Waller & Fawcett, 2013; Siegel, 2016; Davenport, 2006). With predictive models, organizations are able to estimate future demand, customer behavior, as well as market trends (Shmueli & Koppius, 2011; Provost & Fawcett, 2013). Proper forecasting will allow organizations to have the best inventory, resource allocation, and scheduling of production (Murphy, 2012; Domingos, 2012).

As an example, predictive analytics can be applied in a supply chain management to enable organizations to predict demand changes and modify inventory to meet the demand changes (Waller & Fawcett, 2013; Porter & Heppelmann, 2014). This allows cutting stock-out and oversupply that will result in cost savings and higher customer satisfaction (Davenport, 2006; Siegel, 2016).

Another important field of risk management where predictive analytics can be of great use is risk management (Shmueli & Koppius, 2011; Provost & Fawcett, 2013). Through historical analysis and pattern identification, the organizations are able to notice future risks prior to their occurrence (Murphy, 2012; Domingos, 2012). In finance, predictive modeling can be applied to measure credit risk, detect fraud and track suspicious behavior (Waller & Fawcett, 2013; Siegel, 2016). In a similar fashion, predictive maintenance models in manufacturing use equipment data to detect warning indicators of a failure early enough to allow early intervention and minimize downtime (Lee et al., 2015; Zhou et al., 2015).

Predictive analytics also facilitates scenario analysis and simulation, which help organizations to estimate alternative possibilities in different potential conditions (Provost & Fawcett, 2013; Davenport, 2006). As an illustration, a firm will be able to model the consequences of a market alteration, disruption in the supply, or pricing and select the most efficient course of action (Shmueli & Koppius, 2011; Domingos, 2012).

Moreover, resilience and adaptability can be improved with predictive analytics, as it allows the organization to be ready to meet uncertainties (Siegel, 2016; Lu et al., 2020). Businesses will be able not to respond to the issues as they arise but to foresee and avoid them (Davenport, 2006; Provost & Fawcett, 2013).

The integrity of the data flow is the main element of this integration (Xu et al., 2014; Provost & Fawcett, 2013). IoT devices gather the continuous real-time data about physical systems, i.e. machines, infrastructure, and environments (Zanella et al., 2014; Mehmood et al., 2017). This information is then sent to Digital Twin models and simulates the physical systems in an imaginary area (Kritzinger et al., 2018; Fuller et al., 2020). This data is analyzed by AI algorithms and generates insights, detects patterns, and predicts the future (Goodfellow et al., 2016; Jordan & Mitchell, 2015). The findings are looped back into the system thereby allowing the system to be optimized and improved continuously (Shmueli & Koppius, 2011; Domingos, 2012). This establishes a closed loop system with physical and digital environments in a dynamic interaction (Porter & Heppelmann, 2014; Lu et al., 2020).

Figure 4. Integrated Intelligent Ecosystem

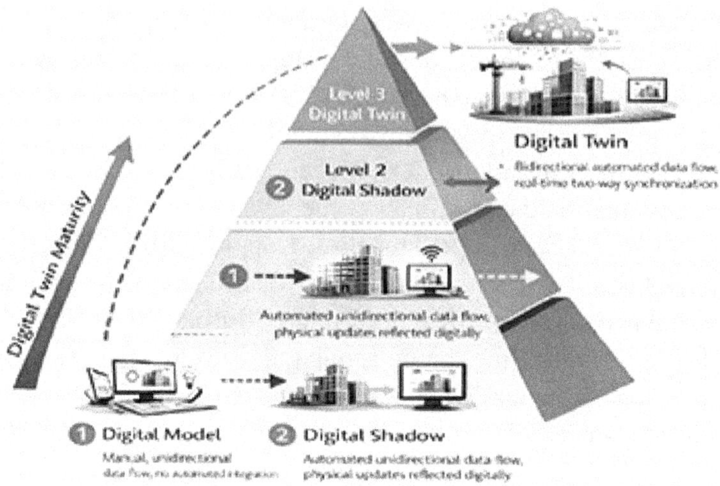

6. SUGGESTED COGNITIVE ENTERPRISE FRAMEWORK

The constraints of the current solutions in the Artificial Intelligence (AI) integration, Internet of Things (IoT), Digital Twins, and Predictive Analytics put on the focus of the necessity of a comprehensive and functioning framework. In line with this, this chapter introduces a comprehensive Cognitive Enterprise Framework that allows real-time sensing, intelligent analysis, virtual simulation, and adaptive decision-making in an enterprise in a closed-loop environment(Tao et al., 2018; Provost & Fawcett, 2013; Lu et al., 2020).

The suggested framework focuses on close integration, permanent feedback, and self-education, which are unavailable to the traditional models, which view the existing technologies separately and allow organizations to develop into fully cognitive enterprises(Kagermann et al., 2013; Porter & Heppelmann, 2014).

6.1 Framework Architecture Overview

The suggested framework is organized into four interrelated layers, which carry out a certain function in the data-to-decision pipeline:

1. Data Centering Layer (Databases Layer)

This layer gathers real-time the information of the physical systems through the IoT device, which are sensors, actuators, and embedded systems. It advances various data types such as temperature, pressure, movement, energy usage and working measures(Gubbi et al., 2013; Xu et al., 2014).

2. Intelligent Processing and Data (AI Layer)

This layer involves machine learning and deep learning algorithms within which the obtained data is processed. The system performs:

Preprocessing and data cleaning.
Feature extraction
Pattern recognition
Anomaly detection
Predictive modeling

3. Digital Twin Layer (Virtual Simulation Layer)

The layer produces a virtual replica of the physical system which is dynamic. The Digital Twin has the ability to synchronous with real-time numbers and allows:

System behavior simulation
Scenario analysis
Performance optimization

4. Decision and Optimization Layer (Predictive Analytics Layer)

This level transforms observations into practical decisions. It supports:

Forecasting future outcomes
Risk assessment
Prescriptive recommendations
Computer-aided or manual decision-making.

6.2 Data Flow and System Operation

The efficiency of the framework is that it has the end-to-end data flow and the closed interaction between physical and digital environment.

Operational Flow

IoT Sensors → Data Ingestion → Data Storage → AI Processing → Digital Twin Simulation → Prediction → Decision → Feedback → System Update

Step-by-Step Explanation

1. Data Acquisition

IoT sensors are constant gathering of real-time physical assets data(Atzori et al., 2010).

2. Data Transmission and Data storage.

The communication networks (ex: 5G, Wi-Fi) are used to transmit the data which is stored on the cloud or an edge system(Shi et al., 2016; Satyanarayanan, 2017).

3. AI-Based Processing

The data are analysed using machine learning models and patterns, future, and abnormality are detected(Goodfellow et al., 2016; Murphy, 2012).

4. Digital Twin Synchronization

The resulting digital twin is demonstrated by updating the digital model with the processed information, thereby making the digital model reflect the actual situation of the physical system(Tao et al., 2018).

5. Scenario Analysis, simulation.

The digital twin plays out others working scenarios to determine possible consequences(Fuller et al., 2020).

6. Predictive Decision-Making

Predictive analytics produces predictions and offers the most effective courses of action(Provost & Fawcett, 2013).

7. Feedback Loop Execution

The physical system implements decisions and generates new data, and the process repeats itself(Lu et al., 2020).

6.3 Feedback Loop Self Learning Mechanism

One of the main innovations of the proposed framework is its closed-loop feedback mechanism and it allows always continuous learning and system adaptation.

- New incoming information is constantly fed into the model AI.
- Performance of the systems is monitored and optimized in the long run.
- The decision-related feedback enhances future predictions.

This is changing the system to:

- Static → Dynamic
- Reactive → Predictive
- Predictive → Prescriptive

6.4 Analytical Model Integration

The framework also includes the use of analytical modeling in order to improve scientific rigor.

In predictive maintenance, in an example:

Input: sensor data of time-series data.
Model: Random Forest or Long Short-Term Memory (LSTM)?
Output: Failure probability

Prediction mathematically can be formulated as:

$$P(failure)=f(Xt, Xt-1,..., Xt-n)$$

Where:

- Xt represents sensor readings at time ttt
- f is the trained machine learning model

Such inclusion of the models of analysis makes sure that the framework is not only purely conceptual, but also operational and implementable.

6.5 Highlight the Main Characteristics of the Framework

The Cognitive Enterprise Framework suggested has a number of peculiarities:

Real-Time Intelligence

Immediate responses and responses are possible because of the continuous data collection and processing(Atzori et al., 2010).

Closed-Loop Learning

Through feedback mechanisms systems are able to enhance themselves(Lu et al., 2020).

Scalability

The modular architecture is allowing integration of various systems and domains(Shi et al., 2016).

Interoperability

Standardized interfaces allow a smooth flow of information between internet of things, machine intelligence and areas of digital twin(Xu et al., 2014).

Predictive and Prescriptive Ability.

It is not only a system that predicts what lies ahead, this is coupled with suggestions to what is best to do(Provost & Fawcett, 2013).

6.6 Differentiation of the Platform vs. Existing Ones

The proposed model: Contrary to the current systems, which are oriented to single technologies.

Offers sense-to-sense and sense-to-service IoT, AI, Digital Twin, and Predictive Analytics integration.

Clarifies data flow and system interchange.

Integrates mechanisms of learning that are based on feedback.

Assists with the operational and strategic decision-making.

This renders the framework more realistic, scalable and viable to actual enterprise transformation in the real world application(Kagermann et al., 2013; Lu et al., 2020).

7. EMERGENCE OF COGNITIVE ENTERPRISES

The dawn of cognitive enterprises is a revolutionary stage in the development of contemporary organizational structures in which intelligence is well integrated into systems, processes and decision making procedures (Lu et al., 2020; Russell & Norvig, 2021; Porter & Heppelmann, 2014). Though digital transformation allows organizations to digitize operations and make them more efficient, the cognitive enterprises would go a step further to use more advanced technologies, including Artificial Intelligence (AI), Internet of Things (IoT), Digital Twins, and Predictive Analytics, to develop systems capable of learning, reasoning, and changing independently (Kagermann et al., 2013; Tao et al., 2018; Atzori et al., 2010; Provost & Fawcett, 2013).

Cognitive enterprise is inherently knowledge based and intelligence-enabled (Davenport, 2006; Siegel, 2016). It manages data as a strategic asset and uses it to create real-time insights and predict future outcomes and automate complex decisions (Shmueli & Koppius, 2011; Domingos, 2012). In comparison to the traditional organization which depends on the periodic reporting and manual intervention, the cognitive enterprises work in the cycle of the constant feedback when the data are constantly gathered and processed and applied to improvement of the functioning (Waller & Fawcett, 2013; Provost & Fawcett, 2013).

The integration of AI, IoT, and Digital Twins is one of the important facilitators of cognitive enterprises (Atzori et al., 2010; Tao et al., 2018; Russell & Norvig, 2021). IoT devices produce real-time data of physical systems, Digital Twin produces virtual models to be simulated and observed and AI uses these to produce actionable insights (Gubbi et al., 2013; Kritzinger et al., 2018; Goodfellow et al., 2016). This cohesive ecosystem enables organizations to attain a great degree of operational brain and reactivity (Lee et al., 2015; Zhou et al., 2015).

7.1 Characteristics of Cognitive Organizations

Cognitive organizations are also characterized by a number of distinct features that distinguish them from traditional and digitally transformed organizations.

One of the primary characteristics of a cognitive organization is the capability of making decisions in real-time. Real-time decision-making facilitates data processing and provides instant results. Such capabilities are essential for responding to changing conditions (Russell & Norvig, 2021; Satyanarayanan, 2017), particularly in areas such as financial markets, supply chains, and manufacturing (Waller & Fawcett, 2013).

Another feature of a cognitive organization is the data-driven culture. In a data-driven culture, decisions are made based on data rather than relying on intuitions. Advanced data analysis models ensure data-driven decisions are accurate, consistent, and aligned with organizational goals (Davenport, 2006; Provost & Fawcett, 2013).

Thirdly, a cognitive organization places a significant emphasis on automation and intelligence. AI systems play a vital role in performing tasks and providing advanced capabilities such as forecasting, anomaly detection, and optimization (Kaplan & Haenlein, 2019; Goodfellow et al., 2016).

Lastly, a cognitive organization is also context-aware. Such awareness provides a system with the capability to interpret the context of the situation and respond accordingly. Such capabilities are essential for improving the efficiency of a system (Jordan & Mitchell, 2015; Lu et al., 2020).

7.2 Self-Learning and Adaptive Systems

One of the characteristics of cognitive enterprises is that of creating self-learning and adaptive systems (Jordan & Mitchell, 2015; Goodfellow et al., 2016; Lu et al., 2020). Such systems are based on machine learning algorithms that are constantly being improved by new information and experiences (Bishop, 2006; Murphy, 2012).

The functioning of self-learning systems is based on detecting patterns in data and changing their models (Domingos, 2012; Provost & Fawcett, 2013). As an example, e-commerce recommendation system learns as a result of the user interactions and as time progresses, the system advances its recommendations (Davenport, 2006; Siegel, 2016). In manufacturing likewise, predictive maintenance systems based on the equipment data learn to identify the early signs of breakdown (Lee et al., 2015; Zhou et al., 2015).

On the other hand, adaptive systems are dynamic in nature and react to a dynamic environment (Russell & Norvig, 2021; Lu et al., 2020). They will be able to adjust their behavior according to live feeds making them perform best in different conditions (Satyanarayanan, 2017; Shi et al., 2016). An example of this is in the supply chain management where adaptive systems are able to adapt inventory levels and logistics plan to demand fluctuations or disruptions (Waller & Fawcett, 2013; Porter & Heppelmann, 2014).

Continuous improvement is an attainment of organizations using these capabilities (Davenport, 2006; Provost & Fawcett, 2013). Cognitive systems are developed automatically as opposed to periodical updates or manual interventions and as such processes are efficient and effective (Goodfellow et al., 2016; Jordan & Mitchell, 2015).

Besides, adaptive systems and self-learning increase organization resilience (Lu et al., 2020; Siegel, 2016). Organizations are able to prepare in advance and act before such changes occur in order to reduce the impact of any of them and even be stable in a volatile environment (Shmueli & Koppius, 2011; Domingos, 2012).

7.3 Human-AI Collaboration

Human involvement is still important even with the development of cognitive systems (Russell & Norvig, 2021; Kaplan & Haenlein, 2019). The term human-AI collaboration focuses on the unique abilities of each entity. AI systems have the ability to process large amounts of data, recognize patterns, and perform repetitive tasks with speed and precision (Goodfellow et al., 2016; Jordan & Mitchell, 2015). On the other hand, human beings have the ability to be creative and have a moral compass, which AI systems lack by design (Nilsson, 2010; Russell & Norvig, 2021).

In cognitive enterprises, AI systems act as a decision-support tool rather than replacing human intelligence (Davenport, 2006; Provost & Fawcett, 2013). For example, in the healthcare sector, AI systems process complex medical information and provide possible diagnoses. However, it is the responsibility of human beings to make the ultimate decision regarding treatment (Topol, 2019; Raghupathi & Raghupathi, 2014). In business settings, AI systems provide useful insights and predictions to guide managers in strategic planning (Siegel, 2016; Domingos, 2012).

The collaboration of human beings and AI systems increases productivity in various organizations by automating processes. This allows human beings to concentrate on other important tasks such as innovation and problem-solving (Lu et al., 2020; Porter & Heppelmann, 2014). In addition, the integration of human beings with AI systems increases trust and ethics in AI systems in various organizations (Kaplan & Haenlein, 2019; Lu et al., 2020).

8. USE CASES AND CASE STUDY ANALYSIS IN INDUSTRY

Artificial Intelligence (AI), Internet of Things (IoT), Digital Twins, and Predictive Analytics would be most easily perceived in the context of the real-life examples. In contrast to generic descriptions, analytical case studies as presented in this section show how the proposed framework works in practice, such as the definition of the problem, system architecture, and quantifiable results(Tao et al., 2018; Lu et al., 2020).

Figure 5. Applications of Intelligent Systems Across Industries

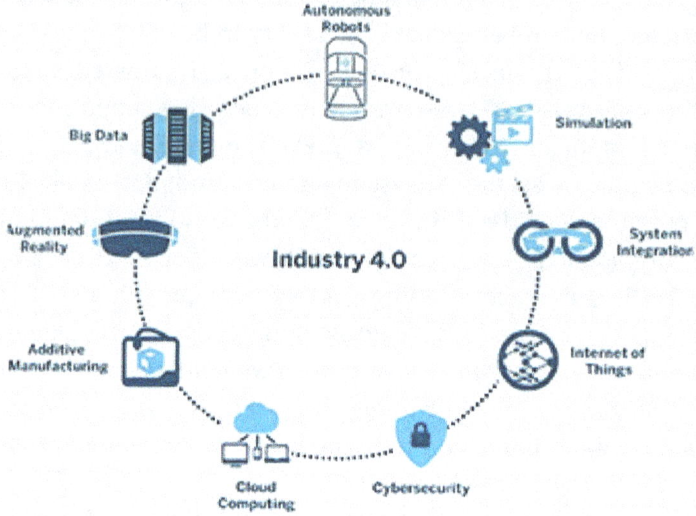

8.1 Case Study 1: Smart Manufacturing (Predictive Maintenance System)

◆ Problem Statement

Conventional manufacturing systems are based on reactive maintenance which results in:

Unexpected machine failures
Increased downtime
High maintenance costs(Lee et al., 2015; Zhou et al., 2015).

◆ System Architecture

The suggested framework is used in the following way:

IoT Layer: Sensors receive vibration, temperature, and pressure information on machines(Gubbi et al., 2013).
AI Layer: The machine learning models (e.g., Random Forest, LSTM) are trained on time-series data(Goodfellow et al., 2016;)
Digital Twin Layer: An artificial image of the machine is used to simulate the working conditions(Fuller et al., 2020)

Predictive Analytics Layer: Predicts failure and suggests maintenance(Provost & Fawcett, 2013; Siegel, 2016)

◆ Analytical Model

The prediction of failure is formulated to be:

P(failure)=f(X1, X2,...,Xn)

Where:

- Xn = sensor features (temperature, vibration, etc.)
- F = trained ML model

◆ Results and Impact

Cutdown of downtime by 20-30 percent.
Maintenance saved 1525% of the cost.
Improved asset lifespan

◆ Key Insight

This example illustrates the fact that closed-loop integration can be used to make proactive decisions rather than reactive ones.(Porter & Heppelmann, 2014).

8.2 Case Study 2: Healthcare (Personalized Digital Twin for Patient Monitoring).

◆ Problem Statement

Healthcare systems tend to be deficient in:

Continuous monitoring
Personalized treatment strategies
Early disease prediction(Topol, 2019; Raghupathi & Raghupathi, 2014)

◆ System Architecture

IoT Layer: Patient vitals (heart rate, oxygen and activity) are gathered using wearable devices(Gubbi et al., 2013)

AI Layer: The deep learning models identify anomalies and foresee the risk of disease(Goodfellow et al., 2016)

Digital Twin Layer: Virtual patient model is a simulation of treatment situations(Fuller et al., 2020)

Predictive Analytics Layer: Gives personalized treatment recommendations(Provost & Fawcett, 2013)

◆ Analytical Approach

AI models classify patient conditions:

Y=f(Xvitals, Xhistory)

Where:

- Y = predicted health condition
- X = patient data

◆ Results and Impact

Improvement in the early detection of the disease by 25% was made.

Accuracy in personalized treatment was heightened.

Less hospital readmission rate.

◆ Key Insight

In the incorporation, preventive care is facilitated, and treatment is replaced with prediction.

8.3 Case Study 3: Smart Cities (Intelligent Traffic Management System)

◆ Problem Statement

Urban environments face:

Traffic congestion

Energy inefficiency

Poor resource utilization(Batty et al., 2012; Zanella et al., 2014)

◆ System Architecture

IoT Layer: Traffic and environmental data is gathered by sensors and cameras(Zanella et al., 2014)

AI Layer: Traffic flow is studied by the use of computer vision and ML models(Goodfellow et al., 2016)

Digital Twin Layer: Simulates traffic in a virtual city model(Kritzinger et al., 2018)

Predictive Analytics Layer: Routing and optimizing traffic signals(Provost & Fawcett, 2013)

◆ Analytical Model

Traffic flow optimization:

Topt = argmin(Cdelay+Cfuel)

Where:

- Topt = optimal traffic signal timing
- CCC = cost functions
  - ◆ Results and Impact
    - Traffic jam cut by 1525 percent.
    - Fuel consumption decreased
    - Improved urban mobility
  - ◆ Key Insight

Adaptive urban systems with real-time simulation + AI.

8.4 Case Study 4: Supply Chain and Logistics Optimization.

◆ Problem Statement

Supply chains face:

Demand uncertainty
Inventory mismanagement
Inefficient routing(Waller & Fawcett, 2013)

◆ System Architecture

IoT Layer: Monitors the location and condition of shipment(Atzori et al., 2010)
AI Layer: Predicts demand with the help of ML models(Jordan & Mitchell, 2015)
Digital Twin Layer: Modeling supply chain operations(Tao et al., 2018)
Predictive Analytics Layer: streamlines inventory and logistics (Provost & Fawcett, 2013)

◆ Analytical Model

Demand forecasting:

Dt=f(Dt−1, St, Et)

Where:

- Dt = demand
- St = seasonal factors
- Et = external variables
    - ◆ Results and Impact

        Inventory expenses decreased by 1020 percent.

        Delivery efficiency improved

        Reduced stockouts
    - ◆ Key Insight

Integration facilitates end-to-end visibility and optimization.

9. CHALLENGES AND IMPLEMENTATION BARRIERS

Although the combination of Artificial Intelligence (AI), Internet of Things (IoT), Digital Twins, and Predictive Analytics has a great potential, there are a number of difficulty that organizations may experience when introducing such technologies successfully (Lu et al., 2020; Kagermann et al., 2013; Porter & Heppelmann, 2014). These are not only technological barriers but organizational, financial, and cultural barriers. When it comes to successful intelligent organizational transformation, it is necessary to understand and address such challenges (Davenport, 2006; Provost & Fawcett, 2013).

9.1 Data Privacy and Security

Provision of data privacy and security is one of the most imperative issues in the implementation of intelligent systems (Atzori et al., 2010; Xu et al., 2014; Lu et al., 2020). The risk of data breaches and cyberattacks is growing as well as organizations continue to depend on data provided by a variety of sources where IoT devices and cloud services are among them (Gubbi et al., 2013; Shi et al., 2016).

Internet of Things, especially IoT devices is susceptible to attacks because of its high adoption rates and, in many cases, low security protection (Zanella et al., 2014; Mehmood et al., 2017). By accessing such devices without official authorization, data can be stolen, systems can be manipulated, or even have their operations interrupted. On the same note, the sensitive information like customer data, financial data, and operational data have to be secured in order to meet the regulatory demands (Davenport, 2006; Provost & Fawcett, 2013).

Companies should adopt strong cybersecurity standards, which are encryption, authentication procedures, and intrusion detection tools (Shi et al., 2016; Satyanarayanan, 2017). Moreover, the data protection regulations and standards should be met to ensure trust and prevent the legal implications (Lu et al., 2020; Porter & Heppelmann, 2014).

9.2 Integration Complexity

The next important obstacle is that it is not as easy as it seems to combine several technologies and systems (Lu et al., 2020; Kagermann et al., 2013). Smart organizational change demands a smooth integration of AI, IoT, Digital Twins and analytics platforms, which can have varied architectures and standards behind them (Atzori et al., 2010; Tao et al., 2018; Provost & Fawcett, 2013).

Organizations have numerous old systems that have not been developed to accommodate the new technologies (Davenport, 2006; Porter & Heppelmann, 2014). The process of integrating these systems with new platforms may not be easy and may take some time. The silos of data also complicate it further because the data is kept in separate systems that are not in effective communication with each other (Waller & Fawcett, 2013; Xu et al., 2014).

In order to overcome these challenges, organizations must embrace standardized protocols, interoperable platforms as well as scalable architectures (Shi et al., 2016; Satyanarayanan, 2017). Integration can be facilitated by middleware solutions and APIs, but one has to plan carefully and implement so smoothly (Lu et al., 2020; Porter & Heppelmann, 2014).

9.3 Cost and Infrastructure

Another significant obstacle is the expensive nature of the implementation (Kagermann et al., 2013; Lu et al., 2020). Implementation of intelligent systems involves a lot of investment, both in the hardware, software, infrastructure and human resource (Porter & Heppelmann, 2014; Davenport, 2006). IoT, cloud services, AI tools, and data storage are all additional elements of the total cost (Atzori et al., 2010; Xu et al., 2014).

Besides start-up cost, organizations need to take into account recurrent expenses on system maintenance, upgrading, and cybersecurity (Shi et al., 2016; Satyanarayanan, 2017). These costs may prove to be a big deterrent to adoption to the small and medium sized enterprises (Lu et al., 2020; Provost & Fawcett, 2013).

There are also problems of infrastructure needs. To facilitate real-time data processing and analytics, organizations require networks that are reliable, high-performance computing systems, and scale-able clouds (Andrews et al., 2014; Shi et al., 2016). The efficiency of the intelligent systems cannot be as effective without proper infrastructure (Satyanarayanan, 2017; Porter & Heppelmann, 2014).

9.4 Skill and Talent Gap

The lack of qualified specialists is one of the largest hindrances facing the adoption of modern technologies (Lu et al., 2020; Russell & Norvig, 2021). Such disciplines as AI, machine learning, data science, IoT, and cybersecurity were among the criteria of intelligent systems (Goodfellow et al., 2016; Jordan & Mitchell, 2015). Nevertheless, the number of professionals possessing such skills is a debilitating issue across the globe (Davenport, 2006; Provost & Fawcett, 2013).

Companies need to invest on training and development programs to establish internal capabilities (Siegel, 2016; Lu et al., 2020). The gap in skills can be bridged with the help of collaboration with academic institutions and technology partners as well. Moreover, lifelong learning should be encouraged in order to stay up-to-date with the fast changing technologies (Jordan & Mitchell, 2015; Russell & Norvig, 2021).

9.5 Organizational Resistance and Change Management

The process of technological change can be resisted by the organizational unit (Kagermann et al., 2013; Lu et al., 2020). Employees can be hesitant to use the new technologies because they will lose their jobs or they can lack familiarity with the new technologies (Davenport, 2006; Kaplan & Haenlein, 2019). Such resistance may decelerate the implementation process and decrease the efficiency of transformation.

The implementation of effective strategies in change management is necessary in order to solve these problems (Porter & Heppelmann, 2014; Provost & Fawcett, 2013). Organizations need to convey the positive aspects of change, engage the workers, and train them and support them. Leadership is essential in the implementation of change and creation of an innovative culture (Lu et al., 2020; Davenport, 2006).

9.6 Data Quality and Data Management Problems

The quality of data is the most crucial factor of intelligent systems (Provost & Fawcett, 2013; Davenport, 2006). Lack of good data such as missing, inconsistent or inaccurate data may give a wrong conclusion and resulting decisions (Shmueli & Koppius, 2011; Domingos, 2012).

Big data is also difficult to manage especially when addressing data in various points of origin (Waller & Fawcett, 2013; Xu et al., 2014). Organizations need to bring data governance frameworks that promote accuracy, consistency and reliability of data. High-quality data is maintained by taking several measures such as data cleaning, validation and standardization (Murphy, 2012; Bishop, 2006).

9.7 Scalability and System Complexity

Scalability is a very important issue as intelligent systems are spread to more parts of the organization (Lu et al., 2020; Shi et al., 2016). Systems should be made to accommodate the rising amounts of information as well as the rising number of interconnected devices (Atzori et al., 2010; Gubbi et al., 2013).

Complex systems may be hard to maintain and control particularly when there are several technologies involved (Porter & Heppelmann, 2014; Xu et al., 2014). Planning and strong architecture design is necessary to ensure consistency, speed, and scale of the system (Satyanarayanan, 2017; Andrews et al., 2014).

10. FUTURE TRENDS AND NEW TECHNOLOGIES

With organizations still on their way to intelligent transformation, a number of technologies and trends are on the horizon of digital ecosystems (Lu et al., 2020; Russell & Norvig, 2021). Artificial Intelligence (AI), Internet of Things (IoT), Digital Twins, and Predictive Analytics are becoming increasingly integrated and is creating more sophisticated, autonomous, and connected systems (Atzori et al., 2010; Tao et al., 2018; Provost & Fawcett, 2013). Such trends are not only augmenting existing competencies, but they are also re-inventing organizational operations, innovativeness and competitiveness in the international arena (Porter & Heppelmann, 2014; Kagermann et al., 2013).

The future of smart enterprise is to develop systems that are based on faster, smart, and more adaptive (Lu et al., 2020; Shi et al., 2016). Edge computing, 5G, autonomous systems and expanded Digital Twin ecosystems are some of the technologies that are revolutionizing it (Satyanarayanan, 2017; Andrews et al., 2014).

10.1 Edge Computing and 5G

The development of edge computing is one of the most notable trends as it implies providing data processing in areas of its origin instead of depending on only centralized cloud solutions (Shi et al., 2016; Satyanarayanan, 2017). Conventional cloud computing has a scenario where data is transmitted to distant servers to be processed thus leading to latency and delay in making decisions.

Edge computing offers a solution to this problem by allowing data to be processed in real-time at or close to its source (Satyanarayanan, 2017; Shi et al., 2016). It is especially significant in applications with immediate responses like autonomous cars, automation in the industrial sector, and medicine monitoring machines (Andrews et al., 2014; Lu et al., 2020).

These capabilities are also increased by the use of 5G technology (Andrews et al., 2014; Zanella et al., 2014). Combined with 5G, edge computing is an effective framework that facilitates real-time analytics, quicker decision-making processes, and enhanced operations of smart systems (Shi et al., 2016; Satyanarayanan, 2017).

10.2 Expansion of Digital Twins Ecosystems

The Digital Twin technology is likely to evolve to cover not only assets and systems, but also ecosystems (Tao et al., 2018; Fuller et al., 2020; Xu et al., 2021). The Digital Twins of the future will be complex systems like the whole organizations, supply chains, cities, and even global systems (Lu et al., 2020; Porter & Heppelmann, 2014).

Such advanced Digital Twin ecosystems will combine data in many aspects, such as IoT devices, enterprise systems, and other external data platforms (Atzori et al., 2010; Xu et al., 2014). It will facilitate the broad scale simulation, analytics, and optimization (Kritzinger et al., 2018; Provost & Fawcett, 2013).

As an example, a Digital Twin of a smart city may combine data of the transportation systems, energy systems, and healthcare and infrastructure systems to improve the organization of cities and managing resources (Batty et al., 2012; Zanella et al., 2014). A similar scenario is that a Digital Twin of a supply chain could mean end-to-end visibility as well as real-time optimization of logistics and inventory (Waller & Fawcett, 2013; Porter & Heppelmann, 2014).

The combination of AI and Digital Twins will also benefit their functions since they will be able to make predictive and prescriptive insights (Goodfellow et al., 2016; Russell & Norvig, 2021; Provost & Fawcett, 2013). Organizations will be in a position to simulate future scenarios, evaluate strategies and make informed decisions with much more precision (Shmueli & Koppius, 2011; Domingos, 2012).

11. STRATEGIC FRAMEWORK FOR ADOPTION

Intelligent technologies including Artificial Intelligence (AI), Internet of Things (IoT), Digital Twins, and Predictive Analytics should be implemented as a successful move that cannot be conducted without a clearly outlined strategic framework (Lu et al., 2020; Kagermann et al., 2013). Companies need to remember to not only implement the technology in solitary fashion but they should exercise a holistic change management approach where technological undertakings are coordinated with corporate goals (Davenport, 2006; Porter & Heppelmann, 2014). The systematic nature of transformation efforts is supported with a structured framework and it would result in making it scalable and sustainable (Provost & Fawcett, 2013; Lu et al., 2020).

11.1 Roadmap for Organizations

There should be a clear roadmap to plan the organization through the transformation journey (Kagermann et al., 2013; Lu et al., 2020). It usually starts with the identification of a vision and objectives which are in line with organizational goals (Porter & Heppelmann, 2014; Davenport, 2006). These involve determining the main areas where smart technologies can add value, which can be the operational efficiency, customer experience, or innovation.

The second step is the analysis of readiness that is used to assess the existing competencies of the organization regarding technology, infrastructure, data management, and human capabilities (Provost & Fawcett, 2013; Siegel, 2016). This can be used to determine the gaps and areas to be improved.

Then the approach that the organizations ought to take is a gradual implementation (Lu et al., 2020; Kagermann et al., 2013). They do not need to roll out all the technologies simultaneously, they can start with pilot projects or proofs-of-concepts to prove that it is feasible and has value (Porter & Heppelmann, 2014; Davenport, 2006). The successful pilots can be then scaled throughout the organization.

The main role in this roadmap is played by data (Provost & Fawcett, 2013; Waller & Fawcett, 2013). Development of a strong data strategy will also provide efficient data collection, storage, and management (Davenport, 2006; Shmueli & Koppius, 2011). This involves the adoption of data governance models, data quality and data integration among systems.

Lastly organizations have to keep an eye and review their progress (Lu et al., 2020; Siegel, 2016). The impact of transformation initiatives must be measured with performance metrics and key performance indicators (KPIs) and be used to improve in the future (Provost & Fawcett, 2013; Davenport, 2006).

11.2 Change Management Strategies

Organizational change management is considered as one of the most important aspects of intelligent transformation (Kagermann et al., 2013; Lu et al., 2020). Implementation of new high-tech technologies usually interfere with the routine processes and workflows and people have to adjust to new models of working (Davenport, 2006; Kaplan & Haenlein, 2019).

Good leadership and vision lead to proper change management (Porter & Heppelmann, 2014; Lu et al., 2020). The leaders need to articulate the reason and the advantages of transformation so that all the stakeholders begin to see the relevance (Davenport, 2006; Siegel, 2016).

It is necessary to train employees and develop their skills (Russell & Norvig, 2021; Jordan & Mitchell, 2015). Organisations have to invest in upskilling and reskilling programs, which will provide the employees with knowledge that will allow them to deal with new technologies. One should be encouraged to learn continuously to stay at par with changes in technology.

It is also important in terms of cultural change (Lu et al., 2020; Davenport, 2006). Organizations should promote an environment of innovation and teamwork and make decisions based on data evidence. Transformation can be increased through the promotion of experimentation and loss as learning capacity.

Moreover, organizations are supposed to develop feedback systems to collect responses on both the employees and the stakeholders (Provost & Fawcett, 2013; Siegel, 2016). This facilitates challenges recognition, process enhancement and guarantee transformation initiatives remain organizational driven.

12. CONCLUSION

The present chapter offered an integrated approach to cognitive enterprise development through the application of AI, IoT, Digital Twins, and Predictive Analytics. Unlike previous approaches that considered these technologies individually, this study offered a unified approach that would allow for real-time decision-making, adaptive learning, and optimization(Lu et al., 2020; Porter & Heppelmann, 2014).

The results showed that organizational intelligence is a product of technology integration rather than its application individually. The offered approach is significant for its theoretical and practical value for organizations that seek to become intelligent(Kagermann et al., 2013; Tao et al., 2018).

Future research is recommended to test and apply the offered model

REFERENCES

Andrews, J. G., Buzzi, S., Choi, W., Hanly, S. V., Lozano, A., Soong, A. C. K., & Zhang, J. C. (2014). What will 5G be? *IEEE Journal on Selected Areas in Communications, 32*(6), 1065–1082. DOI: 10.1109/JSAC.2014.2328098

Ashton, K. (2009). *That 'Internet of Things' thing*. RFID Journal.

Atzori, L., Iera, A., & Morabito, G. (2010). The Internet of Things: A survey. *Computer Networks, 54*(15), 2787–2805. DOI: 10.1016/j.comnet.2010.05.010

Batty, M., Axhausen, K. W., Giannotti, F., Pozdnoukhov, A., Bazzani, A., Wachowicz, M., Ouzounis, G., & Portugali, Y. (2012). Smart cities of the future. *The European Physical Journal. Special Topics, 214*(1), 481–518. DOI: 10.1140/epjst/e2012-01703-3

Bishop, C. M. (2006). *Pattern Recognition and Machine Learning*. Springer.

Davenport, T. H. (2006). Competing on analytics. *Harvard Business Review, 84*(1), 98–107.

Domingos, P. (2012). A few useful things to know about machine learning. *Communications of the ACM, 55*(10), 78–87. DOI: 10.1145/2347736.2347755

Fuller, A., Fan, Z., Day, C., & Barlow, C. (2020). Digital twin: Enabling technologies, challenges and open research. *IEEE Access : Practical Innovations, Open Solutions, 8*, 108952–108971. DOI: 10.1109/ACCESS.2020.2998358

Goodfellow, I., Bengio, Y., & Courville, A. (2016). *Deep Learning*. MIT Press.

Grieves, M., & Vickers, J. (2017). Digital twin: Mitigating unpredictable, undesirable emergent behavior in complex systems. In *Transdisciplinary Perspectives on Complex Systems* (pp. 85–113). Springer. DOI: 10.1007/978-3-319-38756-7_4

Gubbi, J., Buyya, R., Marusic, S., & Palaniswami, M. (2013). Internet of Things (IoT): A vision, architectural elements, and future directions. *Future Generation Computer Systems, 29*(7), 1645–1660. DOI: 10.1016/j.future.2013.01.010

Jordan, M. I., & Mitchell, T. M. (2015). Machine learning: Trends, perspectives, and prospects. *Science, 349*(6245), 255–260. DOI: 10.1126/science.aaa8415

. Kagermann, H., Wahlster, W., & Helbig, J. (2013). *Recommendations for implementing Industry 4.0.*

Kaplan, A. M., & Haenlein, M. (2019). Siri, Siri, in my hand: Who's the fairest in the land? *Business Horizons, 62*(1), 15–25. DOI: 10.1016/j.bushor.2018.08.004

Kritzinger, W., Karner, M., Traar, G., Henjes, J., & Sihn, W. (2018). Digital Twin in manufacturing: A categorical literature review and classification. *IFAC-PapersOnLine*, *51*(11), 1016–1022. DOI: 10.1016/j.ifacol.2018.08.474

LeCun, Y., Bengio, Y., & Hinton, G. (2015). Deep learning. *Nature*, *521*(7553), 436–444. DOI: 10.1038/nature14539

Lee, J., Bagheri, B., & Kao, H. A. (2015). A cyber-physical systems architecture for Industry 4.0. *Manufacturing Letters*, *3*, 18–23. DOI: 10.1016/j.mfglet.2014.12.001

Lu, Y., Liu, C., & Wang, K. I.. (2020). Digital Twin-driven smart manufacturing. *Journal of Manufacturing Systems*, *58*, 319–331.

Mehmood, Y., Ahmad, F., Yaqoob, I., Adnane, A., Imran, M., & Guizani, S. (2017). Internet of Things-based smart cities: Recent advances and challenges. *IEEE Communications Magazine*, *55*(1), 16–24. DOI: 10.1109/MCOM.2017.1600514

Murphy, K. P. (2012). *Machine Learning: A Probabilistic Perspective*. MIT Press.

Nilsson, N. J. (2010). *The Quest for Artificial Intelligence*. Cambridge University Press.

Porter, M. E., & Heppelmann, J. E. (2014). How smart, connected products are transforming competition. *Harvard Business Review*, *92*(11), 64–88.

Provost, F., & Fawcett, T. (2013). *Data Science for Business*. O'Reilly Media.

Raghupathi, W., & Raghupathi, V. (2014). Big data analytics in healthcare. *Health Information Science and Systems*, *2*(1), 3. DOI: 10.1186/2047-2501-2-3

Rosen, R., von Wichert, G., Lo, G., & Bettenhausen, K. D. (2015). About the importance of autonomy and digital twins for the future of manufacturing. *IFAC-PapersOnLine*, *48*(3), 567–572. DOI: 10.1016/j.ifacol.2015.06.141

Russell, S., & Norvig, P. (2021). *Artificial Intelligence: A Modern Approach* (4th ed.). Pearson.

Satyanarayanan, M. (2017). The emergence of edge computing. *Computer*, *50*(1), 30–39. DOI: 10.1109/MC.2017.9

Schmidhuber, J. (2015). Deep learning in neural networks: An overview. *Neural Networks*, *61*, 85–117. DOI: 10.1016/j.neunet.2014.09.003

Shi, W., Cao, J., Zhang, Q., Li, Y., & Xu, L. (2016). Edge computing: Vision and challenges. *IEEE Internet of Things Journal*, *3*(5), 637–646. DOI: 10.1109/JIOT.2016.2579198

Shmueli, G., & Koppius, O. R. (2011). Predictive analytics in information systems research. *Management Information Systems Quarterly*, *35*(3), 553–572. DOI: 10.2307/23042796

Siegel, E. (2016). *Predictive Analytics: The Power to Predict Who Will Click, Buy, Lie, or Die*. Wiley.

Tao, F., Zhang, M., Liu, Y., & Nee, A. Y. C. (2018). Digital twin in manufacturing: A review. *Journal of Manufacturing Systems*, *48*, 157–169. DOI: 10.1016/j.jmsy.2018.01.006

Topol, E. (2019). *Deep Medicine: How Artificial Intelligence Can Make Healthcare Human Again*. Basic Books.

Waller, M. A., & Fawcett, S. E. (2013). Data science, predictive analytics, and big data. *Journal of Business Logistics*, *34*(2), 77–84. DOI: 10.1111/jbl.12010

Xu, L. D., He, W., & Li, S. (2014). Internet of Things in industries: A survey. *IEEE Transactions on Industrial Informatics*, *10*(4), 2233–2243. DOI: 10.1109/TII.2014.2300753

Xu, X., Lu, Y., Vogel-Heuser, B., & Wang, L. (2021). Industry 4.0 and digital twin. *Annual Reviews in Control*, *51*, 1–15.

Zanella, A., Bui, N., Castellani, A., Vangelista, L., & Zorzi, M. (2014). Internet of Things for smart cities. *IEEE Internet of Things Journal*, *1*(1), 22–32. DOI: 10.1109/JIOT.2014.2306328

Zhou, K., Liu, T., & Zhou, L. (2015). Industry 4.0: Towards future industrial opportunities. *Procedia CIRP*, *33*, 214–219.

Chapter 9
Digital Twin-Based Multi-Objective Production Optimization in Smart Factories

Aníbal López
http://orcid.org/0000-0003-4103-3944
ISEG, University of Lisbon, Portugal

Zornitsa Yordanova
http://orcid.org/0000-0002-6056-8445
University of National and World Economy, Bulgaria

Hamed Nozari
http://orcid.org/0000-0002-6500-6708
University of National and World Economy, Bulgaria

ABSTRACT

Smart factories, as one of the main pillars of the fourth-generation industry, require advanced tools for analyzing, monitoring, and optimizing manufacturing operations. In this study, an integrated framework based on digital twins for multi-objective optimization of operations in smart manufacturing systems is presented. The proposed model is designed considering objectives such as reducing production costs, reducing energy consumption, and increasing system efficiency and is solved using NSGA-II and MOPSO algorithms. To evaluate the performance of the model, analyses including Pareto front examination, sensitivity analysis to changing demand

DOI: 10.4018/979-8-3373-9998-0.ch009

levels, energy constraints, and machinery utilization have been conducted. The results show that the combination of digital twins and multi-objective optimization can help improve decision-making in smart factories.

1. INTRODUCTION

The rapid evolution of digital technologies in recent decades has fundamentally transformed the structure and functioning of manufacturing systems. The emergence of concepts such as smart manufacturing, cyber-physical systems, and data-driven factories has led traditional manufacturing environments to move towards intelligent, flexible, and data-driven structures. In such environments, operational decisions are no longer based solely on human experience or static models, but rather on real-time data, advanced simulations, and analytical algorithms. One of the most important technologies that has played a key role in realizing this transformation in recent years is the concept of the digital twin. As a dynamic virtual model of a physical system, the digital twin enables the monitoring, analysis, and prediction of the behavior of real systems in a digital environment, thereby creating a suitable platform for intelligent decision-making in manufacturing systems (Lin et al., 2026).

Smart factories, as one of the most important pillars of the fourth-generation industry, are based on the integration of information technologies, physical systems and industrial data analysis. In this type of factory, machinery, control systems and production infrastructure are continuously connected to each other and produce a large amount of operational data (Nozari et al., 2025). Analyzing this data can provide valuable information about the status of the production system, the efficiency of equipment and the performance of production processes. However, simply accessing production data is not enough to improve system performance and it is necessary to use this data in the form of analytical and decision-making models. In the meantime, the use of digital twins allows for the creation of an accurate virtual view of the production system in which different operational scenarios can be examined and evaluated before actual implementation (Li et al., 2026).

One of the important challenges in managing smart factories is the existence of multiple and sometimes conflicting goals in production planning. Industrial managers are often faced with problems in which they must simultaneously consider several different objectives, such as reducing production costs, reducing energy consumption, increasing machine efficiency, and reducing production completion time (Yordanova et al., 2026). Achieving these objectives simultaneously is often not possible, and therefore it is necessary to establish a balance between them. Multi-objective optimization methods are recognized as one of the important tools in analyzing such complex problems. These methods are able to provide a set of efficient solutions in the form of a Pareto front, each of which represents a compromise between different system objectives (Peng et al., 2026).

Combining digital twin technology with multi-objective optimization methods can create new capacities for improving the performance of manufacturing systems. Digital twin allows for the simulation of system behavior under different conditions, while optimization algorithms are able to identify the best operational decisions among different options (Nozari, 2026). Such a combination can lead to the creation of an advanced decision-support framework for manufacturing operations management. In this framework, real production data is received from the physical system and analyzed in the digital environment, and then optimization algorithms are used to find the best operational solutions (Son, 2026).

In recent years, researchers and industries have increased their attention to the use of digital twins in various manufacturing areas. Applications of this technology include equipment condition monitoring, machinery failure prediction, energy consumption optimization, and intelligent production planning. However, many existing studies have focused more on the simulation or system monitoring aspects and have paid less attention to the development of comprehensive decision-support frameworks based on multi-objective optimization. On the other hand, many of the models presented in this area lack detailed analytical structures to examine the interaction between different system performance indicators.

Given these challenges, it is of particular importance to develop analytical models that can simultaneously manage multiple operational objectives in smart manufacturing environments. The use of metaheuristic algorithms in multi-objective optimization problems has attracted much attention due to their ability to search a large solution space and identify diverse Pareto fronts. Algorithms such as NSGA-II and MOPSO have been widely used in complex engineering and management problems and have shown a high ability to find a set of efficient solutions.

Accordingly, the present study aims to develop an integrated framework for optimizing operations in smart factories based on digital twins. In this study, a multi-objective mathematical model for planning and optimizing manufacturing operations is presented and two metaheuristic algorithms, NSGA-II and MOPSO, are used to solve it. Also, in order to examine the performance of the proposed model, various analyses have been conducted, including Pareto front analysis, demand sensitivity analysis, energy constraint analysis, and machinery utilization analysis. The results show that combining digital twin with multi-objective optimization methods can provide an effective tool for improving operational decisions in smart factory environments and pave the way for the development of smarter and more efficient manufacturing systems in the future.

2. LITERATURE REVIEW

The expansion of digital technologies in the field of industrial production has led to concepts such as smart factories, cyber-physical systems, and data-driven manufacturing being widely considered in scientific research. In this regard, digital twins have been proposed as one of the key technologies in the digital transformation of industries (Li et al., 2026). By creating a dynamic virtual model of physical systems, this technology enables continuous monitoring, data analysis, and prediction of the behavior of real systems. Early research in this area has mainly focused on developing conceptual frameworks and technical architectures for implementing digital twins in industrial environments. These studies have shown that the use of digital twins can improve the visibility of manufacturing systems, increase the transparency of operational processes, and improve the quality of decision-making in industrial organizations (Nozari & Yordanova, 2026).

In the continuation of this research stream, several studies have investigated the application of digital twins in optimizing manufacturing processes. In these studies, digital twins have been used as a platform for simulating various manufacturing scenarios so that managers can evaluate the consequences of operational decisions before they are actually implemented (Shen et al., 2026). The results of these studies show that the use of digital twin-based simulation models can play a significant role in reducing operating costs, increasing the efficiency of manufacturing systems, and improving production planning. In addition, some studies have emphasized the use of real-time data in the digital twin environment and have shown that combining sensor data with analytical models can help to more accurately predict the performance of manufacturing systems (Fu & Zhu, 2026).

On the other hand, multi-objective optimization has attracted much attention in recent years as one of the important tools in analyzing complex engineering and management problems. In many industrial problems, decision-making based on a single objective is not possible and several different objectives need to be considered simultaneously (Yordanova & Nozari, 2026). For example, in production planning, objectives such as reducing production costs, reducing energy consumption, increasing machine efficiency, and reducing order completion time may be considered simultaneously. Multi-objective optimization methods, by providing a set of Pareto solutions, enable decision-makers to balance different system objectives and select the best option based on operational conditions (Paul et al., 2026).

In recent years, combining multi-objective optimization methods with digital simulation environments has been proposed as a new approach in manufacturing system management. In this approach, simulated models of the manufacturing system are used as a platform for evaluating the performance of different solutions, and optimization algorithms are responsible for searching for the best operational decisions (Bordbar et al., 2026). Such an approach can help identify more efficient production policies and increase the flexibility of industrial systems. Various studies have shown that the combination of simulation and optimization can provide effective results in complex problems such as production planning, machine scheduling, and production resource management (Nozari & Yordanova, 2025).

Another important topic that has been considered in the research literature is the role of energy management in manufacturing systems. With increasing energy costs and environmental concerns, many industries have tried to reduce energy consumption in manufacturing processes. In this context, several studies have developed optimization models for managing energy consumption in smart factories. The results of these studies show that the use of analytical methods and optimization algorithms can lead to a significant reduction in energy consumption in manufacturing systems. Some studies have also emphasized that integrating energy management with production planning can play an important role in improving the overall efficiency of industrial systems (Kolate et al., 2026).

In addition to energy management, effective utilization of machinery is also considered one of the key factors in improving the performance of manufacturing systems. Several studies have shown that proper planning for the use of production equipment can increase productivity, reduce waiting times, and reduce operating costs. In the meantime, the use of analytical models and optimization methods to determine the appropriate level of utilization of machinery has been widely investigated. These studies show that determining a balanced level of equipment utilization can prevent the creation of production bottlenecks and improve the overall performance of the system (Nozari, 2025).

Despite significant advances in the field of digital twins and multi-objective optimization, there are still several challenges in integrating these two areas. Many existing studies have focused more on developing conceptual models or optimization algorithms, and have not provided comprehensive frameworks for incorporating these technologies into real-world manufacturing environments. Furthermore, some studies lack comprehensive analyses of the impact of various operational factors, such as demand fluctuations, energy constraints, and machine utilization levels, on the performance of manufacturing systems (Luo et al., 2026).

Accordingly, there is an increasing need to develop integrated analytical frameworks that can simultaneously utilize digital twin capabilities and multi-objective optimization algorithms. Such frameworks can enable more accurate analysis of manufacturing systems, evaluation of different operational scenarios, and identification of optimal solutions for managing production resources. In this regard, the present study has attempted to provide an analytical framework for optimizing operations in digital twin-based smart factories by presenting a multi-objective mathematical model and using meta-heuristic algorithms, and to evaluate the efficiency and capabilities of this approach through various analyses.

3. MULTI-OBJECTIVE OPTIMIZATION IN SMART MANUFACTURING SYSTEMS

Modern manufacturing environments, especially in the form of smart factories, are faced with a set of complex and multidimensional decisions that often have conflicting objectives. In such systems, production managers and decision support systems must simultaneously pay attention to different objectives such as reducing operating costs, increasing equipment productivity, reducing order delivery time, improving product quality, and reducing energy consumption. Achieving all of these objectives simultaneously is usually not possible, and for this reason, the decision-making problem in these environments is naturally defined in the form of multi-objective optimization problems.

In traditional manufacturing systems, many production planning models are designed based on single-objective optimization; for example, the main focus may be solely on minimizing cost or minimizing production completion time. However, in smart factories operating within the framework of the Fourth Industrial Revolution, such an approach no longer responds to the existing complexities. In these environments, manufacturing systems are faced with a large volume of real-time data, dynamic interactions between machines, and rapid changes in market demand. As a result, effective decision-making requires considering multiple objectives simultaneously and finding solutions that strike a good balance between these objectives.

One of the fundamental concepts in multi-objective optimization is the concept of Pareto optimality. In this framework, a solution is considered optimal when an improvement in one of the objectives is not possible without worsening at least one of the other objectives. A set of such solutions is known as a Pareto front and represents a set of decision-making options, each of which offers a compromise between different objectives. In manufacturing environments, this front can represent different scenarios of resource allocation, production planning, or energy management, each with its own advantages and limitations.

In smart factories, multi-objective optimization problems are usually addressed in various areas. One of the most important of these areas is production scheduling, where goals such as reducing order completion time, increasing machine utilization, and reducing order delivery delays must be addressed simultaneously. Another area is energy consumption optimization in production lines, where efforts are made to reduce energy consumption and related costs while maintaining the desired level of production. In addition, issues related to production resource allocation, maintenance planning, and material flow management in the factory are also often modeled in the form of multi-objective problems.

Due to the complexity of these problems, the use of classical mathematical programming methods in many cases faces limitations, especially when the dimensions of the problem are large or the relationships between variables are nonlinear and dynamic. For this reason, in recent years, the use of metaheuristic and evolutionary algorithms in the field of production optimization has received widespread attention. These algorithms are able to identify a set of Pareto solutions in the search space without the need for severe model simplification.

Among these methods, algorithms such as NSGA-II (Non-dominated Sorting Genetic Algorithm II), MOPSO (Multi-Objective Particle Swarm Optimization), and MOEA/D (Multi-Objective Evolutionary Algorithm based on Decomposition) are among the most widely used methods in manufacturing problems. These algorithms use evolutionary mechanisms, such as selection, combination, and mutation, to gradually guide a population of solutions towards optimal regions of the search space. The main advantage of these approaches is their ability to find a diverse set of Pareto solutions that can help decision makers choose the right option according to the operational conditions and organizational priorities.

In the context of smart factories, multi-objective optimization is often combined with advanced technologies such as industrial data analytics, the Internet of Things, and digital twins. These technologies provide access to accurate and real-time data from production equipment and processes, and as a result, optimization models can be run based on real-time and up-to-date information. Such a capability paves the way for the creation of dynamic decision support systems that are able to continuously monitor the state of the production system and propose optimal solutions.

In summary, multi-objective optimization is one of the key tools for managing complexity in smart factories. This approach allows for the design of more efficient and flexible production policies by providing a framework for the simultaneous analysis of different operational objectives. Combined with digital twin technology, this approach can lead to the creation of intelligent manufacturing systems that are able to continuously evaluate their performance and adjust operational decisions to achieve the best balance between different objectives.

4. DIGITAL TWIN-DRIVEN OPTIMIZATION ARCHITECTURE FOR SMART FACTORIES

In smart factories, operational decision-making is no longer based solely on historical data or static models, but requires a dynamic and data-driven framework that can reflect the real state of the production system at any moment. In this regard, digital twin technology is recognized as one of the key tools in integrating physical data, analytical models, and decision-making algorithms. A digital twin is actually a virtual and dynamic representation of the real system that is continuously updated using data from sensors and industrial information systems, enabling analysis, prediction, and optimization of production processes.

The digital twin-based optimization architecture in smart factories usually consists of several main layers, each of which has a specific task in data management and decision-making. The first layer is the physical factory layer, which includes production machinery, robots, assembly lines, material handling systems, and other industrial equipment. These devices are connected to a set of industrial sensors and controllers that record data such as temperature, pressure, production speed, energy consumption and equipment operating status.

Next, the collected data is transmitted to the data processing layer via industrial communication infrastructures such as the Industrial Internet of Things (IIoT). This layer is responsible for storing, pre-processing and integrating production data. In many modern factories, this data is stored in industrial data platforms or manufacturing data management systems to enable advanced analytics and modeling.

Next comes the digital twin modeling layer, where a virtual model of the production system is created. This model can include process simulation models, equipment performance models, energy consumption models and even failure prediction models. By receiving real-time data from the real system, the digital twin reflects the current state of the factory and allows for the examination of various operational scenarios.

The next layer is the data analysis and learning layer, where data analysis methods, machine learning and predictive models are used to extract knowledge from production data. This layer can identify patterns in system performance, equipment behavior and production trends, providing valuable information for the decision-making process.

Finally, there is the optimization and decision-making layer, where multi-objective optimization algorithms are implemented. Using the data and models available in the digital twin, these algorithms evaluate various operational scenarios and propose a set of optimal solutions. The optimization results can be sent directly to the factory control systems or used as a decision support tool for production managers. The general structure of this architecture is shown in Figure 1.

Figure 1. Digital Twin-Based Optimization Architecture in Smart Factories

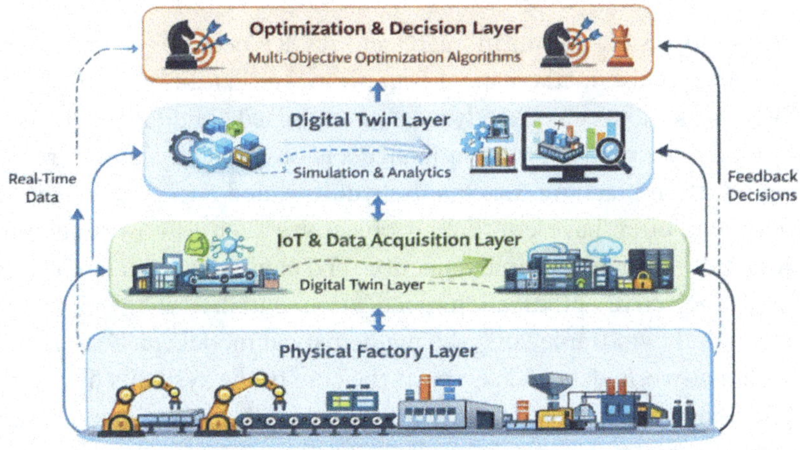

After deploying such an architecture, the optimization process in the factory operates as a dynamic cycle. First, operational data is collected from equipment and sensors and transferred to the digital twin model. Then, the virtual model of the manufacturing system is updated based on this data and represents the current state of the factory. Next, analytical and optimization algorithms are run on this model and a set of operational scenarios are evaluated.

One of the most important advantages of this approach is the ability to analyze different scenarios without disrupting the real system. In other words, production managers can first test different scheduling policies, resource allocation, or process parameter settings in the digital twin environment and then implement the best option in the real factory. This capability significantly reduces decision-making risk and enables continuous improvement of the performance of the manufacturing system.

In addition, the digital twin architecture enables the creation of an adaptive decision-making system that can react quickly to environmental changes or production disruptions. For example, in the event of a machine failure or a sudden increase in demand, the digital twin model can quickly evaluate alternative scenarios and propose a new production plan. Such a capability plays an important role in increasing the flexibility and resilience of smart factories.

Overall, the digital twin optimization architecture provides a unified framework for connecting physical data, analytical models, and decision-making algorithms. This framework allows smart factories to continuously monitor their production processes using real-time data and advanced models and adjust operational decisions to achieve the best balance between different production objectives.

5. MATHEMATICAL MODEL

To support decision-making in smart factories, it is necessary to model operational processes in a precise mathematical framework so that different objectives of the manufacturing system can be analyzed and optimized simultaneously. In advanced manufacturing environments, operational decisions typically involve resource allocation, production planning, machine scheduling, and energy management. Since these decisions often have conflicting objectives such as cost reduction, energy reduction, order completion time reduction, and equipment efficiency increase, the use of multi-objective optimization models is essential.

In the digital twin framework, the mathematical model can be dynamically updated with real-world data and serves as the core of the system's decision-making. In the following, the structure of a multi-objective optimization model for operations management in smart factories is presented.

Sets:

$i \in I$: Set of machines in the smart factory

$j \in J$: Set of products

$t \in T$: Set of time periods in the planning horizon

$k \in K$: Set of objective functions

Parameters:

$D_{j,t}$: Demand of product j during period t

$C_{i,j}$: Production cost of product j on machine i

$E_{i,j}$: Energy consumption rate for producing product j on machine i

$PT_{i,j}$: Processing time of product j on machine i

Cap_i: Available production capacity of machine i

EC_t: Energy cost during time period t

M_i: Maximum production capability of machine i

Decision Variables:

$x_{i,j,t} \geq 0$: Quantity of product j produced on machine i during period t
$y_{i,t} \in \{0,1\}$: Binary variable indicating whether machine i is active in period t
$I_{j,t} \geq 0$: Inventory level of product j at the end of period t
Objective Functions:

$$Z_1 = \sum_{i \in I} \sum_{j \in J} \sum_{t \in T} C_{i,j} x_{i,j,t} \tag{1}$$

$$Z_2 = \sum_{i \in I} \sum_{j \in J} \sum_{t \in T} E_{i,j} EC_t x_{i,j,t} \tag{2}$$

$$Z_3 = \sum_{i \in I} \sum_{j \in J} \sum_{t \in T} PT_{i,j} x_{i,j,t} \tag{3}$$

$$Z_4 = \sum_{i \in I} \sum_{j \in J} \sum_{t \in T} x_{i,j,t} \tag{4}$$

S.t:

$$\sum_{i \in I} x_{i,j,t} + I_{j,t-1} - I_{j,t} \geq D_{j,t} \ \forall j \in J, t \in T \tag{5}$$

$$\sum_{j \in J} PT_{i,j} x_{i,j,t} \leq \text{Cap}_i \ \forall i \in I, t \in T \tag{6}$$

$$\sum_{j \in J} x_{i,j,t} \leq M_i y_{i,t} \ \forall i \in I, t \in T \tag{7}$$

$$\sum_{i \in I} \sum_{j \in J} E_{i,j} x_{i,j,t} \leq \text{EnergyCap}_t \ \forall t \in T \tag{8}$$

$$I_{j,t} = I_{j,t-1} + \sum_{i \in I} x_{i,j,t} - D_{j,t} \ \forall j \in J, t \in T \tag{9}$$

$$x_{i,j,t} \leq M_i \ \forall i \in I, j \in J, t \in T \tag{10}$$

$$x_{i,j,t} \geq 0$$
$$I_{j,t} \geq 0 \tag{11}$$
$$y_{i,t} \in \{0,1\}$$

Objective function (1) represents the minimization of the total cost of production in the smart factory. This function attempts to reduce the total costs associated with producing different products on different machines over the planning horizon. In fact, each unit of production manufactured in the system has a specific cost that can include operating costs, machine usage costs, labor costs, or other costs associated with the production process. Therefore, by aggregating all these costs at the system level, this objective function guides the production policy towards selecting combinations that create the lowest overall cost for the factory. Objective function (2) represents the minimization of the costs resulting from energy consumption in the production process. In smart factories, energy consumption is considered one of the important factors in operational efficiency and system sustainability. Different machines consume energy when producing products, and this energy consumption can vary depending on the type of machine, type of product, and production time. This objective function attempts to adjust the production mix in such a way that energy consumption and related costs are reduced at the system level, taking into account energy costs at different time periods. Objective function (3) is concerned with minimizing the total production time in the system. In competitive manufacturing environments, reducing the time for performing production operations and delivering orders faster is of great importance. This objective function seeks to reduce the total time required to produce different products on existing machinery. In other words, the manufacturing system is directed towards programs in which processing times are managed more efficiently and the total duration of production operations in the factory is reduced. Objective function (4) is dedicated to maximizing the utilization of machinery. In many modern factories, production equipment has a high investment cost, and its effective use plays an important role in increasing productivity. This objective function tries to increase the level of machine utilization so that the capacities available in the production system are better utilized and equipment is prevented from being idle. Constraint (5) is related to the supply of product demand. This constraint ensures that the production quantity of each product in different time periods is sufficient to meet the needs of customers. If there is inventory from previous periods in the system, this inventory is also considered in supplying demand. Therefore, this constraint plays an important role in ensuring that the production system responds to market needs. Constraint (6) represents the capacity constraint of the machines. Each machine in the factory has a certain production capacity in each time period and cannot operate beyond this capacity. This constraint ensures that the total production activities assigned to each machine do not exceed its operating capacity. Compliance with this constraint is essential to maintain the model's realism and prevent unfeasible production plans. Constraint (7) is related to the active or inactive state of the machinery. This constraint specifies that production on a machine is only possible if that machine is active during the given time period. In other words, if a machine is not active during a time period, no production activity can be assigned to it. This constraint allows the model to take into account the on or off state of the equipment in the production planning process. Constraint (8) expresses the energy consumption constraint in the production system. Modern factories usually face energy consumption constraints that may be due to the capacity of the power grid, environmental constraints, or energy management policies. This constraint ensures that the amount of energy consumed in any time period does not exceed a certain limit and that the production system operates within the energy constraints. Constraint (9) balances the inventory of products over different time periods. According to this constraint, the inventory of each product at the end of each period is equal to the inventory of the previous period plus the amount of new production minus the amount of satisfied demand. This relationship maintains the logical flow of materials in the production system and ensures that inventories are managed consistently over time. Constraint (10) is related to production feasibility and ensures that the amount of production assigned to each machine does not exceed its production capacity. This constraint defines an upper operating limit for production on each machine and prevents the creation of unrealistic production schedules. Constraint (11) specifies the range of decision variables. According to this constraint, the values related to production and inventory cannot be negative, and the variable related to machine activity can only take the values of zero or one. These constraints ensure that the variables in the model have logical values that can be interpreted within the framework of the production system.

6. DIGITAL TWIN-BASED SIMULATION AND OPTIMIZATION WORKFLOW

In smart factories, operational decision-making is not only based on predetermined plans, but has become a dynamic process that is continuously fed by real data from the production system. In such an environment, the digital twin acts as an analytical platform that is able to reflect the real state of the factory, predict the future behavior of the system, and evaluate different decision-making scenarios before actual implementation. For this reason, the simulation and optimization process in the digital twin environment is usually defined as a continuous cycle of data acquisition, model update, scenario analysis, and operational decision implementation.

In the first step of this cycle, operational data is collected from production equipment and machinery. This data is transmitted to data management systems via sensors, industrial controllers, and industrial IoT infrastructure. Information such as machine operating status, production rates, processing times, energy consumption, and environmental conditions are among the data used to monitor the status of the manufacturing system. After collection, this data is pre-processed and stored in industrial databases for later analysis.

Next, the processed data is used to update the digital twin model. A digital twin is a virtual model of a manufacturing system that represents the structure, behavior, and operational status of the factory in a digital environment. By receiving real-time data, this model can provide an accurate picture of the current state of the system.

As a result, the digital twin becomes a virtual laboratory where the performance of the manufacturing system can be examined without disrupting real operations.

After updating the twin model, the simulation phase of operational scenarios begins. In this phase, different production scenarios, such as changes in the production schedule, changes in resource allocation, or changes in process parameters, are tested in the digital twin environment. The goal of these simulations is to evaluate the impact of different decisions on the performance indicators of the manufacturing system. These indicators can include production cost, order completion time, equipment utilization, and energy consumption.

After evaluating the scenarios, multi-objective optimization algorithms are run to identify suitable solutions. Using the mathematical model of the manufacturing system and updated digital twin data, these algorithms examine a set of possible solutions and propose solutions that create the best balance between the different system objectives. The output of this phase is usually a set of Pareto solutions, each of which represents a different operating policy in the manufacturing system. The general structure of this process is shown in Figure 2.

Figure 2. Digital Twin-Based Simulation and Optimization Workflow in Smart Factories

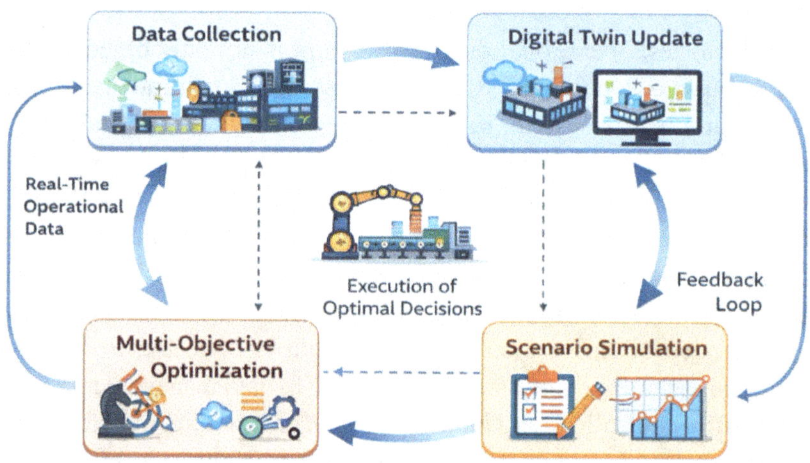

In this framework, the decision-making process operates as a feedback loop. After the optimal decisions are implemented in the real system, new data is generated from the factory performance and this data is transmitted back to the digital twin environment. In this way, the twin model always remains in sync with the real state of the system and can provide new analyses at any time.

One of the important advantages of this approach is that it allows for the examination of different scenarios before their actual implementation. In other words, production managers can first test different operational policies in the digital twin environment and only after evaluating the results, implement the best option in the real system. This capability significantly reduces decision-making risk and prevents disruptions to production operations.

In addition, the use of such a cycle allows the production system to continuously learn and improve. Each time new data is entered into the system, the twin model becomes more accurate and the optimization algorithms can provide more efficient solutions. As a result, the factory gradually moves towards an intelligent and adaptive production system that is able to react quickly and make optimal decisions in the face of environmental changes, demand fluctuations or operational disruptions.

7. SOLUTION APPROACHES

Solving the presented optimization model requires the use of efficient metaheuristic methods due to the multi-objective nature and relatively large dimensions of the problem. In multi-objective optimization problems, the goal is to find a set of efficient solutions that can strike a good balance between different objectives. For this reason, two well-known algorithms in the field of multi-objective optimization, namely NSGA-II (Non-dominated Sorting Genetic Algorithm II) and MOPSO (Multi-Objective Particle Swarm Optimization), were used in this research. These algorithms have been used in many engineering problems and manufacturing systems due to their high ability to search the solution space, maintain diversity in the response set, and generate an appropriate Pareto front.

The Python programming language version 3.10 was used to implement the algorithms. The algorithms were implemented in the PyCharm 2023 environment, and standard scientific libraries including NumPy, Pandas, and Matplotlib were used to process data and analyze the results. In order to achieve stable results and reduce the random effects in metaheuristic algorithms, each algorithm was tested in 30 independent runs and the best Pareto response set in each run was recorded.

To validate the results obtained from the metaheuristic algorithms, the mathematical model was implemented in GAMS version 40 and the CPLEX solver was used to solve the model on a small scale. The results obtained from the exact solution of the model in GAMS were compared with the output of the proposed algorithms to evaluate the accuracy of the performance of the metaheuristic methods.

The NSGA-II algorithm is one of the widely used evolutionary methods in multi-objective optimization that uses the non-dominated sorting mechanism and the concept of crowding distance to maintain population diversity. In this algorithm, a population of solutions is randomly generated and improved in each generation using selection, crossover, and mutation operators. Then, a non-dominated sorting process is performed and the best solutions are selected for the next generation based on the Pareto surface and the crowding distance. This process continues until a stopping criterion is reached (Nozari et al., 2025).

The MOPSO algorithm is also a multi-objective version of the particle swarm optimization algorithm that simulates the collective behavior of particles in the search space (Albelwi, 2026). In this method, each particle represents a potential solution and its position in the search space is updated based on the particle's personal experience as well as the best solutions in the Pareto repository. Using an external repository to store non-dominated solutions helps the algorithm maintain a diverse set of Pareto solutions during the search process. The general steps of the model solving process using metaheuristic algorithms are presented in Figure 3.

Figure 3. Metaheuristic Optimization Framework for Solving the Smart Factory Model

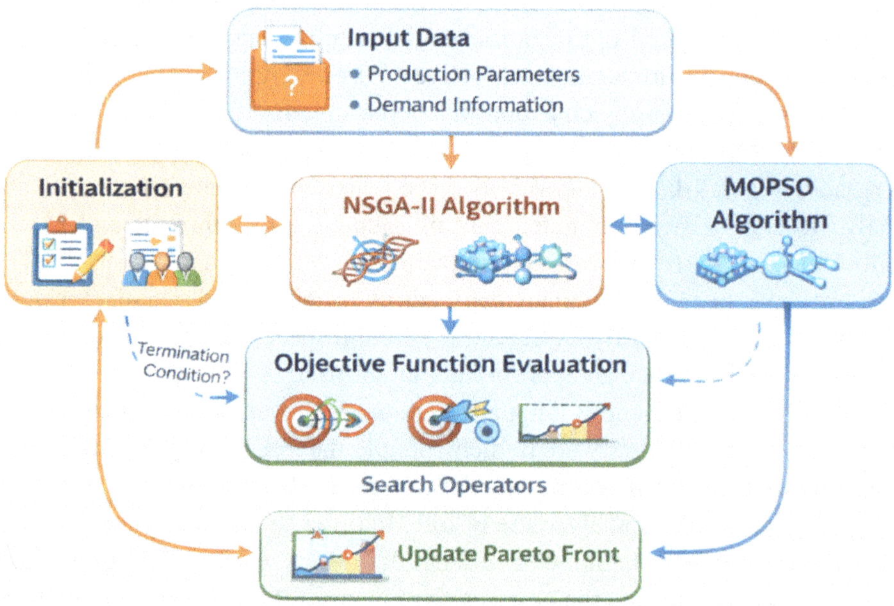

In this framework, first, input data including production system parameters and demand information are received. Then, the initial population of solutions is randomly generated. The optimization algorithms then explore the solution space by evaluating the objective functions and applying search operators. At each iteration, the set of non-dominated solutions is updated and finally the final Pareto front is extracted.

The parameter settings of the metaheuristic algorithms play an important role in the quality of the obtained answers. The parameters used for each of the NSGA-II and MOPSO algorithms are presented in Table 1.

Table 1. Parameter Settings of the Optimization Algorithms

Parameter	NSGA-II	MOPSO
Population Size	100	100
Number of Iterations	200	200
Crossover Probability	0.8	—
Mutation Probability	0.1	—
Inertia Weight	—	0.7
Cognitive Coefficient	—	1.5
Social Coefficient	—	1.5
Archive Size	—	100

The parameters presented in Table 1 were adjusted based on previous studies and initial experiments to create a good balance between the speed of convergence and the diversity of the answers. The population size and the number of iterations were chosen so that the algorithms could explore the problem search space effectively. In the NSGA-II algorithm, the crossover and mutation probabilities were adjusted to create diversity in the population and prevent premature convergence. In the MOPSO algorithm, inertia weight and cognitive and social coefficients were also considered to create a balance between global search and local search in the solution space.

After running the algorithms, the Pareto solution set was extracted and the performance of the algorithms was evaluated based on criteria such as the quality of the Pareto front, the diversity of responses, and the value of the objective functions. Comparing the results with the responses obtained from the exact solution of the model in the GAMS environment showed that the metaheuristic algorithms were able to provide solutions with appropriate quality and acceptable computational time. This indicates that the use of metaheuristic methods can be an effective approach to solving complex optimization problems in the environment of smart factories and digital twin-based systems.

8. ANALYSIS OF RESULTS

The analysis of the results of this study was based on a set of simulated data designed to represent the operating conditions of a smart factory. Due to the limited availability of real industrial data and to precisely control the experimental conditions, all parameters used were generated through a structured simulation framework. These data were designed to reflect common features of modern manufacturing systems, including product diversity, machine capacity constraints, differences in processing times, and changes in demand over time. In this way, the experimental environment was set up to represent the real behavior of a multi-product manufacturing system in smart factories and to allow the performance of optimization algorithms to be evaluated under realistic conditions.

The data set included information on manufacturing machines, products, cost parameters, energy consumption, and market demand. The number of machines and products was determined to bring the complexity of the problem to a level that was both solvable by the proposed algorithms and could reflect the structure of real manufacturing problems. Processing times, production costs, and energy consumption rates for each machine and product combination were randomly generated at specified intervals to simulate the natural heterogeneity found in real manufacturing systems. Product demand was also generated for different time periods using appropriate statistical distributions to reflect typical market fluctuations. In addition, machine capacities and energy constraints were determined to maintain a balance between supply and demand in the system while considering realistic operational constraints in the model.

To comprehensively evaluate the performance of the model and the proposed algorithms, several test scenarios were designed, each representing different operating conditions in the smart factory. These scenarios included changes in demand levels, changes in machine production capacities, and changes in system energy constraints. In some scenarios, market demand was increased to examine the system's performance under production pressure, while in other scenarios, stricter energy constraints were imposed to evaluate the model's ability to manage energy resources. Such scenario design allowed for the analysis of system behavior under different operating conditions and helped to more accurately evaluate the efficiency of optimization algorithms in dynamic production environments.

The performance comparison of NSGA-II and MOPSO algorithms was conducted to evaluate their ability to generate a set of efficient solutions for the smart factory optimization problem. Both algorithms were run under identical conditions and with the parameter settings presented in the parameter setting table. To increase the validity of the results, each algorithm was tested in 30 independent runs and the average values of the objective functions and computational time were recorded. The main evaluation criteria included the quality of the Pareto front, the degree of convergence towards better solutions, and the stability of the results across runs.

In order to visually demonstrate the performance of the algorithms, the Pareto front obtained from the execution of the algorithms is presented in Figure 4.

Figure 4. Comparison of Pareto Fronts Generated by NSGA-II and MOPSO

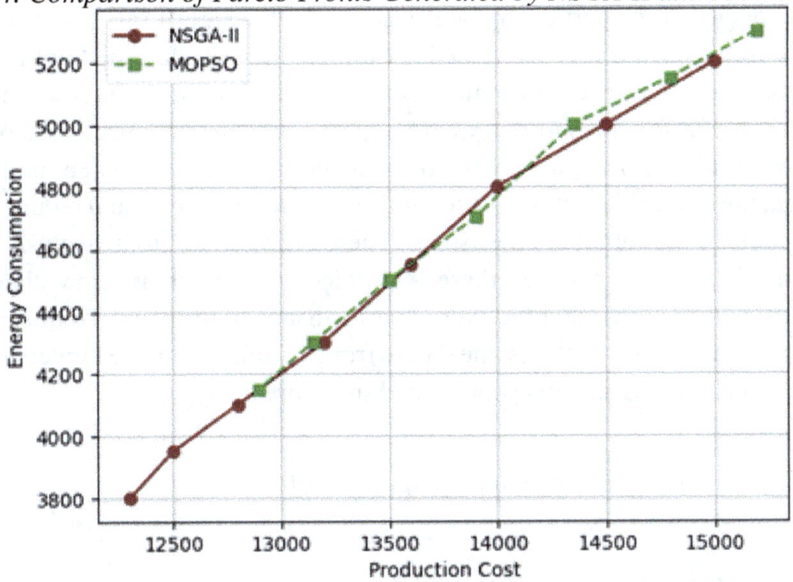

Figure 4 shows the distribution of Pareto solutions obtained by the two algorithms in the objective space. As can be seen, the NSGA-II algorithm was able to produce a more diverse set of responses along the Pareto front and provide a better coverage of the response space. In contrast, the MOPSO algorithm achieved quality responses in some regions of the target space, but the diversity of its generated responses was less than that of NSGA-II. This indicates that the non-dominated sorting mechanism and the use of crowding distance in NSGA-II were effective in maintaining population diversity.

To provide a quantitative comparison between the two algorithms, the numerical results from the runs are presented in Table 2.

Table 2. Performance Comparison of NSGA-II and MOPSO

Algorithm	Avg. Production Cost	Avg. Energy Cost	Avg. Production Time	Computational Time (s)
NSGA-II	12456	3982	842	41.7
MOPSO	12784	4126	865	38.9

The values presented in Table 2 show the average results obtained from independent runs of the algorithms. As can be seen, the NSGA-II algorithm was able to provide better values for the objective functions compared to MOPSO and kept the production cost, energy cost, and production time at a lower level. However, the computational time of the MOPSO algorithm was slightly lower, which is related to the simplicity of the particle update structure in this algorithm.

Pareto front analysis was performed to examine the distribution of optimal solutions in the objective space. In multi-objective optimization problems, the Pareto front represents a set of responses where improvement in one objective is possible only by worsening at least one of the other objectives. In the problem under consideration, the main objectives were to minimize production cost and reduce energy consumption in the production system. Therefore, Pareto front analysis allows examining the balance between these two objectives and shows how changes in production policies can affect the overall performance of the plant. To illustrate the distribution of efficient solutions, the Pareto front resulting from the implementation of the optimization algorithms is presented in Figure 5.

Figure 5. Pareto Front Distribution of Optimal Solutions

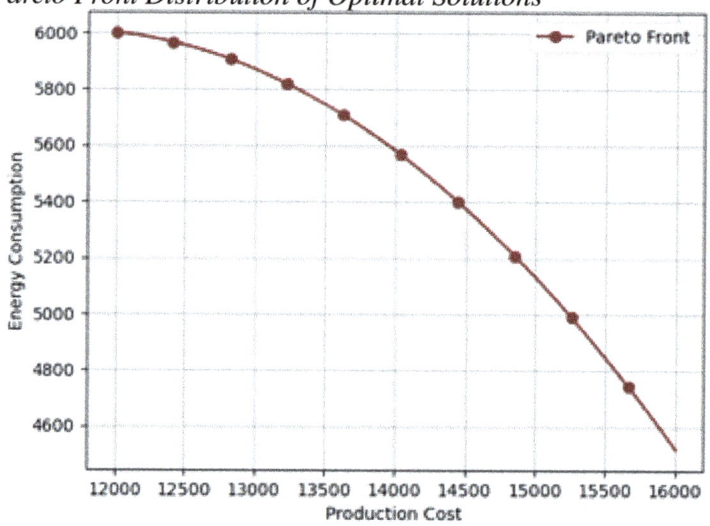

As can be seen in Figure 5, the optimal points are distributed in the objective space as a descending curve. This pattern shows that as production cost decreases, energy consumption usually increases and vice versa. In other words, it is not possible to simultaneously achieve the lowest production cost and the lowest energy consumption, and a compromise must be made between these two objectives. The middle regions of the Pareto front usually provide a better balance between the different objectives and can be more suitable options for operational decision-making in smart factories.

In addition, the relatively uniform distribution of points on the Pareto front indicates that the optimization algorithms have been able to identify a diverse set of efficient solutions in the search space. Such diversity allows decision-makers to select the appropriate option from among the available solutions, given operational conditions, energy constraints, or economic priorities.

Sensitivity analysis with respect to demand level changes was performed to examine the stability of the proposed model and also to evaluate the behavior of the production system under different market conditions. In this analysis, the demand level was changed in several different cases to determine the effect of increasing or decreasing demand on the performance indicators of the production system. For this purpose, the demand amount was changed in a range from 80% to 130% of the base demand and the optimization model was re-run for each demand level. The results provide an opportunity to examine how the production system responds to environmental changes and market pressures. In order to show the behavior of the system against demand changes, the results are presented in Figure 6.

Figure 6. Sensitivity Analysis with Respect to Demand Level

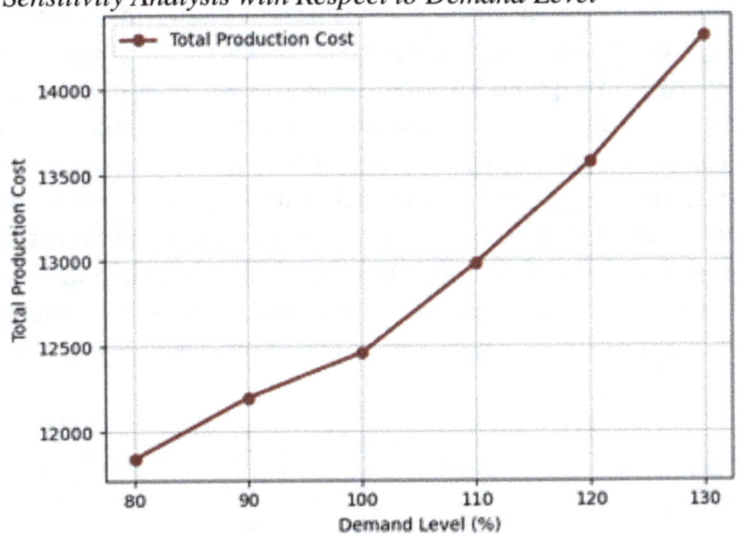

Figure 6 shows that with increasing demand, the total production cost increases gradually. This trend is natural because increasing demand leads to greater utilization of machinery capacity, increased equipment operating hours, and in some cases the use of production resources with higher costs. The slope of the curve increases at higher demand levels, indicating that the production system is facing increased operating costs near its full capacity. For a more detailed quantitative analysis, the results of the change in demand level are presented in Table 3.

Table 3. Impact of Demand Level on System Performance

Demand Level (%)	Production Cost	Energy Consumption	Production Time
80	11840	3725	795
90	12195	3862	812
100	12456	3982	842
110	12980	4210	875
120	13575	4458	910
130	14310	4725	948

The values presented in Table 3 show that increasing demand level not only increases production cost, but also significantly increases energy consumption and production time. This indicates that at higher demand levels, the production system is forced to use more of the available resources and capacities. However, the trend of changes in all indicators has been relatively uniform, indicating that the proposed model has been able to provide stable performance under different demand conditions.

The energy constraint impact analysis was conducted to investigate how the manufacturing system responds to different energy resource availability conditions. In many smart factories, energy consumption is a key factor in production planning, and energy constraints can directly affect operational decisions and production costs. To assess this, the energy capacity was varied at several different levels, and the optimization model was rerun for each energy level. In this experiment, the energy capacity was adjusted in a range from 70% to 120% of the baseline value to examine the system's performance under severe energy constraints as well as under conditions of greater energy availability. The results of this analysis are presented in Figure 7.

Figure 7. Sensitivity Analysis with Respect to Energy Constraints

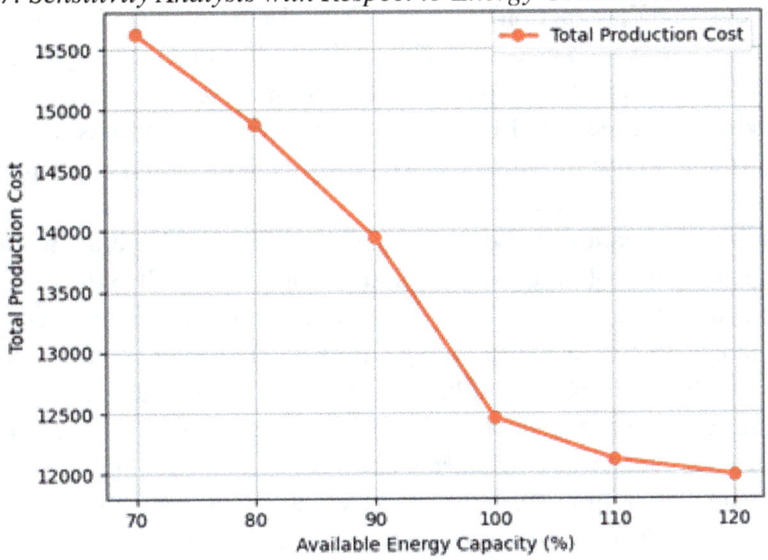

As can be seen in Figure 7, as the available energy capacity increases, the total production cost decreases. Under severe energy constraints, the manufacturing system is forced to use less efficient production schedules, which results in increased production costs. Increasing energy capacity allows for more efficient use of machinery and more efficient production schedules, thereby reducing the total cost of the system. The downward trend of the curve indicates that greater access to energy increases the flexibility of the production system and allows for the selection of more optimal solutions. For a more detailed numerical analysis, the results of changing energy capacity are presented in Table 4.

Table 4. Impact of Energy Constraints on System Performance

Energy Capacity (%)	Production Cost	Energy Consumption	Production Time
70	15620	3185	980
80	14875	3520	942
90	13940	3795	905
100	12456	3982	842
110	12110	4155	828
120	11980	4320	820

The values presented in Table 4 show that with increasing energy capacity, production costs and production operation times decrease, while the total energy consumption of the system increases. This indicates that under energy constraints, the production system is forced to reduce the activity level of some machinery or change production schedules. In contrast, when energy constraints are reduced, the system is able to use the full capacity of the equipment and implement more efficient production schedules.

The machine utilization analysis was conducted to investigate the relationship between the utilization of production equipment and the overall system efficiency. In a smart factory environment, the effective utilization of machines is considered one of the key factors in increasing productivity and reducing operating costs. To assess this, the level of machine utilization was set at several different levels and the performance of the manufacturing system was examined in each case. The system efficiency index was calculated based on a combination of criteria such as production completion time, machine capacity utilization, and system operational efficiency. The results of this analysis are presented in Figure 8.

Figure 8. Impact of Machine Utilization on System Efficiency

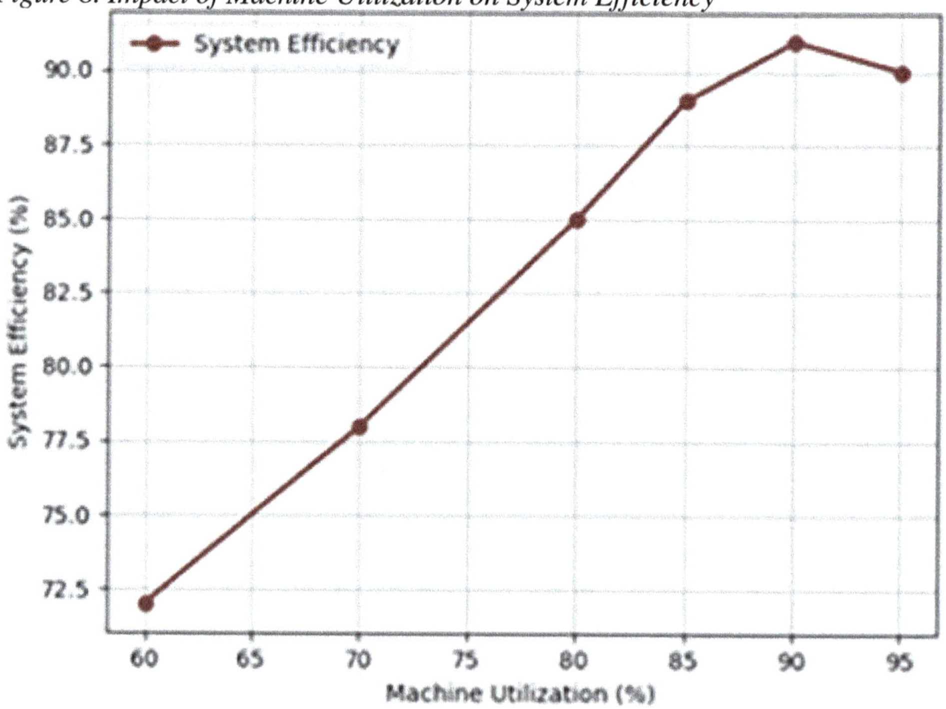

As can be seen in Figure 8, as the level of machine utilization increases, the efficiency of the manufacturing system increases significantly. At low levels of equipment utilization, a significant portion of the system capacity remains unused, resulting in a decrease in operational efficiency. As machine utilization increases, the efficient use of production resources increases and system performance improves.

However, at very high levels of utilization, the rate of increase in efficiency slows down and, in some cases, even drops slightly. This usually occurs when machines are approaching capacity and the likelihood of production bottlenecks or increased waiting times in the system increases.

9. CONCLUSION

The results of this study showed that the combination of digital twin with multi-objective optimization methods can be used as an effective approach for managing and optimizing operations in smart factories. The development of an integrated framework in which production data, digital simulation, and optimization algorithms are combined together allows for more accurate analysis of the behavior of production systems and more informed decision-making. Such a framework allows industrial managers and decision-makers to examine different operational scenarios before actual implementation in the production environment and select the best operational solutions.

The mathematical model presented in this study was designed by considering multiple objectives, including reducing production costs, reducing energy consumption, increasing machine productivity, and improving system efficiency. These objectives were simultaneously modeled in the form of a multi-objective optimization problem to create a proper balance between different system performance indicators. In real production environments, operational decisions are usually accompanied by several conflicting objectives, and therefore, the use of multi-objective approaches seems essential to analyze such complex problems.

In order to solve the presented model, two widely used metaheuristic algorithms, namely NSGA-II and MOPSO, were used. The results obtained showed that both algorithms are able to produce a suitable set of Pareto solutions and can provide diverse solutions for managerial decision-making. However, the comparison of the results showed that the NSGA-II algorithm in many cases was able to provide a more uniform distribution of optimal solutions on the Pareto front, while the MOPSO algorithm also showed a suitable convergence speed in some cases. Such results indicate that the use of a combination of different optimization methods can provide a more comprehensive view of the solution space.

Pareto front analysis showed that there is a trade-off between production cost and energy consumption. Reducing production cost is usually accompanied by increasing energy consumption and vice versa. This shows the importance of using multi-objective methods in production planning, because decision makers have to balance different system objectives. Examination of the shape of the Pareto front also showed that optimization algorithms were able to identify a diverse set of efficient solutions that can be the basis for decision-making under different operating conditions.

The results of the sensitivity analysis also provided important insights into the behavior of the system under different conditions. Examination of the changing demand level showed that increasing demand increases production cost, energy consumption, and operation time. This indicates that at higher demand levels, the production system will be forced to use more of the capacity of the equipment and available resources. On the other hand, energy constraint analysis showed that greater access to energy resources can help improve system efficiency and reduce production costs, while severe energy constraints may reduce the flexibility of the production system.

Also, the analysis of machine utilization showed that increasing the level of equipment utilization can significantly increase the efficiency of the manufacturing system. However, the results showed that excessive use of machines may also lead to the creation of production bottlenecks and reduced operational efficiency. Therefore, achieving a balanced level of equipment utilization is of great importance to maintain stable system performance.

Overall, the results of this research show that the use of digital twins along with multi-objective optimization algorithms can provide a powerful tool for improving the performance of smart factories. Such an approach allows analyzing different manufacturing scenarios, predicting system behavior, and selecting optimal solutions in complex industrial environments. In addition, the use of this framework can help improve resource efficiency, reduce operating costs, and increase the flexibility of manufacturing systems.

Future research could extend this framework using real industrial data and explore its relationship with technologies such as the Industrial Internet of Things, big data analytics, and advanced decision support systems. Also, developing dynamic models that are able to react in real time to changes in the production environment could be an important step towards realizing fully intelligent and self-organizing factories.

REFERENCES

Albelwi, N. (2026). DT-LCAF: Digital Twin-Enabled Life Cycle Assessment Framework for Real-Time Embodied Carbon Optimization in Smart Building Construction. *Sustainability (Basel)*, *18*(5), 2321. DOI: 10.3390/su18052321

Bordbar, A., Tadros, M., Nazemian, A., Aung, M. Z., Georgoulas, K., Louvros, P., & Boulougouris, E. (2026). Digitalisation of shipyard production planning: A review of simulation, optimisation, AI, and digital twin methods (2010–2025). *Journal of Marine Science and Engineering*, *14*(4), 396. DOI: 10.3390/jmse14040396

Fu, T., & Zhu, H. (2026). Digital-twin-based reinforcement learning method for flexible assembly job-shop scheduling with dynamic material kitting. *Computers & Industrial Engineering*, *214*, 111903. DOI: 10.1016/j.cie.2026.111903

Kolate, V. D., Chaudhary, M. K., Mane, S., & Devadhe, M. (2026). Digital twin–enabled model predictive control in additive manufacturing: Critical review, research challenges, and future directions. *Materials and Manufacturing Processes*, *41*(1), 1–17. DOI: 10.1080/10426914.2025.2586498

Li, J., Yan, W., Zhang, M., Zhu, S., Jiang, Z., & Fan, Z. (2026). Digital twin-based multi-view energy efficiency prediction for machining systems. Digital Twin, 2634493.

Li, M., Yang, C. M., Lo, W., & Kao, Y. W. (2026). A Digital-Twin-Enabled AI-Driven Adaptive Planning Platform for Sustainable and Reliable Manufacturing. *Machines (Basel)*, *14*(2), 197. DOI: 10.3390/machines14020197

Lin, C. Y., Tseng, T. L., & Tsai, T. H. (2026). A Digital Twin Framework With Deep Feature Extraction and Gaussian Process for Multi-Objective Optimization in Semiconductor Manufacturing. *IEEE Transactions on Automation Science and Engineering*, *23*, 1928–1949. DOI: 10.1109/TASE.2025.3650620

Luo, R., Zhou, S., Nie, L., Dong, B., & Guo, W. (2026). Digital twin-based resistance spot welding control. *International Journal of Advanced Manufacturing Technology*, •••, 1–14.

Nozari, H. (2025). Integrating Neuromorphic Intelligence with Fuzzy Multi-Objective Models in Resilient Green Supply Chain Design. Process Integration and Optimization for Sustainability, 1-14.

Nozari, H. (2026). Digital twin-based predictive maintenance in cold chain logistics. *Operations Research*, *60*(1), 481–499. DOI: 10.1051/ro/2025167

Nozari, H., Abdi, H., Szmelter-Jarosz, A., & Rahmaty, M. (2025). A digital twin-based neutrosophic multi-objective optimization model for smart supply chains in the food industry. *Journal of Intelligent Manufacturing*, •••, 1–15. DOI: 10.1007/s10845-025-02689-z

Nozari, H., Szmelter-Jarosz, A., & Weiland, D. (2025). A Fuzzy Multi-Objective Sustainable and Agile Supply Chain Model Based on Digital Twin and Internet of Things with Adaptive Learning Under Environmental Uncertainty. *Applied Sciences (Basel, Switzerland)*, *15*(19), 10399. DOI: 10.3390/app151910399

Nozari, H., & Yordanova, Z. (2025). An intelligent digital twin approach for optimizing multi-channel supply chains in uncertain environments. Green Technologies and Sustainability, 100309.

Nozari, H., & Yordanova, Z. (2026). An Adaptive Fuzzy Multi-Objective Digital Twin Framework for Multi-Depot Cold-Chain Vehicle Routing in Agri-Biotech Supply Networks. *Logistics (Basel)*, *10*(2), 27. DOI: 10.3390/logistics10020027

Paul, S., Manna, N., Roy, S., & Jana, T. K. (2026, January). A Machine Tool Digital Twin to Implement Smartness in Discrete Production Environment. In Recent Advances in Industrial and Systems Engineering: Selected Papers from International Conference on Industrial Engineering and Analytics (ICONIEA) 2024 (pp. 223-247). Singapore: Springer Nature Singapore. DOI: 10.1007/978-981-96-8323-9_14

Peng, L., Zhaojin, D., Disheng, Z., Hui, L., Xujiang, L., Weichao, C., & Wang, D. (2026). A Multi-Objective Optimization Framework for Energy–Efficiency Balance in Intelligent Tobacco Logistics Parks Based on NSGA-II. *International Journal of Pattern Recognition and Artificial Intelligence*.

Shen, B., Zeng, Y., Yu, H., Hu, P., Han, Z., & Cai, H. (2026). A Verifiable Digital Twin-aided AI (DTAI) Agent-based Production System Framework with Causally Consistent Symbiotic Simulation. IEEE Transactions on Industrial Cyber-Physical Systems.

Son, Y. H. (2026). Digital twin–enabled hybrid scheduling framework for multi-product cellular manufacturing systems. International Journal of Computer Integrated Manufacturing, 1-23.

Yordanova, Z., & Nozari, H. (2026). An Agentic Digital Twin Framework for Fuzzy Multi-Objective Optimization in Dynamic Humanitarian Logistics. *Algorithms*, *19*(3), 198. DOI: 10.3390/a19030198

Yordanova, Z., & Nozari, H. (2026). Cross-layer optimization for energy efficiency in super-smart cities of the future. In *Energy-Efficient Transformative Technologies for Data-Driven Smart Cities* (pp. 125–144). Elsevier. DOI: 10.1016/B978-0-443-27618-7.00013-3

Chapter 10
Digital Twins as an Enabler of Cognitive Enterprise Architecture:
Reconfiguring Organizational Systems and Decision Intelligence

Doni Sugianto Sihotang
http://orcid.org/0009-0008-5222-4475
Universitas Negeri Jakarta, Indonesia

ABSTRACT

This chapter analyzes the function of digital twins in facilitating Cognitive Enterprise Architecture (CEA) to revolutionize organizational systems and improve decision intelligence. Although current research mostly focuses on the technical and engineering dimensions of digital twins, there is a paucity of attention about their incorporation into corporate architecture and cognitive decision-making frameworks. This chapter bridges the gap by establishing a conceptual connection among digital twins, cognitive capacities, and decision intelligence. It examines critical concerns such as integration complexity, data governance, cybersecurity, and organizational preparedness, and delineates scalable architectural and strategic solutions. This chapter theoretically enhances enterprise design perspectives by integrating cognitive digital twin capabilities, providing a basis for intelligent, adaptable, and data-driven organizational transformation.

DOI: 10.4018/979-8-3373-9998-0.ch010

INTRODUCTION

1. Digital Transformation and the Rise of Cognitive Enterprises

Digital transformation has emerged as a pivotal catalyst for organizational change, allowing organizations to restructure processes, enhance capabilities, and innovate value generation through sophisticated digital technology. This transition transcends technical adoption, signifying a fundamental alteration in organizational operations, competition, and innovation within increasingly intricate and data-driven environments. The amalgamation of artificial intelligence (AI), the Internet of Things (IoT), and sophisticated analytics enables the merging of physical and digital systems, hence empowering organizations to attain improved operational efficiency, agility, and real-time responsiveness (Wan et al., 2023). As digital infrastructures advance, enterprises are increasingly shifting towards data-centric and intelligence-driven operational frameworks.

Digital transformation fundamentally requires the reorganization of organizational structures and decision-making frameworks. Conventional hierarchical and static models are being supplanted by dynamic, interrelated systems that facilitate ongoing learning and adaptive responses. This transition allows firms to progress from automation to the intelligent orchestration of processes and resources, integrating digital capabilities with strategic goals to maintain a competitive edge in unpredictable situations (Erkan et al., 2024). Nevertheless, current research mostly focuses on technology adoption and operational efficiency, with insufficient investigation into how digital transformation alters corporate architecture into cognitively adaptable systems.

The cognitive enterprise represents an advanced level of digital maturity, defined by the incorporation of cognitive technologies, including machine learning, predictive analytics, and intelligent automation, into organizational frameworks. Cognitive organizations have the potential to observe, learn, and adapt through integrated data-driven intelligence across business processes, converting raw data into actionable insights (Elia & Margherita, 2022). Notwithstanding this progress, the synergy between cognitive talents and enterprise architecture is still conceptually immature, especially with real-time decision intelligence and holistic flexibility.

Cognitive digital twins serve as a crucial facilitator in bridging this gap by offering dynamic virtual representations of physical assets and systems that perpetually synchronize with real-world data. These technologies facilitate simulation, prediction, and prescriptive decision-making, hence augmenting organizational intelligence and resilience (Al Faruque et al., 2021). Nevertheless, previous studies have predominantly concentrated on digital twins from a technical and operational standpoint, neglecting their significance in facilitating Cognitive Enterprise Architecture (CEA) and the integration of decision intelligence.

This chapter establishes digital twins as a strategic conduit between digital transformation and cognitive enterprise development by presenting an integrated viewpoint that connects digital twin capabilities with enterprise architecture and decision intelligence. It additionally establishes a conceptual framework for comprehending how digital twins enable the shift towards adaptive, intelligent, and changeable organizational structures, serving as the foundation for the framework elaborated in the next parts.

2. Role of Digital Twins in Organizational Reconfiguration

Digital twins (DTs) have become a crucial technology framework for facilitating organizational restructuring in complex, volatile, and data-rich situations. Digital twins provide dynamic, real-time digital representations of physical assets, processes, and systems, establishing a continuous feedback loop between the physical and virtual realms. This bidirectional interface allows firms to oversee operations, model various situations, and execute optimized decisions with enhanced accuracy and diminished risk. Consequently, digital twins are acknowledged as essential facilitators of the transition from conventional organizational frameworks to adaptive, intelligence-driven systems (Rosen & Pattipati, 2023).

The primary function of digital twins in organizational restructuring is to improve decision support via real-time analytics and simulation functionalities. Organizations can employ digital twins to assess various operational scenarios prior to enacting modifications in real surroundings, thus reducing inefficiencies and enhancing resource allocation. This feature is especially beneficial in production systems and workforce planning, as predicted insights provide proactive modifications and performance enhancement. Thus, digital twins facilitate the shift from reactive to predictive and prescriptive decision-making frameworks (Soylu & Yildiz, 2023). Nevertheless, current research predominantly emphasizes operational optimization and system efficiency, with insufficient consideration of how these skills may be systematically integrated into business design to enhance organization-wide decision intelligence.

Moreover, digital twins substantially enhance organizational agility by facilitating ongoing system reconfiguration in reaction to internal and external dynamics. In the framework of Industry 5.0, which prioritizes human-centricity, sustainability, and resilience, digital twins enable the synchronization of technology systems with changing organizational objectives. Their capacity to amalgamate diverse data sources and deliver comprehensive system visibility enables firms to swiftly adapt to market fluctuations, technological upheavals, and operational ambiguities (Imandi et al., 2025). Notwithstanding these benefits, the research has inadequately explored the structural integration of digital twin-enabled agility inside Cognitive Enterprise Architecture (CEA) to facilitate adaptable and intelligent organizational behavior.

A fundamental part of digital twins is their function in facilitating modular and reconfigurable system architectures. Digital twins facilitate flexible system design and the creation of reconfigurable industrial and enterprise systems by disaggregating complicated systems into interoperable components. This flexibility improves scalability and enables ongoing innovation by permitting businesses to dynamically modify both physical and informational elements in real time (de Cunha et al., 2021). Nonetheless, previous studies often regard modularity as a technological attribute rather than a strategic architectural tool for comprehensive organizational reform.

This chapter rectifies these deficiencies by framing digital twins as essential components of Cognitive Enterprise Architecture, rather than merely operational instruments. It presents a comprehensive viewpoint wherein digital twin functionalities are synchronized with cognitive processes and decision intelligence frameworks, establishing a conceptual model that elucidates how organizations can attain intelligent, adaptive, and reconfigurable systems via digital twin-enabled architectures.

3. Chapter Objectives and Scope

This chapter seeks to deliver a thorough and comprehensive analysis of digital twins as a pivotal facilitator of Cognitive Enterprise Architecture (CEA), emphasizing the transformation of physical assets into intelligent, adaptive, and data-driven systems within enterprises. Amidst the rapid digital revolution, firms must increasingly reconfigure their structures, processes, and decision-making frameworks to maintain competitiveness. Although previous research has examined digital twins mainly from technical and operational viewpoints, there has been insufficient focus on their strategic function in transforming corporate design and facilitating decision intelligence. This chapter fills this gap by establishing digital twins as essential elements in the progression towards cognitive and self-optimizing organizational systems.

The main aim of this chapter is to elucidate the connection between digital twins and cognitive technologies, such as artificial intelligence, machine learning, and advanced analytics, as fundamental components of enterprise systems. This integration is crucial for facilitating real-time data processing, predictive modeling, and autonomous decision-making across organizational functions. This chapter enhances current viewpoints by demonstrating how digital twins transition from mere monitoring instruments to fundamental components of decision intelligence frameworks (Lezoche & Torres, 2024). It creates a theoretical connection between digital twin functionalities and cognitive enterprise processes.

Another purpose is to examine the structural ramifications of digital twin implementation on organizational design and enterprise architecture. Digital twins synchronize physical assets with digital infrastructures, allowing for uninterrupted data flows throughout organizational tiers. This alignment facilitates the creation of intelligent workflows and adaptive systems that can dynamically adjust to environmental changes. Nevertheless, the current literature has inadequately explored how this alignment might be systematically integrated into corporate design models. This chapter offers an integrative perspective linking technology infrastructure with organizational structures to facilitate cognitive enterprise transformation (Nast et al., 2022).

This chapter aims to critically analyze the problems of adopting digital twins in cognitive enterprise environments, encompassing integration complexity, interoperability concerns, and organizational preparedness. These issues underscore the necessity for scalable and resilient architectural methodologies that synchronize technological capabilities with strategic goals (Babar et al., 2019). By tackling these difficulties, the chapter offers a more thorough comprehension of the prerequisites for successful digital twin implementation.

This chapter covers theoretical and practical aspects, including conceptual development, architectural concerns, and example applications in various industries. It additionally presents a conceptual framework that elucidates how digital twins facilitate intelligent workflow adaptation and ongoing organizational learning (Panneerselvam, 2021). These contributions collectively form a conceptual framework that connects digital twins, Cognitive Enterprise Architecture, and decision intelligence as catalysts for organizational transformation.

BACKGROUND

1. Conceptual Foundations of Digital Twins

Digital twins (DTs) have become a fundamental idea in cyber-physical systems, facilitating the integration of physical assets with dynamic, data-driven virtual representations. A digital twin is typically characterized as a perpetually updated virtual representation that mirrors the state, behavior, and performance of a physical system via real-time data exchange (Cao & Bai, 2024). This reciprocal link facilitates monitoring, modeling, and optimization throughout system lifecycles. Nonetheless, although this description is broadly acknowledged, it predominantly embodies a technical and engineering-focused viewpoint, frequently neglecting the wider organizational and cognitive ramifications of digital twin deployment.

The progression of digital twins illustrates a shift from static simulation models to adaptive, intelligent systems proficient in predictive and prescriptive analytics (Kantaros et al., 2025). Initial methodologies focused on mathematical modeling and system replication, but modern research underscores real-time synchronization and interaction with sophisticated digital infrastructures. Notwithstanding this advancement, a conceptual gap persists between digital twin applications in engineering fields and their implementation in enterprise and organizational settings. For example, engineering-centric digital twins emphasize system performance and operational efficiency, whereas new enterprise-focused digital twins seek to encapsulate organizational complexity and decision-making processes (Lyytinen et al., 2024). This gap signifies the lack of a cohesive theoretical framework that integrates technical and organizational viewpoints.

Recent research has commenced to bridge this gap by expanding digital twin applications into enterprise systems and socio-technical contexts. Digital twins are progressively utilized to enhance predictive maintenance, optimize logistics, and bolster system resilience, showcasing their applicability outside conventional industrial environments (Nozari, 2026a). Moreover, the advancement of urban digital twins underscores their significance in overseeing intricate, data-driven ecosystems in the framework of Economy 5.0 (Nozari, 2026b). Although these studies expand the range of digital twin applications, they frequently remain confined to certain domains and lack connection with business architectural frameworks.

A significant advancement is the integration of cognitive and intelligent functionalities into digital twin systems. The amalgamation of artificial intelligence, machine learning, and neuromorphic intelligence empowers digital twins to execute sophisticated analytics and adaptive decision-making in intricate situations (Nozari, 2025; Nawaz Khan & Ahmad, 2025). Nonetheless, these methodologies present new issues with data interoperability, computational complexity, and system scalability. Furthermore, current research mostly emphasizes improving analytical performance while inadequately considering the integration of these talents into organizational frameworks and governance systems.

The conceptual basis of digital twins demonstrate substantial progress in technological and analytical capacities. Nonetheless, challenges remain in synthesizing these advancements into a unified framework that links digital twin technologies with organizational systems, cognitive processes, and business architecture. Mitigating these limitations is crucial for unlocking the complete potential of digital twins as facilitators of intelligent and adaptable corporate transformation.

2. Cognitive Enterprise Architecture (CEA)

Cognitive Enterprise Architecture (CEA) signifies a sophisticated advancement of conventional enterprise architecture through the integration of cognitive capabilities into organizational systems, facilitating intelligent, adaptable, and data-driven operations. Traditional enterprise architecture frameworks predominantly emphasize the alignment of business processes with information technology infrastructure to guarantee efficiency and standardization. Conversely, CEA incorporates cognitive principles like sensing, reasoning, and learning into its structural and functional design, enabling companies to perform in dynamic and uncertain settings (Moisescu et al., 2019). This transition signifies the increasing necessity for organizations to evolve from static architectures to systems that can continuously adapt.

CEA is theoretically based on computational cognitive architectures that replicate human-like intelligence in decision-making and problem-solving (Sun, 2007). These designs integrate techniques for knowledge representation, learning, and adaptive behavior, allowing enterprise systems to process substantial data volumes and produce context-aware insights. Cognitive architectures facilitate ongoing learning and system enhancement, in contrast to conventional rule-based systems. Nonetheless, current implementations frequently prioritize technology, focusing on algorithmic efficacy while inadequately examining their incorporation into wider organizational and strategic frameworks.

A primary advantage of CEA is its capacity to augment decision intelligence through the integration of data, processes, and technology across several organizational tiers. Advanced cognitive models allow organizations to simulate intricate scenarios, assess options, and forecast outcomes, thus enhancing agility and resilience (Mukherjee, 2022). However, the literature indicates a discrepancy between theoretical frameworks of cognitive companies and their actual execution. Theoretical frameworks emphasize the significance of cognitive abilities, although actual applications frequently encounter obstacles concerning system interoperability, data governance, and organizational preparedness.

Furthermore, CEA advocates for a human-centric methodology in corporate systems, harmonizing technical capabilities with human cognition and decision-making processes (Dumitrache et al., 2019). This viewpoint highlights the interplay between human agents and intelligent systems, which is essential in intricate socio-technical contexts. Nonetheless, current research often neglects the incorporation of future technologies like digital twins into CEA frameworks, hence constraining opportunities for real-time synchronization and adaptive intelligence.

Recent advancements indicate that the incorporation of sophisticated analytical models, such as neuromorphic intelligence and multi-objective optimization, can markedly improve the cognitive functions of enterprise systems (Nozari, 2025).

Simultaneously, digital twin applications in data-centric and urban systems exhibit the capacity for scalable, real-time corporate architectures (Nozari, 2026b). Notwithstanding these developments, a deficiency persists in unified frameworks that integrate digital twins, cognitive architectures, and corporate systems into a coherent paradigm.

Although CEA offers a robust theoretical framework for intelligent enterprise systems, challenges remain in connecting conceptual models with real execution and developing technology. Rectifying these deficiencies is crucial to fully utilize CEA as a framework for digital twin-facilitated organizational transformation.

3. Literature Review on Digital Twins and Organizational Intelligence

Digital Twin Evolution and Engineering Foundations

The discourse on digital twins (DTs) has progressed beyond engineering-focused applications to encompass more intricate and integrated system representations. Initial research defines digital twins as dynamic, data-driven virtual representations of physical assets, principally utilized for monitoring, simulation, and lifecycle management (Cao & Bai, 2024; Kantaros et al., 2025). These methodologies prioritize technical precision and system enhancement, especially within manufacturing and industrial environments. This engineering perspective offers a robust technological base but is predominantly centered on physical systems, hence constraining its relevance to wider organizational dynamics.

Digital Twins in Enterprise Systems

Recent research expands the applications of Digital Twins (DT) to corporate settings, presenting the notion of Digital Twins of Organizations (DTOs), which encapsulate the structural, behavioral, and operational dimensions of organizations (Lyytinen et al., 2024). Enterprise-level digital twins facilitate cohesive data ecosystems that enhance analytics, compliance, and strategic planning (Frerichs & Nüttgens, 2022). Moreover, domain-specific applications, such as predictive maintenance in logistics systems, illustrate how digital twins can improve operational resilience and efficiency (Nozari, 2026a). Nevertheless, these studies frequently regard corporate digital transformations as mere extensions of technological systems, failing to achieve a holistic integration with enterprise architecture frameworks and organizational cognition.

AI-Driven Digital Twins and Cognitive Capabilities

The amalgamation of artificial intelligence (AI) with digital twins (DTs) signifies a substantial progression towards intelligent and autonomous systems. AI-driven digital twins utilize machine learning, predictive analytics, and adaptive algorithms to facilitate real-time decision assistance and system optimization (Alghamdi et al., 2025). Innovative methodologies increasingly include sophisticated computational frameworks, like neuromorphic intelligence and fuzzy multi-objective models, to improve decision-making in intricate and unpredictable contexts (Nozari, 2025). These advancements establish DTs as cognitive systems proficient in learning and adaptability. Nonetheless, current research predominantly emphasizes the augmentation of analytical capacities, with insufficient investigation into the structural integration of these cognitive processes inside corporate structures.

Digital Twins and Organizational Intelligence

From an organizational standpoint, digital twins enhance organizational intelligence through real-time data integration, simulation-based reasoning, and adaptive decision-making (Alghamdi et al., 2025). The socio-technical aspect of digital technologies emphasizes the necessity of harmonizing technology infrastructures with human, cultural, and governance elements (Bunjaridh et al., 2025). Moreover, urban-scale digital twins demonstrate the capabilities of digital twins in data-centric frameworks that facilitate intricate, interrelated systems under the Economy 5.0 paradigm (Nozari, 2026b). Notwithstanding these developments, modeling emergent organizational behaviors and decision-making processes continues to pose a considerable difficulty.

Gap Analysis and Research Positioning

An analytical synthesis of the literature indicates that current studies may be classified into three primary categories: engineering-centric digital twins, AI-augmented digital twins, and organizationally-focused digital twin applications. Although each stream provides useful insights, they remain predominantly disjointed. A deficiency exists in integrative frameworks that link digital twin capabilities with Cognitive Enterprise Architecture (CEA) and decision intelligence. This chapter tackles the gap by presenting a cohesive conceptual framework that connects digital technologies, cognitive skills, and enterprise design to facilitate intelligent, adaptable, and data-driven organizational transformation.

4. Conceptual Framework: Digital Twins for Cognitive Enterprise Architecture and Decision Intelligence

This chapter presents a conceptual framework that establishes digital twins as essential facilitators of Cognitive Enterprise Architecture (CEA) and decision intelligence. The framework consolidates technological, cognitive, and organizational aspects into a cohesive, stratified design that elucidates how digital twins enable intelligent and adaptive enterprise systems. Although previous research has predominantly focused on digital twins as instruments for simulation and operational enhancement, there is a paucity of studies that systematically link their functionalities to corporate architecture and decision-making processes. This concept bridges the gap by connecting digital twin capabilities with cognitive functions and organizational change.

The Digital Twin Layer is fundamental to the system, signifying real-time synchronization between physical assets and their virtual equivalents. This layer facilitates ongoing data collection and surveillance via IoT sensors and integrated infrastructures (Pop et al., 2024). The created data is sent to the Data Integration Layer, where diverse data sources are amalgamated into a cohesive and compatible framework. This layer guarantees data governance, interoperability, and scalability, which are crucial for managing intricate digital twin ecosystems (Ouedraogo et al., 2025).

The Cognitive Processing Layer utilizes artificial intelligence, machine learning, and sophisticated analytics to convert structured data into actionable insights. This layer facilitates predictive analytics, anomaly detection, and adaptive learning, aiding the shift towards intelligent and self-optimizing systems (Alghamdi et al., 2025). These cognitive talents correspond with the tenets of cognitive enterprise growth, wherein firms perpetually learn and adapt according to real-time data (Elia & Margherita, 2022).

The Decision Intelligence Layer transforms insights into strategic and operational actions via modeling, optimization, and automated decision-making procedures. This layer facilitates scenario analysis and prescriptive decision-making, enabling businesses to respond adeptly to dynamic conditions (Soylu & Yildiz, 2023). The Organizational Transformation Layer signifies the reorganization of enterprise systems into flexible, modular, and resilient frameworks, facilitating agility and strategic alignment (de Cunha et al., 2021; Nast et al., 2022).

The framework is additionally reinforced by essential enablers, such as cybersecurity, data governance, and organizational competencies, along with a perpetual feedback mechanism that promotes learning and adaptation at all levels.

Figure 1. Conceptual Framework of Digital Twins for Cognitive Enterprise Architecture and Decision Intelligence

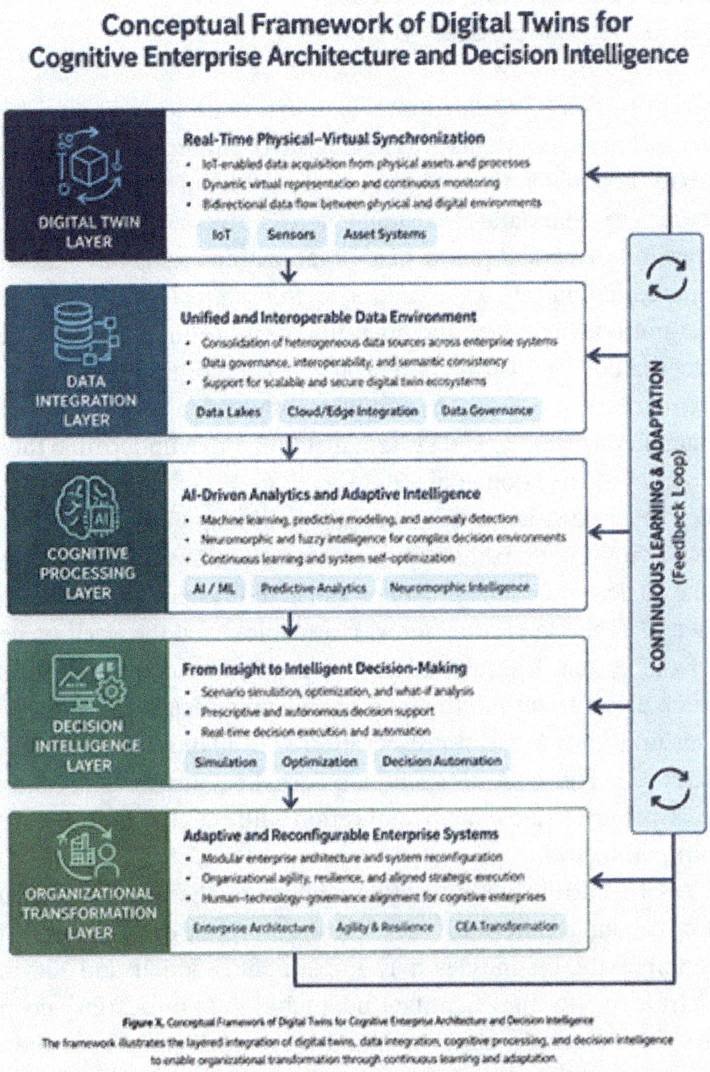

Source: Developed by Authors (2026)

ISSUES, CONTROVERSIES, PROBLEMS

1. Integration Complexity Between Physical and Digital Systems

The integration of physical and digital systems continues to be a primary problem in the deployment of digital twins within Cognitive Enterprise Architecture (CEA). This complexity originates from the necessity to maintain ongoing synchronization, interoperability, and data consistency across diverse systems, including older infrastructures and dispersed platforms. Organizations must navigate various data formats, communication protocols, and system architectures, which substantially heightens integration challenges and operational risk (Human et al., 2023). The difficulty is exacerbated by real-time synchronization, as digital twins rely on constant data flow to accurately represent the condition of physical systems. Challenges like as latency, data inconsistency, and system instability can undermine the efficacy of digital twin deployments (Pop et al., 2024).

Alongside synchronization issues, scalability and adaptability provide considerable limitations. As firms broaden digital twin implementations across various assets and operations, the intricacy of managing interconnected systems significantly escalates. In the absence of scalable architectures, companies face the peril of performance deterioration and system fragmentation. Moreover, the incorporation of cognitive capacities, such as artificial intelligence and machine learning, adds further complexity concerning knowledge representation and adaptive learning mechanisms (Jinzhi et al., 2022). These problems underscore the constraints of solely technical methodologies that prioritize system integration while neglecting wider architectural and organizational factors.

Nevertheless, the current literature often exaggerates these issues while inadequately investigating organized alternatives based on enterprise design theory. To mitigate integration complexity, businesses may implement modular and service-oriented architectural frameworks that facilitate adaptable system design and progressive scalability. Service-oriented architectures and microservices enhance interoperability by enabling separate system components to communicate via standardized interfaces, thus diminishing integration obstacles (Kruger et al., 2021). This methodology corresponds with the tenets of composable enterprise architecture, wherein systems are structured as interoperable modules capable of dynamic reconfiguration.

Furthermore, the layered digital twin architecture suggested in this chapter offers a systematic approach by delineating data collecting, integration, cognitive processing, and decision-making activities. This stratified method improves system manageability and facilitates scaling by compartmentalizing complexity inside designated architectural elements. The implementation of data governance frameworks enhances data consistency and interoperability among systems, tackling significant integration difficulties (Ouedraogo et al., 2025).

Dynamic capacity theory provides a significant framework for comprehending how businesses might navigate integration difficulty. Organizations can adapt digital twin systems to evolving surroundings and technological demands by enhancing their capacities to sense, integrate, and reconfigure resources. This viewpoint transitions the emphasis from technological limitations to organizational flexibility and strategic coherence.

Integration complexity poses a considerable problem; nevertheless, it can be alleviated through modular architectures, layered frameworks, and dynamic organizational capabilities. This balanced strategy allows firms to convert integration obstacles into opportunities for developing scalable and adaptive digital twin ecosystems.

2. Data Governance, Security, and Ethical Concerns

The integration of digital twins into Cognitive Enterprise Architecture (CEA) presents considerable hurdles with data governance, cybersecurity, and ethical issues. Digital twin ecosystems depend on ongoing data streams from various sources, necessitating the assurance of data quality, consistency, and interoperability among dispersed systems. Challenges related to data ownership, lifecycle management, and standardization get progressively intricate when firms include numerous digital twins into interconnected ecosystems (Ouedraogo et al., 2025). The diversity of data formats and platforms hinders smooth data interchange, hence restricting the scalability and efficacy of digital twin systems (Chaves et al., 2025).

Cybersecurity becomes a significant challenge, as the incorporation of digital twins broadens the attack surface of organizational systems. The utilization of IoT devices, cloud infrastructures, and interconnected platforms presents vulnerabilities to cyber threats, such as data breaches, illegal access, and ransomware assaults. Ensuring effective cybersecurity necessitates sophisticated processes including encryption, identity management, and continuous monitoring systems (Jain et al., 2026). The dependence on real-time data sharing heightens the danger of system breakdowns, potentially undermining operational continuity and the precision of decision-making.

Ethical problems hamper the implementation of digital twins. The pervasive utilization of data engenders apprehensions over privacy, permission, and data exploitation, especially when sensitive or personal information is implicated. Furthermore, the incorporation of AI-driven analytics presents challenges about algorithmic bias, transparency, and accountability in decision-making processes. These difficulties underscore the inadequacies of solely technical strategies that tackle security and governance while neglecting ethical and organizational aspects.

Nevertheless, the current literature frequently highlights these dangers while inadequately considering integrated solutions. Organizations can address governance and security concerns by implementing structured data governance frameworks that include established protocols, data lifecycle management, and interoperability rules. Data spaces and federated data architectures offer scalable methods for facilitating secure and consistent data sharing across distant systems (Chaves et al., 2025). Moreover, compliance-focused maturity models can assist firms in systematically improving their data governance competencies, aligning technical practices with legal mandates.

From a cybersecurity standpoint, zero-trust architectures and cybersecurity mesh frameworks provide sophisticated methods for safeguarding digital twin ecosystems. These frameworks provide decentralized and adaptive security procedures that safeguard interconnected systems while ensuring scalability (Achuthan et al., 2025). Blockchain technologies augment data integrity and transparency by offering immutable and verifiable data management frameworks (Putz et al., 2021).

The incorporation of ethical governance systems is equally essential. Human-centered methodologies that prioritize transparency, equity, and responsible data utilization can mitigate ethical issues while cultivating confidence in digital twin systems. Effectively balancing governance, security, and ethics necessitates a comprehensive approach that synthesizes technological, organizational, and regulatory viewpoints to guarantee sustainable and secure digital change.

3. Organizational Readiness and Capability Gaps

The effective execution of digital twins in Cognitive Enterprise Architecture (CEA) relies significantly on organizational preparedness and the capacity to bridge current capability deficiencies. Organizational preparation includes strategy alignment, technological infrastructure, leadership commitment, and cultural flexibility necessary for supporting digital transformation activities. Numerous firms undervalue the multifaceted aspect of preparedness, concentrating mostly on technical implementation while disregarding organizational and human elements (Bandara & Buics, 2025). Consequently, digital twin programs frequently fail to achieve anticipated results due to a misalignment between technology and organizational strategy.

A significant issue resides in leadership and strategic coherence. In the absence of explicit strategic direction and leadership endorsement, digital twin activities may become disjointed and fail to generate organizational value. Furthermore, opposition to change and cultural inertia may impede adoption, especially in traditional or heavily regulated sectors (Hilminata & Alamsjah, 2025). Organizations sometimes lack requisite knowledge in areas such as IoT integration, data analytics, and system compatibility. These technical limitations are exacerbated by shortcomings in non-technical competencies, such as process management, cross-functional collaboration, and change management. Empirical research indicates that legacy systems and data silos are substantial obstacles, hindering the integration and scalability of digital twin solutions (Möhring et al., 2022).

A significant challenge is the difficulty in extending digital twin initiatives beyond pilot programs. Although some firms effectively deploy small-scale digital twin applications, they frequently have difficulties in scaling these solutions throughout organizational systems. This constraint is generally due to the lack of standardized frameworks and inadequate architectural design, leading to disjointed implementations and diminished effectiveness (Edrisi et al., 2024).

Nonetheless, the current research often highlights these issues while insufficiently investigating organized solutions. To rectify organizational readiness and capability deficiencies, organizations may use enterprise architecture-driven transformation strategies that synchronize technical activities with strategic goals. Enterprise architecture frameworks offer systematic approaches for the integration of corporate processes, data, and technologies, facilitating scalable and cohesive digital twin ecosystems (Edrisi et al., 2024).

Dynamic capacity theory provides a significant framework for improving organizational preparedness. By cultivating the ability to identify possibilities, capitalize on technological advancements, and reorganize organizational resources, organizations may adeptly navigate the intricacies of digital twin deployment. Furthermore, capability maturity models can assist firms in evaluating their readiness levels and methodically enhancing their digital competencies.

Workforce development constitutes another essential solution. Organizations must invest in upskilling and reskilling initiatives to furnish personnel with the technical and cognitive competencies necessary for operating digital twin systems. Moreover, cultivating a digital culture that promotes innovation and cooperation can diminish resistance to change and facilitate enduring transformation.

Despite the considerable challenges posed by organizational readiness and capability deficiencies, these can be alleviated through strategic alignment, enterprise architecture frameworks, and capability enhancement, allowing organizations to maximize the potential of digital twins in cognitive enterprise transformation.

SOLUTIONS AND RECOMMENDATIONS

1. Developing Scalable Digital Twin Architecture

Creating scalable digital twin architectures is crucial for facilitating Cognitive Enterprise Architecture (CEA) that can adjust to rising complexity, data volume, and operational requirements. Current methodologies prioritize modular and composable system architecture, enabling enterprises to progressively construct and enhance digital twin ecosystems without interrupting ongoing operations (Villegas et al., 2025). This pragmatic viewpoint emphasizes flexibility and scalability but frequently lacks a robust theoretical foundation that elucidates how such architectures enhance enduring organizational performance and transformation.

From an enterprise architectural viewpoint, scalable digital twin systems can be perceived as organized layers that synchronize business processes, data, and technological infrastructures. Enterprise architecture theory underscores the integration of organizational elements to guarantee coherence and strategic alignment among systems. Organizations can establish interoperable digital twin ecosystems that facilitate real-time data integration, analytics, and decision-making by using layered and modular architectures. This alignment guarantees that digital twin deployments are not standalone technical solutions but essential elements of enterprise-wide transformation (Ahvanouee & Fay, 2024).

Microservices-based designs promote scalability by allowing loosely linked system components to function independently while interacting via standardized interfaces. This methodology facilitates dynamic system reconfiguration and robustness, essential prerequisites for digital twin ecosystems functioning in intricate contexts (Stalidi et al., 2025). Moreover, in addition to technological advantages, microservices architectures may also be analyzed within the framework of dynamic capability theory. These architectures facilitate businesses in swiftly reconfiguring digital resources and system functionalities, hence fostering the development of capacities to perceive, seize, and transform in reaction to environmental changes.

Cloud and edge computing infrastructures are essential for scalable digital twin architecture, offering distributed computing capabilities that facilitate real-time data processing and low-latency operations (Picone et al., 2021). From a decision intelligence standpoint, these infrastructures facilitate ongoing data streams and analyses that guide strategic and operational choices. Decision intelligence theory underscores the amalgamation of data, analytics, and decision-making processes, whereas scalable digital twin architectures furnish the technological basis for this integration.

Moreover, interoperability and standardization are crucial for guaranteeing scalability across enterprise systems. The implementation of standardized protocols and verification frameworks facilitates seamless communication between digital twins and other enterprise components, hence diminishing integration complexity and improving system coherence (Ahvanouee & Fay, 2024). These methods correspond with enterprise architecture principles that emphasize uniformity and integration throughout organizational tiers.

2. Enhancing Data Governance and Cybersecurity Frameworks

Improving data governance and cybersecurity frameworks is crucial for guaranteeing the dependability, scalability, and integrity of digital twins within Cognitive Enterprise Architecture (CEA). Digital twin ecosystems depend on ongoing data interchange within remote contexts, necessitating robust governance and security measures to ensure data quality, interoperability, and system resilience. Although current methodologies prioritize technological solutions like established protocols and sophisticated security technologies, they frequently lack a robust theoretical framework that links these mechanisms to overarching organizational competencies and decision-making processes.\

From an enterprise architecture viewpoint, data governance is a structural mechanism that matches data management practices with business goals and system integration needs. Enterprise architectural theory emphasizes the significance of consistency, interoperability, and governance throughout organizational tiers. Implementing standardized data governance frameworks enables enterprises to assure consistent data flows, minimize fragmentation, and facilitate the integration of digital twins across organizational systems (Ouedraogo et al., 2025). Moreover, data spaces and federated data architectures offer scalable solutions that facilitate secure and interoperable data transmission among diverse systems (Chaves et al., 2025).

Cybersecurity frameworks gain advantages from an enterprise architecture perspective, since they should be integrated into system design rather than seen as external controls. The implementation of zero-trust architectures and cybersecurity mesh models facilitates decentralized and adaptive security methods that improve system resilience in intricate digital twin contexts (Achuthan et al., 2025). These methodologies conform to business architecture principles by embedding security controls inside each architectural layer, guaranteeing that protective measures advance in tandem with system complexity.

From a dynamic capacity standpoint, data governance and cybersecurity are organizational competencies that empower organizations to perceive, react to, and alleviate risks in swiftly evolving contexts. Organizations must consistently modify their governance and security protocols to respond to changing risks and regulatory mandates. Capability maturity models offer systematic methodologies for evaluating and advancing these competences, allowing businesses to incrementally refine their data management and security skills (Yan & Jones, 2026).

Decision intelligence theory enhances governance and cybersecurity by underscoring the need of dependable and secure data in decision-making processes. Digital twins function as data-driven decision-making platforms, with the quality of judgments reliant on the accuracy and accessibility of the foundational data. Advanced security mechanisms, such as blockchain-based solutions, augment data transparency and trust by offering immutable and verifiable records of data transactions (Putz et al., 2021).

Alongside technical and organizational factors, ethical governance frameworks are crucial for guaranteeing responsible data utilization. Incorporating ethical concepts like transparency, justice, and accountability into governance frameworks fosters trust and ensures long-term sustainability.

3. Building Cognitive Capabilities and Organizational Alignment

Developing cognitive talents and attaining organizational alignment are essential requirements for utilizing digital twins as facilitators of cognitive enterprise architecture. Cognitive capabilities denote an organization's proficiency in intelligently processing data, adapting to dynamic circumstances, and making informed decisions using integrated digital systems. The capabilities are chiefly propelled by the integration of new technologies, including artificial intelligence (AI), machine learning, and the Internet of Things (IoT), which transform digital twins from mere monitoring instruments into intelligent, autonomous systems. The incorporation of semantic technologies and knowledge-based systems augments the capacity of digital twins to analyze intricate relationships and facilitate context-aware decision-making (Lezoche & Torres, 2024).

A crucial option for enhancing cognitive capacities is the creation of cognitive digital twin architectures that facilitate lifecycle management and predictive analytics. These architectures allow enterprises to model situations, predict system behaviors, and enhance operations in real time. Integrating learning processes into digital twin systems enables firms to perpetually enhance performance and bolster resilience in dynamic circumstances. These qualities are especially pertinent in Industry 5.0 environments, where human-machine collaboration and adaptive intelligence are crucial for operational success (Yitmen, 2023).

Nonetheless, the advancement of cognitive capacities must be matched with robust organizational alignment. This entails aligning technical initiatives with company plans, organizational frameworks, and sustainability goals. Enterprise architectural frameworks are essential for enabling alignment by offering systematic methods for integrating digital twin technologies throughout organizational levels. These frameworks facilitate the alignment of business processes, data streams, and technology infrastructures, ensuring that digital twin implementations advance overarching company objectives (Schnellmann, 2025).

A crucial element of organizational alignment is the necessity to dismantle silos and promote cross-functional communication. Digital twin ecosystems necessitate seamless collaboration among several departments, including operations, IT, and management. Inconsistent aims and disjointed data architectures can impede the efficacy of digital twin initiatives. Consequently, enterprises must advocate for cohesive workflows, unified performance indicators, and collaborative decision-making procedures. Moreover, workforce development is crucial for providing personnel with the necessary skills to engage with cognitive systems, analyze data insights, and facilitate intelligent operations.

Governance is essential for connecting cognitive capacities with organizational goals. Robust governance structures guarantee that data use, AI implementation, and decision-making processes comply with ethical norms and regulatory mandates. This alignment is crucial in intricate supply chains and fluctuating settings, where autonomous systems must function within explicitly delineated boundaries and accountability frameworks (Kalaboukas et al., 2023).

Enhancing cognitive skills and attaining organizational alignment necessitates a comprehensive strategy that incorporates modern technology, business design, workforce development, and governance. These components combined empower firms to convert digital twins into strategic assets for informed decision-making and lasting organizational transformation.

4. Theoretical Implications

This chapter offers multiple theoretical contributions by enhancing the integration of digital twin technologies, Cognitive Enterprise Architecture (CEA), and decision intelligence into a cohesive conceptual framework. This chapter enhances existing theoretical approaches in digital transformation and enterprise systems by systematically linking previously researched domains independently.

This chapter advances the digital twin literature by transitioning the focus from engineering-centric applications to organizational and cognitive aspects. Current research predominantly defines digital twins as instruments for the monitoring, simulation, and optimization of physical systems (Cao & Bai, 2024; Kantaros et al., 2025). This chapter presents digital twins as strategic facilitators of organizational intelligence, highlighting their function in enabling real-time data integration, predictive analytics, and adaptive decision-making inside corporate systems (Alghamdi et al., 2025). This viewpoint broadens the notion of digital twins beyond mere technical applications to their role as essential elements of intelligent organizational frameworks.

This chapter advances enterprise architecture theory by presenting the concept of Cognitive Enterprise Architecture (CEA) as a progression of conventional frameworks. This chapter incorporates cognitive capabilities, including learning, reasoning, and adaptation, into architectural design, contrasting with traditional enterprise architecture, which emphasizes the alignment of business processes with

IT infrastructure (Moisescu et al., 2019; Elia & Margherita, 2022). The suggested layered framework illustrates the integration of digital twins into business architecture to facilitate continuous data flows, intelligent processes, and system-wide adaptability (Nast et al., 2022). This paper establishes a theoretical framework for comprehending the evolution of enterprise architecture in support of cognitive and data-driven businesses.

This chapter enhances decision intelligence theory by defining digital twins as essential platforms for data-driven decision-making. Decision intelligence underscores the amalgamation of data, analytics, and decision-making processes to enhance organizational results. This chapter elaborates on how digital twins facilitate real-time scenario simulation, predictive modeling, and prescriptive decision-making, thus improving organizational responsiveness and performance (Soylu & Yildiz, 2023). The incorporation of cognitive processing capacities enhances decision intelligence by facilitating adaptive and autonomous decision-making systems.

This chapter ultimately proposes an integrative paradigm that unifies digital twins, enterprise architecture, and decision intelligence into a cohesive model of cognitive enterprise transformation. This paradigm resolves current fragmentation in the literature and establishes a foundation for forthcoming theoretical and empirical study. This chapter provides a thorough grasp of how digital twins might enhance intelligent, adaptive, and sustainable company systems by integrating technological, organizational, and cognitive perspectives.

FUTURE RESEARCH DIRECTIONS

1. Emerging Trends in AI-Driven Digital Twins

The amalgamation of artificial intelligence (AI) and digital twin (DT) technologies is establishing a novel paradigm in Cognitive Enterprise Architecture (CEA), with substantial prospects for future study. Although current research emphasizes the progression of AI-driven digital twins from descriptive and predictive frameworks to prescriptive and autonomous functionalities, these developments are predominantly theoretical and disjointed (Alghamdi et al., 2025). Subsequent research ought to advance beyond broad debates by concentrating on the formulation of structured models that delineate the systematic integration of AI capabilities into digital twin infrastructures.

A crucial research agenda encompasses the creation of models for AI-driven digital twins. Future research should focus on developing multi-tiered frameworks that clearly delineate the connections among data collecting, cognitive processing, and decision intelligence. These models must include sophisticated AI methodologies, like deep learning and reinforcement learning, to improve adaptive system functionality and real-time decision-making abilities (Rojek et al., 2025). Moreover, the incorporation of multimodal data sources into digital twin models necessitates additional theoretical and computational enhancement to guarantee scalability and precision in intricate situations.

Empirical testing constitutes a significant avenue for the progression of AI-driven digital twin research. Despite the growing number of proposed conceptual frameworks, empirical validation of their efficacy in practical organizational settings remains few. Future research should undertake case-based and experimental investigations to assess the efficacy of AI-enabled digital twins in domains such as predictive maintenance, operational optimization, and strategic decision-making. Empirical studies can elucidate the practical challenges and performance results of digital twin implementations, thereby reinforcing the theoretical underpinnings of the discipline.

Cross-industry validation is crucial for guaranteeing the generalizability and scalability of AI-driven digital twin models. Contemporary research is frequently specialized, concentrating on manufacturing, logistics, or intelligent urban environments. Digital twins possess the capability to be utilized across various sectors, including healthcare, banking, and public administration. Future research must investigate the adaptation and validation of AI-driven digital twin frameworks across many organizational contexts, taking into account differences in data architecture, operational procedures, and regulatory environments (Kameswari et al., 2025).

The emergence of interconnected and federated digital twin ecosystems offers novel study options. Future research should examine the interaction of several digital twins inside integrated platforms to facilitate sophisticated, multi-domain systems. This necessitates tackling issues with interoperability, standardization, and governance, especially within extensive organizational settings.

2. Digital Twins for Sustainable and Resilient Enterprises

The integration of artificial intelligence (AI) and digital twin (DT) technologies is creating a new framework in Cognitive Enterprise Architecture (CEA), presenting significant opportunities for future research. Current research highlights the evolution of AI-driven digital twins from descriptive and predictive models to prescriptive and autonomous capabilities; yet, these advancements remain mostly theoretical and fragmented (Alghamdi et al., 2025). Future research should progress beyond general discussions by focusing on the development of structured models that outline the systematic incorporation of AI capabilities into digital twin frameworks.

An essential research agenda is the development of models for AI-driven digital twins. Future research should concentrate on creating multi-tiered frameworks that explicitly define the relationships between data collection, cognitive processing, and decision intelligence. These models must incorporate advanced AI techniques, such as deep learning and reinforcement learning, to enhance adaptive system performance and real-time decision-making capabilities (Rojek et al., 2025). Furthermore, integrating multimodal data sources into digital twin models requires further theoretical and computational advancements to ensure scalability and accuracy in complex scenarios.

Empirical testing represents a crucial pathway for advancing AI-driven digital twin research. Despite the increasing number of proposed conceptual frameworks, empirical validation of their effectiveness in practical organizational contexts remains limited. Future research should conduct case-based and experimental studies to evaluate the effectiveness of AI-enabled digital twins in areas such as predictive maintenance, operational optimization, and strategic decision-making. Empirical research can clarify the practical obstacles and performance outcomes of digital twin implementations, thereby strengthening the theoretical foundations of the field.

Cross-industry validation is essential for ensuring the generalizability and scalability of AI-driven digital twin models. Current research is often specialized, focusing on production, logistics, or smart urban environments. Digital twins can be employed across multiple areas, including healthcare, banking, and public administration. Subsequent research should examine the adaption and validation of AI-driven digital twin frameworks across various organizational contexts, considering disparities in data architecture, operational procedures, and regulatory environments (Kameswari et al., 2025).

The advent of interconnected and federated digital twin ecosystems presents innovative research opportunities. Future study should investigate the interplay of multiple digital twins inside integrated platforms to enable complex, multi-domain systems. This requires addressing challenges related to interoperability, standardization, and governance, particularly in large organizational contexts.

3. Research Opportunities in Cognitive Enterprise Transformation

The shift to cognitive enterprises facilitated by digital twins offers substantial study prospects in technological, organizational, and strategic areas. Although current research emphasizes the significance of merging digital twins with cognitive technology, the domain remains predominantly theoretical, characterized by a scarcity of structured models and empirical validation. Subsequent research should concentrate on creating comprehensive frameworks that comprehensively elucidate how digital twins facilitate cognitive enterprise transformation.

A primary research focus entails the development of models for cognitive enterprise transformation. Future research should develop cohesive frameworks that link digital twin structures with organizational processes, cognitive capacities, and decision-making intelligence. These models must clearly delineate the connections among data, analytics, and organizational decision-making, facilitating a more precise comprehension of how digital twins enhance intelligent workflows and adaptive systems (Elia & Margherita, 2022). Furthermore, the integration of digital twins with sophisticated technologies like artificial intelligence, big data analytics, and intelligent workflow systems might improve model resilience and relevance in intricate organizational settings (Panneerselvam, 2021).

Empirical testing is crucial to validate these conceptual models and evaluate their efficacy in practical organizational settings. Theoretical frameworks offer significant insights; nevertheless, empirical data is lacking about the practical contributions of digital twins to cognitive enterprise transformation. Subsequent study ought to undertake case studies, experiments, and longitudinal analyses to assess the influence of digital twins on organizational performance, decision-making efficacy, and system adaptability. Empirical research can reveal implementation obstacles and contextual elements that affect the effectiveness of digital twin programs, hence enhancing the practical applicability of theoretical models.

Cross-industry validation constitutes a significant research avenue. Contemporary research frequently confines itself to particular sectors, such as manufacturing or supply chain management, so constraining the generalizability of its conclusions. Future research should investigate the application of cognitive enterprise transformation frameworks across several sectors, including healthcare, finance, and public organizations. This necessitates analyzing differences in organizational frameworks, data ecosystems, and regulatory landscapes to guarantee that digital twin models are flexible and scalable across many contexts (Chrusciak et al., 2023).

Furthermore, subsequent research ought to examine human and organizational elements in cognitive company change. The integration of digital twins and cognitive systems necessitates new competencies, governance structures, and cultural adaptations. Research should examine workforce development methods, digital literacy, and the impact of human–machine collaboration on improving organizational intelligence (Hull & Nezhad, 2016).

CONCLUSION

This chapter has analyzed the transformational function of digital twins as facilitators of Cognitive Enterprise Architecture (CEA), highlighting their ability to restructure organizational systems and improve decision-making intelligence. The investigation reveals that digital twins have progressed from mere virtual representations of physical assets to sophisticated, adaptive systems that enable real-time synchronization, predictive analytics, and autonomous decision-making support. Digital twins create continuous feedback loops by merging physical and digital worlds, hence improving operational visibility, optimizing processes, and facilitating proactive, data-driven decision-making (Alghamdi et al., 2025).

This chapter significantly contributes by establishing an integrative conceptual framework that connects digital twins, data integration, cognitive processing, and decision intelligence within a cohesive business architecture. This chapter presents a comprehensive viewpoint that positions digital twins as essential elements of intelligent organizational systems, in contrast to previous research that mostly emphasize technical or domain-specific applications. This viewpoint expands the current digital twin literature, predominantly limited to engineering and operational optimization contexts (Cao & Bai, 2024; Kantaros et al., 2025), by illustrating their strategic function in facilitating adaptable and cognitively driven organizations.

This chapter advances enterprise architecture theory by presenting a layered model of Cognitive Enterprise Architecture that integrates learning, reasoning, and adaptive capabilities into organizational design. This paradigm integrates technical infrastructures with business processes and decision-making systems, hence enabling ongoing organizational transformation (Moisescu et al., 2019; Elia & Margherita, 2022). The chapter further develops decision intelligence theory by demonstrating how digital twins serve as platforms for real-time scenario simulation, predictive modeling, and prescriptive decision-making, hence improving organizational responsiveness and performance (Soylu & Yildiz, 2023).

The results underscore significant problems pertaining to integration complexity, data governance, cybersecurity, and organizational preparedness. By implementing modular architectures, dynamic capabilities, and governance frameworks, businesses may proficiently tackle these difficulties and utilize digital twins as strategic assets for change (Ouedraogo et al., 2025; Kruger et al., 2021). These findings offer both theoretical and practical ramifications for businesses aiming to evolve into intelligent and adaptive enterprise systems.

Digital twins should be regarded not solely as technology instruments but as essential facilitators of cognitive enterprise change. Their capacity to assimilate data, model intricate systems, and facilitate informed decision-making establishes them as pivotal components in the advancement of next-generation corporate architectures. As enterprises traverse increasingly intricate and unpredictable settings, the incorporation of digital twins, cognitive skills, and decision intelligence will be crucial for attaining agility, resilience, and enduring competitive advantage.

ACKNOWLEDGMENT

The authors acknowledge financial support from the Indonesian Ministry of Higher Education, Science, and Technology (Kemendiktisaintek) through the PMDSU (Pendidikan Magister menuju Doktor untuk Sarjana Unggul) program under Grant Numbers 0419/C3/DT.05.00/2025 and 083/C3/DT.05.00/PL/2025.

REFERENCES

Achuthan, K., Gupta, B. B., & Raman, R. (2025). Bridging cybersecurity with digital twin technology: A thematic analysis. *International Journal of Information Security, 24*(5), 207. DOI: 10.1007/s10207-025-01115-y

Ahvanouee, H. R., & Fay, A. (2024, December). Trace-driven verification framework for interoperable digital twins in distributed control systems. In *2024 IEEE 3rd Industrial Electronics Society Annual On-Line Conference (ONCON)* (pp. 1-6). IEEE. DOI: 10.1109/ONCON62778.2024.10931261

Al Faruque, M. A., Muthirayan, D., Yu, S. Y., & Khargonekar, P. P. (2021). Cognitive digital twin for manufacturing systems. In *2021 Design, automation & test in Europe conference & exhibition (DATE)* (pp. 440-445). IEEE. DOI: 10.23919/DATE51398.2021.9474166

Alghamdi, W. Y., Alshamrani, R. M., Aloufi, R. K., Ba Lhamar, S. O., Altwirqi, R. A., Alotaibi, F. S., & Alazwari, A. S. (2025). Exploring the Synergy Between Digital Twin Technology and Artificial Intelligence: A Comprehensive Survey. *International Journal of Advanced Computer Science and Applications, 16*(3). Advance online publication. DOI: 10.14569/IJACSA.2025.0160399

Babar, Z., Yu, E., Carbajales, S., & Chan, A. (2019). Managing and Simplifying Cognitive Business Operations Using Process Architecture Models. In *International Conference on Advanced Information Systems Engineering* (pp. 643-658). Cham: Springer International Publishing. DOI: 10.1007/978-3-030-21290-2_40

Bandara, L. V., & Buics, L. (2025). Toward a Theoretical Framework for Digital Twin Readiness Assessment in Logistics: Conceptualization and Model Development. *Engineering Proceedings, 113*(1), 66. DOI: 10.3390/engproc2025113066

Bunjaridh, Y., Rahman, R. A., Yusof, L. M., & Papadonikolaki, E. (2025). Modeling the organizational attributes and strategies for developing accurate digital twins: the case of constructed facilities. *International Journal of Building Pathology and Adaptation*. DOI: 10.1108/IJBPA-12-2024-0281

Cao, G., & Bai, J. (2024). Design Optimisation and Implementation of an Industrial Robot System Based on Digital Twin Technology. In *2024 4th International Conference on Machine Learning and Intelligent Systems Engineering (MLISE)* (pp. 461-464). IEEE. DOI: 10.1109/MLISE62164.2024.10674459

Chaves, A. C., Alonso, A. N., & Soares, A. L. (2025). Data Spaces as Enablers of Digital Twin Ecosystems: Challenges and Requirements. In *IFIP International Conference on Advances in Production Management Systems* (pp. 340-354). Cham: Springer Nature Switzerland. DOI: 10.1007/978-3-032-03546-2_23

Chrusciak, C. B., Szejka, A. L., & Canciglieri, O., Junior. (2023). A Preliminary Digital Transformation Framework to Support Business Management Processes and Human Factors Impacts: Systematic Review and Gap Analysis. In *Conference on e-Business, e-Services and e-Society* (pp. 308-329). Cham: Springer Nature Switzerland. DOI: 10.1007/978-3-031-50040-4_23

da Cunha, C., Cardin, O., Gallot, G., & Viaud, J. (2021). Designing the digital twins of reconfigurable manufacturing systems: Application on a smart factory. *IFAC-PapersOnLine*, *54*(1), 874–879. DOI: 10.1016/j.ifacol.2021.08.103

Dumitrache, I., Caramihai, S. I., Moisescu, M. A., & Sacala, I. S. (2019). Neuro-inspired Framework for cognitive manufacturing control. *IFAC-PapersOnLine*, *52*(13), 910–915. DOI: 10.1016/j.ifacol.2019.11.311

Edrisi, F., Perez-Palacin, D., Caporuscio, M., & Giussani, S. (2024). Developing and evolving a digital twin of the organization. *IEEE Access : Practical Innovations, Open Solutions*, *12*, 45475–45494. DOI: 10.1109/ACCESS.2024.3381778

Elia, G., & Margherita, A. (2022). A conceptual framework for the cognitive enterprise: Pillars, maturity, value drivers. *Technology Analysis and Strategic Management*, *34*(4), 377–389. DOI: 10.1080/09537325.2021.1901874

Erkan, E. F., Uygun, Ö., & Demir, H. İ. (2024). Assessing digital transformation using fuzzy cognitive mapping supported by artificial intelligence techniques. *Applied Soft Computing*, *166*, 112199. DOI: 10.1016/j.asoc.2024.112199

Frerichs, M., & Nüttgens, M. (2022). Modeling the enterprise digital twin: Towards an open platform for analytics & compliance operations. In *Modellierung 2022* (pp. 65-75). Gesellschaft für Informatik eV. DOI: 10.18420/modellierung2022-008

Hilminata, A. N., & Alamsjah, F. (2025) Exploring Digital Mindset and Organizational Readiness in ISO-Based Information Systems: A Systematic Literature Review. In *2025 10th International Conference on Information Technology and Digital Application (ICITDA)* (pp. 1-6). IEEE. DOI: 10.1109/ICITDA68167.2025.11332422

Imandi, R., Chethana, B., Prasad, B. P., Sethi, K., & Kumar, B. P. (2025). Enhancing data management in industry 5.0: the role of digital twins in optimizing industrial operations. In *Industry 5.0: Key Technologies and Drivers* (pp. 211-236). Cham: Springer Nature Switzerland. DOI: 10.1007/978-3-031-87837-4_9

Jain, K., Gupta, S., & Behare, N. (2026). Safeguarding Digital Transformation: Cybersecurity for Digital Twin and IoT Ecosystems. In *Generative AI Applications and Intelligent Systems: From Chatbots to Cybersecurity* (pp. 243-274). IGI Global Scientific Publishing. DOI: 10.4018/979-8-3373-8011-7.ch010

Jinzhi, L., Zhaorui, Y., Xiaochen, Z., Jian, W., & Dimitris, K. (2022). Exploring the concept of Cognitive Digital Twin from model-based systems engineering perspective. *International Journal of Advanced Manufacturing Technology, 121*(9), 5835–5854. DOI: 10.1007/s00170-022-09610-5

Kalaboukas, K., Kiritsis, D., & Arampatzis, G. (2023). Governance framework for autonomous and cognitive digital twins in agile supply chains. *Computers in Industry, 146*, 103857. DOI: 10.1016/j.compind.2023.103857

Kameswari, Y. L., Jagan, B. O. L., Mohammed, T. K., & Aleem, S. H. A. (2025). Future trends and research challenges in digital twins. *Digital Twins for Smart Cities and Villages*, 81-101. DOI: 10.1016/B978-0-443-28884-5.00004-X

Kantaros, A., Ganetsos, T., Pallis, E., & Papoutsidakis, M. (2025). From mathematical modeling and simulation to digital twins: Bridging theory and digital realities in industry and emerging technologies. *Applied Sciences (Basel, Switzerland), 15*(16), 9213. DOI: 10.3390/app15169213

Khan, M. N., & Ahmad, I. (2025). Harnessing digital twins: Advancing virtual replicas for optimized system performance and sustainable innovation. *Babylonian Journal of Mechanical Engineering, 2025*, 18–33. DOI: 10.58496/BJME/2025/002

Kruger, K., Human, C., & Basson, A. (2021, November). Towards the integration of digital twins and service-oriented architectures. In *International Workshop on Service Orientation in Holonic and Multi-Agent Manufacturing* (pp. 131-143). Cham: Springer International Publishing. DOI: 10.1007/978-3-030-99108-1_10

Lezoche, M., & Torres, D. (2024, June). What the Semantic Web Can Do for Cognitive Digital Twins: Challenges and Opportunities. In *International Workshop on Collaboration in Knowledge Discovery and Decision Making* (pp. 224-237). Cham: Springer Nature Switzerland. DOI: 10.1007/978-3-031-91690-8_18

Lyytinen, K., Weber, B., Becker, M. C., & Pentland, B. T. (2024). Digital twins of organization: Implications for organization design. *Journal of Organization Design*, *13*(3), 77–93. DOI: 10.1007/s41469-023-00151-z

Möhring, M., Keller, B., Radowski, C. F., Blessmann, S., Breimhorst, V., & Müthing, K. (2022, June). Empirical insights into the challenges of implementing digital twins. In *Human Centred Intelligent Systems: Proceedings of KES-HCIS 2022 Conference* (pp. 229-239). Singapore: Springer Nature Singapore. DOI: 10.1007/978-981-19-3455-1_18

Moisescu, M. A., Sacala, I. S., Dumitrache, I., Caramihai, S. I., Barbulescu, B., & Danciuc, M. (2019). A cyber-physical systems approach to cognitive enterprise. *Periodicals of Engineering and Natural Sciences*, *7*(1), 337. Advance online publication. DOI: 10.21533/pen.v7i1.378

Mukherjee, P. K. (2022, February). Artificial intelligence based smart government enterprise architecture (AI-SGEA) framework. In *International Symposium on Artificial Intelligence* (pp. 325-333). Cham: Springer Nature Switzerland. DOI: 10.1007/978-3-031-22485-0_30

Nast, B., Reiz, A., Sandkuhl, K., & Stirna, J. (2022). Integrating Organizational and Technological Aspects of Digital Twin Engineering. In *PoEM Workshops*.

Nozari, H. (2026). Digital twin-based predictive maintenance in cold chain logistics. *Operations Research*, *60*(1), 481–499. DOI: 10.1051/ro/2025167

Nozari, H. (2026). Urban digital twins and data-centric architectures for the emergent economy 5.0. In *Industry 5.0's impact on economic innovation* (pp. 51–70). IGI Global Scientific Publishing., DOI: 10.4018/979-8-3693-4525-2.ch004

Nozari, H. (2025). Integrating neuromorphic intelligence with fuzzy multi-objective models in resilient green supply chain design. *Process Integration and Optimization for Sustainability*, 1–14. DOI: 10.1007/s41660-025-00598-5

Ouedraogo, E. B., Hawbani, A., Wang, X., Liu, Z., Zhao, L., Al-qaness, M. A., & Alsamhi, S. H. (2025). Digital twin data management: A comprehensive review. *IEEE Transactions on Big Data*, *11*(5), 2224–2243. DOI: 10.1109/TBDATA.2025.3533891

Panneerselvam, A. (2021). Intelligent workflow adaptation in cognitive enterprise: design and techniques. In *Operationalizing Multi-Cloud Environments: Technologies, Tools and Use Cases* (pp. 309–324). Springer International Publishing., DOI: 10.1007/978-3-030-74402-1_17

Picone, M., Mamei, M., & Zambonelli, F. (2021). WLDT: A general purpose library to build IoT digital twins. *SoftwareX*, *13*, 100661. DOI: 10.1016/j.softx.2021.100661

Pop, E., Iliuţă, M. E., & Moisescu, M. A. (2024, October). Digital twin architecture based on services interoperability. In 2024 15th International Conference on Communications (COMM) (pp. 1-6). IEEE. DOI: 10.1109/COMM62355.2024.10741458

Putz, B., Dietz, M., Empl, P., & Pernul, G. (2021). Ethertwin: Blockchain-based secure digital twin information management. *Information Processing & Management, 58*(1), 102425. DOI: 10.1016/j.ipm.2020.102425

Rojek, I., Mikołajewski, D., Dostatni, E., Cybulski, J., & Kozielski, M. (2025). Personalization of ai-based digital twins to optimize adaptation in industrial design and manufacturing. *Applied Sciences (Basel, Switzerland), 15*(15), 8525. DOI: 10.3390/app15158525

Rosen, K. M., & Pattipati, K. R. (2023). Operating digital twins within an enterprise process. In *The digital twin* (pp. 599–659). Springer International Publishing., DOI: 10.1007/978-3-031-21343-4_22

Schnellmann, M. (2025, May). Towards an Enterprise Architecture Based Approach for the Development of Digital Twins for Sustainable Real Estate Management. In *International Conference on Research Challenges in Information Science* (pp. 207-217). Cham: Springer Nature Switzerland. DOI: 10.1007/978-3-031-92471-2_17

Soylu, B., & Yildiz, G. B. (2023, May). A Digital Twin-Based Decision Support System for Dynamic Labor Planning. In *International Symposium On Intelligent Manufacturing And Service Systems* (pp. 214-223). Singapore: Springer Nature Singapore. DOI: 10.1007/978-981-99-6062-0_20

Stalidi, C., Popovici, E. C., & Suciu, G. (2025, August). Real-Time Digital Ecosystems: Integrating Virtual Personas and Digital Twins Through Microservices. In *International Conference on Availability, Reliability and Security* (pp. 128-141). Cham: Springer Nature Switzerland. DOI: 10.1007/978-3-032-00642-4_8

Sun, R. (2007). The challenges of building computational cognitive architectures. In *Challenges for Computational Intelligence* (pp. 37–60). Springer Berlin Heidelberg., DOI: 10.1007/978-3-540-71984-7_3

Villegas, L. F., Macchi, M., & Polenghi, A. (2025). Conceptualization of a Platform Architecture for the Rapid Development of Digital Twins in Manufacturing. *Proceedings of the XXIX SUMMER SCHOOL "Francesco Turco"—Industrial Systems Engineering, Lecce, Italy*, 10-12.

Wan, J., Lin, S., & Wu, Q. (2023, May). The Concept and Connotation of Enterprise Digital Transformation. In *Wuhan International Conference on E-business* (pp. 315-324). Cham: Springer Nature Switzerland. DOI: 10.1007/978-3-031-32299-0_27

Yan, S., & Jones, J. (2026). Ensuring Compliance in Digital Transformation: Developing and Validating the Data Management Stage Model (DMSM). *IEEE Transactions on Engineering Management*, *73*, 1402–1428. DOI: 10.1109/TEM.2026.3653511

Yitmen, I. (2023). *Cognitive Digital Twins for Smart Lifecycle Management of Built Environment and Infrastructure*. CRC Press. DOI: 10.1201/9781003230199

Chapter 11
From Digital Twins to Cognitive Enterprise: AI-Driven Organizational Transformation and Intelligent Decision Ecosystems

Manoj Govindaraj
http://orcid.org/0000-0003-2830-7875
Vel Tech Rangarajan Dr. Sagunthala R&D Institute of Science and Technology, India

H. Mohamed Shahil
Vel Tech Rangarajan Dr. Sagunthala R&D Institute of Science and Technology, India

Jenifer Lawrence
http://orcid.org/0000-0002-4115-1521
Woldia University, Ethiopia

ABSTRACT

The emergence of Artificial Intelligence and advanced data ecosystems is transforming traditional organizations into cognitive enterprises. This paper examines the evolution from Digital Twins to AI-driven intelligent decision ecosystems, where real-time data, predictive analytics, and machine learning enable adaptive, resilient, and self-learning organizational systems. Digital Twins are no longer limited to physical assets but are increasingly applied to business processes, supply chains, and customer interactions to enhance strategic and operational decision-making. The study proposes a conceptual framework for AI-enabled organizational transformation, highlighting the role of human–AI collaboration, automation, and

DOI: 10.4018/979-8-3373-9998-0.ch011

intelligent platforms in improving agility, innovation, and sustainability. It also discusses challenges related to governance, ethics, data security, and workforce readiness. The paper contributes to the understanding of cognitive enterprises as a foundation for competitive advantage in the era of Industry 5.0.

1. INTRODUCTION

The modern business environment is evolving very fast due to the changes in technology and globalization that means that the firms have to accommodate the changes or risk being sidelined. The customers have developed quite sophisticated expectations, thus exerting pressure on the need to be constantly creative. In the last ten years, many organizations have implemented digitalization programs like automation, data analytics and cloud computing. Nevertheless, artificial intelligence is expressing these shifts at an even greater pace, the primitive computerized infrastructure replacing it with active intelligent systems that can help businesses to self-guide and self-optimize.

Digital Twins originated within the manufacturing sector as virtual replicas of physical equipment. These digital architectures forecast when failures will occur, optimize and simulate performance in live systems without interfering with them. They were very useful as far as real-time management of the assets and early identification of the fault. The concept later became inclusive of the whole supply-chain and in order to model customer behavior and organizational processes. Their predictive accuracy and prescriptive capacity were further expanded on the basis of the integration of IoT sensors, real-time analytics, and machine learning.

The high flow of both structured and unstructured information demand advanced decision-making tools that are beyond the traditional descriptive analytics. Continuous learning and autonomous execution is offered by adaptive algorithms, predictive models and deep learning structures therefore paving the way to what is referred to as Cognitive Enterprises. Artificial intelligence in these organizations becomes closely embedded in the strategic planning process, the workflow, and the interaction with customers.

The difference between Cognitive Enterprises is their frequent combination of technological and human cognition in order to support changing decisions. They are dynamic unlike the old systems that do not change with modifications in contexts, optimize workflow with limited human touch, and customize offerings in a way that is natural to the customer. This is a significant change over and above the one where the tools are adopted to an embodiment of ubiquitous intelligence.

Industry 5.0 is the next development of this paradigm with an increased focus on human-machine interaction. Whereas, Industry 4.0 was about the automation and connectivity, Industry 5.0 accommodates human innovativeness, sustainability, and ethical aspects. Cognitive Enterprises are a perfect example of this change because they can use artificial intelligence as an aid to human knowledge instead of its substitute.

This paper investigates the progression from Digital Twins to Cognitive Enterprises and analyzes how AI ecosystems reshape organizational operations. It examines the intellectual underpinnings, managerial applications, and governance issues and the direction, which take place with this change.

Integrating empirical and discourses of theory, the existing literature proves that powered transfers contributed greatly and, at the same time, reveals the existing shades of uncertainty in figuring out the best variability between human participation and automated intelligence.

2. BACKGROUND OF THE STUDY

Digital technology has changed the way things are conducted in organizations in an unprecedented pace over the last decade. Modern companies are strongly adopting the use of artificial intelligence, big data analytics, cloud computing, and the Internet of Things to automate businesses and improve the decision-making process. Such technologies give an upper hand and force the traditional companies that used to use manual labor and traditional systems to switch to the smart infrastructures that can learn and automatically change their behavior.

Digital Twins emerged initially within the manufacturing sector as virtual representations of physical assets. These models predictively maintain and optimize performance of the machinery by simulating the performance and keeping an eye on the actual conditions of operation. Sensors will broadcast data to the analytical engines, hence minimizing unplanned downtimes and enhancing production efficiency. The idea has come to an extent of not just hardware but business processes; dynamics of supply chain; model of customer interaction, and even strategic planning on a company-wide perspective over time and is the next step in simulation as compared to a one-isolated simulation.

Artificial intelligence is seen as an inseparable part of the contemporary business. The combination of machine learning algorithms and natural language processing software with predictive analytics enables companies to deal with huge amounts of structured and unstructured data. The outcome is faster decision prolongs and better precision, which essentially turns to simple automation to feature of producing continuous self-evolution systems. The application of AI to the regular operations of the organization gives the whole organization a high degree of analytical cognition.

The fusion of Digital Twins and AI gives rise to what is termed Cognitive Enterprises. These organizations use sophisticated systems and automated platforms which operate in harmony with human resources and AI elements. The observed architecture is very versatile and robust, unlike the former legacy digitized workflows that only digitized individual actions. In this model, intelligence is incorporated in the working processes as well as in strategy planning, which enables the prediction and autonomous optimization.

Industry 5.0 represents a new paradigm of integrating a human being into the center of technology and focusing on the concepts of sustainability and resilience. Unlike the past industrial structure that focused on automation to save time and energy, the current interest aims at synergistic cooperation of human actors and intelligent machines. Artificial intelligence would be used to enhance human resource ingenuity and not replace its power in this environment, augmenting potentials in creative ideation and solving complex problems, which, although prominent, is still subject to the circumstances of particular organizations.

3. REVIEW OF LITERATURE

The Digital Twin technology has experienced an interest in academic literature over the last few years becoming a central facilitator of digital transformation in various sectors of the industry. First designed as electronic substitutes of tangible resources, including machinery and equipment, these models helped to monitor the activities of the operating performance and implement simulations and forecast the maintenance requirements. Michael Grieves (2014) described the principle of a digital replica which embodies the complete lifecycle of a physical object first. Later conceptualization by Fei Tao and others (2019) augmented this model to include incorporation of the physical system, virtual worlds, and real-time information, and in such a way show how it could complement operational efficiency and decision-making.

Further empirical research has been added to the taxonomy and maturity evaluation of Digital Twin systems. Kritzinger et al. (2018) also categorized Digital Twins based on the level of information connectivity and integration, marking a series that runs between the range of fully autonomous digital systems to the fixed digital models. This taxonomy gives a taxonomic structure of the evolution and implementation of the technology. The digital twin concept has expanded over time due to the evolving nature of Digital Twins which now encompasses manufacturing, supply chains, logistic networks, and customer experience. Fuller et al. (2020) stressed that Digital Twins assist in predictive analytics, operational optimisation and process innovation in diverse sectors, hence is quite corresponding with the digital transformation agenda in organizations as a whole (Vial, 2019).

The strategic relevance of Digital Twin architectures is further exaggerated by the need to have Artificial Intelligence (AI) included. The artificial intelligence methodologies, such as machine learning, neural network, and predictive analytics, assist in processing large amounts of structured and unstructured information in the organization, Stuart Russell and Peter Norvig (2021) argue. This allows firms to shift from descriptive to predictive and prescriptive decision-making. Davenport and Ronanki (2018) point out that the implementation of AI in the business environment boosts efficiency in operations, customer-focused deepening, and makes innovations. Brynjolfsson and McAfee (2017) argue that AI is a means of supplementing human working capacity as opposed to substituting it, thus allowing the knowledge workers to make faster and better informed choices. Agencies that manage to embrace the use of AI-based tactics become more agile, competitive, and form more value (Ransbotham et al., 2017).

Digital Twins and AI intersect have led to the birth of the idea of Cognitive Enterprises, where organizational processes are constantly updated and optimized using data-driven knowledge. As defined by Johnk et al. (2021), these organizations are the ones that integrate AI into the main business practices hence facilitating the unlimited learning and the ability to make relevant decisions. The enterprises are using cloud computing, automation, analytics, and Digital Twin platforms to build intersecting intelligent digital ecosystems. These changes are in line with the overall shift to Industry 4.0 and Industry 5.0 paradigms which place emphasis on digitalization, sustainability, and human-centered innovation (Schwab, 2017; Nahavandi, 2019).

However, the successful implementation of Digital twins and AI is still subject to strengthened human-technology collaboration. According to Davenport (2018), although AI is quite effective in working with data and detecting patterns, it will never replace human judgment in ethical regards, creativity, and strategic thinking. Brynjolfsson and McAfee (2017) also state that companies should invest in workforce retraining as well as restructure job descriptions to combine human knowledge and AI into their job descriptions. Such a human-AI partnership creates innovation, flexibility, and resilience, which facilitate organizations to maintain competitiveness in the dynamic environments that are volatile and uncertain.

Together, available literature highlights the fact that Digital Twins and Artificial Intelligence are a revolutionizing nexus, which is helpful in promoting efficiency, decision-making, and innovation in organizations. Further studies need to focus on the problem of integrations and ethical aspects, data regulations, and human-oriented implementation to achieve the full potential of AI application in creating sustainable and inflexible business ecosystems.

3.1 Objectives for the Chapter

1. To examine the evolution of Digital Twins from physical asset-based models to enterprise-wide intelligent systems within modern organizations.
2. To explore how Artificial Intelligence affects the organizational decision-making and how AI helps in at least making intelligent, data-driven, and predictive management practices.
3. To find out the roles of AI-based analytics, automation, and real-time data integration to develop intelligent decision systems in business processes, supply chains and customer engagement systems.
4. To examine the importance of human-AI partnership in raising organizational agile, innovativeness, sustainability and strategic performance.
5. To determine the obstacles, governance problems, ethical considerations, risks of data security and workforce readiness factors related to the shift to cognitive enterprises.

4. RESEARCH QUESTIONS

a. How have Digital Twins evolved from physical asset-based simulations to enterprise-wide intelligent systems within modern organizations?
b. How does Artificial Intelligence improve intelligent decision-making, as well as how does it help to create adaptable and self-learning organizational ecosystems?
c. How do AI based technologies like predictive analytics, machine learning, and automation facilitate the change of traditional enterprises to cognitive enterprises?
d. How can the human-AI collaboration enhance organizational agility, innovativeness, and sustainability?
e. What are the governing, ethics, data security, and algorithmic transparency, and workforce preparedness issues in the shift to cognitive enterprises?
f. How does the integration of Digital Twins with AI influence organizational performance in terms of cost efficiency, productivity, and strategic decision-making?
g. How can the maturity of an organization be evaluated to become a cognitive enterprise?

5. METHODOLOGY FOR THIS STUDY

This paper takes a close look at how Digital Twins have evolved into Cognitive Enterprises, all powered by AI-driven intelligent decision ecosystems. The research draws from a wide range of existing sources—academic journals, conference papers, books, industry reports, technical white papers, and reputed online publications that explore Digital Twins, Artificial Intelligence (AI), predictive analytics, intelligent automation, and organizational transformation. Combining the research establizhed by the interplay between scholarly and practitioner-related literature, the paper will attempt to develop a detailed picture on the managerial and technological aspects of this development.

The research primarily follows a qualitative, conceptual research design based on an extensive literature review. Rather, instead of primary data (surveys and interviews), this study uses secondary sources of data to analyze the existing theories and frameworks and real-life case examples. Peer-reviewed databases, which included Scopus, Web of Science, IEEE Xplore and Google Scholar were consulted to find out the pertinent academic contribution. Moreover, surveys provided by top consulting companies and technology organizations were consulted to learn about the practices used in the industry nowadays and novelties.

The main goal of this methodology is to trace the developmental journey of Digital Twins—from basic digital representations of physical assets to sophisticated, enterprise-wide intelligent systems. The identification of the major themes which constitute the basis of the review process included the lifecycle management, the integration of real-time data, the predictive capabilities using AI, and the interoperability of different systems. Special attention was given to foundational theoretical models and classification frameworks that explain the maturity levels of Digital Twins and their integration with AI technologies.

6. ISSUES AND TRENDS

The transition from Digital Twins to Cognitive Enterprises is fraught with challenges. Cybersecurity and data governance prove to be the main challenges. The Smart ecosystems rely on the concepts of AI strongly require extensive amount of real time and high velocity information collected by sensors, enterprise systems, cloud computing and customer interfaces. The increased reliance on data increases the risks associated with breach of privacy, data hacking, ransomware, and data breach to significant extents. Companies should adhere to the current data-protection standards and conduct and be accountable in gathering, processing, and storage of information. The lack of a good governance structure minimizes trust and minimizes the credibility of AI-driven insights.

Ethical issues bring on board another element of complexity. With algorithmic decisions playing an ever-greater role in strategic and operational decision-making, such questions as the existence of bias, their unaccountability, and unpredictability become particularly important. Should the AI systems be developed based on biased or insufficient data, they might perpetuate injustices or make inaccurate suggestions. Therefore, clarifiable AI (XAI), understandable model design, and strict ethical audit systems should be critical elements of Cognitive Enterprises. Lack of proper human control can result in the development of the unintended push and pull consequences of automated decision systems on employees, customers and stakeholders.

Another significant challenge is that of organizational preparedness. The issues of skill deficits are widespread within many companies, especially in such areas as data science, AI engineering, cybersecurity, and digital governance. The conventional workforce models might not be in line with the AI-centered operating models. Unless provided with ongoing upskilling and reskilling initiatives as well as systematic change-management, the employees might fail to adapt to new technologies or become unable to cooperate with intelligent systems. The cultural change is also of the same importance as the implementation of technology. To effectively transform into a design of cognitive models, organizations need to develop the mentality of innovation, experimentation, and ongoing learning.

The integration issues also make the process of transformation difficult. Connecting Digital Twins to enterprise resource planning (ERP) systems, customer relationship management (CRM) platforms, cloud infrastructures, and AI engines requires robust interoperability frameworks and standardized data architectures. Historical systems usually cannot be interconnected with the new AI-based solutions, which makes their implementation very expensive and disrupts the workflow. The financial cost of the infrastructure upgrade, the cybersecurity, and the preparation of AI can be a barrier especially to small and medium-sized enterprises (SMEs).

Despite these challenges, several transformative trends are shaping the future of Digital Twins and Cognitive Enterprises. Digital Twins are no longer confined to physical assets; they now encompass entire value chains, supply networks, business workflows, healthcare ecosystems, and customer engagement models. Organizations are building real time, dynamic, digital versions of operations, which are used to simulate scenarios, predictive maintenance, and demand as well as risk modelling.

It also has a pronounced trend as to human-centric innovation, which fits perfectly well with Industry 5.0 principles. In contrast to Industry4.0 in which the core focus was made on automation and efficiency, Industry5.0 focuses on human interaction with intelligent machines. It aims at complimenting and not replacing human expertise. AI systems provide an element of analytical volume, speed whereas for humans, creativity, empathy, and ethical thinking, as well as strategy. The synergy produces more balanced and sustainable decision-making processes.

The other new development is the usage of predictive analytics and intelligent automation that is taking root. Organizations are using machine-learning models to predict disruptions, smarter resource allocation, and smart customer experiences. Robot process automation (RPA), which is a subtype of intelligent automation together with AI, reduces workload and other routine activities and improves the efficiency of operations. Concurrently, sustainable digital strategies are gaining prominence; Digital Twins are employed to monitor energy consumption, reduce waste, and support environmentally responsible decision making.

The technologies of cloud computing, edge computing, and the Internet of Things (IoT) contribute to the increased growth of intelligent decision ecosystems. These technologies create the possibilities of real-time processing of data, fast processing of analytics and better system scalability. With more organizations having access to and affordability of computational power, more of them can explore cognitive modeling and Digital Twin-simulations.

7. THE IMPACT OF AI-DRIVEN DIGITAL TWINS ON ORGANIZATIONAL PERFORMANCE

The transition from Digital Twins to Cognitive Enterprises is fraught with challenges. Cybersecurity and data governance prove to be the main challenges. The Smart ecosystems rely on the concepts of AI strongly require extensive amount of real time and high velocity information collected by sensors, enterprise systems, cloud computing and customer interfaces. The increased reliance on data increases the risks associated with breach of privacy, data hacking, ransomware, and data breach to significant extents. Companies should adhere to the current data-protection standards and conduct and be accountable in gathering, processing, and storage of information. The lack of proper governance structures undermines the trust and the credibility of AI-driven insights.

Ethical issues bring on board another element of complexity. With algorithmic decisions playing an ever-greater role in strategic and operational decision-making, such questions as the existence of bias, their unaccountability, and unpredictability become particularly important. Should the AI systems be developed based on biased or insufficient data, they might perpetuate injustices or make inaccurate suggestions. Therefore, clarifiable AI (XAI), understandable model design, and strict ethical audit systems should be critical elements of Cognitive Enterprises. Lack of proper human control can result in the development of the unintended push and pull consequences of automated decision systems on employees, customers and stakeholders.

Another significant challenge is that of organizational preparedness. The issues of skill deficits are widespread within many companies, especially in such areas as data science, AI engineering, cybersecurity, and digital governance. The conventional workforce models might not be in line with the AI-centered operating models. Unless provided with ongoing upskilling and reskilling initiatives as well as systematic change-management, the employees might fail to adapt to new technologies or become unable to cooperate with intelligent systems. The cultural change is also of the same importance as the implementation of technology. To effectively transform into a design of cognitive models, organizations need to develop the mentality of innovation, experimentation, and ongoing learning.

The integration issues also make the process of transformation difficult. Connecting Digital Twins to enterprise resource planning (ERP) systems, customer relationship management (CRM) platforms, cloud infrastructures, and AI engines requires robust interoperability frameworks and standardized data architectures. Historical systems usually cannot be interconnected with the new AI-based solutions, which makes their implementation very expensive and disrupts the workflow. The financial cost of the infrastructure upgrade, the cybersecurity, and the preparation of AI can be a barrier especially to small and medium-sized enterprises (SMEs).

Despite these challenges, several transformative trends are shaping the future of Digital Twins and Cognitive Enterprises. Digital Twins are no longer confined to physical assets; they now encompass entire value chains, supply networks, business workflows, healthcare ecosystems, and customer engagement models. Organizations are building real time, dynamic, digital versions of operations, which are used to simulate scenarios, predictive maintenance, and demand as well as risk modelling.

It also has a pronounced trend as to human-centric innovation, which fits perfectly well with Industry 5.0 principles. In contrast to Industry4.0 in which the core focus was made on automation and efficiency, Industry5.0 focuses on human interaction with intelligent machines. It aims at complimenting and not replacing human expertise. AI systems provide an element of analytical volume, speed whereas for humans, creativity, empathy, and ethical thinking, as well as strategy. Such synergy produces more harmonious and longer-term decision-making processes.

The other new development is the usage of predictive analytics and intelligent automation, which is taking root. Organizations are leveraging machine-learning applications to forecast disruption, optimize company resources, and customize the experiences of their customers. Robot process automation (RPA), which is a subtype of intelligent automation together with AI, reduces workload and other routine activities and improves the efficiency of operations. Concurrently, sustainable digital strategies are gaining prominence; Digital Twins are employed to monitor energy consumption, reduce waste, and support environmentally responsible decision-making.

The technologies of cloud computing, edge computing, and the Internet of Things (IoT) contribute to the increased growth of intelligent decision ecosystems. These technologies create the possibilities of real-time processing of data, fast processing of analytics and better system scalability. With more organizations having access to and the affordability of computational power, more of them can explore cognitive modeling and Digital Twin simulations.

8. CURRENT STATE OF COGNITIVE ENTERPRISE DEVELOPMENT ACROSS INDUSTRIES

Industries are developing differently from cognitive enterprise, and the rate at which this is done will depend on factors such as digital maturity, technological framework, leadership thinking, investment potential, organizational culture, and regulatory limitations. The leadership of this shift belongs to data-intensive, technology-based sectors, namely, finance, manufacturing, telecommunications, healthcare, and e-commerce, which took the initiative to integrate the system based on artificial intelligence in their decision-making and introduced tools of intelligent automation, sophisticated analytics, and cloud computing infrastructures to coordinate operational integrations that have hitherto been impossible.

Cognitive capabilities are used in the financial services industry to detect fraud, as well as algorithmic trading and credit-risk assessment, as well as expert financial advice that is personalized. It means that AI systems are always analyzing transactional data, customer behaviour, and fluctuations of the market to implement real-time decisions.

Manufacturing industries, building upon the foundations of Industry 4.0, are integrating AI-powered Digital Twins, predictive maintenance, robotics, and intelligent supply chains to enhance productivity and reduce operational costs. Telecommunication companies are using AI to maximize network performance, predict the occurrence of service disasters and enjoy a personalized customer experience.

Healthcare too has been quick in implementing the cognitive enterprise principles. AI-based analytics are implemented by hospitals and health-care providers to monitor their patients, diagnose them in advance, and optimize their operations. Digital platforms combine patient data, electronic health records and monitoring systems that are real-time to enhance the quality of care and decision-making. As a reflection of this, e-commerce platforms are relying on AI to predict demand, issue recommendations, provide price dynamism and control inventory, thus developing extremely reactive and customer-focused ecosystems.

The international upheavals that were experienced in 2020 fastened digital transformation programs in industries. Companies had no choice but to employ distant working, electronic group work machines, and automatic mechanisms and sturdy virtual chains of supply. Risk monitoring which was carried out a real time, scenario modelling and data-based forecasting were now necessities and not options. As a result, a lot of businesses accelerated their AI assimilation approaches, including clever frameworks into the fundamental business models. Enterprise Resource Planning (ERP), Customer Relationship Management (CRM), Human Resource Management (HRM) and supply twenty-first century systems are being more and more interconnected, to create data-driven ecosystems.

The ability to learn continuously and adapt is one of the characteristics of cognitive enterprises. In contrast to other conventional organizations with have a fixed set of reports and periodical reviews, cognitive enterprises are based on dynamic feedback loops. AI algorithms handle real time data streams, detect patterns and semi autonomously or autonomously recalibrate processes. This learning capabilities would improve the responsiveness to the changes in the market, demand of the customers and the operational upsets.

The other prominent trend in question is the combination of both structured and unstructured data. The cognitive enterprises are characterized by the integration of different traditional datasets into unstructured ones such as social media communications, customer feedback, e-mail messages, images, and the analysis of market sentiments. Natural-language and machine-learning tools deliver superior means of deriving meaningful insights off all kinds of information, which in turn helps organizations come up with more holistic and contextual information on making decisions.

However, development rates are greatly different in terms of regions and industries. Big multinational companies might have access to funds and technologies necessary to invest in new advanced AI platforms and cloud, and small and medium-sized enterprises (SMEs) might face financial limitations, personnel issues, and integration problems. However, barriers to entry are gradually reduced by increasing the prominence of cloud-based AI software and solutions and software-as-a-service (SaaS) solutions.

Both leadership commitment and organizational culture are very important in promoting cognitive enterprise development. Companies that support experimentation, innovation, and cross-functional cooperation have more chances to be successful in implementing AI between departments. The business culture of strategic alignment can be achieved between IT teams and business executives so that AI projects will result in quantifiable improvements of performance instead of technological explorations.

9. GLOBALIZATION, STAKEHOLDER EXPECTATIONS, AND MAR- KET DYNAMICS SHAPING COGNITIVE ENTERPRISES

Globalization has completely changed the way life is structured and functioned in the contemporary organizations. Modern businesses are encountering very interconnected world systems marked by international trade, digital technologies, multinational relations, and dense supply-chain systems. The period between 2015 to 2024 is associated with the acceleration in digital globalization due to the development of e-commerce between countries, cloud-based systems, and internationally integrated financial systems. As a result, organizations find themselves dealing with large amounts of real-time information and have to deal with different regulatory, cultural, and economic conditions. The old models of decision making that depended on periodic reporting and approvals that were based on hierarchy could not work in such a dynamic environment. The growing pace of the market transformation, geopolitical unpredictability, and digital disturbances require the application of smart and changeable systems. Based on this, organizations are moving to AI-capable cognitive enterprise designs to facilitate real-time analytics, predictive prognostication, and strategic responsiveness.

9.1 Effect of Globalization on Complexity of the Organization

Globalization has played a key role in making operation more complex in enterprises. Companies are now dealing with multinational transactions, their worldwide procurement net-works, decentralized factories, and customers spread globally. This complexity is further complicated by divergent systems of taxation, trade imposture, compliance and data-protection laws.

New digital transformation has compounded this since it has merged international activities based on cloud services and systems powered by IoT. On the one hand, these technologies will increase the efficiency and communication network; they will also increase vulnerability to cybersecurity risks, supply-chain interruptions, and regulatory risks. The approach to addressing these issues by cognitive enterprises is to rely on AI-driven analytics to constantly monitor the business across the world, identify abnormalities, and provide early warning of potential risk.

9.2 Dynamics of Stakeholder Expectation

The organizations are now required to go beyond its financial performance as is expected by its stakeholders. Shareholders require transparency and sustainability measures which are long term. The regulators demand that the data-privacy and ethical standards of AI be adhered to. The customers expect individualized services, speediness of response and being socially responsible. Inclusive, forthcoming and technologically-oriented workplace environments are desired by the employees.

These changing expectations offer enterprises a challenge of including Environmental, Social, and Governance (ESG) in their strategic decisions. Intelligent platforms that make use of AI help organizations to measure their level of sustainability, their compliance needs, and increase transparency in their reporting. Intelligence can be applied in enterprise systems to enable organizations to react proactively to the demands of the stakeholders and build trust.

9.3 Market Volatility and Technological Disruption

The current markets are described to have fast cycles of innovation, technology breakthrough, and unforeseeable discontinuities. The traditional business models have become exposed to fragility owing to the economic crisis, global pandemics, geopolitical tensions, and the digital rivalry. Businesses have to keep on changing with the changing demand patterns, competition, and technological changes.

AI-driven Digital Twins and predictive analytics enable organizations to simulate market scenarios and evaluate strategic alternatives before implementation. Live-time data analysis also allows businesses to predict demand shifts, tune pricing, manage inventory, and strengthen the supply-chain. All these abilities decrease the level of uncertainty and support evidence-based decisions in unstable settings.

9.4 Application in Consonance With Industry 5.0 Principles

The movement towards cognitive businesses is similar to the concepts of Industry 5.0. Compared to other industrial revolutions in the past where the main agenda was on enterprise automation and efficiency, Industry 5.0 is keen on human-oriented innovation, resiliency, and sustainability.

This change has been embodied by cognitive enterprises where people have incorporated AI systems to improve instead of substitute their decision-making process. Data-driven insights come in through intelligent platforms, whereas human knowledge offers a strategic perspective as well as ethical judgment and understanding of the context. Such a cooperative strategy enhances organizational flexibility and encourages innovativeness in a globalized economy.

9.5 Strategic Requirements of AI-Based Cognitive Enterprises

The artificial intelligence-based cognitive companies have ceased to be side effects but rather top-down requirements of the present-day global setting. Companies that do not embrace smart systems face the risk of being left behind the competition, which takes advantage of predictive analytics and a real-time decision ecosystem.

Using AI-based platforms, businesses can become more transparent, more responsible, agile, and sustainable. The forces of globalization and the pressure of stakeholders, as well as the dynamic forces of the market in totality, affirm the need to have intelligent, adaptable, and resilient organizational systems that can flourish in the complex global environments.

10. CHALLENGES AND OPPORTUNITIES IN BUILDING AI-DRIVEN COGNITIVE ENTERPRISES

Shifting an organization from the past to an AI-driven cognitive enterprise is quite a difficult task that has both challenges and opportunities. Although smart technologies can bring more efficiency, new technology, and competitiveness, their implementation process demands careful planning, strong governance, and cultural change.

10.1 Data Governance and Cybersecurity Challenges

One of the most important issues is to have robust data control and cybersecurity. Cognitive enterprises are very strict in real-time data that is being gathered and obtained through internal systems, the Internet of Things, and cloud and external providers. The growth of the data ecosystem also increases the vulnerability to cybercrime like data leakage, ransomware intrusions, and unauthorized access.

Firms should take serious data-management policies to be able to guarantee the presence of accuracy, consistency, and integrity. It is necessary to comply with data-protective laws and privacy principles, especially in the highly regulated sectors like the financial and healthcare industries. Lack of effective governance can cause AI systems to be based on incorrect or insecure data, which will lead to inaccurate decisions and loss of reputation. This invests in encryption technologies, zero-trust security-based architectures, and constant monitoring systems one of the priorities.

10.2 Explainability and Ethical AI

The other issue of great concern is AI systems' explainability. Most modern machine-learning and deep-learning algorithms are black boxes that cannot give answers to the reasoning behind the result. When managed like this, such an opaque nature may be legally and ethically hazardous.

The organizations shall have to implement explainable AI (XAI) models that give them understandable insights into the algorithms. Open decision-making is a source of trust to the customers, employees, and regulators. In addition, ethical issues, including bias in algorithms, fairness, discrimination, and accountability, are to be taken care of. Advocates of AI systems should train them on unbiased data, they can give unfair results, which can have a social and legal impact. These risks can be addressed through the formulation of ethical review boards and guidelines on responsible AI.

10.3 Workforce Transformation and Skill Gaps

Human dimension is one of the most complicated areas of cognitive enterprise construction. Facing resistance to changes, the employees will need to obtain new digital skills, such as data literacy, collaboration with AI, and analysis, but still have to overcome the opposition to change. There is always worry of having no jobs and adapting to the new set up.

Organizations must have reskilling and upskilling initiatives organized to reduce these obstacles. The continuous learning programs, online learning, and leadership should be supported to enable the smooth transitions. The approach towards change management ought to focus on both human and AI cooperation and accentuate the ways in which intelligent systems are used to enrich, not eliminate human abilities. When there is a positive organizational culture, it encourages innovation and less opposition.

10.4 Integration and Infrastructure Complexity

The incorporation of AI systems with the current enterprise systems, including ERP, CRM, supply-chain, and finance systems, is not always a straightforward undertaking. The legacy systems might fail to integrate with the latest AI-based structures, which will require expensive upgrades or new designs. This implies that the interoperability of different digital platforms is crucial to ensure that there is a single data model and a scaled cloud infrastructure.

Nevertheless, these technical challenges do not mean that organizations that are able to integrate AI into their various departments do not enjoy unrestricted flow of information, faster decision making, and enhanced coordination of operations.

10.5 Financial Investment and Return on Investment (ROI)

The construction of a cognitive enterprise will have high financial expenditure in the domains of technology infrastructure, AI design, cybersecurity systems, and employee training. These costs are prohibitive for smaller organizations. In addition, the ROI of AI initiatives may be hard to measure, particularly when benefits may be in the long-term (or intangible), i.e., the increased customer satisfaction or the improved innovation capabilities.

However, when organizations effectively match AI programs with business goals, they tend to reap major returns in the long term in terms of optimization of costs, increased productivity, and a competitive edge.

10.6 Opportunities for Innovation and Competitive Advantage

Still, the challenges are immensely high, but the opportunities are transformative as well. Predictive analytics, intelligent automation, and real-time simulation tools can be used by AI-based cognitive enterprises to make themselves more efficient in their operations and masterful in their strategy. They allow taking ahead decisions, predicting risks, and engaging with the customer in a personal way.

Sustainable development goals are also facilitated through cognitive enterprises through maximization of energy consumption, minimization of waste products and increased transparency of supply chains. Smart information stems by AI will encourage equal prudence in resource distribution and sustainable operations. Besides, the innovative nature of cognitive systems is encouraged by the ability of the system to continually learn. Companies will be able to test new business models, products and services in the simulated digital environment before they can be rolled out in real life thus minimizing risk and shortening time-to-market.

10.7 Strategic Leadership and Organizational Culture

Leadership dedication is crucial in putting challenges into opportunities. The leaders that focus more on digital transformation, ethical use of AI, and empowerment of employees are visionary leaders who are able to develop an environment that promotes innovation. The culture which promotes experimentation, cross-functional coordination and data-based thinking, enhances the basis of a cognitive enterprise.

11. RISKS ASSOCIATED WITH AI-ENABLED DECISION ECOSYSTEMS

Decision ecosystems based on artificial intelligence create a range of technical, ethical, strategic and organizational risks. On the one hand, such systems increase productivity and intelligence, but, at the same time, the complexity and interconnectivity inherent in this specific category of systems are a source of vulnerability that must be consciously addressed.

Algorithms bias and the lack of quality data is one of the major concerns. The quality, diversity, and representativeness of training data are some of the fundamental components of AI models. Unfinished, old-fashioned, or prejudiced data leads to the decision which can be unjust, discriminating, or inaccurate. Biased results in areas like employee recruitment, credit rating, medical diagnosis, or profitability of customers, could cause lawsuits, loss of reputation, and a decline in confidence of stakeholders. Besides, any mistakes in training data can spread quickly within a network of interconnected systems, amplifying the negative consequences.

The second important threat is an overreliance on automation. With more sophisticated AI systems, there is a threat of companies depending on automated recommendations more than they should be regulated without proper human intervention. This has the ability to negate reasoning and limit the judgment of the manager. Automated systems would not necessarily record the subtlety of situations, ethical matters, or any emerging risk in complicated or unforeseeable situations. Having minimal human control over the process, small technical failure will become a significant process interruption. It is important to have a human in the loop paradigm at the right balance to avoid blindly following the outputs of the automated process.

The security of the data and the cybersecurity threats are especially significant in AI-based ecosystems. The cognitive enterprises rely on an interconnected platform, cloud services, Internet of Things (IoT), and real-time data streams. The increased online presence increases vulnerability to online attacks, ransomware, phishing, and hacking of the system. The one point of weakness in the network could destroy the whole ecosystem. Breach of data not just interrupts business but also builds a negative reputation in the organization, and can culminate in regulatory action. In turn, the constant security vigilance and strong encryption measures, as well as zero-trust designs, form the required defenses.

System failures, as well as technical instability is also a significant threat. The platforms provided by AI require a stable infrastructure, quality connectivity, and adaptable computational power. Decision-making processes can be disrupted by hardware failures, software malfunctions, integration issues, or cloud failures. Such failures could have extremely financial and social consequences for the healthcare, finance, transportation, or energy sectors, which are all mission-critical. The process of risk mitigation includes redundancy plans, backup plans, and disaster recovery plans, all of which are essential.

The other current issue is regulatory and compliance uncertainty. AI governance systems are still at the stage of development throughout the world, and AI implementations at the organizational level might fail to comply with the currently changing legal frameworks. Various jurisdictions can use divergent policies on data privacy, the transparency of algorithms, and accountability. This regulatory fragmentation is problematic with regard to cross-border operations and increases the cost of compliance. The issue of proactive policy monitoring and adoption of versatile governance arrangements by organizations should be an active agenda.

The other risk is strategic misalignment. When AI systems are not implemented with a clear business purpose and performance goals, quantifiable performance metrics, and alignment between administration and other key players, they can lead to system inefficiencies instead of productivity. Failing to plan before investing in

AI technologies may result in disjointed systems, redundant activities, or a wasted platform. The effective implementation of AI needs to be coupled with organizational strategy in the long run, operational objectives, and performance-management systems.

There is also a major risk of organizational resistance and cultural barriers. Employees could not trust AI systems or think that they will be pushed out of work, which will make them less collaborative and decrease the adoption rate. Without effective training and clear communication, AI efforts will come across in favoritism in the internal environment. A sustainable implementation requires the building of trust, the development of cultures of digital literacy, and the development of collaborative cultures.

Ethical and accountability issues are still high. It becomes complicated when the errors of the AI systems are held by the accountable one when the decisions are being made. The question arises on whether the person in accountability is the developer, it is the organization, or it is the automated system itself. The lack of clarity in accountability systems will lead to court and reputational risk when it comes to enterprises.

In order to address these risks, organizations ought to embrace a system of continuous validation, model auditing, real-time monitoring, and strong governance systems. Reliability and trust can be improved through the creation of multidisciplinary oversight groups, the use of explainable AI models, and frequently updating the system. Decision ecosystems should also continue to be human-centered, especially in high-impact areas.

12. FUTURE TRENDS IN DIGITAL TWINS AND COGNITIVE ENTERPRISE TRANSFORMATION

The transition from Digital Twins to fully developed cognitive enterprises enters a new phase driven by rapid technological innovation, intelligent automation, and strategic integration of artificial intelligence across enterprise systems. The trends also point to the fact that organizations will advance beyond digital replication and come to a completely adaptive, predictive and self-optimizing ecosystems. These innovations can be viewed in line with the Industry 5.0 ideology where technology improves human creativity, survival, and, consequently, sustainability instead of replacing human abilities.

12.1 Evolution Toward Enterprise-Wide Digital Twins

Future Digital Twins will extend beyond individual assets and operational units to represent entire organizational ecosystems. Enterprise Digital Twins will integrate supply-chain operations, financial systems, customer-behavior analytics, human-resource dynamics, and strategic-planning models into a unified digital environment.

This integrated modelling will play out in terms of organizations having the ability of simulating a scenario, stress testing and long term forecasting to a greater degree of precision. The decision-makers can analyze the what-if situations prior to applying action on the ground, and hence will lessen the risks and boost persuasion of the strategic programs.

12.2 Autonomous and Prescriptive Decision-Making Systems

This paper will identify the various types of autonomous and prescriptive decision-making systems and explain their role within the operational workflows of a business or organization.

Another significant trend is the development of intelligent autonomous AI that can make prescriptive decisions. Counter to the old models of analytics to provide descriptive or predictive information, future systems will be advising from particular actions and may be suggested to implement operational changes without the necessity of human intervention.

Machine-learning and deep-learning algorithms will be constantly educated by real-time data and, as such, allow businesses to react immediately to any disruptive forces like delays in the supply chain, market variability or demand changes. However, there will still be the need of human control as accountability and ethical governance.

12.3 Human–AI Collaboration and Augmented Intelligence

The human and intelligent systems are going to be focused on in the future of cognitive enterprises. Artificial intelligence will assist managers and staff with information, trend identification and optimization recommendations regarding performance.

This is not a replacement of human functions; AI will help in decision-making. Mankind's experience will continue to play a significant role in terms of moral judgment, vision, and situational interpretation. This team approach fosters the element of trust and provides balanced decision-making in complicated environments.

12.4 Integration of Emerging Technologies

The convergence in technology is estimated to have a significant impact on the direction in which the transformation of the enterprise is moving. It can be expected that the collaboration between edge computing, cloud platforms, blockchain, and 5G connections will make Digital Twin systems highly efficient and scalable. Edge computing supports real-time data processing in the places that are adjacent to the sources of operation, and in this manner, latency is overcome. At the same time, blockchain technology can support transparency and ensure data transfer between distributed enterprise networks. It is anticipated that when these technologies are converged, the result will be decentralized but interconnected intelligent ecosystems.

12.5 Sustainability and ESG-Driven Intelligence

The need to develop cognitive enterprises towards sustainability is becoming a crucial goal. Digital Twins based on AI allow companies to calculate the impact of the environment, optimal energy use, and the efficiency of resources in general. Businesses are increasingly becoming a part of the intelligence-based decision-making systems that incorporate the Environmental, Social, and Governance (ESG) considerations. This business change encourages sustainable innovation and operational orientation that matches corporate development with long-term sustainability objectives.

12.6 Ethical Governance and Explainable AI

Due to the increased sophistication of artificial intelligence systems, the need of explainability and the necessity to govern ethical aspects gain additional importance. Companies are embracing open AI systems that define the process of making decisions in a very clear way. Some of the areas that regulatory compliance, data-privacy protection, and algorithmic fairness are impacting enterprise strategy in are these. Further cognitive business networks will also establizh the platform of governance to control the performance of AI, prevent bias, and keep the data usage accountable. The ethical AI practices are thus expected to strengthen the stakeholder trust and organizational credibility.

12.7 Workforce Transformation and Skill Development

The shift to the smart enterprises would require the ongoing workforce change. There is a need to develop digital literacy, analytical skills, and abilities to work well with AI technologies among the employees. This will be facilitated by the organizational investment in the training programs, AI literacy programs, and cultures that are innovation-focused, to name a few. This is because the issue of developing a future-ready workforce is critical to ensuring that cognitive technologies are implemented sustainably.

13. DISCUSSION AND FINDINGS

This research does show that the Digital Twins have not only undergone a transformation in that of a digital enterprise but a complete paradigm shift in business approach. Once organizations combine AI with Digital Twins, they cease to operate passively by monitoring their operation, but build on the creation of intelligent systems to make decisions. The new structures combine real-time values, predictive analytics, and machine learning capabilities, and therefore allow organizations to react quickly and allow it to be flexible when addressing different contingencies.

The Digital Twins have changed significantly in terms of their usage. The Digital Twins have been used in a range of applications (simulations of business processes, supply-chain dynamics, financial systems, and customer experiences) rather than just limited to tracking machinery and equipment in smart factories, which is a characteristic of Industry 4.0. This has resulted in the fact that creating the marginal efficiency gains is becoming less significant and shifting to the overall improvement of organizational intelligence and adaptability.

Artificial intelligence-based decision-making systems contribute to the ability of the organization to be resilient. Real-time analytics enable the prevention of the consequences that unexpected events may cause, as teams can respond in advance. Predictive models would help the leaders to gauge the risk and come up with coalition plans, thus minimizing the exposure to a fluctuating market environment. Besides, harmonious work between automation and human skills improves productivity without compromising ethical practices and vision.

The cooperation between humans and AI becomes one of the crucial factors. Within the paradigm of Industry 5.0, it is not the role of people to be replaced but rather to gain more abilities as human beings. Smart platforms give business managers software feedback and advice, but it is up to humans to drive the operations, bring creativity, and guarantee moral behavior. These collaborations breed the level of trust and a better quality of decision-making.

There is the issue of governance and ethics. Institutional trust is put at risk by data privacy, cybersecurity, the bias of algorithms, and black box AI models. Companies that move towards putting a strong system of governance, AI transparency, and empowering the staff with the necessary skills are also well placed to make sure that the trust of stakeholders is not compromised.

Online maturity has a great impact on company agility. Companies that are defined by a lean IT architecture, defined data management, and an innovation-driven culture move faster towards cognitive maturity. On the other hand, dysfunctional systems and a shortage of skills will impede change processes, and they might lead the organization into the back stage.

14. SUGGESTIONS

Organizations need to consider grounding their AI strategies on human capital to move on to adopting Digital Twins to fully operationalize cognitive enterprises. In general, instead of seeking technological improvements with the aim of satisfying themselves, it is worth doing it gradually, starting with a clear alignment to the overall strategic purposes. Piloting initiatives helps teams to learn, improve, and eliminate threats before the extension of implementation.

Good cybersound and data governance are grounded. Development of elaborate privacy and compliance measures would be a critical aspect in ensuring trust, as opposed to meeting the regulatory requirements.

The collaboration between humans and AI must be kept in the middle. Delegating analytical and predictive tasks to AI systems and retaining human judgments regarding the important decisions will result in contextual relevance and stewardship. Constant development of principles of digital capabilities, AI solutions, and analytics keeps pace with the workforce and drives the culture of progress and change.

It is necessary to be transparent. The provision of explorable and moral-congruent AI systems can guarantee the understanding of all the stakeholders of decision-making processes and responsible agents. The spread of Digital Twin to supply chains, finance, and customer services, as well as physical assets, makes the organization more agile.

Lastly, it is essential to make AI plans sustainable. The use of advanced analytics to determine resource optimization keeps the long-term social and environmental responsibility. A balanced approach of future-readiness involves the application of superior technology, sound governance, effective human resources, and a concise code of ethics, which allows organizations to overcome the changing challenges.

15. IMPLICATIONS OF THE STUDY

This research plays a significant role in the literature. Its contribution to the theoretical development can be termed as expanding our understanding of Artificial Intelligence and Digital Twin technology by connecting Digital Twins and the new paradigm of cognitive enterprises. Besides, it advances the topic of digital transformation by showing how AI-based decision ecosystems are the foundations of more intelligent organizations, especially with Industry 5.0 coming into view. The offered framework provides the researchers with a new outlook on enterprise intelligence and human-AI partnership and flexible reorganization of corporate hierarchies.

To managerial audiences, it is quite categorical that Digital Twins should not be treated as additional tools of operation. Instead, they are to be viewed as central figures as far as making a better decision is concerned. The leaders can only consider the full-scale adoption of AI in the organization if they are willing to increase the agility of the organization, develop innovative ideas, and restore order immediately after facing the disruption. The paper emphasizes that organizations must ensure that the AI programs are aligned with the organizational goals, active governance frameworks, and declare significant investments in the development of the workforce skills as the only conditions for the continuity of change. Not only is the approval of leadership and the mastery of digital competencies not optional, but it is also decisive in terms of the euphoria of reform.

Technologically, this is highly focused on legendary data infrastructure, real-time analytics, and reliable digital systems. The issues of data governance, cybersecurity, and explainable artificial intelligence are not minor support aspects but should hold a pivotal role in maintaining the trustworthiness of intelligent managed systems. Similarly, in the area of predictive analytics, automation, and Digital Twin platforms, they must be designed with scalability and durability in mind, as opposed to simply being added on.

Without reservations, the wider implications of society are tackled. Ethical AI and responsible innovation are not only trendy terms, but they are also necessary conditions. Companies working in cognitive firms should make sure automation is not propagated irresponsibly. A human intervention is still necessary to reduce the potential bias, protect the privacy, and ensure the integrity of such a decision. Finally, since intelligent systems are going to be a part and parcel of the daily process, automatic learning and adaptation is a requirement but not an option.

16. CONCLUSION

The shift in Digital Twins to cognitive enterprises is a significant transformation in how businesses conduct operations and compete, as well as value creation in the business. Digital Twins are not restricted to machine monitoring applications anymore; they have developed to become enterprise-wide tools that can be used to monitor the whole strategy as well as to make day-to-day decisions. With the integration of Artificial Intelligence, real-time analytics and machine learning, organizations develop adaptive ecosystems that are able to learn by themselves. Such organizations do not just follow the movement of the market dynamics but predict and influence them.

The strong advantage offered by artificial intelligence in the process of decision-making is high responsiveness rates, quick recovery, and new ideas. The intelligent automation and predictive analytics allow companies to anticipate problems and prevent them instead of reacting to them, putting them in a proactive strategy mode. However, the transformation of the organizational substantive core requires the further than acquiring new technologies. Strong governance, responsibility in AI endeavors, strong cybersecurity, and employees willing to work with AI and not fight it are required. The power of human agency still prevails, and the interdependence between humans and AI is the real solution to excellence.

Cognitive enterprises go hand in hand with Industry 5.0, which focuses on the prioritizing of human capital, sustainability, and responsible digital evolution. The ability of organizations to precisely incorporate Digital Twins and AI in the main business processes can survive and, when done well, actually flourish in more and more intricate environments. Finally, the shift to the cognitive enterprise is not merely a technological upgrade but a new step in the evolution of organizations in the digital world. Companies developing smart, ethical, and cooperative AI regimes are building a sustainable basis of success and survival.

REFERENCES

Brynjolfsson, E., & McAfee, A. (2017). *Machine, platform, crowd: Harnessing our digital future*. W. W. Norton & Company.

Davenport, T. H. (2018). *The AI advantage: How to put the artificial intelligence revolution to work*. MIT Press. DOI: 10.7551/mitpress/11781.001.0001

Davenport, T. H., & Ronanki, R. (2018). Artificial intelligence for the real world. *Harvard Business Review*, *96*(1), 108–116.

Fuller, A., Fan, Z., Day, C., & Barlow, C. (2020). Digital twin: Enabling technologies, challenges and open research. *IEEE Access : Practical Innovations, Open Solutions*, *8*, 108952–108971. DOI: 10.1109/ACCESS.2020.2998358

Grieves, M. (2014). Digital twin: Manufacturing excellence through virtual factory replication.

Jöhnk, J., Weißert, M., & Wyrtki, K. (2021). Ready or not, AI comes: An interview study of organizational AI readiness factors. *Business & Information Systems Engineering*, *63*(1), 5–20. DOI: 10.1007/s12599-020-00676-7

Kritzinger, W., Karner, M., Traar, G., Henjes, J., & Sihn, W. (2018). Digital twin in manufacturing: A categorical literature review and classification. *IFAC-PapersOnLine*, *51*(11), 1016–1022. DOI: 10.1016/j.ifacol.2018.08.474

Nahavandi, S. (2019). Industry 5.0: A human-centric solution. *Sustainability (Basel)*, *11*(16), 4371. DOI: 10.3390/su11164371

Ransbotham, S., Kiron, D., Gerbert, P., & Reeves, M. (2017). Reshaping business with artificial intelligence. *MIT Sloan Management Review*, *59*(1), 1–17.

Russell, S., & Norvig, P. (2021). *Artificial intelligence: A modern approach* (4th ed.). Pearson.

Schwab, K. (2017). *The fourth industrial revolution*. World Economic Forum.

Tao, F., Zhang, H., Liu, A., & Nee, A. Y. C. (2019). Digital twin in industry: State-of-the-art. *IEEE Transactions on Industrial Informatics*, *15*(4), 2405–2415. DOI: 10.1109/TII.2018.2873186

Vial, G. (2019). Understanding digital transformation: A review and research agenda. *The Journal of Strategic Information Systems*, *28*(2), 118–144. DOI: 10.1016/j.jsis.2019.01.003

Chapter 12
Rule Design in Digital Twin Decision Systems:
A Game-Theoretic Perspective on Strategic Behaviour and Cognitive Enterprises

Rithika Voruganti
http://orcid.org/0009-0005-3044-3915
Christ (Deemed to be) University, India

Rajveer S. Rawlin
http://orcid.org/0000-0003-4359-3363
Christ (Deemed to be) University, India

Amisha Bawa
Christ (Deemed to be) University, India

Ritisha Gulati
Christ (Deemed to be) University, India

Tiitikksha Singh
Christ (Deemed to be) University, India

ABSTRACT

The chapter analyzes the role of rule design in the strategy and strategic behavior of game-theoretic models, equilibrium, and efficiency of decisions and then generalizes findings to digital twin-driven cognitive enterprises. Digital twins are becoming smart decision-support systems, which mimic real-world situations and demand powerful rule-based systems to direct strategic engagements between agents. Based

DOI: 10.4018/979-8-3373-9998-0.ch012

on combinatorial and economic game theory, this paper is going to examine how the differences in information structures, payoff mechanisms, action space and rules of enforcement influence strategic behavior. The article uses a systematic literature review. The results point to the fact that flexible rule systems are helpful in the process of strategic richness, but they also make computation more difficult. The chapter offers a theoretical model that connects the design of the rules, which can help enhance the decision-making processes in cognitive businesses.

1. INTRODUCTION

The use of the accelerated digital transformation, artificial intelligence, and cyber-physical systems has transformed the way organizations work and make decisions significantly. The appearance of digital twins, or the virtual models of real-world systems, processes, or organizations, is one of the most significant changes in this sphere. Such systems are also being applied in strategic decision-making and optimization as well as monitoring and simulation. With the development of digital twins into more intelligent and adaptive systems, they become the basis of what is called cognitive enterprises- organizations that are capable of learning, adaptable and responsive to changes in their environment. The decision in such systems is mainly influenced by predetermined rules that dictate the interaction between agents, information exchange, and the determination of results. Such interactions basing on rules can be analysed based on game theory as it offers a powerful theoretical perspective. Nonetheless, most traditional models presuppose rigid regulations, and the reality, particularly digital twins, has to rely on flexible and adaptable rule sets. Even minor modifications in regulations can change incentives, strategy and outcomes considerably. The proposed study will help in filling this gap by looking at the effects of changes in rules on the strategic behaviour and performance of various game types. The paper has demonstrated the significance of rule design in the creation of decision systems that are both intelligent and efficient by combining information on game theory with its application in the digital twin setting. In the context of digital twins, such rule-based environments become programmable and adaptive, enabling real-time experimentation with strategic interactions and decision policies.

1.1 Contribution of the Chapter

The chapter is an interrelated theoretical and methodological contribution at the crossroads of game theory, mechanism design, and decision systems based on digital twins. Its greatest contribution has been to redefine the form of rules, not as constraints (passive or otherwise), but as the design variables that form the basis of strategic behavior, equilibrium properties and system-level performances in both classical and digital spaces. To begin with, the chapter has added to the body of game theory literature, providing a synthesis of rule-dependence in several theoretical traditions, in a systematized fashion. Although previous literature has studied the structure of the rules in particular areas, like in combinatorial games, or in refining equilibria, or in mechanism design, these lessons have been scattered. This chapter incorporates these strands into a single analytical system, illustrating that action-space regulations, payoff structures, information protocols and enforcement mechanisms all play a role in the determination of strategic results.

The systematic arrangement of the literature into a coherent structure helps the chapter to move past the descriptive review and give a structured explanation of how various kinds of rules work by different causality processes. Second, the chapter advances the literature with a gap between classical games with insight into game-theoretic and digital twin environment, a field where research has not yet gone. Although the use of digital twins has mostly been based on technological architectures and optimization of operations, the explicit application of game-theoretic principles of operational strategic interaction has not been implemented so far. This chapter bridges that gap by demonstrating that programmable rule environments in digital twins can operationalize notions like equilibrium selection, incentive compatibility, and information design, which are theoretical constructs. By so doing, it will prove to convert abstract theoretical knowledge into practical principles to be applied in the design of decision-making systems in both cyber-physical and organizational settings. Third, the chapter creates a new conceptual framework that connects rule architectures to strategic results in digital twin architectures. In contrast to the current frameworks that present components separately, the proposed model clearly identifies the connection between the type of rules (action, payoff, information, and enforcement) and the dimensions of the outcomes (equilibrium stability, efficiency, fairness, and computational tractability). This framework offers a systematic approach to the analysis of the propagation of changes in the rule configurations through the multi-agent systems, which is why it has explanatory and predictive utility.

Fourth, the chapter is methodologically relevant, as the PRISMA-informed application of a structured narrative review has been applied to a highly theoretical field. The chapter shows that the formation of methodological transparency is possible even in non-empirical research contexts by integrating systematic search processes with conceptual synthesis. The method enhances reproducibility and credibility of theoretical integration, which is a typical limitation of interdisciplinary studies. Fifth, the chapter also provides a practical contribution by operationalizing the design of the rules of digital twins. The chapter opens a channel through which theory and practice can be connected by showing how one can simulate and assess the impact of modifications to rules, including information sharing, incentive systems, or co-ordination procedures, in digital twins.

This is specifically applicable to new organizations that are becoming cognitive in nature, where the decision-making systems need to be responsive, evidence-based, and strategically focused. Lastly, the chapter is beneficial in that it introduces a clear research agenda at the nexus of game theory and digital twin systems. It specifies the necessity of empirical validation, experimentation based on simulations, and creation of rule-learning mechanisms--adaptive. By presenting these directions, the chapter is not only putting itself in a position of being a synthesis of the existing knowledge, but also a starting point of future interdisciplinary study. Overall, the extensive contribution of the chapter is the development of the rule design as the analytical prism that establishes the theoretical game models with the actual digital decision-making environments. The chapter has incorporated various works and translated them into cohesive and functioning system, which has given the chapter conceptual clarity as well as practical relevance in advancing the study of strategic behaviour in programmable and adaptive systems.

2. LITERATURE REVIEW

2.1 Stream 1: Rule Structure as the Foundation of Strategic Behaviour

The literature on the combinatorial game theory offers the most telling understanding of what rules are since it shows that rules do not just constrain the strategic interaction but constitute it. John Horton Conway defines games as formal mathematical objects, the values of which, their outcomes, and their strategic dominance relations, are all products of rules. *Winning Ways for Your Mathematical Plays* by (Berlekamp, Conway, & Guy, 2001), this ontological viewpoint is applied systematically to demonstrate that changes in move sets, termination conditions and structural constraints refold optimal strategies in predictable yet non-trivial ways. The results of equivalence that were proved by Roland Sprague and Patrick Grundy also support this opinion, as they demonstrate that every neutral game can be reduced to a Nim heap that depends only on the structure of its rule and, therefore, that any small change in the set of available moves is such that it creates a completely different strategic system instead of a minor variation of an old one (Sprague, 1935; Grundy, 1939).

The basic assertion is reinforced by later research that explores the effects of varying aspects of rule design on strategic behaviour. (Gale, 1974) illustrates that minor alteration of the rules of the game played in Nim can cause discontinuous changes in equilibrium choice, meaning that the choice of strategies is so sensitive to the formulation of the rules. (Milnor, 1953) demonstrates that the rules of aggregation, such as how individual games are configured to form an aggregate, have emergent strategic effects that are not determined by the structure of components only, thus bringing in a systems-level point of view on the interaction of rules. (Fraenkel, 1996) goes further to explain trade-offs between expressiveness and tractability by illustrating that transitions between impartial and partisan rule structures dramatically enlarge the strategy space while simultaneously raising the complexity of analysis.

The further contributions made by those who think more recently clarify these observations by identifying processes by which propagation of rule changes happens in strategic systems. Yuki Suetsugu demonstrates that when dominance-order rules are introduced in Emperor Nim, it changes the applicability of the classical Sprague–Grundy theory, thus demonstrating that some changes to the rules alter fundamentally the analytical framework (Suetsugu, 2018, 2020). However, Robbert Fokkink and Jan Rust show that geometric constraints in Wythoff Nim leave the underlying structural properties intact but shift winning positions, implying that the location and nature of rule changes determine whether the change will be incremental or transformational (Fokkink & Rust, 2010).

Asymmetric rule structures are predicted to produce systematic biases in the outcome and introduce foreseeable strategic benefits, as shown by Masashi Abuku and others (Abuku, Hasegawa, & Yamada, 2024). Enforcement rules are found to play this role by showing that the reestablishment of fairness and a change of incentive structures are possible by relaxing compliance with rules.

An analogous point is demonstrated by Endre Boros, that rule forms dictate not only the strategic result but also the computational solvability (Boros, Gurvich, & Tserkovnyak, 2006), and an important synthesis of these insights is given by Aaron Siegel, who argues that even localized changes in the rules produce strategic backwash on the rest of the system (Siegel, 2013).

Notably, computational schools also enhance this analysis. It has been shown that computational hardness is directly proportional to the structure of rules, and therefore that strategic design has a direct relationship with algorithmic feasibility, by work by Erik Demaine and Robert Hearn (Demaine & Hearn, 2009), and complexity results by Theodore Schaefer, Larry Stockmeyer, and Christos Papadimitriou (Schaefer, 1978; Stockmeyer & Chandra, 1979; Papadimitriou, 1994). All these findings establish an overall view that structures of rules concomitantly define strategy space, equilibrium, and optimal strategy computability.

In the context of digital twin systems, this stream offers a crucial conceptual base: if the interaction between strategies is completely determined by rules, then programmable environments like digital twins can support the creation and manipulation of whole strategic systems through adjustments in rule structures. The shortcoming however of this stream is that it has limited itself to finite, well-defined, and often two-player games, and it is unclear how these lessons can be applied to complex, multi-agent, and dynamically changing environments.

2.2 Stream 2: Rule-Dependent Equilibrium and Strategic Stability

Although it has been established in the combinatorial game theory literature that game strategies are defined by rules, the broader game theory literature demonstrates that rules also establish the existence, selection, and stability of equilibria. Equilibrium results are determined by the joint specification of the action spaces and the payoff structures as John Nash has demonstrated (Nash, 1950), implying that any change in these factors will result in a different equilibrium set.

This observation is developed by Reinhard Selten who introduces the concept of subgame perfection, showing that credibility constraints (rules that define which strategies are feasible) directly influence equilibrium selection by eliminating non-credible strategies (Selten, 1975). The dynamic and informational aspects of rules are further developed in the work of David Kreps and Robert Wilson, who demonstrate that belief-update rules play a central role in shaping strategic behaviour in sequential environments (Kreps & Wilson, 1982).

Roger Myerson presents trembling-hand perfection, explaining that robustness requirements in rule systems refine equilibria and make predictions more reliable (Myerson, 1978). Elon Kohlberg and Jean-Francois Mertens further show that the stability of equilibrium is conditional on the structure of rules and that some rule structures remain stable under perturbations while others do not (Kohlberg & Mertens, 1986).

Eric van Damme synthesizes these insights and suggests that institutional and informational rules can determine which equilibria are practically achievable (van Damme, 1991). The role of information and uncertainty is further developed by John Harsanyi whose Bayesian approach demonstrates that the rules governing information distribution fundamentally redefine the logic of strategy (Harsanyi, 1967). Ehud Kalai and Dov Samet reveal that the structure of beliefs determines equilibrium persistence (Kalai & Samet, 1984), whereas Partha Dasgupta and Eric Maskin show that payoff discontinuities can influence the existence of equilibria regardless of other rule characteristics (Dasgupta & Maskin, 1986).

Recent work has extended these insights into more practical and probabilistic settings. Zhe Jiang demonstrates that disclosure rules refine equilibria in evidence-based games (Jiang, 2021), Yutaka Kamijo illustrates that procedural rules influence focal equilibria in bargaining environments (Kamijo, 2011), and Jun Pei shows that payoff distribution rules affect equilibrium robustness in uncertain environments

(Pei & Takahashi, 2019). Additional evidence of interactions between bounded rationality and rule structures influencing observed outcomes has been confirmed through behavioural game theory (Camerer, 2003) and quantal response models (McKelvey & Palfrey, 1995).

In digital contexts, this stream implies that equilibrium properties in simulated environments are not inherent features but are immediate consequences of programmable rule configurations. Digital twins therefore provide an environment in which organizations can simulate outcomes and systematically study the impact of rule design on equilibrium stability and predictability. However, this stream remains largely analytical and does not fully address how rules can be deliberately engineered to generate desired outcomes.

2.3 Stream 3: Mechanism and Information Design as Rule Engineering

The analysis of rules is transformed into a problem of deliberate institutional construction through mechanism design. The work of Dirk Bergemann and Stephen Morris demonstrates that robust mechanisms can achieve desirable equilibrium properties under uncertainty, thereby showing that rule systems can be systematically optimized (Bergemann & Morris, 2005). Yuta Hishida and Takuro Kumano similarly show that carefully designed allocation rules can produce stable and incentive-compatible outcomes (Hishida & Kumano, 2021).

Information design extends this idea by treating information structures themselves as controllable variables. As Vincent Crawford and Joel Sobel demonstrate, communication protocols determine the efficiency of information transmission (Crawford & Sobel, 1982), while Emir Kamenica and Matthew Gentzkow show that strategic information disclosure can systematically influence behaviour (Kamenica & Gentzkow, 2011). Trade-offs between coordination and manipulation are highlighted by Luis Rayo and Ilya Segal, while information aggregation rules analysed by George-Marios Angeletos and Alessandro Pavan demonstrate how coordination and efficiency depend on information structures (Angeletos & Pavan, 2007).

The importance of rule engineering is also evident in collective decision-making applications. Pedro Amorós shows that voting rules determine the existence of feasible equilibria (Amorós, 2024), while Sanford Grossman and Oliver Hart demonstrate that disclosure rules affect incentives in financial markets (Grossman & Hart, 1980).

Algorithmic game theory further connects rule design with systemic inefficiencies. As introduced by Noam Nisan and Tim Roughgarden, the concept of the price of anarchy highlights how poorly designed rules can produce inefficient outcomes (Roughgarden, 2005; Nisan et al., 2007). This stream therefore establishes that rules can be deliberately engineered to achieve efficiency, fairness, and robustness.

This perspective is particularly relevant for digital twins, where rule design can be implemented as an iterative optimization process within simulation environments. However, traditional mechanism design often assumes relatively stable institutional environments, limiting its applicability to dynamic and data-driven systems.

The implications of rule design for computational aspects also reinforce its centrality in strategic systems. The work of Papadimitriou (1994), Schaefer (1978), and Stockmeyer and Chandra (1979) shows that the rule structure of a game directly influences computational tractability, and even small changes may cause exponential increases in complexity. Similarly, Daskalakis, Goldberg, and Papadimitriou (2009) and Goldberg and Papadimitriou (2006) demonstrate that computing Nash equilibria can become computationally intractable depending on rule configurations.

Conitzer and Sandholm (2006) further show that mechanism design itself can be computationally complex, revealing a trade-off between strategic richness and practical feasibility. Algorithmic game theory (Nisan et al., 2007; Roughgarden, 2005) complements these insights by integrating incentives with computational considerations in large-scale systems.

At the same time, multi-agent systems research (Russell & Norvig, 2021; Wooldridge, 2009; Shoham & Leyton-Brown, 2009) provides the operational foundations for implementing rule-based strategic interactions among autonomous agents. Together, these strands demonstrate that rule design is not only an economic and strategic issue but also a computational and architectural one, directly relevant to the construction of scalable digital twin environments.

2.4 Stream 4: Digital Twins as Dynamic Rule Design Platforms

Digital twin research introduces a new paradigm of programmable, adaptive, and simulation-driven rule environments. Digital twins, as envisioned by Michael Grieves, represent continuously updated virtual replicas of physical systems that enable monitoring, prediction, and optimization (Grieves, 2014). Later contributions by Fei Tao and colleagues demonstrate how digital twins integrate real-time data, simulation, and analytics to support decision-making in complex systems (Tao et al., 2018; Tao et al., 2019).

Unlike traditional game-theoretic environments, digital twins allow dynamic adjustments to action spaces, payoff structures, information flows, and enforcement mechanisms. The computational foundations for modelling such interactions are provided by multi-agent system research (Wooldridge, 2009; Shoham & Leyton-Brown, 2009) and artificial intelligence frameworks (Russell & Norvig, 2021).

More importantly, digital twins transform rule design into an experimental process. Alternative rule configurations can be simulated, their performance evaluated, and rules iteratively refined based on performance metrics. This enables organizations to test alternative strategic environments before implementing them in real-world systems.

This capability creates a direct bridge between theoretical game models and real-world decision systems. Nevertheless, despite this potential, the digital twin literature remains largely disconnected from game-theoretic rule design. Existing research focuses primarily on technical implementation and operational capabilities rather than on the strategic structure of rules governing agent interaction (Negri et al., 2017; Kritzinger et al., 2018; Fuller et al., 2020).

As a result, there remains a significant gap between theoretical rule design frameworks and their practical application in digital twin environments.

Synthesis and Research Gap

There is overall coherent cumulative argument in the four streams. Combinatorial game theory already proves that strategic systems are defined by rules; equilibrium theory shows that rules define stability and result; mechanism design provides a way to design rules to obtain desired results; and programmable environments that come with digital twins can operationalize the rule design in real time. Despite this development, these insights are still being divided along the disciplinary lines and therefore there is an absence of oneness between theoretical knowledge and practical applications.

The following are the research gaps identified:

- Absence of a coherent model of how to connect rule design and the strategic outcomes of various kinds of games.
- The connection between combinatorial game theory and equilibrium-based methods has been limited in existing literature.
- Lack of emphasis on dynamic and adaptive rule regimes in changing environments.
- The lack of exploration of behavioural aspects that include limited rationality and learning.
- Very little use of game-theoretical design of rules in digital twins and cognitive enterprises.
- Lack of focus on practical application and empirical testing of theoretical models.
- Increment of complexity of rule systems and lack of care to computational feasibility.

3. METHODOLOGY

3.1 Research Design

The chapter uses a narrative review organized systematically to review the evidence of the impact of rule design on strategic behaviour in a variety of game-theoretic traditions and apply these results to digital twin decision architecture. In contrast to a pure narrative review, a structured narrative review uses explicit inclusion and exclusion criteria, records the search and selection process, and does its analysis based on an a priori thematic framework (Grant and Booth, 2009). Compared to a full systematic review or meta-analysis, it does not involve quantitative aggregate and is suitable where there is a focus of conceptual integration across heterogeneous theoretical areas. The research is conceptual and theoretical in nature. The main goal of it is to find causal relationships between rule forms and strategic performance, generalize discoveries in different lines of game theory, and establish a single framework of analysis that can be applied to digital twin systems, in which rule sets can be deployed and experimented with.

3.2 Search Strategy and Data Sources

In January 2026, the literature search was undertaken through three large academic databases, including Scopus, Web of Science, and Google Scholar. The choice of these databases was due to the requirement to cover interdisciplinary research in the fields of economics, computer science, and engineering. The Boolean search strings were the following: (game theory) or (combinatorial game) and (rule design) or (rule change) or (rule structure) and (strategic behavior) or (equilibrium) or (mechanism design) "digital twin" or "cyber-physical system" and (decision making or strategic interaction or agent-based). (information design) OR (mechanism design), and (equilibrium) OR (strategic outcome) OR (rule). Peer-reviewed journal articles, books, and conference proceedings that were written in English were restricted to the search. There was no time limit to include contributions in the field (e.g., Sprague, 1935; Nash, 1950; Conway, 1976), which are used to form the theoretical background of the study. The first search had 70 unique records after deduction was done by machine. 3.3 Study Selection: PRISMA-Informed Process. To promote transparency and reproducibility, study selection took place through the four stages informed by PRISMA.

Identification (n = 70): The search query in the database provided 50 Scopus, 5 Web of Science, and 15 Google Scholar. Following deduplication 70 distinct records were left. Screening and Eligibility (n = 70): Abstracts and titles were filtered on inclusion criteria. Records that were excluded because of are forty-five records. (b) non-formal empirical focus (n = 5), (c) issues not directly related to strategic interaction (n = 5). Inclusion (n = 50): They were ten studies that were eliminated in the thematic coding as their contributions were duplicated or could not be uniformly mapped with the analysis framework. The last synthesis comprises 50 studies. Such a sequence of filtering provides internal consistency and prevents overlapping exclusion criteria.

3.3 Inclusion and Exclusion Criteria

The studies were eligible when they fulfilled the following criteria:

(1) English-written peer-reviewed publication.
(2) that it contains an expressive game-theoretic or formal analytical model.
(3) direct investigation of rule structures (action, payoff, information, or enforcement);
(4) adequate conceptual clarity so that the concept can be conceptually replicated. Articles about digital twins were considered to have met the criteria provided they defined the structure of agent interaction, the decision rule, or coordination mechanism at the system level.

The studies were not included in case they:

1) lacked formal modelling. There was no rule-based strategic interaction that took place between (2). (3) did not belong to the categories of defined rules. The minimum requirements of theoretical rigor were not satisfied in (4).

3.4 Thematic Coding

The chosen studies were coded in two dimensions in terms of analysis. The former dimension was the type of rule structure under analysis: action-space rules, payoff rules, information-disclosure rules and enforcement rules. The second dimension was used to categorize the outcomes of strategic impacts, which were equilibrium existence, equilibrium stability, strategic complexity, efficiency and fairness and the computational tractability. The author used a structured protocol to code. The coding scheme was developed to achieve the reliability of cross-checking of studies across categories and ambiguous cases were reconsidered to achieve internal consistency.

3.5 Development of Framework and Approach to Analysis

A constant-comparative approach was used to synthesize the coded studies. The results of the findings in various classes of games such as combinatorial, strategic-form and extensive-form and mechanism design were compared to determine recurring patterns and boundary conditions. It is based on this synthesis that the conceptual framework in Section 5 was built that connects rule structures to strategic outcomes. The framework is then applied to the digital twin systems where the rule configurations can be simulated and optimized dynamically and in multi-agent systems.

3.6 Limitations

Three main limitations are present in this study. One, it is a theoretical foundation of literature and lacks empirical verification in actual digital twins. Second, the literature of game-theory is exhaustively presented but the literature of digital twins is selectively provided to define the relevance of application. Third, the typology of rule structures is one way to analyze them; other typologies can produce supplementary information.

4. PRISMA (PREFERRED REPORTING ITEMS TO SYSTEMATIC REVIEWS AND META-ANALYSES) ANALYSIS

The PRISMA Analysis of the performed Systematic literature review consists of Identification, Screening, Eligibility, and Inclusion stages, as demonstrated in the following diagram: Explanation The PRISMA flow diagram reflects the systematic process that was used in identifying, screening, assessing the eligibility of the studies and the ultimate inclusion of the studies to the qualitative synthesis. The systematic methodology provides clarity, logical consistency and repeatability of the study selection procedure, thus reducing selection bias.

The search of databases with preset search strings in the identification stage resulted in retrieving a total of 70 records. These documents were the first source of the possible related studies. Database filtering tools and manual cross-verification were used to detect any duplicates, and no such duplicates were detected. As such, the entire 70 records were brought to the screening phase.

All the 70 records were screened on the basis of titles and abstracts to determine their fit with the research objectives during the screening stage. At this point, 10 articles were filtered out because they were not relevant to the rule-based strategic interaction, had an inadequate study design (e.g., was strictly empirical, not modelled theoretically), or were not conceptually compatible with the study subject. This left 60 records at the stage of eligibility. The rest of the 60 articles were retrieved and thoroughly examined in the eligibility stage. Each study was evaluated based on predetermined criteria, such as the existence of an explicit game-theoretic or analytical model, explicit interactions with rule structures (action, payoff, information, or enforcement), and being theoretically rigorous enough. At this point, ten articles were filtered out because of the methodological constraints, the absence of the formal modelling or the inability to directly answer the research questions.

After this procedure, an ultimate group of 50 studies was included and integrated in the qualitative synthesis because they fulfilled all the inclusion criteria. Such studies are the basis of analysis of thematic coding and conceptual framework development that is going to take place in the following passages. Altogether, PRISMA-based selection procedure offers an intuitive and logically coherent way to go through the initial search to the eventual inclusion and make the process of the review systematic and reproducible. Thematic Findings The fourth rule is known as Structures of rules and Strategic Behaviour.

The synthesis shows that rule structures affect strategic behaviour by specific and distinguishable mechanisms and not by an overall series of changes in the incentives. In combinatorial games, strategic-form games, and mechanism design environments, rule change is a phenomenon that causes the feasibility of a strategy set, as well as dominance relations and best-response mappings, to change, redefining equilibrium paths. In combinatorial games, game tree is redefined directly by changes of rules.

To give an example, the Sprague-Grundy values change with alterations in move sets (as presented in variants with Nim rules), thus changing the winning strategies completely. Conversely, in strategic-form games, the increase in the action space leads to new best responses, which can cause old best responses to become dominated, or multiple equilibria to be generated. In mechanism design, the adjustments of the rules, including incentive-compatible changes in the payoffs, can redesign the strategy choice, by harmonizing the individual incentives towards the overarching system-wide goals.

One lesson that has been learned during this comparison is that strategic behaviour is rule endogenous but the mechanism varies according to the type of game: structural in combinatorial games, payoff-based in strategic-form games and incentive-based in mechanism design. In digital twin settings, this means that a change of the operational rules, which can include resource allocation priorities or agent permissions, can be used to systematically reform agent behaviour through simulation to enable the designers to predict and optimize strategic responses before acting.

4.1 Rule Changes and Equilibrium

The review shows that the equilibrium properties, existence, uniqueness, and stability are extremely sensitive to configurations of rules, yet such sensitivity varies across domains of theory. In classical strategic games, the existence of equilibria is based on the continuity of payoffs as well as on compact strategy spaces as demonstrated in the original equilibrium theory. Adjustments of payoff rules may either create or destroy equilibria without changing actions available in the case. In dynamic games, changes in the rules with respect to credibility or sequential rationality optimize the choice of equilibrium, typically wiping out non-credible ones. The equilibrium outcomes in mechanism design are designed: the rules are designed in a manner that desired results be the equilibrium strategies. This is however contrary to combinatorial games where although equilibrium is implicit in optimal play it cannot be externally designed. A comparative lesson is that equilibrium is not a property inherent to the game, it is a property of rule configuration and various rule elements (payoff vs information vs enforcement) are felt at various dimensions of equilibrium. Under digital twin systems, this means that the balanced behaviour, which is constant production schedules or synchronized resource utilisation, may be proactively influenced by adjusting rule parameters and simulating the performance in the regulated environment.

4.2 Information Structures and Uncertainty of Strategy

Information rules become an important factor of strategic complexity and predictability. The results indicate that the information structures play a role in determining not only the results but also the kind of reasoning agents, in this case. In perfect-information games, tactics are matched at predictable equilibria by common knowledge.

Conversely, the incomplete-information settings provide with the formation of belief, signalling, and screening strategy. Information design literature also demonstrates that equilibrium can change without altering payoffs or behaviour by having controlled disclosure. Combinatorial games are played via perfect information and deterministic outcomes compared to strategic and mechanism design games which have uncertainty in terms of information asymmetry.

This opposition guides toward the idea that information rules add another strategic dimension that does not exist in structural games only. Information structures in digital twin applications are dynamic in nature instead of being static because real time data streams continuously. Changes in access to information, such as making system states visible, or adding delays in signals, can change coordination, predictability and efficiency of a system dramatically. The fourth rule is called Complexity and Tractability of the Rule. One similarity that can be observed throughout the literature is the trade-off between richness and computational viability of rules.

The more the rule systems are expressive the more difficult is the solving of the corresponding game. Combinatorial games have the property that simple modifications in rules can move the problems in the games to either tractable or computationally hard classes. The equilibrium calculation in the algorithmic game theory is not always practical especially in large or complex systems and hence the use of approximation or heuristic techniques. Likewise, in mechanism design, the more complex the rules are, the more the efficiency of the outcome will be achieved, but the higher the complexity of implementation. This analogy demonstrates that strategic considerations are not the only limiting factor to rule design, but also computational limits.

This trade-off is put into practice in digital twin systems: very detailed rule simulations can give good predictions but can be too costly to compute in real-time decision-making scenarios. So, rule design must be realistically and at the same time compute efficiently.

4.3 Fairness, Cooperation, and Incentives Alignment

The results show that fairness and cooperation are not an emergent phenomenon but are the result of design of rules. In cooperative environments and bargaining environments, incentive-congruent rules enhance stability and mutual gainful results, and badly designed rules create inefficiency or war.

Models of mechanism design explicitly introduce the considerations of fairness via incentive compatibility and participation constraints, whereas behavioural game theory demonstrates that perceived fairness influences the actual strategic behaviour. Conversely, fairness is not often considered in combinatorial games and instead the emphasis is placed on optimal play, which is a contrast to theoretical simplicity and practical application in the real world. In digital twins, multi-agent coordination is an important issue of fairness, particularly in an organizational or platform context. The cooperation and stability of the system in the long run depend directly on the rule settings that control the allocation of resources, the access to priorities, or reward distribution.

4.4 System Level Effects and Emergent Dynamics

The concluding synthesis shows that designing of rules is system wide in its implications than what individual interactions show. Local rule changes have the potential to have system-level non-linear and emergent effects in multi-agent systems. In combinatorial games, and strategic games, interactions are usually studied as a system in isolation, whereas in complex systems, there are feedback loops, and cascading effects because of interconnected decision processes. Part of this is dealt with by mechanism design, which assumes optimization across the system, although usually under the assumptions of a static environment. Digital twin systems build upon this analysis by being able to simulate these dynamics in real-time. Not only can rule changes be tested in the local effects of the strategies, but also in their system-wide effects, such as the existence of bottlenecks or failures in coordination, or efficiency. This contributes to an important integrative fact: the design of rules must be assessed in the micro (agent) and macro (system) level, especially in the digital twin setting where feedback and adaptation are both dynamic.

5. CONCEPTUAL FRAMEWORK

5.1 Framework Overview

The theoretical framework created during the current research makes rule design the main analytical motor of the strategic interaction and the results of the system level. In contrast to the descriptive approach where rules are viewed as background conditions, in this framework a definite causal framework is established where rule configurations are the causal factor that influences strategic behaviour which subsequently decides observable outcomes. It is thus structured in a directional relation; rule structures dictate how agents will act, and the collective action of such responses in creating equilibrium features, efficiency levels, and system performance. By allowing the framework to be used as a conceptual summary but also as an analytical model that can be applied in both traditional game-theoretic scenarios and digital twins.

5.2 Structures of Rules as Analytical Drivers

Rule structures are at the basis of the framework and stipulate the space where agents will interact. These rules are broken down to four analytically distinct elements: action-space rules, payoff rules, information rules, and enforcement rules. All the components have a particular causal pathway. Action-space rules define the collection of viable strategies open to the agents, and thus directly limit or widen the range of the strategies. Payoff rules determine the form of rewarding and punishments on the outcomes and thus determine the desirability of various strategies. Rules of information regulate the knowledge possessed by agents, when they possess it and the way that they make prediction about other agents to bring uncertainty or lessen uncertainty in strategic interaction. The rules of enforcement establish the degree of credibility of the commitments and the effects of breaking the rules and, as such, have an impact on the sustainability of some strategies over the long run. These parts divide the structures of rules so that the framework does not describe rules as an abstract idea but as a collection of different and manipulable design variables. The decomposition is essential to analysis and application, since it enables researchers and practitioners to isolate what rule changes lead to particular strategic effects.

5.3 Strategic Behaviour as an Intermediating Process

The strategic behaviour has occupied the main mediating position within the framework that converts rule settings into visible results. The connection between rules and outcomes is not direct but rather changes in the rules reconfigure the rationales by which the agents make decisions. This is done in three major ways. To begin with, the action-space rules vary the set of possible strategies, allowing or disabling some courses of action. Second, the alterations of payoff and information regulations restructure best-response processes by altering incentives and expectations, thus affecting the way agents react to each other. Third, it has rules of enforcement that influence the plausibility of strategies and commitment, which actions are in equilibrium. This stratified insight brings out the fact that strategic behaviour is rule-endogenous in nature. The rules do not cause the agents to act independently of rules; by the structure of the environment, in which they act, they are constantly molded. This means that the changes that occur in the strategy behaviour due to minor changes in rules can cause major changes especially in the complex or multi-agent systems.

5.4 Dimensions and Analytical Mapping of Outcomes

The results of the strategic interaction are determined based on four major dimensions, namely equilibrium properties, efficiency, fairness and computational tractability. All these outcome dimensions are associated with certain elements of rule structure. In the example, payoff rules are dominant in setting efficiency and fairness in positioning or mispositioning incentives among agents. The predictability and coordination are affected by the information rules which determine the extent to which the system is uncertain. Action-space rules influence the variety and attainability of equilibria by increasing or restricting strategic alternatives. Enforcement rules, on the other hand, make the stability to be measurable by making equilibrium strategies credible and sustainable.

Such mapping identifies an analytical linkage between the rule design and system outcomes. It shows that various kinds of rules affect various performance areas, and thus, to achieve effective rule design, one would need to have a combined knowledge of the way these parts relate instead of focusing on them separately. 5.5 System-level Feedback and Dynamic Effects. The addition of system-level feedback effects is also an important extension of the framework. The results of strategic interaction in multi-agent environments may affect future behavior, as well as result in modifications in rules settings. This forms a self-organizing feedback loop where behaviour is influenced by the design of rules, results give rise to an enhancement of the rule design process, and rule changes are also influenced by behaviour. The emergent patterns produced by such feedback mechanisms can be coordination, inefficiencies or instability depending on the structure of the rules. The dynamic view is especially applicable when the interactions of a complex system are non-linear and interdependent. It emphasizes the rule design is not an event but a continuous process that needs to consider the adaptation and evolution as time goes by.

5.5 Digital Twin Environment Operationalization

The framework is fully functional in digital twin settings, where the structures of rules can be programmed, simulated, and refined. These systems have a configurable parameter, which is represented by every component of the framework. The action-space-rules are embodied in the form of system constraints or options in the decision space, the payoff-rules are embodied by the performance measures and reward systems, the information-rules are embodied by the data access and visibility schemes, and the enforcement-rules are embodied by the system control and compliance schemes.

As an example, machines in a digital twin of a manufacturing system could be represented as agentic in making scheduling decisions. The system can be used to simulate the performance of different agents by changing the parameters of the various rules, such as priority assignment, information-sharing schemes, or performance rewards. The resultant outcomes- production efficiency, bottlenecks, or the level of coordinations can then be assessed and thereafter changes in the actual system can be implemented. This shows how the framework offers a useful tool of analysis and optimization in decision-making in real-life settings.

5.6 The Framework Contribution

. The theoretical framework has its contribution to the literature because it passes a wide range of theoretical knowledge into a structured and operational model. It goes beyond descriptive synthesis because it explicitly outlines causal relationships between rule structures, strategic behavior, and outcomes as well as provides a generalizable tool of analysis. It combines the knowledge of combinatorial game theory, equilibrium analysis and mechanism design, and applies them to programmable and adaptive programmable settings, like digital twins. By so doing, the framework helps in closing the gap between abstract theory and practice so that both researchers and practitioners can engage in a systematic and systematic analysis of decision environments, create more effective rules, and enhance performance in systems.

6. DIGITAL TWINS AND COGNITIVE ENTERPRISE APPLICABILITY

6.1 The Conceptual Potential to Operational Modeling

The introduction of game-theoretic rule design to digital twins is a milestone in the organizational decision-making process by converting the abstract strategic concepts into functional processes. Digital twins being real-time virtual models of physical systems and organizational processes offer an environment where agent interactions can be modeled, simulated, and optimized explicitly. In this context, rules are not fixed constraints but dynamic design variables which organize decision-making by defining action spaces, payoff functions, access to information and enforcement. By instantiating these features into digital twin systems, organizations can be able to rationally explore the effects of alternative rule settings on strategic behavior and system level performance, thus transforming the theoretical implications of game theory into decision support systems.

6.2 System Specification: Agents, Strategies and Rules

As an example of operationalizing the framework, a smart manufacturing digital twin can be considered, whereby a set of machines act as autonomous agents who vie over common resources in the form of processing time, energy, and raw materials. Every agent must have a strategic decision between high-speed production that maximizes the output in the short run and energy-efficient production that minimizes costs and consumption of resources. These agents can be described as a non-cooperative game whereby the result is contingent on the joint strategy profile. The rule framework used to govern this system is made up of four elements. Action-space rules constitute the options of all machines, payoff rules constitute the performance rewarding or punishment, information rules determine the visibility of system states and other actions of other agents, and enforcement rules define compliance mechanisms. Collectively, these regulations dictate the strategic context in which agents act, either individually or as a group.

6.3 Baseline Set-Up and Inefficient Equilibrium

The system in the baseline arrangement is poorly coordinated. Machines have a limited action space (high-speed or energy-efficient production), however, payoff structures are aimed at maximizing individual output only. There is lack of information, in the sense that agents are not aware of the decisions or use of resources made by other agents and there is no form of control-to-control behaviours. In this case, the dominant strategy of every agent is to adopt the high-speed production which will provide short-term personal gains independent of the behaviour of others. The ensuing equilibrium represents a classic coordination failure, in which every agent rallies around the high-speed production, which causes the resource congestion, energy consumption, and overall lack of efficiency. This finding indicates that individually rational actions may produce suboptimal outcomes in a collection, should there not be properly crafted rules governing such actions. Notably, such inefficiency is not an internal process of the system but the direct result of the current rule set-up.

6.4 Modification of Payoff Rule and Incentive Realignment

The initial intervention is the adjustment of rules of payoff that will lead to the establishment of incentive alignment. The payoff structure is restructured, by introducing dynamic pricing mechanisms or punishments against excessive energy use; an approach that would manifest system-wide goals, not necessarily on pure self-interest. The change in best-response functions of the agents is caused by this change since high-speed production would no longer be so tempting when related to high costs. Consequently, the balance between mass-scale-high speed production and a more balanced strategy profile, with the agents choosing to display energy-efficient behaviours selectively, is disrupted. This illustrates the way specific adjustments in the rules of payoffs can alter the incentive framework resulting in a better coordination and the performance of the system in general. This transition can be simulated and assessed in the digital twin to make sure that the new equilibrium is effective and stable.

6.5 Information Rule Modification and Coordination Enhancement

The second intervention is about information regulations where there is more transparency in the system. The real-time information about queues, resources usage, and the activity of other machines is offered to the agents. The change will modify the informational structure of the game so that the agents are able to develop more accurate expectations and change their strategies based on these expectations. As the information improves, the system becomes no longer a environment of uncertainty, but that of partial observability, where coordination mechanisms will appear without forced effort on their part. Agents are also able to predict congestion and change their production strategies, which leads to more predictable and efficient performance.

This depicts that information design is very crucial in the formation of strategic interaction and can even supplement complete incentive mechanisms or replace them. 6.6 Design of the Rule of Enforcement and Equilibrium Stability. In the third intervention, enforcement rules will be implemented to provide compliance and stabilize the results. Priorities to compliant agents or fines on a rule breaker are some of the mechanisms that establish plausible incentives to comply with the goal of a system. Game theoretically, this implies the introduction of credibility constraints that destroy unstable or non-cooperative equilibria. Cooperative behaviour is supported by the existence of mechanisms of enforcement so that the agents are not tempted to engage in unilateral deviations. Not only is the ensuing equilibrium efficient but it is also stable since it is underpinned by plausible commitments instilled in the rule structure. This brings the relevance of enforcement as a separate and required element of rule design.

6.6 Digital Twin as a Recurrent Rule Optimization Platform

One of the benefits of digital twin systems is their capability to act as a platform of iterative experimentation to design rules. Every rule setup is stimulable and its effects on both the strategy behaviour and the performance of the systems can be evaluated systematically. Measures that include the efficiency of the equilibrium, throughput, resource utilization, and stability can be contrasted among the situations and data-driven decision-making becomes possible.

This is done in a systematic cycle where the rules are designed, simulated, performance criteria are used to evaluate the rules, and the process of refinement is done. The digital twin can therefore be seen as a risk-free platform in testing other possible strategic setups enabling organizations to determine the best rule systems before its application in the real world.

6.7 Expansion to Cognitive Enterprises and Adaptive Systems

The rule design has more expansive functions in cognitive enterprise settings that are supported by artificial intelligence and machine learning. Roles are not fixed but dynamic and change according to the real-time statistics and feedback. Payoff structures can be tuned automatically to changing goals, data analytics can be used to optimize information flow and enforcement mechanisms may be tuned by predictive models. This forms a closed-loop loop where the strategic behaviour, outcomes and rule configurations interact. The framework therefore does not only help in the situation of the perfect fit but also the adaptive learning making organizations fit well to respond to uncertainty and to the changing environment. Game-theoretic rule design in this kind of systems is a constant process of coordinating the agent action with the organizational objective.

6.8 Major Implications on the Decision System Design

The implementation of the game-theoretic rule design into digital twins shows that the strategic results can be rationally designed by configuring rules. The framework stipulates the clear definition of agents, strategies, and the rule elements, as well as their connection to the equilibrium results, which allows offering an efficient, stable, and adaptive decision system design. Digital twins implement this methodology by making rule structure simulation, comparison, and optimization a possibility, thus closing the gap between theoretical modeling and practice.

7. FUTURE RESEARCH DIRECTIONS

Future studies need to seek to establish research in integrated and comprehensive frameworks that can help to systematically relate rule design and strategic behaviour and performance of results under a broad variety of game-theoretic environments. Specifically, both the necessity to investigate more dynamic and adaptive rule systems, capable of developing in response to changing environments, is increasing, particularly in the realms of digital twins and cognitive enterprises, where real-time data redefines decision spaces. The other important direction is incorporating the behavioural dimensions in existing models since such aspects as bounded rationality, learning, trust, and agent heterogeneity play an important role in the process of real world decision making, but are not represented in the theoretical models.

Further research should be also aimed at improvement of computation and algorithm techniques to deal with the growing complexity of flexible rule systems. The use of efficient methods of solutions, such as approximation algorithms, strategy optimization method based on machine learning, and methods that are driven by simulation, is required as the strategic environment grows more complex. The role of empirical validation will help also to reinforce the applicability of theoretical insights. Experimental studies, simulations, and real-world case studies should be done to determine the effectiveness of rule changes in a real world context, market, supply chain or digital world.

Moreover, the application of game theory can be combined with artificial intelligence, data analytics and systems engineering, which can contribute to the development of smart decision systems significantly. The research of how automated agents interact with human decision-makers in a rule-based environment can also be insightful to the field of hybrid decision systems. Lastly, the research on the design of the rules and how they can be used to enhance equity, transparency, and ethical decision-making can also be expanded, especially in digital ecosystems of scale. The research directions will help to develop strong, dynamic and effective strategic systems that have the potential to respond to complexities of today organizational and technology landscapes.

The flowchart offered represents a systematic and repeatable procedure in which the rule design may be applied to make the most of decision-making in the digital twin setting. It embodies the shift in defining the system towards continuous improvement which focuses on the dynamism of the rule-based strategic systems. This starts with the definition of system environment where the important aspects of decision context are established. This involves identifying the concerned agents (e.g. individuals, departments, or automated systems), establishing their goals, as well as knowing their limitations under which they can work. This action provides the background of strategic interplay.

8. CONCLUSION

This paper analyses the importance of the design of rules in determining strategic behavior and outcomes in game-theoretic models and applies these to contexts of digital twins-driven decision-making. The discussion indicates that the underlying changes in the properties of equilibrium and strategic action, fairness and the level of complexity are all tightly linked to changes in the structure of rules, such as information protocols, payoff mechanisms, action spaces and enforcement schemes.

As opposed to being peripheral constraints, the rules seem to serve as constitutive factors that organize strategic interaction. One of the major contributions of this chapter is that a conceptual framework is created which connects the rule design, strategic behavior, and outcome dimensions in a systematic way. The framework can be used to analyze and compare various rule configurations and does so in an ordered manner. Although it is mostly purely theoretical, it can provide a systematic reason of examining the manner in which the change of rules can impact decision-making in both digital and traditional game-theoretic contexts.

This view is further applied to digital twin systems and cognitive enterprises in the study and their possibility to be used as a platform to apply and test rule-based decisions architecture. It is mentioned in the discussion that digital twins could potentially allow organizations to experiment with alternative rule designs, get strategic reactions, and progressively enhance decision-making mechanisms.

But these implications are merely conceptual and illustrative, since no empirical validation or even large-scale simulation analysis is carried out in the current study. In that regard, even though the results are indicative of the possible advantages of introducing the game-theoretic design of rules and the digital twin technologies, e.g., enhanced coordination and better-informed decision-making, one should take those results with a grain of salt. Practical considerations such as system complexity, agent behavior and implementation constraints are likely to be context-related concerns that determine how well rules are designed. There are also a few future research directions that are brought out in this study. The proposed framework could be empirically validated with the help of real-world digital twins applications or simulated experiments that would help to better support its practical applicability. Also, more research may be done on adaptive rule systems, behavioral aspects of strategic interaction, and how artificial intelligence can be used in rule design. Finally, this chapter also adds to the existing literature on the interface between game theory and digital systems in that it suggests an organized way to think about rule design. Instead of making concrete assertions, it offers a theoretical backbone which can be used to develop more theory and scientific research towards the design of intelligent and adaptive decision-making systems.

8.1 Declaration of Generative AI and AI-Assisted Technologies in the Writing Process

During the preparation of this work, the author(s) used ChatGPT to assist in brainstorming and generating initial drafts for specific sections of the manuscript. Following this process, the author(s) manually reviewed, substantially revised, and edited the content to ensure accuracy and original scholarly contribution. The author(s) take full responsibility for the final content and the integrity of the research presented.

REFERENCES

Abuku, M., Hasegawa, T., & Yamada, K. (2024). A complete solution for the partisan chocolate game. *Integers: Electronic Journal of Combinatorial Number Theory.*

Abuku, M., Hasegawa, T., & Yamada, K. (2024). Enforce and selective operators of combinatorial games. *Theoretical Computer Science.*

Amorós, P. (2024). Nash implementation of supermajority rules. *Journal of Economic Theory.*

Angeletos, G. M., & Pavan, A. (2007). Efficient use of information and social value of information. *Econometrica, 75*(4), 1103–1142. DOI: 10.1111/j.1468-0262.2007.00783.x

Bergemann, D., & Morris, S. (2005). Robust mechanism design. *Econometrica, 73*(6), 1771–1813. DOI: 10.1111/j.1468-0262.2005.00638.x

Berlekamp, E. R., Conway, J. H., & Guy, R. K. (2001). *Winning ways for your mathematical plays* (2nd ed.). Academic Press.

Boros, E., Gurvich, V., & Tserkovnyak, Y. (2006). Impartial games with decreasing Sprague–Grundy function and their hypergraph compound. In *Games of No Chance 3* (pp. 105–120). Cambridge University Press.

Camerer, C. F. (2003). *Behavioral game theory: Experiments in strategic interaction.* Princeton University Press.

Conitzer, V., & Sandholm, T. (2006). Complexity of mechanism design. In *Proceedings of the 18th Conference on Uncertainty in Artificial Intelligence* (pp. 103–110).

Conway, J. H. (1976). *On numbers and games.* Academic Press.

Crawford, V. P., & Sobel, J. (1982). Strategic information transmission. *Econometrica, 50*(6), 1431–1451. DOI: 10.2307/1913390

Dasgupta, P., & Maskin, E. (1986). The existence of equilibrium in discontinuous economic games. *The Review of Economic Studies, 53*(1), 1–26. DOI: 10.2307/2297588

Daskalakis, C., Goldberg, P. W., & Papadimitriou, C. H. (2009). The complexity of computing a Nash equilibrium. *SIAM Journal on Computing, 39*(1), 195–259. DOI: 10.1137/070699652

Demaine, E. D., & Hearn, R. A. (2009). Playing games with algorithms: Algorithmic combinatorial game theory. In *Games of No Chance 3* (pp. 3–56). Cambridge University Press. DOI: 10.1017/CBO9780511807251.002

Fokkink, R., & Rust, J. (2010). Queen reflections: A modification of Wythoff Nim. *Integers: Electronic Journal of Combinatorial Number Theory*, *10*, A29.

Fraenkel, A. S. (1996). Scenic trails ascending from sea-level Nim to alpine chess. In *Games of No Chance* (pp. 13–42). Cambridge University Press.

Fuller, A., Fan, Z., Day, C., & Barlow, C. (2020). Digital twin: Enabling technologies, challenges and open research. *IEEE Access : Practical Innovations, Open Solutions*, *8*, 108952–108971. DOI: 10.1109/ACCESS.2020.2998358

Gale, D. (1974). A curious Nim-type game. *The American Mathematical Monthly*, *81*(8), 876–879. DOI: 10.1080/00029890.1974.11993683

Goldberg, P. W., & Papadimitriou, C. H. (2006). Reducibility among equilibrium problems. In *Proceedings of the 38th ACM Symposium on Theory of Computing* (pp. 61–70).

Grieves, M. (2014). Digital twin: Manufacturing excellence through virtual factory replication. *White Paper, Florida Institute of Technology.*

Grossman, S. J., & Hart, O. D. (1980). Disclosure laws and takeover bids. *The Journal of Finance*, *35*(2), 323–334. DOI: 10.1111/j.1540-6261.1980.tb02161.x

Grundy, P. M. (1939). Mathematics and games. *Eureka (Asunción)*, *2*(5), 6–8.

Harsanyi, J. C. (1967). Games with incomplete information played by "Bayesian" players. *Management Science*, *14*(3), 159–182. DOI: 10.1287/mnsc.14.3.159

Hishida, Y., & Kumano, T. (2021). Dominant strategy implementation of the doctor-optimal stable rule with bilateral contracts. *Journal of Economic Theory*, *194*, 105241.

Jiang, Z. (2021). Equilibrium refinement in finite action evidence games. *Games and Economic Behavior*, *128*, 163–183.

Kalai, E., & Samet, D. (1984). Persistent equilibria in strategic games. *International Journal of Game Theory*, *13*(3), 129–144. DOI: 10.1007/BF01769811

Kamenica, E., & Gentzkow, M. (2011). Bayesian persuasion. *The American Economic Review*, *101*(6), 2590–2615. DOI: 10.1257/aer.101.6.2590

Kamijo, Y. (2011). A note on the risk dominance of the Nash demand game. *Journal of Economic Theory*, *146*(2), 794–802.

Kohlberg, E., & Mertens, J. F. (1986). On the strategic stability of equilibria. *Econometrica*, *54*(5), 1003–1037. DOI: 10.2307/1912320

Kreps, D. M., & Wilson, R. (1982). Sequential equilibria. *Econometrica, 50*(4), 863–894. DOI: 10.2307/1912767

Kritzinger, W., Karner, M., Traar, G., Henjes, J., & Sihn, W. (2018). Digital twin in manufacturing: A categorical literature review and classification. *IFAC-PapersOnLine, 51*(11), 1016–1022. DOI: 10.1016/j.ifacol.2018.08.474

McKelvey, R. D., & Palfrey, T. R. (1995). Quantal response equilibria for normal form games. *Games and Economic Behavior, 10*(1), 6–38. DOI: 10.1006/game.1995.1023

Milnor, J. (1953). Sums of positional games. *Contributions to the Theory of Games, 2*, 291–301.

Myerson, R. B. (1978). Refinements of the Nash equilibrium concept. *International Journal of Game Theory, 7*(2), 73–80. DOI: 10.1007/BF01753236

Nash, J. F.Jr. (1950). Equilibrium points in n-person games. *Proceedings of the National Academy of Sciences of the United States of America, 36*(1), 48–49. DOI: 10.1073/pnas.36.1.48

Negri, E., Fumagalli, L., & Macchi, M. (2017). A review of the roles of digital twin in CPS-based production systems. *Procedia Manufacturing, 11*, 939–948. DOI: 10.1016/j.promfg.2017.07.198

Nisan, N., Roughgarden, T., Tardos, É., & Vazirani, V. V. (Eds.). (2007). *Algorithmic game theory*. Cambridge University Press. DOI: 10.1017/CBO9780511800481

Papadimitriou, C. H. (1994). On the complexity of the parity argument and other inefficient proofs of existence. *Journal of Computer and System Sciences, 48*(3), 498–532. DOI: 10.1016/S0022-0000(05)80063-7

Pei, J., & Takahashi, S. (2019). Nash equilibria in random games with right fat-tailed distributions. *Economic Theory, 68*, 813–845.

Roughgarden, T. (2005). *Selfish routing and the price of anarchy*. MIT Press.

Russell, S., & Norvig, P. (2021). *Artificial intelligence: A modern approach* (4th ed.). Pearson.

Schaefer, T. J. (1978). On the complexity of some two-person perfect-information games. *Journal of Computer and System Sciences, 16*(2), 185–225. DOI: 10.1016/0022-0000(78)90045-4

Selten, R. (1975). Reexamination of the perfectness concept for equilibrium points in extensive games. *International Journal of Game Theory, 4*(1), 25–55. DOI: 10.1007/BF01766400

Shoham, Y., & Leyton-Brown, K. (2009). *Multiagent systems: Algorithmic, game-theoretic, and logical foundations*. Cambridge University Press.

Siegel, A. N. (2013). *Combinatorial game theory*. American Mathematical Society. DOI: 10.1090/gsm/146

Sprague, R. P. (1935). Über mathematische Kampfspiele. *Tohoku Mathematical Journal, 41*, 438–444.

Stockmeyer, L. J., & Chandra, A. K. (1979). Provably difficult combinatorial games. *SIAM Journal on Computing, 8*(2), 151–174. DOI: 10.1137/0208013

Stone, P., & Veloso, M. (2000). Multiagent systems: A survey from a machine learning perspective. *Autonomous Robots, 8*(3), 345–383. DOI: 10.1023/A:1008942012299

Suetsugu, Y. (2018). Emperor Nim and emperor sum: A new sum of impartial games. *Discrete Mathematics, 341*(7), 1907–1916.

Suetsugu, Y. (2020). Universal partisan rulesets and a universal partisan dicotic ruleset. *Theoretical Computer Science, 806*, 260–273.

Tao, F., Qi, Q., Liu, A., & Kusiak, A. (2018). Data-driven smart manufacturing. *Journal of Manufacturing Systems, 48*, 157–169. DOI: 10.1016/j.jmsy.2018.01.006

Tao, F., Zhang, M., Liu, Y., & Nee, A. Y. C. (2019). *Digital twin driven smart manufacturing*. Academic Press.

van Damme, E. (1991). *Stability and perfection of Nash equilibria* (2nd ed.). Springer. DOI: 10.1007/978-3-642-58242-4

Wooldridge, M. (2009). *An introduction to multiagent systems* (2nd ed.). Wiley.

Chapter 13

Transforming Physical Assets Into Cognitive Enterprises With Digital Twins:

A Governance-Enabled Architecture for SME Cyber-Physical Transformation

Daniela Nikolaeva Ilieva
http://orcid.org/0000-0002-5987-5499
University of Insurance and Finance, Bulgaria

Angelika Kokkinaki
University of Nicosia, Cyprus

ABSTRACT

Building on design science research, we propose the Governance-Enabled Digital Twin (GEDT) architecture, a five-layer model that integrates an explicit governance and compliance layer with the conventional asset, data, modeling/simulation, and analytics/AI layers. The governance layer operationalizes "governance-by-design" through policy management, risk assessment, privacy and security controls, auditability, and mechanisms for human oversight. We demonstrate and assess GEDT using evidence from European R&I initiatives – iDriving (road safety), ACTING (federated cyber ranges), and MaaSAI (manufacturing-as-a-service) – showing how governance enables trustworthy experimentation, cross-organizational data sharing, and sustainable value creation. The chapter contributes a regulatory-aware reference

DOI: 10.4018/979-8-3373-9998-0.ch013

architecture for digital twin systems and derives implications for researchers, system designers, SME managers, and policy makers seeking to accelerate the digital-and-green ("twin") transition while maintaining legal compliance and societal trust.

1. INTRODUCTION

In the context of digital transformation, the concept of a digital twin has emerged as a vital component, integrating digital models of physical entities to analyze the current state, recreate the past, and predict future possibilities through simulation and advanced analytics. A digital twin goes beyond simple models because it involves mental and physical integration of entities at a defined frequency and precision, allowing for continuous learning and decision making in real time, and throughout the entire value chain of an asset (Digital Twin Consortium, 2023; International Organization for Standardization [ISO], 2021). The mental-physical integration of entities is made possible by the Omnipresence of smart devices, the Industrial Internet of Things (IIoT), and data-driven models and machine learning (Lu et al, 2020; Huang et al, 2021).

The possible strategies for Digital Twins align with the cognitive enterprise concept. This describes an enterprise capable of continuously monitoring its operational ecosystem, transforming data into actionable information, and continuously evolving its processes through human-AI interaction. The phrase "cognitive enterprise" appears in both managerial and technical discourse and can be described as a socio-technical system for closed-loop learning and optimization, where decisions are made based on virtual models of assets, processes, and the environment. Digital twins are the fundamental closed-loop framework that integrates real-time data with predictive analytics and decision support (Fuller et al. 2019).

While there is clear potential for utilization of digital twins, their assimilation into small and medium-sized enterprises (SMEs) is often discouraged by deficits in competencies (specifically, operational data, infrastructure, and funding) as well as the growing complexities of regulatory governance (privacy, safety, and cybersecurity). This is most profoundly the case in SMEs in Europe, where the adoption gap relative to larger businesses in cloud and AI technologies is most evident, notwithstanding European legislation aimed at digitalization (European Commission, 2025). The simultaneous "twin transition" (that is, combined digital and green transitions) increases the burden on digital twins for the purposes of evaluating and optimizing the sustainability of resources and the efficiency of the overall system (Aklilu et al., 2025; Breque et al., 2021).

An essential paradox presents itself: while Digital Twins are generally viewed as innovative and performative technologies, their most significant use cases are within high risk and high data sensitive environments (transport, construction, energy, health) where the potential for damaging errors exists. Legal studies show that Digital Twins are unexplored in the context of the current legal frameworks, leaving important questions around ownership, liability, and responsibility unaddressed (Stapleton & Stapleton, 2022; Bostwick, 2023). Research on health care and intelligent urbanism highlights the need for governance of Digital Twins, as the benefits are shown to be negated by the potential for infractions of privacy, inequitable outcomes, and the implementation of Digital Twins without appropriate control mechanisms (Ghosh & Banerji, 2023).

This chapter explores the context of digital twin systems, where governance should not be seen as an afterthought, but an integral part of the digital twin system. Governance has begun to be incorporated in European legislation that sets boundaries on the use of data in systems. Examples of such legislation include the General Data Protection Regulation (GDPR) (European Parliament & Council, 2016), the Data Governance Act (European Parliament & Council, 2022a), the Data Act (European Parliament & Council, 2023), Cybersecurity legislation like the NIS 2 Directive (European Parliament & Council, 2022b) as well as the Artificial Intelligence Act (European Parliament & Council, 2024). For SMEs, the necessity to comply is not only a legal requirement, but part of a social contract that allows for the establishment of trust, the acquisition of data partnerships, and participation in the rapidly evolving data ecosystems and digital ecosystems.

To address the gap between technical design and the requirements of governance, we propose a governance-relevant reference architecture we call the Governance-Enabled Digital Twin (GEDT). This chapter answers three research questions that guide the design and evaluation of GEDT. First, how can digital twins be designed in such a way that SMEs can progress from isolated automation to cognitive enterprises? Second, what governance, legal, and ethical considerations should be incorporated as design elements rather than as after-the-fact restrictions? Finally, what architectural framework can balance the integration of governance and accountability through AI analytics and simulation, while preserving the configurability and extensibility of the system?

To respond to these questions, we use a design science approach in which GEDT is conceived as an artefact that responds to the problem of the lack of an architectural framework to support the integration of governance in digital twin systems. The next step is to present and analyze the architecture through data from several large European R&I projects: iDriving (road safety), ACTING (federated cyber ranges for defense), and MaaSAI (manufacturing-as-a-service). This caters for two things: (i) a comprehensive reference architecture that makes governance operational, and (ii) a transversal study that illustrates the balanced operationalization of governance in relation to the preservation of value and innovation.

The parts of the chapter are structured as follows: Section 2 reviews basic and recent literature concerning digital twins, reference architectures, cognitive enterprise capabilities and the challenges of governance; Section 3 outlines the conceptual framework and the research methodology; Section 4 introduces the GEDT architecture and its 5 layers. Section 5 uses case evidence to illustrate GEDT; Section 6 discusses the theoretical and practical implications; Section 7 outlines the future research directions; and Section 8 is a conclusion.

2. BACKGROUND AND LITERATURE REVIEW

This section contextualizes our approach by reviewing key literature. We begin by tracing the evolution of digital models into advanced digital twins. We clarify definitional and developmental dimensions, then discuss reference models, the cognitive enterprises strand, and governance.

2.1 From Digital Models to Digital Twins: Definitions and Maturity

Digital twins build on the historical "mirror world" perspective. As computing technology improves, the virtual copies that can be created and manipulated become more precise (Gelernter, 1991). In the context of engineering and manufacturing, the digital twin became important due to work that viewed the digital twin to control undesirable emergent behavior in complex systems by maintaining an integrated connection between the real and the virtual (Grieves & Vickers, 2017). Modern definitions of digital twins agree on three aspects: (i) a digital representation of some entity or process, (ii) the ability to model and/or predict behavior, and (iii) a real-time data alignment with, and control of, the model or process at a specified frequency (Digital Twin Consortium, 2023; ISO, 2021).

Not every type of "digital replica'" is eligible to be called a digital twin, as the literature further emphasizes. Kritzinger et al. (2018) state that there is a digital model (no active automated data exchange), a digital shadow (one-way data transfer from physical to digital), and a digital twin (two-way data transfer and feedback). As systems progress from offline modeling to real-time operational integration, governance risk and value proposition significantly shift. The Inter-American Development Bank classifies component twins (single components), asset twins (single machines), system twins (sets of interconnected components), and process twins (whole operational processes), which indicates the demand for flexible, scalable systems that can evolve from localized setups to system-wide configurations (Latorre et al., 2024).

2.2 Reference Architectures and Standards: Technical Integration Versus Trustworthiness

Numerous studies have focused on digital twin reference designs in the context of Industry 4.0 and cyber-physical systems. These designs typically focus on: sensor and data collection; data management and semantic interoperability; modeling and simulation; analytics and optimization; and operational technology (OT) and enterprise information systems (EIS) interfaces. Standardization efforts and reference models like ISO 23247 concerning digital twin frameworks in manufacturing (ISO, 2021) and holistic industrial IoT reference architectures propagate the same approaches for interoperability and practical use.

The Digital Twin Consortium's Platform Stack Architectural Framework provides the first iteration of the "security, trust, and governance" as integral, fundamental, and thus non-optional framework elements of digital twin systems (Digital Twin Consortium, 2023). The framework defines "trustworthiness" as an umbrella term for privacy, safety, resilience, and reliability. These frameworks may acknowledge some aspects of trust, but they do little to guide the integration of legal, ethical, and accountability mechanisms as operational system functions – especially in the asynchronous regulatory environments of multiple jurisdictions. This creates a distinct area of concern for SMEs and project teams that wish to translate trusting constructs.

2.3 Digital Twins as Engines of Cognitive Enterprise Capability

Digital twins have been used for designing socio-technical systems for organization modeling. Once augmented with AI, they enable organizations to shift from descriptive monitoring to predictive and prescriptive decision support. Evaluations and analyses of AI-enabled digital twins highlight an increased focus on machine learning for anomaly detection, prognosis and optimization, and human-robot teaming (Huang et al., 2021; Lu et al., 2020). Fuller et al. (2019), claim that the most breakthrough digital twins implementations involve cross-iterative model and data stream evolution and model-data pipeline evolution over time.

From capabilities perspective, digital twins support cognitive functions of the enterprise in a minimum of three ways. First, they provide an integrated "digital thread" that connects different data sources across the entire lifecycle of an asset. They also enable in silico testing of strategies and policies before actual implementation. Lastly, they support closed-loop control when an automated decision, or a decision made by a human, is re-entered into the physical system. These capabilities mark the shift from traditional automation to more adaptive, learning organizations, while also increasing the stakes of governance when the outcomes of decisions may affect safety, equitable resource allocation, and the rights of individuals.

2.4 Governance and Regulation: Privacy, Liability, and Accountability Challenges

The first distinction discussed by Stapleton and Stapleton (2022) is the lack of clarity regarding regulation of digital twins and simulations vis-a-vis the real and the digital, the distinctions of data and property, and the distinctions of simulation and operational control. Digital twins, according to the authors, obscure the effects of digital twins on the real and digital property bar, and intellectual property rights as a consequence of the collaborative contribution of data, models, and expertise of a number of actors. Bostwick (2023) suggests that the utilization of digital twins has implications that current liability theories do not adequately address, and that further development of liability law to avoid digital twins based decisions, especially where the outcomes of the decisions relate to the design of the system or the control of the system's operations, is warranted.

Regarding digital transformation, O'Leary and Armfield (2020) noted that when organizations rapidly adopt digitization, it is often the case that the digitization progresses develop more rapidly than the governance and control. This usually results in ambiguity in the legal and operational areas, especially if governance does not keep pace with the digitization. Regulatory concerns are most pronounced in domains containing personal or sensitive information. Story (2023) states that unless privacy, security, and discrimination concerns are managed, the potential of digital twins in prediction and personalization in healthcare may lead to unregulated adoption. Similarly, techno-legal analyses of smart cities warn that, in the absence of regulations on the collection, retention, and secondary use of data, digital twins may intensify existing surveillance systems (Ghosh & Banerji, 2023).

These concerns are far broader than privacy and include cybersecurity and safety of the system as a whole: a compromised digital twin, for instance, can be a substantial attack route on critical infrastructure and mobility. This is what the NIS 2 Directive is all about as it expands the cybersecurity obligation for different sectors and reinforces the need for risk and incident reporting (European Parliament & Council, 2022b). With respect to the European level, the manifestation of governance concerns becomes evident with the design of explicit constraints. The GDPR divides the legality, fairness, transparency, purpose limitation, data minimization, integrity, confidentiality, and accountability, and sets out "data protection by design and by default" (European Parliament & Council, 2016). The Data Governance Act sets out provisions concerning the data intermediaries and data altruism to promote trust in the sharing and reuse of data, while the Data Act sets out provisions on the rights and obligations of access and use of data generated by connected devices and services, especially concerning sensors in digital twins (European Parliament & Council, 2022a, 2023). The AI Act states the responsibilities of high-risk AI systems and promotes human oversight, risk control, record keeping and post-market monitoring (European Parliament & Council, 2023). In this regard, the aforementioned tools shift the consideration of compliance from the legal sphere to the domain of engineering.

2.5 SMEs and the European "Twin Transition": Contextual Constraints and Opportunities

Small and medium-sized enterprises are key contributors to the European economies and national innovation targets; however, they often face structural barriers to the implementation of advanced digital systems. The Digital Decade 2025 country report for Bulgaria describes this problem numerically: in 2024, 49.93% of Bulgarian SMEs achieved at least a basic level of digital intensity, which is 22.98% lower than the EU average of 72.91%. Additionally, only 16.46% of SMEs achieved a high or very high digital intensity level compared to 32.66% in the EU. Furthermore, the adoption of key enabling technologies is very low; in 2023, only 14.22% of Bulgarian SMEs used cloud services (EU average 38.90%), and only 6.47% used AI technology, which is lower than the EU average of 13.48% (European Commission, 2025). These gaps are underscored by the fact that modern digital twins are built upon cloud and edge computing, data flow, and analytics toolchains that are difficult to operate and maintain without specialized expertise. Because SMEs are subject to the same regulatory frameworks as large businesses, they face unique compliance challenges. For digital twin systems targeting SMEs, this means governance systems must be designed modularly, be cost effective, and be reusable to address compliance concerns. This is especially true concerning the "twin transition" regulatory framework, as digital advancements are now designed to achieve environmental goals. OECD data suggests the emerging digital innovations designed to meet environmental goals are still a small marketplace. This demonstrates the urgent need and opportunity to develop accessible integrated digital and sustainable solutions (Aklilu et al., 2025). Digital twins can support predictive maintenance, resource optimization, and a full lifecycle assessment of assets. For these benefits to be realized, there must be effective systems for data sharing and measuring, as well as accountability and governance systems for actions derived from data.

3. CONCEPTUAL FRAMEWORK OR METHODOLOGY

Based on this synthesized background, the next step consists of articulating clearly the conceptual lens informing our architectural decisions and interpretations of the cases. In this regard, Section 3 presents the framework in broad terms, beginning with our characterization of digital twins as governed socio-technical systems.

3.1 Conceptual Framing: Digital Twins as Governed Socio-Technical Systems

This chapter presents digital twins as socio-technical systems. Their performance and legitimacy are shaped by techniques such as data integration, modeling, analytics, and control, as well as governance techniques centered on legal, ethical, accountability, and security oversight. Framed this way, governance is not an external "context" but an internal design variable. It shapes what data is permitted, how models are trained and validated, how automated decisions are made, and how responsibility is allocated among multiple actors. We outline three propositions that result from this perspective and connect the design choices of governance and the outcomes of its implementation. These propositions are not meant to be universally applicable but remain as relevant-to-design assertions that inform the development of the GEDT architecture and the parameters to be tested.

Proposition P1: Governance Integration Reduces Adoption Risk and Increases Trust

According to P1, the integrated approach to the digital twin architecture's governance and compliance structures reduces risks associated with deployment and strengthens stakeholder trust. This has been built on legal appraisals, where uncertainty about accountability, ownership, and compliance is likely to limit the uptake and increase the risk (Bostwick, 2023). This is in harmony with the GDPR's design requirements that force the inclusion of certain measures in privacy system designs and the Digital Twin Consortium advocating that governance and compliance are primary concerns in digital twin systems (European Parliament & Council, 2016; Digital Twin Consortium, 2023).

Proposition P2: Modeling and AI Integration Enables Cognitive Enterprise Performance Gains

P2 claims that a digital twin architecture which integrates modelling and simulation with analytics and AI, shows measurable improvements in performance and strengthens cognitive capabilities of an enterprise. This assertion builds upon the digital twin literature that relates two-way synchronization and predictive modelling to optimization, maintenance, and decision assistance (Kritzinger et al., 2018; Lu et al., 2020; Huang et al., 2021). It also shows an understanding that the creation of value is not only in going beyond dashboards but also in the ability to engage in experimentation and adaptive control, with appropriate human oversight in decision making that is critical to safety.

Proposition P3: Trustworthy Governance Enables Cross-Organizational Data Sharing and Ecosystems

P3 claims that the trust mechanisms facilitated by governance systems allow for the sharing of data across organizations and the involvement of ecosystems, both of which are critical for federated and composable digital twin systems. In the case of digital twins for cyber ranges, mobility corridors and supply chains, the digital twins can even cross organizational boundaries, and therefore, regulated data sharing is needed. The Data Governance and the Data Acts aim to establish trust in data sharing by defining the rights, duties, and the roles of intermediaries, while the AI and cybersecurity Acts impose elements of risk management and accountability for governance in AI (European Parliament & Council, 2022a, 2023, 2024).

3.2 Research Design: Design Science Research and Multi-Case Demonstration

We employ Design Science Research (DSR) methodology to construct and assess an artefact that responds to a specific practical problem (Hevner et al., 2004; Peffers et al., 2007). In DSR, knowledge contributions stem from the design and evaluation of artefacts that comprise both the organizational and the technical aspects of the problem.

In this regard, our research aligns with the fundamental DSR cycles, which cover: (i) problem identification and motivation (the governance gap in digital twin frameworks for SMEs), (ii) hypothesizing objectives for a potential solution (advocating a modular structure with governance-by-design), (iii) the design and development of the GEDT structure, (iv) the demonstration by use in relevant contexts, and (v) evaluation through a governance and value creation reflective analysis of the architecture in the selected disparate case areas (Peffers et al., 2007).

3.3 Evidence Base and Evaluation Strategy

To illustrate GEDT and to conduct an evaluative study, we utilize documentary and project-based evidence from European initiatives in research and innovation concerning the creation and/or implementation of digital twin systems within governance-sensitive areas. The primary case of our study includes the following projects: (1) iDriving, a Horizon Europe project using digital twins and AI analytics to monitor and evaluate road safety and infrastructure (iDriving Consortium, 2025a, 2025b); (2) ACTING, the project focused on the development of cyber range federations and simulations in a context of defense (ACTING Consortium); and (3) MaaSAI, a Horizon Europe project that aims to create a working digital ecosystem for manufacturing as a service (MaaSAI Consortium, 2025) that includes digital twins, AI, and mechanisms of trust.

These cases were chosen because they (i) cover multiple industries (mobility, cybersecurity, manufacturing), (ii) present significant high-stakes governance challenges (privacy, security, responsibility), and (iii) offer extensive documentation on architectures and compliance practices. The evaluation is interpretive and comparative: we attempt to align the elements and practices of each case to the GEDT layers and attempt to determine how governance frameworks facilitate or restrict data flows, modeling options, and operational frameworks. Although this methodology lacks the ability to quantify results, it still offers the potential of analytic generalization by recognizing multiple reusable patterns of architecture and governance frameworks in each domain (Yin, 2018).

4. DIGITAL TWIN ARCHITECTURE / MODEL / APPROACH

The conceptual framing prepares us to present the centerpiece of this research, which is a governance-enabled reference architecture for digital twins. Section 4 introduces the GEDT model, starting with its designing principles, followed by a description of its high-level structure.

4.1 Design Principles and Overview of the Governance-Enabled Digital Twin (GEDT)

GEDT architecture is proposed as a benchmarking model for digital twin systems development concerning cognitive organizational transformation for SMEs with a focus on compliance to governance structures. The architecture is "governance-enabled" in that compliance, accountability, and trust, are considered system features, as opposed to system restrictions. GEDT is designed to be modular so that SMEs can begin with a sufficiently limited scope, for example, an asset twin for predictive maintenance, and then build up to system and process twins, thereby increasing autonomy and ecosystem integration as the capabilities evolve (Latorre et al., 2024; Kritzinger et al., 2018).

GEDT has five levels. The first four layers create the technical foundation for the detection, representation, and optimization of physical assets. These layers are: (1) Physical Layer; (2) Data Layer; (3) Analytics/ AI Layer; and (4) Cognitive Layer. Layer 5, the Governance and Compliance layer, has a unique, dual-functioning role that both constrains and enables the other layers in terms of policy, risk and accountability. This layer aligns with the Digital Twin Consortium's position that for digital twin systems, the governance of security, trust, and compliance is critical, although this layer takes a more extensive, operationalized view on governance, especially in terms of ethics and compliance in the European Union (Digital Twin Consortium, 2023).

GEDT is illustrated in Table 1 (conceptual) as a closed-loop system. With this system, data flows from physical assets to models and analytics, and decisions and actions flow back to operational systems. The governance layer manages and directs these flows through policy, whether on data governance (access and retention), model approval, accountability, and manual intervention, which facilitates audits.

Table 1. Summary of the GEDT layers and their governance touchpoints.

GEDT layer	Main purpose	Typical components	Governance touchpoints
Physical Layer Asset and sensing	Observe and (optionally) influence physical assets and processes.	Sensors, UAVs/cameras, edge devices, actuators, OT interfaces.	Data minimization; safe actuation limits; secure device management; safety constraints.
Data Layer Data acquisition and management	Ingest, integrate, contextualize, and store real-time and historical data.	Streaming/batch pipelines; message brokers; databases; metadata/semantics; data quality services.	Lawful basis/purpose limitation; access control; retention; provenance and logging; data sharing controls.
Analytics/ AI Layer Modeling and simulation	Represent asset/process behavior and support what-if experimentation.	Physics/process models; 3D/ semantic models; hybrid models; scenario engines; model management.	Model validation and documentation; change control; IP protection; constraints on safety-critical use.
Cognitive Layer Analytics and intelligence	Generate insights and recommendations; support optimization and decision-making.	ML/AI models; anomaly detection; forecasting; optimization; agent orchestration; dashboards.	Human oversight; bias/ impact assessment; explainability where needed; monitoring and post-deployment controls.
Governance & Compliance Layer Compliance and trustworthiness	Provide a control plane for compliance, accountability, security, and sustainability.	Policy management; risk registers; DPIA workflows; IAM; audit trails; cybersecurity controls; sustainability metrics.	Cross-layer enforcement; accountability allocation; regulatory updates; incident response; audit readiness.

4.2 Layer 1: Physical Layer – Asset and Sensing

This layer consists of the physical entities and processes that are being twinned and the instrumentation that is necessary to create usable data. Depending on the use case, assets could consist of machinery, vehicles, components of infrastructure, buildings, elements of networks, and human-machine interactions. Examples of instrumentation include fixed sensors, embedded controllers, cellular phones, videos, unmanned aerial vehicles, and telemetry from enterprise systems. In the simplest case, this layer can perform one-way sensing, and in more developed cases, it includes actuators or control interfaces that allow for two-way interactions (Kritzinger et al., 2018).

The main design choice on this layer from an architectural perspective involves the questions of observability and controllability. Which parameters can be tracked, to what level of detail, and what operational knobs can be manipulated in an unsafe manner? These choices impact on governance, given that the choice of sensors can capture personal data (e.g., video of people) and can increase the risk of cyberattacks. Therefore, "data minimization" and "security by design" principles should guide the design of sensors, rather than being an afterthought once the data is collected (European Parliament & Council, 2016; European Parliament & Council, 2022b).

4.3 Layer 2: Data Layer – Data Acquisition, Integration, and Management Layer

The data layer acts as the digital twin's conceptual building block. It includes data ingestion pipelines (both streaming and batch), integration middleware, storage (time-series, relational, graph, and object storage), metadata, data quality services, and more. In many cases, message brokers and event streaming applications offer low latency and data lakes and warehouses provide the ability to do analysis over time. The data layer keeps critical contextual elements required to make sense of data (time, location, asset IDs, and semantics). This adds to the data layer's digital thread. The digital thread interlinks various stages and silos of an organization (Lu et al, 2020).

For SMEs, one of the most significant architectural challenges is balancing scalability and operational ease. GEDT conceptualizes data management as a set of reusable services which can be deployed in cloud spaces, on-premises, or at the edge based on latency and sovereignty considerations. In inter-organizational situations, the data layer must facilitate controlled sharing according to standardized and contractual frameworks. European data governance policies have increasingly developed concepts around „data spaces" and trusted intermediaries to facilitate data sharing. The Data Governance Act and the Data Act provide a regulatory framework for the establishment of reusable and shareable rights, which can be operationalized through a combination of identity, access, and usage control (and monitoring) frameworks at the data layer (European Parliament & Council, 2022a, 2023).

4.4 Layer 3: Analytics/ AI Layer – Modeling and Simulation Layer

The modeling and simulation layer adds a unique representation to a digital twin as compared to pure data platforms. It stores models of assets and processes which may include models based on the laws of physics, discrete event simulation, and hybrid models comprising a mechanistic part and a data-driven part. Models may represent geometry (e.g., a 3D model of an asset), behavior (e.g., a model of traffic), or performance (e.g., a model representing various degradation and failure modes). The simulation functionality (or default mode) of models supports the modeling of different scenarios to explore the impacts of proposed actions, the comparison of alternative policy actions, and the evaluation of the results of model simulations in the face of uncertainty (Digital Twin Consortium, 2023).

This layer is responsible for model versioning, model calibration, and model validation. These tasks become paramount when the model is used to make decisions impacting individuals' safety, in which case model governance is a priority. For GEDT, managing the model's lifecycle is a core function of governance that defines the establishment of model lifecycle management in conjunction with governance to model governance and model validation in anticipation of compliance with regulatory frameworks, particularly the AI Act, for systems classified as high-risk (European Parliament & Council, 2024).

Nozari and Yordanova (2026) exemplify this in food logistics, where agentic AI within an adaptive DT dynamically reprioritizes fuzzy objectives (cost, waste, service), achieving 45% cost reduction and 13% waste minimization via self-regulating loops. This validates GEDT's cognitive layer for SMEs in perishable supply chains, aligning with Industry 5.0 resilience.

4.5 Layer 4: Cognitive Layer - Analytics and Intelligence Layer

This analytical and intelligence layer offers mechanisms for converting data and model results into decisions. Three analyses are performed: descriptive (monitory and visualization), predictive (forecast and risk), prescriptive (optimize and advise). When it comes to AI-enabled digital twins, this layer typically uses ML for perception (computer vision), anomaly detection, prognostics, and RL or agent-based decision support frameworks (Huang et al., 2021; Lu et al., 2020).

In GEDT, the concept of intelligence involves working with AI. In many SMEs and public sector contexts, ideal complete autonomy may not be feasible or even desired. This preference is for the design to accommodate incremental autonomy: analytics may propose, model impacts, and issue captures, but human operators have the final say in the actions with the greatest consequences. This design concept also resonates with emerging regulations.

4.6 Layer 5: Governance, Compliance, and Trustworthiness Layer

GEDT's singular and distinctive features are governance, compliance, and trustworthiness framework. It applies governance-by-design through a set of services and processes that both constrain and enable the technical tiers. This layer comprises six interlinked groups of capabilities.

First, legal and regulatory compliance management pertains to the translation of external requirements and obligations into internal policies and procedures. This involves maintaining a regulatory inventory, mapping obligations to system elements, and implementing policy-as-code where possible (e.g. retention regulations, consent and lawful basis documents, access permissions). This capacity under the GDPR hinders accountability proof, including records of processing and data protection impact assessments (European Parliament and Council, 2016), along with the data protection accountability framework, retrospectively.

Second, data governance and stewardship allocate responsibilities pertaining to the quality, ownership, and authorized use of data. Digital twins often integrate data from multiple entities (vendors, operators, public agencies), and as such can raise competing claims regarding the rights to the data generated by the models and the outputs produced by the models. The governance layer responds to the property-rights ambiguities identified in the legal literature (Stapleton & Stapleton, 2022) by integrating stewardship, usage rights, and accountability frameworks to facilitate data sharing agreements as prescribed in European data law (European Parliament & Council, 2022a, 2023).

Third, the management of cybersecurity and resilience provides protective measures regarding the digital twin and the physical system. This includes, but is not limited to, threat modeling, secure-by-design approaches, identity and access management, encryption, segmentation, vulnerability management and incident management in accordance with NIS 2's risk management framework (European Parliament & Council, 2022b). In critical safety contexts, cyber resilience is linked with physical safety because attacks on the digital twin can lead to dangerous consequences in the physical domain.

Fourth, ethical oversight and accountability mechanisms ensure that there is a process to contest an AI decision and that there is attribution of blame. This includes bias and impact assessments, human oversight mechanisms, and frameworks for negative impact mitigation. In fields like health care and criminal justice, scholars suggest that ethical oversight must be proactive due to the fast-paced nature of digital twin technology (Story, 2023).

Fifth, auditability and transparency provide compliance and accountability's evidential foundation. Digital twin systems are required to maintain records that are permanent and unchangeable regarding data ingestion, modeling, decisions, and interventions. This aids and supports internal audits, compliance audits, and investigations regarding incidents. Relating to Bostwick's (2023) liability concerns, these audit trails demonstrate the strongest accountability, allowing activities to be assigned to people and/or systems.

Sixth, sustainability and lifecycle responsibility extends governance to consider the social and environmental dimensions. In the context of the twin transition and Industry 5.0, the use of digital twin systems is becoming increasingly compulsory to report on sustainability and to enable the evaluation of the lifecycle, circularity, and efficient use of resources (Breque et al., 2021; Aklilu et al., 2025). This addition to the governance framework reduces "greenwashing" and ensures that the optimization of processes is aligned with the true purpose and value for the stakeholders.

Layer 5 functions as a governance "control plane" and "communicates" with other layers through functional interfaces by controlling what can be collected and shared (Layer 2), what types of models can be applied and changed (Layer 3), what analytics can be done and the oversight of automation (Layer 4), and what actions can be done at the asset level (Layer 1). Such a control plane approach is valuable for SMEs as it allows the transversal reuse of governance capabilities across multiple use cases and therefore reduces the marginal cost of compliance.

4.7 Implementation Considerations for SMEs

The GEDT model does not require SMEs to develop each of the levels internally. The design, in fact, allows integration of modular services, open standards, and platform ecosystems. SMEs may use managed cloud services for data pipelines and analytics, while retaining governance through contracts, access control, and auditing. European initiatives such as digital innovation hubs and regulatory sandboxes offer testing and compliance support, which is particularly important considering the AI Act's emphasis on compliance assessments and documentation for certain AI systems (European Parliament & Council, 2024).

Having said that, GEDT requires a shift to digital twin initiatives, in which governance design is prioritized. Initial steps include design choices made with respect to the identification of the legal basis for data governance, the mapping of data flows, risk and impact assessments, and the identification of accountability. These governance elements are the minimum for ensuring engagement, scalability, and transformative cognitive enterprise sustainability.

5. CASE STUDY OR APPLICATION

This section describes the implementation of the GEDT architecture from the perspective of cross-domain use cases. Rather than viewing these activities as holistic assessments, the activities provide examples of the real-world application of the different layers of the GEDT and the layered governance interaction with data, modeling, and AI-driven decision support. Overall, the cases illustrate the relevant trends for SMEs with a focus on the safe scaling of digital twins and the safe immersion in novel digital ecosystems.

5.1 iDriving: Governance-Sensitive Digital Twins for Enhanced Road Safety and Infrastructure

iDriving is a Horizon Europe initiative (2024–2027; Grant Agreement No. 101147004) which contributes to the development of a TRL 6 prototype for improving the safety of urban and secondary rural road infrastructure. The project is built around seven interrelated pillars, including the development of a Safety Criteria Catalogue (SCC) defining key safety indicators, the establishment of interoperable communication solutions, and the integration of compact, deployable sensor systems across vehicles and road infrastructure.

These components enable advanced monitoring services, such as road condition assessment, vehicle behavior analysis, and weather monitoring, alongside intelligent maintenance and traffic management tools. The system further incorporates AI-based warning mechanisms to provide real-time alerts to both infrastructure operators and road users. At its core, iDriving integrates these elements through a digital twin of the road infrastructure, combining sensor data, AI-driven analytics, and simulation capabilities to support real-time risk detection, prediction, and decision-making for enhanced road safety and maintenance.(iDriving). The project encompasses multiple pilots in various parts of Europe, including urban and rural road settings. Beyond technical innovation, iDriving's approach to governance innovation is noteworthy, as the project relies on the use of videos and sensors for data collection which may affect individuals (drivers, pedestrians), and the outcome of the project may be used to support enforcement, traffic management, and control infrastructure governance.

From a GEDT standpoint, iDriving demonstrates a road-safety digital twin evolving into an operational decision support system instead of merely a descriptive dashboard. The project features include real-time traffic monitoring and notifications (via variable message signs and mobile/ in-vehicle apps), administration and dangerous behavior detection, and road repair scheduling through pothole and debris detection (iDriving). These activities correspond to the cognitive enterprise conceptual framework of sensing-learning-adapting loops, where organizational interventions and learning are based on data-driven insights.

5.1.1 iDriving and the GEDT Layers

Compared to the sensing layer, iDriving merges multiple sources, including UAVs equipped with high-resolution cameras, roadside stationary cameras and sensors, weather stations, and sensors on vehicles. This configuration enhances observation across a wide area, allowing for rapid assessments of road safety and infrastructure condition.

The project integrates raw information at the data layer, the inputs from these sources are processed through platform services designed to manage, store, index, and contextualize information. Through the use of metadata – such as geolocation, time, and provenance of the sensor(s) – event histories of the roadway can be constructed and made available for analysis. Because of the diverse sources of the data layer, including on-site and mobile sensors, UAVs, and administrative and city datasets, considerations related to data stewardship and access control are likely to arise.

In the modeling and simulation layer, iDriving integrates digital twin of road segments and traffic flow, and the traffic flow dynamics. In the maintenance use cases, the twin supports the analysis of the evolution of a problem and the assessment of repair alternatives within the bounds of the potential traffic disruption. In safety applications, the twin can represent localized threats (e.g. water, trees) and simulate traffic re-routing or real-time notification (iDriving).

The analytics and intelligence layer uses computer vision and data analytics methods for the detection of objects, the classification of behaviors, and the analysis of risks. This allows the system to assess risks and compliance and to generate dangerous situation reports, critical area heatmaps, and recommendations for focused intervention and notifications (iDriving). The project framework emphasizes assistance for decisions made by traffic engineers and authorities, who are ultimately responsible for the implementation of the decisions with the greatest impact.

Within governance and compliance, iDriving employs governance-by-design approaches. Project materials illustrate the importance of data protection and ethical oversight detailing the need for data protection impact assessments (DPIAs) for UAV videos as well as the need for the use of technical measures such as anonymization or blurring where possible (iDriving). Governing practices include setting retention periods, implementing access restrictions for sensitive data, and monitoring frameworks for possible biased and disproportionate effects that could arise from AI systems used for risk detection and safety monitoring.

5.1.2 Value Creation Versus Governance

Even though iDriving is still under development, prototype reports show how the digital twin technology can drive operational value while also clarifying the governance trade-offs. For instance, predictive maintenance and defect identification can reduce inspection costs and improve targeting for repairs, while real-time alerts can improve the situational awareness and reaction times of traffic management (iDriving). The experiment shows that governance is not a given. Enhanced sensing (e.g., aerial video) can improve the detection of real threats while also increasing the need for privacy and compliance. GEDT is the systematic means to address the prospect of considering sensing, data, model, and decision management as a governance and collaborative means.

5.2 ACTING: Federated Cyber Ranges and Simulation for Defense-Relevant Contexts

ACTING is a EDF program initiative (2022 – 2026; Grant Agreement No. 101103208). It also pertains to cyber ranges and federated simulations in defense-related use cases where data, access, and ethics become critical. The project showcased materials at the ACTING validation workshops that describe federated cyber range and scenario-driven simulation methods that enable collaborative training and assessment across multiple organizations (ACTING Consortium, 2024).

From the GEDT perspective, ACTING emphasizes governance concerns with respect to federation: as multiple cyber ranges function in unison, governance must address issues of identity management, access control, auditing, and regulations governing the exchange of scenario-based artefacts and telemetry. Given that the simulations may involve attack scenarios, ethical oversight is critical. The guiding principle is that governance stems from the design; for federation, a governing control plane is indispensable, defining what can be shared, the conditions under which sharing occurs, and what auditing mechanisms are in place.

5.3 MaaSAI: Manufacturing-as-a-Service and Governance-Enabled Industrial Ecosystems

MaaSAI is a Horizon Europe Initiative (2024–2027; Grant Agreement No. 101177368) that outlines an architecture for Manufacturing-as-a-Service (MaaS) using AI autonomous agents, digital twins, and platform-based marketplace systems (MaaSAI Consortium, 2025). The MaaSAI architecture combines various reference models and consists of components such as digital twin designers, data analytics service, predictive maintenance toolkits, lifecycle assessment (LCA/LCC) tools, smart contract tool as well as blockchain-based trust tools.

MaaSAI, from the GEDT perspective, is the most refined and comprehensive representation of the technical layers. The asset layer captures the manufacturing resources and the shop-floor data sources; the data layer integrates various operational data; the modelling layer enables digital copies of machines and production capacity; and the analytics layer provides optimization and predictive maintenance. MaaSAI integrates sustainability instruments (e.g. repair-reuse-recycle toolkits and lifecycle assessment) reinforcing the importance of sustainability as a governing concern (MaaSAI).

In the context of integrating the GEDT) framework into the MaaSAI concept, it is particularly noteworthy how GEDT integrates governance as an element that connects the technical competencies and the regulatory and accountability aspects. The governance of the elements within the industrial ecosystems involves the contractual division of labor, the rights to access and control data, the protection of trade secrets, the cybersecurity of interconnected systems, and the accountability for the decisions made by AI agents. While MaaSAI implements smart contracts and blockchain technology, which cover some governance aspects (e.g., agreements that can be traced and usage monitoring), the arrangements for legal, ethical compliance, and governance require purposeful design and organizational processes, which coincide with P1 and P3.

5.4 Cross-Case Synthesis: Governance as a Design Facilitator

From the four cases, three main points can be developed. **First**, governance mechanisms, in some form, are present in all domains: privacy and data protection impact assessments (DPIAs) in the mobility sector, data isolation and synthetic data in cyber ranges, federation governance and access control in defense related simulations, and contractual and lifecycle governance within manufacturing ecosystems. **Second**, governance mechanisms are most effective when designed as reusable services and processes, rather than ad hoc project documentation. **Finally**, the cases illustrate that when the government creates "safe spaces" for experimentation, innovation can be encouraged. For example, providing cyber ranges for realistic attack simulations, and road safety twins where focus improvements can be made without continuous surveillance.

These details underpin the basic principle of GEDT: Ascending governance as a separate architectural layer enables the ethical expansion of digital twins from pilot initiatives to fully functional systems and from solo organizational implementations to more extensive ecosystems.

Table 2. Illustrative governance mechanisms across the cases (mapped to GEDT Layer 5).

Case	Illustrative governance mechanisms
iDriving (road safety)	DPIAs; data minimization and anonymization/blurring; role-based access control for sensitive feeds; retention limits; human oversight for enforcement-relevant decisions; ethics and safety review processes.
ACTING (federated cyber ranges)	Federated identity and authorization; governance for scenario sharing; auditing across federation; constraints for dual-use/ethical risks; handling of classified or sensitive information.
MaaSAI (manufacturing-as-a-service)	Contractual allocation of responsibilities; smart contracts and traceable agreements; protection of trade secrets and IP; cybersecurity for interconnected production resources; lifecycle/sustainability metrics and reporting.

6. DISCUSSION AND IMPLICATIONS

Having demonstrated the GEDT architecture through concrete cases, this section now evaluates its theoretical and practical implications. We begin by systematically assessing how the evidence relates to our core propositions P1–P3.

6.1 Evidence Assessment Relating to P1 – P3

The cross-case evidence speaks to the viability and parameters of the design proposals. P1 (Governance integration reduces adoption risk and increases trust) case studies provide evidence that governance systems are not just barriers to solutions; they also promote the feasibility and societal acceptance of technical means. For example, in the case of iDriving, governance related to user privacy and accountability impacts the selection of operational sensors, data retention and enforcement, and the level of automation in analytic enforcement (iDriving). In ACTING, governance-related constraints are tied to cybersecurity; effective training, in the context of these projects, is related to the structured use of sensitive systems and techniques that are used in attacks (Rebecchi et al., 2022; ACTING Consortium, 2024). In MaaSAI, the governance framework is crucial for the sustainability of the ecosystem, as trust (and transparency in contractual arrangements) is essential for effective data sharing and coordination of AI agents (MaaSAI). These patterns correlate with legal studies that have found that the absence of clarity with respect to rights and obligations is a barrier to the acceptance of new systems (Stapleton & Stapleton, 2022; Bostwick, 2023).

With respect to P2 (Modeling and AI integration enables cognitive enterprise performance gains), these cases exemplify the fact that value creation is fundamentally based on the fusion of representation with analytics, rather than the reductive view of digital twins as merely visualization tools. Value proposition of iDriving pivots on the fusion of sensing technology with predictive analytics and scenario analytics for maintenance and hazard response. Specifically, the architecture of MaaSAI incorporates digital twins coupled with predictive maintenance and optimization, including sustainability-related decision support tools. The cases support the claim that integrated modeling and AI foster higher order cognitive processes in the corporate environment. However, they reveal an important boundary condition: the higher the autonomy and integration, the greater the need for governance, making P2 dependent on P1.

Regarding P3 (Trustworthy governance enables cross-organizational data sharing and ecosystems), the examples illustrate that advanced digital twin systems require inter-organizational relations as part of their fundamental infrastructure. In this regard, the combination of cyber ranges and platform-oriented manufacturing requires the controlled flow of information, models, and scenario artefacts. European data legislation, unlike preceding initiatives, progressively clarifies the foundational parameters of data sharing by describing access and intermediary rights, though the exercise of these rights is subject to structural limitations that include identity management, policy enforcement, auditing, and contract control (European Parliament & Council, 2022a, 2023). GEDT improves the architecture by clarifying these limitations instead of leaving them to project negotiations.

6.2 Government-Enabled Digital Twin Systems

The chapter contributes to digital twin research in three ways. **First**, it reframes governance as a constitutive architectural layer, extending the "trustworthiness" emphasis in recent reference architectures into a concrete control-plane model that maps to legal and ethical requirements (Digital Twin Consortium, 2023). **Second**, it integrates a regulatory-aware perspective into digital twin design, which is often absent from engineering-centric frameworks. By linking governance mechanisms to EU instruments such as GDPR, the Data Act, and the AI Act, the chapter shows how legal regimes shape technical architectures and thereby should be treated as design parameters (European Parliament & Council, 2016, 2023, 2024). **Third**, architecture situates digital twins within the broader shift from Industry 4.0 toward Industry 5.0, where stakeholder value, human-centricity, and sustainability become explicit objectives (Breque et al., 2021).

These contributions also highlight an underexplored research agenda: the co-evolution of technical architecture and regulatory regimes. Legal scholars note that legislation often falls behind technological change (Bostwick, 2023), while technology designers may treat law as external compliance. Governance-enabled architectures provide a mechanism to bridge this gap by enabling adaptive compliance – updating policy rules and controls as regulatory interpretations evolve.

6.3 Managerial Implications for SMEs and System Developers

The GEDT architecture suggests SME managers view digital twin investments as building capabilities rather than acquiring a new piece of technology. To be effective, scoping governance initiatives begin with identifying potential sources of data, analyzing risks for exposure of personal data, determining the need for cyber protections, and defining roles and responsibilities for accountability. Such approach can mitigate governance rework and increase the likelihood that pilots will be integrated into working systems.

For system developers and SME technology providers, the GEDT recommends that "governance services" be built as a modular layer in parallel with data and analytics services. This includes governance services such as DPIA templates and workflows, retention and access policy engines, audit logging and provenance capturing, and governance tools for model lifecycle management. For SMEs, these services are especially useful because they help to control the marginal costs of compliance for a variety of different use cases. Developers are encouraged to implement the AI Act's (European Parliament & Council, 2024) risk-based human oversight approach to the creation of "combined" capabilities of graduated autonomy and human oversight.

6.4 Policy Implications: Supporting Responsible Experimentation and Growth

Digital twin technology developers want to identify and overcome obstacles to rapid deployment. While there are challenges to the creation of a new technology, establishing trust and protecting rights are equally difficult. GEDT shows that the balanced governance approach is needed. Policy makers can develop control mechanisms to empower SMEs within frameworks like regulatory sandboxes, Digital

Innovation Hubs, and cross-border testing facilities, especially when they integrate governance frameworks with empirical technological infrastructure.

With the European Data Strategy, the European Parliament and the European Council (2022, 2023) aim to promote the sharing of data "under" the conditions of a trusted ecosystem. Digital twin technology with governance frameworks can serve as the basis for the proposed data ecosystem in the European Data Strategy, as this technology implements the required governance frameworks, including policy enforcement, usage audits, and accountability mechanisms. Therefore, there is potential for European policies to build digital twin technology governance frameworks and establish cross-border data flow of digital twin technologies as a valid approach to cybersecurity.

6.5 Constraints

There are constraints that will be brought to the assessment of the chapter that guides the scope of the assessment. Generally, the scenarios are based on work-from research and innovation activities and the associated documentation, which are different from documented industrial practices. Evidence of outcomes is often described in terms of the performance of a prototype or projected impact as opposed to a sustained operational measure. Additionally, laws are constantly changing and there are different interpretations across industries and Member States. Further work should therefore be of a longitudinal, empirical nature, after this design-science-type study, that examines the effects of governance-driven architectures on the gradual acceptance, performance, and trust over time.

7. FUTURE RESEARCH DIRECTIONS

The future of this field of study promises a solid return on expanding and evaluating the GEDT design construct. For example, there is the design impact of governance-enabled frameworks on the adoption outcomes of SMEs. This impact must first be empirically validated. In addition, the adoption of reusable governance mechanisms such as policy engine audits, trail audits, and DPIAs may provide a basis for comparative analyses in terms of expansion, efficiency and compliance blockage.

Also of interest is the need for a metric system that can quantify a digital twin's trustworthiness, in a holistic view that encompasses elements of technology and elements of compliance with the law and morality. Though there are frameworks for evaluating trustworthiness (Digital Twin Consortium, 2023), operational data, necessary to evaluate and benchmark trustworthiness, are unavailable in most discipline domains. Evaluations may address issues such as the completeness of data provenance, versioning of the model, test coverage, and oversight.

Concerning the automation of governance-by-design, policy-as-code approaches may take steps toward transforming a legal demand for a more automated approach, such as control, retention, and sharing of data. However, automation can hamper some legal flexibility and misinterpret sociotechnical design, thus requiring oversight.

Further study on interoperability and federation remains ongoing. As digital twin systems evolve to operate as systems-of-systems over multiple organizations, design systems will need standardized interfaces for the governance and data models, including policies, consent, audits, and risk governance registries. Integrating GEDT with the emerging European data spaces, including sector-specific data standards, could accelerate this development.

Sustainability digital twins require integrated approaches to lifespan assessment, circularity, and the alignment of optimization with stakeholder value. Research on digital twins and sustainability should examine measurement and governance accountability to ensure Digital Twins optimizations contribute to the twin transition (Aklilu et al., 2025; Breque et al., 2021).

8. CONCLUSION

Digital twins are becoming prominent as key infrastructures for cognitive enterprises because they support continuous data detection, learning, and optimization in the lifecycle of physical assets and processes. The most profitable applications of digital twins are often controversial in terms of governance, as they involve personal or proprietary data and important proprietary decisions. The chapter argues that governance should not be viewed as an external restriction, rather, it should be internalized in digital twin systems as a core design element.

This chapter moves the discussion forward by proposing the Governance-Enabled Digital Twin (GEDT) architecture, a five-layer reference model that includes a separate governance and compliance layer in addition to the conventional asset, data, modeling/simulation, and analytics/AI layers. The governance layer provides compliance control with respect to law, data stewardship, cyber security, ethics, audit, and accountability to sustain governance. The data from European projects in mobility, cyber security, and manufacturing shows that governance frameworks support dependable experimentation, engagement with ecosystems, and the creation of scalable value.

Combining governance-by-design with respect to the European regulations on data, AI, and cybersecurity and digital twin engineering, provides GEDT with a means to promote cognitive enterprise transformation for SMEs and their partners.

The scaling of digital twins is just as dependent on institutional and governance frameworks as it is on technological frameworks. The focus of subsequent studies should be on the experimental refinement of the architecture, enhancement of operational dependability, and the provision of governance frameworks that are interoperable across multiple industry ecosystems.

REFERENCES

Aklilu, A. Z., Dussaux, D., & Verrier, A. (2025). *Quantifying digital innovation for the twin transition: Historical trends, current landscape and links with environmental innovation* (OECD Environment Working Papers No. 261). OECD Publishing. DOI: 10.1787/19970900

Bostwick, B. (2023). Lagging legislation: The use of digital twins calls by manufacturers calls for new legal regulations. *Journal of High Technology Law, 23*(2), 440–478.

Breque, M., De Nul, L., & Petridis, A. (2021). *Industry 5.0: Towards a sustainable, human-centric and resilient European industry.* European Commission, Directorate-General for Research and Innovation. DOI: 10.2777/308407

Digital Twin Consortium. (2023). *Platform Stack Architectural Framework: An Introductory Guide.* Digital Twin Consortium.

European Commission. (2025). *Digital Decade 2025: Country report—Bulgaria* (Commission Staff Working Document SWD(2025) 294 final). Publications Office of the European Union.

European Parliament & Council. (2016). *Regulation (EU) 2016/679 of the European Parliament and of the Council of 27 April 2016 on the protection of natural persons with regard to the processing of personal data and on the free movement of such data (General Data Protection Regulation).* Official Journal of the European Union.

European Parliament & Council. (2022a). *Regulation (EU) 2022/868 of the European Parliament and of the Council of 30 May 2022 on European data governance (Data Governance Act).* Official Journal of the European Union.

European Parliament & Council. (2022b). *Directive (EU) 2022/2555 of the European Parliament and of the Council of 14 December 2022 on measures for a high common level of cybersecurity across the Union (NIS 2 Directive).* Official Journal of the European Union.

European Parliament & Council. (2023). *Regulation (EU) 2023/2854 of the European Parliament and of the Council of 13 December 2023 on harmonised rules on fair access to and use of data (Data Act).* Official Journal of the European Union.

European Parliament & Council. (2024). *Regulation (EU) 2024/1689 of the European Parliament and of the Council laying down harmonised rules on artificial intelligence (Artificial Intelligence Act).* Official Journal of the European Union.

Fuller, A., Fan, Z., Day, C., & Barlow, C. (2019). *Digital twin: Enabling technologies, challenges and open research* (arXiv:1911.01276). arXiv. https://arxiv.org/abs/1911.01276

Gelernter, D. (1991). *Mirror worlds: Or the day software puts the universe in a shoebox—How it will happen and what it will mean.* Oxford University Press. DOI: 10.1093/oso/9780195068122.001.0001

Ghosh, J., & Banerji, O. (2023). Excavating the role of digital twins in upgrading cities and homes amidst 21st century: A techno-legal perspective. *Indian Journal of Law and Justice, 14*(2), 248–270.

Grieves, M., & Vickers, J. (2017). Digital twin: Mitigating unpredictable, undesirable emergent behavior in complex systems. In Kahlen, F.-J., Flumerfelt, S., & Alves, A. (Eds.), *Transdisciplinary perspectives on complex systems: New findings and approaches* (pp. 85–113). Springer., DOI: 10.1007/978-3-319-38756-7_4

Hevner, A. R., March, S. T., Park, J., & Ram, S. (2004). Design science in information systems research. *Management Information Systems Quarterly*, *28*(1), 75–105. DOI: 10.2307/25148625

Huang, Z., Shen, Y., Li, J., Fey, M., & Brecher, C. (2021). A survey on AI-driven digital twins in Industry 4.0: Smart manufacturing and advanced robotics. *Sensors (Basel)*, *21*(19), 6340. DOI: 10.3390/s21196340

iDriving Consortium. (2025a). *D1.5 Mid-term review & progress report* (Horizon Europe Project iDriving; public deliverable).

iDriving Consortium. (2025b). *D5.1 First iDriving Prototype* (Horizon Europe Project iDriving; public deliverable).

International Organization for Standardization. (2021). *ISO 23247-1:2021 Digital twin framework for manufacturing — Part 1: Overview and general principles.* ISO.

Kritzinger, W., Karner, M., Traar, G., Henjes, J., & Sihn, W. (2018). Digital twin in manufacturing: A categorical literature review and classification. *IFAC-PapersOnLine*, *51*(11), 1016–1022. DOI: 10.1016/j.ifacol.2018.08.474

Latorre, L., Rego, E., & de Leo, L. (2024). *Tech report: Digital twins.* Inter-American Development Bank (IDB) TechLab.

Lu, Y., Liu, C., Wang, K. I.-K., Huang, H., & Xu, X. (2020). Digital twin-driven smart manufacturing: Connotation, reference model, applications and research issues. *Robotics and Computer-integrated Manufacturing*, *61*, 101837. DOI: 10.1016/j.rcim.2019.101837

MaaSAI Consortium. (2025). *MaaSAI Deliverable D5.1: MaaSAI Architecture* (Horizon Europe Project MaaSAI; public deliverable).

Nozari, H., & Yordanova, Z. (2026). A self-deciding adaptive digital twin framework using agentic AI for fuzzy multi-objective optimization of food logistics. *Algorithms, 19*(3), Article 218. DOI: 10.3390/a19030218[file:49]

O'Leary, T., & Armfield, T. (2020). Adapting to the digital transformation. *Alberta Law Review, 58*(2), 249–272. DOI: 10.29173/alr2618

Peffers, K., Tuunanen, T., Rothenberger, M. A., & Chatterjee, S. (2007). A design science research methodology for information systems research. *Journal of Management Information Systems, 24*(3), 45–77. DOI: 10.2753/MIS0742-1222240302

Stapleton, D., & Stapleton, K. M. (2022). Digital twins and Industry 4.0: A review of legal implications regarding property rights in physical and virtual spaces. *Journal of Transportation Law. Logistics and Policy, 89*, 95–113.

Story, B. (2023). Digital twins in healthcare: Proactive regulation to prevent a "runaway train". *North Carolina Journal of Law & Technology, 25*(2), 315–343.

Yin, R. K. (2018). *Case study research and applications: Design and methods* (6th ed.). SAGE.

Compilation of References

Abdessadak, A., Ghennioui, H., Thirion-Moreau, N., Elbhiri, B., Abraim, M., & Merzouk, S. (2025a). Digital twin technology and artificial intelligence in energy transition: A comprehensive systematic review of applications. In *Energy Reports* (Vol. 13, pp. 5196–5218). Elsevier Ltd., DOI: 10.1016/j.egyr.2025.04.060

Abuku, M., Hasegawa, T., & Yamada, K. (2024). A complete solution for the partisan chocolate game. *Integers: Electronic Journal of Combinatorial Number Theory.*

Abuku, M., Hasegawa, T., & Yamada, K. (2024). Enforce and selective operators of combinatorial games. *Theoretical Computer Science.*

Achuthan, K., Gupta, B. B., & Raman, R. (2025). Bridging cybersecurity with digital twin technology: A thematic analysis. *International Journal of Information Security, 24*(5), 207. DOI: 10.1007/s10207-025-01115-y

Ahvanouee, H. R., & Fay, A. (2024, December). Trace-driven verification framework for interoperable digital twins in distributed control systems. In *2024 IEEE 3rd Industrial Electronics Society Annual On-Line Conference (ONCON)* (pp. 1-6). IEEE. DOI: 10.1109/ONCON62778.2024.10931261

Aklilu, A. Z., Dussaux, D., & Verrier, A. (2025). *Quantifying digital innovation for the twin transition: Historical trends, current landscape and links with environmental innovation* (OECD Environment Working Papers No. 261). OECD Publishing. DOI: 10.1787/19970900

Al Faruque, M. A., Muthirayan, D., Yu, S. Y., & Khargonekar, P. P. (2021). Cognitive digital twin for manufacturing systems. In *2021 Design, automation & test in Europe conference & exhibition (DATE)* (pp. 440-445). IEEE. DOI: 10.23919/DATE51398.2021.9474166

Alam, K. M., & El Saddik, A. (2017). C2PS: A digital twin architecture reference model for the cloud-based cyber-physical systems. *IEEE Access : Practical Innovations, Open Solutions, 5*, 2050–2062.

Albelwi, N. (2026). DT-LCAF: Digital Twin-Enabled Life Cycle Assessment Framework for Real-Time Embodied Carbon Optimization in Smart Building Construction. *Sustainability (Basel), 18*(5), 2321. DOI: 10.3390/su18052321

Alcácer, V., & Cruz-Machado, V. (2019). Scanning the Industry 4.0: A Literature Review on Technologies for Manufacturing Systems. *Engineering Science and Technology, an International Journal, 3*(3), 899–919. https://linkinghub.elsevier.com/retrieve/pii/S2215098618317750. DOI: 10.1016/j.jestch.2019.01.006

Alghamdi, W. Y., Alshamrani, R. M., Aloufi, R. K., Ba Lhamar, S. O., Altwirqi, R. A., Alotaibi, F. S., & Alazwari, A. S. (2025). Exploring the Synergy Between Digital Twin Technology and Artificial Intelligence: A Comprehensive Survey. *International Journal of Advanced Computer Science and Applications, 16*(3). Advance online publication. DOI: 10.14569/IJACSA.2025.0160399

Ali, J. A., Gaffinet, B., Panetto, H., & Naudet, Y. (2024). Cognitive systems and interoperability in the enterprise: A systematic literature review. *Annual Reviews in Control, 57*, 100954. Advance online publication. DOI: 10.1016/j.arcontrol.2024.100954

Alokdeh, S. K., Al-Sulaiti, I., Shwedeh, F., Alzoubi, H. M., & Ahmed, G. (2026). Transforming Smart Manufacturing: The Pivotal Role of IOT and Data Integration in Enhancing Operational Efficiency in Manufacturing Sector.

Amirkhanova, G., Adilkyzy, S., Amirkhanov, B., Baizhanova, D., & Chen, S. (2026). A Digital Twin Architecture for Integrating Lean Manufacturing with Industrial IoT and Predictive Analytics. *Information (Basel), 17*(2), 196.

Amirkhanov, B., Kunelbayev, M., Amirkhanova, G., Nurgazy, T., Tyulepberdinova, G., & Tletay, S. (2026). Development of a Digital Twin for a Bakery Line With Predictive Analytics and Adaptive Control Functions. *IET Collaborative Intelligent Manufacturing, 8*(1), e70056. DOI: 10.1049/cim2.70056

Amorós, P. (2024). Nash implementation of supermajority rules. *Journal of Economic Theory.*

Andrews, J. G., Buzzi, S., Choi, W., Hanly, S. V., Lozano, A., Soong, A. C. K., & Zhang, J. C. (2014). What will 5G be? *IEEE Journal on Selected Areas in Communications, 32*(6), 1065–1082. DOI: 10.1109/JSAC.2014.2328098

Andruccioli, M., Girau, R., Mirri, S., & Salomoni, P. (2026, January). Towards declarative deployment and lifecycle orchestration of digital twin ecosystems. In 2026 IEEE 23rd Consumer Communications & Networking Conference (CCNC) (pp. 1-6). IEEE.

Angeletos, G. M., & Pavan, A. (2007). Efficient use of information and social value of information. *Econometrica, 75*(4), 1103–1142. DOI: 10.1111/j.1468-0262.2007.00783.x

Ashton, K. (2009). *That 'Internet of Things' thing*. RFID Journal.

Atzori, L., Iera, A., & Morabito, G. (2010). The Internet of Things: A survey. *Computer Networks, 54*(15), 2787–2805. DOI: 10.1016/j.comnet.2010.05.010

Autor, D. H. (2015). Why are there still so many jobs? The history and future of workplace automation. *The Journal of Economic Perspectives, 29*(3), 3–30. DOI: 10.1257/jep.29.3.3

Babar, Z., Yu, E., Carbajales, S., & Chan, A. (2019). Managing and Simplifying Cognitive Business Operations Using Process Architecture Models. In *International Conference on Advanced Information Systems Engineering* (pp. 643-658). Cham: Springer International Publishing. DOI: 10.1007/978-3-030-21290-2_40

Bagherian, A., Srivastav, A. L., & Mukherjee, S. (2026). Barriers and strategies of smart factory evolution in industry 4.0: An empirical study. *International Journal of Computer Integrated Manufacturing, 39*(1), 65–97. DOI: 10.1080/0951192X.2025.2461055

Bakliwal, K., Dhada, M. H., Palau, A. S., Parlikad, A. K., & Lad, B. K. (2018). A multi agent system architecture to implement collaborative learning for social industrial assets. *IFAC-PapersOnLine, 51*(11), 1237–1242. DOI: 10.1016/j.ifacol.2018.08.421

Banad, Y. M., Sharif, S. S., & Rezaei, Z. (2025). Artificial intelligence and machine learning for smart grids: from foundational paradigms to emerging technologies with digital twin and large language model-driven intelligence. In *Energy Conversion and Management: X* (Vol. 28). Elsevier Ltd., DOI: 10.1016/j.ecmx.2025.101329

Bandara, L. V., & Buics, L. (2025). Toward a Theoretical Framework for Digital Twin Readiness Assessment in Logistics: Conceptualization and Model Development. *Engineering Proceedings, 113*(1), 66. DOI: 10.3390/engproc2025113066

Barata, J., & Kayser, I. (2024). How will the digital twin shape the future of industry 5.0? *Technovation, 134*, 103025. Advance online publication. DOI: 10.1016/j.technovation.2024.103025

Barbuto, V., Savaglio, C., Lee, E. A., & Fortino, G. (2026). Engineering opportunistic digital twins with lingua franca. *Future Generation Computer Systems, 178*, 108262. DOI: 10.1016/j.future.2025.108262

Barykin, S., Shulga, A., Dinets, D., & Mikhaylov, A. (2026). Digital twin-enhanced credit risk prioritization in mortgage portfolios: A hybrid model approach. *Quality & Quantity*, *60*(2), 1–23. DOI: 10.1007/s11135-026-02579-3

Batini, C., & Scannapieco, M. (2006). *Data quality: Concepts, methodologies and techniques*. Springer.

Batty, M., Axhausen, K. W., Giannotti, F., Pozdnoukhov, A., Bazzani, A., Wachowicz, M., Ouzounis, G., & Portugali, Y. (2012). Smart cities of the future. *The European Physical Journal. Special Topics*, *214*(1), 481–518. DOI: 10.1140/epjst/e2012-01703-3

Becker, W. (2016). Digital transformation in manufacturing: Implications for lean management. *International Journal of Operations & Production Management*, *36*(12), 1452–1469.

Bergemann, D., & Morris, S. (2005). Robust mechanism design. *Econometrica*, *73*(6), 1771–1813. DOI: 10.1111/j.1468-0262.2005.00638.x

Berlekamp, E. R., Conway, J. H., & Guy, R. K. (2001). *Winning ways for your mathematical plays* (2nd ed.). Academic Press.

Besnard, F., & Bertling, L. (2010). An approach for condition-based maintenance optimization applied to wind turbine blades. *IEEE Transactions on Sustainable Energy*, *1*(2), 77–83. DOI: 10.1109/TSTE.2010.2049452

Bhatia, M., & Kumar, V. (2026). The role of digital twin in urban infrastructure and building management: A global scientometric perspective. *Cluster Computing*, *29*(1), 38. DOI: 10.1007/s10586-025-05813-z

Bibri, S. E., & Huang, J. (2025). AI and AI-powered digital twins for smart, green, and zero-energy buildings: A systematic review of leading-edge solutions for advancing environmental sustainability goals. *Environmental Science and Ecotechnology*, *28*, 100628. DOI: 10.1016/j.ese.2025.100628 PMID: 41244699

Bishop, C. M. (2006). *Pattern Recognition and Machine Learning*. Springer.

Blazewicz, J., Ecker, K. H., Pesch, E., Schmidt, G., & Weglarz, J. (2019). *Handbook on scheduling: From theory to applications* (2nd ed.). Springer.

BMBF (Bundesministerium fur Bildung und Forschung). (2019). *Mittelstand-Digital: The program for SME digitalization*. Federal Ministry of Education and Research.

Bocken, N. M. P., de Pauw, I., Bakker, C., & van der Grinten, B. (2016). Product design and business model strategies for a circular economy. *Journal of Industrial and Production Engineering*, *33*(5), 308–320. DOI: 10.1080/21681015.2016.1172124

Bommasani, R., Hudson, D. A., Aditi, E., ... (2021). On the opportunities and risks of foundation models. arXiv preprint arXiv:2108.07258.

Bordbar, A., Tadros, M., Nazemian, A., Aung, M. Z., Georgoulas, K., Louvros, P., & Boulougouris, E. (2026). Digitalisation of shipyard production planning: A review of simulation, optimisation, AI, and digital twin methods (2010–2025). *Journal of Marine Science and Engineering, 14*(4), 396.

Boros, E., Gurvich, V., & Tserkovnyak, Y. (2006). Impartial games with decreasing Sprague–Grundy function and their hypergraph compound. In *Games of No Chance 3* (pp. 105–120). Cambridge University Press.

Bosch Group. (2022). *Bosch annual report 2022: Connected manufacturing and sustainability*. Robert Bosch GmbH.

Bostwick, B. (2023). Lagging legislation: The use of digital twins calls by manufacturers calls for new legal regulations. *Journal of High Technology Law, 23*(2), 440–478.

Botín-Sanabria, D. M., Mihaita, A. S., Peimbert-García, R. E., Ramírez-Moreno, M. A., Ramírez-Mendoza, R. A., & Lozoya-Santos, J. (2022). Digital Twin Technology Challenges and Applications: A Comprehensive Review. *Remote Sensing (Basel), 14*(6), 1335. DOI: 10.3390/rs14061335

Box, G. E. P., Jenkins, G. M., Reinsel, G. C., & Ljung, G. M. (2015). *Time series analysis: Forecasting and control* (5th ed.). Wiley.

Breque, M., De Nul, L., & Petridis, A. (2021). *Industry 5.0: Towards a sustainable, human-centric and resilient European industry*. European Commission, Directorate-General for Research and Innovation. DOI: 10.2777/308407

Brown, T. B., Mann, B., & Ryder, N.. (2020). Language models are few-shot learners. *Advances in Neural Information Processing Systems, 33*, 1877–1901.

Brynjolfsson, E., & McAfee, A. (2014). *The second machine age: Work, progress, and prosperity in a time of brilliant technologies*. W. W. Norton.

Brynjolfsson, E., & McAfee, A. (2017). *Machine, platform, crowd: Harnessing our digital future*. W. W. Norton & Company.

Buccoliero, F. O., Corallo, A., Crespino, A. M., Del Vecchio, V., Lezzi, M., & Spennato, A. (2026). Modelling a Process Shop Floor Digital Twin in Smart Manufacturing: Best Practices from a Case Study. *IEEE Transactions on Engineering Management, 73*, 1667–1680. DOI: 10.1109/TEM.2026.3657042

Buer, S. V., Strandhagen, J. O., & Chan, F. T. S. (2018). The link between Industry 4.0 and lean manufacturing: Mapping current research and establishing a research agenda. *International Journal of Production Research, 56*(8), 2924–2940. DOI: 10.1080/00207543.2018.1442945

Bunjaridh, Y., Rahman, R. A., Yusof, L. M., & Papadonikolaki, E. (2025). Modeling the organizational attributes and strategies for developing accurate digital twins: the case of constructed facilities. *International Journal of Building Pathology and Adaptation.* DOI: 10.1108/IJBPA-12-2024-0281

Camerer, C. F. (2003). *Behavioral game theory: Experiments in strategic interaction.* Princeton University Press.

Cao, G., & Bai, J. (2024). Design Optimisation and Implementation of an Industrial Robot System Based on Digital Twin Technology. In *2024 4th International Conference on Machine Learning and Intelligent Systems Engineering (MLISE)* (pp. 461-464). IEEE. DOI: 10.1109/MLISE62164.2024.10674459

Cappiello, G., Casoli, D., Tuan, A., & Visentin, M. (2026). From digital tools to sustainable change: How change agents enable the twin transition in hospitality. *International Journal of Hospitality Management, 134*, 104591. Advance online publication. DOI: 10.1016/j.ijhm.2026.104591

Chaves, A. C., Alonso, A. N., & Soares, A. L. (2025). Data Spaces as Enablers of Digital Twin Ecosystems: Challenges and Requirements. In *IFIP International Conference on Advances in Production Management Systems* (pp. 340-354). Cham: Springer Nature Switzerland. DOI: 10.1007/978-3-032-03546-2_23

Chen, J., Wang, Z., Gao, H., He, Q., Mou, J., & Wang, W. (2026). The Role of Digital Twin in Advancing Industrial Internet of Things: Insights, Applications, and Future Directions. IEEE Internet of Things Journal.

Chopra, S., & Sodhi, M. S. (2004). Managing risk to avoid supply-chain breakdown. *MIT Sloan Management Review, 46*(1), 53–61.

Chrusciak, C. B., Szejka, A. L., & Canciglieri, O., Junior. (2023). A Preliminary Digital Transformation Framework to Support Business Management Processes and Human Factors Impacts: Systematic Review and Gap Analysis. In *Conference on e-Business, e-Services and e-Society* (pp. 308-329). Cham: Springer Nature Switzerland. DOI: 10.1007/978-3-031-50040-4_23

Clemen, T., Ahmady-Moghaddam, N., Lenfers, U. A., Ocker, F., Osterholz, D., Ströbele, J., & Glake, D. (2021, May). Multi-agent systems and digital twins for smarter cities. In *Proceedings of the 2021 ACM SIGSIM conference on principles of advanced discrete simulation* (pp. 45-55). DOI: 10.1145/3437959.3459254

Cong, W., Tao, W., & Jinsong, B. (2026). Agentic digital twin-embedded maintenance methodology for energy equipment: A self-evolving operational paradigm. *Journal of Manufacturing Systems*, *84*, 100–116. DOI: 10.1016/j.jmsy.2025.11.020

Conitzer, V., & Sandholm, T. (2006). Complexity of mechanism design. In *Proceedings of the 18th Conference on Uncertainty in Artificial Intelligence* (pp. 103–110).

Conway, J. H. (1976). *On numbers and games*. Academic Press.

Crawford, V. P., & Sobel, J. (1982). Strategic information transmission. *Econometrica*, *50*(6), 1431–1451. DOI: 10.2307/1913390

da Cunha, C., Cardin, O., Gallot, G., & Viaud, J. (2021). Designing the digital twins of reconfigurable manufacturing systems: Application on a smart factory. *IFAC-PapersOnLine*, *54*(1), 874–879. DOI: 10.1016/j.ifacol.2021.08.103

Daneshvar, A., Golroo, A., Moghadas Nejad, F., Karbalaei, A., Hosseini, P., & Rasti, M. (2026). Cognitive Digital Twins for Pavement Management: A Comprehensive Review. *Archives of Computational Methods in Engineering*, *33*(3), 1–20. DOI: 10.1007/s11831-026-10503-z

Dasgupta, P., & Maskin, E. (1986). The existence of equilibrium in discontinuous economic games. *The Review of Economic Studies*, *53*(1), 1–26. DOI: 10.2307/2297588

Daskalakis, C., Goldberg, P. W., & Papadimitriou, C. H. (2009). The complexity of computing a Nash equilibrium. *SIAM Journal on Computing*, *39*(1), 195–259. DOI: 10.1137/070699652

Das, P., Woods, O., & Kong, L. (2026). Modelling nature? The digital twinning and untwinning of urban farms. *Geoforum*, *170*, 104539. DOI: 10.1016/j.geoforum.2026.104539

Davenport, T. H. (2006). Competing on analytics. *Harvard Business Review*, *84*(1), 98–107.

Davenport, T. H. (2018). *The AI advantage: How to put the artificial intelligence revolution to work*. MIT Press. DOI: 10.7551/mitpress/11781.001.0001

Davenport, T. H., & Patil, D. J. (2012). Data scientist: The sexiest job of the 21st century. *Harvard Business Review*, *90*(10), 70–76.

Davenport, T. H., & Ronanki, R. (2018). Artificial intelligence for the real world. *Harvard Business Review*, *96*(1), 108–116.

de las Morenas, J., Belmonte, L. M., & Morales, R. (2025). Designing an AI-driven digital twin architecture for building energy prediction. *Journal of Building Engineering*, *113*, 113966. Advance online publication. DOI: 10.1016/j.jobe.2025.113966

Delsing, J. (Ed.). (2017). *IoT automation: Arrowhead framework*. CRC Press. DOI: 10.1201/9781315367897

Digital Twin Consortium. (2023). *Platform Stack Architectural Framework: An Introductory Guide*. Digital Twin Consortium.

Digital, G. E. (2016). *Predix: The industrial internet platform*. General Electric Company.

Domingos, P. (2012). A few useful things to know about machine learning. *Communications of the ACM*, *55*(10), 78–87. DOI: 10.1145/2347736.2347755

Doshi-Velez, F., & Kim, B. (2017). Towards a rigorous science of interpretable machine learning. arXiv preprint arXiv:1702.08608.

Duflou, J. R., Sutherland, J. W., Dornfeld, D., Herrmann, C., Jeswiet, J., Kara, S., Hauschild, M., & Kellens, K. (2012). Towards energy and resource efficient manufacturing: A processes and systems approach. *CIRP Annals*, *61*(2), 587–609. DOI: 10.1016/j.cirp.2012.05.002

Dui, H., Wang, H., & Xing, L. (2026). Digital Twin-Enabled Smart Operation and Maintenance Framework With Generative AI Design of Intelligent Manufacturing Systems. *IEEE Transactions on Reliability*, *75*, 504–517. DOI: 10.1109/TR.2025.3646186

Dumitrache, I., Caramihai, S. I., Moisescu, M. A., & Sacala, I. S. (2019). Neuro-inspired Framework for cognitive manufacturing control. *IFAC-PapersOnLine*, *52*(13), 910–915. DOI: 10.1016/j.ifacol.2019.11.311

Edirisinghe, E., Wu, G., Maggo, D., Cheng, C. T., Pang, T. Y., Rahman, A., Avery, A. L., Murphy, K. R., & Lora, C. A. (2026). A Digital Twin-Enabled Framework for Agrivoltaic System Design, Simulation, Monitoring and Control. *Machines (Basel)*, *14*(3), 254. DOI: 10.3390/machines14030254

Edrisi, F., Perez-Palacin, D., Caporuscio, M., & Giussani, S. (2024). Developing and evolving a digital twin of the organization. *IEEE Access : Practical Innovations, Open Solutions*, *12*, 45475–45494. DOI: 10.1109/ACCESS.2024.3381778

Elia, G., & Margherita, A. (2022). A conceptual framework for the cognitive enterprise: Pillars, maturity, value drivers. *Technology Analysis and Strategic Management, 34*(4), 377–389. DOI: 10.1080/09537325.2021.1901874

Ellahi, R. M., Ali, M., Ali Shah, S. A., Qureshi, M. A., Gulzar, S., Wood, L. C., & Ahmed Bekhit, A. E. D. (2026). Harnessing digital twins: transforming livestock supply chain management: a comprehensive review. *Cogent Food & Agriculture, 12*(1), 2611196.

Elshafei, B., Chaplin, J. C., Sanderson, D., & Ratchev, S. (2025). Facilitating interoperability in manufacturing systems using digital twins: A multi-asset AAS system. *International Journal of Advanced Manufacturing Technology*, •••, 1–18. DOI: 10.1007/s00170-025-17178-z

Erkan, E. F., Uygun, Ö., & Demir, H. İ. (2024). Assessing digital transformation using fuzzy cognitive mapping supported by artificial intelligence techniques. *Applied Soft Computing, 166*, 112199. DOI: 10.1016/j.asoc.2024.112199

European Commission. (2025). *Digital Decade 2025: Country report—Bulgaria* (Commission Staff Working Document SWD(2025) 294 final). Publications Office of the European Union.

European Parliament & Council. (2016). *Regulation (EU) 2016/679 of the European Parliament and of the Council of 27 April 2016 on the protection of natural persons with regard to the processing of personal data and on the free movement of such data (General Data Protection Regulation)*. Official Journal of the European Union.

European Parliament & Council. (2022a). *Regulation (EU) 2022/868 of the European Parliament and of the Council of 30 May 2022 on European data governance (Data Governance Act)*. Official Journal of the European Union.

European Parliament & Council. (2022b). *Directive (EU) 2022/2555 of the European Parliament and of the Council of 14 December 2022 on measures for a high common level of cybersecurity across the Union (NIS 2 Directive)*. Official Journal of the European Union.

European Parliament & Council. (2023). *Regulation (EU) 2023/2854 of the European Parliament and of the Council of 13 December 2023 on harmonised rules on fair access to and use of data (Data Act)*. Official Journal of the European Union.

European Parliament & Council. (2024). *Regulation (EU) 2024/1689 of the European Parliament and of the Council laying down harmonised rules on artificial intelligence (Artificial Intelligence Act)*. Official Journal of the European Union.

Fang, L., Shi, J., Wu, L., Tan, J., & Wan, J. (2026). Perspectives and prospects on embodied intelligence-empowered smart manufacturing. *Journal of Intelligent Manufacturing*, •••, 1–20. DOI: 10.1007/s10845-025-02763-6

Fan, H., Chow, E., Lu, T., Fuh, J. Y. H., Lu, W. F., & Li, B. (2026). A unified framework for large language model-guided reinforcement learning in digital twin industrial environments. *Robotics and Computer-integrated Manufacturing*, *99*, 103215. DOI: 10.1016/j.rcim.2025.103215

Farhi, E., Goldstone, J., & Gutmann, S. (2014). A quantum approximate optimization algorithm. arXiv preprint arXiv:1411.4028.

Feng, C., Reed, K. F., Giordano, J. O., & You, F. (2025). Precision decarbonization for clean dairy farming with digital twin and edge intelligence. In *Nexus* (Vol. 2, Number 4). Cell Press. DOI: 10.1016/j.ynexs.2025.100105

Fildes, R., Ma, S., & Kolassa, S. (2022). Retail forecasting: Research and practice. *International Journal of Forecasting*, *38*(4), 1283–1318. DOI: 10.1016/j.ijforecast.2019.06.004

Filinis, N., Spatharakis, D., Dimolitsas, I., Fotopoulou, E., Vassilakis, C., Zafeiropoulos, A., & Papavassiliou, S. (2026). A Scalable and Modular Open-Source Stack for Computing Continuum Digital Twins. *Future Generation Computer Systems*, •••, 108411.

Fokkink, R., & Rust, J. (2010). Queen reflections: A modification of Wythoff Nim. *Integers: Electronic Journal of Combinatorial Number Theory*, *10*, A29.

Fonseca i Casas, P., & Pi i Palomes, X. (2026a). Building Society 5.0: A foundation for decision-making based on open models and digital twins. *Advanced Engineering Informatics*, *69*, 103970. Advance online publication. DOI: 10.1016/j.aei.2025.103970

Fornari, F., Compagnucci, I., Callisto De Donato, M., Bertrand, Y., Beyel, H. H., Carrión, E., Franceschetti, M., Groher, W., Grüger, J., Kilic, E., Koschmider, A., Leotta, F., Li, C. Y., Lugaresi, G., Malburg, L., Mangler, J., Mecella, M., Pastor, O., Riss, U., . . . Valderas, P. (2025). Digital Twins of Business Processes: A Research Manifesto. In *Internet of Things (The Netherlands)* (Vol. 30). Elsevier B.V. DOI: 10.1016/j.iot.2024.101477

Forrester, J. W. (1961). *Industrial dynamics*. MIT Press.

Fraenkel, A. S. (1996). Scenic trails ascending from sea-level Nim to alpine chess. In *Games of No Chance* (pp. 13–42). Cambridge University Press.

Frerichs, M., & Nüttgens, M. (2022). Modeling the enterprise digital twin: Towards an open platform for analytics & compliance operations. In *Modellierung 2022* (pp. 65-75). Gesellschaft für Informatik eV. DOI: 10.18420/modellierung2022-008

Frey, C. B., & Osborne, M. A. (2017). The future of employment: How susceptible are jobs to computerisation? *Technological Forecasting and Social Change*, *114*, 254–280. DOI: 10.1016/j.techfore.2016.08.019

Fuller, A., Fan, Z., Day, C., & Barlow, C. (2019). *Digital twin: Enabling technologies, challenges and open research* (arXiv:1911.01276). arXiv. https://arxiv.org/abs/1911.01276

Fuller, A., Fan, Z., Day, C., & Barlow, C. (2020). Digital Twin: Enabling Technologies, Challenges and Open Research. *IEEE Access : Practical Innovations, Open Solutions*, *8*, 108952–108971. Advance online publication. DOI: 10.1109/ACCESS.2020.2998358

Fu, T., & Zhu, H. (2026). Digital-twin-based reinforcement learning method for flexible assembly job-shop scheduling with dynamic material kitting. *Computers & Industrial Engineering*, *214*, 111903. DOI: 10.1016/j.cie.2026.111903

Fu, X., Qin, M., Pace, P., Savaglio, C., Li, W., & Fortino, G. (2026). Generative AI-Driven Digital Twin in the Manufacturing Internet of Things: A Comprehensive Survey. *IEEE Internet of Things Journal.*

Gahm, C., Denz, F., Dirr, M., & Tuma, A. (2016). Energy-efficient scheduling in manufacturing companies: A review and research framework. *European Journal of Operational Research*, *248*(3), 744–757. DOI: 10.1016/j.ejor.2015.07.017

Gale, D. (1974). A curious Nim-type game. *The American Mathematical Monthly*, *81*(8), 876–879. DOI: 10.1080/00029890.1974.11993683

Galuzin, V., Galitskaya, A., Grachev, S., Larukhin, V., Novichkov, D., Skobelev, P., & Zhilyaev, A. (2022). Autonomous digital twin of enterprise: Method and toolset for knowledge-based multi-agent adaptive management of tasks and resources in real time. *Mathematics*, *10*(10), 1662. DOI: 10.3390/math10101662

Gandomi, A., & Haider, M. (2015). Beyond the hype: Big data concepts, methods, and analytics. *International Journal of Information Management*, *35*(2), 137–144. DOI: 10.1016/j.ijinfomgt.2014.10.007

Garcia-Sabater, J. P., Maheut, J., & Marin-Garcia, J. A. (2017). A two-stage sequential planning scheme for integrated operations planning and scheduling system using MILP: The case of an engine assembler. *Flexible Services and Manufacturing Journal*, *24*(2), 171–209. DOI: 10.1007/s10696-011-9126-z

Garro, A., & Sorrenti, A. (2026). Designing an ISO 23247-compliant Hybrid Digital Twin Architecture for industry. *Information and Software Technology*, •••, 108039.

Geissdoerfer, M., Savaget, P., Bocken, N. M. P., & Hultink, E. J. (2017). The circular economy: A new sustainability paradigm? *Journal of Cleaner Production, 143*, 757–768. DOI: 10.1016/j.jclepro.2016.12.048

Gelernter, D. (1991). *Mirror worlds: Or the day software puts the universe in a shoebox—How it will happen and what it will mean*. Oxford University Press. DOI: 10.1093/oso/9780195068122.001.0001

Ghosh, J., & Banerji, O. (2023). Excavating the role of digital twins in upgrading cities and homes amidst 21st century: A techno-legal perspective. *Indian Journal of Law and Justice*, *14*(2), 248–270.

Goldberg, P. W., & Papadimitriou, C. H. (2006). Reducibility among equilibrium problems. In *Proceedings of the 38th ACM Symposium on Theory of Computing* (pp. 61–70).

Goldratt, E. M. (1990). *Theory of constraints*. North River Press.

Goodfellow, I., Bengio, Y., & Courville, A. (2016). *Deep Learning*. MIT Press.

Grieves, M. (2014). Digital twin: Manufacturing excellence through virtual factory replication.

Grieves, M. (2014). Digital twin: Manufacturing excellence through virtual factory replication. *White Paper, Florida Institute of Technology*.

Grieves, M. (2014). Digital twin: Manufacturing excellence through virtual factory replication. White Paper. Florida Institute of Technology.

Grieves, M., & Vickers, J. (2017). Digital Twin: Mitigating Unpredictable, Undesirable Emergent Behavior in Complex Systems. In *F.-J. Kahlen, S. Flumerfelt, & A. Alves, Transdisciplinary Perspectives on Complex Systems* (pp. 85–113). Springer International Publishing. DOI: 10.1007/978-3-319-38756-7_4

Grossman, S. J., & Hart, O. D. (1980). Disclosure laws and takeover bids. *The Journal of Finance*, *35*(2), 323–334. DOI: 10.1111/j.1540-6261.1980.tb02161.x

Grundy, P. M. (1939). Mathematics and games. *Eureka (Asunción)*, *2*(5), 6–8.

Gubbi, J., Buyya, R., Marusic, S., & Palaniswami, M. (2013). Internet of Things (IoT): A vision, architectural elements, and future directions. *Future Generation Computer Systems*, *29*(7), 1645–1660. DOI: 10.1016/j.future.2013.01.010

Gupta, B., Namireddy, V., Quraishi, A., Begum, A. Y., Rao, K. B., Sundaram, A., & Smerat, A. (2026). Adaptive Resource Scheduling for Digital Twin-Based 6G Communication on Intelligent Computing-Integrated Network. IEEE Communications Standards Magazine.

Hamadache, M., Daho, S., Begg, S., & Lotfi, A. (2019). A comprehensive review of near-zero downtime maintenance approaches for Industry 4.0 predictive maintenance. *IEEE Access : Practical Innovations, Open Solutions*, *7*, 77452–77464.

Hamza, M. F. (2026). Cloud, Edge, and Digital Twin Architectures for Condition Monitoring of Computer Numerical Control Machine Tools: A Systematic Review. *Information (Basel)*, *17*(2), 153.

Harsanyi, J. C. (1967). Games with incomplete information played by "Bayesian" players. *Management Science*, *14*(3), 159–182. DOI: 10.1287/mnsc.14.3.159

Hasan, A., & Nguyen, D. T. (2026). Integrating agentic AI and digital twins for intelligent decision-making systems. *Array (New York, N.Y.)*, *29*, 100721. DOI: 10.1016/j.array.2026.100721

Hausladen, I., & Schosser, M. (2021). Towards a maturity model for digital lean management. *Total Quality Management & Business Excellence*, *32*(9-10), 1035–1053.

Hendricks, K. B., & Singhal, V. R. (2005). An empirical analysis of the effect of supply chain disruptions on long-run stock price performance. *Production and Operations Management*, *14*(1), 35–52. DOI: 10.1111/j.1937-5956.2005.tb00008.x

Hermann, M., Pentek, T., & Otto, B. (2016). Design principles for Industrie 4.0 scenarios. *Proceedings of the 49th Hawaii International Conference on System Sciences*, 3928-3937. DOI: 10.1109/HICSS.2016.488

Hevner, A. R., March, S. T., Park, J., & Ram, S. (2004). Design science in information systems research. *Management Information Systems Quarterly*, *28*(1), 75–105. DOI: 10.2307/25148625

He, Y. (2026a). Rewiring industrial futures: The role of AI-enabled digital twins in energy productivity transitions. *International Review of Economics & Finance*, *105*, 104898. Advance online publication. DOI: 10.1016/j.iref.2026.104898

Hilminata, A. N., & Alamsjah, F. (2025) Exploring Digital Mindset and Organizational Readiness in ISO-Based Information Systems: A Systematic Literature Review. In *2025 10th International Conference on Information Technology and Digital Application (ICITDA)* (pp. 1-6). IEEE. DOI: 10.1109/ICITDA68167.2025.11332422

Hishida, Y., & Kumano, T. (2021). Dominant strategy implementation of the doctor-optimal stable rule with bilateral contracts. *Journal of Economic Theory, 194*, 105241.

Holweg, M. (2007). The genealogy of lean production. *Journal of Operations Management, 25*(2), 420–437. DOI: 10.1016/j.jom.2006.04.001

Hopp, W. J., & Spearman, M. L. (2011). *Factory physics* (3rd ed.). Waveland Press.

Huang, D., & Liu, R. (2026). Research on the Technology–Organization–Environment Matching Mechanism in the Digital Transformation of the Manufacturing Industry: Evidence from Frontline Employees in the Guangdong–Hong Kong–Macao Greater Bay Area. *Administrative Sciences, 16*(1), 43. DOI: 10.3390/admsci16010043

Huang, Z., Shen, Y., Li, J., Fey, M., & Brecher, C. (2021). A survey on AI-driven digital twins in Industry 4.0: Smart manufacturing and advanced robotics. *Sensors (Basel), 21*(19), 6340. DOI: 10.3390/s21196340

Huber, J., Gossmann, A., & Stuckenschmidt, H. (2017). Cluster-based hierarchical demand forecasting for perishable goods. *Expert Systems with Applications, 76*, 140–151. DOI: 10.1016/j.eswa.2017.01.022

Hu, R., Guoyong, M., Abbas, A., & Wattoo, M. U. (2026). Explorative industrial internet promotes open green innovation in manufacturing enterprises. *Scientific Reports, 16*(1), 11312. DOI: 10.1038/s41598-026-40439-0 PMID: 41760707

Iansiti, M., & Lakhani, K. R. (2014). Digital ubiquity: How connections, sensors, and data are revolutionizing business. *Harvard Business Review, 92*(11), 90–99.

Ibrahim, N. I., Vering, C., Giannetti, N., & Kim, M. Sholahudin, Storek, T., Müller, D., & Saito, K. (2026). State-of-the-art of the digital twin concept in HVAC+R systems for thermal management of buildings. In *Renewable and Sustainable Energy Reviews* (Vol. 229). Elsevier Ltd. DOI: 10.1016/j.rser.2025.116601

iDriving Consortium. (2025a). *D1.5 Mid-term review & progress report* (Horizon Europe Project iDriving; public deliverable).

iDriving Consortium. (2025b). *D5.1 First iDriving Prototype* (Horizon Europe Project iDriving; public deliverable).

Iglesias, F., Ros, F., Hoang, L., Thuy, V., Gourcy, L., Moquet, J.-S., Daële, V., & Dupraz, S. (2026a). *A conceptual architecture for AI-assisted Digital Twins in natural resource management.* https://doi.org/DOI: 10.48436/b615a

Iliu ă, M. E., Moisescu, M. A., Pop, E., Ionita, A. D., Caramihai, S. I., & Mitulescu, T. C. (2022). Digital Twin—A Review of the Evolution from Concept to Technology and Its Analytical Perspectives on Applications in Various Fields. *Applied Sciences (Basel, Switzerland)*, *12*(8). Advance online publication. DOI: 10.3390/app14135454

Imandi, R., Chethana, B., Prasad, B. P., Sethi, K., & Kumar, B. P. (2025). Enhancing data management in industry 5.0: the role of digital twins in optimizing industrial operations. In *Industry 5.0: Key Technologies and Drivers* (pp. 211-236). Cham: Springer Nature Switzerland. DOI: 10.1007/978-3-031-87837-4_9

IMDA (Infocomm Media Development Authority). (2022). *SMEs Go Digital programme report*. Singapore Government.

Inmon, W. H., & Linstedt, D. (2014). *Data architecture: A primer for the data scientist*. Morgan Kaufmann.

International Organization for Standardization. (2021). *ISO 23247-1:2021 Digital twin framework for manufacturing — Part 1: Overview and general principles*. ISO.

Ivanov, D. (2026). Agentic digital twins: Bridging model-based and AI-driven decision-making support for a new era of supply chain and operations management. *International Journal of Production Research*, •••, 1–17. DOI: 10.1080/00207543.2026.2630277

Ivanov, D., & Gusikhin, O. (2026a). Supply chain digital twin design and implementation at scale: A case study at the Ford Motor Company and generalizations. *Omega*, *139*, 103447. Advance online publication. DOI: 10.1016/j.omega.2025.103447

Jagatheesaperumal, S. K., & Rahouti, M. (2023). Building digital twins of cyber physical systems with metaverse for industry 5.0 and beyond. *IT Professional*, *24*(6), 34–40.

Jain, K., Gupta, S., & Behare, N. (2026). Safeguarding Digital Transformation: Cybersecurity for Digital Twin and IoT Ecosystems. In *Generative AI Applications and Intelligent Systems: From Chatbots to Cybersecurity* (pp. 243-274). IGI Global Scientific Publishing. DOI: 10.4018/979-8-3373-8011-7.ch010

Janssen, M., van der Voort, H., & Wahyudi, A. (2017). Factors influencing big data decision-making quality. *Journal of Business Research*, *70*, 338–345. DOI: 10.1016/j.jbusres.2016.08.007

Jardine, A. K., Lin, D., & Banjevic, D. (2006). A review on machinery diagnostics and prognostics implementing condition-based maintenance. *Mechanical Systems and Signal Processing*, *20*(7), 1483–1510. DOI: 10.1016/j.ymssp.2005.09.012

Jarzyńska, M., Nierychlok, A., & Olender-Skóra, M. (2026). The Concept of a Hierarchical Digital Twin. *Applied Sciences (Basel, Switzerland)*, *16*(2), 605.

Jiang, Z. (2021). Equilibrium refinement in finite action evidence games. *Games and Economic Behavior*, *128*, 163–183.

Jinzhi, L., Zhaorui, Y., Xiaochen, Z., Jian, W., & Dimitris, K. (2022). Exploring the concept of Cognitive Digital Twin from model-based systems engineering perspective. *International Journal of Advanced Manufacturing Technology*, *121*(9), 5835–5854. DOI: 10.1007/s00170-022-09610-5

Jöhnk, J., Weißert, M., & Wyrtki, K. (2021). Ready or not, AI comes: An interview study of organizational AI readiness factors. *Business & Information Systems Engineering*, *63*(1), 5–20. DOI: 10.1007/s12599-020-00676-7

Jones, D., Snider, C., Nassehi, A., Yon, J., & Hicks, B. (2020). Characterising the Digital Twin: A systematic literature review. *CIRP Journal of Manufacturing Science and Technology*, *29*, 36–52. DOI: 10.1016/j.cirpj.2020.02.002

Jordan, M. I., & Mitchell, T. M. (2015). Machine learning: Trends, perspectives, and prospects. *Science*, *349*(6245), 255–260. DOI: 10.1126/science.aaa8415

Joshi, S., Sharma, M., Gunasekaran, A., & Joshi, T. (2026). Sustainable smart manufacturing through digital Servitization: A systematic literature review using use cases. *International Journal of Computer Integrated Manufacturing*, •••, 1–38. DOI: 10.1080/0951192X.2026.2622987

Kabashkin, I., & Saveljevs, A. (2026). Mathematical Framework for Airport as Cognitive Digital Twin of Aviation Ecosystem. *Mathematics*, *14*(3), 558. DOI: 10.3390/math14030558

Kagermann, H., Wahlster, W., & Helbig, J. (2013). *Recommendations for implementing the strategic initiative Industrie 4.0. National Academy of Science and Engineering*. Acatech.

Kalaboukas, K., Kiritsis, D., & Arampatzis, G. (2023). Governance framework for autonomous and cognitive digital twins in agile supply chains. *Computers in Industry*, *146*, 103857. DOI: 10.1016/j.compind.2023.103857

Kalai, E., & Samet, D. (1984). Persistent equilibria in strategic games. *International Journal of Game Theory*, *13*(3), 129–144. DOI: 10.1007/BF01769811

Kalyani, Y., & Collier, R. (2024). The role of multi-agents in digital twin implementation: Short survey. *ACM Computing Surveys*, *57*(3), 1–15. DOI: 10.1145/3697350

Kamenica, E., & Gentzkow, M. (2011). Bayesian persuasion. *The American Economic Review, 101*(6), 2590–2615. DOI: 10.1257/aer.101.6.2590

Kameswari, Y. L., Jagan, B. O. L., Mohammed, T. K., & Aleem, S. H. A. (2025). Future trends and research challenges in digital twins. *Digital Twins for Smart Cities and Villages*, 81-101. DOI: 10.1016/B978-0-443-28884-5.00004-X

Kamijo, Y. (2011). A note on the risk dominance of the Nash demand game. *Journal of Economic Theory, 146*(2), 794–802.

Kantaros, A., Ganetsos, T., Pallis, E., & Papoutsidakis, M. (2025). From mathematical modeling and simulation to digital twins: Bridging theory and digital realities in industry and emerging technologies. *Applied Sciences (Basel, Switzerland), 15*(16), 9213. DOI: 10.3390/app15169213

Kaplan, A. M., & Haenlein, M. (2019). Siri, Siri, in my hand: Who's the fairest in the land? *Business Horizons, 62*(1), 15–25. DOI: 10.1016/j.bushor.2018.08.004

Kelton, W. D., Sadowski, R. P., & Zupick, N. B. (2015). *Simulation with Arena* (6th ed.). McGraw-Hill.

Khan, M. N., & Ahmad, I. (2025). Harnessing digital twins: Advancing virtual replicas for optimized system performance and sustainable innovation. *Babylonian Journal of Mechanical Engineering, 2025*, 18–33. DOI: 10.58496/BJME/2025/002

Khojasteh, Y., Mousavi Jahan Abadi, S. M., & Ng, C. (2026). Leveraging digital transformation in supply chains: Strategies for agility, performance, and resilience. In *Digital Transformation of Supply Chains: Business Objectives and Applications* (pp. 3–39). Springer Nature Switzerland. DOI: 10.1007/978-3-032-01206-7_1

Kleijnen, J. P. C. (2015). *Design and analysis of simulation experiments* (2nd ed.). Springer. DOI: 10.1007/978-3-319-18087-8

Kleindorfer, P. R., & Saad, G. H. (2005). Managing disruption risks in supply chains. *Production and Operations Management, 14*(1), 53–68. DOI: 10.1111/j.1937-5956.2005.tb00009.x

Kohlberg, E., & Mertens, J. F. (1986). On the strategic stability of equilibria. *Econometrica, 54*(5), 1003–1037. DOI: 10.2307/1912320

Kolate, V. D., Chaudhary, M. K., Mane, S., & Devadhe, M. (2026). Digital twin–enabled model predictive control in additive manufacturing: Critical review, research challenges, and future directions. *Materials and Manufacturing Processes, 41*(1), 1–17. DOI: 10.1080/10426914.2025.2586498

Kookalani, S., Green, S., Luo, P., Alavi, H., Parn, E., Sun, Z., & Brilakis, I. (2026a). Mapping digital twin applications in infrastructure and the built environment across research types, methods, sectors, phases, and scales. *Automation in Construction, 182*, 106778. DOI: 10.1016/j.autcon.2026.106778

Kreps, D. M., & Wilson, R. (1982). Sequential equilibria. *Econometrica, 50*(4), 863–894. DOI: 10.2307/1912767

Kreuzer, T., Papapetrou, P., & Zdravkovic, J. (2024). Artificial intelligence in digital twins—A systematic literature review. *Data & Knowledge Engineering, 151*, 102304. Advance online publication. DOI: 10.1016/j.datak.2024.102304

Kristoffersen, E., Blomsma, F., Mikalef, P., & Li, J. (2020). The smart circular economy: A digital-enabled circular strategies framework for manufacturing companies. *Journal of Business Research, 120*, 241–261. DOI: 10.1016/j.jbusres.2020.07.044

Kritzinger, W., Karner, M., Traar, G., Henjes, J., & Sihn, W. (2018). Digital Twin in manufacturing: A categorical literature review and classification. [Elsevier.]. *IFAC-PapersOnLine, 51*(11), 1016–1022. DOI: 10.1016/j.ifacol.2018.08.474

Kroese, D. P., Taimre, T., & Botev, Z. I. (2011). *Handbook of Monte Carlo methods.* Wiley. DOI: 10.1002/9781118014967

Kruger, K., Human, C., & Basson, A. (2021, November). Towards the integration of digital twins and service-oriented architectures. In *International Workshop on Service Orientation in Holonic and Multi-Agent Manufacturing* (pp. 131-143). Cham: Springer International Publishing. DOI: 10.1007/978-3-030-99108-1_10

Kulkarni, V., Barat, S., & Clark, T. (2019). *Towards adaptive enterprises using digital twins. In 2019 winter simulation conference (WSC).* IEEE.

Kumar, D., Addula, S. R., Lind, M., Brown, S., & Odion, S. (2026). AI-Driven Hybrid Deep Learning and Swarm Intelligence for Predictive Maintenance of Smart Manufacturing Robots in Industry 4.0. *Electronics (Basel), 15*(3), 715. DOI: 10.3390/electronics15030715

Lan, X., Hu, Z., Pei, X., & Wen, C. (2026). Does Digital Infrastructure Promote the Upgrading of Manufacturing Enterprises? Evidence From China. *Growth and Change, 57*(1), e70101. DOI: 10.1111/grow.70101

Lasi, H., Fettke, P., Kemper, H. G., Feld, T., & Hoffmann, M. (2014). Industry 4.0. *Business & Information Systems Engineering, 6*(4), 239–242. DOI: 10.1007/s12599-014-0334-4

Latorre, L., Rego, E., & de Leo, L. (2024). *Tech report: Digital twins*. Inter-American Development Bank (IDB) TechLab.

Law, A. M. (2015). *Simulation modeling and analysis* (5th ed.). McGraw-Hill.

LeCun, Y., Bengio, Y., & Hinton, G. (2015). Deep learning. *Nature*, *521*(7553), 436–444. DOI: 10.1038/nature14539

Lee, E. A., & Seshia, S. A. (2017). *Introduction to embedded systems: A cyber-physical systems approach* (2nd ed.). MIT Press.

Lee, H. L., Padmanabhan, V., & Whang, S. (1997). Information distortion in a supply chain: The bullwhip effect. *Management Science*, *43*(4), 546–558. DOI: 10.1287/mnsc.43.4.546

Lee, J., Bagheri, B., & Kao, H. A. (2015). A cyber-physical systems architecture for Industry 4.0-based manufacturing systems. *Manufacturing Letters*, *3*, 18–23. DOI: 10.1016/j.mfglet.2014.12.001

Lee, J., Wu, F., Zhao, W., Ghaffari, M., Liao, L., & Siegel, D. (2014). Prognostics and health management design for rotary machinery systems. *Mechanical Systems and Signal Processing*, *42*(1-2), 314–334. DOI: 10.1016/j.ymssp.2013.06.004

Lehmann, J., Lober, A., Häußermann, T., Rache, A., Ollinger, L., Baumgärtel, H., & Reichwald, J. (2023). The anatomy of the internet of digital twins: A symbiosis of agent and digital twin paradigms enhancing resilience (not only) in manufacturing environments. *Machines (Basel)*, *11*(5), 504. DOI: 10.3390/machines11050504

Lei, Y., Yang, B., Jiang, X., Jia, F., Li, N., & Nandi, A. K. (2020). Applications of machine learning to machine fault diagnosis: A review and roadmap. *Mechanical Systems and Signal Processing*, *138*, 106587. DOI: 10.1016/j.ymssp.2019.106587

Leng, J., Wang, D., Shen, W., Li, X., Liu, Q., & Chen, X. (2021). Digital twins-based smart manufacturing system design in Industry 4.0: A review. *Journal of Manufacturing Systems*, *60*, 119–137. DOI: 10.1016/j.jmsy.2021.05.011

Leng, J., Zhang, H., Yan, D., Liu, Q., Chen, X., & Zhang, D. (2019). Digital twin-driven manufacturing cyber-physical system for parallel controlling of smart workshop. *Journal of Ambient Intelligence and Humanized Computing*, *10*(3), 1155–1166.

Leng, S., Yang, X., Jiang, Z., Wei, Y., & Wang, C. (2026). Dynamic simulation and optimization approach for coevolutionary intelligent manufacturing cell with digital twin. *International Journal of Advanced Manufacturing Technology*, •••, 1–16.

Lezoche, M., & Torres, D. (2024, June). What the Semantic Web Can Do for Cognitive Digital Twins: Challenges and Opportunities. In *International Workshop on Collaboration in Knowledge Discovery and Decision Making* (pp. 224-237). Cham: Springer Nature Switzerland. DOI: 10.1007/978-3-031-91690-8_18

Li, J., Yan, W., Zhang, M., Zhu, S., Jiang, Z., & Fan, Z. (2026). Digital twin-based multi-view energy efficiency prediction for machining systems. Digital Twin, 2634493.

Li, Y. (2025). AI-Enhanced Digital Twins for Energy Efficiency and Carbon Footprint Reduction in Smart City Infrastructure. *Applied and Computational Engineering*, 42-47.

Lian, M., Li, L., Wang, S., Wang, C., & Li, M. (2026). Design and research of IIoT intelligent automatic production line security monitoring system based on digital twin. *International Journal of Computer Applications in Technology*, *78*(1), 13–24.

Li, J., Song, H., & Ma, Y. (2026). The mechanism and impact of digital transformation on supply chain resilience in the manufacturing industry. *Scientific Reports*, *16*(1), 7635. DOI: 10.1038/s41598-026-38930-9 PMID: 41652069

Liker, J. K. (2004). *The Toyota way: 14 management principles from the world's greatest manufacturer*. McGraw-Hill.

Liker, J. K., & Meier, D. (2006). *The Toyota way fieldbook*. McGraw-Hill.

Li, M., Yang, C. M., Lo, W., & Kao, Y. W. (2026). A Digital-Twin-Enabled AI-Driven Adaptive Planning Platform for Sustainable and Reliable Manufacturing. *Machines (Basel)*, *14*(2), 197.

Lim, B., Arik, S. O., Loeff, N., & Pfister, T. (2021). Temporal fusion transformers for interpretable multi-horizon time series forecasting. *International Journal of Forecasting*, *37*(4), 1748–1764. DOI: 10.1016/j.ijforecast.2021.03.012

Lin, C. Y., Tseng, T. L., & Tsai, T. H. (2026). A Digital Twin Framework With Deep Feature Extraction and Gaussian Process for Multi-Objective Optimization in Semiconductor Manufacturing. *IEEE Transactions on Automation Science and Engineering*, *23*, 1928–1949. DOI: 10.1109/TASE.2025.3650620

Lin, C. Y., Tseng, T. L., & Tsai, T. H. (2026). Adaptive Reinforcement Learning-Driven Digital Twin for Multi-Objective and Multi-Machine Process Optimization. *IEEE Transactions on Artificial Intelligence*, 1–15. DOI: 10.1109/TAI.2026.3655629

Lin, T. Y., Ming-Fang Yen, A., Li-Sheng Chen, S., Hsu, C. Y., Yeh, Y. P., & Hsiu-Hsi Chen, T. (2025a). Artificial intelligence for precision viral surveillance of emerging infectious disease (EID): Data-driven digital twin metaverse-envisioned study. *Computers in Biology and Medicine*, *196*, 110877. Advance online publication. DOI: 10.1016/j.compbiomed.2025.110877 PMID: 40773996

Lin, Y. C., & Dang, J. F. (2026). From product specifications to smart manufacturing: Generative AI-driven process innovation for BOM digitization and its applications. *Advanced Engineering Informatics*, *71*, 104451. DOI: 10.1016/j.aei.2026.104451

Liu, C., Zhang, X., & Song, X. (2022). A survey of deep reinforcement learning for intelligent production scheduling. *Journal of Manufacturing Systems*, *64*, 579–596.

Loia, F., Perillo, C., & Gravili, G. (2026a). Unleashing the power of digital twin and big data as a new frontier for smart mobility: An ecosystem perspective. *Big Data Research*, *43*, 100576. Advance online publication. DOI: 10.1016/j.bdr.2025.100576

Lundberg, S. M., & Lee, S. I. (2017). A unified approach to interpreting model predictions. *Advances in Neural Information Processing Systems*, *30*, 4765–4774.

Luo, R., Zhou, S., Nie, L., Dong, B., & Guo, W. (2026). Digital twin-based resistance spot welding control. *International Journal of Advanced Manufacturing Technology*, •••, 1–14.

Lu, Y., Liu, C., & Wang, K. I.. (2020). Digital Twin-driven smart manufacturing. *Journal of Manufacturing Systems*, *58*, 319–331.

Lu, Y., Liu, C., Wang, K. I.-K., Huang, H., & Xu, X. (2020). Digital twin-driven smart manufacturing: Connotation, reference model, applications and research issues. *Robotics and Computer-integrated Manufacturing*, *61*, 101837. DOI: 10.1016/j.rcim.2019.101837

Lu, Y., Xu, X., & Wang, L. (2022). Smart manufacturing process and system automation: A critical review of the standards and envisioned scenarios. *Journal of Manufacturing Systems*, *56*, 312–325. DOI: 10.1016/j.jmsy.2020.06.010

Lyytinen, K., Weber, B., Becker, M. C., & Pentland, B. T. (2024). Digital twins of organization: Implications for organization design. *Journal of Organization Design*, *13*(3), 77–93. DOI: 10.1007/s41469-023-00151-z

MaaSAI Consortium. (2025). *MaaSAI Deliverable D5.1: MaaSAI Architecture* (Horizon Europe Project MaaSAI; public deliverable).

Macal, C. M., & North, M. J. (2010). Tutorial on agent-based modelling and simulation. *Journal of Simulation*, *4*(3), 151–162. DOI: 10.1057/jos.2010.3

Makridakis, S., Spiliotis, E., & Assimakopoulos, V. (2018). Statistical and machine learning forecasting methods: Concerns and ways forward. *PLoS One*, *13*(3), e0194889. DOI: 10.1371/journal.pone.0194889

Manyika, J., Chui, M., Bughin, J., Dobbs, R., Bisson, P., & Marrs, A. (2013). *Disruptive technologies: Advances that will transform life, business, and the global economy*. McKinsey Global Institute.

Marah, H., & Challenger, M. (2024). Adaptive hybrid reasoning for agent-based digital twins of distributed multi-robot systems. *Simulation*, *100*(9), 931–957. DOI: 10.1177/00375497231226436

Marfoglia, A., D'Errico, C., Mellone, S., & Carbonaro, A. (2026). A Knowledge Graph-Driven Framework for Deploying AI-Powered Patient Digital Twins. *Future Generation Computer Systems*, *108380*, 108380. Advance online publication. DOI: 10.1016/j.future.2026.108380

Márquez, A. C., & Fernández, J. F. G. (2026). Agentic AI for autonomous preventive maintenance policy governance: A multi-agent framework for dynamic industrial environments. *Expert Systems with Applications*, *314*, 131767. DOI: 10.1016/j.eswa.2026.131767

McKelvey, R. D., & Palfrey, T. R. (1995). Quantal response equilibria for normal form games. *Games and Economic Behavior*, *10*(1), 6–38. DOI: 10.1006/game.1995.1023

McKone, K. E., Schroeder, R. G., & Cua, K. O. (1999). Total productive maintenance: A contextual view. *Journal of Operations Management*, *17*(2), 123–144. DOI: 10.1016/S0272-6963(98)00039-4

Mehmood, Y., Ahmad, F., Yaqoob, I., Adnane, A., Imran, M., & Guizani, S. (2017). Internet of Things-based smart cities: Recent advances and challenges. *IEEE Communications Magazine*, *55*(1), 16–24. DOI: 10.1109/MCOM.2017.1600514

Meller, R. D., & Dobson, K. (2022). Optimizing Amazon fulfillment center layouts with simulation and machine learning. *IISE Transactions*, *54*(5), 445–461.

Meng, T., & Song, S. (2026). Environmental regulation, greenization pressure and enterprise digital transformation: The role of government subsidy policies in China. *Post-Communist Economies*, •••, 1–28. DOI: 10.1080/14631377.2026.2634634

Milnor, J. (1953). Sums of positional games. *Contributions to the Theory of Games*, *2*, 291–301.

Mnih, V., Kavukcuoglu, K., Silver, D., Rusu, A. A., Veness, J., Bellemare, M. G., Graves, A., Riedmiller, M., Fidjeland, A. K., Ostrovski, G., Petersen, S., Beattie, C., Sadik, A., Antonoglou, I., King, H., Kumaran, D., Wierstra, D., Legg, S., & Hassabis, D. (2015). Human-level control through deep reinforcement learning. *Nature, 518*(7540), 529–533. DOI: 10.1038/nature14236

Mobley, R. K. (2002). *An introduction to predictive maintenance* (2nd ed.). Butterworth-Heinemann.

Mohammed, S. K., Singh, S., Mizouni, R., Otrok, H., & Damiani, E. (2026). Digital Twins Paradigm: A Systematic Review from the Reinforcement Learning Perspective. *ACM Computing Surveys*, *58*(7), 1–33. DOI: 10.1145/3777367

Möhring, M., Keller, B., Radowski, C. F., Blessmann, S., Breimhorst, V., & Müthing, K. (2022, June). Empirical insights into the challenges of implementing digital twins. In *Human Centred Intelligent Systems: Proceedings of KES-HCIS 2022 Conference* (pp. 229-239). Singapore: Springer Nature Singapore. DOI: 10.1007/978-981-19-3455-1_18

Moisescu, M. A., Sacala, I. S., Dumitrache, I., Caramihai, S. I., Barbulescu, B., & Danciuc, M. (2019). A cyber-physical systems approach to cognitive enterprise. *Periodicals of Engineering and Natural Sciences*, *7*(1), 337. Advance online publication. DOI: 10.21533/pen.v7i1.378

Montgomery, D. C. (2019). *Introduction to statistical quality control* (8th ed.). Wiley.

MOTIE. (Ministry of Trade, Industry and Energy). (2021). Korea smart factory support program annual report. Government of the Republic of Korea.

Mourtzis, D. (2020). Simulation in the design and operation of manufacturing systems: State of the art and new trends. *International Journal of Production Research*, *58*(7), 1927–1949. DOI: 10.1080/00207543.2019.1636321

Movahed, A. B., Aliahmadi, A., Parsanejad, M., & Nozari, H. (2023). A systematic review of collaboration in supply chain 4.0 with meta-synthesis method. *Supply Chain Analytics*, *4*, 100052. DOI: 10.1016/j.sca.2023.100052

Mukherjee, P. K. (2022, February). Artificial intelligence based smart government enterprise architecture (AI-SGEA) framework. In *International Symposium on Artificial Intelligence* (pp. 325-333). Cham: Springer Nature Switzerland. DOI: 10.1007/978-3-031-22485-0_30

Murphy, K. P. (2012). *Machine Learning: A Probabilistic Perspective*. MIT Press.

Myerson, R. B. (1978). Refinements of the Nash equilibrium concept. *International Journal of Game Theory*, *7*(2), 73–80. DOI: 10.1007/BF01753236

Nahavandi, S. (2019). Industry 5.0: A human-centric solution. *Sustainability (Basel)*, *11*(16), 4371. DOI: 10.3390/su11164371

Nakajima, S. (1988). *Introduction to TPM: Total productive maintenance*. Productivity Press.

Nash, J. F.Jr. (1950). Equilibrium points in n-person games. *Proceedings of the National Academy of Sciences of the United States of America*, *36*(1), 48–49. DOI: 10.1073/pnas.36.1.48

Nast, B., Reiz, A., Sandkuhl, K., & Stirna, J. (2022). Integrating Organizational and Technological Aspects of Digital Twin Engineering. In *PoEM Workshops*.

Nee, A. Y. C., Ong, S. K., Chryssolouris, G., & Mourtzis, D. (2012). Augmented reality applications in design and manufacturing. *CIRP Annals*, *61*(2), 657–679. DOI: 10.1016/j.cirp.2012.05.010

Negri, E., Fumagalli, L., & Macchi, M. (2017). A review of the roles of digital twin in CPS-based production systems. *Procedia Manufacturing*, *11*, 939–948. DOI: 10.1016/j.promfg.2017.07.198

Netland, T. H., & Powell, D. J. (Eds.). (2017). *The Routledge companion to lean management*. Routledge.

Nilsson, N. J. (2010). *The Quest for Artificial Intelligence*. Cambridge University Press.

Nisan, N., Roughgarden, T., Tardos, É., & Vazirani, V. V. (Eds.). (2007). *Algorithmic game theory*. Cambridge University Press. DOI: 10.1017/CBO9780511800481

Nozari, H. (2025). Integrating Neuromorphic Intelligence with Fuzzy Multi-Objective Models in Resilient Green Supply Chain Design. Process Integration and Optimization for Sustainability, 1-14.

Nozari, H. (2025). Integrating neuromorphic intelligence with fuzzy multi-objective models in resilient green supply chain design. *Process Integration and Optimization for Sustainability*, 1–14. DOI: 10.1007/s41660-025-00598-5

Nozari, H. (2026). Neuromorphic Computing and Cognitive Economics. In Industry 5.0's Impact on Economic Innovation (pp. 17-34). IGI Global Scientific Publishing.

Nozari, H. (2026). Urban Digital Twins and Data-Centric Architectures for the Emergent Economy 5.0. In Industry 5.0's Impact on Economic Innovation (pp. 51-70). IGI Global Scientific Publishing.

Nozari, H., & Nassar, S. (2025). Real-time data-driven multi-objective optimization in B2B marketing using digital twins. OPSEARCH, 1-27.

Nozari, H., & Yordanova, Z. (2025). A fuzzy–digital twin optimization framework for simultaneous management of waste and energy consumption in sustainable manufacturing. An International Journal of Optimization and Control: Theories & Applications, 25360152.

Nozari, H., & Yordanova, Z. (2025). An intelligent digital twin approach for optimizing multi-channel supply chains in uncertain environments. Green Technologies and Sustainability, 100309.

Nozari, H., & Yordanova, Z. (2026). A self-deciding adaptive digital twin framework using agentic AI for fuzzy multi-objective optimization of food logistics. *Algorithms, 19*(3), Article 218. DOI: 10.3390/a19030218[file:49]

Nozari, H., & Yordanova, Z. (2026). Digital twin–driven decision support for human capital management under uncertainty. Green Technologies and Sustainability, 100353.

Nozari, H., & Yordanova, Z. (2026). Green and Circular Supply Chain Finance Supported by Carbon-Twin Accounting. In Industry 5.0's Impact on Economic Innovation (pp. 99-116). IGI Global Scientific Publishing.

Nozari, H. (2025). *Artificial Intelligence of Everything and Sustainable Development*. Springer. DOI: 10.1007/978-981-96-7202-8

Nozari, H. (2026). Digital twin-based predictive maintenance in cold chain logistics. *Operations Research, 60*(1), 481–499. DOI: 10.1051/ro/2025167

Nozari, H. (2026). Urban digital twins and data-centric architectures for the emergent economy 5.0. In *Industry 5.0's impact on economic innovation* (pp. 51–70). IGI Global Scientific Publishing., DOI: 10.4018/979-8-3693-4525-2.ch004

Nozari, H. (Ed.). (2023). *Building smart and sustainable businesses with transformative technologies*. IGI Global. DOI: 10.4018/979-8-3693-0210-1

Nozari, H., Abdi, H., Szmelter-Jarosz, A., & Rahmaty, M. (2025). A digital twin-based neutrosophic multi-objective optimization model for smart supply chains in the food industry. *Journal of Intelligent Manufacturing*, •••, 1–15. DOI: 10.1007/s10845-025-02689-z

Nozari, H., Ghahremani-Nahr, J., & Najafi, E. (2023). The role of Internet of things and Blockchain in the development of agile and sustainable supply chains. In *Digital supply chain, disruptive environments, and the impact on retailers* (pp. 271–282). IGI Global Scientific Publishing. DOI: 10.4018/978-1-6684-7298-9.ch015

Nozari, H., Nassar, S., & Szmelter-Jarosz, A. (2025). Fuzzy multi-objective optimization model for resilient supply chain financing based on blockchain and IoT. *Digital*, *5*(3), 32. DOI: 10.3390/digital5030032

Nozari, H., & Szmelter-Jarosz, A. (2025). A Predictive Maintenance Approach for Composting Plants Based on ERP and Digital Twin Integration. *Machines (Basel)*, *13*(12), 1123.

Nozari, H., Szmelter-Jarosz, A., & Weiland, D. (2025). A Fuzzy Multi-Objective Sustainable and Agile Supply Chain Model Based on Digital Twin and Internet of Things with Adaptive Learning Under Environmental Uncertainty. *Applied Sciences (Basel, Switzerland)*, *15*(19), 10399. DOI: 10.3390/app151910399

Nozari, H., & Yordanova, Z. (2026). An Adaptive Fuzzy Multi-Objective Digital Twin Framework for Multi-Depot Cold-Chain Vehicle Routing in Agri-Biotech Supply Networks. *Logistics (Basel)*, *10*(2), 27.

Nozari, H., & Yordanova, Z. (2026a). Fuzzy multi-objective digital twin framework for dynamic pricing and assortment optimization in metaverse-based retail environments. *Journal of Revenue and Pricing Management*. Advance online publication. DOI: 10.1057/s41272-026-00586-5

Nozari, H., & Yordanova, Z. (2026b). A self-deciding adaptive digital twin framework using agentic AI for fuzzy multi-objective optimization of food logistics. *Algorithms*, *19*(3), 218. DOI: 10.3390/a19030218

O'Leary, T., & Armfield, T. (2020). Adapting to the digital transformation. *Alberta Law Review*, *58*(2), 249–272. DOI: 10.29173/alr2618

OECD. (2019). *OECD going digital: Shaping policies, improving lives*. Organisation for Economic Cooperation and Development.

Ohno, T. (1988). *Toyota production system: Beyond large-scale production*. Productivity Press.

Okegbile, S. D., Cai, J., Niyato, D., & Shen, X. (2026). Leveraging Knowledge-Driven Large Language Models-Enabled Intent-Based Security Architectures for Human Digital Twin Networks. *IEEE Network*, 1–9. DOI: 10.1109/MNET.2025.3649156

Olawade, D. B., Oisakede, E. O., Bello, O. J., Analikwu, C. C., Egbon, E., & Ojo, A. (2026). Digital twins in oncology: From predictive modelling to personalised treatment strategies. *Critical Reviews in Oncology/Hematology, 220*, 105171. Advance online publication. DOI: 10.1016/j.critrevonc.2026.105171 PMID: 41621635

Oreshkin, B. N., Carpov, D., Chapados, N., & Bengio, Y. (2020). N-BEATS: Neural basis expansion analysis for interpretable time series forecasting. *International Conference on Learning Representations (ICLR).*

Oroojlooy, A., & Nazari, M. (2021). A review of cooperative multi-agent deep reinforcement learning. *Applied Intelligence, 53*(11), 13677–13722. DOI: 10.1007/s10489-022-04105-y

Ouedraogo, E. B., Hawbani, A., Wang, X., Liu, Z., Zhao, L., Al-qaness, M. A., & Alsamhi, S. H. (2025). Digital twin data management: A comprehensive review. *IEEE Transactions on Big Data, 11*(5), 2224–2243. DOI: 10.1109/TBDATA.2025.3533891

Padhamnath, P. (2026). AIoT-Driven Robotics System in Smart Manufacturing Sectors. In *AIoT-Driven Sustainable Manufacturing and Operational Initiatives* (pp. 174–193). CRC Press. DOI: 10.1201/9781003503323-10

Palmarini, R., Erkoyuncu, J. A., Roy, R., & Torabmostaedi, H. (2018). A systematic review of augmented reality applications in maintenance. *Robotics and Computer-integrated Manufacturing, 49*, 215–228. DOI: 10.1016/j.rcim.2017.06.002

Panneerselvam, A. (2021). Intelligent workflow adaptation in cognitive enterprise: design and techniques. In *Operationalizing Multi-Cloud Environments: Technologies, Tools and Use Cases* (pp. 309–324). Springer International Publishing., DOI: 10.1007/978-3-030-74402-1_17

Pan, Y., Huang, Z., Lev, B., Xu, L., & Olson, D. (2026). A literature review on the artificial intelligence in manufacturing systems under industry 5.0. *International Journal of Production Research*, •••, 1–42. DOI: 10.1080/00207543.2026.2623537

Papadimitriou, C. H. (1994). On the complexity of the parity argument and other inefficient proofs of existence. *Journal of Computer and System Sciences, 48*(3), 498–532. DOI: 10.1016/S0022-0000(05)80063-7

Patel, U. R., Ghaffarianhoseini, A., GhaffarianHoseini, A., & Burgess, A. (2026). Towards a well-being-oriented framework for urban digital twins. *Cities (London, England), 169*, 106579. DOI: 10.1016/j.cities.2025.106579

Pater, J., & Stadnicka, D. (2021). Towards Digital Twins Development and Implementation to Support Sustainability Systematic Literature Review. *Management and Production Engineering Review*, 63-73.

Paul, S., Manna, N., Roy, S., & Jana, T. K. (2026, January). A Machine Tool Digital Twin to Implement Smartness in Discrete Production Environment. In Recent Advances in Industrial and Systems Engineering: Selected Papers from International Conference on Industrial Engineering and Analytics (ICONIEA) 2024 (pp. 223-247). Singapore: Springer Nature Singapore.

Paul, S., Manna, N., Roy, S., & Jana, T. K. (2026, January). A Machine Tool Digital Twin to Implement Smartness in Discrete Production Environment. In Recent Advances in Industrial and Systems Engineering: Selected Papers from International Conference on Industrial Engineering and Analytics (ICONIEA) 2024 (pp. 223-247). Singapore: Springer Nature Singapore. DOI: 10.1007/978-981-96-8323-9_14

Pavleska, T. (2026a). Taxonomy of digital twins for power grids. *Advanced Engineering Informatics*, *70*, 104124. DOI: 10.1016/j.aei.2025.104124

Pearl, J. (2009). *Causality: Models, reasoning, and inference* (2nd ed.). Cambridge University Press. DOI: 10.1017/CBO9780511803161

Peffers, K., Tuunanen, T., Rothenberger, M. A., & Chatterjee, S. (2007). A design science research methodology for information systems research. *Journal of Management Information Systems*, *24*(3), 45–77. DOI: 10.2753/MIS0742-1222240302

Pei, J., & Takahashi, S. (2019). Nash equilibria in random games with right fat-tailed distributions. *Economic Theory*, *68*, 813–845.

Peng, L., Zhaojin, D., Disheng, Z., Hui, L., Xujiang, L., Weichao, C., & Wang, D. (2026). A Multi-Objective Optimization Framework for Energy–Efficiency Balance in Intelligent Tobacco Logistics Parks Based on NSGA-II. *International Journal of Pattern Recognition and Artificial Intelligence*.

Peng, Y., Dong, M., & Zuo, M. J. (2010). Current status of machine prognostics in condition-based maintenance. *International Journal of Advanced Manufacturing Technology*, *50*(1-4), 297–313. DOI: 10.1007/s00170-009-2482-0

Picone, M., Mamei, M., & Zambonelli, F. (2021). WLDT: A general purpose library to build IoT digital twins. *SoftwareX*, *13*, 100661. DOI: 10.1016/j.softx.2021.100661

Pinedo, M. L. (2016). *Scheduling: Theory, algorithms, and systems* (5th ed.). Springer. DOI: 10.1007/978-3-319-26580-3

Pop, E., Iliuţă, M. E., & Moisescu, M. A. (2024, October). Digital twin architecture based on services interoperability. In 2024 15th International Conference on Communications (COMM) (pp. 1-6). IEEE. DOI: 10.1109/COMM62355.2024.10741458

Porter, M. E., & Heppelmann, J. E. (2014). How smart, connected products are transforming competition. *Harvard Business Review, 92*(11), 64–88.

Pratitajati, E., Lestari, Y. D., & Okdinawati, L. (2026). Reframing innovation adoption in high compliance sectors: A multi-level perspective on digital twins for circular economy in pharmaceuticals. *International Journal of Innovation Science*, •••, 1–26. DOI: 10.1108/IJIS-07-2025-0344

Preskill, J. (2018). Quantum computing in the NISQ era and beyond. *Quantum : the Open Journal for Quantum Science, 2*, 79. DOI: 10.22331/q-2018-08-06-79

Provost, F., & Fawcett, T. (2013). *Data Science for Business*. O'Reilly Media.

Putz, B., Dietz, M., Empl, P., & Pernul, G. (2021). Ethertwin: Blockchain-based secure digital twin information management. *Information Processing & Management, 58*(1), 102425. DOI: 10.1016/j.ipm.2020.102425

Pu, Y., Pan, X., Shang, X., Li, M., & Zhang, M. (2024). Cyber Physical Integrated Digital Twin Network Model for Enterprise Producing High-Performing Logistics. *Wireless Personal Communications*, •••, 1–18.

Qian, C., Liu, X., Ripley, C., Qian, M., Liang, F., & Yu, W. (2022). Digital twin—Cyber replica of physical things: Architecture, applications and future research directions. *Future Internet, 14*(2), 64.

Qiu, P. (2014). *Introduction to statistical process control*. CRC Press.

Qiu, S., Zaheer, Q., Ali, F., Wajid, S., Chen, H., Ai, C., & Wang, J. (2025). EXPLORING THE IMPACT OF DIGITAL TWIN TECHNOLOGY IN INFRASTRUCTURE MANAGEMENT: A COMPREHENSIVE REVIEW. *Journal of Civil Engineering and Management, 31*(4), 395–417. Advance online publication. DOI: 10.3846/jcem.2025.23718

Qu, Y., Zhao, N., & Zhang, H. (2026). Digital Twin-Driven Joint predictive and optimization scheduling Method for Parcel Sorting Systems. Digital Engineering, 100092.

Raghupathi, W., & Raghupathi, V. (2014). Big data analytics in healthcare. *Health Information Science and Systems, 2*(1), 3. DOI: 10.1186/2047-2501-2-3

Ransbotham, S., Kiron, D., Gerbert, P., & Reeves, M. (2017). Reshaping business with artificial intelligence. *MIT Sloan Management Review, 59*(1), 1–17.

Rasheed, A., San, O., & Kvamsdal, T. (2020). Digital Twin: Values, Challenges and Enablers From a Modeling Perspective. *IEEE Access : Practical Innovations, Open Solutions*, *8*, 21980–22012. Advance online publication. DOI: 10.1109/ACCESS.2020.2970143

Rathore, M. M., Shah, S. A., Shukla, D., Bentafat, E., & Bakiras, S. (2021). The Role of AI, Machine Learning, and Big Data in Digital Twinning: A Systematic Literature Review, Challenges, and Opportunities. *IEEE Access : Practical Innovations, Open Solutions*, *9*, 32030–32052. Advance online publication. DOI: 10.1109/ACCESS.2021.3060863

Ren, L., Cui, J., Sun, Y., & Cheng, X. (2018). Multi-bearing remaining useful life collaborative prediction: A deep learning approach. *Journal of Manufacturing Systems*, *43*, 248–256. DOI: 10.1016/j.jmsy.2017.02.013

Reuther, A., Plesker, C., Bassauer, D., & Schleich, B. (2026). A Digital Twin Framework for Programmable Logic Controllers in Industrial Automation Systems. *Procedia CIRP*, *139*, 446–452. DOI: 10.1016/j.procir.2025.08.193

Riedl, M., Zipper, H., Meier, M., & Diedrich, C. (2017). Cyber-physical systems alter automation architectures. *Annual Reviews in Control*, *38*(1), 123–133. DOI: 10.1016/j.arcontrol.2014.03.012

Rojek, I., Mikołajewski, D., Dostatni, E., Cybulski, J., & Kozielski, M. (2025). Personalization of ai-based digital twins to optimize adaptation in industrial design and manufacturing. *Applied Sciences (Basel, Switzerland)*, *15*(15), 8525. DOI: 10.3390/app15158525

Romero, D., Bernus, P., Noran, O., Stahre, J., & Fast-Berglund, A. (2016). The operator 4.0: Human cyber-physical systems and adaptive automation. *IFIP Advances in Information and Communication Technology*, *488*, 677–686. DOI: 10.1007/978-3-319-51133-7_80

Rosen, K. M., & Pattipati, K. R. (2023). Operating digital twins within an enterprise process. In *The digital twin* (pp. 599–659). Springer International Publishing., DOI: 10.1007/978-3-031-21343-4_22

Rosen, R., von Wichert, G., Lo, G., & Bettenhausen, K. D. (2015). About the importance of autonomy and digital twins for the future of manufacturing. *IFAC-PapersOnLine*, *48*(3), 567–572. DOI: 10.1016/j.ifacol.2015.06.141

Rossmann, A., & Hertweck, D. (2022). Digital Twins: A Meta-Review on Their Conceptualization, Application, and Reference Architecture. *Hawaii International Conference on System Sciences.* DOI: 10.24251/HICSS.2022.550

Rother, M., & Shook, J. (1998). *Learning to see: Value stream mapping to add value and eliminate muda*. Lean Enterprise Institute.

Roughgarden, T. (2005). *Selfish routing and the price of anarchy*. MIT Press.

Rusal, A., Iqbal, M., Anwar, W., & Gul, M. (2019). Industry 4.0: Technological revolution and its impact on value chain. *International Journal of Supply Chain Management*, *8*(6), 921–935.

Russell, S., & Norvig, P. (2020). *Artificial intelligence: A modern approach* (4th ed.). Pearson.

Russell, S., & Norvig, P. (2021). *Artificial Intelligence: A Modern Approach* (4th ed.). Pearson.

Russom, P. (2011). Big data analytics. *TDWI Best Practices Report*, *19*(4), 1–34.

Sacoto-Cabrera, E. J., Perez-Torres, A., Tello-Oquendo, L., & Cerrada, M. (2025). IoT, AI, and Digital Twins in Smart Cities: A Systematic Review for a Thematic Mapping and Research Agenda. *Smart Cities*, 175.

Salinas, D., Flunkert, V., Gasthaus, J., & Januschowski, T. (2020). DeepAR: Probabilistic forecasting with autoregressive recurrent networks. *International Journal of Forecasting*, *36*(3), 1181–1191. DOI: 10.1016/j.ijforecast.2019.07.001

Sanders, A., Elangeswaran, C., & Wulfsberg, J. P. (2016). Industry 4.0 implies lean manufacturing: Research activities in industry 4.0 function as enablers for lean manufacturing. *Journal of Industrial Engineering and Management*, *9*(3), 811–833. DOI: 10.3926/jiem.1940

San, O., Rasheed, A., Bozdemir, E., & Deng, J. (2026). The evolution of digital twins from reactive to agentic systems. *Nature Computational Science*, *6*(1), 6–10. DOI: 10.1038/s43588-025-00944-0 PMID: 41612013

Santos, R., Piqueiro, H., Dias, R., & Rocha, C. D. (2024). Transitioning trends into action: A simulation-based Digital Twin architecture for enhanced strategic and operational decision-making. *Computers & Industrial Engineering*, *198*, 110616. DOI: 10.1016/j.cie.2024.110616

Satyanarayanan, M. (2017). The emergence of edge computing. *Computer*, *50*(1), 30–39. DOI: 10.1109/MC.2017.9

Schaefer, T. J. (1978). On the complexity of some two-person perfect-information games. *Journal of Computer and System Sciences*, *16*(2), 185–225. DOI: 10.1016/0022-0000(78)90045-4

Scheffer, C., & Girdhar, P. (2004). *Practical machinery vibration analysis and predictive maintenance*. Newnes.

Schink, A., Gutmann, T., & Brenk, S. (2026a). Transforming B2B platforms through interconnected digital twins: Enhancing situation awareness for decision-making. *Technovation, 149*, 103368. Advance online publication. DOI: 10.1016/j.technovation.2025.103368

Schluse, M., Priggemeyer, M., Atorf, L., & Rossmann, J. (2018). Experimentable digital twins: Streamlining simulation-based systems engineering for Industry 4.0. *IEEE Transactions on Industrial Informatics, 14*(4), 1722–1731. DOI: 10.1109/TII.2018.2804917

Schmidhuber, J. (2015). Deep learning in neural networks: An overview. *Neural Networks, 61*, 85–117. DOI: 10.1016/j.neunet.2014.09.003

Schmitt, A. J., & Singh, M. (2012). A quantitative analysis of disruption risk in a multi-echelon supply chain. *International Journal of Production Economics, 139*(1), 22–32. DOI: 10.1016/j.ijpe.2012.01.004

Schnellmann, M. (2025, May). Towards an Enterprise Architecture Based Approach for the Development of Digital Twins for Sustainable Real Estate Management. In *International Conference on Research Challenges in Information Science* (pp. 207-217). Cham: Springer Nature Switzerland. DOI: 10.1007/978-3-031-92471-2_17

Schwab, K. (2016). The fourth industrial revolution. World Economic Forum.

Schwab, K. (2017). *The fourth industrial revolution*. World Economic Forum.

Scolamiero, V., & Boccardo, P. (2026). A BIM-Based Digital Twin Framework for Urban Roads: Integrating MMS and Municipal Geospatial Data for AI-Ready Urban Infrastructure Management. *Sensors (Basel), 26*(3), 947. DOI: 10.3390/s26030947

Selten, R. (1975). Reexamination of the perfectness concept for equilibrium points in extensive games. *International Journal of Game Theory, 4*(1), 25–55. DOI: 10.1007/BF01766400

Serpanos, D., & Wolf, M. (2018). *Industrial internet of things*. Springer.

Shah, R., & Ward, P. T. (2007). Defining and developing measures of lean production. *Journal of Operations Management, 25*(4), 785–805. DOI: 10.1016/j.jom.2007.01.019

Sharda, R., Delen, D., & Turban, E. (2018). *Business intelligence, analytics, and data science: A managerial perspective* (4th ed.). Pearson.

Sharma, A., Kosasih, E., Zhang, J., Brintrup, A., & Calinescu, A. (2022). Digital Twins: State of the art theory and practice, challenges, and open research Questions. *Journal of Industrial Information Integration*, *30*, 100383. Advance online publication. DOI: 10.1016/j.jii.2022.100383

Sheffi, Y. (2005). *The resilient enterprise: Overcoming vulnerability for competitive advantage*. MIT Press.

Shen, B., Zeng, Y., Yu, H., Hu, P., Han, Z., & Cai, H. (2026). A Verifiable Digital Twin-aided AI (DTAI) Agent-based Production System Framework with Causally Consistent Symbiotic Simulation. IEEE Transactions on Industrial Cyber-Physical Systems.

Shewhart, W. A. (1931). *Economic control of quality of manufactured product. D.* Van Nostrand.

Shingo, S. (1989). *A study of the Toyota production system from an industrial engineering viewpoint*. Productivity Press.

Shi, W., Cao, J., Zhang, Q., Li, Y., & Xu, L. (2016). Edge computing: Vision and challenges. *IEEE Internet of Things Journal*, *3*(5), 637–646. DOI: 10.1109/JIOT.2016.2579198

Shmueli, G., & Koppius, O. R. (2011). Predictive analytics in information systems research. *Management Information Systems Quarterly*, *35*(3), 553–572. DOI: 10.2307/23042796

Shoham, Y., & Leyton-Brown, K. (2009). *Multiagent systems: Algorithmic, game-theoretic, and logical foundations*. Cambridge University Press.

Siegel, A. N. (2013). *Combinatorial game theory*. American Mathematical Society. DOI: 10.1090/gsm/146

Siegel, E. (2016). *Predictive Analytics: The Power to Predict Who Will Click, Buy, Lie, or Die*. Wiley.

Siemens, A. G. (2019). *Amberg electronics plant: Where digitalization meets reality*. Siemens Communications.

Simchi-Levi, D., Kaminsky, P., & Simchi-Levi, E. (2014). *Designing and managing the supply chain: Concepts, strategies, and case studies* (3rd ed.). McGraw-Hill.

Simchi-Levi, D., Wang, H., & Wei, Y. (2018). Increasing supply chain robustness through process flexibility and inventory. *Production and Operations Management*, *27*(8), 1476–1491. DOI: 10.1111/poms.12887

Singamsetty, S., Singamsetty, S., Satyanarayana, S., & Kumar, P. R. (2026, February). Next-Generation Digital Twin Analytics in Smart Manufacturing using Cross-Layered Edge Cloud Deep Learning. In 2026 IEEE 5th International Conference on AI in Cybersecurity (ICAIC) (pp. 1-6). IEEE. DOI: 10.1109/ICAIC67076.2026.11395731

Sisinni, E., Saifullah, A., Han, S., Jennehag, U., & Gidlund, M. (2018). Industrial internet of things: Challenges, opportunities, and directions. *IEEE Transactions on Industrial Informatics*, *14*(11), 4724–4734. DOI: 10.1109/TII.2018.2852491

Sivarethinamohan, R., Elamurugan, B., & Aranganathan, P. (2026). Benefits and Challenges of Industrial Robotics in Smart Manufacturing. In Industrial Robotics in Smart Manufacturing (pp. 119-136). CRC Press.

Skobelev, P., Laryukhin, V., Simonova, E., Goryanin, O., Yalovenko, V., & Yalovenko, O. (2020, September). Multi-agent approach for developing a digital twin of wheat. In 2020 IEEE international conference on smart computing (SMARTCOMP) (pp. 268-273). IEEE.

Sompolgrunk, A., Golzad, H., Liu, H., Banihashemi, S., & Najafi, M. (2026). The evolution of digital twins within the big BIM data landscape. Smart and Sustainable Built Environment, 1-28.

Son, Y. H. (2026). Digital twin–enabled hybrid scheduling framework for multi-product cellular manufacturing systems. International Journal of Computer Integrated Manufacturing, 1-23.

Soylu, B., & Yildiz, G. B. (2023, May). A Digital Twin-Based Decision Support System for Dynamic Labor Planning. In *International Symposium On Intelligent Manufacturing And Service Systems* (pp. 214-223). Singapore: Springer Nature Singapore. DOI: 10.1007/978-981-99-6062-0_20

Sprague, R. P. (1935). Über mathematische Kampfspiele. *Tohoku Mathematical Journal*, *41*, 438–444.

Stalidi, C., Popovici, E. C., & Suciu, G. (2025, August). Real-Time Digital Ecosystems: Integrating Virtual Personas and Digital Twins Through Microservices. In *International Conference on Availability, Reliability and Security* (pp. 128-141). Cham: Springer Nature Switzerland. DOI: 10.1007/978-3-032-00642-4_8

Stapleton, D., & Stapleton, K. M. (2022). Digital twins and Industry 4.0: A review of legal implications regarding property rights in physical and virtual spaces. *Journal of Transportation Law. Logistics and Policy*, *89*, 95–113.

Stark, J., Anderl, R., & Schleich, B. (2019). Digital twin: Research and applications in manufacturing. *Procedia Manufacturing*, *28*, 1–9.

Sterman, J. D. (2000). *Business dynamics: Systems thinking and modeling for a complex world.* McGraw-Hill.

Stockmeyer, L. J., & Chandra, A. K. (1979). Provably difficult combinatorial games. *SIAM Journal on Computing*, *8*(2), 151–174. DOI: 10.1137/0208013

Stone, P., & Veloso, M. (2000). Multiagent systems: A survey from a machine learning perspective. *Autonomous Robots*, *8*(3), 345–383. DOI: 10.1023/A:1008942012299

Story, B. (2023). Digital twins in healthcare: Proactive regulation to prevent a "runaway train". *North Carolina Journal of Law & Technology*, *25*(2), 315–343.

Stouffer, K., Falco, J., & Scarfone, K. (2015). Guide to industrial control systems (ICS) security. NIST Special Publication 800-82 Revision 2. National Institute of Standards and Technology.

Suetsugu, Y. (2018). Emperor Nim and emperor sum: A new sum of impartial games. *Discrete Mathematics*, *341*(7), 1907–1916.

Suetsugu, Y. (2020). Universal partisan rulesets and a universal partisan dicotic ruleset. *Theoretical Computer Science*, *806*, 260–273.

Sun, R. (2007). The challenges of building computational cognitive architectures. In *Challenges for Computational Intelligence* (pp. 37–60). Springer Berlin Heidelberg., DOI: 10.1007/978-3-540-71984-7_3

Tang, C. S. (2006). Perspectives in supply chain risk management. *International Journal of Production Economics*, *103*(2), 451–488. DOI: 10.1016/j.ijpe.2005.12.006

Tang, C. S., & Musa, S. N. (2011). Identifying risk issues and research advancements in supply chain risk management. *International Journal of Production Economics*, *133*(1), 25–34. DOI: 10.1016/j.ijpe.2010.06.013

Tao, F., Qi, Q., Wang, L., & Nee, A. Y. C. (2019). Digital twins and cyber–physical systems toward smart manufacturing and industry 4.0: Correlation and comparison. *Engineering*, *5*(4), 653–661.

Tao, F., Zhang, H., Liu, A., & Nee, A. (2019). Digital Twin in Industry: State-of-the-Art. *IEEE Transactions on Industrial Informatics*, *15*(4), 2405–2415. Advance online publication. DOI: 10.1109/TII.2018.2873186

Tao, F., Zhang, M., Liu, Y., & Nee, A. Y. C. (2018). Digital twin in manufacturing: A review. *Journal of Manufacturing Systems*, *48*, 157–169. DOI: 10.1016/j.jmsy.2018.01.006

Tao, F., Zhang, M., Liu, Y., & Nee, A. Y. C. (2019). *Digital twin driven smart manufacturing*. Academic Press.

Teece, D. J. (2018). Business models and dynamic capabilities. *Long Range Planning, 51*(1), 40–49. DOI: 10.1016/j.lrp.2017.06.007

Teng, X., Shen, Z., & Zhang, Y. (2025). Rule-based symbolic AI computing-driven digital twin model for ex-ante energy evaluation of task-ambience air conditioning systems in zero-energy buildings. *Sustainable Cities and Society, 134*, 106947. Advance online publication. DOI: 10.1016/j.scs.2025.106947

Tonelli, F., Paolucci, M., Giovannetti, A., Mosca, M., & Torterolo, L. (2026). Integrated 3D Simulation and Digital Twin Framework for Collaborative Production Process Design and Planning in Small and Medium Enterprises: A Use Case Analysis. *Procedia CIRP, 138*, 48–53. DOI: 10.1016/j.procir.2026.01.010

Topol, E. (2019). *Deep Medicine: How Artificial Intelligence Can Make Healthcare Human Again*. Basic Books.

Tordecilla, R. D., Juan, A. A., Montoya-Torres, J. R., Quintero-Araujo, C. L., & Panadero, J. (2021). Simulation-optimization methods for designing and assessing resilient supply chain networks under uncertainty scenarios: A review. *Simulation Modelling Practice and Theory, 106*, 102166. DOI: 10.1016/j.simpat.2020.102166

Toyota Motor Corporation. (2023). *Annual report 2023: Woven by Toyota*. Toyota Motor Corporation.

van Damme, E. (1991). *Stability and perfection of Nash equilibria* (2nd ed.). Springer. DOI: 10.1007/978-3-642-58242-4

Vial, G. (2019). Understanding digital transformation: A review and research agenda. *The Journal of Strategic Information Systems, 28*(2), 118–144. DOI: 10.1016/j.jsis.2019.01.003

Villegas, L. F., Macchi, M., & Polenghi, A. (2025). Conceptualization of a Platform Architecture for the Rapid Development of Digital Twins in Manufacturing. *Proceedings of the XXIX SUMMER SCHOOL "Francesco Turco"—Industrial Systems Engineering, Lecce, Italy*, 10-12.

Waller, M. A., & Fawcett, S. E. (2013). Data science, predictive analytics, and big data. *Journal of Business Logistics, 34*(2), 77–84. DOI: 10.1111/jbl.12010

Wan, J., Lin, S., & Wu, Q. (2023, May). The Concept and Connotation of Enterprise Digital Transformation. In *Wuhan International Conference on E-business* (pp. 315-324). Cham: Springer Nature Switzerland. DOI: 10.1007/978-3-031-32299-0_27

Wang, R. (2026). A Data-Driven Predictive Maintenance Framework for Smart Buildings: Integrating Digital Twin and Machine Learning in HVAC Systems. Journal of Building Engineering, 115416. Aklashie, S., Agyekum, K., Tchao, E. T., Adinyira, E., & Nani, G. (2026). Blockchain-digital twin integration in construction material passports: preparing for digital product passport implementation. Built Environment Project and Asset Management, 1-18. Nozari, H., & Yordanova, Z. (2026). Digital twin–driven decision support for human capital management under uncertainty. Green Technologies and Sustainability, 100353.

Warke, V., Kumar, S., Bongale, A., & Kotecha, K. (2021). Sustainable Development of Smart Manufacturing Driven by the Digital Twin Framework: A Statistical Analysis. *Sustainability (Basel)*, *13*(18), 10139. Advance online publication. DOI: 10.3390/su131810139

Watson, K. J., Blackstone, J. H., & Gardiner, S. C. (2007). The evolution of a management philosophy: The theory of constraints. *Journal of Operations Management*, *25*(2), 387–402. DOI: 10.1016/j.jom.2006.04.004

Weimer, D., Scholz-Reiter, B., & Shpitalni, M. (2016). Design of deep convolutional neural network architectures for automated feature extraction in industrial inspection. *CIRP Annals*, *65*(1), 417–420. DOI: 10.1016/j.cirp.2016.04.072

Westerman, G., Bonnet, D., & McAfee, A. (2014). *Leading digital: Turning technology into business transformation*. Harvard Business Review Press.

Wickremasinghe, G., Frost, S., Rafferty, K., & Sharma, V. (2025a). Sustainable business decision modelling with blockchain and digital twins: A survey. *Blockchain: Research and Applications*, *100312*. Advance online publication. DOI: 10.1016/j.bcra.2025.100312

Womack, J. P., & Jones, D. T. (1996). *Lean thinking: Banish waste and create wealth in your corporation*. Simon & Schuster.

Wooldridge, M. (2009). *An introduction to multiagent systems* (2nd ed.). Wiley.

World Economic Forum. (2020). The future of jobs report 2020. World Economic Forum.

Wu, J., Zhou, M., Xu, M., Zhang, J., Guo, Y., Zhang, Y., & Zhang, C. (2021, October). Research and design of a digital twin-based enterprise architecture digital control platform for provincial electrical power company. In 2021 6th international conference on control, robotics and cybernetics (CRC) (pp. 186-191). IEEE. DOI: 10.1109/CRC52766.2021.9620120

Wu, X., Yu, T., Liu, X., Yue, C., Jiang, X., Li, J., & Li, Z. (2026). Design of laser-assisted processing digital twin system. *Journal of Manufacturing Systems, 85*, 155–174. DOI: 10.1016/j.jmsy.2026.01.001

Xu, L. D., He, W., & Li, S. (2014). Internet of Things in industries: A survey. *IEEE Transactions on Industrial Informatics, 10*(4), 2233–2243. DOI: 10.1109/TII.2014.2300753

Xu, L. D., Xu, E. L., & Li, L. (2018). Industry 4.0: State of the art and future trends. *International Journal of Production Research, 56*(8), 2941–2962. DOI: 10.1080/00207543.2018.1444806

Xu, X., Lu, Y., Vogel-Heuser, B., & Wang, L. (2021). Industry 4.0 and digital twin. *Annual Reviews in Control, 51*, 1–15.

Xu, Z., Shan, X., Pan, R., Wu, W., & Liu, N. (2026). Nonlinear relationship between innovation input and intelligent manufacturing from an absorptive capacity perspective. *Scientific Reports, 16*(1), 7269. DOI: 10.1038/s41598-026-37926-9 PMID: 41639162

Yang, M., Pu, Z., Tavera, C., & Liu, G. (2026). Digital transformation and corporate financialization: Evidence against the tech bubble hypothesis. *Financial Innovation, 12*(1), 7. DOI: 10.1186/s40854-025-00800-0

Yan, S., & Jones, J. (2026). Ensuring Compliance in Digital Transformation: Developing and Validating the Data Management Stage Model (DMSM). *IEEE Transactions on Engineering Management, 73*, 1402–1428. DOI: 10.1109/TEM.2026.3653511

Yin, R. K. (2018). *Case study research and applications: Design and methods* (6th ed.). SAGE.

Yitmen, I. (2023). *Cognitive Digital Twins for Smart Lifecycle Management of Built Environment and Infrastructure*. CRC Press. DOI: 10.1201/9781003230199

Yoon, S., Ye, W., Snell, J., Best, H., & Tarvainen, M. (2020). Wearable sensors for human activity recognition and health assessment. *IEEE Reviews in Biomedical Engineering, 14*, 45–62.

Yordanova, Z., & Nozari, H. (2026). An Agentic Digital Twin Framework for Fuzzy Multi-Objective Optimization in Dynamic Humanitarian Logistics. *Algorithms, 19*(3), 198. DOI: 10.3390/a19030198

Yordanova, Z., & Nozari, H. (2026). Cross-layer optimization for energy efficiency in super-smart cities of the future. In *Energy-Efficient Transformative Technologies for Data-Driven Smart Cities* (pp. 125–144). Elsevier. DOI: 10.1016/B978-0-443-27618-7.00013-3

Zakaria, L., Akil, I., Dhiana, A., & Prayitno, E. (2025). Designing the SiMiTi Architecture: A Framework for Sustainable Digital Transformation in Intelligent Enterprises. *Jurnal ilmiah Sistem Informasi dan Ilmu Komputer, 5*(3). DOI: 10.55606/juisik.v5i3.1775

Zanella, A., Bui, N., Castellani, A., Vangelista, L., & Zorzi, M. (2014). Internet of Things for smart cities. *IEEE Internet of Things Journal, 1*(1), 22–32. DOI: 10.1109/JIOT.2014.2306328

Zhang, C., Song, W., Cao, Z., Zhang, J., Tan, P. S., & Chi, X. (2020). Learning to dispatch for job shop scheduling via deep reinforcement learning. *Advances in Neural Information Processing Systems, 33*, 1621–1632.

Zhang, C., & Xu, Y. (2026). How Does Digital Intelligence Empower Green Transformation in Manufacturing Companies? A Case Study Based on FAW-Volkswagen. *Sustainability (Basel), 18*(2), 1045. DOI: 10.3390/su18021045

Zhang, H. (2026). Research on enterprise digital strategy in the context of intelligent manufacturing: The application and impact of AIGC. *Technology Analysis and Strategic Management*, 1–15. DOI: 10.1080/09537325.2026.2620060

Zhang, J., Sun, J., Zhao, H., Huang, F., Xu, B., & Wang, Q. (2026). Toward Smart and Green Energy Stations: A Cognitive Digital Twin Framework for Intelligent Management. *IEEE Internet Computing*, 1–10. DOI: 10.1109/MIC.2025.3649567

Zheng, X., Lu, J., & Kiritsis, D. (2022). The emergence of cognitive digital twin: Vision, challenges and opportunities. *International Journal of Production Research, 60*(24), 7610–7632. DOI: 10.1080/00207543.2021.2014591

Zhong, R. Y., Xu, X., Klotz, E., & Newman, S. T. (2017). Intelligent manufacturing in the context of Industry 4.0: A review. *Engineering (Beijing), 3*(5), 616–630. DOI: 10.1016/J.ENG.2017.05.015

Zhou, K., Liu, T., & Zhou, L. (2015). Industry 4.0: Towards future industrial opportunities. *Procedia CIRP, 33*, 214–219.

Zsidisin, G. A., Ellram, L. M., Carter, J. R., & Cavinato, J. L. (2004). An analysis of supply risk assessment techniques. *International Journal of Physical Distribution & Logistics Management, 34*(5), 397–413. DOI: 10.1108/09600030410545445

About the Contributors

Zornitsa Yordanova is an academic, entrepreneur, and digital transformation expert specializing in AI, innovation management, digital twins, ICT, and organizational digitization. She currently serves as an Associate Professor at the University of National and World Economy (UNWE) in Sofia—the largest economic university in the Balkans—where she teaches Innovation & Technology Management and Digital Transformation / MIS. Her academic work includes more than 120 publications, with over 70 indexed in Scopus and Web of Science, and she holds an H-index of 12. She has successfully led multiple national research projects in education, innovation, and digital transformation. Beyond academia, Dr. Yordanova works at the intersection of research and industry. She has extensive experience as a project manager in international ICT initiatives, a trainer and consultant supporting organizations in their innovation and digital transformation journeys, and a founder of technology-driven ventures.

***

Infant Kavin F is an aspiring Computer Science engineer currently pursuing a Bachelor of Engineering in Computer Science under Anna University. As a dedicated learner with a strong interest in emerging technologies, programming, and research, he strives to build a solid foundation in both theoretical concepts and practical skills. He is passionate about exploring areas such as artificial intelligence, software development, and problem-solving. With a curiosity-driven approach to learning, he actively engages in academic projects, coding practice, and technical activities that help strengthen his engineering mindset. Committed to continuous growth, he aims to contribute to innovative solutions and pursue opportunities that connect technology with real-world impact. As he advances in his engineering journey, he looks forward to expanding his knowledge, participating in research, and shaping a promising career in the field of computing.

Silambarasan G possesses a comprehensive academic foundation, holding a Bachelor of Computer Applications (BCA) and a Master of Computer Applications (MCA), and is currently pursuing a Ph.D. (Full-Time) in the Department of Computer Science at Periyar University, Salem, Tamil Nadu, India. With over 08 years of teaching experience and 02 years of industry exposure, he has consistently demonstrated excellence in both academic and technical domains. His professional journey reflects a strong commitment to research, innovation, and pedagogical advancement in the rapidly evolving field of computer science. Renowned for his expertise in network administration, system architecture, virtualization, and emerging computing technologies, Silambarasan G continues to contribute significantly to the integration of theory and practical application. His academic and research pursuits exemplify a passion for technological innovation and a steadfast dedication to advancing the frontiers of computer science education.

Mohamed Shahil H is an independent researcher specializing in Artificial Intelligence and digital transformation. His work focuses on intelligent enterprise systems and data-driven decision-making strategies. He is passionate about innovation, sustainability, and human–AI collaboration. His research aims to develop adaptive and future-ready organizational frameworks.

Manickam I is an emerging researcher and technologist with a strong academic foundation in computer science. He is currently pursuing a Bachelor of Engineering in Computer Science under Anna University, where he has developed a keen interest in advancing the frontiers of computational intelligence and innovative system design. His research interests include Artificial Intelligence, Machine Learning, Data Science, and Intelligent Systems, with a focus on developing technologies that integrate efficiency, ethics, and social impact. Through his academic projects and self-driven explorations, Manickam has demonstrated a commitment to research excellence, critical inquiry, and interdisciplinary collaboration. Motivated by a vision to contribute to the growing body of research in intelligent computing, He aspires to pursue postgraduate studies and engage in impactful research addressing real-world challenges through technology-driven solutions.

Daniela Ilieva, PhD, is a distinguished Bulgarian professor in Management, renowned for bridging academia, business training, and nonprofit leadership. She excels in business communication, process management, and personal development, authoring Bulgaria's pioneering mentoring guide. She holds a Bachelor's in Business Administration (European University), Master's in Marketing, and Expert degree in International Tourism and Hospitality Management. Her 2015 PhD from UNWE focused on "Methodology for Perfecting Presentation Skills" in Social Management.

Promoted to Associate Professor in 2016 (Administration and Business Process Management) and full Professor in 2022 (Business Communication and Personal Development). Since 2015, she serves as Executive Director and Management Board Member at Law and Internet Foundation, leading EU projects as team lead and communication expert. Full-time Professor at VUZF University (head of Business Management and Marketing Research Department since 2018); guest lecturer at Sofia University "St. Kliment Ohridski", UNIBIT, and others. Founder of daniela.bg (2009) for corporate training. Prof. Daniela Ilieva, PhD, merges her academic expertise in management and business process optimization with her leadership at the Law and Internet Foundation to pioneer governance frameworks for digital transformation technologies like digital twins. As Executive Director since 2015, she has spearheaded projects addressing legal and ethical challenges in cyber-physical systems, directly informing her research on governance-enabled architectures for SME adoption of AI-IoT-digital twin ecosystems. This synergy positions her chapter in Transforming Physical Assets into Cognitive Enterprises with Digital Twins to offer practical, regulation-aware strategies for cognitive enterprises amid EU digital decade goals.

Anish K is currently pursuing a Bachelor of Engineering in Computer Science and Engineering with a strong interest in Artificial Intelligence and emerging technologies. He is passionate about exploring how AI can be applied to solve real-world problems, particularly in digital systems and medical imaging applications. He has successfully published a research paper in the International Journal of Science, Engineering and Technology (IJSET), reflecting his growing involvement in research and innovation. He has developed skills in programming, data analysis, and problem-solving through academic learning and practical exposure. Anish is a quick learner who enjoys working in collaborative team environments and continuously strives to enhance his technical and analytical abilities. His career goal is to design intelligent and innovative solutions that improve efficiency, accuracy, and user experience in modern digital platforms.

Daniel Raj K is a faculty member in the Department of Computer Science and Engineering (AI & ML) at Kalaignar Karunanidhi Institute of Technology, Coimbatore. He holds a B.Tech in Information Technology and an M.E in Computer Science Engineering. His work includes journal publications on neuromorphic computing and intelligent systems, as well as reviewing contributions for IEEE, IGI Global, and other SCOPUS-indexed venues. He has authored book chapters and continues to work on applied projects in machine learning and resilient communication systems.

Angelika Kokkinaki currently holds the position of Dean of the School of Business and serves as the MBA Director at the University of Nicosia. Her academic credentials are focused on Information Systems, with a PhD in Computer Science from the University of Louisiana at Lafayette (1995), a M.Sc. in Computer Science from Northeastern University (1991), and a Diploma in Computer Engineering and Informatics (5 year curriculum) from Patras University (1987). Prof. Kokkinaki's professional journey is marked by significant international exposure, having contributed to academia in the USA, the UK, and the Netherlands. Her expertise primarily spans across inter- and intra-organizational information systems, including e-business, e-government, e-learning, and e-innovation. Prof. Kokkinaki has been an integral part of over thirty national and European Union-funded projects, showcasing her commitment to advancing knowledge and practical applications in her field. Her recent scholarly activities have been focused on the domain of Smart Cities, where she has played pivotal roles in several high-impact projects.

Aprajita Parihar, 1st year student at NIFT Kannur, pursuing a Bachelor's in fashion technology; interests lay upon apparel manufacturing and designing as well as lean management; believes in sustainable, environment-friendly and animal-cruelty-free fashion.

Rajveer Rawlin received his Ph.D. from Bharathiar University, Tamil Nadu, India, and his MBA in finance from the Cardiff Metropolitan University, Wales, UK. He teaches in the Department of Business & Management at CHRIST University. His research interests include areas of Capital Markets, Investment Analysis, and Portfolio Management, and he has more than 25 years of experience in the above, covering the US and Indian Markets. He is the author of the popular financial blog Ahead of the Curve. He reviews for Emerald and Sage.

Rupayan Roy is an Assistant Professor in the Department of Fashion Technology at the National Institute of Fashion Technology (NIFT), Kannur. He holds a Ph.D. in Textile Engineering from IIT Delhi, with research focused on fibre orientation and nonwoven structures. His expertise includes technical textiles, composites, filtration, and IoT applications in apparel. He has extensive teaching and research experience, with numerous publications in reputed international journals and book chapters. Dr. Roy has received multiple fellowships and international travel grants, and actively contributes to advancing sustainable and high-performance textile technologies through research and academic engagement.

Gautam Shivaraj, with a comprehensive academic background including a Bachelor's in Mechanical Engineering, Master of Engineering Management (Australia), MBA,and is currently pursuing a Ph.D. brings an impressive 07 years of teaching experience alongside a brief stint in the industry of 5 years. Currently serving as an Assistant Professor at the Adarsh Institute of Management and Information Technology in Bangalore, Karnataka, India, he has distinguished himself in the academic and research fields. Prof.Gautam Shivaraj professional journey is a testament to his dedication to academia, research, in the evolving world.

Doni Sihotang is a doctoral student in Marketing at Jakarta State University, Indonesia. His academic background combines a Bachelor's degree in Social Anthropology from Universitas Sumatera Utara and a Master's degree in Marketing Management from Jakarta State University. His research interests focus on consumer behavior, digital marketing, tourism marketing, and behavioral analytics. He has actively contributed to several peer-reviewed publications, exploring topics such as consumer decision-making, destination branding, and electric vehicle adoption. He also serves as a Graduate Teaching Assistant and Research Assistant at Jakarta State University, supporting research in marketing and behavioral sciences. Doni has received several national awards, including the BIMA DRTPM Research Grant from the Indonesian Ministry of Education and the PMDSU Fast-Track Scholarship for outstanding young researchers. His interdisciplinary background in anthropology and marketing enables him to integrate cultural and behavioral insights into the study of consumer decision processes and sustainable tourism development.

Manoj Tiwari is associated with the Department of Fashion Technology of National Institute of Fashion Technology, Kannur, India. Prof. Tiwari is a Textile Engineer (batch of 2003, University of Rajasthan), Masters of Fashion Technology, and a Ph.D. from the National Institute of Fashion Technology, New Delhi. He has more than 17 years of industry and academic experience including teaching, industrial training, research and development, and consultancy in India and abroad. He has contributed to several consultancy projects including experience in leading an international project involving capacity building and consultancy in manufacturing and production management. He has presented and published over 60 research papers and articles in conferences and journals. The books "Industrial Engineering in Apparel Manufacturing: Practitioner's Handbook" (ISBN: 9788193247204) and "Lean Tools in Apparel Manufacturing" (ISBN: 9780128194270, published by Elsevier, UK) have been co-authored and co-edited with Prof. Prabir Jana, NIFT Delhi. He has also been involved in the prestigious INDIAsize project (National Sizing Survey of India) as a Core Team member. His key areas of interest include Industrial Engineering, Lean Manufacturing, Ergonomics, Sizing & Anthropometry, Apparel Technology Management, and Natural Textiles.

Index

A

B

C

D

E

G

I

K

L

M

O

P

R

S

www.ingramcontent.com/pod-product-compliance
Lightning Source LLC
LaVergne TN
LVHW062329300926
849161LV00007B/1632
* 9 7 9 8 3 3 7 3 9 9 9 8 0 *